CRAIG CALHOUN, PAUL PRICE, AND ASHLE[...]
JUERGENSMEYER: RELIGIOUS TERROR AND [...]
THE STRUGGLE FOR THE SOUL OF ISLAM. BA[...]
ALIST" ISLAMIC ACTIVISM: DEOBAND, TABLI[...]
THE RELIGIOUS UNDERTOW OF MUSLIM ECO[...]NCES. ROBERT O.
KEOHANE: THE GLOBALIZATION OF INFORMAL VIOLENCE, THEORIES OF
WORLD POLITICS, AND "THE LIBERALISM OF FEAR". DAVID HELD: VIOLENCE,
LAW, AND JUSTICE IN A GLOBAL AGE. SASKIA SASSEN: GOVERNANCE HOTSPOTS:
CHALLENGES WE MUST CONFRONT IN THE POST-SEPTEMBER 11 WORLD.
BARRY EICHENGREEN: THE UNITED STATES AND THE WORLD ECONOMY AFTER
SEPTEMBER 11TH. JACK A. GOLDSTONE: STATES, TERRORISTS, AND THE CLASH
OF CIVILIZATIONS. MARY KALDOR: BEYOND MILITARISM, ARMS RACES, AND
ARMS CONTROL. JAMES DER DERIAN: 9-11: BEFORE, AFTER, AND IN BETWEEN.
DOROTHY E. DENNING: IS CYBER TERROR NEXT? BRUCE CUMINGS: BLACK
SEPTEMBER, INFANTILE NIHILISM, AND NATIONAL SECURITY. SUSAN L. WOOD-
WARD: ON WAR AND PEACE-BUILDING: UNFINISHED LEGACY OF THE 1990s.
SEYLA BENHABIB: UNHOLY WARS: RECLAIMING DEMOCRATIC VIRTUES AFTER
SEPTEMBER 11. PETER ALEXANDER MEYERS: TERRORISM AND THE ASSAULT
ON POLITICS. RONALD DWORKIN: THE THREAT TO PATRIOTISM. ARISTIDE R.
ZOLBERG: GUARDING THE GATES. MARC HOWARD ROSS: THE POLITICAL PSY-
CHOLOGY OF COMPETING NARRATIVES: SEPTEMBER 11 AND BEYOND. RAJEEV
BHARGAVA: ORDINARY FEELINGS, EXTRAORDINARY EVENTS: MORAL COM-
PLEXITY IN 9/11. NILÜFER GÖLE: CLOSE ENCOUNTERS: ISLAM, MODERNITY,
AND VIOLENCE. IMMANUEL WALLERSTEIN: AMERICA AND THE WORLD: THE
TWIN TOWERS AS METAPHOR. SABA GUL KHATTAK: VIOLENCE AND HOME:
AFGHAN WOMEN'S EXPERIENCE OF DISPLACEMENT. MARITA STURKEN: MEMO-
RIALIZING ABSENCE. CRAIG CALHOUN, PAUL PRICE, AND ASHLEY TIMMER:
INTRODUCTION. MARK JUERGENSMEYER: RELIGIOUS TERROR AND GLOBAL
WAR. ROBERT W. HEFNER: THE STRUGGLE FOR THE SOUL OF ISLAM. BARBARA D.
METCALF: "TRADITIONALIST" ISLAMIC ACTIVISM: DEOBAND, TABLIGHIS, AND
TALIBS. TIMUR KURAN: THE RELIGIOUS UNDERTOW OF MUSLIM ECONOMIC
GRIEVANCES. ROBERT O. KEOHANE: THE GLOBALIZATION OF INFORMAL VIO-
LENCE, THEORIES OF WORLD POLITICS, AND "THE LIBERALISM OF FEAR".
DAVID HELD: VIOLENCE, LAW, AND JUSTICE IN A GLOBAL AGE. SASKIA SASSEN:
GOVERNANCE HOTSPOTS: CHALLENGES WE MUST CONFRONT IN THE POST-
SEPTEMBER 11 WORLD. BARRY EICHENGREEN: THE UNITED STATES AND THE
WORLD ECONOMY AFTER SEPTEMBER 11TH. JACK A. GOLDSTONE: STATES,
TERRORISTS, AND THE CLASH OF CIVILIZATIONS. MARY KALDOR: BEYOND
MILITARISM, ARMS RACES, AND ARMS CONTROL. JAMES DER DERIAN: 9-11:
BEFORE, AFTER, AND IN BETWEEN. DOROTHY E. DENNING: IS CYBER TERROR
NEXT? BRUCE CUMINGS: BLACK SEPTEMBER, INFANTILE NIHILISM, AND
NATIONAL SECURITY. SUSAN L. WOODWARD: ON WAR AND PEACE-BUILDING:
UNFINISHED LEGACY OF THE 1990s. SEYLA BENHABIB: UNHOLY WARS: RECLAIM-
ING DEMOCRATIC VIRTUES AFTER SEPTEMBER 11. PETER ALEXANDER MEYERS:
TERRORISM AND THE ASSAULT ON POLITICS. RONALD DWORKIN: THE THREAT
TO PATRIOTISM. ARISTIDE R. ZOLBERG: GUARDING THE GATES. MARC HOWARD
ROSS: THE POLITICAL PSYCHOLOGY OF COMPETING NARRATIVES: SEPTEMBER

UNDERSTANDING SEPTEMBER 11

UNDERSTANDING SEPTEMBER 11

CRAIG CALHOUN, PAUL PRICE, AND
ASHLEY TIMMER, EDITORS

PROJECT COORDINATED BY THE
SOCIAL SCIENCE RESEARCH COUNCIL, NEW YORK

THE NEW PRESS
NEW YORK

Published in the United States by The New Press, New York, 2002
Distributed by W. W. Norton & Company, Inc., New York

ISBN 1-56584-774-1 (pbk.)
CIP data available

The New Press was established in 1990 as a not-for-profit alternative to the large,
commercial publishing houses currently dominating the book publishing industry.
The New Press operates in the public interest rather than for private gain, and is committed
to publishing, in innovative ways, works of educational, cultural, and community value
that are often deemed insufficiently profitable.

The New Press, 450 West 41st Street, 6th floor, New York, NY 10036
www.thenewpress.com

Printed in Canada

2   4   6   8   10   9   7   5   3   1

CONTENTS

Acknowledgments ix

Introduction
Craig Calhoun, Paul Price, and Ashley Timmer 1

I. ISLAMIC RADICALISM

1. Religious Terror and Global War
Mark Juergensmeyer 27

2. The Struggle for the Soul of Islam
Robert W. Hefner 41

3. "Traditionalist" Islamic Activism: Deoband, Tablighis, and Talibs
Barbara D. Metcalf 53

4. The Religious Undertow of Muslim Economic Grievances
Timur Kuran 67

II. GLOBALIZATION

5. The Globalization of Informal Violence, Theories of World Politics,
and "the Liberalism of Fear"
Robert O. Keohane 77

6. Violence, Law, and Justice in a Global Age
David Held 92

7. Governance Hotspots: Challenges We Must Confront in the
Post-September 11 World
Saskia Sassen 106

8. The United States and the World Economy After September 11th
Barry Eichengreen 121

III. NEW WAR/NEW WORLD ORDER?

9. States, Terrorists, and the Clash of Civilizations
Jack A. Goldstone   139

10. Beyond Militarism, Arms Races, and Arms Control
Mary Kaldor   159

11. 9/11: Before, After, and In Between
James Der Derian   177

12. Is Cyber Terror Next?
Dorothy E. Denning   191

13. Black September, Infantile Nihilism, and National Security
Bruce Cumings   198

14. On War and Peace-building: Unfinished Legacy of the 1990s
Susan L. Woodward   212

IV. TERRORISM AND DEMOCRATIC VIRTUES

15. Unholy Wars. Reclaiming Democratic Virtues After September 11
Seyla Benhabib   241

16. Terrorism and the Assault on Politics
Peter Alexander Meyers   254

17. The Threat to Patriotism
Ronald Dworkin   273

18. Guarding the Gates
Aristide R. Zolberg   285

V. COMPETING NARRATIVES

19. The Political Psychology of Competing Narratives:
September 11 and Beyond
Marc Howard Ross   303

20. Ordinary Feelings, Extraordinary Events: Moral Complexity in 9/11
Rajeev Bhargava   321

21. Close Encounters: Islam, Modernity, and Violence
Nilüfer Göle   332

22. America and the World: The Twin Towers as Metaphor
Immanuel Wallerstein   345

23. Violence and Home: Afghan Women's Experience of Displacement
Saba Gul Khattak   361

24. Memorializing Absence
Marita Sturken   374

Notes   385
Contributors   433
Index   435

ACKNOWLEDGMENTS

The September 11 tragedy made all of us in New York pay attention to the social fabric within which we carry out our individual work. Certainly this book could not have been produced without the support of the Social Science Research Council as an institution, and a wide range of its staff members, committee members, and colleagues around the world. We are indebted especially to our colleagues Beverlee Bruce and Eric Hershberg who joined us in an early committee to develop the website which preceded this book and who have helped with a range of intellectual connections and contributions. Other program directors and officers at the SSRC have read manuscripts and offered a range of suggestions. We are especially grateful to Ron Kassimir, Kevin Moore, and Joe Karaganis for their help. Anne Lally has been an indefatigable support as the program coordinator for the larger project of which this book is one product. She also played an important role in developing teaching resources available on our "After September 11" website and is likely to be of help to those who use this book in classes. The Spencer Foundation provided timely and much appreciated financial support. The editors and staff of The New Press have been exceptionally supportive as we worked to shorten the usual publication times.

In addition to those who helped directly in the production of this book, we would like to thank all our colleagues who gave time and blood and money to aid others in the immediate aftermath of the tragedy. The Council's main role is intellectual, but we are glad that Council members responded in human ways as well—not just in New York, but in the Middle East and Central Asia and a range of places around the world where these events had personal implications for scholars who are part of the Council's broad networks and programs.

INTRODUCTION

CRAIG CALHOUN, PAUL PRICE, AND ASHLEY TIMMER

The morning of September 11 was clear and bright in New York, the sky especially blue and the breeze light. The flames that shot from the gaping holes in the twin towers were oddly beautiful. The air shimmered with what I suppose were fragments of shattered glass. Occasionally a bit of debris fell from a high floor, dark against the generally bright background. Only after I had stared for three or four minutes did my mind accept what my eyes were really seeing: falling bodies, human beings leaping to one certain death because another seemed worse. And eventually the towers fell and the bright day turned darker than midnight, with ash billowing around and blocking the sun.

To be across the street from the cinematic horror was to be an eyewitness, perhaps, but not to grasp the whole picture. My memories are still startlingly clear, but they are fragments. They do not go to the center of the events of September 11, though they weave my connection to them. Standing alone they do not give the events meaning. Some of the images I saw on TV are as indelible as those formed while I was close enough for the smoke to sting my eyes. My understanding of what happened depends on far more than what I saw that day. The sense of having *seen* it is still powerful, though. Indeed, the visual images are basic to the very idea that there was a singular "it" to be apprehended, that the complex chains of events could be contained into such a specific package. I can try critically to distinguish what I saw firsthand from what I saw only on television (though I fear the operation is inevitably incomplete). It is still harder to separate what I know because I saw it from what I know because someone or another provided words to give shape to that knowledge. It was a terrorist attack. It was war. It was a moment when everything changed. It was simple human tragedy.

Though there were sirens and screams, my aural memories are oddly of quiet. There were no sounds commensurate with the visual shock; there were gasps from horrified onlookers; the principal victims seemed silent. And New York was quiet for days, lower Manhattan because traffic was restricted and the whole city because no one wanted to speak out loud of what had happened and no one could speak of anything else. Yet the dust was everywhere, and everyone knew it was more than gypsum and steel. And one could choke with a sixth sense that was not premonition of something outside but connection to one's very viscera, a rising sickness, or tears.

Ten minutes into the chain of events, standing in the street just north of the World Financial Center and looking up, I heard from passersby that the damage came from a plane and not a bomb or a gas explosion. Five minutes later I learned that the crash was not an accident—because a second plane hit, certainly, but I was on the other side of the building and didn't see the crash itself; I heard the explanation from people who shouted as they ran away. And then I heard a radio report. And nothing I saw or felt after that was free from the influence of the media and commentary and discussion.

—*C. C.*

INTERPRETING SEPTEMBER 11

Through varying removes of media and interpretation, the events of September 11 became part of the common memory of people around the world. They were more important and more immediate to some and more distant to others. They were framed in very different ways and connected to other memories of different sorts. Before George Bush ever called this an act of war, World War II veterans in a "senior" residence near the scene were saying "not again." And of course it wasn't precisely *that* again. Indeed, trying to take hold of the events through the language of war rather than crime was a fateful decision—or impulse—and one that shaped the U.S. response and continues to reverberate, encouraging a search for military victories, for example, and discouraging reliance on international criminal law.

During the days, weeks, and months after September 11 the work of interpretation was carried on disproportionately by government officials and by the press, though also by everyone who stopped to think about what had happened and what it meant. Interpretation was the project of newspaper "op ed" columns, official pronouncements, and coffee-shop discussions. Each led into angry quarrels. Was looking for meaning in global inequality or Middle East politics to dignify the terrorists? Was praying for peace failing in patriotism? Was focusing on causes and effects obscuring the tragedies of the victims and their families?

The press and the conversations also led to a rough consensus in the United States: The *country* had been attacked, not just symbols of its global power. The attack dramatized a threat we had been complacently ignoring and demanded new vigilance from us. We had been "innocent" and now we needed to be "realistic." The world was a dangerous place.

This was an American consensus, of course, and other collective understandings of what had happened and was likely to happen next formed elsewhere. European allies scrambled to discern where they fit in—to U.S. military plans that were described as "unilateral multilateralism," and to a U.S.–dominated "West" that included them, but seemed to subordinate them symbolically, militarily, and economically. Sympathy for the U.S. was widespread. The U.S. had to act, a broad consensus suggested, but there was anxiety both in America and around the world lest the response be an overreaction, a dangerous escalation.

The events affected other countries directly through the loss of nationals working in New York and through exacerbated economic recession, as well as indirectly through new lines of global conflict. In Latin America, events helped shift the balance of power among different approaches to civil conflicts; the Colombian government was not alone in emphasizing that its rebels should be called "terrorists." There was a consensus that Americans failed to recognize the extent to which others had lived through similar horrors before, with perpetrators sometimes supported by the U.S., but there was also an expectation that Americans would forget this—forget even that the date September 11 was the anniversary of the 1973 overthrow of Salvador Allende in Chile. And despite this, there was widespread sympathy for the U.S. and rejection of what was seen as the reactionary antimodernism of Islamist terrorists. In Russia the new circumstances presented an opportunity to solidify alliance, renew a sense of importance to world affairs, and reframe the war against Chechen rebels as part of the global war against terrorism. In South Asia, even before the actual fighting in Afghanistan and its repercussions in Pakistan and India, the September 11 events were woven into regional histories of struggles over Islam. In much of Asia—not least in China—there was a complex mix of recognition that terror was always terrible and yet a certain satisfaction that the United States got a taste of what others had endured and a bit of a comeuppance.

None of these views simply encapsulated the truth. Nor was there a global consensus, but rather varying degrees of regional and local similarity of opinion. And nowhere, in fact, was the consensus simply spontaneous. Everywhere, there were arguments about what the events meant, and everywhere there were pressures to stop those arguments and adopt views backed by governments, or the press, or religious leaders, or public opinion. In the United States, the rough consensus of press and coffee shops was consolidated by political leaders who condemned peace marches, university presidents who tried to stop faculty members from making public criticism of U.S. policies, and a broad willingness to portray any effort to question the standard interpretation as somehow sympathetic to terrorism.

At the same time, though, in other parts of the world, consensus demanded that Osama bin Laden be considered a hero—or that the U.S. contention that he was behind the terrorist attack be dismissed as unfounded, or the possibility entertained that Israel's Mossad had staged the whole thing. The point is not that one consensus was right and another wrong, but rather that the production of conventional wisdom was everywhere shaped by crowd pressures and media simplifications and political manipulations. In some places it was based more on empirical evidence, and in some places there was greater respect for those who questioned that evidence. Some versions proved more responsive to correction by new information than others. But in no case was the consensus primarily the result of critical inquiry, reflection, and debate. Nowhere was it easy to question either the empirical claims or the categories through which they were presented. In the U.S., for example, it was hard to question the idea that the attacks were acts of "war," even to argue that this label dignified a criminal network with a kind of respect it did not deserve, implicitly treating it as the sort of international actor that can declare war. It was controversial to wonder aloud whether speaking of terrorists as individuals and networks distracted attention from governments who sometimes used violence to terrify civilians for political purposes.

The attacks are not simply a set of discrete and idiosyncratic events. They are part of complex patterns at several levels—from the very local suffering of families and efforts to rebuild lower Manhattan to the very global projects of peace and prosperity. Both the pain of individuals and the course of history are in some sense infinite; no scale can be calibrated to weigh one against the other. And yet they are interconnected.

It is precisely because the pain of individuals can be so sharp, and because it extends through the networks of family and friendship, and because each of us can identify at some level with victims, that terrorism is a possibility. Civilians—ordinary people engaged in ordinary life projects—are made to suffer to make a point, to weaken a government, to express a grievance. Civilians in a literal sense are also inhabitants of a city, and the city itself suffers. The ruptured relationships were part of its social fabric, the disrupted commerce its sustenance, the destroyed buildings and damaged streets its scars. The city has a reality of its own, just as the family does, not altogether contained by the nation. Those killed on September 11—the immediate, physical victims of the tragedy—came from dozens of countries. New York is part of the United States and yet connected to the world in ways that are not all about being American. And 9/11 has become one of those ways, just as the finance industry, migration and tourism, and global media are others.

Of course, the attackers struck not only New York, but also the U.S. Department of Defense at its famous home base, the Pentagon, outside Washington, D.C. And they struck using airplanes and thus killing people who had no other immediate connections to New York or Washington, and attacking and changing a transportation system that transcended specific localities. Inadvertently, they struck a field in rural Pennsylvania; they struck the earth in literal and metaphorical senses. By including the Pentagon among their targets, they connected all the other targets to U.S. military might and global domination. In some ways, the U.S. military response to 9/11 further stressed that very connection. But even if the attackers and the U.S. government agreed to stress this connection—to frame the events as war—this frame could never contain the events and their diverse implications.

The 9/11 attacks were also part of the causal sequence that brought devastation to Afghan villages, increased violence in Israel and the Palestinian Territories, and resulted in an individual, but not an isolated, loss to the family of Daniel Pearl, a reporter kidnapped and killed by terrorists in Pakistan. The experience of violence is not necessarily unifying, but much violence is nonetheless connected. People's experience has a local history and local effects that may be more powerful than the international connections (though that does not mean these are never made).

Some of the implications of 9/11 involved not so much material change as shifting perspectives. Thus the events came to crystallize issues and clashes that have existed for years: terrorist tactics, for example, and tensions between established states and groups without states to represent them. The events refocused attention and encouraged us to see things differently, to pay central attention to what earlier looked like peripheral concerns. Amid enthusiasm for the spread of information technology, a few observers had recognized the potential for cyberterrorism, and indeed a few relatively minor cases had occurred. But after September 11 the issue moved to the forefront of attention—along with the more straightforward way in which the Internet and improved communications technology could aid the communication of terrorists just as much as anybody else. The fact that police were able to trace Mohammed Atta and others to specific cybercafes, and unearth copies of what they must have thought were private and even long-since-erased communications, gave pause not just to would-be terrorists but to all who use the Internet to send messages they think are private. That security agencies in the U.S. and around the world now propose to increase their routine monitoring of electronic communications makes certain questions more pressing: How should the tension between civil liberties and effective law enforcement, especially antiterrorist policing, be managed? It is a question that arises especially in the use of special military tribunals instead of civilian courts, in large-scale use of detention without public announcement or other aspects of due process, and in debates over racial or ethnic profiling. In Peter Meyers's terms, the struggle to defend politics from terrorism is not only a matter of overcoming material dangers but also of protecting the possibility of the free and engaged speech without which there can be no democratic politics.

Likewise, the 9/11 attacks focused attention on the vulnerabilities of various sorts of infrastructure and the weaknesses of government preparedness for terrorist attacks. This was most acute in the U.S., not surprisingly, but versions of these concerns were nearly worldwide. The use of civilian aircraft as the mechanisms in terrorist violence called forth new security measures in air travel. But it also and rightly called forth attempts to think through the ways in which all sorts of complex systems might be vulnerable. If an older sort of thinking about what is now called "homeland security" had stressed bridges linking major segments of the highway system, thinkers now added questions about water supplies, mail delivery, energy production, and the power grid. The very infrastructure on which modern economic activity and social integration depend had been improved dramatically, and not least by information technology, yet with the very improvements and the growing interconnection came new vulnerabilities. In the United States, civil defense had long been neglected in the complacent assumption that the real threats lay in more distant military "theaters." Military strategists had begun to raise questions about new threats to "homeland security" years earlier, but these only commanded attention throughout the bureaucratic hierarchy—let alone from the public—after 9/11. Questions about preparedness reached well beyond military planning, though, as the anthrax scare that followed 9/11 called attention to the public health system. Parts of the system, like the Centers for Disease Control, operated at a high level even while other parts, like local-level primary care including vaccinations, were problematic (not least because based on high-cost private providers in a country where a fifth of the population lacked health insurance).

Ironically, while the talk of technology focused on vulnerability in the U.S., a widespread response in the Middle East, even among people who condemned the attacks, was a certain pleasant surprise that for once technology had been mastered by Arabs and not by their enemies. Yet, at the same time, the U.S. intelligence and defense leadership indicated that they would attempt to defend against threats by adding to their technological capabilities. Few seemed to appreciate that one of the prime ironies of 9/11 had been the way in which advanced technology had been turned against its makers.

The 9/11 events raised questions about how well the finance industry could respond after being hit so directly—and for the most part the answer is in. It responded extremely well. The question of whether the finance industry would continue to be comparably centered in New York is not yet so clearly answered, though, and firms are still wrestling with their own questions about how to prepare for possible future disruptions, whether and how to decentralize, how much to invest in redundancy of computer systems, and what kinds of training employees need for emergencies. Charities were challenged by 9/11 and have played a major part in helping victims, from the families of lost firefighters to workers laid off because their employers were closed or destroyed. Rock stars staged benefit concerts; millions of people gave donations small and large; long-established philanthropic foundations made major grants; voluntary organizations mobilized citizens and created support systems. If the main religious story in the wake of 9/11 focused on the beliefs of perpetrators and whether these were representative of some broader pattern in Islam, the back pages of newspapers carried another less commonly remarked: the centrality of religious organizations to providing assistance after the disaster. Where, one might ask, would such assistance come from if American society were as secular as some of its critics assert?

At the same time, though, systems of charity and voluntary organization were under stress. The performance of some charitable organizations, like the American Red Cross, seemed confused and problematic and led to management upheavals. Numerous new organizations were created to handle new donations, and provisions for public oversight were revealed to be marginal. Worries surfaced that there would be high levels of support for some victims and their survivors while others would fall through the cracks—huge sums were raised for lost policemen, for example, but lost security guards were initially ineligible, no matter that many were among the first to respond and equally heroic.

More generally, practical action raised ethical questions: Should victims' families be compensated in proportion to victims' highly unequal salaries, for example, or should the government and charities treat lost lives as equally valuable? The list of questions could go on and on: How should plans for redeveloping the site of the tragedy take account of the horror; what provisions should be made for mourning and commemoration; and how should these relate to aesthetic, financial, and political concerns? How should one balance the huge amount of money spent to help the victims of tragedy in New York with the lesser sums made available to equally innocent victims of tragedies in less rich countries? How should one balance the very level of attention to 3,000 dead in the World Trade Center attacks to the comparable number dying daily of AIDS?

These questions, though specific to 9/11, reveal ongoing themes. Many of the events that followed, indeed the attacks themselves, are in ways episodes in other, longer-term stories. In some cases, they come to symbolize a trend; in others they mark a turning point. Perhaps the most important of the latter cases is the whole complex cluster of phenomena grouped together as "globalization." Globalization communicates not only increasing international flows of people, ideas, and goods, but also the increasing interdependence of well-being, governance, and power.

There is another burden carried by the term "globalization." To many people around the world, it has seemed not a neutral process of internationalization, but the imposition of an "American" or "Western" model. It has been true that the rich countries have often become so through global investment and trade, seemingly at the expense of the poor. This is part of the complaint. But so is the idea that Western cultural ideas—and sometimes ideologies, like perhaps neoliberalism itself—ride on the back of economic and technological and other forces of globalization to which they are not necessary. In the background of 9/11 is the complaint that it should not be necessary to accept secularism, mass merchandising, pornography, or new gender roles just to be global or modern. There are those that say everyone must take the whole package. And there are those who want to reject all of it—some Qaeda leaders may have been among these. But many more people, all around the world, would like to pick and choose.

Globalization certainly does not explain 9/11, though it is an important context for understanding the events and their repercussions. The events and the response to them raise questions about economic and political inequalities, about migration and freedom of movement, and about the role of the media. They mark a sharp counterpoint to the celebratory discussions of globalization that dominated during the 1990s; they are in the foreground of a gloomier discourse about its dangers.

But this is not just a matter of shifting discussions about globalization; material realities have shifted in important ways as well. September 11 shone a spotlight on some changes, but also played a part in producing or furthering many. Consider, for example, the prominence—sudden to Europeans and Americans—of the Arabic news service Al Jazeera. This has a longer history, including notably the decision of the BBC to disband its Arabic broadcast service in the late 1990s. That was itself partly a story of globalization, including both Britain's reduced geopolitical presence and the spread of neoliberal ideology that called for reducing state expenditure. Staff released from the BBC (but carrying certain parts of the BBC model with them) formed the core of the new service, which received financial support and a base from the Emir of Qatar. Relying especially on broadcast media, the new service reached both the literate and the illiterate, though it also supplemented its broadcasts with an effective website. Its well-trained and often incisive interviewers surprised many of their international subjects (including, in the wake of the U.S. attacks on Afghanistan, Defense Secretary Donald Rumsfeld). But, even to many Arabs, it first became famous during the post–9/11 war on terrorism. It emerged that no other news service really operated effectively in Afghanistan. If CNN or ABC wanted to show local footage, buying it from Al Jazeera was usually the best approach. And at the same time, Al Jazeera was broadcasting the story throughout the Arabic world—and in Arabic, not simply reaching the English-speaking elites who might tune in to CNN (itself a symbol of globalization, but a monolingual channel in a polyglot world). The initial U.S. government response was to treat Al Jazeera as though it were somehow part of the problem, a threat because it seemed to tell other sides of the story and especially to provide Osama bin Laden with a media outlet (though the U.S. security services were glad to have the Al Jazeera tape to analyze, and U.S. networks were eager to broadcast extracts from it). After a few weeks, as the U.S. administration saw more need to strengthen alliances in the Arab world and possibly even to try to appeal to Arab public opinion, this position changed. Al Jazeera then looked like a useful tool, and Rumsfeld and others were happy to be interviewed (even if likely a bit ambivalent about some of the results). What 9/11 did, in brief, was to reveal the gulf between the English-language version of media globalization and the demand for information in other languages, and also to strengthen the position of Al Jazeera as a new and important international media network.

Similarly, an important dimension of the 9/11 attacks was the place of international migration, especially of a European sojourn in the background of individual terrorists and European connections in the Qaeda network. Osama bin Laden had briefly studied at Oxford, and several others in Germany; cells were uncovered in Spain and France—and indeed in Malaysia and Singapore. International migration has been part and parcel of globalization for generations, and its acceleration in the late twentieth century had certainly been noted. Likewise, the growth of a Muslim minority in several European countries has gained both public and academic attention. But the two issues come together in important ways in relation to 9/11. In the first place, the events highlight the fact that migration is not a simple movement from one place to another but often a (dis)location into a diasporic flow in which the meanings of both "home" and "away" are changed. The place of European experience in the formation of many apparent terrorists upsets easy accounts of the West vs. the rest, the modern vs. the traditional, the advanced vs. the backward, and even the rich vs. the poor. The terrorists often came from local elites in majority Muslim (and mostly Arab) countries. Whether the attempt of many to claim the Umma Islam as a transnational home reflected an alternative vision of modernity or a rejection of modernity, it revealed dissatisfaction with the actual conditions of majority Muslim nation-states—not least Saudi Arabia. Some had apparently embarked on careers they expected Western education to advance, and many had become devout in the context of their European experience, not in advance of it. Yet all were joined in a communication circuit that drew sustenance from resentment of Israeli occupation of Arab lands in the Middle East and helped to mobilize volunteers against Soviet-backed rule in Afghanistan. Relatively few were recruited directly from "home" without some apparently triggering experience of "away." And so migration is revealed to be not merely a matter of closed vs. open doors, access to economic opportunity, or even the struggle to maintain native culture in new settings.

At the same time, the response to 9/11 is likely to close some doors, shift access to economic opportunity, and put new pressures on those who want to maintain at least aspects of the cultures into which they were born and make them available to their children born in distant lands. Certainly one of the important results of 9/11 is a tightening of U.S. immigration policy—and also its integration into a new security regime. As often in its history, the U.S. has seen a tide of nativism—with children and grandchildren of immigrants visible in the vanguard. Yet the contrary is also prominent—self-conscious efforts to reach across ethnic and religious divisions, to renew appreciation of diversity, at least within the bounds of patriotism. In international as well as domestic policy the response to 9/11 is frequently nationalistic, reinscribing the importance of national identity and solidarity in the face of unsettling globalization. Yet this is precisely not the "clash of civilizations" predicted by Samuel Huntington and others who expected transnational alliances of Judeo-Christian West against Muslims and other versions of East (including the lands of Orthodox Christianity and both Confucian and non-Confucian Asia). Ironically or not, it may have looked like that more to Osama bin Laden than to most Western observers. The Bush administration's first impulses seemed to lean toward such a view, yet quickly a contrary wisdom gained the upper hand and the president importantly visited a mosque and began to retune his speeches to try to make clear that the U.S. did not regard Muslims in general as its enemies.

Nonetheless, after 9/11 it became clear that American self-understanding was not easily meshed with the views of many groups around the world, perhaps most notably Muslims. Where Americans saw openness—including in trade—others saw dominance. Where Americans saw aid, others saw influence. Where Americans saw a "reluctant sheriff" others saw self-appointed police who made the law to suit their own purposes. There is no easy parceling of the truth in these clashing perspectives. They reflect differences in vantage points, in experience, in analytic frameworks, in values, in evidence considered. What is clear is that they are important and, whatever their truth, are factors to be considered in world affairs. And it is clear also that America's rapid military success in Afghanistan has not ended the battle for public opinion. As late as February 2002, the Gallup poll found that 61 percent of Muslims in nine countries doubted that Arabs were responsible for the 9/11 attacks. Osama bin Laden may have lost face for seeming to hide, but in victory, the public significance of an image of American strength remains at best ambivalent. Is this just vengeance, necessary restoration of order, righteous advocacy of democracy, or the lashing out of a bully after briefly being bested? One of the things Americans find hardest to consider is that strength and dominance are resented, simply as such, and that good intentions do little if anything to temper this.

The point goes even to the dramatically superior military technology the Americans displayed in Afghanistan. The pinpoint bombings were impressive. But while to the American media this was a story mainly about a "clean" war and minimizing of civilian casualties, to much of the world it was a story about the radical asymmetry of power. Americans were willing to inflict but not suffer casualties. And the very sense that the U.S. will not place the lives of American soldiers at risk, and that Americans enter wars only when their computers and airplanes give them a sense of distance, may make America into Goliath in all conflicts and offer the kid with the slingshot and rock some sense of justification in striking first. Indeed, part of the poignancy in the images of 9/11 comes from the marvels of modern technology—the technology in which America has excelled and reveled—being turned into weapons against those who usually wield the technology, those with the economic and military power to benefit disproportionately from such technology.

There is no end to competing narratives. There is no moment when we can say that September 11 meant one and only one thing and must mean the same thing to everyone (nor will it necessarily mean the same thing to any one of us all the time). It will necessarily mean different things to those who lost loved ones and those who think of it as a strategic problem, for those who witnessed devastation first hand and those for whom it is an abstraction. It will mean different things to those in the Middle East and those in the Midwest. It is important to see, though, that the conflicting narratives do not line up into just two or three sides, certainly not into just ours and theirs. It is easy for Americans to forget that there are arguments among Muslims, different theologies and views of the relationship between religion and public life, different histories, different mixings of Islamic and nationalist identities, different projects of modernization and of the preservation of tradition. There is no more a singular Muslim view of September 11 or of whether modernity is clearly a good thing than there is a singular Christian view or a singular secular view. Yet there is a worrying division between the dominant partial consensuses in the West and those in the Middle East. The recurrence of rhetorical flourishes recalling the Crusades is only evidence of the power of half-unconscious historical memories, renewed by continuing geopolitical divisions.

Indeed, from the point of view of the Middle East, the September 11 attacks are not so much an issue in themselves as one important moment in a longer series of conflicts. This itself can be framed in terms of Islam generally or Arabs more specifically or Palestinians still more specifically—and in terms of Israel, or the United States, or the West as a whole. The September 11 attacks not only reflected roots in this context, among others, but also have influenced the course of further tragic struggles in the Middle East. Sympathies and analyses have both shifted. Israeli actions to "root out the terrorist infrastructure" in the occupied Palestinian territories sounded to many Americans like an extension of President Bush's own war on terrorism. For Palestinians to have even a fraction of the arms the occupying army had seemed evidence of "Arab terrorism." Suicide bombings that may have seemed legitimate tactics of struggle to some were mere terrorist acts to others—and the September 11 attacks could be understood as simply suicide bombings with unusually large and complex "bombs."

Yet the Bush administration tried to play down the increasing violence in Palestine in order to build a coalition for an attack on Iraq—a project that the administration thought flowed directly from the post-September 11 war on terrorism. It had its own account of what kinds of action the September 11 tragedies legitimated. At the same time, the very deepening of the conflict over Palestine reduced the efficacy of September 11 as the anchor to a legitimating narrative for "war against terrorism."

Still, there are a host of other divisions in the world. The 9/11 tragedies may shape future conflicts far from Palestine or from renewed terrorism by Islamists against the West. Among the most worrying flashpoints is Kashmir and the struggle over a beautiful mountain region that has become the most potent symbol for the unresolved tensions that grew out of the mixture of Islamic and British conquests of South Asia. This embeds 9/11 as a moment in a different history, one that includes the extraordinary civilization of Mughal India, and the civilizations that preceded the Mughal Empire in India. It is a history that included British acts of terrorism and British achievements that remain among the triumphs of the West, a history into which Jews and Catholics also wandered but in which the dominant religious conflicts (and syncretisms) are not Christian and Muslim but Hindu and Muslim and Sunni and Shi'a within Islam. It is a history that should remind us that civilizations are not hermetically sealed but interrelated. And that such kinship has never stopped bloodshed.

September 11 brought Afghanistan to the forefront of American attention and toppled the Taliban, militant Islamist students who came to power after conflicts with the former USSR and aid from Americans, who then imposed a crude vision of Islamic puritanism on their country, and sheltered and ultimately lost control to their foreign allies, Al Qaeda. September 11 transformed the strategic calculations for Pakistan's rulers and made General Musharaff into a president whose American counterpart wanted him as a friend. This worried Indian rulers who conceivably would prefer the advantage that American enmity to Pakistan offered them over the possibilities of regional peace. It fanned the flames of tensions over Kashmir because it made some groups think they had better seize the moment before being undercut and others think they had a new chance to win once and for all.

The implications of September 11 are not limited to the world's "hotspots." In Europe, questions of how to respond brought Germany's Green Party a parliamentary defeat that could yet prove fatal, for reasons ancillary to the environmentalism that brought it to power. It refused to back its own coalition government partners, the Social Democrats, in taking up arms internationally for the first time since the defeat of the Third Reich. September 11 was intertwined, in other words, with the complex histories of Nazism and pacifism as well. Britain's Tony Blair played his special American relationship to a triumphant crescendo, eagerly appearing as America's European partner (and neatly also using American alliance to keep distance from Europe). Even while it introduced its new currency, the European Union revealed its difficulties forging a common foreign policy. Europeans grumbled at America's disdain for allies' opinions, and at the Bush administration's bellicose rhetoric culminating in its denunciation of an alleged "axis of evil" joining Iraq to Iran and North Korea. Yet European governments, unable to forge their own collective military stance, experienced the meaning of American hegemony as they faced the choice of jumping on the American bandwagon or sitting on the sidelines.

One might have thought that September 11 strikingly revealed the need for strong multilateral institutions. What better argument could be offered for the value of multinational law enforcement and the creation of an International Criminal Court than the dramatic violence of terrorist actions that lacked the backing of any recognized nation-state and benefited from a variety of criminal activities from forged passports to illegal financial transfers? Yet, the American administration—already hostile to such multilateral institutions for fear that they might try American criminals and diminish national sovereignty—was steadfastly opposed. With minimal gestures to forging an alliance, it chose its own, mainly military, response. Despite the Bush administration's call for a collective struggle of all the world against terrorism, ironically enough, the actual building of multilateral institutions to carry out such a struggle—along with the rest of law enforcement—seems further away than before.

In fact, there are even debates over how much damage terrorism can do. Obviously it can do a lot. But is the real lesson of September 11 perhaps how quickly markets bounced back, how effective the human and technological systems were that sustained trading and communications? Cantor Fitzgerald, a firm integral to the global bond market, lost two-thirds of its employees in the World Trade Center attacks. Perhaps as important as the human story of its recovery and the care of owners and living employees for lost colleagues and their families is the fact that the firm was able to get its bond trading back to full strength within a week. Clearly the global economy was shaken, but it was not brought to its knees. Of course, this means only that it works—within certain terms of reference—not that it works as well as it might or that it works for good in all respects. It doesn't settle disputes over the proclaimed neutrality of the market vs. the dominance of an American (mostly free-market) model, over economic productivity vs. environmental damage, or over growth vs. inequality.

During all this, newspaper readers discovered that there were more Muslims in India than in Saudi Arabia; that there were perhaps more Muslims than Jews in America (though the number has been debated); and that Muslims were the largest minority in many European countries. But this was also a discovery that any simple account of the secularization of the world was misleading, and that religion matters, in both radical and moderate forms. As Robert Keohane makes clear in this volume, one of the important weaknesses of international relations theory—and it is true of much political and social theory—is its unexamined secularism and failure to appreciate the continuing importance of religion in the world. Fundamentalists, puritans, and extremists of various sorts dominate our concerns for security, but as in lower Manhattan, so too in other parts of the world are religious convictions deployed for peace and care for the needy.

This is one of the challenges to democracies in the wake of 9/11. They must discern effective ways to embrace diversity but also to achieve solidarity in the face of both internal and external pressures. Focus just on America for a moment: A sad teenage boy in Florida flew an airplane into a tall building in imitation of Al Qaeda, though surely he understood little of what that meant. It is still unclear whether anthrax was spread by a more informed sympathizer or simply someone criminally deranged. But it is certain that America faces a range of internal threats, including ones who, like Timothy McVeigh, claim to speak as Christians and patriots while they cause mass destruction. Democracy depends not merely on tolerance, and not merely on legal procedures, though both are important. It depends also on the virtues of its citizens, on informed public life, and on respect for these conditions of both freedom and self-rule. It is crucial to ask whether the actions taken to protect America in the wake of 9/11 actually protect its democracy, and likewise whether they make democracy more likely elsewhere.

Few doubt that September 11, 2001 was an important day. Their reasons, however, are both varied and contested. It was an attack on America. It was a reminder to America. It brought death to thousands of innocent people and sorrow to their families. It avenged death and suffering elsewhere. It brought economic shocks. It challenged economic hegemony. It produced a new sense of insecurity. It opened American eyes to the insecurity of the world. It renewed American unity and resolve. It called forth American vengeance. And it was not only an American story.

The editorial and "op ed" pages of newspapers touch on all of these issues but usually do not clarify the information, theoretical perspectives, and intellectual commitments that inform different conclusions. How can they, when columnists are limited to 600 words? As a result, there is a need for well formulated and clearly presented analyses that reveal rather than hide their intellectual underpinnings. This book is an attempt to meet this need, and to help in the intellectual task—as basic to science as to democracy—of revising conventional wisdom by bringing forward new evidence, filling in the context that makes facts meaningful, asking questions about received categories of understanding, and clarifying the theoretical assumptions and arguments that support different conclusions.

The work that led to this book started within days of September 11. It was clear that many people recognized a need to move beyond the easy simplifications of the attacks themselves, their perpetrators, and the U.S. response, to explore the wide range of global and local affairs that provided the context to them. There was a sudden desire for more information—about political Islam, about Afghanistan, about the different ways in which the United States might be vulnerable to further terrorist acts, and about how the attacks and the "war on terrorism" would affect the economy, migration, civil rights, and a range of other concerns. Some U.S. newspapers and magazines (and others around the world) did begin to provide this information, and indeed one of the byproducts of the events was an impressive public education about important issues. There was a shortage, however, of analytic writing, and especially writing that would draw effectively on the knowledge social scientists had developed before by research on related issues. Our first step was to create a website and invite distinguished social scientists from the U.S. and around the world to write short essays; many of the chapters in this book are developed out of these essays, revising and expanding early hurried efforts. Even in the present version, they are rushed into print rather faster than the usual academic process—which would devote a few more years to working out details. This seems important because public discussion needs the deepened sense of context, critical analysis of categories, and reexamination of assumptions they provide.

As is evident throughout these pages, social scientists have no unified view of the 9/11 attacks or responses to them. Anthropologists, economists, historians, political scientists, and sociologists emphasize different aspects; specialists on Islam and on information technology rightly raise different issues. Nor do all of these together offer a complete and final analysis. The course of events is still unfolding; as we write, it is not clear whether the U.S. will attack Iraq or whether there will be some new major strike against America or Americans. It is not clear whether the 9/11 events will be part of a story of new war in Israel and Palestine or of new peace.

Not only is history open-ended; there is no limit to the range of different analytic questions that could be posed. We think the chapters in this book point to most of the major ones. We also hope that the way we have organized them helps the reader to organize her own thoughts. Below we offer some introductions to the sections of the book. The categories we have employed—Islamic Radicalism, Globalization, New War/New World Order?, Terrorism and Democratic Virtues, and Competing Narratives—are not intended as containers for analysis or boundaries of understanding. It is precisely testimony to the significance of the 9/11 events that their repercussions ripple outward in many directions. Information demonstrates its risible untidiness, to paraphrase Adrienne Rich. In this volume, we have done our best to commission and arrange essays in a way that they speak to each other. In so doing, we run the risk of reifying divisions between the subject headings within which they fall. But the reader will note, we hope, that contributors to the volume range widely in their concerns, and that essays speak across the categories we have constructed as well as within them.

OVERVIEW OF THE VOLUME

ISLAMIC RADICALISM

In achieving a deeper understanding of September 11, it is impossible to ignore the role of religion, and Islam in particular, in the attacks and subsequent events. So, like much of the discussion of September 11 in the West, we start with Islam.

But simply saying Islam only begs deeper questions. What is specific to Islam and what is general to religious radicalism, for example? After all, fundamentalist Christians, and Hindus, and Jews have been killers of civilians in the present era. More specifically, how do the versions of Islam linked to the September 11 attacks fit into Islamic history—which has often been peaceful and tolerant—and contemporary Islam—in which theology and politics are both hotly contested?

The attacks were made in the name of God, and the attackers were apparently supported by a group of religious students turned government. But these facts do not simply speak for themselves. The essays in this section provide necessary context. Mark Juergensmeyer helps us understand comparatively the assault on the secular state by religious radicals, and how terrorism developed as a strategy within Islamist movements. He has interviewed (failed) suicide bombers, members of the Taliban, and other Islamic extremists, and thus helps us understand the context of Islamic terrorism. But religious radicalism is not limited to Islam. Other religions are involved in the current events, as the recurring rhetoric of "crusades" and the escalating conflict in Israel/Palestine and Kashmir demonstrate. Juergensmeyer examines the deeply embedded link between violence and religion that exists in almost all major religions, and the link between violence and political support that makes terrorism so attractive.

The entanglement of politics with religion is deep in Islam, but hardly limited to it. Neither is there a single pattern of political movement or political ideal that is universal to Islam. As Barbara Metcalf and Robert Hefner document in their essays, claims about the relationship of religion to worldly power are intensely contested. Not only are there "moderates" and "extremists," there are also divisions among regions and countries, between Shi'ites and Sunnis, and simply between different lines of faith. Metcalf's historical analysis explores the rise of the Deobandi movement, which established the first *madrasas* in South Asia at which the Taliban were schooled, in comparison with the Tablighi movement, which has maintained a separation from politics and the state while attracting Muslim faithful at a phenomenal rate. Thus she highlights a point made explicit by Robert Hefner—there is not one Islam which presents itself in opposition to the West. There are many Islams, of which the fundamentalist, radical variety is a small subset. Hefner further argues that Islam has a long history of cycling between religious conservatism and more secular modernism.

Timur Kuran builds on Hefner's insights by examining the current and historical relationship between Islam and modern market economies. The Taliban and Osama bin Laden aligned themselves against modern society, and although they are not alone in supporting an Islamic world free from certain materialisms and modern developments, Kuran argues that historical roots of Islam include the fostering of wide-reaching trade networks, and where Muslims have had the opportunity to compete successfully in modern economies, they have overwhelmingly chosen to do so. But the fundamentalist movements do purport to offer an alternative, and they may be attractive where the market-economy is seen to be unfairly structured.

GLOBALIZATION

Globalization helped to create the conditions for the September 11 attacks; it shaped how people saw them, and, in turn, it will itself be influenced for decades to come not just by the attacks but by responses to them. The essays in this section explore these interactions.

At one level, globalization means simply that a range of social processes are becoming more closely interconnected around the world. Globalization has a long history and was aided by steamships and telegraphs long before television and the Internet. It involves increasing flows of people, money, information, and even diseases across national borders. But further, it captures the organization of power and production on a global scale by corporations, governments, and multilateral organizations in which governments and private companies combine their force. We are increasingly interconnected thus, and our fortunes linked; neither local communities nor national economies are autonomous and self-sufficient.

September 11 was very much a product of this trend—shaping the individuals involved and allowing for the attacks themselves. It thus presents a challenge for globalization as well as demonstrating how profound these global interdependencies have become. On the one hand, as David Held points out in his essay, trends in interconnectedness have offered the opportunity for global institutions of law and justice, so that individuals no longer need depend solely on their home regime for their moral standing. The attacks can be viewed as a crime in this global context, against humanity and its potential for peaceful, cosmopolitan unity, not merely as a crime against New Yorkers and Americans. But from the reverse perspective, Robert Keohane argues that as useful and necessary as such international institutions are and will be, they respond in part to the fact that violence itself has become globalized. The terrorist networks that now cause domestic insecurity and threaten human rights do not themselves respect any boundaries. The new shape of violence challenges us to rethink the appropriate relationships between states, world politics, and justice, and to ask how well democracies are able to protect their citizens from fear.

The term globalization is not simply a neutral synonym for interconnections, though, but takes on more controversial meaning. It has also become a shorthand for *capitalist modernization*. In the process of being drawn into global markets, economies are transformed by new divisions of labor, industrialization, and openness to new sources of capital, labor, and natural resources. Globalization in this sense means the implementation of new economic systems that emphasize free trade, markets, and protections for private property rights. While historically this structural transformation of economies has dramatically increased incomes, life expectancy, and other measures of basic well-being, economic development has also brought increasing disparities of income and disparities of how well basic needs are met. Even if on balance most people in the world are better off (it-self much debated), they are also more unequal—and accordingly, many com-plain. Thus the processes of globalization are blamed for exacerbating the sense of deprivation that often breeds discontent.

As Saskia Sassen argues, we must at least pay attention to the charge, if not for the sake of equity and human rights, then for the sake of the self-interest of "the north." If the massive debt burden that poor economies face, and the abject poverty connected to it continue to underlie mass migrations, the spread of dis-ease, and the spread of violence, then the United States and its allies in the devel-oped countries of the global north need to evolve more effective multilateral mechanisms to deal with these "governance hotspots." But security concerns could also drive both private-sector economic activity and international eco-nomic policy in ways that only add to the charges against globalization. Barry Eichengreen points out that international financial institutions, like the Interna-tional Monetary Fund (IMF), face new pressures to be the solution in places like Afghanistan, while at the same time, private markets may be going the other di-rection—eschewing politically risky economies in favor of the stable. This may only further widen the gap between rich and poor. Eichengreen argues, as does Sassen, that the West needs to support policies to encourage globalization to do more good than harm.

Globalization has also become shorthand for the increasing international dominance of Western culture, media, and ideologies. Among the many critics of this process are Al Qaeda and Osama bin Laden, but they are the more extreme elements of a pervasive sense throughout the world that this dominance is both unnecessary and unwanted. Timur Kuran and Mark Juergensmeyer, in their chapters in the preceding section, locate specific versions of these complaints in the context of Islamist movements.

NEW WAR/NEW WORLD ORDER?

Terrorism and the events of September 11 present new complexities for global se-curity as well as domestic security. While terrorists exploit their transnational status and demonstrate the globalization of violence, responses to terrorism will likewise challenge national boundaries and state-centered interests. While it is clear that contemporary armed conflict is increasingly less about armed combat for geographical domination between states, what other features of "new wars" stand out post–September 11? And has September 11 challenged us, as some have claimed, to find a New World Order—a post–Cold War, post "unipolar" relationship among states? Or, after a brief hiatus, have familiar patterns of relations between nations reasserted themselves? These are some of the central issues addressed in this section.

Jack Goldstone explores how the political and economic forces in the Middle East and Central Asia gave rise to an international Islamic terror network and Al Qaeda. In doing so, he demonstrates the complexity of motivations of the terrorists and he defines the challenges for creating peace out of this new war. Solutions must go beyond states and nation-building, he argues, to the level of individuals on whom the terror networks rely. But "new war" is not only about a new kind of enemy. It is also about new weapons and strategies. James Der Derian argues that the war on terrorism is as much about Internet and media networks as about terrorist ones. The battlefields are not all physical, but virtual as well. His sees in September 11 a "mimetic war"—a battle of images and representation where bin Laden issues videos that counter the statements made by Secretary of Defense Rumsfeld and President Bush. Dorothy Denning surmises that the Internet may be the next network to be engaged in the battle. As our infrastructures increasingly depend on technology, there are expanding possibilities to inflict real harm through computer networks. Although cyberterror, as she notes, has yet to be realized in any deadly capacity, Al Qaeda claims indicate that it may be a reality soon.

Mary Kaldor, echoing Der Derian's observation about the media, suggests that contemporary wars are often prosecuted as much for the purpose of political mobilization as for any strategic military victory. Networks wage war to recruit supporters to their cause, and thus modern communications are central. In response, the United States has been developing its capacity to fight *asymmetric warfare*—responding to the weapons of the weak—but simultaneously committed to perfecting the bloodless war. But perhaps more challenging for the international community, civilian casualties and violation of non-combatants' rights are not merely unfortunate side effects, but are often the central point of the warfare of the weak.

Do events since September 11, both in the prosecution of the war on terrorism and in relations within the community of nations, suggest fundamental change in world order? Many observers, including essayists in this volume, have noted that the U.S. had a newfound appreciation for multilateralism in the weeks that followed September 11. But Bruce Cumings argues that as much as 9/11 seemed to force a break from past policy, in the end little will have changed. His historical perspective on U.S. engagements around the world leads him to suspect that the U.S. will try to stabilize the Central Asian region—and perhaps overstay its welcome. But more generally, the tougher battle for the U.S. will be to try to maintain public enthusiasm for a world presence when its rationale is little understood by the American public.

Susan Woodward also casts doubt on the proposition that the war in Afghanistan has represented a qualitatively new approach, citing continuities that extend back to the "tortured conflicts" of the 1990s. She shows that while reconstruction efforts in Afghanistan have been informed by the lessons learned about peace-building in the 1990s in Kosovo, Bosnia, and Somalia, many lessons have been forgotten, especially when concerns for military victory have taken precedence over concerns for an effective peace to follow.

While initial indications were that September 11 had introduced new thinking about international relations, global security, and peace-building, Woodward and Cumings share the view that there may be little that is new in the New World Order.

TERRORISM AND DEMOCRATIC VIRTUES

What challenges confront liberal democracies at home, as they face non-state threats of violence? The attacks on the Pentagon and the World Trade Center brought to the U.S. what had been an ongoing concern in Europe, Israel, and elsewhere of assuring safety (or at least order) for citizens at home, not just abroad. The U.S. response, expanding federal investigative powers, suspending court trials for suspected terrorists, and cracking down on immigration, struck many as appropriate, necessary, and reassuring. For many others, it seemed that the terrorist threat had succeeded in shutting down some of the most central aspects of American identity and values—freedom of thought, freedom of movement, civil liberties. So how is a liberal, democratic country to respond when—as Robert Keohane points out (citing Judith Shklar)—the first right we have in a liberal regime is to be protected from fear?

Seyla Benhabib elaborates how the new violence—no longer the monopoly of the state—forces us to fight a war without ever declaring war, where the enemy wants to bring down our way of life, not just our government. And in creating the everyday fear, terrorism challenges our government to new forms of security. But she argues that our systems of protection cannot handle an internal enemy. We are not capable of recognizing the possibility of threat from within our borders without suspiciously eyeing everyone who seems unlike us. We become wary of the other, and suspicious of dissent. But this distrust of dissent, as Peter Meyers argues, is precisely what the attacks have generated, and in so doing, made democracy falter. Without conversation and argument, he maintains, there can be no politics. Without disagreement, no progress in our views. Thus the terrorists succeed in breaking down our way of life by making us fear the very values on which our society was built.

Ronald Dworkin details the progress that the U.S. government has made in tearing down our civil liberties, arguably one such foundational value. Since September 11, the U.S. has planned for military tribunals that sidestep due-process requirements and expanded government power to conduct secret searches. Echoing Peter Meyers, Dworkin notes the overwhelming approval of the American public for these actions. He recognizes that the public is scared and is being presented with a trade-off: security or liberty. But he, like the other authors in this section, argues that it is a false trade-off.

U.S. society was built, of course, on the fact of immigration as well, and that too is under challenge. In the U.S., immigration has been contentious for centuries, reaching its most hostile discourse in the 1990s. But as Aristide Zolberg demonstrates, critics of a liberal immigration policy needed no prompting to use the events of September 11 to bolster their cause. It reflects the problem that Benhabib points out—we do not know how to handle the enemy—or possible enemy—among us. We can only keep him out, or watch him more closely when he is here. But to distinguish the lawful citizens and foreign-born residents from those who do not have such authorization would be to markedly alter the balance between freedom and control. Again, terrorism challenges liberalism.

COMPETING NARRATIVES

In the preceding chapters of this volume, the authors elaborate on the factors that have facilitated, exacerbated, dramatized, and avenged the events of September 11. But as Marc Ross explains in the first chapter of this section, these factors are at play only in the context of the stories that are told. The way that we recount events—even such seemingly unassailable tragedies as September 11—depends deeply on the world we inhabit as we witness them. What September 11 was to a New Yorker is not exactly what it was to a poor Muslim on the streets of Jakarta. More generally, the value of what the United States does in/to the world depends on where one stands.

Although we may agree on the simple facts, we often construct narratives attributing motives and implications very different from those whose perspectives derive from other situations in the world. This section of the book offers some attempts to examine these divides in perspective.

After 9/11 many Americans repeated a perhaps naïve question: "Why do they hate us?" There was apparently a national expectation to be loved. But the question did also call for a deeper look at America's symbolic as well as material place in the world. Rajeev Bhargava and Immanuel Wallerstein take up this question. Bhargava writes from a non-Western perspective about September 11, with sympathy for the individuals lost in a horrific event. But he also notes a collective dimension of resentment toward the U.S. found in a commonly expressed satisfaction that even the mighty are sometimes humbled. From within the U.S., Wallerstein looks critically at America's view of itself, seeing in the twin towers a metaphor for our unlimited aspirations, and yet asking also what that means about American power in the world and how America will respond to a possibly declining hegemony. Nilüfer Göle argues for capturing these events and holding them still before proceeding. Her snapshots are taken mostly from within the Muslim Middle East; they are personal, but also help us locate how perspectives come to differ.

These conflicting perspectives are not confined to North–South and the "clash of civilizations" between Islam and the West. Nor are they so stark as we might think. As Rajeev Bhargava argues, to think at the level of the individual— the victim in the tower—versus the collective—U.S. actions in the world—can itself muddle the moral verdict. Further, if you stand in South Asia and feel that these events confirm your instinct that you do not count, but you are among the academic elite, you need only look around to find those who do not count to you. In Afghanistan, those who may not have counted are the women. As Saba Gul Khattak elaborates, war is a very male activity, and what women take from it is not at all what men may take from it. In the widespread displacement of Afghan refugees from their homes, Khattak finds voices of women for whom September 11, or the twin towers, or the Pentagon, "are as remote from their lives as Mars," even as their lives are intimately caught up with the competing narratives these terms evoke.

Marita Sturken reflects on the memorialization of the victims of September 11 in New York in the final essay of the volume. This process, necessarily private and public, individual and collective, will shape how these events resonate into the future. While Sturken recognizes that memorializing is centrally about grieving for the dead, she also reminds us of the importance of not "smoothing over" the search for meaning, or trying to bring closure to an event that is riven with conflict.

As with memorialization, our readings of September 11 necessarily depend on both the very singular, particular experience we have of that day and the broader contexts and ideas we carry with us. They depend on how we connect to the personal stories of victims and the loss felt by families, and how we commit to building a better society and achieving greater security. The terrorist attacks have stimulated public soul-searching. Both the attacks and responses to them have raised a host of questions about social organization, basic social institutions, and how people mobilize amid crises. This book offers insight into these questions and others. We offer it in hope that it will encourage deeper thinking and more determined search and eventually better answers.

We dedicate it to the grandchildren of all who died September 11 and after, not just in New York or Washington or Pennsylvania but around the world, with wishes that they will see less of sadness and carnage than their grandparents.

—C. C., P. P., A. T.

PART I

ISLAMIC RADICALISM

1. RELIGIOUS TERROR AND GLOBAL WAR

MARK JUERGENSMEYER

Though the horrific images of the aerial assaults on the World Trade Center and the Pentagon on September 11, 2001 were shocking, the headlines of American newspapers on September 12 contained another surprise: how quickly the rhetoric of warfare entered into public consciousness. "The world at war," pronounced one headline. "The first war of the twenty-first century," President George W. Bush proclaimed. The September 11, 2001 assaults were in fact the most spectacular of a decade-long series of attempts by Osama bin Laden's Al Qaeda network to bring the rest of the world into his view of global war. An earlier, less devastating attack on the World Trade Center in 1993 received scarcely a shrug from the American populace. But in 2001 he was more successful, both in the enormity of the event and in the change in America's mindset that it created.

Yet even though it seemed palpably to be an act of war, it was not clear what kind of war it was. The instant comparisons to Pearl Harbor seemed forced. The Japanese attack that signaled America's entry into World War II was, after all, the military act of a sovereign state. Osama bin Laden's Al Qaeda network was essentially a rogue band of transnational activists based in distant caves but spread throughout the world. What united them was neither a state-centered organization nor a political ideology, but the ties of a certain form of politicized religion and the riveting image of an evil secular foe.

The Al Qaeda network has not been alone in the religious assault on the secular state. In the last fifteen years of the post–Cold War world, religion seems to have been connected with violence everywhere: from the World Trade Center bombings to suicide attacks in Israel and Palestine; assassinations in India, Israel, Egypt, and Algeria; nerve gas in the Tokyo subways; abortion clinic killings in Florida; and the bombing of Oklahoma City's federal building. What unites these disparate acts of violence is their perpetrators' hatred of the global reach of the modern secular state.

Thus in many ways the September 11 attacks were part of a global confrontation. In the minds of many on both sides this confrontation is increasingly viewed as a war—though the enemies in this engagement are less like the axis of powers engaged in World War II than the ideological foes of the Cold War.[1] Like the old Cold War, the confrontation between these new forms of culture-based politics and the secular state is global in its scope, binary in its opposition, occasionally violent, and essentially a difference of ideologies; and, like the old Cold War, each side tends to stereotype the other. The image of war mobilizes the animosities of both sides. The major differences between the old Cold War and the new one is that the present war is in a sense imaginary—it entails very little state support—and the various forms of religious opposition are scarcely united. Yet when they do lash out in acts of terrorism, as September 11 demonstrated, the results can be as awesome as they are destructive.

THE ROLE OF RELIGION

What is odd about this new global war is not only the difficulty in defining it and the non-state, transnational character of the opposition, but also the opponents' ascription to ideologies based on religion. The tradition of secular politics from the time of the Enlightenment has comfortably ignored religion, marginalized its role in public life, and frequently co-opted it for its own civil religion of public religiosity. No one in the secular world could have predicted that the first confrontations of the twenty-first century would involve, of all things, religion—secularism's old, long-banished foe.

Religious activists are puzzling anomalies in the secular world. Most religious people and their organizations are either firmly supportive of the secular state or quiescently uninterested in it. Osama bin Laden's Al Qaeda network, like most of the new religious activists, comprises a small group at the extreme end of a hostile subculture that itself is a small minority within the larger world of their religious cultures. Osama bin Laden is no more representative of Islam than Timothy McVeigh is of Christianity, or Japan's Shoko Asahara is of Buddhism.

Still, one cannot deny that the ideals and ideas of activists like bin Laden are authentically and thoroughly religious and could conceivably become popular among their religious compatriots. The authority of religion has given bin Laden's cadres the moral legitimacy of employing violence in their assault on the very symbol of global economic power. It has also provided the metaphor of cosmic war, an image of spiritual struggle that every religion has within its repository of symbols—the fight between good and bad, truth and evil. In this sense, then, the attack on the World Trade Center was very religious. It was meant to be catastrophic, an act of biblical proportions.

Though the World Trade Center assault and many other recent acts of religious terrorism have no obvious military goal, they are meant to make a powerful impact on the public consciousness. These are acts meant for television. They are a kind of perverse performance of power meant to ennoble the perpetrators' views of the world and to draw us into their notions of cosmic war. In my comparative study of cases of religious terrorism around the world I have found a strikingly familiar pattern.[2] In all of these cases, concepts of cosmic war are accompanied by strong claims of moral justification and an enduring absolutism that transforms worldly struggles into sacred battles. It is not so much that religion has become politicized, but that politics have become religionized. Worldly struggles have been lifted into the high proscenium of sacred battle.

This is what makes religious warfare so difficult to combat. Its enemies have become satanized—one cannot negotiate with them or easily compromise. The rewards for those who fight for the cause are transtemporal, and the time lines of their struggles are vast. Most social and political struggles look for conclusions within the lifetimes of their participants, but religious struggles can take generations to succeed. When I pointed out to political leaders of the Hamas movement in Palestine that Israel's military force was such that a Palestinian military effort could never succeed, I was told that "Palestine was occupied before, for two hundred years." The Hamas official assured me that he and his Palestinian comrades "can wait again—at least that long," for the struggles of God can endure for eons.[3] Ultimately, however, they knew they would succeed.

Insofar as the U.S. public and its leaders embraced the image of war following the September 11 attacks, America's view of this war was also prone to religionization. "God Bless America" became the country's unofficial national anthem. President George W. Bush spoke of the defense of America's "righteous cause," and the "absolute evil" of its enemies. Still, the U.S. military engagement in the months following September 11 was primarily a secular commitment to a definable goal and largely restricted to limited objectives in which civil liberties and moral rules of engagement, for the most part, still applied.

In purely religious battles, waged in divine time and with heaven's rewards, there is no need to compromise one's goals. There is no need, also, to contend with society's laws and limitations when one is obeying a higher authority. In spiritualizing violence, therefore, religion gives the resources of violence a remarkable power.

Ironically, the reverse is also true: Terrorism can give religion power. Although sporadic acts of terrorism do not lead to the establishment of new religious states, they make the political potency of religious ideology impossible to ignore. The first wave of religious activism, from the Islamic revolution in Iran in 1978 to the emergence of Hamas during the Palestine *intifada* in the early 1990s, was focused on religious nationalism and the vision of individual religious states. Increasingly, religious activism has a more global vision. Such disparate groups as the Christian militia, the Japanese Aum Shinrikyo, and the Al Qaeda network all target what their supporters regard as a repressive and secular form of global culture and control.

GLOBAL WAR

The September 11 attack and many other recent acts of religious terrorism are skirmishes in what their perpetrators conceive to be a global war. This battle is global in three senses. The choices of targets have often been transnational. The World Trade Center employees killed in the September 11 assault were citizens of 86 nations. The network of perpetrators was also transnational: The Al Qaeda network, which was implicated in the attack—though consisting mostly of Saudis—is also actively supported by Pakistanis, Egyptians, Palestinians, Sudanese, Algerians, Indonesians, Malaysians, Filipinos, and a smattering of British, French, Germans, Spanish, and Americans. The incident was global in its impact, in large part because of the worldwide and instantaneous coverage of transnational news media. This has been terrorism meant not only for television but for global news networks such as CNN—and especially for Al Jazeera, the Qatar-based news channel that beams its talk-show format throughout the Middle East.

Increasingly terrorism has been performed for a televised audience around the world. In that sense it has been as real a global event as the transnational activities of the global economy, and as vivid as the globalized forms of entertainment and information that crowd satellite television channels and the Internet. Ironically, terrorism has become a more efficient global force than the organized political efforts to control and contain it. No single entity, including the United Nations, possesses the military capability and intelligence-gathering capacities to deal with worldwide terrorism. Instead, consortia of nations have been formed to handle the information-sharing and joint operations required to deal with forces of violence on an international scale.

This global dimension of terrorism's organization and audience, and the transnational responses to it, give special significance to the understanding of terrorism as a public performance of violence—as a social event that has both real and symbolic aspects. As the late French sociologist Pierre Bourdieu observed, our public life is shaped by symbols as much as by institutions. For this reason, symbolic acts—the "rites of institution"—help to demarcate public space and indicate what is meaningful in the social world.[4] In a striking imitation of such rites, terrorism has provided its own dramatic events. These rites of violence have signaled alternative views of public reality: not just a single society in transition, but a world challenged by strident religious visions of transforming change.

What is extraordinary about such performances is their success in bringing the rest of the world into their world view—specifically their view of the world at war. War is an enticing conceptual construct, an all-embracing view of the world that contains much more than the notion of forceful contestation. It points to a dichotomous opposition on an absolute scale. War suggests an all-or-nothing struggle against an enemy who is determined to destroy. No compromise is deemed possible. The very existence of the opponent is a threat, and until the enemy is either crushed or contained, one's own existence cannot be secure. What is striking about a martial attitude is the certainty of one's position and the willingness to defend it, or impose it on others, to the end.

Such certitude may be regarded as noble by those whose sympathies lie with it and dangerous by those who do not agree with it. But either way it is not civil. One of the first rules of conflict resolution is the willingness to accept the notion that there are flaws on one's own side as well as on the opponent's side. This is the sensible stand to take if one's goal is to get along with others and avoid violence.[5] But often that is not the goal. In fact, a warring attitude implies that the one who holds it no longer thinks compromise is possible or—just as likely—does not want an accommodating solution to the conflict in the first place. In fact, if one's goals are not harmony but the empowerment that comes with using violence, it is in one's interest to be in a state of war. In such cases, war is not only the context for violence but also the excuse for it. This reasoning holds true even if the worldly issues that are at heart in the dispute do not seem to warrant such an extreme and ferocious position.

This logic may explain why acts of terrorism seem so puzzling to people outside the movements that perpetrate them and entirely understandable to those within them. The absolutism of war makes compromise unlikely, and those who suggest a negotiated settlement can be excoriated as the enemy. In the Palestinian situation, the extreme religious positions on both sides loathed the carefully negotiated compromise once promised by Israel's Yitzhak Rabin and Palestine's Yasir Arafat. "There is no such thing as coexistence," a Jewish activist in Israel told me, explaining that there was a biblical requirement for Jews to possess and live on biblical land. This was why he despised the Oslo and Wye River accords and regarded Rabin and Benjamin Netanyahu as treasonous for signing them.[6] Hamas leaders told me essentially the same thing about the necessity for Arab Muslims to occupy what they regarded as their homeland. They expressed anger toward their own secular leader—Yasir Arafat—for having entered into what both Jewish and Muslim extremists regarded as a dangerous and futile path toward an accommodation deemed by them to be impossible.[7] The extremes on both sides preferred war over peace.

One of the reasons why a state of war is often preferable to peace is that it gives moral justification for acts of violence. Violence, in turn, offers the illusion of power. The idea of warfare implies more than an attitude; ultimately it is a world view and an assertion of identity. To live in a state of war is to live in a world in which individuals know who they are, why they have suffered, by whose hand they have been humiliated, and at what expense they have persevered. It provides cosmology, history, and eschatology, and offers the reins of political control. Perhaps most importantly, it holds out the hope of victory and the means to achieve it. In the images of religious war this victorious triumph is a grand moment of social and personal transformation, transcending all worldly limitations. One does not easily abandon such expectations. To be without such images of war is almost to be without hope itself.

The idea of warfare has had an eerie and intimate relationship with religion. History has been studded with overtly religious conflicts such as the Crusades, the Muslim conquests, and the Wars of Religion that dominated the politics of France in the sixteenth century. These have usually been characterized as wars in the name of religion, rather than wars conducted in a religious way. However, the historian Natalie Zemon Davis has uncovered what she calls "rites of violence" in her study of religious riots in sixteenth-century France. These constituted "a repertory of actions, derived from the Bible, from the liturgy, from the action of political authority, or from the traditions of popular folk practices, intended to purify the religious community and humiliate the enemy and thus make him less harmful." Davis observed that the violence was "aimed at defined targets and selected from a repertory of traditional punishments and forms of destruction."[8] According to Davis, "even the extreme ways of defiling corpses—dragging bodies through the streets and throwing them to the dogs, dismembering genitalia and selling them in mock commerce—and desecrating religious objects," had what she called "perverse connections" with religious concepts of pollution and purification, heresy and blasphemy.[9]

Anthropologist Stanley Tambiah showed how the same "rites of violence" were present in the religious riots of South Asia.[10] In some instances innocent bystanders would be snatched up by a crowd and burned alive. According to Tambiah, these horrifying murders of defenseless and terrified victims were done in a ritual manner, in "mock imitation of both the self-immolation of conscientious objectors and the terminal rite of cremation."[11] In a macabre way, the riotous battles described by Davis and Tambiah were religious events. But given the prominence of the rhetoric of warfare in religious vocabulary, both traditional and modern, one could also turn this point around and say that religious events often involve the invocation of violence. One could argue that the task of creating a vicarious experience of warfare—albeit one usually imagined as residing on a spiritual plane—is one of the main businesses of religion.

Virtually all cultural traditions have contained martial metaphors in their symbols, myths, and legendary histories. Ideas such as the Salvation Army in Christianity or a Dal Khalsa ("army of the faithful") in Sikhism characterize disciplined religious organizations. Images of spiritual warfare are even more common. The Muslim notion of jihad is the most notable example, but even in Buddhist legends great wars abound. In Sri Lankan culture, for instance, virtually canonical status is accorded the legendary history recorded in the Pali Chronicles, the Dipavamsa and the Mahavamsa, that related the triumphs of battles waged by Buddhist kings. In India, warfare contributes to the grandeur of the great epics, the Ramayana and the Mahabharata, which are tales of seemingly unending conflict and military intrigue. More than the Vedic rituals, these martial epics defined subsequent Hindu culture. Whole books of the Hebrew Bible are devoted to the military exploits of great kings, their contests related in gory detail. Though the New Testament does not take up the battle cry, the later history of the Church does, supplying Christianity with a bloody record of crusades and religious wars.

What is unusual about contemporary acts of terrorism is that the vision of religious war is not confined to history and symbols but is a contemporary reality. Politics have become religionized as struggles in the real world become baptized with the absolutism of religious fervor. Acts of violence are conducted not so much to wage a military campaign as to demonstrate the reality of the war to a unknowing public. In such cases, the message is the medium in which it is sent: The bombings provide moments of chaos, warfare, and victimage that the perpetrators want a slumbering society to experience. These acts make the point that war is at hand by providing a bloody scene of battle in one's own quiet neighborhoods and everyday urban streets.

What is buttressed in these acts of symbolic empowerment is not only the credibility of their cause. These acts, for the moment, place the perpetrators on a par with the leaders of governments that they target, and equate the legitimacy of the secular state with their own vision of religious social order. Through the currency of violence they draw attention to what they believe to be significant and true about the social arena around them. In the language of Bourdieu they create a perverse "habitus," a dark world of social reality, forcing everyone to take stock of their perception of the world.[12] Thus the very act of performing violence in public is a political act: It announces that the power of the group is equal or superior to that of the state. In most cases this is exactly the message that the group wants to convey.

The establishment of political rule based on religious law has been the primary aim of many Muslim groups. Members of Hamas regarded this as the main difference between their organization and the secular ideology of Fateh and other groups associated with Yasir Arafat's Palestinian Authority. A similar argument has been made by activists associated with Egyptian groups. Mahmud Abouhalima told me that President Hosni Mubarak could not be a true Muslim because he did not make *shari'a*—Islamic law—the law of the land.[13] A cleric in Cairo's conservative Al-Azhar theological school told me he resented his government's preference for Western law. "Why should we obey Western laws when Muslim laws are better?" he asked me.[14] It is this position that has been assumed by many Muslim activists: that Western political institutions and the ideology on which they were based should be banished from their territories. They want to rebuild their societies on Islamic foundations.

Yet the images of political order that these activists yearn to create have been deliberately fuzzy. Sometimes the goals have appeared to be democratic, sometimes socialist, sometimes a sort of religious oligarchy. Sometimes the goals have been nationalist, at other times international in scope. A Hamas leader told me that what distinguished his organization from Yasir Arafat's Fateh movement was that Fateh was waging a "national struggle" whereas Hamas was "transnational."[15] The Al Qaeda network of Osama bin Laden has been especially striking in its global reach and curious in its lack of a specific political program. It is as if the idea of global struggle is sufficient, its own reward. Although it is clear who the supporters of Al Qaeda hate, nowhere have they given a design for a political entity—Islamic or otherwise—that could actually administrate the results of a victory over American and secular rule and the emergence of a religious revolution, should they achieve it.

My conclusion is that acts of religious terrorism are largely devices for symbolic empowerment in wars that cannot be won and for goals that cannot be achieved. The very absence of thought about what the activists would do if they were victorious is sufficient indication that they do not expect to win, nor perhaps even want to do so. They illustrate a peculiar corollary to the advice of the French theorist, Frantz Fanon, during Algeria's war of independence some years ago, when he advocated terrorism as the Algerians' mobilizing weapon. Fanon reasoned that even a small display of violence could have immense symbolic power by jolting the masses into an awareness of their own potency.[16] What Fanon did not realize was that for some activist groups the awareness of their potency would be all that they desired.

Yet these acts of symbolic empowerment have had an effect beyond whatever personal satisfaction and feelings of potency they have imparted to those who supported and conducted them. The very act of killing on behalf of a moral code is a political statement. Such acts break the state's monopoly on morally sanctioned killing. By putting the right to take life in their own hands, the perpetrators of religious violence have made a daring claim of power on behalf of the powerless, a basis of legitimacy for public order other than that upon which the secular state relies. In doing so, they have demonstrated to everyone how fragile public order actually is, and how fickle can be the populace's assent to the moral authority of power.

EMPOWERING RELIGION

Such religious warfare not only gives individuals who have engaged in it the illusion of empowerment, but it also gives religious organizations and ideas a public attention and importance that they have not enjoyed for many years. In modern America and Europe, the recent warfare has given religion a prominence in public life that it has not held since before the Enlightenment, more than two centuries ago.

Although each of the violent religious movements around the world has its own distinctive culture and history, I have found that they have three things in common regarding their attitudes toward religion in society. First, they reject the compromises with liberal values and secular institutions that most mainstream religion has made, be it Christian, Muslim, Jewish, Hindu, Sikh, or Buddhist. Second, radical religious movements refuse to observe the boundaries that secular society has set around religion—keeping it private rather than allowing it to intrude into public spaces. And third, these movements try to create a new form of religiosity that rejects what they regard as weak modern substitutes for the more vibrant and demanding forms of religion that they imagine to be essential to their religion's origins.

During a prison interview, one of the men accused of bombing the World Trade Center in 1993 told me that the critical moment in his religious life came when he realized that he could not compromise his Islamic integrity with the easy vices offered by modern society. The convicted terrorist, Mahmud Abouhalima, claimed that the early part of his life was spent running away from himself. Although involved in radical Egyptian Islamic movements since his college years in Alexandria, he felt there was no place where he could settle down. He told me that the low point came when he was in Germany, trying to live the way that he imagined Europeans and Americans carried on: where the superficial comforts of sex and inebriates masked an internal emptiness and despair. Abouhalima said his return to Islam as the center of his life carried with it a renewed sense of obligation to make Islamic society truly Islamic—to "struggle against oppression and injustice" wherever it existed. What was now constant, Abouhalima said, was his family and his faith. Islam was both "a rock and a pillar of mercy." [17] But it was not the Islam of liberal, modern Muslims: They, he felt, had compromised the tough and disciplined life the faith demanded. In Abouhalima's case, he wanted his religion to be hard, not soft like the humiliating, mind-numbing comforts of secular modernity. Activists such as Abouhalima—and, for that matter, Osama bin Laden—have imagined themselves to be defenders of ancient faiths. But in fact they have created new forms of religiosity: Like many present-day religious leaders they have used the language of traditional religion in order to build bulwarks around aspects of modernity that have threatened them, and to suggest ways out of the mindless humiliation of modern life. It is vital to their image of religion, however, that it be perceived as ancient.

The need for religion—a "hard" religion as Abouhalima called it—was a response to the soft treachery they had observed in the new societies around them. The modern secular world that Abouhalima and the others inhabited was a dangerous and chaotic sea, in which religion was a harbor of calm. At a deep level of their consciousnesses they sensed their lives slipping out of control, and they felt both responsible for the disarray and a victim of it. To be abandoned by religion in such a world would mean a loss of their own individual locations and identities. In fashioning a "traditional religion" of their own making, they exposed their concerns not so much with their religious, ethnic, or national communities, but with their own personal, perilous selves.

These intimate concerns have been prompted by the perceived failures of public institutions. As Pierre Bourdieu observed, social structures never have a disembodied reality; they are always negotiated by individuals in their own strategies for maintaining self-identity and success in life. Such institutions are legitimized by the "symbolic capital" they accrue through the collective trust of many individuals.[18] When that symbolic capital is devalued, when political and religious institutions undergo what the German social philosopher Jurgen Habermas has called a "crisis of legitimacy," this devaluation of authority is experienced not only as a political problem but as an intensely personal one, as a loss of agency.[19]

It is this sense of a personal loss of power in the face of chaotic political and religious authorities that is common, and I believe critical, to Osama bin Laden's Al Qaeda group and most other movements for Christian, Muslim, Jewish, Sikh, Buddhist, and Hindu nationalism around the world. The syndrome begins with the perception that the public world has gone awry, and the suspicion that behind this social confusion lies a great spiritual and moral conflict, a cosmic battle between the forces of order and chaos, good and evil. The government—already delegitimized—is perceived to be in league with the forces of chaos and evil.

Secular government is easily labeled as the enemy of religion, because to some degree it is. By its nature, the secular state is opposed to the idea that religion should have a role in public life. From the time that modern secular nationalism emerged in the eighteenth century as a product of the European Enlightenment's political values, it did so with a distinctly antireligious, or at least anticlerical, posture. The ideas of John Locke about the origins of a civil community, and the "social contract" theories of Jean-Jacques Rousseau required very little commitment to religious belief. Although they allowed for a divine order that made the rights of humans possible, their ideas had the effect of taking religion—at least Church religion—out of public life. At the time, religious "enemies of the Enlightenment" protested religion's public demise.[20] But their views were submerged in a wave of approval for a new view of social order in which secular nationalism was thought to be virtually a natural law, universally applicable and morally right.

Post-Enlightenment modernity proclaimed the death of religion. Modernity signaled not only the demise of the Church's institutional authority and clerical control, but also the loosening of religion's ideological and intellectual grip on society. Scientific reasoning and the moral claims of the secular social contract replaced theology and the Church as the bases for truth and social identity. The result of religion's devaluation has been "a general crisis of religious belief," as Bourdieu has put it.[21]

In countering this disintegration, resurgent religious activists have proclaimed the death of secularism. They have dismissed the efforts of secular culture and its forms of nationalism to replace religion. They have challenged the notion that secular society and the modern nation-state are able to provide the moral fiber that unites national communities, or give it the ideological strength to sustain states buffeted by ethical, economic and military failures. Their message has been easy to believe and has been widely received, because the failures of the secular state have been so real.

The moral leadership of the secular state was increasingly challenged in the last decade of the twentieth century following the breakup of the Cold War and the rise of a global economy. The Cold War provided contesting models of moral politics—communism and democracy—that were replaced with a global market that weakened national sovereignty and was conspicuously devoid of political ideals. The global economy became controlled by transnational businesses accountable to no single governmental authority and with no clear ideological or moral standards of behavior. But while both Christian and Enlightenment values were left behind, transnational commerce did transport aspects of Westernized popular culture to the rest of the world. American and European music, videos, and films were beamed across national boundaries, where they threatened to obliterate local and traditional forms of artistic expression. Added to this social confusion were convulsive shifts in political power that followed the break-up of the Soviet Union and the collapse of Asian economies at the end of the twentieth century.

The public sense of insecurity that came in the wake of these cataclysmic global changes was felt not only in the societies of those nations that were economically devastated by them—especially countries in the former Soviet Union—but also in economically stronger industrialized societies. The United States, for example, saw a remarkable degree of disaffection with its political leaders and witnessed the rise of right-wing religious movements that fed on the public's perception of the inherent immorality of government.

Is the rise of religious terrorism related to these global changes? We know that some groups associated with violence in industrialized societies have had an antimodernist political agenda. At the extreme end of this religious rejection in the United States were members of the American antiabortion group Defensive Action; the Christian militia and Christian Identity movement; and isolated groups such as the Branch Davidian sect in Waco, Texas. Similar attitudes toward secular government emerged in Israel—the religious nationalist ideology of the Kach party was an extreme example—and, as the Aum Shinrikyo movement has demonstrated, in Japan. As in the United States, contentious groups within these countries were disillusioned about the ability of secular leaders to guide their countries' destinies. They identified government as the enemy.

The global shifts that have given rise to antimodernist movements have also affected less-developed nations. India's Jawaharlal Nehru, Egypt's Gamal Abdel Nasser, and Iran's Reza Shah Pahlavi once were committed to creating versions of America—or a kind of cross between America and the Soviet Union—in their own countries. But new generations of leaders no longer believe in the Westernized visions of Nehru, Nasser, or the Shah. Rather, they are eager to complete the process of decolonialization and build new, indigenous nationalisms.

When activists in Algeria who demonstrated against the crackdown against the Islamic Salvation Front in 1991 proclaimed that they were continuing the war of liberation against French colonialism, they had the ideological rather than political reach of European influence in mind. Religious activists such as the Algerian leaders, the Ayatollah Khomeini in Iran, Sheik Ahmed Yassin in Palestine, Sayyid Qutb and his disciple, Sheik Omar Abdul Rahman, in Egypt, L. K. Advani in India, and Sant Jarnail Singh Bhindranwale in India's Punjab have asserted the legitimacy of a postcolonial national identity based on tradi-tional culture.[22]

The result of this disaffection with the values of the modern West has been a "loss of faith" in the ideological form of that culture—secular nationalism, or the idea that the nation is rooted in a secular compact rather than religious or ethnic identity.[23] Although a few years ago it would have been a startling notion, the idea has now become virtually commonplace that secular nationalism is in crisis. In many parts of the world it is seen as an alien cultural construction, one closely linked with what has been called "the project of modernity."[24] In such cases, reli-gious alternatives to secular ideologies have had extraordinary appeal.

This uncertainty about what constitutes a valid basis for national identity is a political form of postmodernism. In Iran it has resulted in the rejection of a modern Western political regime and the creation of a successful religious state. Increasingly, even secular scholars in the West have recognized that religious ide-ologies might offer an alternative to modernity in the political sphere.[25] Yet, what lies beyond modernity is not necessarily a new form of political order, religious or not. In nations formerly under Soviet control, for example, the specter of the future beyond the socialist form of modernity has been one of cultural anar-chism.

The Al Qaeda network associated with Osama bin Laden takes the challenge to secularism to yet another level. The implicit attack on global economic and political systems that are leveled by religious nationalists from Algeria to Indone-sia are made explicit: America is the enemy. Moreover, it is a war waged not on a national plane but a transnational one. Their agenda is not for any specific form of religious nation-state, but an inchoate vision of a global rule of religious law. Rather than religious nationalists, transnational activists like bin Laden are guer-rilla antiglobalists.

POSTMODERN TERROR

Bin Laden and his vicious acts have a credibility in some quarters of the world be-cause of the uncertainties of this moment in global history. The fear that there will be a spiritual as well as a political collapse at modernity's center has, in many parts of the world, led to terror. Both violence and religion have appeared at times when authority is in question, since they are both ways of challenging and replacing authority. One gains its power from force and the other from its claims to ultimate order. The combination of the two in acts of religious terrorism has been a potent assertion indeed. Regardless of whether the perpetrators con-sciously intend them to be political acts, all public acts of violence have political consequences. Insofar as they have been attempts to reshape the public order, these acts have been examples of what Jose Casanova has called the increasing "deprivatization" of religion.[26] In various parts of the world where attempts have been made by defenders of religion to reclaim the center of public attention and authority, religious terrorism is often the violent face of these attempts.

The postmodern religious rebels such as those who rally to the side of Osama bin Laden are therefore neither anomalies nor anachronisms. From Algeria to Idaho, they are small but potent groups of violent activists who represent masses of potential supporters, and they exemplify currents of thinking and cultures of commitment that have risen to counter the prevailing modernism. The enemies of these groups have seemed to most people to be both benign and banal: such symbols of prosperity and authority as the World Trade Center. The logic of this kind of militant religiosity has therefore been difficult for many people to comprehend. Yet its challenge has been profound, for it has contained a fundamental critique of the world's post-Enlightenment secular culture and politics.

Acts of religious terrorism have thus been attempts to use violence to purchase public recognition of the legitimacy of this view of the world at war. Since religious authority can provide a ready-made replacement for secular leadership, it is no surprise that when secular authority has been deemed morally insufficient, the challenges to its legitimacy and the attempts to gain support for its rivals have often been based in religion. When the proponents of religion have asserted their claim to be the moral force undergirding public order, they sometimes have done so with the kind of power that even a confused society can graphically recognize: the force of terror.

What the perpetrators of such acts of terror expect—and indeed welcome—is a response as vicious as the acts themselves. By goading secular authorities into responding to terror with terror, they hope to accomplish two things. First, they want tangible evidence for their claim that the secular enemy is a monster. Second, they hope to bring to the surface the great war—a war that they have told their potential supporters was hidden, but real. When the American missiles began to fall in Afghanistan on October 7, less than a month after the September 11 attacks, the Al Qaeda forces must initially have been exhilarated, for the war they had anticipated for so long had finally arrived. Its outcome, however, likely gave them less satisfaction: Their bases were routed, their leadership demolished, and the Muslim world did not rise up in support in the numbers and enthusiasm they had expected. Yet the time line of religious warfare is long, and the remnant forces of Al Qaeda most likely still yearn for the final confrontation. They are assured that the glorious victory will ultimately be achieved, for they are certain that it is, after all, God's war, not theirs.

2. THE STRUGGLE FOR THE SOUL OF ISLAM

ROBERT W. HEFNER

Six hundred years ago the great Arab historian, Ibn Khaldun, observed that popular religion in Muslim societies tends to oscillate between moments of strict religious observance and other periods of devotional laxity. An astute observer of social life, Khaldun attributed this cultural cycle to features of ecology and social organization peculiar to the Middle East. Urban settlements across the region, he noted, are located amidst grasslands and deserts inhabited by nomads only nominally controlled by urban-based rulers. In principle, the nomads share the townspeople's faith. Tempted by the pleasures of cosmopolitan living, however, town dwellers tend over time to relax their moral guard and sink into what is, from a zealot's perspective, decadent impiety. Immunized by the spartan demands of desert living, the nomadic population is more resistant to this moral slide. The result is that nomads have the potential to serve as a reserve army if and when an Islamic reformer arises, decrying urban decadence and demanding a return to the purity of the Word. Where he can tap popular resentments in this manner, Khaldun remarked, the reformer may succeed in pressing the urban population into scriptural piety for a generation or two. Eventually, however, urban temptations lure the townspeople back to their old ways, preparing the way for yet another cycle of religious reform.[1]

Khaldun never traveled outside the Middle East, and his model was never really applicable to the entire Muslim world or all periods in Muslim history. The incidence of far-reaching religious reform was actually less common than this model implies. Equally important, the great Muslim kingdoms in Mesopotamia, Turkey, Islamic Spain, and Southeast Asia were, relatively speaking, nomad free. Yet they too experienced occasional movements for religious reform, a fact that suggests that the nomadic population was not as central to the reform process as Khaldun's remarks imply.

It is nonetheless true that, in one striking sense, Khaldun's model contains insights still relevant for understanding the Muslim world today. Its central insight lies not so much in its details on desert living, but in its twin recognition that religious contestation has long been a feature of Muslim society and that movements for Islamic reformation typically involve the efforts of pious preachers to link their religious ambitions to some disadvantaged or aggrieved social class. Where such a linkage is created, movements of Islamic reform may extend their horizons beyond the aim of heightening piety toward the goal of social and political transformation.

Directed as they were at the United States, the attacks of September 11 prompted a blizzard of speculation in the media on the nature of Islam and the scale of the "Islamic" threat. The bold-lettered title on the cover of the October 15 edition of *Newsweek* captured this concern vividly: "Why They Hate Us: The Roots of Islamic Rage and What We Can Do About It." In the aftermath of a tragedy as great as the September 11 attacks, defensive and self-centered reflections of this sort are perhaps an inevitable part of the public discussion of tragedy, especially where dialogue is conducted in mass-media as competitively commercialized as our own. Nonetheless, the Western public will have missed a great opportunity for insight into the Muslim world if it fails to appreciate that the September violence was directed not merely at the United States, but against moderate and democratic-minded Muslims around the world. The attack was but another chapter in a long struggle between moderate Muslims and Islamist hardliners for the hearts and minds of Muslim believers.

PLURALIZATION AND AUTHORITY IN MODERN ISLAM

Although, as Khaldun observed, competition between rival visions of Islam is nothing new, over the past thirty or forty years the struggle has assumed a new form. To understand why this is so, and what it implies for intra-Islamic struggles and Muslim interaction with the West, it is helpful to stand back and reflect on the nature of the Muslim world's passage into the modern era.

Although scholars of Western Christianity sometimes think of religious reformation as a single event that marked the passage from the late Middle Ages to the early modern era, Ibn Khaldun reminds us that Muslim civilization has known a long history of intermittent revival and reformation. The modern era has added several new twists, however, to the long-established pattern of Islamic reformation. First, and quite unlike the experience of Western Christianity, the modern age brought heightened competition with, and (for most but not all of the Muslim world) eventual colonization by, Western powers. Whereas the Protestant reformation in early modern Europe bore the optimistic imprint of northern Europe's growing political and economic muscle, religious reform in the modern Muslim world was haunted by Muslims' relative backwardness in matters of science, military technology, and state administration. The affront to Muslim dignity was all the greater because, by most of these measures, the central territories in the Muslim world were, until the fourteenth or fifteenth century, more advanced than their counterparts in Western Europe. Worse yet, the Europeans who enjoyed this late civilizational advantage were descendants of crusaders who had laid waste to Muslim lands just a few centuries earlier. The arrival of the Western powers, then, revived memories of another era in which the West promoted its interests in an anything-but-peaceful manner.

A second influence on modern movements of Islamic reform is that they arose at a time when the old ideal of a united pan-Islamic kingdom, or caliphate, was in precipitous decline while new, Western-inspired ideals of nations and nationalism were on the rise. Established in 1281, the Ottoman Empire was the last kingdom to inherit the mantle of the Islamic caliphate. Following the disastrous defeat of the Ottomans in the First World War, the secular nationalist founder of modern Turkey, Mustafa Kemal, abolished what remained of the institution, replacing it with the modern Republic of Turkey. Some Muslim leaders outside of Turkey protested Kemal's actions and appealed for the caliphate's restoration. A handful of individuals, like Osama bin Laden, even dream of its revival still today. However, by the mid–twentieth century, most religious scholars and Muslim leaders had accepted the legitimacy of the modern ideas of nationhood and nationalism.[2] This change in political organization meant that the Islamic reformation of the twentieth century would take place within a political order dominated by the institutions of the nation-state.

Although nationalism and nationhood dominated modern Muslim imaginings of politics, the *content* of nationalist discourse in the Muslim world has proved considerably more permeable to religious influences than has nationalism in most of the modern West. The rise of ethno-nationalisms in the nineteenth-century West took place against a backdrop of the declining influence of the Church in public life. Critics have rightly pointed out that authors like Benedict Anderson and Ernest Gellner exaggerate the secularity of modern Western nationalism.[3] After all, Irish, English, Polish, and Spanish nationalism, among others, have regularly drawn on religious symbolism to strengthen their appeals. It is nonetheless true, however, that cultural constructs of nationalism in the modern West have depended rather less significantly on religious idioms than they have secular markers of social identity like language, culture, and ethnicity. Since the end of the Second World War, the trend has become all the more pronounced, with religious symbolism becoming less salient even in countries like Britain, Ireland, and Spain, where religion had once been given pride of place among the symbols of nation.[4]

In the Muslim world at the middle of the twentieth century, it seemed for a while as if secular nationalism were about to experience a triumph as dramatic as that in the West, consigning Islamic discourse to the margins of the nation. With the notable exception of countries like Pakistan and Saudi Arabia, the dominant political discourse in most of the Muslim world at that time was nationalist, lightly inflected, at best, by references to the past glories of Islam. From the late 1960s on, however, much of the Islamic world was swept by an Islamic resurgence deeper and more socially pervasive in its penetration than any prior reformation. Although nationalist rulers in most Muslim countries managed to maintain their grip on power, many did so by altering received symbols of nationhood so as to incorporate more Islamic motifs. In a few Muslim countries, like Indonesia and Egypt most notably, nationalist rulers went even further. Having attempted but failed to suppress the resurgence, they then switched tack and promoted state-sponsored programs of conservative Islamization. These aimed to implement some of the cultural demands of the Islamic movement, while blocking any significant reformation of the political order itself.[5]

As these last examples imply, in some countries the Islamic advance was helped along by the failure of nationalist regimes to make good on their promises of national development and clean government. There were other, more complex influences on the resurgence as well, however, several of which illustrate important differences in the role played by religion in the modern West and Muslim worlds.

During the first years of the twentieth century, most Muslims still lived in agrarian societies, some of which were under Western colonial rule. In the aftermath of World War II and national independence, all this changed. Developmentalist regimes introduced new roads, markets, and mass media, along with state administrations capable of reaching into even remote areas of the countryside. Most countries also saw unprecedented urban growth. In the large and impersonal landscapes of the Muslim world's cities, ties of kinship and locality proved ineffective at providing a meaningful compass for social life. In this fast changing world, some among the populace turned to Islam for moral and practical guidance.

There was an important educational influence on the Islamic resurgence as well. After the Second World War, states across the Muslim world launched ambitious programs of school-building and mass education. Between 1950 and 1979, the populace in most countries went from being largely illiterate to being predominantly literate.[6] Enrollments in high school and universities also soared. As this change in literacy and education progressed, a mass market in inexpensive Islamic books and magazines developed. The publishing market served as a populist Islamic counterpart to the "print capitalism" the political scientist Benedict

Anderson has identified as a central element in the development of nationalism in the West.[7] Popular religious literature offered commentaries on everything from how to pray or cleanse oneself to the need for an Islamic state. Although the nationalist elite may have hoped otherwise, mass education was having a social impact anything but secularizing.

Another feature of this revolution in knowledge and authority was that the classically educated scholars (*ulama*) who long acted as stewards of Islamic tradition found themselves challenged by a new and less conventionally educated class of religious notables. Earlier, in the secular nationalist heyday of the 1950s and 1960s, traditional *ulama* were often targets of popular derision because they were identified with a backward profession of the faith. In the aftermath of the Islamic resurgence in the 1970s, all this changed, as expertise in religious matters came to be respected once again. However, much more than had been the case fifty years earlier, the guardians of religious knowledge now included people from a diverse array of social backgrounds. Many of the "new Muslim intellectuals," as they are sometimes called, had no formal training in Islamic scholarship and were barely, if at all, able to read the classical Arabic used in the Quran, Hadith, and religious commentaries. What they lacked in religious training, however, the new intellectuals made up for in topical range. Some incorporated socialist and nationalist ideals into their thinking. Others, like the famous Dr. Ali Shariati of Iran,[8] drew on French existentialism and Third-Worldist radicalism. In the wake of East Asia and Eastern Europe's democracy movements in the late 1980s, still others drew on liberal or social-democratic thought. Rather than ushering in a new and colorless uniformity, then, the Islamic resurgence of the late twentieth century brought heightened "competition and contest over both the interpretation of [religious] symbols and control of the institutions, formal and informal, that produce and sustain them."[9]

Mass education and new religious media, then, combined to shatter the monopoly of cultural authority earlier enjoyed by classically trained *ulama*. Astute observers of Muslim politics, Dale F. Eickelman and James Piscatori have emphasized that some new intellectuals' interpretations of Muslim texts can be dogmatic and authoritarian. Nonetheless, these authors believe that, over the long run, the fragmentation of religious authority in Islam is bound to create "multiple centers of power and contenders for authority" and this in turn will enhance the prospects for a broader democratization of Muslim society and culture.[10]

In support of Eickelman and Piscatori's thesis, one can note that a similar democratization of religious authority took place in American Protestantism in the early twentieth century, a period marked, like the Muslim world today, by fierce competition between fundamentalists and liberals. In the case of the United States, this pluralization of religious authority is thought to have made a significant contribution to the democratization of American public life as a whole.[11] The questions remain, however, whether this is always or necessarily the case and whether the Muslim world is really on the verge of a broader reformation of religion and politics.

A CLASH OF CULTURES

At the very least, we can say that recent developments in the Muslim world show clearly that, contrary to the claims of hard-line Islamists and some reports in the Western media, there is no uniform political disposition to the modern Islamic resurgence. Recent developments would also seem to indicate that, if Islam is to be a positive force for democratic change, further progress toward that goal will require the organization of civic organizations and movements dedicated to a democratic reorientation of Muslim politics.

Unfortunately, however, the attacks of September 11, 2001, have reminded many observers of the Muslim world that the pluralization of religion and society is itself not sufficient to guarantee this progress toward democratization. Some in the ranks of new resurgents insist that Islam knows nothing of democracy, human rights, or civil society. Confronted by the conflict between Israelis and Palestinians, the plight of Muslims in Bosnia, and other international developments, still other Muslim leaders speak in a manner reminiscent of Western policy analysts, warning of a "clash of civilizations" between Islam and the West.[12]

Some among the most militant of these anti-Western Islamists identify themselves as "Salafy." The phrase refers to a long-established movement in Islam that aims to model profession of the faith on the example of the first generation of followers of the Prophet. The variant of Islam professed in Saudi Arabia is also referred to by some of its followers as Salafy. This fact should remind us that not all variants of this puritanical Islam are fiercely anti-Western—even if, as with the Saudis, most variants see democracy as antithetical to Islam. However, in the form promoted by individuals like Osama bin Laden or the *Laskar Jihad* (jihad militias) in Indonesia, the movement is best understood as neofundamentalist or "neo-Salafy," because it emphasizes concerns not associated with earlier variants of Salafism. The most important of these is the firm belief that there is a worldwide conspiracy led by the United States and Israel to destroy Islam. The claim that there is such a conspiracy, and that the participants in that conspiracy will stop at nothing to get their way, allows neo-Salafis to portray the United

States and Israel as *kafir harbi,* or nonbelievers aiming to destroy the Muslim community. Classical Islamic law makes clear that military violence is not merely allowed against such enemies of Islam, but required.

Others among the new Muslim leadership, however, have come to see their faith as deeply consistent with ideas of democracy, civic freedom, the rule of law, and partnership with the West.[13] This stream within modern Muslim politics has been given a number of names, including neomodernism, Islamic liberalism, or, simply, democratic Islam. The precise strength and ideological emphases of democratic Islam vary in different national settings. In general, however, Muslim democrats embrace the concepts of constitutional government, a balance of state powers, civic freedoms, and a separation of religious and state authority. The civic freedoms they emphasize include three directly opposed to neofundamentalist Islamism: freedom and equality in the profession of religion, rather than the relegation of non-Muslims to the second-class status of "protected minorities" (*dhimmi*); equal citizen rights for men and women, rather than the hierarchical subordination of women to male authority; and the freedom of Muslims to dissent from established religious opinion, rather than risk banishment or death as apostates.[14]

While rejecting the claim that Islam requires an "Islamic" state, which is to say a state based on Islamic law (*shari'a*) rather than democratic constitutionalism, Muslim democrats typically do not support religion's retreat from the public realm and relegation to the status of something purely private. During the years following the Second World War, it was an article of faith in Western policy circles that modernization required that religion retire from public life so that politics could be conducted on purely secular grounds. Today most specialists of religion in the West realize that, in fact, religious traditions in countries like the United States continued to play a vital role in public life, without necessarily undermining democracy.[15] The only way believers can do so, however, is by repudiating any ambition of fusing religion and state, and instead concentrating their religious energies in civil society and the public sphere. Consistent with this Tocquevillian model of religious-minded citizenship, Muslim democrats like Abdolkarim Soroush in Iran or Nurcholish Madjid in Indonesia insist their faith is compatible with civic habits—if and when it strengthens the public's commitments to freedom, equality, and tolerance. By strengthening democratic values, religion can help to provide the social resources needed, in Robert Putnam's words, "to make democracy work."[16]

Like Judaism, Islam is a religion of divine law or *shari'a.* Over the long run, the democratic reformation of Islam will require painstaking intellectual labors of Muslim jurists and intellectuals willing and able to bring their tradition into dialogue, not just with the sources of the law, but also with the demands of the late modern world. The long-term success of this effort will in turn depend not just on the cogency of intellectual arguments, but also on a balance of powers among rival Muslim groupings in state and society.

Two recent examples from the Muslim world, Iran and Indonesia, remind us of the scale of the challenge involved in achieving just such a balance. Iran is interesting because it is the only country in the Muslim world to have gone through the full process of an Islamic revolution, the establishment of an Islamic republic, and the postrevolutionary maturation of that polity. The third of these phases has proved to be the most revealing. The Islamic Republic managed to expand higher education and create a new Muslim middle class. The election of President Khatami in May 1997 demonstrated, however, that the youth wing of this new middle class has grown deeply disaffected with the reigning conservative interpretation of Muslim politics. The children of the revolution seem more interested in the creation of a civil society with real intellectual, social, and political pluralism than they do the old shibboleths of *ulama* leadership. Architect of the revolutionary purges at the University of Teheran in the mid–1980s, Abdolkarim Soroush's evolution from Islamist militant to a courageous spokesperson for democracy and secular freedom provides just one of the many indices of this breathtaking transformation.

However, like many of his reform-minded cohorts, Soroush's personal travails in recent years remind us of the difficulties of taking the Muslim democratic ideal from intellectual aspiration to political reality. Although the elections of 1997 and 2001 showed an overwhelming majority of the population in favor of a more civil and open political system, the conservatives who control the courts, military, and presidency have effectively blocked all steps toward reform. Worse yet, regime hard-liners have actually reversed several previous reforms, such as, most notably, those affecting press freedom.[17] Strong support in civil society for a democratic and pluralist profession of Muslim politics, it seems, is not alone sufficient to overrule the dictates of well-entrenched state officials.

The Southeast Asian nation of Indonesia, the largest majority-Muslim country in the world (population 215 million) offers a similarly sobering lesson concerning the challenges of a democratic reform of Muslim politics. Indonesia is a Sunni country, vastly poorer and less educated than the Iran of 1979 or today. Nonetheless, in the final years of the Suharto* regime, a military-dominated government that ruled Indonesia from 1966 through 1998, this country created a

---

* To remain consistent with English conventions, I do not spell Suharto's name in the way he preferred: *Soeharto.*

movement for a democratic reorientation of Muslim political thinking that, after Iran, was arguably the Muslim world's most vibrant. This democracy movement succeeded in toppling President Suharto in May 1998. The movement itself was a multireligious coalition that included many Christians (9 percent of the country's population) and secular Muslims in its ranks. Among the movement's core theorists, however, was a diverse group of Muslim intellectuals interested in devising good Islamic grounds for pluralism, democracy, religious tolerance, and civil society.[18]

Although hard-nosed political observers may dismiss such efforts, it is important to remember that a key feature of Muslim politics is that political initiatives must be justified in relation to divine injunctions and religious commentaries. Indonesia in the 1990s had an efflorescence of just such thinking. Moreover, quite unlike similar efforts by Muslim intellectuals in Egypt, Morocco, or Syria, this reorientation of Muslim politics was not just the work of a few isolated intellectuals. On the contrary, the initiative showed one of the key features political theorists like Guillermo O'Donnell and Philippe Schmitter identify as vital for a successful transition from authoritarian rule: a coalitional structure linking "exemplary individuals" and intellectuals to mass-based organizations in society.[19] Measured according to its intellectual vitality and prospective mass base, Indonesia in the late 1990s was one of the most vibrant centers for new Muslim political thinking the modern world has seen.

Sadly, Indonesia's great achievement may never get the credit it deserves, because the movement for a democratic Muslim politics was quickly overtaken by events on the ground that were anything but civil or democratic. The reform coalition that toppled Suharto failed to hold itself together after the dictator was gone. The single most important reason for the coalition's collapse was that, aside from Suharto and his closest allies, most of the old regime remained in place after the president's departure. "The 'Reformation Order' which had come into being was not much more than the New Order minus the Soeharto family."[20] While continuity of this sort might lead some observers to expect that old-regime stalwarts would unite against the forces of reform, what happened in fact was not nearly so simple. Old-regime holdovers did obstruct the reform program, but they were far from united in their efforts. At both the national and local level, political elites responded to the ideological and administrative vacuum created by Suharto's departure by reaching out to groupings in society in an effort to mobilize popular support against rival elites. In some parts of the country, such as Yogyakarta and East Kalimantan, the local administration demonstrated great skill at keeping this patronage-cum-ideological competition within civil bounds. In Maluku, Central Kalimantan, and Central Sulawesi (all provinces that have seen fierce violence in the past two years), however, rival contestants resorted to mobilizing against their competitors by appealing to ethnic and religious divisions.

In several notable instances, this populist sectarianism was made worse by rival elites' reliance on another category of social actor that had come to prominence during the Suharto era: the organized gangsters known in Indonesian as *preman*. Gangsterism in the New Order had always tended to display an ideological face, in large part so as to give the organizations' activities an air of legitimacy. Whereas the dominant groups in the early New Order were nationalist, by the end of the New Order period some of the largest groups had adopted an Islamist garb. Where, as in Maluku or Central Sulawesi, rivalries among local bosses involved this flammable mixture of elite factionalism, extralegal gangsterism, and ethnoreligious tensions, the result could be deadly. The explosion of ethnoreligious violence in these provinces dealt a severe blow to the fledgling democracy movement and seemed to lend credibility to the military's claim that civilians were incapable of holding Indonesia together.

Whether in Iran, Indonesia, or other Muslim countries, one can find many examples like these of powerful elites in state and society who choose to ignore Islam's civil-democratic precedents and, instead, amplify uncivil sentiments and animosities. These examples also demonstrate how it is that violent groupings with a small base can exercise an influence vastly out of proportion with their actual representation in society, because they enjoy the support of well-endowed elites intent on obstructing political reform whatever the price.

The example recalls an insight into transitions from authoritarian rule offered by the California political sociologist Peter Evans.[21] Evans has observed that for a transition from authoritarianism to take hold, it is not enough for there to be a democratic majority or a tolerant and participatory civil society. For a transition to move forward, civil and democratic precedents in society have to be "scaled up" into governmental institutions capable of defending freedoms and promoting democratic habits in society. It is this type of democratic synergy that has proved so elusive in parts of the Muslim world where movements for a democratic reform of Muslim politics have taken hold. Rather than building on and amplifying dispositions in the Muslim community for democracy and participation, conservatives intent on holding power have often provided hard-line Islamists with an influence vastly out of proportion with their numbers in society.

CONCLUSION: A SHARED FUTURE

It is these last points that make the United States campaign against Al Qaeda so serious and weighty a mission. Throughout the Muslim world, *jihadi* radicals have attempted to use the campaign to mobilize public sentiment, not just against the United States, but against their moderate rivals as well. Even if the U.S.'s long-term military campaign should prove a technical success, the battle between these two visions of Muslim politics and society is likely to rage for some years to come.

Over the long term, an outcome favorable to a pluralist and democratic Muslim politics will require that the United States and other countries dedicate themselves to resolving once and for all the Israel–Palestine conflict. As long as this impasse remains, Muslim democrats' appeals for peace and tolerance across civilizations will receive a cool reception in many circles. A positive outcome to the struggle for Islam will also depend on the West's long-term commitment to educational and economic programs in the Muslim world. These are needed to insure that the majority of Muslims realize that they have a stake in their government, as well as in a global political order in which they are treated as valued and equal partners.

Perhaps the most important conclusion to be drawn from this brief review, however, is that there is no inevitable clash of civilizations between Islam and the West. In both the Western and Muslim worlds, politics in recent years have seen "culture wars" marked by fierce debates over the values and practices appropriate to public life. However, in both of these cases, the really decisive cultural conflict is taking place *within* each civilization's horizons, not beyond them. In the West, there is a debate raging among politicians and the public as to the nature of citizenship under conditions of growing cultural pluralism. One part of this debate concerns the question of what Islam is and what policies the West should adopt toward Muslims. This discussion has been made all the more urgent by the recognition that, with 15 million Muslims in Europe and perhaps 6 million in the United States, its outcome will influence the way in which Western publics welcome their new Muslim citizens.

There is, of course, an equally bitter clash of cultures unfolding in the Muslim world. There, ultraconservatives intent on forcing the Muslim world's diversity back into a repressive iron cage are squaring off against moderate democrats for the heart and soul of the Muslim public. If Iran and Indonesia are at all indicative, the evidence clearly suggests that higher education and economic growth work decisively to the advantage of democratic reformers. Unfortunately, poverty and political repression may have a different effect, especially where they converge with the efforts of rulers to hold on to power by promoting neoconservative Islamization.

In sum, the tragedy of September 11 provided, among many other things, an important reminder that the globalization so widespread in our age will never bring about an "end to history" or a world-wide homogenization of culture and politics. But the tragedy also made clearer the basic interests democratic Westerners share with the great majority of Muslims. People on both sides of this civilizational divide are still in an early phase of mutual familiarization. One hopes that those of us who are Americans, in particular, will not lose sight of this fact as we move beyond the events of September 11 and the campaign in Afghanistan. The lesson to keep in mind is that many Muslims saw the violence of September 11 as an attack on their hopes and aspirations as well as those of the United States. Today these same Muslims look to us with the hope and expectation that we recognize just how much we share with them a sense of common moral challenge, pluralist civility, and, above all else, humanity.

3. "TRADITIONALIST" ISLAMIC ACTIVISM: DEOBAND, TABLIGHIS, AND TALIBS

BARBARA D. METCALF

When the Afghan Taliban emerged into the international spotlight at the end of the twentieth century, no image was more central than what seemed to be their rigid and repressive control of individual behavior, justified in the name of Islam. They set standards of dress and public behavior that were particularly extreme in relation to women, limiting their movement in public space and their employment outside the home. They enforced their decrees through public corporal punishment. Their image was further damaged, particularly after the bombings of the East African American embassies in 1998, when they emerged as the "hosts" of Osama bin Laden and other "Arab Afghans" associated with him.[1]

Many commentators described the Taliban with generic, catchall phrases like "fanatic," "medieval," and "fundamentalist."[2] The Taliban identified themselves, however, as part of a Sunni school of thought that has its origins in the late–nineteenth-century colonial period of India's history. The school is named after Deoband, the small country town northeast of Delhi, where the original *madrasa* or seminary of the movement was founded in 1867. Many of the Taliban had, indeed, studied in Deobandi schools, but one spokesman for the movement in its final months went so far as to declare "Every Afghan is a Deobandi."[3] This comment may be disconcerting to those familiar with the school in its Indian environment where its *'ulama*—those learned in traditional subjects and typically addressed as "maulana"—were not directly engaged in politics and were primarily occupied in teaching and providing both practical and spiritual guidance to their followers. The comment might be disconcerting as well, moreover, since it was suggestive of a regime shaped by ideals more than reality, given, for example, the substantial *Shi'a* element in the Afghan population.

Another movement linked to Deoband came to international attention at the same time, an apolitical, quietist movement of internal grassroots missionary renewal, the Tablighi Jama'at. It gained some notoriety when it appeared that a young American who had joined the Taliban first went to Pakistan through the encouragement of a Tablighi Jama'at missionary.[4] This movement was intriguing, in part by the very fact that is was so little known, yet, with no formal organization or paid staff, sustained networks of participants that stretched around the globe.

The variety of these movements is in itself instructive. Clearly, all Islamic activism is not alike, and each of these movements deserves attention on its own. Together, however, for all their variety, these Deoband movements were, in fact, alike in one crucial regard that set them apart from other well-known Islamic movements. What they shared was an overriding emphasis on encouraging a range of ritual and personal behavioral practices linked to worship, dress, and everyday behavior. These were deemed central to *shari'a*—divinely ordained morality and practices, as understood in this case by measuring current practice against textual standards and traditions of Hanafi reasoning. The anthropologist Olivier Roy calls such movements "neo-fundamentalist" to distinguish them from what can be seen as a different set of Islamic movements, often called "Islamist."[5] Limited, as he puts it, to "mere implementation of the *shari'a*" in matters of ritual, dress, and behavior, "neo-fundamentalist" movements are distinguishable from Islamist parties primarily because, unlike them, they have neither a systematic ideology nor a global political agenda. A more precise label for them is, perhaps, "traditionalist," because of their continuity with earlier institutions, above all those associated with the seminaries and with the *'ulama* in general.

The contrasting Islamist movements include the Muslim Brothers in Egypt and other Arab countries, and the Jama'at-i Islami in the Indian subcontinent, as well as many thinkers involved in the Iranian revolution. All these movements constructed ideological systems and systematically built models for distinctive polities that challenged what they saw as the alternative systems: nationalism, capitalism, and Marxism.[6] Participants were Western educated, not seminary educated. They were engineers and others with technical training, lawyers, doctors, and university professors, and, generally speaking, they had little respect for the traditionally educated *'ulama*. These "Islamist" movements sought to "do" modernity in ways that simultaneously asserted the cultural pride of the subjects and avoided the "black" side of Western modernity. Many of the *jihad* movements that arose in Afghanistan in opposition to the Soviets were heirs of Islamist thought (although over time they also moved to define their Islamic politics primarily as encouragement of a narrow range of Islamic practices and symbols).[7] Participants in militant movements, including bin Laden's Al Qaeda, often belonged to extremist, break-away factions of Islamist parties.

What is perhaps most striking about the Deoband-type movements is the extent to which politics is an empty "box," filled expediently and pragmatically depending on what seems to work best in any given situation. Islam is often spoken of as "a complete way of life"—arguably a modernist and misleading distinction from other historical religious traditions—so that political life must be informed by Islamic principles. In fact, as these Deobandi movements illustrate, virtually any strategy is accepted that allows the goal of encouraging what is defined as core *shari'a*-based individual practice, coupled with a range of mundane goals that may or may not be explicit—from protection of life and property to social honor and political power to the dignity that comes from pious adherence to what are taken as divine commands. Indeed, these movements often work well in the context of secular regimes where they can pursue their emphasis on disseminating adherence to correct practice with relative freedom.

Secondly, the movements illustrate another important corrective. A great deal is written about modern Muslim societies being consumed with antipathy toward America, American values, and American international political activities. No one, especially after September 11, 2001 would deny that that anger exists. However, anger may well be very specific; for example, it may be directed at specific American international policies and not at American "freedom" or "values" in general. Moreover, Islamic movements like the ones discussed here may have many goals and offer a range of social, moral, and spiritual satisfactions that are positive and not merely a reactionary rejection of modernity or "the West." Quite simply, these movements may, in the end, have much less to do with "us" than is often thought. In all their complexity, the Deobandi movements serve as an example of one important model of contemporary Islamic thought and action, a major example of what can be called "traditionalist" Islamic activism.

THE DARU'L-'ULUM AND "CULTURAL STRENGTHENING"

The origin of the Deobandi school of thought is literally a school, a *madrasa* or seminary, founded in the late nineteenth century at the height of colonial rule in the Delhi region of northern India.[8] Indeed, the key institution of the movement would prove to be the seminary. The *madrasa* does not appear to have been a major institution in the precolonial period. Instead, those who wished to be specialists in the great classic disciplines studied through Arabic—Qur'an, Qur'anic recitation and interpretation, *hadith,* jurisprudential reasoning based on these holy sources, and ancillary sciences like logic, rhetoric, and grammar—would sit at the feet of one or more teachers, traveling often from place to place, seeking not a degree but a certificate of completion of particular books and studies. The modern *madrasa,* in contrast, as a formal institution, organized by classes, offering a sequential curriculum, staffed by a paid faculty, and supported by charitable campaigns, was a product of the colonial period and the result of familiarity with European educational institutions. The founders of the school gained support by utilizing all manner of new technologies—from printing presses to the post office to railroads—as they turned from reliance on increasingly constrained princely patronage to popularly based contributions. Deoband spun off some two dozen other seminaries across the subcontinent by the end of the nineteenth century.[9]

Boys who came to the school were provided their basic necessities. They lived modestly and were expected to adhere to a serious schedule of discipline. They did not learn English or other "modern" subjects. They did use Urdu as a lingua franca, enhancing links among students from Bengal to Central Asia to the south. The 'ulama who founded this school were above all specialists in prophetic *hadith*, the narratives which constitute the Prophet Muhammad's sayings and practices and which serve either directly or analogously to guide every aspect of moral behavior. Their lives were meant to embody their teachings. Through the giving of *fatawa*, they responded to inquiries with advisory opinions to guide their followers as well. By the end of the nineteenth century, Deoband formalized the position of a chief *mufti* at the school. Increasingly, the Deobandi *fatawa*, like the *fatawa* of other groups, were disseminated through print. *Fatawa* were judgments, attempts to fit sanctioned precedent to present circumstances, and it was well accepted that there could be differences of opinion about what was correct. Islamic law at its core is not rigid but profoundly contextual.

Focus on *hadith* was not only central to the desire to live in external conformity to certain behavioral patterns. It was also a route to cultivating spiritual relationship through practice, love and devotion to the Prophet Muhammad and, through the bonds of Sufism, to those guides and elders who were his heirs in chains of initiation that stretched back through time. Many of the teachers at Deoband shared Sufi bonds, and many students sought initiation into the charisma-filled relationship of discipleship. The Deobandis cherished stories about the Sufis. They practiced the disciplines and meditations that opened them to what was typically imagined as a relationship that developed from one focused on their teacher, to one engaged with the Prophet, and, ultimately, with the Divine. The bonds among students and teachers in this largely male world were profound and enduring, based on shared experience, commitments, and affection.

The 'ulama as a class were new in the modern period, much as the *madrasas* that produced them were. There of course had been learned people in Mughal times, but the emergence of a distinctive class, one that over time became professionalized (for example with "degrees" recognized by state authorities), was very new. The role of the 'ulama was distinctive as well. Instead of being trained, as the learned had been in the past, for specific state functions in such areas as the judiciary, these scholars went out to take up positions as teachers themselves, writers, debaters with rival Muslims and non-Muslims, publishers in the expanding vernacular marketplace, prayer leaders, and guardians at mosques and shrines.

The Deobandis were "reformists" in a way that, with broad strokes, was shared across a whole range of Muslim, Sikh, and Hindu movements in the colonial period. Characteristic were movements that recognized a lack of worldly power and looked to earlier periods or pristine texts as a source of cultural pride and a possible roadmap to resurgence. Armed with their studies of *hadith*, the Deobandis, for example, deplored a range of customary celebrations and practices, including what they regarded as excesses at saints' tombs, elaborate life-cycle celebrations, and practices attributed to the influence of the *Shi'a*.

There were rival Islamic reformist schools in the quest for true Islamic practice. One group, the Ahl-i Hadith, for example, in their extreme opposition to such practices as visiting the Prophet's grave, rivaled that of the Arabians typically labeled "Wahhabi." The Wahhabis were followers of an iconoclastic late eighteenth century reform movement associated with tribal unification who were to find renewed vigor in internal political competition within Arabia in the 1920s.[10] From colonial times until today, it is worth noting, the label "Wahhabi" is often used to discredit any reformist or politically active Islamic group.

Another group that emerged in these same years was popularly known as "Barelvi," and although engaged in the same process of measuring current practice against *hadith*, was more open to many customary practices. They called the others "Wahhabi." These orientations—"Deobandi," "Barelvi" or "Ahl-i Hadith"— would come to define sectarian divisions among Sunni Muslims of South Asian background to the present. Thus, *'ulama*, mosques, and a wide range of political, educational, and missionary movements were known by these labels at the end of the twentieth century, both within the South Asian countries of India, Pakistan, and Bangladesh, as well as in places like Britain, where South Asian populations settled.[11] Beginning in the colonial era, *'ulama* competed in public life to show themselves as the spokesmen or defenders of "Islam" to their fellow Muslims. This was a new understanding of Islam, as a corporate identity in competition with others, and it created a new role in public life for religious leaders.

That role in the colonial period was not overtly political. The brutal repression of the so-called Mutiny of 1857 against the British had fallen very hard on north Indian Muslims. In the aftermath, the *'ulama*, not surprisingly, adopted a stance of apolitical quietism. As the Indian nationalist movement became a mass movement after World War I, the Deobandi leadership did something of an about-face. They were never a political party as such, but, organized as the Association of the 'Ulama of India (Jamiat 'Ulama-i Hind), they threw in their lot with Gandhi and the Indian National Congress in opposition to British rule. Deobandi histories written before 1920 insisted that the *'ulama* did not participate in the anticolonial rebellion of 1857; those written after, give "freedom-fighters" pride of place. Like much of the orthodox Jewish leadership in the case of the Zionist movement, most Deobandis opposed the creation of what in 1947 would become the independent state of Pakistan—a separate state for Muslims to be led by a Westernized, secular leadership.[12] They preferred operating in an officially secular context, apart from the government, in pursuit of their own goals.

Despite a serious dispute over control of the institution in the early 1980s, Deoband at the end of the twentieth century continued to thrive, with more than 3,000 students enrolled, although in the mid-1990s the government of India terminated visas that allowed foreign students to enroll. The seminary's web page displays a monumental marble mosque, still being built and intended to accommodate more than 30,000 worshippers. Links provide further information in English, Hindi, Arabic, and Urdu.[13] Visitors to the school reported remarkable continuity in the content and mode of teaching characteristics of the school,[14] and the web page itself stresses its enduring role: the training "of Ulama, Shaikhs, traditionists, jurisconsults, authors and experts." Its network of schools, moreover, are "stars of this very solar system by the light of which every nook and corner of the religious and academic life of the Muslims of the sub-continent is radiant." Among these, presumably would be the humble Deobandi *madrasas* along the Pakistan-Afghan frontier and in southern Afghanistan, which were the original Taliban base.[15] But within India at least, the *'ulama* of Deoband continued their preindependence pattern: They did not become a political party and they justified political cooperation with non-Muslims as the best way to protect Muslim interests. For "millions of Muslim families . . . ," the website writes, "[their] inferiority complex was removed. . . ."

TABLIGHI JAMA'AT

The Tablighi Jama'at was an offshoot of the Deoband movement. In some ways, it represented an intensification of the original Deobandi commitment to individual regeneration apart from any explicit political program. All reform movements strike some balance between looking to individual regeneration on the one hand and intervention from above on the other. The Tablighis put their weight wholly at the end of reshaping individual lives. They were similar in this regard to an organization like Alcoholics Anonymous—to pick a familiar example which began at about the same period—in its rejection of progressive-era government politics in favor of individual bootstraps. Like AA, the heart of Tablighi Jama'at strategy was the belief that the best way to learn is to teach and encourage others.

Always closely tied to men with traditional learning and the holiness of Sufis, Tablighi Jama'at nonetheless took its impetus from a desire to move dissemination of Islamic teachings away from the *madrasa,* the heart of Deobandi activity, toward inviting "lay" Muslims, high and low, learned and illiterate, to share the obligation of enjoining others to faithful practice. It also differed from the original movement because it eschewed debate with other Muslims over jurisprudential niceties and resultant details of practice. The movement began in the late 1920s when Maulana Muhammad Ilyas Kandhlawi (d. 1944), whose family had long associations with Deoband and its sister school in Saharanpur, Mazaahiru'l-'Ulum, sought a way to reach nominally Muslim peasants who were being targeted by a Hindu conversion movement.

Maulana Ilyas's efforts took place in an atmosphere of religious violence and the beginnings of mass political organization. His strategy was to persuade Muslims that they themselves, however little book learning they had, could go out in groups, approaching even the *'ulama,* to remind them to fulfill their fundamental ritual obligations. Participants were assured of divine blessing for this effort, and they understood that through the experiences of moving outside their normal everyday enmeshments and pressures, in the company of like minded people bent on spending their time together in scrupulous adherence to Islamic behavior, they themselves would emerge with new accomplishments, dignity, and spiritual blessing. Tablighis not only eschewed debate, but also emulated cherished stories, recalling prophetic *hadith* of withdrawing from any physical attack, an experience mission groups periodically encountered. No word resonates more in Tablighi reports of their experiences than *sukun,* the "peace" they experience as a foretaste of the paradise they believe their efforts (*jihad*), in this path of Allah, help merit.

A pattern emerged of calling participants to spend one night a week, one weekend a month, 40 continuous days a year, and ultimately 120 days at least once in their lives engaged in *tabligh* missions. Women would work among other women or travel, occasionally, with their menfolk on longer tours.[16] Although Tablighis in principle preferred to use any mosque as their base while traveling, over time specific mosques throughout the world have come to be known as "Tablighi mosques." Periodic convocations also came to be held. With no formal bureaucracy or membership records, it is hard to calculate the number of participants over time, but at the end of the twentieth century, annual meetings of perhaps two million people would congregate for three-day meetings in Raiwind, Pakistan and Tungi, Bangladesh; large regional meetings were regularly held in India; and other convocations took place in North America and Europe, for example in Dewsbury, the site of a major seminary associated with Tablighi activities in the north of England. These convocations were considered moments of intense blessings as well as occasions to organize for tours. They also gave evidence of the vast numbers touched by the movement.

Even though there are publications specific to the movement, above all those associated with Maulana Muhammad Zakariyya Kandhlawi (d. 1982) of the Mazaahiru'l-'Ulum *madrasa* at Saharanpur, the stress in the movement was not at all on book learning but rather on face-to-face, or "heart to heart," communication.[17] Their cherished books included topically arranged prophetic traditions, used as a stimulus to everyday behavior. In invoking and embodying those traditions, participants felt themselves part of dense networks of Muslims, both dead and alive, and aspired to relive the Prophet's own time when he too was part of a faithful few among a population sunk in ignorance. Participation thus gave meaning and purpose to everyday life. It is important to see that participation in such a movement, often explained as a response to the failure of the corrupt, underdeveloped, or alienating societies in which Muslims perhaps find themselves, in fact offered a positive, modern solution to people who were geographically and socially mobile. Participants in principle made a "lifestyle" choice; they found a stance of cultural dignity; they opted for a highly disciplined life of sacrifice; they found a moral community of mutual acceptance and purpose. That community would be reinvented and reformed in the course of missions, and replaced if participants themselves relocated. Other contemporary Islamic movements of the *'ulama* or, indeed, of Sufi cults, provided many of the same satisfactions.

As noted above, the original Deobandis were both *'ulama* and Sufis, offering "a composite" form of religious leadership. Indeed Pnina Werbner has recently argued that the fact that Muslims in South Asia (in contrast to those in other parts of the Muslim world) have not had to choose between Sufism and a learned, often reformist, leadership in the modern period accounts for the vitality of Sufism and, indeed, for the continued role of the *'ulama*.[18] Tablighis continued to offer the *'ulama* a respected role. The place of Sufism was more complex. Although what were seen as deviant customs around holy men were discouraged, Sufism in no sense disappeared. Indeed, among Tablighis, the holiness associated with the Sufi *pir* was in many ways defused into the charismatic body of the *jama'at* so that the missionary group itself became a channel for divine intervention. The kind of story typically told about a saint—overcoming ordeals, being blessed with divine illumination, triumphantly encountering temporal authority—was in fact often told about a group engaged in a mission. Thus, as in the initial Deoband movement and in many other Sufi and sectarian movements in modern South Asia, it was not necessary to choose between the devotional power of Sufism and the conviction of reformist imitation of prophetic teaching.

Participants in *tablighi* activities define their efforts as *jihad*. This word is, of course, widely translated as "holy war" but its root meaning is "effort" or "struggle." Following prophetic *hadith*, *jihad* may be classified as "the greater *jihad*," the inner struggle to discipline and moral purification that a person exerts upon the individual self, or as "the lesser *jihad*" of militancy or violence. For both kinds of *jihad*, the focus transcends the nation-state to a global *umma*. Tablighis use the same discourse of *jihad* as do those engaged in militant action. Their leaders are *amirs*, their outings are "sorties" or "patrols"; the merit for actions are exponentially multiplied as they are during a military campaign; a person who dies in the course of *tabligh* is a *shahiid*. Finally, the obligation to mission is not negotiable: on fulfilling it hinges nothing less than one's own ultimate fate at the Day of Judgment. Both militants and Tablighis, moreover, stress the obligation of the individual believer, not (in the case of mission) the *'ulama*, nor (in the case of militancy) the state.[19] One of the fundamental characteristics of the reform movements of the colonial period and after was a diffusion of leadership and authority, a kind of "laicization," evident here.

The key difference in the two kinds of *jihad* is, of course, that one is the *jihad* of personal purification, the other of warfare. In the words of an annual meeting organizer at Raiwind, "Islam is in the world to guide people, not to kill them. We want to show the world the correct Islam."[20] As noted above, the oft-told tales of the movement are tales of meeting opposition, even violence, and of unfailingly withdrawing from conflict—and of so gaining divine intervention and blessing.

Effectively by this focus, as in the original Deoband movement, religion, in practice, became a matter of personal, private life, separate from politics. This division, albeit untheorized, has worked well in the context of a wide variety of state structures, including the modern liberal state. The Sufi tradition, moreover, here as elsewhere, always engages with, but imagines itself morally above, worldly power. This attitude further encourages an apolitical or detached stance toward government.

THE TALIBAN AND THEIR TEACHERS,
THE JAMIAT ULEMA-I-ISLAM (JUI)

In the final years of colonial rule, a minority group among the Deobandi *'ulama* dissented from support for the secular state and the privatization of religion espoused by the Indian nationalist movement. They organized, instead, as the Jamiat Ulema-i-Islam to support the Muslim League and the demand for a separate Muslim state. In independent Pakistan after 1947 they became a minor political party led by *'ulama* and a voice in the ongoing debate over the nature of the Pakistani state. Should it be the secular state presumably intended by its founders, or a state meant to be shaped in accordance with Islam? The JUI has never had more than minute popular support, and the content of the party's programs over the years, it is probably fair to say, has been a fairly simplistic call for the primacy of Islam in public life.[21]

Like other Pakistani parties, the JUI has been subject to factional splits coalescing around personalities more than issues, and there were perhaps a half-dozen factions and reorganizations over its first half century.[22] The JUI struck alliances with any party that would win them influence. In the 1970s, for example, they allied with a Pashtun regionalist party in opposition to Bhutto's Pakistan People's Party (PPP), a party that was, in principle, socialist. In the mid-1990s, in contrast, they allied with that same PPP, now led by Bhutto's Harvard- and Oxford-educated daughter. Its *'ulama* were given to realpolitik with a vengeance and, like just about every party in Pakistan, not shielded from corruption, in this case because they were clerics. Their most famous leader at one point, for example, was referred to as "Maulana Diesel" because of his reputed involvement in fuel smuggling earlier in the 1990s.[23] When the JUI was excluded from power, its Islamic rhetoric became a language of opposition, often invoking a discourse of "democracy" and "rights."

At the same time, the *'ulama* of the JUI were engaged with the *madrasas* that furthered Deobandi teachings. From the 1980s on, the number of seminaries in Pakistan soared, used as a tool of conservative influence by the military dictator Ziaul Haq (in power from 1977 through 1988), who was, in fact, particularly sympathetic to the Deobandi approach. The seminaries were not only a resource in domestic politics but at times found themselves engaged in a kind of "surrogate" competition between Saudis and Iranis, as each patronized religious institutions likely to support their side.[24] It was in this atmosphere of politics and education that the origin of the Taliban is to be found.

The surge in the number of *madrasas* in the 1980s coincided with the influx of some three million Afghan refugees, for whose boys the *madrasas* located along the frontier frequently provided the only available education. One school in particular, the Madrasa Haqqaniya, in Akora Kathak near Peshawar, trained many of the top Taliban leaders. These sometime students (*talib;* plural, *taliban*) were shaped by many of the core Deobandi reformist causes, all of which were further encouraged by Arab volunteers in Afghanistan. These causes, as noted above, included rigorous concern with fulfilling rituals; opposition to custom-laden ceremonies like weddings and pilgrimage to shrines, along with practices associated with the Shi'a minority; and a focus on seclusion of women as a central symbol of a morally ordered society. Theirs was, according to Ahmed Rashid, a long-time observer, "an extreme form of Deobandism, which was being preached by Pakistani Islamic parties in Afghan refugee camps in Pakistan."[25] This focus on a fairly narrow range of *shari'a* law, which emphasized personal behavior and ritual, was something the Taliban shared with other Deobandi movements, even while the severity of the Taliban approach made them unique.

The Taliban emerged as a local power in Afghanistan starting in 1994 because they were able to provide protection and stability in a context of warlordism, raping, and corruption. They found ready support from elements within the Pakistani state, which welcomed an ally likely to protect trade routes to Central Asia and to provide a friendly buffer on the frontier. Similarly, the Taliban also appeared, in the mid-1990s, to serve a range of U.S. interests, above all in securing a route for an oil pipeline to the Central Asian oilfields outside Iranian control. The Taliban, on their part, like their teachers, were not ideologically driven as they determined with whom they were willing to work as allies and supporters. Indeed, the scholar Olivier Roy suggests that while they could not be manipulated easily—for example in relation to issues related to women—they were profoundly expedient when it came to securing a power base. They worked with the Pakistani state, the United States, and, anti-Shi'a or not, he argues, they would have dealt with Iran had it served their advantage.[26] The United States' interest in the Taliban shifted away from them, however, first because of what were seen as human rights abuses in relation to women, and second because the East African embassy bombings in August 1998 were linked to the presence of terrorist activists within Taliban-controlled areas, with Osama bin Laden as their most visible supporter. That alliance would, after the World Trade Center bombing of September 11, 2001, be the Taliban's undoing. Bin Laden's charisma, his access to wealth, and his networks had been invaluable to the Taliban in achieving their success, and his anti-Americanism found fertile soil among the Taliban already inclined to disapproval of "the West." There is an irony in the fact that links to him brought the Taliban down, since the Taliban's driving force at core had *not* been abhorrence of Western culture but the specific goal of prevailing within Afghanistan, and, in so doing, fostering Islamic behavior.

The Taliban, for all their extremism and the anomaly of their rise to power on the basis of dual levels of support from Pakistan and Arabs, nonetheless throw into relief an important dimension of Deobandi strategy in the school's early years and later. None of the Deobandi movements has a theoretical stance in relation to political life. They either expediently embrace the political culture of their time and place or withdraw from politics completely. For the Taliban, that meant engaging with the emerging ethnic polarities in the country and seeking allies wherever they could find them.[27] For the JUI, it meant playing the game of realpolitik in Pakistani political life. For the Deobandis in India and the Tablighi Jama'at, it meant fostering benign relations with existing regimes—necessary even in the latter case to receive permits for meetings, travel visas, and protection.

DEOBANDIS, TALIBS, AND TABLIGHIS

Deobandis, Talibs, and Tablighis demonstrate pragmatic responses to the varying environments in which they find themselves. The Taliban surely represent an exceptional case both in their rigor—criticized, for example, in relation to women even by leading *'ulama* of the JUI—and in the deal they struck with Arab extremists, who were like them in embracing Islamic rituals and social norms, but so unlike them in their vision of global *jihad*. Even the Taliban, arguably, had moderate voices, as well as pragmatism in their alliances, that might one day have made their society more acceptable in terms of international standards, had that possibility not been foreclosed by the attacks of September 11, and the American "war on terrorism."[28]

The other Deobandi movements—the JUH in India, the JUI in Pakistan, Tablighi Jama'at everywhere—although they tend to see the world in black and white, have in fact all played a largely moderate role by participating in or accepting ongoing political regimes. The recent exceptions were some students and teachers in the *madrasas* of Pakistan, as well as Pakistanis in other walks of life, who were drawn to the heady rhetoric, demonizing America and Jews on the one hand and imagining the triumph of global Islam on the other, symbolized by the *jihad* in Afghanistan.[29] Deobandi *madrasas* on the Pakistani frontier at the turn of the twenty first century periodically closed to allow their students to support Taliban efforts.[30]

Nevertheless, the historical pattern launched by the Deoband *'ulama* for the most part treated political life on a primarily secular basis, typically, *de facto* if not *de jure,* identifying religion with the private sphere and in that sphere foster-ing Islamic teachings and interpretations that proved widely influential. Aside from Deoband's enduring influence, it exemplifies a pattern, represented in gen-eral terms in a range of Islamic movements outside South Asia as well, of "tradi-tionalist" cultural renewal on the one hand coupled with political adaptability on the other. This tradition, seen over time and across a wide geographic area, illus-trates that there are widespread patterns of Islamic apoliticism that foster a *modus vivendi* with democratic and liberal traditions. It also demonstrates, most notably in the teaching and missionary dimensions of their activities, that the goals and satisfactions that come from participation in Islamic movements may well have little to do with opposition or resistance to non-Muslims or "the West." Their own debates or concerns may well focus on other Muslims—an internal foe, and not an external "Other" at all.[31] And what they offer participants may be the fulfillment of desires for individual empowerment, transcendent meaning, and moral sociality that do not engage directly with national or global political life at all.

As for political life, recently the commentator Nicholas Lemann has argued that particularly in contexts of weak or nonexistent states, alliances typically re-flect estimates of who will prevail, not who is "right." As Lemann puts it, "in the real world people choose to join not one side of a great clash of civilizations but what looks like the winning team in their village."[32] The JUI would seem almost a textbook case of this kind of argument. In the fragmented, factionalized world of Pakistan's gasping democracy, the winning side seems to be whichever party—regional interest, secular, or Islamic—offers some leverage. In the aftermath of the terrorist attacks of September 11, along with the Jama'at-i Islami, the JUI was at the forefront of anti-American protest. Were they motivated, particularly given their support base among Pashtuns along the Afghan border, by the expec-tation that the "winning team" would be transnational Islamic militants (and their funding sources), and, in the end, that they would gain the support of the presumed majority of Pakistanis who do not support religious parties but do re-sent American foreign policy? As for the Deobandis in India, sometimes the win-ning team seemed to be the British colonial power, sometimes the Indian National Congress, sometimes other parties.

Tablighi Jama'at is particularly striking in regard to its accommodationist strategy since it implicitly fosters the privatization of religion associated with the modern liberal state. Political leaders of all stripes in Pakistan and Bangladesh at least since the mid-1980s have invariably appeared at the annual convocations and been welcomed accordingly. Some observers and political figures claim that the movement is in fact covertly political; others, that it is a first stage on the way to militancy. This argument is made particularly in Pakistan, since the majority of Tabligh participants there belong to the frontier province adjoining Afghanistan. All of this is, however, speculation. What is clear is that the formally apolitical missionary tours, gatherings in local mosques and homes, and annual gatherings continue to be the routine of the movement, one that clearly offers meaning and dignity to many who participate. In the many goals fostered by these movements—social, psychological, moral, and spiritual—as well as in the political strategies adopted with such virtuosity, Islamic movements, in the end, turn out to be less distinctive than either they or outsiders often assume they are.

4. THE RELIGIOUS UNDERTOW OF MUSLIM ECONOMIC GRIEVANCES

TIMUR KURAN

Many of the arguments heard since September 11 have invoked the economic underdevelopment of the Islamic world to explain why so many Muslims appear angry at the West and particularly at the United States. Economic globalization has benefited the West and harmed vast segments of the Islamic world, it is said. Some add that Islam has exacerbated the conflict by transforming economic grievances into mistrust of Westernization, even into antagonism toward modernity. This hostility is consistent, we are told, with the emergence of an Islamic banking system and with Al Qaeda's use of *hawala*, an old Middle Eastern credit delegation instrument, to finance its deadly operations.

Other observers, trying to counter the perception that such acts of economic separatism represent broad trends, note that mainstream Islam has been, and remains, supportive of markets, technological creativity, and material prosperity. Nothing in Islam conflicts with economic development or global economic integration, say the latter group of commentators. The 19 Arab hijackers of September 11 hardly spoke for the millions of Muslims who yearn to participate in the global economy as equals.

Whatever their inconsistencies, none of these interpretations can be dismissed out of hand. Each captures important truths that we ignore at our peril.

MISGIVINGS ABOUT GLOBALIZATION

Widespread Muslim misgivings about globalization are not a figment of anyone's imagination; just as there exist antiglobalists all across America and Europe, so there are many in Egypt, Pakistan, and Indonesia. But, for the most part, the observed Muslim resentment is less an expression of opposition to modern capitalism than it is a cry of desperation. Middle Easterners who have acquired skills to compete in the global economy, when given opportunities to participate in the exchange process, usually prefer peaceful production to hateful destruction. The Hebron crowd that danced in the streets on September 11 consisted overwhelmingly of people pushed by modern technologies to the fringes of the global economy.

Does it follow that poverty is responsible for whatever clash we observe between Islam and the West? Will the current tensions subside if measures are taken to uplift the Islamic world's desperately poor sectors? While it would be comforting to possess a quick fix, it is doubtful that the problems will respond to economic incentives alone. After all, the hijackers of September 11 were not unemployable souls living at the margins of subsistence. Holding university degrees, some of them were perfectly capable of achieving prosperity through legitimate means. What motivated *them* was not material deprivation, but an all-consuming ideology that has been allowed to spread. They were not just Muslims but also Islamists pursuing goals they considered higher than life itself.[1] The difference is critical. Just as Timothy McVeigh belonged to a small minority of Americans consumed by hatred against their government, so Islamists, whether or not they are prone to violence, differ from most Muslims by a commitment to radical global transformation.

RETURNING TO ISLAM

Islamists believe that to be a good Muslim is to lead a distinctly Islamic lifestyle.[2] In principle, every facet of one's existence must be governed by Islamic rules and regulations—marriage, family, dress, politics, economics, and much more. In every domain of life, they believe, a clear demarcation exists between "Islamic" and "un-Islamic" behaviors. Never mind that in all but a few ritualistic matters the Islamists themselves disagree on what Islam prescribes. They have been educated to dismiss their disagreements as minor and to expect a bit more study of God's commandments to produce a consensus about the properly Islamic way to live.

The march of history, Islamists are also trained to believe, is going their way. Earlier generations of Islamists had predicted that the two major economic systems of the modern era, capitalism and communism, were doomed to fail, because in their own ways they both bred injustice, inequity, and inefficiency.[3] One part of this prediction was borne out by the collapse of the Soviet Union in 1991. Now it is the turn of capitalism, which is far less stable than the pace of its arrogant global expansion might suggest. Just as communism collapsed like a house of cards as soon as communist societies discovered it was safe to revolt, so capitalism will self-destruct when its vulnerability finally shows through. Capitalism has failed humanity because it breeds emptiness, mistrust, dissatisfaction, and despair even among the materially successful.

What Islamists offer as an improvement is an Islamic economic system.[4] The key components of the envisioned Islamic economy are an Islamic banking system that avoids interest, an Islamic redistribution system based on Quranic principles of sharing and equity, and a set of norms to ensure fairness and honesty in the marketplace. To anyone familiar with the complexities of modern economic relations, this list will seem hopelessly truncated. In fact, the "Islamic" elements of the planned economic transformation do not go much beyond these three elements.

Consequently, there exists no workable Islamic economic system. Official "economic Islamization" programs in Sudan, Pakistan, and Iran have all ended in failure.[5] Leading Islamist writers rationalize these disappointments by arguing that no properly Islamic economy can exist so long as the world is rife with corruption. Some add that none has existed in history, except during the initial few decades of the first Islamic state founded 14 centuries ago in Western Arabia. After that "Golden Age," corruption took over, breeding unfairness, injustice, and inefficiency.

There is, of course, a massive contradiction here. How can the march of history be favoring the Islamist agenda if that agenda has repeatedly been frustrated for the last 14 centuries, since shortly after the birth of Islam? And why should anyone believe in the viability of Islam's economic agenda if its proponents cannot cite a single contemporary example of successful implementation? Yet, within the Islamist mind set, observed failures establish merely the need to redouble efforts to defeat the offending sources of corruption. Today, so goes the argument, the principal source of corruption is Westernization, which masquerades as globalization and whose chief instruments are the military, cultural, and economic powers of the United States. Americans have been corrupting people everywhere, including Muslims, through seductive advertising and the dominance of their Godless media. They have also been propping up client regimes that are committed, despite appearances to the contrary, to frustrating Islamist goals.

Not that this tendency to blame outside forces for various sorts of failures is limited to terrorists. Islamists with no affinity for violence attribute sundry domestic problems, including failures of their own movements and initiatives, to the prevailing moral standards. Articulated incessantly in diverse contexts, such excuses foster an intellectual climate that enables violent groups to justify their destructiveness as essential to ridding the world of evil and building an Islamic utopia. It also aids these groups in finding recruits.

CULTURAL ROOTS OF ECONOMIC ISLAMIZATION

Contrary to common understandings, the notion that Islam offers the world a workable economic system destined to outperform its alternatives is a recent creation. This belief emerged in late-colonial India, in the 1930s, a time when Muslim Indians were debating whether the dominant element of their communal identity was their Muslim faith or their Indian nationality. Some Muslim leaders proposed that to be a Muslim was to live differently from Hindus and Westerners, and that their Westernized coreligionists were Muslims only in name. To substantiate these views, they undertook to show that Islam offers distinct prescriptions in *all* domains of life, including economics. Concepts such as Islamic economics, Islamic finance, Islamic banking, and Islamic redistribution emerged in the course of a sustained campaign they launched to differentiate what they considered the properly Muslim lifestyle from other lifestyles.[6]

Many clerics in South Asia and elsewhere endorsed this campaign, partly because the elevation of religious values promises to enhance their own authority. Weak governments, including those run by essentially secular Muslims, have had their own reasons to support Islamist efforts to define, articulate, and, where necessary, invent an Islamic way of life. To stay in power, they have found it convenient to trumpet their Islamic virtues through Islamist pet projects. Thus, Saudi agencies have bankrolled Islamic universities in numerous countries, sponsored conferences on the Islamization of knowledge, and built institutes to train Islamic bankers. For their part, Pakistani leaders known to have a low opinion of Islamic economics have paid lip service to the ideal of economic Islamization, supported a ban on non-Islamic forms of banking, and founded an Islamic redistribution system.

Neither individually nor collectively have the economic measures taken in the name of Islam revolutionized the economies they were supposed to cleanse and perfect. This is hardly surprising when one considers that they were inspired by cultural goals rather than efforts to stimulate economic development. In any case, whatever the economic successes of Islamic history, it is patently unrealistic to expect the Quran or early Islamic precedents to yield a viable blueprint for contemporary economic life. A modern economy is far more complex than the seventh-century Arabian desert economy that contemporary Islamists treat as their model. In practice, the inspiration for economic development must come primarily from outside Islam and Islamic precedents.

Forced to confront this plain fact, even some Islamists grant the necessity of basing the design of modern economic institutions at least partly on nonreligious experiences and human judgment. Yet, such recognition does not amount to a discarding of their Islamist beliefs. Their capacity for mental compartmentalization (a capacity we all share) allows them to revert to Islamist thought patterns in contexts where it is convenient to have clear and simple answers to complex problems. Their mental compartmentalization is facilitated by the prevalence of Islamist discourse and by the paucity of challenges to its premises, assertions, and arguments.

The economic grievances that contribute to Muslim resentment of the global economic order have, then, an unmistakable cultural, and specifically religious, dimension. Muslims who are angry at the United States and at the modernizing regimes of the Islamic world are propelled by more than their own poverty or that of their societies. They are driven also by a vision that treats Islam as the answer to every conceivable problem and attributes all failures to non-Islamic influences.

WHAT CAN BE DONE?

If I am right, there can be no immediate solution to the current world crisis. Catching Arab terrorists hiding in Afghani caves and destroying remnants of the Taliban will do nothing to alleviate nightmarish conditions in the Afghan countryside or the slums of Cairo. Nor will it keep Pakistani and Saudi youths from being taught that capitalism is evil and that an oversimplified form of Islam is a source of unrivaled economic wisdom.

A lasting solution to our crisis requires an arduous two-pronged strategy of economic development and cultural repair. Out of both compassion and self-interest, the developed countries must take steps to assist the Islamic world in ways that go beyond window dressing. For starters, the United States and the European Community should lift barriers to the industrial and agricultural exports of the Islamic countries, especially the poorest. Equally important, the developed world must lend a helping hand to the secular education systems of the Middle East and South Asia. Within the Islamic world itself, governments and civil organizations can join the struggle through a dual program of their own. Making a renewed and credible commitment to poverty reduction, they must also be willing to counter the nonsensical and destructive elements of Islamist discourse.

Regardless of their faith or creed, the world's intellectuals can also help out by abandoning the relativist strains of modern multiculturalism. Although all major cultures, including those associated with Islam, offer much that is valuable and instructive, they are not equally successful at producing viable economic solutions. In particular, whatever other comforts Islamism gives its adherents, it is clearly an inferior instrument of economic development. In fact, some of its variants, including that of the Taliban, have proven to be positively harmful, even hostile, to material prosperity. The laudable goal of cherishing the achievements of diverse cultures and respecting cultural differences does not absolve us of the responsibility to acknowledge failures, dead ends, and dangers where they are noticed.

Well before multiculturalism became a cherished ideal, Muslims were struggling to define what Islam represents and what it means to be a believer in good standing within a modernizing social environment. Ever since the nineteenth century, when crafting a response to Western domination became a pressing concern throughout the Islamic world, Muslims have pursued a wide variety of social agendas. They have ranged from unabashed, unfiltered, and uncritical Westernization to reactionary cultural isolationism.[7] In our own time, Turks who crave acceptance by Europe, secular Iraqis and Syrians committed to Arab nationalism, and Pakistanis devoted to the pragmatic Islam of Mohammad Ali Jinnah have competed with Islamists for the hearts and minds of their coreligionists. If multiculturalism is to remain true to its guiding principles, it must recognize the visions of Islam embodied in non-Islamist movements of the Islamic world as surely as it demands respect for the anti-Western and backward-looking interpretations of Islam that grab headlines. It must hear all Muslim voices, including those with no scores to settle with the West.

Denying legitimacy to the wide range of Westernization movements formed by Muslims is not to stay out of the struggle to define Islam. It amounts to siding with conservative and regressive Muslim movements by giving them a free rein in interpreting Islam and setting its social agenda.

TURNING ISLAM INTO A FORCE FOR GLOBAL DEVELOPMENT AND INTEGRATION

None of this implies that the sole challenge is to restrict Islam's social role. Some interpretations of Islam are perfectly compatible with economic growth and cultural exchange. Moreover, Islam's historical legacy offers abundant precedents for flexibility, reform, openness, tolerance, and material enrichment. Most of the early Islamic jurists who produced the canonical compilations of Islamic law were investors who appreciated the need for reducing the costs of doing business.[8] In the period known as Europe's Dark Age, the Arab Middle East boasted libraries far larger than any the West would see until the Renaissance. Under Islamic rule Spain became a center of intellectual creativity. In its high period Ottoman Turkey welcomed the Jews fleeing the Spanish Inquisition, not just out of compassion but also because they commanded valuable skills. There is no evidence that Ottoman rulers of the time feared the resulting cross-cultural interactions or that they considered Islam in need of protection against Judeo-Spanish influences.

Devoting greater attention to such aspects of the Islamic heritage will help to correct the distortions that Islamists have inflicted on Islam's image. They will ensure that the ongoing struggle over Islam's future is based on a balanced interpretation of its past, rather than on a one-sided view that denies the pragmatism and rationality it has shown in diverse contexts.

Globalization itself, particularly the growth of international trade, is justifiable through hallowed Islamic institutions. Until modern times Islam encouraged long-distance trade through one of its five basic requirements, the duty, incumbent on all Muslims of means, to make at least one pilgrimage to Mecca (*hajj*). In the Quran, the pilgrimage duty is described in a passage that goes on to encourage commerce (2:198), suggesting that one of its functions, if not its primary role, was economic integration. In practice, the annual pilgrimage, which can be performed only during three specified days of the year, served as an occasion for intercontinental commerce on a grand scale. A disproportionate share of the pilgrims were professional merchants, and most of the others financed their journeys at least partly by participating in buying and selling on the road to and from Mecca.[9]

Even the officers responsible for protecting the pilgrims traded on their own accounts. Significantly, through the nineteenth century a Muslim ruler's legitimacy depended partly on how well he guarded the major pilgrimage routes from brigands who preyed on pilgrim caravans loaded with merchandise. Commerce was so integral to the Islamic pilgrimage that a pilgrim would often be blessed through the formula: "May God accept your pilgrimage, condone your sins and let you find a good market for your wares."[10] The annual pilgrimage also provided opportunities for the exchange of knowledge among people from far-flung places.

In today's global economy trade relations are too complex, of course, for Islam's annual pilgrimage to carry the commercial significance it held in the past. The value of this historical account lies not in its implications for the commercial potential of the Islamic pilgrimage but, rather, in its significance for debates over Islam's place in the modern world. In providing a religious justification for essentially unsupervised and decentralized trade, it counters the authoritarian and isolationist interpretations of Islam that have grabbed enormous attention.

Publicizing the openness and flexibility found in Islam's heritage will not end Muslim grievances about globalization. Just as there exist antiglobalist movements at Western universities that provide ample access to Adam Smith's writings about the virtues of free trade, so Islam's protectionist face may exert an appeal even where early Islam's encouragement of long-distance trade is widely appreciated. However, such information may give Muslims seeking Islamic answers to their problems alternatives to those offered by Islamist leaders. In particular, it can convince disaffected Muslims that the world's growing economic interdependence does not conflict with Islamic teachings or Islamic history.

PART II
GLOBALIZATION

5. THE GLOBALIZATION OF INFORMAL VIOLENCE, THEORIES OF WORLD POLITICS, AND "THE LIBERALISM OF FEAR"

ROBERT O. KEOHANE[1]

The attacks on the United States on September 11, 2001 have incalculable consequences for domestic politics and world affairs. Reliable predictions about these consequences are impossible. However, it may be worthwhile, even at this early point, to reflect on what these acts of violence reveal about the adequacy of our theories of world politics. In what respects have our assumptions and our analytical models helped us to understand these events and responses to them? And in what ways have we been misled by our theories?

In this short chapter, I will not attempt to be comprehensive. Instead, I will focus on specific issues on which my commentary may be of some value, without presuming that these are the most important issues to address. For instance, the attacks of September 11 reveal that all mainstream theories of world politics are relentlessly secular with respect to motivation. They ignore the impact of religion, despite the fact that world-shaking political movements have so often been fueled by religious fervor. None of them takes very seriously the human desires to dominate or to hate—both so strong in history and in classical realist thought. Most of them tend to assume that the world is run by those whom Joseph Schumpeter called "rational and unheroic" members of the bourgeoisie.[2] After September 11 we need also to keep in mind another motivation: the belief, as expressed by Osama bin Laden, that terrorism against "infidels" will assure one "a supreme place in heaven."[3] However, since I have few insights into religious motivations in world politics, I will leave this subject to those who are more qualified to address it.

In the next section of this chapter I define the phrase, "the globalization of informal violence." In referring to a general category of action, I substitute this phrase for "terrorism," since the latter concept has such negative connotations that it is very difficult to define it in an analytically neutral and consistent way that commands general acceptance.[4] Even as the United Nations Security Council has passed resolutions against terrorism, it has been unable to define the term. Since everyone is against terrorism, the debate shifts to its definition, as each party seeks to define its enemy's acts, but not its own, as terrorist. Nevertheless, deliberately targeted surprise attacks on arbitrarily chosen civilians, designed to frighten other people are clearly acts of terror. The attacks on the World Trade Center of September 11, 2001 were therefore terrorist acts, and I refer to them as such.

This chapter has three themes. First, the events of September 11 illustrate starkly how our assumptions about security are conceived in terms of increasingly obsolescent views of geographical space. Secondly, the globalization of informal violence can be analyzed by exploring patterns of asymmetrical interdependence and their implications for power. Thirdly, United States responses to the attacks tell us quite a bit about the role of multilateral institutions in contemporary world politics.

My argument is that our theories provide important components of an adequate post–September 11 conceptualization of world politics, but that we need to alter some of our assumptions in order to rearrange these components into a viable theoretical framework. Effective wielding of large-scale violence by non-state actors reflects new patterns of asymmetrical interdependence, and calls into question some of our assumptions about geographical space as a barrier. Responses to these actions reveal the significance of international institutions as well as the continuing central role of states. In thinking about these issues, students of world politics can be usefully reminded of Judith N. Shklar's concept of the "liberalism of fear," and her argument that the most basic function of a liberal state is to protect its citizens from the fear of cruelty.[5]

1. THE GLOBALIZATION OF INFORMAL VIOLENCE AND THE RECONCEPTUALIZATION OF SPACE

The various definitions of globalization in social science all converge on the notion that human activities across regions and continents are being increasingly linked together, as a result of both technological and social change.[6] Globalism as a state of affairs has been defined as "a state of the world involving networks of interdependence at multicontinental distances, linked through flows of capital and goods, information and ideas, people and force, as well as environmentally and biologically relevant substances."[7]

When globalism is characterized as multidimensional, as in these definitions, the expansion of terrorism's global reach is an instance of globalization.[8] Often, globalism and globalization have been defined narrowly as economic integration on a global scale; but whatever appeal such a definition may have had, it has surely disappeared after September 11. To adopt it would be to imply that globalized informal violence, which takes advantage of modern technologies of communication, transportation, explosives, and potentially biology, somehow threatens to *hinder* or *reduce the level of* globalism. But like military technology between 1914 and 1945, globalized informal violence strengthens one dimension of globalism—the networks through which means of violence flow—while potentially weakening globalism along other dimensions, such as economic and social exchange. As in the past, not all aspects of globalization go together.

I define informal violence as violence by non-state actors, capitalizing on secrecy and surprise to inflict great harm with small material capabilities. Such violence is "informal" because it is not wielded by formal state institutions and it is typically not announced in advance, as in a declaration of war. Such violence becomes globalized when the networks of non-state actors operate on an intercontinental basis, so that acts of force in one society can be initiated and controlled from very distant points of the globe.

The implications of the globalization of *formal* violence were profound for traditional conceptions of foreign policy in an earlier generation, particularly in the United States, which had so long been insulated by distance from invasion and major direct attack. The great expositors of classical realist theories of foreign policy in the United States, such as Walter Lippmann, began with the premise that defense of the "continental homeland" is "a universally recognized vital interest." Before World War II, threats to the homeland could only stem from other states that secured territory contiguous to that of the United States or that controlled ocean approaches to it. Hence the Monroe Doctrine of 1823 was the cornerstone of American national security policy. As Lippmann recognized in 1943, changes in the technologies of formal violence meant that security policy needed to be more ambitious: The United States would have to maintain coalitions with other great powers that would "form a combination of indisputably preponderant power."[9] Nevertheless, Lippmann was able to retain a key traditional concept: that of a geographically defined defensive perimeter, which can be thought of as a set of concentric circles. If the United States were to control not only its own area but the circle surrounding that area, comprising littoral regions of Europe and Asia, its homeland would be secure.

The American strategists of the 1950s—led by Bernard Brodie, Thomas Schelling, and Albert Wohlstetter—had to rethink the concept of a defensive perimeter, as intercontinental ballistic missiles reduced the significance of distance: that is, as formal violence became globalized. John Herz argued that nuclear weapons forced students of international politics to rethink sovereignty, territoriality, and the protective function of the state:

> With the advent of the atomic weapon, whatever remained of the impermeability of states seems to have gone for good. . . . Mencius, in ancient China, when asked for guidance in matters of defense and foreign policy by the ruler of a small state, is said to have

counseled: "dig deeper your moats; build higher your walls; guard them along with your people." This remained the classical posture up to our age, when a Western sage, Bertrand Russell, could still, even in the interwar period, define power as a force radiating from one center and diminishing with the distance from that center until it finds an equilibrium with that of similar geographically anchored units. Now that power can destroy power from center to center everything is different.[10]

September 11 signifies that informal violence has become globalized, just as formal, state-controlled violence became globalized for the superpowers during the 1950s. The globalization of informal violence was not *created* by September 11. Indeed, earlier examples, extending back to piracy in the seventeenth century, can be easily found. But the significance of globalization—of violence as well as economically and socially—is not its absolute newness but its increasing magnitude as a result of sharp declines in the costs of global communications and transportation.[11]

Contemporary theorists of world politics face a challenge similar to that of this earlier generation: to understand the nature of world politics and its connections to domestic politics, when what Herz called the "hard shell" of the state has been shattered.[12] Geographical space, which has been seen as a natural *barrier* and a locus for human barriers, now must be seen as a *carrier* as well.

The obsolescence of the barrier conception of geographic space has troubling implications for foreign policy. One of the strengths of Realism in the United States has always been that it imposed limitations on American intervention abroad. By asking questions about whether vital national interests are involved in a particular situation abroad, Realists have sought to counter the moralistic and messianic tendencies that periodically recur in American thinking. For Lippmann, the key to a successful foreign policy was achieving a "balance, with a comfortable surplus of power in reserve, [between] the nation's commitment and the nation's power".[13] Going abroad "in search of monsters to destroy" upset that balance.[14] Realism provided a rationale for "just saying no" to advocates of intervening, for their own ideological or self-interested reasons, in areas of conflict far from the United States. It is worthwhile to be reminded that Lippmann, Hans J. Morgenthau, and Kenneth N. Waltz were all early opponents of the war in Vietnam. Unfortunately, this Realist caution, salutary as it has been, is premised on the barrier conception of geographical space. In the absence of clear and defensible criteria that American leaders can use to distinguish vital from non-vital interests, the United States is at risk of intervening throughout the world in a variety of conflicts bearing only tangential relationships to "terrorism with a global reach."

The globalization of informal violence, carried out by networks of non-state actors, defined by commitments rather than by territory, has profoundly changed these fundamental foreign-policy assumptions.[15] On traditional grounds of national interest, Afghanistan should be one of the least important places in the world for American foreign policy—and until the Soviet invasion of 1979, and again after the collapse of the Soviet Union in 1991 until September 11, the United States all but ignored it. Yet in October 2001 it became the theatre of war. Globalization means, among other things, that threats of violence to our homeland can occur from anywhere. The barrier conception of geographical space, already anachronistic with respect to thermonuclear war and called into question by earlier acts of globalized informal violence, was finally shown to be thoroughly obsolete on September 11.

2. INTERDEPENDENCE AND POWER

Another way to express the argument made above is that networks of interdependence, involving transmission of informal violence, have now taken a genuinely global form. Using this language helps us to see how the literature on interdependence and power, which was originally developed to understand international political economy, has become relevant to the globalization of informal violence. In that literature, interdependence is conceptualized as mutual dependence, and power is conceptualized in terms of *asymmetrical interdependence.*[16] This literature has also long made clear that "military power dominates economic power in the sense that economic means alone are likely to be ineffective against the serious use of military force."[17]

September 11 revealed how much the United States could be hurt by informal violence, to an extent that had been anticipated by some government reports but that had not been incorporated into the plans of the government.[18] The long-term vulnerability of the United States is not entirely clear, but the availability of means of mass destruction, the extent of hatred for the United States, and the ease of entering the United States from almost anywhere in the world, all suggest that vulnerability may be quite high.

If the United States were facing a territorial state with conventional objectives, this vulnerability might not be a source of worry. After all, the United States has long been much more vulnerable, in technological terms, to a nuclear attack from Russia. But the United States was not *asymmetrically vulnerable*. On the contrary, the fact that the United States had either superior nuclear capability or "mutual assured destruction" (MAD) kept vulnerability more or less symmetrical. Russia has controlled great *force,* but has not acquired power over the United States from its arsenal.

With respect to terrorism, however, two asymmetries, which do not normally characterize relationships between states, favored wielders of informal violence in September 2001. First, there was an *asymmetry of information*. It seems paradoxical that an "information society" such as that of the contemporary United States would be at an informational disadvantage with respect to networks of individuals whose communications seem to occur largely through handwritten messages and face-to-face contacts. But an information society is also an open society. Potential terrorists had good information about their targets, while before September 11 the United States had poor information about the identity and location of terrorist networks within the United States and other Western societies. Perhaps equally important, the United States was unable to process coherently the information that its various agencies had gathered. Secondly, there is an *asymmetry in beliefs*. Some of Osama bin Laden's followers apparently believed that they would be rewarded in the afterlife for committing suicidal attacks on civilians. Others were duped into participating in the attacks without being told of their suicidal purpose. Clearly, the suicidal nature of the attacks made them more difficult to prevent and magnified their potential destructive power. Neither volunteering for suicide missions nor deliberately targeting civilians is consistent with secular beliefs widely shared in the societies attacked by Al Qaeda.

The United States and its allies have enormous advantages in resources, including military power, economic resources, political influence, and technological capabilities. Furthermore, communications media, largely based in the West, give greater weight to the voices of people in the wealthy democracies than to those of the dispossessed in developing countries. Hence the asymmetries in information and beliefs that I have mentioned are, in a sense, exceptional. They do not confer a permanent advantage on the wielders of informal violence. Yet they were sufficient to give the terrorists at least a short-term advantage, and they make terrorism a long-term threat.

Our failure to anticipate the impact of terrorist attacks does not derive from a fundamental conceptual failure in thinking about power. On the contrary, the power of terrorists, like that of states, derives from asymmetrical patterns of interdependence. Our fault has rather been our failure to understand that the most powerful state ever to exist on this planet could be vulnerable to small bands of terrorists due to patterns of asymmetrical interdependence. We have overemphasized states and we have overaggregated power.

Power comes not simply out of the barrel of a gun, but from asymmetries in vulnerability interdependence—some of which, it turns out, favor certain nonstate actors more than most observers anticipated. The networks of interdependence along which power can travel are multiple, and they do not cancel one another out. Even a state that is overwhelmingly powerful on many dimensions can be highly vulnerable on others. We learned this lesson in the 1970s with respect to oil power; we are relearning it now with respect to terrorism.

3. INSTITUTIONS AND LEGITIMACY

Institutionalist theory implies that multilateral institutions should play significant roles wherever interstate cooperation is extensive in world politics. Yet a reader of the American press immediately after the September 11, 2001 attack on the World Trade Center and the Pentagon might well have thought this claim weirdly divorced from reality. Immediate reactions centered on domestic security, military responses, and the creation of a broad international coalition against terrorism. Although the United Nations Security Council did act on September 12, passing Resolution 1368, its response attracted relatively little attention. Indeed, President Bush's speech to Congress on September 20 did not mention the United Nations, although the President did praise NATO and made a generic reference to international organizations. And coverage of the United Nations was virtually nonexistent in the *New York Times*.

But theory is not tested by the immediate reactions of policymakers, much less by those of the press. Social science theory purports to elucidate underlying structures of social reality, which generate incentives for action. Kenneth Waltz rightly looks for confirmation of his theory of the balance of power "through observation of difficult cases." The theory is confirmed, he claims, where states ally with each other, "in accordance with the expectations the theory gives rise to, even though they have strong reasons not to cooperate with one another." [19] Realists rightly argue that if leaders seem to be compelled toward actions that theory suggests—as, for instance, Winston Churchill was when Britain allied with the Soviet Union in 1941 and American leaders when they built NATO after World War II—this counts for their theory. Indeed, the most demanding test of theory comes when policymakers are initially unreceptive to the arguments on which the theory is based. If they nevertheless turn to the policy measures that the theory anticipates, it gains support.

The terrorist attacks of September 11 therefore pose a fruitful test for institutionalist theory. Before September 11, the Bush Administration had been pursuing a notably unilateralist policy with respect to several issues, including global warming, trade in small arms, money laundering, and tax evasion. Its leading policymakers all had realist proclivities: They emphasized the decisive use of force and had not been public supporters of international institutions. Their initial inclinations, if their public statements and those of the President are any guide, did not lead them to emphasize the role of the United Nations.

Nevertheless, the United States returned to the Security Council. On September 28, 2001 the Security Council unanimously adopted Resolution 1373, on the motion of the United States. This resolution used the mandatory provisions of Chapter VII of the United Nations Charter to require all states to "deny safe haven" both to terrorists and to those who "provide safe haven" to terrorists. Resolution 1373 also demanded that states prevent potential terrorists from using their territories, and "prevent and suppress the financing of terrorist acts." It did not, as noted above, define terrorism. Furthermore, the United States continued to engage the United Nations, indeed delegating to it the task of bringing Afghan factions together in Germany in a meeting that culminated in an agreement in December 2001.

Why should the United States have relied so extensively on the United Nations? The UN, in Stalin's famous phrase, has no divisions. The United States, not the UN, carried out the significant military actions. Transnational banks, central banks, and states, in their capacities as bank regulators, froze funds allegedly belonging to terrorists. Even before the September 28 Security Council resolution, allies of the United States had already invoked Article 5 of NATO's Charter.

Inis L. Claude proposed one answer almost 35 years ago.[20] States seek "collective legitimation" for their policies in the United Nations. Only the UN can provide the breadth of support for an action that can elevate it from the policy of one country or a limited set of countries, to a policy endorsed on a global basis. In contemporary jargon, the "transaction costs" of seeking support from over 150 countries around the world are higher than those of going to the Security Council, ready to meet at a moment's notice. But more important than these costs is the fact that the institution of the United Nations can confer a certain degree of legitimacy on a policy favored by the United States.

What does legitimacy mean in this context? Legally, decisions of the United Nations Security Council on issues involving the use of violence are legitimate since members of the United Nations, through the Charter, have authorized such decisions. In a broader popular and normative sense, decisions are legitimate for a given public insofar as members of that public believe that they should be obeyed. As Weber pointed out, the sources of such legitimacy may include tradition, charisma or rational-legal authority;[21] they may also include appeal to widely accepted norms. People in various parts of the world may believe that their governments should obey decisions of the Security Council because they were made through a process that is normatively as well as legally acceptable. Or they may regard its decisions as legitimate insofar as they are justified on the basis of principles—such as collective opposition to aggression—that they regard as valid.

Why is legitimacy important? In part because people will voluntarily support a legitimate policy, without requiring material inducements.[22] But it would be naïve to believe that leaders of most countries will be persuaded by Security Council action of the wisdom or righteousness of the policy and will therefore support it for normative reasons. To explain the impact of Security Council resolutions, we need also to look for self-interested benefits for leaders.

Even if the leaders are entirely cynical, the adoption of a legitimate UN resolution will change their calculations. If they lead democratic societies in which publics accept the legitimacy of UN action, they will benefit politically more from supporting policies endorsed by the United Nations than from supporting policies not so endorsed. If they exercise rule over people who are unsympathetic to the policies and who do not accept them merely due to UN endorsement, the legal status of Security Council resolutions may change their calculations. Chapter VII decisions are mandatory, which means that states defying the Security Council run the risk of facing sanctions themselves, as in the Gulf War. Leaders of countries with unsympathetic populations can point out that, however distasteful it may be to take action against Osama bin Laden and his network, it could be more costly to be cut off from essential supplies and markets, to suffer disruption of transportation and banking services, or even to become a target of military action.

The general point is one that has often been made by institutional theory: International institutions work largely by altering the costs of state strategies. Of course, there is no guarantee that institutions will be sufficiently important to ensure that strategies change; they are only one element in a mixture of calculations. Yet as the use of the United Nations by the United States indicates, they are an element that should not be overlooked.

How important multilateral instutions will in fact be is another question—one that has been much-debated during the early months of 2002. Several factors seem to work in favor of more reliance on multilateral institutions in the wake of 9/11. As noted, the United States seeks legitimacy for its military actions. Furthermore, it needs help from a number of countries, from Pakistan to the Philippines. Even the very powerful United States needs to negotiate for access to sovereign territory and must provide some reciprocal benefits in return for access and cooperation. Some of these benefits may be provided through concessions in multilateral institutions on a variety of issues, ranging from money-laundering to controls on trade in weapons.

On the other hand, the war against terrorism also increases incentives for unilateral action and bilateral diplomacy. Threats of terrorism generate incentives to retain the ability to act decisively, without long deliberation or efforts at persuasion. The United States government in February 2002 signalled that it might renew its war on Iraq, with or without the endorsement of the United Nations Security Council or even its traditional allies. In the conduct of its war in Afghanistan during the fall of 2001, the United States was notably reluctant to permit the United Nations, or its own allies, to restrict its military freedom of action. In fact, requests by Great Britain to send in troops to protect relief operations were rebuffed by the United States on the advice of its military commanders. A cynical interpretation of United States policy toward multilateral institutions would suggest that American policymakers want to retain freedom of military action for themselves, but to delegate tedious political issues—such as reconstructing Afghanistan—to the United Nations. When the inevitable political failures become evident, blame can be placed at the door of the UN.

One can easily imagine an even more pessimistic scenario for the next few years. The United States government could decide that its security required radical measures that would not be supported even by many of its NATO allies, such as an attack on Iraq without strong evidence of Iraqi complicity in prior attacks on the United States. In such an eventuality, American actions would not be legitimated either by the United Nations or by NATO. Having acted unilaterally, the United States would not be moved to rely more heavily on international institutions, and multilateralism could suffer a serious blow.

Even if the multilateral path is chosen, it is hardly likely to be sufficient. It is unlikely that multilateral organizations will be the key operating agencies in dealing with the globalization of informal violence: They are too cumbersome for that. The state, with its capacity for decisive, forceful action and the loyalty it commands from citizens, will remain a necessary part of the solution to threats of informal violence. Jejune declarations of the "death of the state" are surely among the casualties of the terrorist offensive. But multilateral organizations will be an essential part of the process of legitimizing action by states.

It should be evident that these arguments about multilateral institutions and networks are not "antirealist." On the contrary, they rest on an appreciation of the role of power, and of state action, in world politics; on an understanding that new threats create new alliances; and on a belief that structures matter. Analysts who are sensitive to the role of multilateral institutions need not regard them as operating *independently* from states, nor should they see such institutions as a panacea for our new ills. But sensitivity to the role of multilateral institutions helps us see how these institutions can play a role: not only by reducing transaction costs but also by generating opportunities for signalling commitments and providing collective legitimacy for effective action.

4. THE "LIBERALISM OF FEAR"

Judith Shklar's "liberalism of fear" envisages liberal democracy as "more a recipe for survival than a project for the perfectibility of mankind." It seeks to avoid the worst outcomes, and therefore declares that "the first right is to be protected against the fear of cruelty." [23] The liberalism of fear certainly speaks to our condition today, as it did to that of victims, such as Shklar, of the Nazis. It raises both an analytical and a normative issue. Analytically, it leads us to ask about the protective role of the state, facing the globalization of informal violence. Normatively, it should make us think about our own role as students of world politics.

The erosion of the concept of a protected homeland within a defensive perimeter, discussed above, makes the "liberalism of fear" more relevant to Americans than it has been in almost two centuries. Suddenly, the task of protecting citizens from the fear of cruelty has become a demanding project for the state, not one that a superpower can take for granted.

Shklar looked to the state as the chief threat. "No liberal," she declared, "ever forgets that governments are coercive." [24] In this respect, the "liberalism of fear" shares a blind spot with the most popular theories of world politics, including realism, institutionalism, and some forms of constructivism. All of these views share a common fault: they do not sufficiently take account of how globalization facilitates the agency of non-state entities and networks. After September 11 no liberal should be able to forget that non-state actors, operating within the borders of liberal states, can be as coercive and fear-inducing as states.

Recognition of the dangers of informal violence may lead the United States toward a broader vision of its global interests. As we have seen, classical realist thinking drew a bright line between geographical areas important to the national interest and those parts of the world that were insignificant from the standpoint of interests. Now that attacks against the United States can be planned and fostered within countries formerly viewed as insignificant, this bright line has been blurred.

One of the implications of this blurring of lines is that the distinction between self-defense and humanitarian intervention may become less clear. Future military actions in failed states, or attempts to bolster states that are in danger of failing, may be more likely to be described *both* as self-defense and as humanitarian or public-spirited. When the only arguments for such policies were essentially altruistic ones, they commanded little support, so the human and material price that American leaders were willing to pay to attain them was low. Now, however, such policies can be framed in terms of American self-interest, properly understood. Sound arguments from self-interest are more persuasive than arguments from responsibility or altruism.

More generally, recognition of the dangers of informal violence will force a redefinition of American national interests, which could take different forms. Such a redefinition could lead Americans to support measures to reduce poverty, inequality, and injustice in poor countries. The Marshall Plan is a useful if imperfect analogy. In 1947 the United States redefined its self-interest, taking responsibility for helping to build a democratic and capitalist Europe, open to other capitalist democracies. The United States invested very large resources in this project, with great success. The task now in the less developed countries is much more daunting, both in sheer magnitude and since the political systems of most of these countries are weaker than those of European countries in 1947.[25] But the resources available to the United States and other democratic countries are also much greater than they were in 1947.

Any widely appealing vision of American interests will need to be based on core values that can be generalized. Individual freedom, economic opportunity, and representative democracy constitute such values. The ability to drive gas-guzzling sports utility vehicles (SUVs) does not. In the end, "soft power"[26] depends not merely on the desire of people in one country to imitate the institutions and practices prevailing in another, but also their ability to do so. Exhibiting a glamorous lifestyle that others have no possibility of attaining is more likely to generate hostility and a feeling of "sour grapes" than support. To relate successfully to people in poor countries during the twenty-first century, Americans will have to distinguish between their values and their privileges.

The attachment of Americans to a privileged lifestyle raises the prospect of a defensive and reactionary broadening of American national interests. Recall that a virtue of classical realism was to link commitments to a relatively limited set of interests, defined partly by geography. Ideology and a self-serving attempt to preserve privileges could define a different set of interests. Opponents—not merely those who have attacked the United States—would be demonized. Deals would continue to be cut with corrupt and repressive regimes to keep cheap oil flowing to the United States. The United States would rely exclusively on military power and bilateral deals rather than also on economic assistance, trade benefits, and efforts at cultural understanding. The costs would include estrangement from our democratic allies and hatred of the United States in much of the world. Ultimately, such a vision of national interest is a recipe for isolation and continual conflict—an environment in which liberal democracy could be threatened by the emergence of a garrison state at home.

Normatively, thinking about the "liberalism of fear" reminds our generation that in a globalized world, we cannot take liberal societies for granted. People such as Shklar, who experienced Nazism, understood the fear of cruelty in their bones. Those of us who grew up in the United States during the Cold War experienced such fear only in our imaginations, although nuclear threats and wars such as those in Korea and Vietnam gave our imaginations plenty to work with. The generations that have come of age in the United States since the mid-to-late 1980s—essentially those people under 35—have been able to take the basics of liberalism for granted, as if the United States were insulated from the despair of much of the world's population. The globalization of informal violence means that we are not so insulated. We are linked with hateful killers by real physical connections, not merely those of cyberspace. Neither isolationism nor unilateralism is a viable option.

Hence, the liberalism of fear means that we who study international interdependence and multilateral institutions will need to redouble our efforts. We should pay less attention to differentiating our views from those of other schools of international relations; more to both synthesis and disaggregation. We need to synthesize insights from classical realism, institutionalism, and constructivism, but we also need to take alternative worldviews—including religious worldviews—more seriously. We need to examine how purposes are shaped by ideas and how calculations of power interact with institutions to produce outcomes in world politics. We need, at the same time, to disaggregate strands of asymmetrical interdependence, with their different implications for power, and to differentiate international institutions and networks from one another in their effects and their potential for good or ill.

CONCLUSION

The terrorist attacks on New York and Washington force us to rethink our theories of world politics. Globalism should not be equated with economic integration. The agents of globalization are not simply the high-tech creators of the Internet, or multinational corporations, but also small bands of fanatics travelling on jet aircraft and inspired by fundamentalist religion. The globalization of informal violence has rendered problematic our conventional assumptions about security threats. It should also lead us to question the classical realist distinction between important parts of the world, in which great powers have interests, and insignificant places, which were thought to present no security threats although they may raise moral dilemmas. Indeed, we need to reconceptualize the significance for homeland security of geographical space, which can be as much a carrier of malign informal violence as a barrier to it.

Most problematic are the assumptions in international relations theory about the roles played by states. There has been too much "international relations," and too little "world politics," not only in work on security but also in much work on international institutions. States no longer have a monopoly on the means of mass destruction: More people died in the attacks on the World Trade Center and the Pentagon than in the Japanese attack on Pearl Harbor in 1941. Indeed, it would be salutary for us to change the name of our field, from "international relations" to "world politics." [27] The language of "international" relations enables us to slip back into state-centric assumptions too easily. Asymmetrical interdependence is not merely an interstate phenomenon.

Yet as the state loses its monopoly on means of mass destruction, the response to terrorism is strengthening the powers of states, and the reliance of people on government. Even as states acquire more authority, they are likely to cooperate more extensively with each other on security issues, using international institutions to do so. Ironically, as states acquire more authority, they will be forced to learn better how to relate to networks—both hostile networks and networks that they may use instrumentally—and to rely more heavily on multilateral institutions. These institutions, in turn, will have to define their tasks in ways that emphasize their advantages—in conferring collective legitimacy on actions—while minimizing the impact of their liabilities, as cumbersome organizations without unity of command.

One result of these apparently paradoxical changes is closer linkages between traditional security issues and other issues. The artificial but convenient separation of the field into security and political economy may be one of the casualties of the struggle against terrorism. Areas formerly seen as "non-security areas," such as air transport, transnational finance, and migration, have become more important to security and more tightly subject, therefore, to state regulation.

Finally, the globalization of informal violence indicates how parochial some of the disputes among various schools of international relations theory have been. Analysis of the ramifications of the attacks on the United States must come to grips not only with structures of power, but also with changing subjective ideas and their impact on strategies. It must be concerned with international institutions, and with non-state actors and networks—elements of world politics emphasized by different schools of thought. And it must probe the connections between domestic politics and world politics. We do not face a *choice* between these perspectives, but rather the task of *synthesizing* them into a comprehensive, yet coherent, view.

Our understanding of world politics has often advanced under the pressure of events, such as those of World War II, the Nuclear Revolution, and the growth of economic interdependence over the last fifty years. Perhaps the globalization of informal violence will refocus our attention for a new period of intellectual creativity, as sober thinking about global governance and classic political realism converge on problems identified so well by the "liberalism of fear."

6. VIOLENCE, LAW, AND JUSTICE IN A GLOBAL AGE

DAVID HELD[1]

On Sunday, September 23, 2001, the novelist Barbara Kingsolver wrote in *The Los Angeles Times*:

> It's the worst thing that's happened, but only this week. Two years ago, an earthquake in Turkey killed 17,000 people in a day, babies and mothers and businessmen. . . . The November before that, a hurricane hit Honduras and Nicaragua and killed even more. . . . Which end of the world shall we talk about? Sixty years ago, Japanese airplanes bombed Navy boys who were sleeping on ships in gentle Pacific waters. Three and a half years later, American planes bombed a plaza in Japan where men and women were going to work, where schoolchildren were playing, and more humans died at once than anyone thought possible. Seventy thousand in a minute. Imagine. . . .
>
> There are no worst days, it seems. Ten years ago, early on a January morning, bombs rained down from the sky and caused great buildings in the city of Baghdad to fall down—hotels, hospitals, palaces, buildings with mothers and soldiers inside—and here in the place I want to love best, I had to watch people cheering about it. In Baghdad, survivors shook their fists at the sky and said the word "evil." When many lives are lost all at once, people gather together and say words like "heinous" and "honor" and "revenge." . . . They raise up their compatriots' lives to a sacred place—we do this, all of us who are human—thinking our own citizens to be more worthy of grief and less willingly risked than lives on other soil.[2]

This is an unsettling and challenging passage. When I first read it, I felt angered and unsympathetic to its call to think systematically about September 11 in the context of other disasters, acts of aggression, and wars. A few days later I found it helpful to connect its sentiments to my own strong, cosmopolitan orientations.

Immanuel Kant wrote over two hundred years ago that we are "unavoidably side by side." A violent challenge to law and justice in one place has consequences for many other places and can be experienced everywhere.[3] While he dwelt on these matters and their implications at length, he could not have known how profound and immediate his concerns would become.

Since Kant, our mutual interconnectedness and vulnerability have grown rapidly. We no longer live, if we ever did, in a world of discrete national communities. Instead, we live in a world of what I like to call "overlapping communities of fate" where the trajectories of countries are heavily enmeshed with each other. In our world, it is not only the violent exception that links people together across borders; the very nature of everyday problems and processes joins people in

multiple ways. From the movement of ideas and cultural artifacts to the fundamental issues raised by genetic engineering, from the conditions of financial
stability to environmental degradation, the fate and fortunes of all of us are thoroughly intertwined.

The story of our increasingly global order—"globalization"—is not a singular
one. Globalization is not a one-dimensional phenomenon. For example, there
has been an expansion of global markets which has altered the political terrain,
increasing exit options for capital of all kinds and putting pressure on polities
everywhere.[4] But the story of globalization is not just economic: It is also one of
growing aspirations for international law and justice. From the United Nations
system to the European Union, from changes to the laws of war to the entrenchment of human rights, from the emergence of international environmental
regimes to the foundation of the International Criminal Court, there is also another narrative being told—a narrative which seeks to reframe human activity
and entrench it in law, rights, and responsibilities. In the first section of this essay,
I would like to reflect on this second narrative and highlight some of its strengths
and limitations. Once this background is sketched, elements of the legal and political context of September 11 can be better grasped.

REFRAMING HUMAN ACTIVITY: INTERNATIONAL LAW, RIGHTS, AND RESPONSIBILITIES

The process of the gradual delimitation of political power, and the increasing significance of international law and justice, can be illustrated by reflecting on a
strand in international legal thinking which has overturned the exclusive position of the state in international law and buttressed the role of the individual, in
relation to, and with responsibility for, systematic violence against others.

In the first instance, by recognizing the legal status of conscientious objection,
many states—particularly Western states (I shall return to the significance of this
later)—have acknowledged there are clear occasions when an individual has a
moral obligation beyond that of his or her obligation as a citizen of a state.[5] The
refusal to serve in national armies triggers a claim to a "higher moral court" of
rights and duties. Such claims are exemplified as well in the changing legal position of those who are willing to go to war. The recognition in international law of
the offenses of war crimes, genocide, and crimes against humanity makes clear
that acquiescence to the commands of national leaders will not be considered
sufficient grounds for absolving individual guilt in these cases. A turning point in
this regard was the judgment of the International Tribunal at Nuremberg (and
the parallel tribunal in Tokyo). The Tribunal laid down, for the first time in his-

tory, that when *international rules* that protect basic humanitarian values are in conflict with *state laws,* every individual must transgress the state laws (except where there is no room for "moral choice," i.e. when a gun is being held to someone's head).[6] Modern international law has generally endorsed the position taken by the Tribunal and has affirmed its rejection of the defense of obedience to superior orders in matters of responsibility for crimes against peace and humanity. As one commentator has noted: "Since the Nuremberg Trials, it has been acknowledged that war criminals cannot relieve themselves of criminal responsibility by citing official position or superior orders. Even obedience to explicit national legislation provides no protection against international law."[7]

The most notable recent extension of the application of the Nuremberg principles has been the establishment of the war crimes tribunals for the former Yugoslavia (established by the UN Security Council in 1993) and for Rwanda (set up in 1994).[8] The Yugoslav tribunal has issued indictments against people from all three ethnic groups in Bosnia, and is investigating crimes in Kosovo, although it has encountered serious difficulty in obtaining custody of the key accused. (Significantly, of course, ex-President Slobodan Milosevic has recently been arrested and brought before The Hague war crimes tribunal.) Although neither the tribunal for Rwanda nor the Yugoslav tribunal have had the ability to detain and try more than a small fraction of those engaged in atrocities, both have taken important steps toward implementing the law governing war crimes and, thereby, reducing the credibility gap between the promises of such law on the one hand, and the weakness of its application on the other.

Most recently, the proposals put forward for the establishment of a permanent International Criminal Court are designed to help close this gap in the longer term.[9] Several major hurdles remain to its successful entrenchment, including the continuing opposition from the United States (which fears that its soldiers will be the target of politically motivated prosecutions) and dependency upon individual state consent for its effectiveness.[10] However, it is likely that the Court will be formally established (with or without the United States) and will mark another significant step away from the classic regime of state sovereignty—that is, sovereignty as effective power—toward the firm entrenchment of the "liberal regime of international sovereignty" as I refer to it—sovereignty shaped and delimited by new, broader frameworks of governance and law.[11]

The ground now being staked out in international legal agreements suggests something of particular importance: that the containment of armed aggression and abuses of power can only be achieved through both the control of warfare and the prevention of the abuse of human rights. For it is only too apparent that many forms of violence perpetrated against individuals, and many forms of abuse of power, do not take place during declared acts of war. In fact, it can be argued that the distinctions between war and peace, and between aggression and repression, are eroded by changing patterns of violence.[12] The kinds of violence witnessed in Bosnia and Kosovo highlight the role of paramilitaries and of organized crime, and the use of parts of national armies which may no longer be under the direct control of a state. What these kinds of violence signal is that there is a very fine line between explicit formal crimes committed during acts of national war and major attacks on the welfare and physical integrity of citizens in situations that may not involve a declaration of war by states. While many of the new forms of warfare do not fall directly under the classic rules of war, they are massive violations of international human rights. Accordingly, the rules of war and human rights law can be seen as two complementary forms of international rules which aim to circumscribe the proper form, scope and use of coercive power.[13] For all the limitations in enforcement, these are significant changes which, when taken together, amount to the rejection of the doctrine of legitimate power as effective control, and its replacement by international rules which entrench basic humanitarian values as the criteria for legitimate government.

How do the terrorist attacks on the World Trade Center and the Pentagon fit into this pattern of legal change? A wide variety of legal instruments, dating back to 1963 (the Convention on Offenses and Certain Other Acts Committed on Board Aircraft), enable the international community to take action against terrorism and bring those responsible to justice. If the persons responsible for the September 11 attacks can be identified and apprehended, they could face prosecution in virtually any country that obtains custody of them. In particular, the widely ratified Hague Convention for the Suppression of Unlawful Seizure of Aircraft (1970) makes the hijacking of aircraft an international criminal offense. The offense is regarded as extraditable under any extradition treaty in force between contracting states, and applies to accomplices as well as to the hijackers. In addition, the use of hijacked aircraft as lethal weapons can be interpreted as a crime against humanity under international law (although there is some legal argument about this). Frederic Kirgis has noted that the statute of the International Criminal Court defines a crime against humanity as any of several listed acts "when committed as part of a widespread or systematic attack directed against any civilian population. . . ." The acts include murder and "other inhumane acts of a similar character intentionally causing great suffering, or serious injury to body or to mental or physical health."[14]

Changes in the law of war, human rights law and in other legal domains have placed individuals, governments, and nongovernmental organizations under new systems of legal regulation—regulation which, in principle, recasts the legal significance of state boundaries. The regime of liberal international sovereignty entrenches powers and constraints, and rights and duties in international law which—albeit ultimately formulated by states—go beyond the traditional conception of the proper scope and boundaries of states, and can come into conflict, and sometimes contradiction, with national laws. Within this framework, states may forfeit claims to sovereignty, and individuals their right to sovereign protection, if they violate the standards and values embedded in the liberal international order. Such violations no longer become a matter of morality alone. Rather, they become a breach of a legal code, a breach that may call forth the means to challenge, prosecute and rectify it.[15] To this end, a bridge is created between morality and law where, at best, only stepping stones existed before in the era of classic sovereignty. These are transformative changes which alter the form and content of politics, nationally, regionally, and globally. They signify the enlarging normative reach, extending scope, and growing institutionalization of international legal rules and practices—the beginnings of a "universal constitutional order" in which the state is no longer the only layer of legal competence to which people have transferred public powers.[16]

In short, boundaries between states are of decreasing legal and moral significance. States are no longer regarded as discrete political worlds. International standards breach boundaries in numerous ways. Within Europe, the European Convention for the Protection of Human Rights and Fundamental Freedoms and the European Union create new institutions and layers of law and governance which have divided political authority. Any assumption that sovereignty is an indivisible, illimitable, exclusive, and perpetual form of public power— entrenched within an individual state—is now defunct.[17] Within the wider international community, rules governing war, weapons systems, terrorism, human rights, and the environment, among other areas, have transformed and delimited the order of states, embedding national polities in new forms and layers of accountability and governance (from particular regimes such as the Nuclear Non-Proliferation Treaty to wider frameworks of regulation laid down by the United Nations Charter and a host of specialized agencies).[18] Accordingly, the boundaries between states, nations, and societies can no longer claim the deep legal and moral significance they once had; they can be judged, along with the communities they embody, by general, if not universal, standards. That is to say, they can be scrutinized and appraised in relation to standards which, in principle, apply to each person, each individual, who is held to be equally worthy of concern and respect. Concomitantly, shared membership in a political community, or spatial proximity, is not regarded as a sufficient source of moral privilege.[19]

The political and legal transformations of the last 50 years or so have gone some way toward circumscribing and delimiting political power on a regional and global basis. Several major difficulties remain, nonetheless, at the core of the liberal international regime of sovereignty which create tensions, if not fault-lines, at its center.[20] I shall dwell on just one aspect of these tensions here.

Serious deficiencies can, of course, be documented in the implementation and enforcement of democratic and human rights, and of international law more generally. Despite the development and consolidation of the regime of liberal international sovereignty, massive inequalities of power and economic resources continue to grow. There is an accelerating gap between rich and poor states as well as between peoples in the global economy.[21] The development of regional trade and investment blocs, particularly the Triad (NAFTA, the European Union, and Japan), has concentrated economic transactions within and between these areas.[22] The Triad accounts for two-thirds to three-quarters of world economic activity, with shifting patterns of resources across each region. However, one further element of inequality is particularly apparent: A significant proportion of the world's population remains marginal to these networks.[23]

Does this growing gulf in the life circumstances and life chances of the world's population highlight intrinsic limits to the liberal international order, or should this disparity be traced to other phenomena—the particularization of nation-states or the inequalities of regions with their own distinctive cultural, religious, and political problems? The latter phenomena are contributors to the disparity between the universal claims of the human rights regime and its often tragically limited impact.[24] But one of the key causes of the gulf lies, in my judgment, else-where—in the tangential impact of the liberal international order on the regulation of economic power and market mechanisms. The focus of the liberal international order is on the curtailment of the abuse of political power, not economic power. It has few, if any, systematic means to address sources of power other than the political.[25] Its conceptual resources and leading ideas do not suggest or push toward the pursuit of self-determination and autonomy in the economic domain; they do not seek the entrenchment of democratic rights and obligations outside of the sphere of the political. Hence, it is hardly a surprise that liberal democracy and flourishing economic inequalities exist side by side.

Thus, the complex and differentiated narratives of globalization point in stark and often contradictory directions. On the one side, there is the dominant tendency of economic globalization over the last three decades toward a pattern set by the deregulatory, neoliberal model; an increase in the exit options of corporate and financial capital relative to labor and the state, and an increase in the volatility of market responses, which has exacerbated a growing sense of political uncertainty and risk; and the marked polarization of global relative economic inequalities (as well as doubt as to whether there has been a "trickle down" effect to the world's poorest at all). On the other side, there is the significant entrenchment of cosmopolitan values concerning the equal dignity and worth of all human beings; the reconnection of international law and morality; the establishment of regional and global systems of governance; and growing recognition that the public good—whether conceived as financial stability, environmental protection, or global egalitarianism—requires coordinated multilateral action if it is to be achieved in the long term.

SEPTEMBER 11, WAR, AND JUSTICE

If September 11 was not a defining moment in human history, it certainly was for today's generations. The terrorist violence was an atrocity of extraordinary proportions. The intensity of the range of responses to the atrocities of September 11 is fully understandable. There cannot be many people in the world who did not experience shock, revulsion, horror, anger, and a desire for vengeance, as the Kingsolver passage acknowledges. This emotional range is perfectly natural within the context of the immediate events. It was a crime against America and against humanity; a massive breach of many of the core codes of international law; and an attack on the fundamental principles of freedom, democracy, justice and humanity itself—i.e. those principles which affirm the sanctity of life, the importance of self-determination and of equal rights and liberty.

These principles are not just Western principles. Elements of them had their origins in the early modern period in the West, but their validity extends much further than this. For these principles are the basis of a fair, humane and decent society, of whatever religion or cultural tradition. To paraphrase the legal theorist Bruce Ackerman, there is no nation without a woman who yearns for equal rights, no society without a man who denies the need for deference, and no developing country without a person who wishes for the minimum means of subsistence so that they may go about their everyday lives.[26] The principles of freedom, democracy, and justice are the basis for articulating and entrenching the equal liberty of all human beings, wherever they were born or brought up. These principles are the basis of underwriting the liberty of others, not of obliterating it. Their concern is with the irreducible moral status of each and every person—the acknowledgment of which links directly to the possibility of self-determination and the capacity to make independent choices.[27]

Terrorism does negate our most elementary and cherished principles and values. Thus we are challenged to put the fight against terror on a new footing. Terrorists must be brought to heel, and those who protect and nurture them must be brought to account. Zero tolerance is fully justified in these circumstances. But the justified emotional response cannot be the basis for a more considered and wise response. A considered response attends to those very values that terrorism denies.

The founding principles of our society dictate that we do not over-generalize our response from one moment and one set of events; that we do not jump to conclusions based on concerns that emerge in one particular country at one moment; and that we do not rewrite and rework international law and governance arrangements from one place—in other words, that we do not think and act over-hastily and take the law into our hands. Any defensible, justifiable, and sustainable response to September 11 must be consistent with our founding principles and the aspirations of international society for security, law, and the impartial administration of justice—aspirations painfully articulated after the Holocaust and the Second World War—and embedded, albeit imperfectly, in regional and global law and the institutions of global governance. If the means deployed to fight terrorism contradict these principles and achievements, then the emotion of the moment might be satisfied, but our mutual vulnerability will be deepened.

The fight against terrorism raises tactical as well as moral challenges. President Bush described the attacks of September 11, and the U.S.-led coalition response, as a "new kind of war," and, indeed, the attacks of September 11 can be viewed as a more dramatic version of patterns of violence witnessed during the last decade in the wars in the Balkans, the Middle East, and Africa. These wars are quite different from, for example, the Second World War. They are wars which are difficult to end and difficult to contain, where, typically, there have been no clear victories and many defeats for those who champion the sanctity of human life, human rights, and human welfare. There is much that can be learned from these experiences that is relevant to the situation now unfolding.

The contours of these "new wars" are distinctive in many respects because the range of social and political groups involved no longer fit the pattern of a classical inter-state war; the type of violence deployed by the terrorist aggressors is no longer carried out by the agents of a state (although states, or parts of states, may have a supporting role); violence is dispersed, fragmented, and directed against citizens; and political aims are combined with the deliberate commission of atrocities which are a massive violation of human rights. Such a war is not typically triggered by a state interest, but by religious identity, zeal, and fanaticism. The aim is not to acquire territory, as was the case in "old wars," but to gain political power through generating fear and hatred. War itself becomes a form of political mobilization in which the pursuit of violence promotes extremist causes.[28]

In Western security policy, there is a dangerous gulf between the dominant thinking about security based on "old wars"—like the Second World War and the Cold War—and the reality in the field. The so-called Revolution in Military Affairs, the development of "smart" weaponry to fight wars at long distance, the proposals for the National Missile Defense program, were all predicated on outdated assumptions about the nature of war—the idea that it is possible to protect territory from attacks by outsiders. The language of President Bush, with its emphasis on the defense of America and of dividing the world between those "who are with us or against us," tends to reproduce the illusion, drawn from the experience of World War II, that this is a war between simply "good" states led by the United States and "bad" states. Such an approach is regrettable and, potentially, very dangerous.

Today, a clear-cut military victory is very difficult to achieve because the advantages of supposed superior technology have been eroded in many contexts. As the Russians discovered in Afghanistan and Chechnya, the Americans in Vietnam, and the Israelis in the current period, conquering people and territory by military means has become an increasingly problematic form of warfare. These military campaigns have all been lost or suffered serious and continuous setbacks as a result of the stubborn refusal of movements for independence or autonomy to be suppressed; the refusal to meet the deployment of the conventional means of interstate warfare with similar forces which play by the same set of rules; and by the constantly shifting use of irregular or guerrilla forces which sporadically but steadily inflict major casualties on states (whose domestic populations become increasingly anxious and weary). And the risks of using high-tech weapon systems, carpet bombing, and other very destructive means of inter-state warfare are very high, to say the least.

War and bombing were and are one option in the fight against terrorism. But the risks of concentrating military action against states like Afghanistan are the risks of ratcheting up fear and hatred, of actually creating a "new war" between the West and Islam, a war which is not only between states but within every community in the West as well as in the Middle East. The terrorists likely hoped for air strikes, which would rally more supporters to their cause. They are now likely hoping for a global division between those states who side with America and those who do not. The fanatical Islamic networks that were probably responsible for the attacks have groups and cells in many places including Britain and the United States. The effect of the U.S.-led war might very well be to expand the networks of fanatics, who may gain access to even more horrendous weapons, to increase racist and xenophobic feelings of all kinds, and to increase repressive powers everywhere, justified in the name of fighting terrorism.

An alternative approach existed, and might even be salvaged in some respects, although the longer the forces of the U.S. and its allies have to remain in place to secure foreign lands, the less optimistic one can be. An alternative approach is one which counters the strategy of "fear and hate." What is needed, as Mary Kaldor and I have argued, is a movement for global, not American, justice and legitimacy, aimed at establishing and extending the rule of law in place of war and at fostering understanding between communities in place of terror.[29] Such a movement must press upon governments and international institutions the importance of three things.

First, there must be a commitment to the rule of law, not the prosecution of war. Civilians of all faiths and nationalities need protection, wherever they live, and terrorists must be captured and brought before an international criminal court, which could be either permanent or modeled on the Nuremberg or Yugoslav war crimes tribunals. The terrorists must be treated as criminals and not glamorized as military adversaries. This does not preclude internationally sanctioned military action under the auspices of the United Nations both to arrest suspects and to dismantle terrorist networks. But such action should always be understood as a robust form of policing—as a way of protecting civilians and bringing criminals to trial. Moreover, this type of action must scrupulously preserve both the laws of war and human rights law. Imran Khan put a similar point forcefully in a recent article:

> The only way to deal with global terrorism is through justice. We need international institutions such as a fully empowered and credible world criminal court to define terrorism and dispense justice with impartiality. . . . The world is heading towards disaster if the sole superpower behaves as judge, jury and executioner when dealing with global terrorism.[30]

The news (in October 2001) of an increasingly intense pattern of extrajudicial, outlaw killings (organized, targeted murders) on both sides of the Israeli-Palestine conflict compounds anxieties about the breakdown of the rule of law, nationally and internationally. This way only leads one way; that is, toward Hobbes's state of nature: the "warre of every one against every one"—life as "solitary, poore, nasty, brutish, and short."

Second, a massive effort has to be undertaken to create a new form of global political legitimacy, one which must confront the reasons why the West is so often seen as self-interested, partial, one-sided and insensitive. This must involve condemnation of all human rights violations wherever they occur, renewed peace efforts in the Middle East, talks between Israel and Palestine, and rethinking policy toward Iraq, Iran, Afghanistan, and elsewhere. This cannot be equated with an occasional or one-off effort to create a new momentum for peace and the protection of human rights. It has to be part of a continuous and ongoing emphasis in foreign policy. Many parts of the world will need convincing that the West's interest in security and human rights for all regions and peoples is not just a product of short-term geopolitical or geo-economic interests.

And, finally, there must be a head-on acknowledgment that the ethical and justice issues posed by the global polarization of wealth, income, and power, and with them the huge asymmetries of life chances, cannot be left to markets to resolve. Those who are poorest and most vulnerable, locked into geopolitical situations which have neglected their economic and political claims for generations, will always provide fertile ground for terrorist recruiters. The project of economic globalization has to be connected to manifest principles of social justice; the latter need to reframe global market activity.

To date the U.S.-led coalition, in pursuing first and foremost a military response to September 11, has chosen *not* to prioritize the development of international law and UN institutional arrangements (point 1); and *not* to emphasize the urgency of building institutional bridges between the priorities of social justice and processes of economic globalization (point 3), although one or two coalition politicians have made speeches acknowledging the importance of this question. Peace in the Middle East has been singled out as a priority by some coalition leaders, but there is little sign as yet that this is part of a broader rethinking of foreign policy in the Middle East, and of the role of the West in international affairs more generally (point 2). These are political choices and, like all such choices, they carry a heavy burden of possibility and lost opportunity.

Of course, terrorist crimes of the kind we witnessed on September 11 may often be the work of the simply deranged and the fanatic and so there can be no guarantee that a more just world will be a more peaceful one in all respects. But if we turn our back on this challenge, there is no hope of ameliorating the social basis of disadvantage often experienced in the poorest and most dislocated countries. Gross injustices, linked to a sense of hopelessness born of generations of neglect, feed anger and hostility. Popular support against terrorism depends upon convincing people that there is a legal and pacific way of addressing their grievances. Without this sense of confidence in public institutions and processes, the defeat of terrorism becomes a hugely difficult task, if it can be achieved at all.

Kant was right; the violent abrogation of law and justice in one place ricochets across the world. We cannot accept the burden of putting justice right in one dimension of life—security—without at the same time seeking to put it right everywhere. A socioeconomic order in which whole regions and peoples suffer serious harm and disadvantage independently of their will or consent, will not command widespread support and legitimacy. If the political, social and economic dimensions of justice are separated in the long term—as is the tendency in the global order today—the prospects of a peaceful and civil society will be bleak indeed.

ISLAM, THE KANTIAN HERITAGE, AND DOUBLE STANDARDS

The responsibility for this pursuit of justice does not just fall on the West. It is not simply the United States and Europe that must look critically at themselves in the aftermath of September 11; there is a chronic need for self-examination in parts of Islam as well. The Muslim writer Ziauddin Sardar wrote recently:

> To Muslims everywhere I issue this fatwa: any Muslim involved in the planning, financing, training, recruiting, support or harbouring of those who commit acts of indiscriminate violence against persons . . . is guilty of terror and no part of the *ummah*. It is the duty of every Muslim to spare no effort in hunting down, apprehending and bringing such criminals to justice.
>
> If you see something reprehensible, said the Prophet Muhammad, then change it with your hand; if you are not capable of that then use your tongue (speak out against it); and if you are not capable of that then detest it in your heart. The silent Muslim majority must now become vocal.[31]

Iman Hamza, a noted Islamic teacher, has spoken recently of the "deep denial" many Muslims seem to be in. He is concerned that "Islam has been hijacked by a discourse of anger and a rhetoric of rage."[32] The attacks of September 11 appear to have been perpetrated in the name of Islam, albeit a particular version of Islam. It is this version of Islam which must be repudiated by the wider Islamic community, who need to reaffirm the compatibility of Islam with the universal, cosmopolitan principles that put life, and the free development of all human beings, at their center.

Hugo Young made the same point rather bluntly in *The Guardian* recently:

> [T]he September terrorists who left messages and testaments described their actions as being in the name of Allah. They made this their explicit appeal and defence. Bin Laden himself, no longer disclaiming culpability for their actions, clothes their murders and their suicides in religious glory. A version of Islam—not typical, a minority fragment, but undeniably Islamic—endorses the foaming hatred for America that uniquely emanates, with supplementary texts, from a variety of mullahs.[33]

Accordingly, it is not just enough for the West to look critically at itself in the shadow of September 11. Muslim countries need to confront their own ideological extremists and reject without qualification any doctrine or action which encourages or condones the slaughter of innocent human beings. In addition, they need to reflect on their own failings to ensure minimum standards of living, and a decent, free and democratic life for all their citizens. As Bhikhu Parekh, chair of the Commission on the Future of Multi-ethnic Britain, put it, Muslims must "stop blaming the West for all their ills" and must grapple with the temptation to locate all the main sources of their problems elsewhere.[34]

September 11 can be linked to a new, integrated political crisis developing in West Asia. The crisis has been well analyzed by Fred Halliday:

> In several countries, there has been a weakening, if not collapse, of the state—in the 1970s and 1980s in Lebanon, more recently in Afghanistan and Yemen. . . . It is in these countries, where significant areas are free of government control, or where the government seeks to humour autonomous armed groups, like al-Qaeda, that a culture of violence and religious demagogy has thrived. . . . This is compounded by the way in which the historically distinct conflicts of Afghanistan, Iraq and Palestine have, in recent years, come to be more and more connected. Militants in each—secular nationalist (Saddam) as well as Islamist (Osama bin Laden)—see the cause of resistance to the West and its regional allies as one.[35]

Hence, Osama bin Laden's first target was the government of Saudi Arabia, to which he later added the governments of Egypt and Jordan (and the Shi'ite Republic of Iran). Only later did he formally connect (via a declared *fatwa* in 1998) his war against these governments to the United States, which he came to see as the key source of, and support for, the corruption of Islamic sovereignty in the Middle East.[36]

The fundamental fissure in the Muslim world is between those who want to uphold universal standards, including the standards of democracy and human rights, and want to reform their societies, dislodging the deep connection between religion, culture and politics, and those who are threatened by this and wish to retain and/or restore power to those who represent "fundamentalist" ideals. The political, economic, and cultural challenges posed by the globalization of (for want of a better shorthand) "modernity" now face the counterforce of the globalization of radical Islam. This poses many big questions, but one in particular should be stressed: that is, how far and to what extent Islam—and not just the West—has the capacity to confront its own ideologies, double standards, and limitations. Clearly, the escape from dogma and unvindicated authority— the removal of constraints on the public use of reason—has a long way to go, East and West. The Kantian heritage should be accepted across Islam as well.

It's a mistake to think that this is simply an outsider's challenge to Islam. Islam, like the other great world religions, has incorporated a diverse body of thought and practice. In addition, it has contributed, and accommodated itself, to ideas of religious tolerance, secular political power, and human rights. It is particularly in the contemporary period that radical Islamic movements have turned their backs on these important historical developments and sought to deny Islam's contribution both to the Enlightenment and to the formulation of universal ethical codes. There are many good reasons for doubting the often expressed Western belief that thoughts about justice and democracy have only flourished in the West.[37] Islam is not a unitary or explanatory category.[38] Hence, the call for cosmopolitan values speaks to a vital strain within Islam which affirms the importance of rights and justice.

CONCLUDING REFLECTIONS

It is useful to return to the passage with which I started this chapter. It makes uncomfortable reading because it invites reflection on September 11 in the context of other tragedies and conflict situations, and asks the reader to step outside of the maelstrom of September 11 and put those events in a wider historical and evaluative framework. Uncomfortable as this request is, we have to accept it if we are to find a satisfactory way of making sense of September 11. To begin with, as the passage suggests, it is important to affirm the irreducible moral status of each and every person and, concomitantly, reject the view of moral particularists that belonging to a given community limits and determines the moral worth of individuals and the nature of their freedom. At the center of this kind of thinking is the cosmopolitan view that human well-being is not defined by geographical and cultural locations, that national or ethnic or gendered boundaries should not determine the limits of rights or responsibilities for the satisfaction of basic human needs, and that all human beings require equal moral respect and concern. Cosmopolitanism builds on the basic principles of equal dignity, equal respect, and the priority of vital need in its preoccupation with what is required for the autonomy and development of all human beings.

Cosmopolitan principles are not principles for some remote utopia; for they are at the center of significant post–Second World War legal and political developments, from the 1948 UN Declaration of Human Rights to the 1998 adoption of the Statute of the International Criminal Court. Many of these developments were framed against the background of formidable threats to humankind—above all, Nazism, Fascism and the Holocaust. The framers of these initiatives affirmed the importance of universal principles, human rights, and the rule of law when there were strong temptations to simply put up the shutters and defend the position of some nations and countries only. The response to September 11 could follow in the footsteps of these achievements and strengthen our multilateral institutions and international legal arrangements; or it could take us further away from these fragile gains toward a world of further antagonisms and divisions—a distinctively uncivil society. At the time of writing, the signs are not good, but we have not yet run out of choices—history is still with us and can be made.

7. GOVERNANCE HOTSPOTS: CHALLENGES WE MUST CONFRONT IN THE POST–SEPTEMBER 11 WORLD

SASKIA SASSEN

September 11, 2001 brings to the fore, with perhaps greater urgency than other events, the need for global governance. But it also underlines the fact of place-specific understandings about the event and how different positions in the global system produce different logics for how to proceed. Moving on after September 11 will require more than the U.S. government's focus on eliminating organized terrorist networks and providing humanitarian aid, crucial as these two interventions are. There is a much larger set of issues that needs to be addressed—by world and country leaders, by the supranational system, by NGOs, by global civil society, by corporate economic actors. Many of these issues are specific to each country and inevitably centered in the internal dynamics and struggles of each, as Seyla Benhabib reminds us in her piece for this volume.[1] Others concern the development of global governance institutions discussed by David Held and Robert O. Keohane, also in this volume.[2] Better global governance can take many forms: from improved control over the use of global financial markets and immigration to helping reduce poverty and misery, and hence rage, in the global south. This is a broad field for examination variously taken up by other chapters in this volume.

Here I will confine myself to two subjects which are emerging as major challenges for a well functioning global economic and political system and which demonstrate the sharpening interdependence between the global south and north: the growing debt of governments in the global south and the world immigration regime, with its steady accumulation of contradictions.[3] While these two problems are connected in some ways, each of them calls for specific and distinct governance mechanisms; and although these mechanisms may tend to push in the same direction, they do not overlap, except perhaps in dealing with the rise of illegal trafficking in people, one of the issues I will discuss. Methodologically, these two subjects are interesting both because they capture global interdependence and because each has been largely assigned to the domain of "markets," and hence not to "governance," even as each is subject to very specific regulations in particular moments of the larger processes that they represent.

Both the debt crisis and the contradictions of the immigration regime capture a broad range of intersections between governments, supranational institutions, and markets. Examining them in the context of the events of September 11 helps us reposition these events in a much broader set of dynamics than those of the terrorist acts themselves. Though less so now than then, introducing a broader context in the examination of September 11 is often considered to be putting blame on the victim and even as unpatriotic.[4] But it is also a way of dissecting the nature of the sharpening interdependencies that globalization entails and identifying the corresponding governance deficits. The two cases focused on here show that as the world is more interconnected, we need more multilateralism and internationalism. Both will require innovations in our conceptions of governance. This will have to consist of multiple and often highly specialized cross-border governance regimes—simply relying on overarching institutions will not do. While I confine myself here to the role of governments, it is clear that new forms of collaboration with civil society and supranational institutions are part of this effort.

I examine these two governance hotspots from the perspective of the countries of the global north and their self-interest, rather than broader issues of social justice and humanitarian concern. The latter are crucial, yet utilitarian arguments are more persuasive to many. If there is one general assumption in my argument, it is that misery in the global south is not good for anyone: neither for the suffering global south nor the prosperous global north (*pace* the fact of prosperous elites in the global south and tens of millions of poor in the global north). It is also probably the case that addressing the global debt and immigration as issues of self-interest to the global north, rather than simply a matter of social justice, is the more difficult argument to make. Indeed such an argument has not quite been developed and I do not claim to succeed at it here.[5] What follows are some elements toward the development of such an argument.[6] It is important to emphasize that one's positionality does make a difference. If I were to produce an account from the perspective of a country in the global south, the issues would not be exactly the same.

The kind of socioeconomic devastation I focus on here cannot be seen as a cause for terrorism. But socioeconomic devastation can be seen, and is increasingly so, as a breeding ground for extreme responses, including illegal trafficking in people and successful recruitment of young people for terrorist activity, both random and organized. An example of such an extreme response was what we now know about the militarized gangs in the aftermath of the Bosnian conflict: There were no jobs and no hope for these young men, so the most viable option was continuing warfare. This is also the case with some of the gangs in devastated inner cities in the U.S. (though not all gangs, since now we also know that many in inner cities are actually contributing to social order and making life more manageable in devastated neighborhoods).

In the global south, the growth of poverty and inequality and the disablement of governments—overwhelmed by indebtedness which allows them to put fewer and fewer resources into development—are all part of the broader landscape within which rage and hopelessness thrive. If history is an indication, it is only miniscule numbers who will resort to terrorism, even when rage and hopelessness may engulf billions. But the growth of debt and unemployment, the decline of traditional economic sectors, and other similar trends in the global south are feeding multiple forms of extreme reactions, including political violence and an exploding illegal trade in people, largely directed to the rich countries.

Generally, it is becoming evident that even as we experienced a "decade of unprecedented peace and prosperity" in the language of our leaders, a growing number of countries in the global south experienced accelerated indebtedness, unemployment, decay of health and social services, and of infrastructure. While the spread of misery will largely not touch the global north directly and hence, from a narrow utilitarian logic, can be seen as of little concern to the global north, it can lead to extreme acts by a minority of people and organizations in these countries that may have direct impacts on the global north, partly through the infrastructure for globalization largely developed by the global north. Further, the spread of misery can and is having multiple indirect effects, or effects mediated through other dynamics, such as the spread of diseases once under control in the developed countries, and international criminal activity.

THE DEBT TRAP: BREEDING DESPAIR

There are now about 50 countries recognized as hyper-indebted and unable to redress the situation. It is no longer a matter of loan repayment but a fundamental new structural condition which will require real innovation. The debt cycle for poor countries has changed and debt relief is not enough to address the situation. One of the few ways out, perhaps the only one, is for the governments of the rich countries to take a far more active and innovative part in efforts to address the underlying logic of the debt trap.

It is always difficult to accept that an effort that mobilized enormous institutional and financial resources does not work. But we now know that structural adjustment programs, privatization, and deregulation in the global south will not solve the problem. Even full cancellation of the debt will not necessarily put these countries onto a sustainable development path. Had the Jubilee campaign to cancel all existing debt of poor countries succeeded, it would not necessarily solve the basic structural trap. There is enough evidence now to suggest that a new structural condition has evolved from the combined effect of massive transformations in the global capital market and so-called economic "liberalization" related to globalization. Middle-income countries are also susceptible, as indicated by the financial crises of 1997 and 1998, and the 2001 Argentine default on approximately $141 billion, the largest sovereign default in history.[7]

If key features of the global capital market can have severe impacts on what are some of the richest economies in the world, such as South Korea, Brazil, Argentina, or Mexico, one can imagine the impact on poor countries. While all countries, including the U.S. and the UK, have in fact implemented some version of structural adjustment programs to lower expenditures by states on the social agenda, the impact on poor countries has been devastating. Over the 1980s and 1990s many innovations were launched, most importantly by the IMF and the World Bank through their Structural Adjustment Programs (SAPs) and Structural Adjustment Loans, respectively.[8] SAPs became a new norm for the World Bank and the IMF on grounds that they were one promising way to secure long-term growth and sound government policy. The bundle of new policies imposed on states to accommodate new conditions associated with globalization includes the opening up of economies to foreign firms, the elimination of multiple state subsidies, and financial deregulation. It is now clear that in most of the countries involved, whether Mexico and South Korea or the U.S. and the UK, these conditions have created enormous costs for certain sectors of the economy and of the population.[9] In the poor countries these costs have been overwhelming and have not fundamentally reduced government debt but rather entrapped these countries in a syndrome of growing debt.

There is no definitive proof that globalization is the cause of this outcome, since local inefficiencies and corrupt governments also play a crucial role in many cases. But we can assert, first, that globalization has not reduced these conditions: most countries that became deeply indebted in the 1980s have not been able to overcome their debt.[10] Secondly, as globalization proceeded in the 1990s these conditions worsened. In the 1990s a whole new set of countries became deeply indebted.[11] Third, this holds even for countries which adopted the new regime. The current crisis in Argentina could function as a natural experiment situation insofar as that country dutifully implemented many of the recommendations of the IMF and the World Bank, with extensive privatization and deregulation of its public sector and overall economy.[12] The purpose of much of this effort was and is to make countries more "competitive." While this may sound reasonable to many, it typically has meant sharp cuts in various social programs in countries where these programs are already inadequate in their coverage.

The actual structure of these debts, their servicing, and how they fit into debtor countries' economies, suggests that most of these countries will not be able to pay loans in full under current conditions. According to some estimates, from 1982 to 1998 indebted countries paid four times their original loans, and at the same time their debt stocks went up by four times.[13] Debt-service ratios to GNP in many of the HIPC countries (highly indebted poor countries) exceed sustainable limits. Many of these countries pay over 50 percent of their government revenues toward debt service or 20 to 25 percent of their export earnings. Africa's debt-service payments reached $5 billion in 1998, which means that for every $1 billion in aid received, African countries paid $1.4 billion in debt service in 1998.

What is often overlooked or little known is that many of these ratios are far more extreme than what were considered unmanageable levels in the Latin American debt crisis of the 1980s. Debt to GNP ratios are especially high in Africa, where they stand at 123 percent, compared with 42 percent in Latin

TABLE 7.1

External Debt and Debt Service in Developing Countries,
1991 to 1999, selected years (bn USD)

DEVELOPING COUNTRIES	1991	1995	1998	1999
External Debt	1,269.8	1,714.4	1,965.2	1,969.6
Net Creditor Countries	22.2	29.9	58.9	64.5
Net Debtor Countries	1,247.6	1,684.5	1,906.3	1,905.1
by Official Financing	234.5	286.8	292.9	300.3
by Private Financing	674.1	990.8	1,166.6	1,162.5
by Diversified Financing	338.9	406.9	446.8	442.2
Debt Service Payments	150.1	242.9	316.1	331.8
Net Creditor Countries	1.8	7.1	8.5	8.6
Net Debtor Countries	148.3	235.8	307.5	323.2
by Official Financing	16.5	25.8	22.7	16.8
by Private Financing	99.5	165.2	213.5	240.9
by Diversified Financing	32.2	44.8	71.4	65.5

Source: World Economic Outlook and Staff Studies for the World Economic Outlook, 1992–1999, IMF

Note: Developing countries include different countries in Africa, Asia, Middle East, Eastern and Western Europe.

America and 28 percent in Asia. The IMF asks HIPCs to pay 20 to 25 percent of their export earnings toward debt service. In contrast, in 1953 the Allies cancelled 80 percent of Germany's war debt and only insisted on 3 to 5 percent of export earnings to be paid toward debt service. These are also the terms asked from Central Europe after Communism.

This debt burden inevitably has large repercussions on state spending composition. We can see this in the case of Zambia, Ghana, and Uganda, three countries which have been seen as cooperative and responsible by the World Bank as well as effective in implementing SAPs. Taking 1994 data, for example, Zambia's government paid $1.3 billion in debt but only $37 million for primary education; Ghana's social expenses, at $75 million, represented 20 percent of its debt service; and Uganda paid $9 per capita on its debt and only $1 per capita for health care. In 1994 alone these three countries remitted $2.7 billion to bankers in the north.

THE SOCIAL COSTS

It is perhaps in the social impact of these features of government debt in the global south that new or sharpened interdependencies with the global north emerge. The processes that constitute these interdependencies are specific; some are new, others are older and become stronger or become global where before they may have been regional.

Among the social costs are, prominently, the growth in unemployment, the closure of a large number of firms in often fairly traditional sectors oriented to local or national markets, the promotion of export-oriented cash crops which have increasingly replaced and undermined survival agriculture and food production for local or national markets. The ongoing and mostly heavy burden of government debt in most of these economies has often drastically reduced socially oriented state expenditures and thereby sharpened the crisis of survival. Low public expenditures as share of GNP appear to be accompanied by increases in malnutrition and declines in life expectancy in many of the hyperindebted countries.

There is considerable research showing the detrimental effects of debt on government programs for women and children, notably education and health care—clearly investments necessary to ensure a better future. Further, the increased unemployment typically associated with austerity and adjustment programs implemented by international agencies to address government debt have also been found to have adverse economic effects on women. Unemployment, both of women themselves but also more generally of the men in their households, has added to the pressure on women to find ways to ensure household sur-

TABLE 7.2

Social Spending and Indebtedness: HIPC and Non-HIPC PRGF-Eligible Countries

(In units as indicated; latest year for which data are available)[1]

	EDUCATION SPENDING[2]		HEALTH SPENDING[2]		DEBT SERVICE[3]		Debt Stock	Number of Countries[4]
	In percent of GDP	In percent of total government expenditures	In percent of GDP	In percent of total government expenditures	In percent of GDP	In percent of total government expenditures	In percent of GDP	
HIPCs[5]	3.3	13.2	1.6	6.3	5.1	19.8	117.1	30
of which program countries	3.4	13.5	1.7	6.5	5.1	20.4	130.5	28
Non-HIPC PRGF-eligible countries[6]	4.6	15.3	2.5	8.0	2.9	11.2	56.6	20
of which program countries	3.9	15.4	1.8	7.3	3.0	11.6	58.6	13

Based on data from the World Bank and national authorities; and on IMF staff estimates.

[1] For most countries, the latest year for which data are available is 1997 for debt service and 1998 for health and education spending.

[2] In general, data on local government spending and in-kind donor contributions are not available, thereby understating total public spending.

[3] World Bank Global Development Finance (GDF) estimates of debt service paid, which may be lower than debt service due. However, caution should be exercised in interpreting these ratios due to the misclassification of debt service between cash and accrual.

[4] Sample size may vary across categories.

[5] Excludes Nigeria.

[6] Excludes transition economies (Albania, Armenia, Azerbaijan, Bosnia and Herzegovina, Georgia, the Kyrgyz Republic, the former Yugoslav Republic of Macedonia, Moldova, Mongolia, and Tajikistan) and includes Nigeria.

Source: From *World Economic Outlook, May 2000: Asset Prices and the Business Cycle*, Chapter 4, p. 143. Washington, D.C.: International Monetary Fund.

vival. Subsistence food production, informal work, emigration, and prostitution have all grown as survival options for women.[14]

Perhaps one of the clearest indications of a direct effect of the debt trap in the last few years is the exploding illegal trade in people, largely directed to the rich countries. The United Nations estimates that four million people were trafficked in 1998, producing a profit of $7 billion for criminal groups.[15] Since then, available estimates suggest these levels have grown.

Heavy government debt and high unemployment have brought with them the need to search for survival alternatives; and a shrinking of regular economic opportunities has brought with it the widened use of illegal profit-making by enterprises and organizations. In this regard, heavy debt burdens play an important role in the formation of countergeographies of survival, of profit-making, and of government revenue enhancement. Economic globalization has to some extent added to the rapid increase in certain components of this debt and it has provided an institutional infrastructure for cross-border flows and global markets. We can see economic globalization as facilitating the operation of these countergeographies at a global scale.

HOW THE GLOBAL NORTH CAN HELP

The events of September 11 eventually came to produce a growing recognition of the importance of enabling the global south to develop and to reduce misery as one component in the so-called war against terrorism. One key way in which the highly developed countries can help is to become lenders of first resort to countries in the global south in support of needed imports for development and in order to minimize the incidence of private lenders in these loans.

Poor countries need to import goods for basic needs and for development. Most are heavily dependent on imports of oil, food, and manufactured goods. Few poor countries can avoid trade deficits—of 93 low-and moderate-income countries, only 11 had trade surpluses in 2000. These countries would like to export more, as is evidenced by the setting up recently of a new African Trade Insurance Agency supporting exports to, from, and within Africa. Such specialized and focused efforts hold promise.

HIPCs need loans for these imports. Most exporters, especially from the global north, will only accept payment in dollars or other high-value currencies. This further renders native currencies valueless. Once poor countries have debts, interest payments and other debt servicing costs escalate rapidly and their currencies are likely to devaluate further. Borrowing in the leading foreign currencies is for these countries an important part of the debt trap. Their position is radically different from that of the rich countries, e.g., the U.S. has a $300 billion trade deficit and no problem getting loans at good rates, but foreign lenders are unlikely to want to hold loans denominated in LDC currencies. Further, lenders will ask for much higher interest rates from poor countries. Thus the debt trap reproduces itself.[16]

What is necessary is not a lender of last resort to bail out rich investors but a lender of first resort to help the global south pay for needed, development-linked imports, in their own currencies if at all possible. The logic is that this would make poor governments less dependent on private lenders who demand leading currencies, and even then charge these governments a premium, and would never accept their weak currencies.

The government debt of poor countries, and perhaps increasingly of middle-income countries as well, needs to be taken out of global capital markets and placed in the domain of the inter-state system. The governments of the rich countries could set up a mechanism or institution that would address the debt trap: it would accept the minor currencies of the indebted countries even if private investors will not. A growing number of observers are calling for an international bank, not as a lender of last resort to international banks but as a lender of first resort for payment imbalances between sovereign nations. Keynes already proposed this in the 1940s when the IMF was created. And the IMF has recently gone in this direction with its plan to provide early financing before a crisis, rather than bailouts of rich countries' investors—though its prescriptions to Argentina did not reflect this.

IMMIGRATION: UNSUSTAINABLE CONTRADICTIONS

Immigration is at the intersection of a number of key dynamics that have gained strength over the last decade and in some cases after September 11. Among the most prominent are the conditions described above which are likely to function as inducements for emigration and trafficking in people, much of it directed to the global north.[17] A second set of conditions is the demographic deficit forecast for much of the global north. A third is the increasingly restrictive regulation of immigration in the global north, to which we must now add new restrictions after September 11. A fourth is the shift in the trade-off between the protection of civil liberties and control over immigrant populations, which after September 11 shifted toward the latter.[18]

What I want to extricate from this bundle of issues is the existence of some serious tensions among these different conditions. Here I will briefly focus on two. The first tension is that between the evident preference in much of the global north, perhaps especially after September 11, for greater restrictions over immigrant entries and control over the immigrant population in a context where immigration plays an increasingly important role in demographic and labor force growth. The second tension is that between the consequences of some of the key dynamics of globalization and the growth of illegal trafficking in people as a mechanism for individual and household survival, for profit-making by illegal operators, and for government revenue.

THE DEMOGRAPHIC TURN

Even as the rich countries try harder and harder to keep would-be immigrants and refugees out, they face a growing demographic deficit and rapidly aging populations.[19] The most extreme demographic deficit will take place in Japan. According to a major study,[20] at the end of the current century and under current fertility and immigration patterns, population size in Western Europe will have shrunk by 75 million and almost 50 percent of the population will be over 60 years old—a first in its history.[21] Europe, perhaps more so than the U.S. given its relatively larger intake of immigrants, faces some difficult decisions. Where will they get the new young workers needed to support the growing elderly population and to do jobs considered unattractive by the native born, particularly in a context of rising educational attainment? The numbers of these jobs are not declining, even if the incidence of some of them is; one sector that is likely to add jobs is home and institutional care for the growing numbers of old people. Export of older people and of economic activities is one option being considered now. But there is a limit to how many old people and low-wage jobs an economy can export and a society can tolerate. Immigration is expected to be part of the solution.[22]

In the U.S. the evidence suggests a slightly different pattern. By century's end the forecasted labor shortfall for the U.S. is 34 million people, though this represents a point in the upward slope of the deficit which will not reach its highest level until early in the next century. The evidence shows fairly clearly that a significant component of population and labor-force growth in the U.S. over the last two decades was accounted for by immigrants, both second generation and foreign born.[23] In both cases, immigrants account for a larger component of growth than their share in, respectively, the general population and the total labor force.

Yet the way the countries in the global north are proceeding is not preparing them to handle this future scenario. They are building walls to keep would-be immigrants out. While this is not a new development in Europe, it has taken on a new urgency after September 11.[24] And at a time of growing refugee flows, the UN High Commissioner for Refugees faces an even greater shortage of funds than usual. Given an effective demand for immigrant workers, and indeed families, both of these policy preferences are likely to have negative repercussions for Europe and the United States. The construction of the immigrant and the refugee as a negative and undesirable subject, particularly after September 11, encumbers integration in the north. Further, given firms and households interested in hiring immigrants or determined to do so, for whatever reasons, restrictive policies aimed at the immigrant and the refugee can only be expected to feed the already growing illegal trafficking of people.

This would seem to be especially the case given the incentives built into the conditions described in the preceding section on indebtedness and lack of opportunity in much of the global south. Driven to look for economic security for themselves and their families by increasingly difficult conditions in their countries of origin, individuals are drawn by the opportunities of more developed economies. Through their remittances, emigrants also enter the macro level of development strategies for sending countries. In many countries these represent a major source of foreign exchange reserves for the government. While the flows of remittances may be minor compared to the massive daily capital flows in various financial markets, they are often very significant for developing or struggling economies.

In 1998 global remittances sent by immigrants to their home countries reached over $70 billion. To understand the significance of this figure, it should be related to the GDP and foreign currency reserves in the specific countries involved, rather than compared to the global flow of capital. For instance, in the Philippines, a key sender of migrants generally and of women for the entertainment industry in several countries, remittances were the third largest source of foreign exchange over the last several years. In Bangladesh, another country with significant numbers of its workers in the Middle East, Japan, and several European countries, remittances represent about a third of foreign exchange. Exporting workers and remittances are means for governments to cope with unemployment and foreign debt.[25]

The potential for growth in trafficking also arises from the growing interdependencies brought on by globalization which facilitate trafficking. Cross-border business travel, global tourism, the Internet, and other features of globalization enable multiple global flows not foreseen by the framers and developers of economic globalization. This creates a difficult trade-off in a context where September 11 has further sharpened the will to control immigration and resident immigrants. Neither increased unauthorized immigration and trafficking on the one hand, nor the reduction in civil liberties of immigrants on the other, are satisfactory ways to accommodate more immigration in response to the future demographic turn.

TRAFFICKING

Trafficking in workers for both licit and illegal work (e.g. unauthorized sex work) illuminates a number of intersections between the negative conditions described in the first section and some of the tensions in the immigration regime discussed in this section.[26] Trafficking is a violation of several distinct types of rights: human, civil, political. Trafficking in people appears to be mainly related to the sex market, to labor markets, to illegal migration. Much legislative work has been done to address trafficking: international treaties and charters, UN resolutions, and the establishment of various bodies and commissions.[27] Trafficking has become sufficiently recognized as an issue that it was also addressed in the G8 meeting in Birmingham in May 1998.[28] The heads of the eight major industrialized countries stressed the importance of cooperation against international organized crime and trafficking in persons. U.S. President Clinton issued a set of directives to his administration in order to strengthen and increase efforts against trafficking in women and girls. This in turn generated the legislation initiative by Senator Paul Wellstone; Bill S.600 was introduced in the Senate in 1999.[29] NGOs are also playing an increasingly important role. For instance, the Coalition Against Trafficking in Women has centers and representatives in Australia, Bangladesh, Europe, Latin America, North America, Africa, and Asia Pacific. The Women's Rights Advocacy Program has established the Initiative Against Trafficking in Persons to combat the global trade in persons.

This type of trafficking shows us one of the meanings of interdependence in the current global system. There are two distinct issues here: One is that globalization has produced new conditions and dynamics, especially the growing demand for these types of workers by the expanding high-income professional workforce associated largely, though not exclusively, with globalization.[30] The second issue is that globalization has enabled older trafficking networks and practices which used to be national or regional to become global.

Trafficking in migrants is a profitable business. According to a UN report, criminal organizations in the 1990s generated an estimated $3.5 billion per year in profits from trafficking migrants (excluding most of the women trafficked for the sex industry). The entry of organized crime is a recent development in the case of migrant trafficking; in the past it was mostly petty criminals who engaged in this type of activity. The Central Intelligence Agency of the U.S.[31] reports that organized crime groups are creating intercontinental strategic alliances through networks of co-ethnics throughout several countries; this facilitates transport, local contact and distribution, provision of false documents, etc. The Global Survival Network[32] reported on these practices after a two-year investigation using the establishment of a dummy company to enter the illegal trade. Such networks also facilitate the organized circulation of trafficked women among third countries—not only from sending to receiving countries. Traffickers may move women from Burma, Laos, Vietnam, and China to Thailand, while Thai women may have been moved to Japan and the U.S.[33]

Illegal trafficking is, in this context, a worrisome development in that it introduces a new type of highly aggressive, ruthless, and determined agent with enormous capacity to distort what have historically been key features of migration flows. The patterning of migrations largely reflects older and current bonds between sending and receiving countries and thereby suggests the possibility of developing fruitful bi- and multilateral ways of addressing migration among the particular countries involved. The massive entry of large scale trafficking can introduce completely new patterns that may bear little connection to the other dynamics binding the countries involved. Further, the increasing globalization and organization of these flows by international criminals introduces almost invariably the element of coercion, resulting in the abrogation of migrants' human, civil, and political rights (reflected in forced labor as a condition of fulfillment of contracts, in the sex trade, and in accounts that regularly surface in the news of the suffocation or drowning of migrants in transit).

THE NEED FOR SPECIALIZED MULTILATERALISMS IN IMMIGRATION POLICY

It is in the interest of the developed countries to alter the conditions in the global south promoting the rapid growth in illegal trafficking and the advantages it brings to traffickers and governments in the form of hard currency. If we accept that immigration flows are partly embedded in larger dynamics of poverty and debt, and that they are enabled by the infrastructure of globalization, then we may eventually confront the necessity of a radical rethinking of what it means to govern and regulate them. Putting aside the desirability of it, such a radical policy rethinking has been worked out with trade through the Uruguay round of GATT and the creation of the WTO. Such a policy rethinking is also becoming evident in military operations, with the growing weight of international cooperation, United Nations consent, and multilateral interventions. And it is being done for telecommunications policy and other areas that require compatible standards across the world. But there has been little innovation in immigration policy, a fact often explained by invoking the complexity and intractability of the issues.

In this context it is important to emphasize that many international policy areas that have seen enormous innovation are also extremely complex, that the actual achievements of these policy reformulations could not have been foreseen even a decade ago, and, perhaps most importantly, that the actual changes on the ground (e.g. globalization) in each of these domains forced the policy changes on governments no matter how high their reluctance. From where I look at the immigration reality—which is the freedom of the scholar rather than the day-to-day constraints of immigration policymakers and analysts—the changes brought about by the growing interdependencies in the world will sooner or later force a radical rethinking of how we handle immigration. Taking seriously the evidence about immigration produced by vast numbers of scholars and researchers all over the world could actually help, because it tends to show us that these flows are bounded in size, time, and space, and are conditioned on other processes; they are not mass invasions or indiscriminate flows from poverty to wealth.

We will need regionally focused multilateral approaches involving the governments of both emigration and immigration countries, as well as a range of nongovernmental actors, to develop the capacity to manage migration flows. This means recognizing that migration flows are part of interconnected world functions. This recognition may help reduce the incentives for illegal trafficking. The challenge that lies ahead will demand that all countries involved move beyond current conceptions of immigration policy in the receiving countries and that the governments of sending countries, notorious for their lack of involvement and indifference, join in this effort.

Beyond the crucial objective of effective socioeconomic development that makes it possible for people to stay in their countries, there are specific migration-linked issues. For instance, a very particular and utilitarian beginning that might motivate rich countries concerns precisely the emerging demographic and labor-force asymmetries. We have recognized the emergence of a global labor market for high-tech, financial, and legal experts, and to that end we have set up multilateral systems and institutional protections and guarantees for these workers (e.g. in NAFTA and in GATT).[34] Now it is time to recognize that there is an emerging global labor market for low-wage workers as well (e.g. maids, nannies, and nurses, janitors and industrial service workers), and that they deserve the institutional protections and guarantees given to professional workers. In the long run, it will be to the advantage of the global north, as well as to that of the global south.

CONCLUSION

The world today faces major governance challenges. Growing interconnectedness has given new meaning to old asymmetries as well as creating new ones. The rising debt, poverty, illegal migration, and generalized rage in the global south are beginning to reach deep into the rich countries. They are producing outcomes that are brutalizing for all involved and in the long run produce overall disadvantage in both the global south and north.

The two cases I briefly examined here bring to the fore the need for specialized multilateral collaboration among specific sets of countries. In an era of privatization and market rule we are facing the fact that governments will have to govern a bit more. But it cannot be a return to old forms—countries surrounding themselves with protective walls. It will take genuine multilateralism and internationalism and some radical innovations. National governments will have to get involved along with nongovernmental actors and supranational organizations.

Travelling around the world since September 11, I have found one theme becoming louder and louder in many places outside the U.S., in both the global north and global south, among critics of the attacks who share our horror and do not want to see such attacks ever again anywhere in the world. The theme is, in a nutshell, that the attacks on the U.S. and the war against organized terrorism should not keep us from seeing and remembering all the other struggles going on and the larger landscape of rage and hopelessness engulfing more and more people. Resolving the irrationality of the global debt trap and the accumulation of contradictions in the global immigration regime are by no means the only responses the international community must make after September 11, but they are two important ones if we hope to see global governance that proceeds from global cooperation, not brutality.

8. THE UNITED STATES AND THE WORLD ECONOMY AFTER SEPTEMBER 11

BARRY EICHENGREEN

Without question, the events of September 11 reshaped the debate over economic globalization. A trend that many economists had been inclined to characterize as irresistible suddenly came to appear less so. Foreign assembly operations have become less attractive to U.S. corporations now that there is the fact or even the danger that their trucks will be stuck in mile-long queues at the border. Companies like McDonald's and Starbucks, whose principal opportunities for market growth are abroad, must now factor in extra costs of security and the danger of disruptions when opening an outlet outside the United States. Computer programmers from India and graduate students from Pakistan face additional hurdles when attempting to obtain temporary residency, and American companies will think twice about posting executives abroad. There is good reason to believe that international trade, foreign direct investment, and international migration will all grow less quickly than before the terrorist attacks.

Some have gone further, suggesting that the events of September 11 imply more than just the slower growth of foreign trade, investment, and migration—that they put the very notion of globalization at risk. As Alan Greenspan cautiously put the point in a speech at the Institute of International Economics a little more than a month after September 11, "Terrorism poses a challenge to the remarkable record of globalization."[1] John Gray, the British political scientist and critic of globalization, put it more starkly, writing that "The entire view of the world that supports the markets' faith in globalisation has melted down. . . . Led by the United States, the world's richest states have acted on the assumption that people everywhere want to live as they do. As a result, they failed to recognize the deadly mixture of emotions—cultural resentment, the sense of injustice and a genuine rejection of western modernity—that lies behind the attacks on New York and Washington."[2]

These dire predictions are lent some plausibility by the observation that it was the United States that provided much of the impetus for globalization in the 1990s. The Clinton Administration negotiated the North American Free Trade Agreement, proposed a Free Trade Area of the Americas, urged developing countries to open their economies to trade and financial flows, and pressed the International Monetary Fund to mount emergency rescues when emerging markets encountered financial difficulties.[3] To the extent that globalization is associated with U.S. policies and products (Coca-Cola, McDonald's hamburgers, Starbucks's coffee), anti-Americanism and antiglobalization make obvious, if sometimes strange, bedfellows. To the extent that the United States is under attack, so too is globalization.

Moreover, the initial U.S. reaction to the terrorist attacks was to draw back from international entanglements, on the grounds that the world had suddenly become more dangerous, economically and otherwise. Before long, of course, this instinct gave way to a recognition of the impossibility of security in one country, leading to a commitment to root out the institutions of terrorism wherever they reside. However, the implications of this stance for international economic cooperation are decidedly mixed. Notwithstanding their desire to craft alliances, U.S. political leaders reiterated—for example, in the President's post-attack State of the Union message—their readiness to take unilateral action if the country's allies were reluctant to enlist in the campaign to bring down regimes lending comfort and support to terrorists. To the extent that the United States is prepared to act unilaterally to defend what it perceives as its vital security interests, even if this threatens to disrupt oil shipments from the Middle East or seaborne transport through the Suez Canal, it has become a less attractive economic partner for other governments, who fear being tarred by the same brush in countries that question the effects and effectiveness of the U.S. campaign.

The events of September 11 being superimposed on the first synchronized OECD–wide recession in 30 years, it is not hard to conjure up scenarios of the collapse of globalization. The process of international integration has been reversed before, in the wake of World War I and that mother of all synchronized recessions, the Great Depression of the 1930s.[4] Then the corrosive effect of integration on social structures and traditional ways of life unleashed a political backlash that took the form of destructive nationalism, culminating in both trade warfare and a devastating military conflict.[5] Is there reason to doubt that the same could happen again, this time with cleavages running along religious and ideological as well as national lines?

There are good grounds for thinking that foreign trade, foreign direct investment, and international migration will grow less quickly than before the terrorist attacks. But how much less quickly? Airfreight rates rose by some 15 percent in the aftermath of the attacks. The costs of insuring goods in transit rose even more sharply. But these headline items surely overstate the impact. Only a small fraction of merchandise travels by air. Airfreight is perishable whether it takes the form of legal documents or fresh-cut flowers, therefore justifying whatever additional expenditure on security is required to minimize delays in transit. Insurance costs have risen unusually sharply due to the extraordinary uncertainty that surrounds future terrorist disruptions. At the same time, however, insurance accounts for only a small fraction of transaction and transportation costs.

The OECD has estimated that the additional costs of screening and time in transit will come to perhaps 3 percent of the value of global merchandise trade.[6] Together with the elasticities of the Obstfeld-Rogoff model,[7] which emphasizes the impact of transport costs on trade, this suggests a very large fall in the value of world trade, on the order of 25 percent of benchmark levels. The slump in the rate of growth of world trade in goods and services (in volume terms) from 12.4 percent in 2000 to 1 percent in 2001 is seen by some as an early manifestation of this change.[8]

If these inferences are accurate, then they suggest that the age when world trade expanded more rapidly than production is over. U.S. companies will have to rethink their strategy of minimizing inventories and of sourcing inputs and final products from abroad on a just-in-time basis. It follows that the age when emerging markets can pursue an export-led development strategy may be over as well.

But there are a number of reasons for doubting the OECD estimates and the alarmist conclusions drawn on their basis. In particular, there is a strong incentive to invest in new technologies in order to minimize disruptions to international business.[9] We use infrared scanners on trucks coming in from Mexico and CAT scans on selected luggage at airports. The Dutch have begun to experiment with an iris-recognition system for airline passengers. The U.S. Congress is discussing the possibility of mandating the use of electronic seals on containers. More investment in such technologies will allow international traffic to move more quickly, whether it takes the form of trucks, container ships, or passenger airliners. Technologies that are hard to imagine now, precisely because they have not been invented, will help these lines to move faster, and threats to security to be identified at lower cost.

In addition, relatively modest changes in the organization of foreign trade could contain the security threat to the U.S. homeland at little cost to the country's international transactions. The U.S. government is discussing with its foreign counterparts a plan to funnel container traffic into the United States through a select number of foreign ports which will enjoy preferential access to the U.S. market, and reap corresponding rents, if they allow U.S. officials to subject their cargo to intensive scrutiny prior to embarkation. In a sense, the idea is to extend to container traffic the approach already used for passenger air traffic, whereby carriers prepared to transmit their passenger manifests to U.S. customs and immigration officials prior to departure receive preferential treatment on arrival.

Other countries have a strong incentive to cooperate in these initiatives. The United States is far and away the largest national export market in the world, access to which is prized. Our NAFTA partners have a particularly strong incentive to adapt their economies and trade to avoid losing access to the U.S. market. Soon after September 11, Mexican President Vicente Fox proposed major investments in immigration control on Mexico's southern border in order limit the burden on U.S. immigration officials along the United States' own southern border and thereby to preserve access for Mexican firms and shippers. A survey of 250 Canadian CEOs, taken a little more than a month after the terrorist attacks, similarly yielded an overwhelming consensus that the two neighbors urgently needed to agree on a common set of immigration rules in order to protect Canadian access to the U.S. market. Canada and Mexico have the largest investments in globalization of virtually any countries in the world. They have a strong incentive to make us see the relevant security zone as North America and not simply the United States.

All this suggests a relatively muted impact of the events of September 11 on U.S. and world trade. There will be some reorientation of trade toward middle- and high-income countries with the technological sophistication and administrative capacity to satisfy our security concerns. There will be some reorientation of trade toward countries with which we already have extensive economic and political links and that consequently have a particularly strong incentive to cooperate on such matters. Over time, the United States and other countries that share its security concerns can substitute cost-efficient technological and organizational changes for the laborious human inspection processes implemented after September 11. Although the result will be to throw a bit of sand in the wheels of international trade, there are likely to be fewer such grains than feared in the aftermath of the terrorist attacks.

The personal experience of many readers of this chapter will be consistent with this view. In the weeks following September 11, the lines at the check-in counter and X-ray machines at U.S. airports were endless. Various economists sought to calculate the cost to American corporations of adding four hours of waiting time onto every business trip. Rather quickly thereafter, however, technological and organizational change reduced the length of the lines. Additional X-ray machines were purchased, and curbside check-in of baggage was reinstated. The personnel responsible for security checks were given additional training. Frequent flyers learned to discard heavy belt buckles and shoes with metal clasps in order to avoid activating sensitive metal detectors. The last time I went to the airport the additional time required to clear security had fallen to only a couple of minutes. These changes are not without cost: Every time I fly I now pay an additional $10 to defray the costs of that extra security. But this price is modest compared to four additional hours of time for a $100-an-hour business executive or consultant (or, in my case, the cost of missing an academic conference). It is an example of how technological and organizational change can work to minimize the disruptions to international transactions owing to security concerns.

The terrorists targeted the World Trade Center because it was a symbol of American capitalism in one of its most visible manifestations, global financial markets. Among the victims were a large number of persons who worked for companies, foreign as well as domestic, whose business was international finance. This points up the question of how international investment will be affected by these events.

One widely heard prediction following the events of September 11 was that multinational corporations would rethink their foreign investment plans. Perhaps so, but their retrenchment will have to overcome powerful momentum for outsourcing production and developing global supply chains. Transfers between the foreign affiliates of multilaterals rose nearly twice as fast as global trade in the course of the 1990s. Multinational production and investment proved themselves to be powerful sources of cost savings for U.S. corporations. Some U.S. firms may decide to repatriate production to U.S. soil or to maintain larger inventories in order to insulate themselves from potential terrorist disruptions abroad, but there is little sign of this so far. Rather than building inventories in response to any new uncertainties associated with foreign supply, the fourth quarter of 2001 saw inventory liquidation at an historically unprecedented rate in response to the downturn in the U.S. economy.[10]

In other words, the economic logic for multinational investment is compelling. Nearly half of all U.S. exports (47 percent in 2000, to be precise) is trade within companies, reflecting these deeply entrenched employment and production relationships which require additional investment to sustain. Not long ago, the United Nations reported that 70 percent of the respondents to its survey anticipated expanding investment and employment in their foreign operations in the coming three years.[11] The Institute of International Finance estimates that foreign direct investment flows to emerging markets will fall only marginally between 2001 and 2002, and that any fall that takes place is likely to be due primarily to the global recession that was already evident before September 11 (affecting the electronics sector in particular), and not to the terrorist attacks.[12]

To be sure, the destinations of direct investment will change: U.S. firms are more likely to be attracted to Thailand than Indonesia and to Taiwan than the Philippines—that is, to places where the danger posed by separatist movements and religious conflict is less. As this set of paired comparisons suggests, middle-income countries tend to be viewed as more stable than their low-income counterparts; they have stronger political and social institutions, these being both causes and consequences of economic development. One disturbing implication of the events of September 11, then, is that relatively poor countries will tend to be struck from the list of potential and actual FDI recipients.

Whatever the outlook for foreign direct investment, there are plausible reasons for thinking that portfolio investment will actually be buoyed rather than depressed by the attacks. Buying a bond of a foreign government or a stock issued by a foreign corporation is physically less risky than opening an American factory abroad or checking into the Intercontinental Hotel in the capital city of a country whose government is not a member of the Bush administration's coalition against terrorism. There is still a big world economy out there. Investors still want foreign exposure in their portfolios. They still value international diversification.

Relative to the alternatives, the events of September 11 make portfolio investment a more attractive way of getting it. Portfolio capital flows to emerging markets have fallen precipitously since 1997, reflecting the sobering impact of the Asian crisis, the Russian crisis, the Brazilian crisis, and now the Argentine crisis. But their resilience in the face of recent events—Brazil and Mexico were able to issue global bonds worth some $1.5 billion in January 2002 at the height of the Argentine crisis—suggests that their new attractions may be just the tonic needed by this segment of the international financial market.

In this view, the main impact on capital flows will be not on their level but on their composition and direction. Investors will have an even stronger incentive to differentiate among countries according to the strength of their economic, financial, and political institutions, and the amount of support they are likely to receive from the United States and the international financial institutions. One of the problems of the 1990s was that investors, in their enthusiasm for emerging markets, failed to distinguish adequately among destinations for their funds. This had already begun to change before September 11. Having been burned repeatedly, the markets had begun to distinguish more carefully among emerging-market credits, a trend that manifested itself in the increasing dispersion of emerging-market spreads and a steeper gradient between spreads and country credit ratings.[13] This trend will now accelerate.

Any new tendency for capital to flow even more disproportionately to countries that have built relatively strong financial systems, political institutions, and international alliances is a good thing from the point of view of financial stability. It will sharpen the rewards for countries that build strong democratic institutions, that deal with minorities in ways that minimize ethnic strife, and that build bridges to their neighbors, since these will be the places where Americans will seek to invest. But it also means that the gap between the haves and have-nots will widen. More foreign investment will flow to the first-tier countries of Eastern Europe, attracted by their strong democratic institutions and prospects for accession to the European Union. Investment in sub-Saharan Africa, in contrast, is likely to be seen as even less attractive than before. Note that this is the same conclusion drawn for foreign trade and foreign direct investment—that its reorganization in response to the events of September 11 is likely to favor the middle-income emerging markets at the expense of the poorest countries.

The events of September 11 will also have implications for International Monetary Fund assistance for emerging markets and for U.S. views of that institution's activities. The Bush administration has made clear that it will use every weapon at its disposal to fight terrorism. The IMF is one such instrument, since the United States is the Fund's largest single shareholder. This clearly enhances the prospects for multilateral assistance for countries like Turkey and Pakistan, who are now too geopolitically important to be allowed to default on their debts. On December 7, 2001, the IMF Executive Board approved a three-year, $1.3 billion arrangement for Pakistan under the terms of the Poverty Reduction and Growth Facility. On February 4, 2002, the IMF announced the decision to provide a three-year, $16 billion Standby Credit for Turkey.[14] This favorable treatment is surely not unrelated to the fact that these are "frontline" states in the war against terrorism.

Argentina, on the other hand, is far from the front lines. One is reminded of Henry Kissinger's quip that "Argentina is a dagger pointed straight at the heart of Antarctica." Now that the stakes have been raised, amplifying the voices of those who argue that the United States cannot afford a major disruption to international financial markets, IMF lending will be ramped up. But to demonstrate that the United States is not blindly throwing at emerging markets the hard-earned tax dollars of U.S. plumbers and carpenters (to paraphrase U.S. Treasury Secretary Paul O'Neill), there will also be a temptation to make an example of a problem country. It was never hard to imagine who this might be. The other shoe dropped when the IMF, with the support of its largest shareholders, refused to release an additional tranche of financial assistance for Argentina in December 2001.

The most dramatic development in IMF policy came the week previous, however, when the institution's first deputy managing director, Anne Krueger, raised the idea of an international bankruptcy proposal for sovereign debtors.[15] The idea of an amendment to the IMF Articles of Agreement which would override U.S. securities law by empowering the IMF to authorize a standstill on payments, bar litigation by disgruntled creditors, and allow debts to be restructured by a qualified majority vote of investors was inconceivable before September 11. It would not have been proposed without the tacit support of the U.S. government (which nominates the Fund's first deputy managing director).

To be sure, frustration over their inability to engineer an orderly restructuring of Argentina's debts had more than a little to do with the U.S. Treasury's new-found sympathy for these long-standing ideas. But, in addition, there was a perception that the difficulty of debt restructuring made life intolerably hard for developing countries, something that the world could ill afford if lack of opportunity in highly indebted poor countries was part of what caused disaffected young men to take up weapons and extremist causes. The result of the status quo, in the words of the IMF's director of external relations, is that "the citizens of the defaulting country experience greater hardship than they need to, and the international community has a tougher job helping pick up the pieces. In the end, unsustainable debts have to be restructured. The only question is how painfully."[16] The events of September 11, which suggested a linkage between painful financial disruptions in the Third World and homeland security in the United States, played at least some role in this newfound willingness on the part of the IMF and the Bush administration to consider alternatives to the status quo.

Just as the Asian crisis had forced the Congress to acknowledge the need for an increase in Special Drawing Rights, the current crisis highlights the need for the international financial equivalent of the New York Fire Department. As a result, the extreme view on Capitol Hill that the IMF should be abolished has essentially been extinguished. At the same time, the legitimacy of the IMF and its economic advice will not be enhanced if it is viewed by other countries, more so than before, as an instrument of U.S. foreign policy. Calls for reform of the institution's voting formulas and procedures to enhance the representation of developing countries have traditionally been met in Washington with an unsympathetic response. If the IMF is to become less of a lightning rod in the developing world as well as in the United States, the notion that it is simply a water carrier for the United States and the other high-income countries must be overcome. This means taking seriously the proposals of the Cooper Committee for rethinking quota formulas and voting shares within the institution.[17]

This new enthusiasm for IMF programs is likely to be matched by a greater willingness on the part of the Bush administration and the U.S. Congress to pursue trade liberalization, although the decision to slap anti-dumping duties on imported steel in March 2002—while exempting producers from the poorest countries—raises questions about the depth of that commitment. Be that as it may, the fear dominating commentary in the wake of September 11—that the United States would turn its back on the world economy—has not come to pass. To the contrary, in November, two months after the attacks, the House of Representatives finally passed a bill giving the President fast-track authority to negotiate trade agreements. This was followed by an agreement at Doha to embark on a new round of global trade-liberalization negotiations, something which came as a pleasant surprise to pundits who had widely predicted the collapse of the meeting.

From this point of view, it is no coincidence that the prospects for a successful round of trade negotiations brightened after September 11 or that the focus of the Doha round will be on the problems of the poorest countries. There is a clear appreciation of the extent to which U.S. security rests in the long run on the existence of a peaceful and prosperous world. There is a newfound appreciation in the United States of the fact that the ideology that supports violent political action finds fertile soil in those parts of the world where the prospects for economic growth and prosperity are least. Security concerns thus militate in favor of hard compromises designed to enhance the market access of the poorest countries. This means farm-trade liberalization. It means liberalizing market-access rules for textiles and other labor-intensive goods. It means providing additional technical and financial assistance to poor countries that find it difficult to meet the product and safety standards needed to penetrate international markets.

To be sure, such liberalization will not be received happily by the U.S. steel and textile industries or by other sectors that blame their ills on import competition. It does not spell a happy future for European and Japanese farmers. Agricultural, steel, and textile lobbies are powerful not just in the United States but throughout the OECD. It is far from certain, therefore, that efforts to negotiate new trade agreements enhancing the market access of poor countries will succeed. Revealingly, the House bill renewing the President's fast-track negotiating authority is loaded down with restrictive provisions. It calls for the unilateral withdrawal of trade benefits granted by U.S. law in 2000 to textile exporters in the Caribbean and sub-Saharan Africa. To tie the President's hands, it calls for detailed consultations with the Congress on any and all agricultural tariff cuts. The Senate may yet modify many of these restrictive provisions in the House bill, but this debate makes clear that special interests will not go quietly.

These countercurrents notwithstanding, awareness of the linkages between export orientation, economic development, and political stability have patently increased the interest of the United States in a successful trade round. Vested interests in the high-income countries may yet may block that positive outcome. But the influence of newfound security concerns will force those attempting to stand in the way of further liberalization to go the extra mile.

Not all underdeveloped countries are well positioned to take advantage of the opportunities afforded by economic and financial globalization. The tropics are fertile breeding grounds for disease, of which AIDS and malaria are only the most obvious examples. Tropical climates and desert conditions limit the productivity of agriculture, making it difficult to support the growth of urban centers, where technological progress tends to be concentrated, and to free up labor for industrial employment, much less to export agricultural goods themselves. Afghanistan, like Israel, can grow sweet melons and pomegranates where natural springs make irrigation possible. But in general, water is insufficient for crop growth. Water shortage makes sanitation and hygiene more costly. Together with the impact of high temperatures on infection, this makes for a fecund disease environment and an extra obstacle to economic development.[18]

In addition, landlocked countries in Africa and Asia—again, Afghanistan is a prime example—must surmount special obstacles in the form of high transport costs and a lack of commercial relationships when attempting to substitute out of agriculture and to develop exports of light manufactures.[19] Landlocked countries lacking navigable waterways trade less than otherwise comparable countries.[20] They attract less foreign investment. For both reasons they benefit less from globalization.[21]

This is not a counsel of despair; rather, it is a guide for what kind of policy interventions are needed to support economic development in the poorest countries and to prevent lack of economic opportunity from breeding religious fanaticism and political extremism. Where the productivity of agriculture is low, the logic of comparative advantage suggests promoting the production of light, labor-intensive manufactures—shoes, cloth, and garments, for example—and exporting surplus production in exchange for food.[22] Where transport costs are high, it suggests cultivating trade with one's neighbors, where the obstacle of physical distance is least. Where investment is discouraged by the unreliability of contract enforcement and instability of policy, it suggests building stronger policy-making institutions.

Unfortunately, encouraging the development of stronger policy-making institutions is not something on which the international policy community has a track record of success. The West can attempt to write a constitution for Afghanistan, as the United States did for Japan after World War II. Making rural land reform an integral part of that effort—again, as occurred in East Asia after World War II—can give individuals a real stake in the economy. But writing a constitution is a very different task than implementing it. Redistributing land holdings is of little benefit so long as there remains confusion over property rights.

Indeed, the failure of many such efforts is one reason for the skepticism regarding foreign aid that is pervasive in the United States. The U.S. devotes scarcely one-tenth of one percent of its GDP to foreign aid—the lowest such share of any industrial country. The events of September 11 provide obvious impetus for this stance to be rethought, and the United Nations was quick to see the linkage, proposing a $50 billion increase in foreign aid and a summit conference designed to marshal support.

The war against the Taliban also led, predictably, to calls for a Marshall Plan for Afghanistan and for the developing world generally. Whether the U.S. will be prepared to devote significant resources to such an undertaking is uncertain. The answer lies, in part, on what return we can expect on our investment. The Marshall Plan may have been a great economic and political success, but its history, and the history of foreign aid generally, renders one pessimistic that its success can be replicated in the poorest countries today.[23] Foreign aid has worked only where there has existed a domestic constituency for reform and where multilateral assistance tipped the balance in its direction. This was recognized by one of the IMF's early managing directors, Per Jacobsson, as early as 1959, when he observed that foreign assistance "can only succeed if there is the will in the countries themselves." It is why Marshall Plan funds worked after World War II to help bring about inflation stabilization, fiscal consolidation, and market-friendly reform. Foreign aid could tip the balance because European governments were strongly predisposed to adopt these policies, something with which the Marshall Plan helped by limiting the short-run pain and sacrifices that had to be imposed on their constituents. Europe already had long experience with the market, which inclined it toward the adoption of market-friendly reforms. It had suffered devastating hyperinflations after World War I, which predisposed it to monetary and fiscal stabilization after World War II. It already had relatively strong monetary, fiscal, and exchange-rate policies and, perhaps more importantly, strong policy-making institutions. It had democratic governments with checks and balances that prevented aid from being diverted into the pockets of elites. And many European countries had single-party governments or strong coalitions capable of credibly committing to the relevant reforms.[24]

Where, on the other hand, has foreign aid *not* worked? It has not worked where there did not already exist a strong domestic constituency for reform, and where democracy was absent or the government otherwise lacked the capacity to commit to the relevant reforms. Burnside and Dollar show that aid has had no noticeable effect on growth in countries where policies were poor, governments were weak, and policy-making institutions were underdeveloped.[25] Scholars like Andrew MacIntyre ascribe the failure of IMF assistance to produce quick results in Thailand in 1997–1998 to a flawed constitutional design that generated weak coalition governments and incohesive parties unable to commit to reform.[26] They attribute the severity of Indonesia's crisis to the weakness of democratic institutions, which vested arbitrary decision-making power in the hands of one person, Suharto, who could as easily change his mind as stay the reformist course.[27]

These observations caution against exaggerated hopes that foreign aid conditioned on a laundry list of reforms and policies can play a major role in getting a postwar Afghanistan back onto its feet. They suggest relatively pessimistic conclusions about whether providing sustained U.S. aid, as opposed to dropping dehydrated meals from the skies and hiring U.S. construction companies to rebuild bridges and airstrips, will do much to alleviate the problems of countries where contract enforcement and investor protections are unreliable, and where political checks and balances are too weak to prevent foreign aid from being funneled into the pockets of the elites. They raise doubts about the effectiveness of aid for an interim government that lacks clear political legitimacy and strong domestic support.

One positive lesson of the Marshall Plan suggests, however, how foreign aid— conditioned on a few concrete steps that might be taken by the governments— could yield positive results. As a condition for the receipt of U.S. aid, European countries after World War II agreed to commit to regional integration. The Marshall Planners required them to move toward the construction of a European free trade area, building the institutions of what has become the European Union. This condition was relatively straightforward to monitor. It promoted postwar recovery and growth by allowing European countries to specialize along lines of comparative advantage. And it allowed the European continent to overcome a century of conflict by cultivating economic interests in common and by encouraging the construction of transnational institutions to govern those relationships.

To be sure, a free-trade area between Afghanistan and Pakistan would not deliver equally impressive results. The historical and economic circumstances are different than those of the Marshall Plan. But if Western policymakers are serious about a Marshall Plan for the region, aid conditioned on the negotiation of a free-trade agreement might produce positive results. One of the few factories still standing in Afghanistan in the wake of the American attack produced rubber shoes at a fraction of their cost in neighboring Pakistan.[28] Pakistani firms will be quick to see the advantages of outsourcing production to a neighboring country where labor costs are even lower than at home.[29] If the free-trade area includes not just Afghanistan and Pakistan but also the United States, there will then be more of a market for the final goods.[30] Freer trade will lead, not incidentally, to the freer flow of technologies and political ideas.

Plastic shoes may seem a weak reed on which to hang hopes for economic development and poverty reduction. But, in fact, World Bank studies have shown that textile and apparel exports can be a powerful engine for reducing poverty and unemployment.[31] Significant positive effects from the growth of these industries have been seen in Bangladesh, Madagascar, Mauritius, Pakistan, and Tunisia. Bangladesh, like Afghanistan, is one of the world's poorest countries. Yet between 1975–1980 and 1980–1995, a boom in apparel production and exports played an important role in a one-third reduction in urban poverty rates. The same was true in Pakistan between 1980–1985 and 1986–1990, an even shorter period.

Whether closer economic ties will lead also to ties of political cooperation only time will tell. But there is precedent for the approach.

The aftermath of September 11 saw a flurry of dire predictions regarding the future of globalization. The terrorist threat, it was warned, would cause the United States to withdraw into a protectionist shell. By slowing traffic across the U.S.–Canada and U.S.–Mexico borders, increasing the risks of direct foreign investment, heightening the perceived danger of business travel, and raising the specter of cyber-terrorism, the terrorists, in the words of David Hale, "had implemented the anti-globalizers' agenda."[32]

With time it has become apparent that these reports of the death of globalization were exaggerated. To be sure, the need for more thorough inspection of imported merchandise and the higher price of insurance for international transactions will increase the costs of trade, but the reorganization of security procedures in the short run and the development of new technologies in the longer run show every sign of minimizing the impact. The risks of foreign investment have risen as well, but here too market participants have shown an impressive ability to develop ways of containing those threats without being forced to radically change the way they do business.

More fundamentally, the events of September 11 created a new appreciation of the stake the United States has in economic and political development in the rest of the world. Just as the country turned from shunning military entanglements to spearheading a global war on terrorism and from rejecting state building to embracing alliance building, it can be argued that its political leaders developed a new appreciation of globalization as an engine of growth for developing countries. The evidence that opening to foreign trade and investment boosts growth rates and raises living standards in emerging markets was already compelling to economists.[33] Officials drawn from other disciplinary backgrounds may have been less convinced, but they were forced to acknowledge that economic opening and liberalization comprised the only coherent formula for raising living standards in parts of the world where they were lowest and of giving residents of those countries a stake in global connectivity. This rendered the argument for extending trade concessions to U.S. partners in the Third World all the more compelling. And, if doing so meant goring someone's sacred political cow, so be it. That the collapse of the Doha round of trade talks was averted and a fast-track trade bill was passed by the U.S. House of Representatives—over the objections of special interests—are two clear manifestations of this trend.

Thus, September 11 did not sound the death knell of economic globalization. While introducing additional costs and concerns, it rededicated the U.S. polity to spreading the gospel of globalization and harnessed U.S. technological and organizational resources to overcoming security threats.

None of this is to deny that the events of September 11 and new awareness of the immediacy of terrorist threats have implications for globalization. In particular, the reorientation of international trade and investment that will follow from these events will favor middle-income emerging markets relative to their less-developed brethren. U.S. imports will flow through ports with the technological sophistication and administrative capacity to guarantee the security of containers. The largest investments in guaranteeing the security of trade will be made by countries like Mexico that already trade most heavily with the United States. Foreign direct investment by multinationals will flow to countries with strong democratic institutions that allow religious and cultural disputes to be resolved in the political arena, and with strong social institutions capable of sustaining a distinctive national culture in the face of global media and global markets. Portfolio investment will flow to countries that similarly possess strong institutions and are viewed as reliable allies in the fight against terrorism.

There is a danger that the poorest countries will be left out. Trading with and investing in countries with weak institutions and unstable politics will be seen as riskier than before. This is an alarming prospect, given that poverty, lack of voice, and lack of opportunity make breeding grounds for terrorism.

If trade and investment cannot be counted on to help solve the problems of these countries, is there not an increased political as well as economic case for foreign aid? Here, an opportunity was missed. In the aftermath of September 11,

U.S. politicians and officials failed to make the link between development assistance on the one hand, and foreign aid as an instrument in the war against terrorism on the other. The Bush administration's first post-attack budget included only a very modest increase in foreign aid. At the United Nations' development summit in Monterrey, Mexico in March 2002, the administration did come forth with a commitment to increase foreign aid, but grudgingly, at the last minute, and only for countries that demonstrated an ability to spend aid funds "productively."

To be sure, major obstacles will have to be overcome if there are to be significant benefits from a Marshall Plan for the poorest countries. In countries with weak social and political institutions, there is a danger that aid will not reach its intended recipients but instead be diverted into the pockets of the elites. This is the rationale for the U.S. strategy, articulated at Monterrey, of extending aid only to countries that show an ability to produce results, whether in terms of infants vaccinated or students enrolled. But, in rejecting the case for additional aid for countries that have not yet demonstrated this capacity, the critics dismiss the extent to which the changes in international trade, investment and multilateral policy that flow from the terrorist attacks will make life harder for the poorest countries. They neglect the danger that poverty and lack of economic opportunity will make these countries breeding grounds for terrorism. It is not clear that aid for countries with weak institutions will in fact deliver the desired results, but can we afford not to try?

PART III

NEW WAR/NEW WORLD ORDER?

9. STATES, TERRORISTS, AND THE CLASH OF CIVILIZATIONS

JACK A. GOLDSTONE[1]

On September 11, 2001 the United States was attacked by a foreign adversary on its own mainland for the first time in almost two hundred years; no such attack had taken place since the War of 1812. Yet in the twenty-first century, that adversary was not another state. It was a terrorist "NGO," or nongovernmental organization, the terrorist group Al Qaeda. This attack has raised new questions about the nature of terrorism, and about the role of states and non-state groups in sponsoring and fighting international violence. It has led the United States to develop a foreign policy based on a "war on terrorism." Yet if that war is to be successful, rather than just a moralistic stance, we need to clearly understand our adversary—who they are, why they are fighting, how they operate, and how they might be halted.

UNDERSTANDING TERRORISM: THREE TYPES OF TERRORIST MOVEMENTS

Terrorism—the deliberate attack on civilians through the assassination of leaders or creating mass casualties and/or destruction of property, in order to demonstrate the power of the attacker and to intimidate a population—has been a tactic of war at least since the Huns attacked the Roman Empire. It has been used by both governments and nongovernment organizations, regular militaries and irregular guerrillas. The goal of "ridding the world of terrorism" thus boils down to, in essence, ridding the world of war and civil conflict; as long as the latter occurs, terrorist tactics will likely be used by one side or the other in pursuit of their goals.

However, the terrorist act of September 11 represents something new and distinct from the terrorism that has accompanied conflicts throughout history. It represents an attempt to lift a religious war to a global scale, by striking a highly visible and destructive blow that would herald the "clash of civilizations."[2]

In order to understand the unique threat posed by the group responsible for this action, it is necessary to show how their operations are distinct from other terrorist activity. We can begin by dividing the many and varied terrorist groups operating in the world into roughly three distinct types, according to their composition and their goals:

I. National or regional liberation or other extremist or ethnic movements that use terrorist tactics aimed at regimes deemed to be illegitimate occupiers of territory.

These movements are widespread and numerous and have included the Sendero Luminoso in Peru, the FARC in Colombia, the Tamil Tigers in Sri Lanka, the ETA in Spain, the IRA in Britain, and many of the rebel armies operating in West and East Africa. This category also includes extremists in the United States such as the radical antigovernment groups who inspired Timothy McVeigh's attack on the Oklahoma Federal Building. Some of these groups operate exclusively locally, on the territory in which they reside. Others operate internationally, either obtaining weapons, sanctuary, or other assistance from other countries, or striking across international borders.

However, what is common to all of these groups is that their goal is to liberate a particular territory. It is thus conceivable to negotiate or achieve some settlement relevant to their goals that will not involve the overthrow of many different nations' regimes, nor a wholesale change in international cultural and political norms.

II. International movements aimed at overthrowing widespread systems of social and political organization, and whose goals would necessarily involve the destruction of many nations' regimes.

The most familiar of these movements to Europeans and Americans of the twentieth century were facism and communism. Nazism used terror in its rise to power (against Jews to be sure, but the brownshirts used terror against any adversaries who stood in their way). In addition, international terrorist movements seeking to destroy capitalist regimes ranged from guerrilla fighters in Latin America to such groups as the Red Brigades in Europe and the Red Army Faction in Japan. With such groups, no negotiation over autonomy or governance in a particular nation was more than just a temporary truce. What such movements sought was nothing less than the international overthrow of liberal capitalism and the remaking of governance and authority in their own mold (whether fascist or communist).

In fact, many of these movements had both national liberation and international change as their goals. In some cases, the movements focused on the liberation and reshaping of particular nations (fascism in Italy, communism in Russia) as their primary goal. However, international change always remained a key element in their program, and thus international expansion and power projection were an inevitable accompaniment to their control of specific territories or nations.

While fascism and communism now seem to us to represent "evil" forces, there have also been international movements aimed at overthrowing systems of social and political organization that used terrorist tactics for what now seem to be more noble ends. Anticolonial movements assisted each other throughout Asia and Africa in attacking colonial regimes. While both freedom fighters and colonial regimes might claim to aim strictly to attack the military forces of their opponents, in practice attacks on civilians were often unavoidable and even deliberate elements of these bitter struggles. Today, a variety of national and international NGOs aimed at protecting animal rights and natural ecosystems have conducted terrorist raids on the property of producers of genetically modified crops, energy companies, and laboratories that carry out animal research.

III. Hybrid movements, in which national liberation movements with local territorial aims join forces with international movements with global aims.

In this partnership, the local national liberation movement gains military and financial support for its forces; in return it gives its support to the ideology and operations of the global movements. The global movement thus gains new bases for operations and expansion, and new areas to recruit supporters for its international operations.

The United States has, on some occasions, been deeply concerned with terrorist groups of type I, when they were located in territories deemed critical to U.S. interests. Thus for example the United States fought against terrorist guerrilla movements in the Philippines after both the Spanish-American War and World War II. The United States also fought against terrorist guerrilla movements in Latin America when they threatened U.S. interests (as in Nicaragua in the 1920s). Yet in general, the U.S. has treated most of these movements (including the ETA, the IRA, the Tamil Tigers, and, for most of its existence, the South African ANC) as local problems that are not central to U.S. foreign policy. These movements only became critical when they became *hybrids* of type III, most especially when local national liberation movements allied with international communism. Indeed, much of the Cold War was concerned precisely with identifying and countering type III movements allied with communism throughout the developing world, from Cuba to Vietnam to central America to Africa.

After the collapse of the Soviet Union in 1989–1991, most local national liberation movements lost their identification with any international movement aiming at the widespread destruction of other nations' regimes and sociopolitical systems. There was thus a widespread belief that U.S. foreign policy would no longer be troubled by hybrid terrorist organizations of type III, and that most terrorism would remain linked to local national liberation struggles and thus to groups of type I.

But this is not what has happened. Instead, in the course of the very struggle against communism, indeed in one of the key actions that led to its fall—the support of the liberation of Afghanistan from communist and Soviet control—the United States and other allies fostered a new international terrorist movement aimed at the destruction of Western liberal regimes. Almost without their realizing it, this new international terrorist movement has grown and linked up with a variety of national liberation movements to form new hybrid movements of type III. This new type III movement I shall label *International Islamic Terrorism,* or IIT.

THE NEW WORLD OF INTERNATIONAL ISLAMIC TERRORISM

International Islamic Terrorism aims to reestablish a unified Muslim ascendancy in the world against the current dominance of secular and Western powers. It perceives a wide range of governments as illegitimate occupying powers, including not only the United States, which has armed forces stationed throughout the Muslim world, and Israel, but also those governments of Muslim countries that are avowedly secular or allied with Western powers. These include the majority of governments in countries with large Muslim populations, including Saudi Arabia, Egypt, Turkey, Indonesia, Pakistan, and the Philippines, among others. This broad opposition to both non-Islamic regimes *and* secularized regimes within the Islamic world is something relatively new.

From the 1940s through the 1970s, the Islamic world had many followers of anticolonialist and Arab-nationalist ideologies.[3] However, these ideologies were avowedly secular. The regimes in power in such countries as Egypt, Iraq, and Syria today stem from the Arab-nationalist tide of that era. The regimes of the Shah in Iran, of Suharto in Indonesia, and of various military and democratic leaders in Pakistan endorsed variants of Islam as national religions, but they did not subscribe to any internationalist creed for the expansion of Islam beyond their borders or the reshaping of other governments. The Palestine Liberation Organization—drawing on Palestinians of all religions including Christians, Muslims, and varied sects—was a secular movement for the creation of a free Palestinian state.

These regimes promised to restore the power of Arab and Muslim nations by liberating them from Western colonial control and building powerful, autonomous states. Yet these promises went largely unfulfilled. Even with the enormous development of oil exports to provide a source of wealth and leverage over the West, the Muslim nations stretching from Morocco to Indonesia remained far poorer than their former colonial masters, and dependent on foreign investment and assistance. At the same time, modernization went far enough to create tens of thousands of college-educated youth, acutely aware of the subordinate positions of their countries and their cultures in global affairs.

Although many of these youths were educated as engineers or other professionals, and had parents who had embraced the secular creeds of post–World War II Arab and Muslim liberation, the new generation growing up in the 1960s and 1970s remained frustrated at the position of Muslim countries in the world, and turned to the study of Islam to seek alternative orientations. Teaming up with Muslim clerics who also—for their own reasons—were aggrieved at the secular regimes in their countries and the incursions of Western morals and manners into Muslim lands, these youths energized a movement for a radical Islamicization of Muslim nations.

In this movement, there is something similar to the phenomenon of the 1960s in the United States and Europe. There, many college-educated youths from affluent backgrounds came to question the moral basis for their own society, and challenged the legitimacy of their government's positions on issues ranging from family structures to civil and women's rights to involvement in Vietnam. The openness of U.S. society allowed the "New Left" to spread its views; some were generally adopted and influenced policy. Yet more extreme attacks on capitalist enterprise and private property were not tolerated, and groups like the Yippies became the target of FBI control. In response, some New Left groups became even more extreme, turning in some cases into flat-out terrorist bombers, such as the Weather Underground or the Symbionese Liberation Army.

In most Muslim countries, the openness of American society was absent, for even the anticolonial and secular Arab nationalist movements had given rise to closed and authoritarian, not democratic, regimes. The destruction of those regimes, and their replacement with Islamicized governments, thus became an avowed goal of the Islamicist movements in those countries. As a result, these Islamicist movements were harshly repressed by regimes who saw them as a threat. Just as with the Weather Underground in the U.S., but only after much larger-scale conflicts, repressive campaigns against Islamic terrorist groups in Egypt, in Syria, in Iran, and elsewhere in the Muslim world from the 1970s through the 1990s managed to break up these movements and suppress their activity.

That might have been the end of terrorist Islamist groups, except for three otherwise unconnected developments. First and most important was a series of coups and revolutions in the Kingdom of Afghanistan. Second was a profound shift in the struggle for the liberation of Palestine against Israel. Third was the collapse of the Shah's regime and the rise of an Islamicized regime Iran. Let us consider each of these in turn.

AFGHANISTAN AND THE MUJAHEDEEN[4]

In 1973, after pursuing a decade-long program of modest liberalization and modernization, the regime of King Zahir Shah of Afghanistan was overthrown in a coup d'etat by a former prime minister, Mohammed Daud. Daud sought to create a more firmly centralized and modernized regime. However, Daud had to deal with two competing organized factions among the Afghan elite: the communists, who wanted to aggressively modernize the country under government control on the model of the Soviet Union; and the Islamists, who wanted to halt those aspects of modernization that most impinged on family organization, local tribal autonomy, and clerical authority. After five years of trying to manage these competing interests while increasing his own personal control, Daud was overthrown in 1978 by leftists in the military who brought the communists to power.

Once in power, the communists sought to bring about a revolutionary reorganization of Afghan society by imposing radical land reform, modernizing and secularizing family law, and purging the bureaucracy and military of Islamicist and anticommunist elements. Yet the narrow elite of the communist party had little or no popular support for these actions, and the communists' policies aroused a growing national opposition to their rule. Within a little over a year, armed rebellion had broken out in over half the provinces of Afghanistan. In 1979, the Afghan communists invited the Soviet Army into the country to help them maintain their grip on power. The Soviet "invasion," as it was viewed by most Afghans, turned the domestic struggle against the Afghan communist regime into a national liberation movement with international ramifications.

Two distinct groups came to aid the Afghans in their struggle against the Soviets. From within the Muslim world, especially from Egypt, Saudi Arabia, Iran, and Pakistan, came many youths from the Islamicist movements that had been developing and struggling throughout the Muslim world (including one Osama bin Laden). These individuals, whose departure from their country was often supported by their own regimes as a way of exporting troublemakers, found a battlefield in which they were now strongly encouraged to fight for Islam against a godless and foreign power. The Muslim freedom fighters, or "Mujahedeen," were also given generous assistance by the governments of Iran, Pakistan, and Saudi Arabia. In each case, these regimes could burnish their Islamic credentials by supporting a clearly Islamic struggle. In addition, for Iran and Pakistan, who shared long borders with Afghanistan, support for the Muslim opposition also meant influence in any future liberated Afghan nation.

The second group of supporters were Western powers, chiefly the U.S., who supported the Mujahedeen as a way to attack the Soviet Union and turn back international communism. Western powers gave the Mujahedeen advanced tactical and weapons training, and sophisticated arms including mines and antitank and antiaircraft weapons, making it possible for them to stand up to the massive and well equipped Soviet armies.

Yet instead of using their influence to moderate the Islamicist current in the anti-Soviet opposition and instill a pro-Western and democratic ideology in the Afghan freedom fighters, Western nations—including the U.S.—chose to keep a low profile by funneling their aid through Pakistan. This decision was made in large part because since the 1979 revolution in Iran (discussed below), Iran had become an active enemy of the U.S. In seeking to secure influence in a post–Soviet-occupation Afghanistan, it thus seemed to make sense to work through Pakistan, who was seeking to secure its influence by supporting anti-Soviet groups. Thus Iran supported the Shi'a Islamic groups fighting in Afghanistan, mainly drawn from the Hezara ethnic group of western and central Afghanistan, while Pakistan supported the majority group of Sunni Muslims, drawn from the Pashtun, Uzbek, and Tajik groups in the south, north, and east of the country. The net result was to stamp an Islamic cast even more firmly on the Afghan resistance.

Drawing on nearly unlimited flows of weapons from Saudi Arabian and U.S. funds, and nearly unlimited flows of military recruits from sanctuaries for Afghan refugees in Iran and Pakistan, the Mujahedeen were able to wear down the Soviet occupation forces. In 1989, the Soviet Union withdrew its military, leaving a battleground of ethnically and religiously divided Islamic militias contending for control of the country.

From 1989 to 1994, regional commanders switched alliances with bewildering speed, and local populations were repeatedly prey to warlord struggles for territory. However, in 1994, in the southern city of Kandahar, a religious leader named Muhammed Omar rallied a group of local Mujahedeen and religious students to seize power from the local warlords. Drawing support from the majority Pashtun ethnic group and their tribal forces; from the idealist foreign Mujahedeen fighters, who came to support what they saw as the most truly Islamicized movement in Afghanistan; and above all from Pakistan, who believed it could control this movement, and thus indirectly control Afghanistan; Mohammed Omar's movement—the Taliban—quickly spread out from its base in Kandahar and by 1998 controlled 90 percent of the country.

The way that the liberation of Afghanistan played out was wholly unforeseen. Instead of a national liberation movement of type I, which might have aimed terror operations only at Soviet and Soviet-allied forces within the country, there developed in Afghanistan a type III hybrid terrorist movement, in which the national liberation forces were joined—and indeed largely funded and inspired by—an internationally recruited and organized network of "Islamic fighters" whose goal was to create Islamicized societies and turn back all secular and Westernized forces that threatened Muslim peoples and Muslim lands. Under the Taliban, Afghanistan thus became not merely a new national state, but a home for an international movement aiming to restore Muslim power by overturning secular governments and Western influence throughout the world. Furthermore, this new international Islamic movement had been trained and equipped by the U.S. and its allies, over the course of its struggle against the Soviet military, with the latest armory of lethal weaponry and tactics of stealth and guerrilla attack against its foes. Once the Taliban had established control, Afghanistan thus became the site of sophisticated training operations and communications for a network of Islamic warriors with international aims and ambitions.

PALESTINE AND THE INTIFADA[5]

Since 1948, the Palestine Liberation Organization (PLO) had aimed to return the lands composing the State of Israel to Palestinian settlement and control. After several Arab–Israeli wars from 1948 to 1967, however, Israeli-occupied territories had expanded, and the PLO was reduced to conducting terrorist actions from various external bases, including Lebanon and Tunisia. Dissatisfaction with the efforts of the foreign-based PLO, and again, frustration among a new generation of often college-educated Palestinians with their seemingly permanent second-class status in an occupied Palestine, led to an indigenous struggle against Israeli authority and settlements, known as the *intifada*.

Beginning in 1987, the *intifada* relied on a new generation of Palestinian elites, educated and based in the occupied territories (university education in Palestine increased greatly under the Israeli occupation). Many of these elites, as well as their followers, drew inspiration from the international Islamicist movement and gained their funding and ideological support from the same Iranian, Egyptian, and Saudi organizations—including the Muslim Brethren and Islamic Jihad—that had contributed to the struggle to liberate Afghanistan. There thus grew up a wholly new, Islamicized branch of Palestinian resistance to Israel, the "Islamic Resistance Movement," popularly known as Hamas. This new movement sought to displace the older generation of more secular PLO fighters.

However, after the Oslo Accords of 1993 and the Gaza Jericho Agreement of

1994, the PLO returned to Palestine as the leader of a new territorial entity, the Palestinian Authority (PA). At first, the PA under Yasir Arafat sought to secure its control of territory in Gaza and the West Bank and to reduce that of the new Islamic organizations. Yet from 1994 to 2000, no further progress was made in extending the territory or power of the Palestinian Authority. The prestige and authority of the PA among the Palestinians diminished, while that of the Islamic movements grew.

By late 2000, a confrontation at the al-Asqa mosque in Jerusalem led to the resumption of an active military and terror campaign between Israel and the Palestinian resistance groups. In this new round of struggle, both the secular and Islamic wings of resistance were actively involved, yet the Islamicist movement represented by Hamas, Hezbollah (nurtured by Iran, as noted below), and Islamic Jihad continuously threatened to take control of the resistance away from the more secular PA. As a result, like the Afghan liberation movement, the Palestine liberation movement also became a type III hybrid, in which an international Islamic movement has joined, and even taken the leadership of, what had previously been a more secular movement with strictly local nationalist goals. The campaign for Palestine liberation, in the eyes of these groups, thus becomes just one more battleground in the global competition between the West and Islam.

THE IRANIAN REVOLUTION

In 1979, just a few years after the overthrow of Zahir Shah in Afghanistan, the regime of Shah Reza Pahlevi of Iran also collapsed. Yet while Zahir Shah fell to a coup, the Shah of Iran's regime was replaced by a fundamentalist Islamic movement that immediately aimed to create a base for international challenges to Western influence. The Shah of Iran had been a major recipient of Western aid and, like Zahir Shah of Afghanistan, sought to build a more modern and liberalized nation, but to retain his personal authority. Yet these goals proved incompatible. Modernized elites agitated for more democratic institutions and railed against the corruption of the Shah's regime. At the same time, the Shah of Iran had embarked on a series of land reforms, and curtailments of clerical authority, that antagonized the traditional elites. When in the 1970s excessive debt and oil-financed spending drove up inflation and undermined the position of the urban middle class—while the earlier agricultural reforms had led to huge movements of unemployed rural families to the cities—the foundations were set for a massive cross-class coalition united against the Shah. In the late 1970s, human-rights pressures from the Carter regime in the U.S. encouraged the opposition, and an anti-inflation campaign of imprisonment and harassment by the Shah against traditional business elites (intended to deflect blame for inflation away from the

Shah's government) drove a critical ally over to the opposition. Inspired by militant clerics, led by modernized professionals, funded by traditional merchants and business leaders, and supported by underemployed urban masses, the opposition to the Shah took to the streets in 1978–1979 and brought down his government.

There then ensued a struggle for control of the revolution between its clerical visionary leaders and its modernizing professional organizers. The struggle was won by the former, with the aid of the new Islamic Guard—drawn from urban youth—who terrorized Iranians who sought a more secularized or Western-leaning regime. For the first time in a large and powerful Islamic country, a modernizing secular government had been overthrown and was replaced with an Islamicist regime led by the clergy.

The new Iranian regime was a model for promoters of Islam throughout the Muslim world. Yet its influence was limited for two reasons. First, the brand of Islamic fundamentalism in Iran was that of the Shi'a branch of the faith, which had followers primarily in Iran and contiguous regions. Outside of Iran, the Shi'a were a minority in all other large and populous Muslim states, where Sunnis were generally the dominant branch of Islam. Second, Iran soon became embroiled in a decade-long war with the secular Arab state of Iraq, which fully occupied Iran's energies in regard to international affairs.

However, since the end of the Iraq–Iran war, Iran has again sought to project its support for Islamicized rebellion against Western and non-Muslim forces across international borders. As we noted above, Iran was an important supporter of Mujahedeen forces in Afghanistan, although its influence was confined to the Shi'a groups within that country. Iran has also sponsored anti-Israel terrorist groups, mainly Hezbollah. Iran's actions have thus fostered the transformation of national liberation movements of type I into hybrid movements of type III, and provided a territorial base of operations for international Islamic terrorist movements.

In summary, developments in Afghanistan, Palestine, and Iran gave renewed life to Islamicist movements that had been unable to overcome authorities and establish themselves in such secular Muslim states as Egypt, Saudi Arabia, Syria, or Pakistan. The Afghanistan revolution drew Islamicist supporters together, gave them a mission, combat experience, and sophisticated weapons and training; and under the Taliban, they gained a territorial base. The development of an indigenous *intifada* and the growing role of Hamas in Palestine gave the international Islamicist movement another territorial bridgehead and campaign front against Westernized powers. In addition, the existence of a fundamentalist regime in Iran gives the international Islamicist movement a territorial and funding base controlled by a sovereign nation whose leadership shares their goals. Together, these events from the late 1970s through the 1990s created a formidable basis for an international Islamic movement that is prepared to use terror to advance its goals.

Let us now look more closely at the goals and activity of that movement, to see how these led up to the events of September 11, 2001.

AL QAEDA AND SEPTEMBER 11: WHO, HOW, AND WHY

Al Qaeda was founded during the winding down of the Afghan conflict, in 1988 or 1989, to serve as a clearing-house providing a variety of support, training, and guidance services to those individuals seeking to further the international strengthening of Islam through direct action against the West. Led by Osama bin Laden of Saudi Arabia and Muhammed Atef of Egypt, Al Qaeda became a leading branch of the international Islamic terrorist movement (IIT). The IIT is not a single structure, but rather my label for a loosely linked network of groups with common aims, including, in addition to Al Qaeda, such groups as Islamic Jihad, Hezbollah, Hamas, Abu Sayef, the National Islamic Front, and many other, smaller groups. What the various groups that compose the IIT have in common is a desire to destroy the dominance of Western power and culture in the world, and particularly to drive out all Western forces and allied secular regimes in the Muslim world. Their targets thus include not only Israel, but also the governments of Egypt, Saudi Arabia, and Pakistan, and also the governments and populations of the United States, Britain, Russia, and other European and pro-Western regimes.

The IIT is a new and especially troubling threat to the United States and its allies precisely because its aims are *not* limited to the liberation of a particular region or territories. Rather, it aims at the liberation of a broad swath of territories from Morocco to the Philippines, and believes that such liberation requires attacks to undermine the power and prestige of Western powers around the world. Thus wherever Western forces are to be found—whether on Western countries' territories, in embassies in Africa, at military installations in Saudi Arabia or Lebanon or Somalia, or in any other presence around the world—they are legitimate targets for attack. This is a wholly different mode of terrorist activity and goals than existed with prior anticolonialist or Arab nationalist movements in Islamic countries.

However, while generously distributing support to Islamicist causes in many countries, bin Laden also took Al Qaeda in a direction no other Islamicist group had dared go: planning sophisticated assaults directly targeting U.S. facilities, armed forces, and even U.S. territory. Al Qaeda is suspected of playing a role in almost all the major terrorist assaults on U.S. personnel and facilities carried out by Islamicist groups since 1989. These include the assault on U.S. forces in Somalia in 1993, the attempted bombing of the World Trade Center in 1993, the bombings of U.S. military posts in Saudi Arabia in 1996, the bombings of U.S. embassies in Dar es Salaam and Nairobi in 1998, the attack on the U.S. destroyer the *U.S.S. Cole* in Yemen in 2000, and the September 11 attacks. Each of these attacks displays a willingness to make U.S. forces or territory a primary target, with meticulous planning for complex operations, often simultaneously against multiple targets. So far, I believe these characteristics distinguish Al Qaeda from any other IIT groups, most of which remain hybrids of type II, aiming to combine their Islamicist goals with liberation of specific territories. It thus makes excellent sense, while understanding the broader context of IIT in which Al Qaeda developed, to focus on Al Qaeda and its leadership as the most critical threat to U.S. personnel, facilities, and territory.

Al Qaeda is a truly international organization. Its recruits include thousands of former fighters in the Afghan war, plus other individuals drawn to Al Qaeda through their involvement with other Islamicist organizations, whether those are other terrorist groups such as Egyptian Jihad, or simply mosques or religious schools (*madrasas*) in any number of countries who promote hatred of the West and the goal of restoring the global dominance of Islam. Many Al Qaeda leaders are recruited as college-educated individuals from affluent backgrounds who have been radicalized by experiencing the relative power and wealth of the West, the relative poverty of many of their Islamic compatriots, and the often exclusionary and corrupt nature of the governments in their home countries.

For such educated elites, the goal of restoring the glory of Islam on a global basis is not illusory, but a reasonable extrapolation of past history. From the seventh to the tenth century, Islamic forces swept all enemies—both Christian Western and Asian—before them, creating the vast Islamic empire of the Caliphate. Islamic forces conquered all of Spain, all of North Africa, and all of the Middle East. However, in the eleventh and twelfth centuries, the West struck back. In the Crusades, Christians retook the Holy Lands of the Eastern Mediterranean and embarked on the reconquest of Spain in the Western Mediterranean. Furthermore, in the thirteenth and fourteenth centuries Russia expanded to the north and Spanish kingdoms expanded in the West. Yet at the same time, the Ottoman Turks were building their empire in Turkey. By the seventeenth century, the Ottomans had reestablished an Islamic empire that stretched from Morocco to Iran, and which had pushed the West out of Turkey, Greece, Romania, parts of Hungary, and the Balkans (including the still-Muslim territories of Albania and

Bosnia). Then the West reasserted itself again, and by the early twentieth century, the Ottoman Empire had been dismembered by the European powers. Thus, for Islam to reassert itself and expand at the expense of the West in the twenty-first century would be simply the normal pattern of history. It should be appreciated that however unrealistic this aspiration seems to modern Western peoples, it is not a wholly irrational or unfounded aspiration among Muslims. Moreover, in many regions of the world, the Muslim religion is today the fastest-growing religion, by the peaceful means of conversion and natural population growth.

What is uniquely dangerous about Al Qaeda is that in addition to their goal of achieving Muslim dominance on a global scale, they draw on apocalyptic texts that argue for embracing death and inflicting death upon one's enemies as the favored path to their goal. Whereas mainstream Islam is a peaceful religion that has, through most of its history, advocated peaceful coexistence with other faiths, Al Qaeda draws on and propagates strategies of death and destruction, shaping not only its own operations but the hybrid terrorist/national liberation movements that it has come to influence.

In addition to its elite leaders, Al Qaeda draws followers from throughout the Muslim world, wherever lack of opportunity makes a career as an international terrorist more attractive than menial labor and poverty. In this attraction, Al Qaeda is like gangs in U.S. inner cities or social protest movements throughout the world. It is not poverty per se that gives birth to terrorists (or gangs or protest). Rather, poverty provides a situation in which there is fairly low competition by other occupations when leaders who seek to mobilize supporters against perceived injustices, and who offer attractive short-term rewards, come to recruit. Al Qaeda can draw on veterans of the Afghan liberation and other liberation struggles (Bosnia, Kosovo), as well as the graduates of Islamicist religious schools that preach the evils of Western influence, as recruits for their activities; both of these groups have little opportunity to become anchored in conventional occupations.

It is this combination of educated elites and large numbers of potential recruits with few other opportunities or anchors to "normal" life that allows Al Qaeda to conduct a large number of sophisticated operations. For example, in order to plan and carry out the 9/11 attacks, leaders for each of several groups of hijackers had to be recruited who would pilot the planes and act as the information conduits to the overall leadership. Then followers had to be placed who would provide the "muscle" to overpower the airplane crews and passengers. All of these individuals had to be financed and monitored, and then activated when the time for action came.[6]

The creativity of Al Qaeda in developing methods of conventional massive destruction suggests considerable ingenuity. However, having tried car bombs and now airplanes as guided missiles, it seems likely that Al Qaeda will try to escalate its attacks still further. Its pattern has been to shift targets and methods of destruction in order to keep its adversaries off balance. It is not unreasonable to suppose that Al Qaeda will try to obtain, and use, nonconventional weapons of mass destruction, including nuclear, biological, chemical, or radiological armaments.

In other words, Al Qaeda represents an exceptional and new threat to U.S. and Western interests. It is the most aggressive and sophisticated anti–U.S. spearhead of a broad international Islamic terrorist network that not only conducts direct attacks on U.S. targets but also reshapes various national liberation movements to join its cause. Instead of the world of terrorism that we anticipated after the collapse of the Soviet Union, with almost exclusively type I terrorist groups, we instead face a world with highly active type II and type III groups, with multiple territorial bases and broad international operations.

RESPONDING TO INTERNATIONAL ISLAMIC TERRORISM

It is a futile goal to seek to rid the world of terrorism. Type I terrorist groups will continue to operate as long as there are civil and international conflicts. Yet these become direct threats to Western civilization more broadly, and to the U.S. in particular, only when they are supplanted by terrorist organizations of type II and type III. The reasonable, and necessary, goal of U.S. policy regarding terrorism should therefore be to undermine and disable terrorist groups of type II, and to return the hybrids of type III to more localized goals of type I groups.

However, that is not an easy task. At this point, after allowing the IIT to build up over several decades from the 1970s to the present, an entire generation has grown up in the Islamic world strongly influenced by IIT groups. As with the threat from communism, it may take a decade or more of concerted effort to end this threat. Let us examine possible responses. We should consider both those responses that, although frequently mentioned in the media, would *not* be effective in curtailing ITT—specifically, imposing a settlement on Israel/Palestine and alleviating poverty in the Islamic world—and other responses which promise to be more effective.

Will settling the Israeli–Palestinian conflict end the threat from international Islamic terror?

No. For Al Qaeda and its followers, the goal is the removal of Western influence from as many lands as possible, and the spread of a "purified" Islam into all those

lands occupied by the faithful. Although for the nationalist Palestinian liberation groups, a minimal goal would be the establishment of a secure Palestinian
state—controlling key holy sites and with the economic and political capacity to
preserve its autonomy while coexisting with Israel—for the IIT groups, coexistence with Israel—even if agreed to by Palestinians—is not a satisfactory outcome. The hybridization of Palestinian liberation movements with international
Islamicist movements has produced a mix in which "for the Islamists, Palestine
had been lost in large measure as God's punishment for turning away from Islam.
They believed that Palestine was part of a larger God-given Islamic endowment;
thus no human had the right to cede control of any part of such lands to non-
Muslims. While the PLO . . . focused on gaining control of the lands occupied in
1967, a policy recognized formally in the Oslo Accords, the [Islamists] rejected
any Israeli presence in the Middle East. [Hamas therefore] undertook an ideological campaign devoted to the idea that not one inch of Palestine can be ceded
to Israel."[7] In this view, no negotiation of land for peace, or for anything else, is
possible.

Moreover, even the destruction of Israel would not suffice to satisfy the IIT
goals. That would simply be a victory in one battle, on one battlefront. A liberated Palestine would then be a base for the IIT groups to seek to expand "purified" Islam throughout the Muslim lands of the Near East and North Africa. The
most recent historical manifestation of the Islamic Caliphate, or world empire,
was the Ottoman Empire, which included Turkey, much of the Balkans and
North Africa across Egypt, Algeria, Libya, Tunisia, and Morocco, as well as the
Middle East. The struggle to restore the Caliphate would thus extend from Palestine to seek to undermine all Western-allied Muslim regimes.

In short, no conceivable outcome of the Israeli–Palestinian conflict would reduce the enmity or activity of IIT. Quite the contrary—the only hope for a peaceful resolution of the Israeli–Palestinian conflict is to reduce or remove the
influence of the IIT within the Palestinian liberation movement, so that a resolution to the conflict can be negotiated that focuses strictly on satisfying the interests of Palestinians and Israelis with regard to the lands they inhabit.

Will reducing poverty stem the rise of IIT?

It is well known to social scientists who analyze revolution, rebellion, and political violence that while poorer countries have more of all of these types of conflict, there is no simple relationship between poverty and political violence.[8]
India is far poorer than most Western nations, and most Mexicans are far poorer
than most Americans. But these countries have never provided a direct threat to

the U.S. Saudi Arabia and many Near Eastern states, such as Iran, are richer than many African states; yet the former have provided more anti–U.S. terrorists than the latter.

It is true that poverty, and a lack of opportunity for careers and livelihoods that anchor people in everyday life, increase the number of potential recruits for rebellious and terrorist movements. However, those potential recruits are only activated by the organization, money, weapons, and ideology provided by the leaders of the IIT. Those leaders do not come from poverty. Although much of their resentment is fueled by the relative wealth of the West (and often of their own government leaders), compared to their ordinary coreligionists, there is no reason to believe that raising income levels in poor countries around the world will immediately end the resentment felt by radical Islamists toward the West.

If poor people blame themselves for their condition, they work to overcome it. If they blame a corrupt or evil government for their condition, they may rebel against it. If they blame a foreign power or foreign culture for undermining their society and causing their condition, they may mobilize against that foreign power. It is not poverty as such, but perceptions of *injustice* that motivate political violence. And how those perceptions of justice are shaped is crucial in determining the spread of IIT. If humanitarian assistance is delivered in such a way as to demonstrate the concern of Western powers for Muslim peoples, it may somewhat offset the perception that poverty is an unjust imposition by the West. Or it may simply appear as one more handout from the conqueror to a beaten-down people.

The fact of the relative poverty of many Muslim peoples relative to the West, and indeed the absolute poverty of many peoples in the Muslim world, is not going to be changed in the near future. However, the consequences of that poverty for international terrorism depend on the perceptions that are created and spread regarding the causes of that poverty. If Muslim peoples are persuaded that the corruption of Western morals and the injustice of Western capitalism have imposed their conditions on them from outside, then enmity toward Western civilization will multiply. However, if Muslim peoples are persuaded that they can improve their situation with sound government and hard work, and that Western powers will assist and not hinder that process, then the poverty that exists will not be an extensive breeding ground for terror. Much of that perception depends on education.

EDUCATION IN THE ISLAMIC WORLD

Education is something of a two-edged sword. The Islamic world, like the West, has seen an enormous expansion in university education. Islamic elites have recognized that they cannot run modern military establishments, oil refineries, and financial systems—all foundations of their regimes' power—without university-trained elites. Yet as with other great expansions of university enrollments, as in Western Europe in the nineteenth century, in Russia in the early twentieth century, and in many countries after World War II (including the United States), a certain fraction of university graduates have been drawn to idealism, reform, and rebellion. This has been all the more so in Muslim countries in the late twentieth century for three reasons. First, the narrow oil-based economies of many Muslim countries do not provide the economic opportunities found in more diversified economies for an educated managerial and technical elite. Second, the closed and authoritarian regimes of many Muslim countries do not allow for either reform or a broad array of roles in politics. Third, in order to satisfy the demands of clerics, many universities remain partially or fully staffed by Islamic clergy in order to provide an Islamic education and train a new generation of clergy. The result is a combination of relatively high unemployment and economic frustration among university graduates, relatively high political frustration with the closed and unresponsive nature of the political regime, and an infusion of Islamism absorbed from the study of (often radical) Islamic texts.

At the same time, elementary and secondary education has grown more slowly. In many countries, the public school system is underfinanced. Clergy-run schools (as in many inner cities in the United States) provide the most compelling alternative for education. In many cases, religious schools are attached to charitable foundations that not only pay for the schools but also provide living stipends for students. In the last two decades, there has been a proliferation of Islamic religious schools (*madrasas*), often funded by Saudi and other overseas charitable foundations seeking to show their support for a renewal of Islam. However, many of these schools have taken into their curriculum a particularly venomous anti-Western bias, drawn not from the Quran but from more recent writings of Islamicist writers seeking to exalt Islam and condemn Western powers for the current condition of Muslims and Muslim nations.

The net outcome of these trends in education has been the production of both radicalized elites and willing conscripts to the IIT cause. Although there are moderate Islamic scholars and teachers, they have been increasingly shouted down and displaced by more radical Islamist institutions and leaders. This has been true on the West Bank and in Gaza, in Afghanistan, in Iran, and in parts of Pakistan, Egypt, and Saudi Arabia—even in Indonesia.

To alter these trends in education, there is much the West can do. Free gifts of textbooks in local languages, which adopt neither a Eurocentric nor Islamist anti-Western view, but teach global history as a process of peaceful competition and integration, punctuated by dismal and deplorable episodes of violence, would be useful. Publication of weekly newspapers—or financial support for newspapers, radio and TV stations—that portray a more balanced viewpoint for distribution throughout the Islamic world would also help.

During the struggle against communism, Western powers took it for granted that anti-Western media and propaganda needed to be vigorously countered by media presenting Western viewpoints. Yet in the struggle against Islamic terrorism, the West has been tardy and niggling in its efforts to counter a similar barrage of anti-Western portrayals. IIT is, like communism, a revolutionary movement with global aims and operations. It can only be countered by similar measures.

However, delivering a better-balanced education requires an adequately funded and staffed public education system with secular leadership. This requires competent and capable states.

State Building

One of the first policy declarations of the Bush administration regarding the struggle with the Taliban, since sensibly retracted, is that the United States would not be drawn into "state building." We also initially resisted the idea of being drawn into state building in Bosnia. Yet we should ask ourselves why this is so. In the struggle against communism, the chief approach to countering its international spread was precisely efforts at state building, whether in West Germany and Western Europe more generally; in South Korea; in Taiwan; or less successfully in many other nations. Strong states—if not also anti-Western—are a critical element in the struggle against IIT. Such states can suppress terrorist training and activity in their territories; deliver educational services and provide employment for educated elites; and maintain legitimate banking and financial systems. Weak or failed states are unable to fulfill these functions and thus provide a vacuum in which IIT can flourish.

It is important to recognize that IIT is a nongovernmental organization, or NGO (or more accurately, a loosely linked network of allied NGOs). NGOs may operate beyond state boundaries, but they need physical locations in which to operate, train, hold and disburse funds, have leaders meet, and plan operations. Destroying one state refuge or territory of operations will not destroy IIT, however much it may diminish their operations in the short term, as long as IIT can find other territories in which to operate. Strong states that control their territories can curtail or terminate the activity of NGOs on their territory. But it requires an alliance of states cooperating to effectively end the operations of an international NGO.

States also compete with IIT for the loyalty, energy, and support of their peoples. Where IIT groups are more successful than states in providing such basic services as protection, education, and welfare, they are naturally more influential over the local population than states. Strong and successful states who provide these services thus reduce the scope for IIT to gain support by taking up roles that states fail to fulfill.

It is not a novelty for states to compete against NGOs—the international antislavery movement and the European democratic/constitutional movement of the nineteenth century targeted states, as did the Communist International of the twentieth century. Clearly, in some cases the NGOs outlasted their state opponents; in other cases they did not. However, in recent years the proliferation of NGOs with international financial and other operations make it all too easy for IIT to shelter itself by blending in with the host of international Islamic charitable and religious NGOs. It thus makes heavy demands on intelligence and state cooperation to locate and target the supporting operations of IIT activity.

TOWARD A CONCLUSION

It is important in this struggle, as in all such struggles, to know our adversary. It is not the Muslim world, or Arab nations, or Islamic peoples. Most Muslims are *not* fundamentalists or aiming at global domination by Islam. Not all Islamic fundamentalists, much less many Muslims, believe that terror, suicidal sacrifice, and violence are the best way to secure the future of Islam or combat Western influence. Most Muslims, like most people everywhere, are interested in taking care of their families, in surviving each day and living in peace. Yet it is the goal of international Islamic terrorists to turn all Muslims against the West and against Westernized governments and elites in Muslim countries, and to convince as many Muslims as possible to take up arms against Western powers and Western influence.

The key to defeating the threat of IIT is thus to demonstrate to Muslims that support of IIT goes *against* their own best interests and to isolate IIT groups from the mainstream of Muslim populations. This can best be achieved by showing the world that IIT is *not effective* against the West, and is *illegitimate* as a force for Islam.

The first goal is largely a military and police task. It involves military action against nations that support and harbor IIT groups and hybrids; it involves police action to track down IIT cells wherever they are operating and to neutralize them; and it involves homeland security measures to prevent effective operations by IIT in the future. As the Al Qaeda network has been the most effective and dangerous IIT group, it is reasonable to make elimination of that organization's leaders and operatives a chief priority. On this goal, once galvanized by the events of September 11, the United States and its allies appear to be making good progress.

The second goal, however, is equally if not more important. Unless the injustice and illegitimacy of IIT is made manifest, unless their propaganda that Western powers and Western culture are responsible for the suffering of all Muslims anywhere in the Islamic world is refuted, the destruction of particular Al Qaeda leaders and operatives will only result in others taking their place. The power of IIT to recruit suicide bombers and terrorists lies in their claim to be acting on behalf of all Muslims. Undermine that claim, and their power will fade. A sustained and systemic effort to support Muslim leaders, clerics, and lay elites who call for coexistence with the West, who emphasize self-strengthening of Islamic peoples, and who decry the wasteful suicide and violence by Muslims is needed.

The war against international Islamic terrorism is not a war against Islam. Nor is it a war against all terrorism full stop. It is a war against a specific and recently developed international movement that threatens U.S. and Western populations and interests on a global scale. It is not a war that can be won by military means alone. It is not a war that can be ended by sacrificing Israel. It is not a war that can be ended without the cooperation of Muslim countries and their governments. But it is a war that can be won by the cooperation of Western and Muslim peoples and nations who treasure peace, if they will focus on isolating, defeating, and delegitimizing their common enemy.

10. BEYOND MILITARISM, ARMS RACES, AND ARMS CONTROL

MARY KALDOR[1]

INTRODUCTION

Since the end of the Cold War, a profound restructuring of armed forces has taken place. During the Cold War period, armed forces tended to resemble each other all over the world. They were disciplined, hierarchical, and technology intensive. There were, of course, guerrilla and/or terrorist groups, but they were considered marginal and their demand for weapons was small in relation to the overall demand for weapons.

The Cold War could be described as the final stage of what has come to be known as modernity, or to use Anthony Giddens's terminology, the final stages of the first phase of modernity.[2] By modernity, I mean that period of human development that began somewhere between the fifteenth and the eighteenth centuries, characterized by the development of science and technology, the nation-state, modern industry, and, I would argue, Clausewitzean or modern war. By modern war, I mean war between states, fought by armed forces, for state interest; the type of war that was theorized so brilliantly by Clausewitz. The development of modern war cannot be disentangled from the development of modern states. It was in war that European states, which were to provide the model for other states, established their monopoly of organized violence within the territorial confines of the state; they eliminated competitors, centralized administration, increased taxation and forms of borrowing, and, above all, created an idea of the state as the organization responsible for protection of borders against other states and for upholding a rule of law within the state. The sharp distinctions between the military and civilians, public and private, internal and external, are a product of these developments. As Charles Tilly put it in a famous phrase: "States made war and war made the state."[3]

After 1945, the whole world was parceled up into individual states, each with their own currency and their own armed forces. Each state was a member of a bloc (West, East, and non-aligned) and within each bloc, there were transfers of weapons and other types of military assistance according to a very similar model of warfare. The idea of war and of preparations for war was bound up with the ways in which states established their political legitimacy.

Since the end of the Cold War, military spending by governments has fallen substantially. But what we have witnessed is less a contraction of military forces than a restructuring and increased diversity of types of military forces. There is a parallel with the premodern period, which was also characterized by a diversity of military forces—feudal levies, citizen militias, mercenaries, pirates, for example—and by a corresponding variety of types of warfare.

Two interlinked developments have been critical, in my view, in bringing about these changes. One is the sheer destructiveness of modern warfare. As all types of weapons have become more lethal and/or more accurate, decisive military victory has become more and more difficult. The scale of destruction in World War II (some 50 million dead) is almost unbearable to contemplate. The Cold War could be understood as a way of evading or psychologically suppressing the implications of that destructiveness. Through the system of deterrence, the idea of modern war was kept alive in the imagination and helped to sustain the legitimacy and discipline of modern states. The military planners and scenario builders imagined wars, even more destructive than World War II, and developed competitive new technologies that, in theory, would be used in such wars. There were, of course, real wars and some five million people have died in wars in every decade since 1945 but, among the dominant powers, these were regarded as "not-war" or marginal to the main contingency—a global inter-state clash. With the end of the Cold War, we have to come to terms with the impossibility of wars of the modern type.

The second development is the process known as globalization. By globalization, I mean increasing interconnectedness, the shrinking of distance and time, as a result of the combination of information and communications technology (ICT) and air travel. A central issue for theorists of globalization has to do with the implications for the modern state.[4] Some argue that the state has become an anachronism and that we are moving toward a single world community. Some take the opposite view, that globalization is an invention of the state and can easily be reversed. Yet others insist that globalization does not mean the end of the state but rather its transformation. I share the last position, but I would argue that there is no single method of transformation. States are changing in a variety of ways and, moreover, these changes, I shall argue, are bound up with changes in the types of armed forces and the forms of warfare.

The terms "militarism," "arms races," and "arms control" are expressions drawn from the Cold War era and before. Militarism refers to excessive levels of military spending by the state and excessive influence of armed forces over civilian life. "Arms races" refer to the competition between similar types of military forces. "Arms control" refers to the process of treaty-making between states, based on the assumption that stability can best be preserved through a "balance of power (or terror)" between states.

In this chapter, I shall distinguish between the different types of armed forces that are emerging in the post–Cold War world, only some of which can be characterized in terms of militarism and arms races, and discuss how they are loosely associated with different modes of state transformation and different forms of warfare. I have identified four different types of armed forces. They could be described as Weberian ideal types. They are probably not comprehensive and no single example exactly fits a particular type. There is also a lot of overlap. The point is to provide a schematic account of what is happening in the field of warfare so as to be able to offer some new ways of thinking about the possibilities for controlling or limiting the means of warfare and why we need a new terminology beyond militarism, arms races, and arms control. I shall suggest that the emphasis that has been increasingly accorded to international law, particularly humanitarian law, offers a possible way forward.

NETFORCE: INFORMAL OR PRIVATIZED ARMED FORCES

A typical new phenomenon is armed networks of nonstate and state actors. They include: paramilitary groups organized around a charismatic leader, warlords who control particular areas, terrorist cells, fanatic volunteers like the Mujahedeen, organized criminal groups, units of regular forces or other security services, as well as mercenaries and private military companies.

The form of warfare that is waged by these networks is what I call "new war." [5] New wars, which take place in the Balkans, Africa, Central Asia, and other places, are sometimes called internal or civil wars to distinguish them from inter-state or Clausewitzean war. I think this terminology is inappropriate for a number of reasons. First, the networks cross borders. One of the typical features of the "new wars" is the key role played by diaspora groups either far away (Sudanese or Palestinian workers in the Gulf states, former Yugoslav workers in Western Europe, immigrant groups in the new "melting pot" regions like North America or Oceania) or in neighboring states (Serbs in Croatia and Bosnia, Tutsis in Burundi or the Democratic Republic of Congo). Secondly, the wars involve an array of global actors—foreign mercenaries and volunteers, diaspora supporters, neighboring states, not to mention the humanitarian actors such as aid agencies, NGOs or reporters.

And thirdly, and most importantly, the "new wars" tend to be concentrated in areas where the modern state is unraveling and where the distinctions between internal and external, public and private, no longer have the same meaning. Such areas are characterized by what are called frail or failing states, quasi or shadow states. These are states, formally recognized by the outside world, with some of the trappings of statehood—an incomplete administrative apparatus, a flag, sometimes a currency—but where those trappings do not express control over territory and where access to the state apparatus is about private gain not public policy. In particular, these are states where the monopoly of legitimate organized violence is eroding.

In many of the areas where new wars take place, it is possible to observe a process that is almost the reverse of the process through which modern states were constructed. Taxes fall because of declining investment and production, increased corruption and clientelism, or declining legitimacy. The declining tax revenue leads to growing dependence both on external sources and on private sources, through, for example, rent seeking or criminal activities. Reductions in public expenditure as a result of the shrinking fiscal base as well as pressures from external donors for macroeconomic stabilization and liberalization (which also may reduce export revenues) further erode legitimacy. A growing informal economy, associated with increased inequalities, unemployment and rural-urban migration, combined with the loss of legitimacy, weakens the rule of law and may lead to the reemergence of privatized forms of violence: organized crime and the substitution of "protection" for taxation; vigilantes; private security guards protecting economic facilities, especially international companies; or paramilitary groups associated with particular political factions. In particular, reductions in security expenditure, often encouraged by external donors for the best of motives, may lead to breakaway groups of redundant soldiers and policemen seeking alternative employment.

Of course, the networks that engage in new wars are not all to be found in these failing states. They include nodes in advanced industrial countries and, in the inner cities of the West, it is possible to observe gang warfare that has many of the characteristics of new wars. Nevertheless, this type of state provides a fertile environment for these types of network.

There are three main characteristics of the new wars. First of all, I use the term "war" to emphasize the political character of the new wars, even though they could also be described as organized crime (illegal or private violence) or as massive violations of human rights (violence against civilians). Because networks are loose horizontal coalitions, unlike vertical disciplined armies of the past, a shared narrative—often based on a common identity, ethnic or religious—is an important organizing mechanism. In the case of the netforce, the networks engaged in the new wars, what holds them together is generally an extreme political ideology based on the exclusive claim to state power on the basis of identity—ethnic chauvinism or religious communalism. I stress access to state power because these ideologies are not about substantive grievances, such as language rights or religious rights, although these may be indirectly important; rather they are about control of power and resources for an exclusively defined group of people.

I take the view that these ideologies are politically constituted. Even though they are based on preexisting cleavages of tribe, nation, and religion, and even though they may make use of memories and experiences of past injustices, they are constructed or accentuated for the purpose of political mobilization.

Modern communications are important for the new networks both as a way of organizing the network and as a form of mobilization. Constructions of the past are developed and disseminated through radio, videos, and television. Thus hate radio was of key importance in Rwanda. In Serbia, television was effectively used to remind people of the injustices of the past—the defeat of the Serbs by the Turks in 1389 and the fascist Croat treatment of Serbs during World War II. In the Middle East, videocassettes of bin Laden's speeches circulate widely. The effect of television and radio in speeding up mobilization especially in the countryside or among newly arrived urban migrants, who do not have the reading habit, should not be underestimated. There is an important contrast here with nineteenth-century "imagined communities" which were propagated through the print media and involved the intellectual classes. The more populist electronic media are designed to appeal primarily to the least-educated members of the public. In general, it is states that control radio and television. But non-state groups can make use of other forms of media: diaspora broadcasts through satellite television, which were important in Kosovo; the circulation of videos; or local radio in areas under political control.

A second characteristic of the new wars is that war itself is a form of political mobilization. In what I have called wars between states, the aim of war was, to quote Clausewitz, "to compel an opponent to fulfill our will." In general this was achieved through the military capture of territory and victory in battle. People were mobilized to participate in the war effort—to join the army or to produce weapons and uniforms. In the new wars, mobilizing people is the aim of the war effort; the point of the violence is not so much directed against the enemy; rather the aim is to expand the networks of extremism. Generally the strategy is to control territory through political means, and military means are used to kill, expel, or silence those who might challenge control. This is why the warring parties use techniques of terror, ethnic cleansing, or genocide as deliberate war strategies. In the new wars, battles are rare, and violence is directed against civilians. Violations of humanitarian and human rights law are not a side effect of war but the central methodology of new wars. Over 90 percent of the casualties in the new wars are civilian, and the number of refugees and displaced persons per conflict has risen steadily.

The strategy is to gain political power through sowing fear and hatred, to create a climate of terror, to eliminate moderate voices, and to defeat tolerance. The political ideologies of exclusive nationalism or religious communalism are generated through violence. It is generally assumed that extreme ideologies, based on exclusive identities—Serb nationalism, for example, or fundamentalist Islam—are the cause of war. Rather, the spread and strengthening of these ideologies are the consequence of war. "The war had to be so bloody," Bosnians will tell you, "because we did not hate each other; we had to be taught to hate each other."

A third characteristic of the new wars is the type of economy they generate. Because these networks flourish in states where systems of taxation have collapsed and where little new wealth is being created, and where the wars destroy physical infrastructure, cut off trade, and create a climate of insecurity that prohibits investment, they have to seek alternative, exploitative forms of financing. They raise money through loot and plunder, through illegal trading in drugs, illegal immigrants, cigarettes and alcohol, through "taxing" humanitarian assistance, through support from sympathetic states, and through remittances from members of the networks. All of these types of economic activity are predatory and depend on an atmosphere of insecurity. Indeed, the new wars can be described as a central source of the globalized informal economy—the transnational criminal and semi-legal economy that represents the underside of globalization.

The logical conclusion that can be drawn from these three characteristics is that the new wars are very difficult to contain and very difficult to end. They spread through refugees and displaced persons, through criminal networks, and through the extremist viruses they nurture. We can observe growing clusters of warfare in Africa, the Middle East, Central Asia, or the Caucasus. The wars represent a defeat for democratic politics, and each bout of warfare strengthens those networks with a vested political and economic interest in continued violence. There are no clear victories or defeats, because the warring parties are sustained both politically and economically by continuing violence. The wars speed up the process of state unraveling, they destroy what remains of productive activities, they undermine legitimacy, and they foster criminality. The areas where conflicts have lasted longest have generated cultures of violence, as in the jihad culture taught in religious schools in Pakistan and Afghanistan or among the Tamils of Sri Lanka, where young children are taught to be martyrs and where killing is understood as an offering to God. In the instructions found in the car of the hijackers in Boston's Logan Airport, it is written: "If God grants any one of you a slaughter, you should perform it as an offering on behalf of your father and mother, for they are owed by you. If you slaughter, you should plunder those you slaughter, for that is a sanctioned custom of the Prophet's."

It should be noted that there are other private or informal forces that do not correspond to this analysis. For example, in many of the new wars, villages or municipalities establish citizens' militias to defend local people—this was the case among some groups in Rwanda and also in Tuzla and Zenica during the Bosnian war. There are also more traditional guerrilla groups, whose strategy is to gain political control through winning hearts and minds rather than through sowing fear and hatred; hence they attack agents of the state and not civilians, at least in theory. Finally, there are numerous private security companies, often established to protect multinational companies in difficult places, and mercenaries, who fight for money; tactics and forms of warfare, in these cases, depend largely on the paymasters.

THE NEW AMERICAN MILITARISM

It could be argued that if September 11 had not happened, the American military-industrial complex might have had to invent it. Indeed, what happened on September 11 could have come out of what seemed to be the wild fantasies of "asymmetric threats" that were developed by American strategic analysts as they sought a new military role for the United States after the end of the Cold War. A reporter for the London *Observer* claimed to have found, in one of the headquarters for terrorist training in Afghanistan, a photocopy of a "terrorist cookbook," some of which circulates among the American fundamentalist right.

World military spending declined by one-third in the decade after 1989. America military spending also declined, but by less than the global average, and began to rise again after 1998. As of the year 2000, American military spending in real terms was equivalent to its spending in 1980, just before the Reagan military build-up. More importantly, what took place during the 1990s was a radical shift in the structure of U.S. military expenditure. Spending on military research and development declined less than overall military spending and has increased faster since 1998. As of 2000, U.S. military research and development (R&D) spending was 47 percent higher in real terms than in 1980.[6] Instead of ushering in a period of downsizing, disarmament and conversion (although some of that did take place at local levels in the U.S.), the end of the Cold War led to a feverish technological effort to apply information technology to military purposes, known as the Revolution in Military Affairs (RMA).

Indeed, it can be argued that the cuts of the early 1990s are equivalent to the reductions that can be expected in the normal post-1945 U.S. military procurement cycle. The high points in the procurement cycle were in the early 1950s, late 1960s, early 1970s, and the early 1980s. During the downturns, military R&D is always sustained, designing and developing the systems to be procured in the next upturn. As new systems reach the more expensive development and procurement phases, this has always coincided with renewed preoccupations with threats of various kinds. The North Korean invasion of South Korea in 1950, for example, occurred at a moment when pressure to increase military spending was mounting as a result of overcapacity in the arms industry, especially the aircraft industry, and of fears about the return of mass unemployment after the end of the postwar consumer boom. NSC 68, the famous report which recommended an increase in military spending to meet the Soviet threat, was published just before the Korean invasion. A parallel can be drawn with the current situation since the systems developed under the rubric of the RMA are reaching the development and production phase, and there is overcapacity in the aerospace industry.

During the 1990s, great efforts were expended in "imagining" new "worst-case scenarios" and new post-Soviet threats. With the collapse of the Soviet military-industrial complex, strategic planners have come up with all sorts of inventive new ways of attacking America, through spreading viruses, poisoning water systems, causing the collapse of the banking system, disrupting air-traffic control or power transmission. Of particular importance has been the idea of state-sponsored terrorism and the notion of "rogue states" who sponsor terrorism and acquire long-range missiles as well as WMD (weapons of mass destruction). These new threats emanating from a collapsing Russia or from Islamic fundamentalism are known as "asymmetric" threats, as weaker states or groups develop WMD or other horrific techniques to attack U.S. vulnerabilities to compensate for conventional inferiority. Hence what happened on September 11, and the subsequent anthrax scare, seems like a confirmation of these anticipations of horror.

RMA consists of the interaction between various systems for information collection, analysis, and transmission and weapons systems—the so-called "system of systems." It has spawned a suitably sci-fi jargon—"battlespace" to replace "battlefield," connoting the three-dimensional character of contemporary battle; "dominant battlespace knowledge," "precision violence," "near-perfect mission assignment," C4I/BM (command, control, communications, computers, intelligence, and battle management); "cooperative engagement capability" (Navy); "digitalized ground forces" (Army); and (one of my favorites) "just-in-time warfare" (referring to reduced logistical requirements).[7]

The cruise missile, the target of peace-movement campaigns in the 1980s, can be described as the paradigmatic weapon of RMA. It is a "system that can be delivered by a variety of platforms (i.e. all three services can use it) and strike in a precise manner and with low collateral damage."[8] It was the cruise missile that was used in the summer of 1998 against terrorist camps in Afghanistan and an alleged chemical-weapons factory in Sudan after the bombings of the U.S. embassies in Kenya and Uganda.

Enthusiasts for RMA suggest that the introduction of information technology is akin to the introduction of the stirrup or gunpowder in its implications for warfare. Unlike these earlier innovations, however, RMA takes place within the traditional force structures inherited from the past. Earlier innovations were adopted only when force structures changed in such a way as to be capable of assimilating the new technologies. Thus the introduction of the stirrup depended on the evolution of feudal relations and the emergence of knights, while gunpowder was applied to warfare only after capitalist development made possible the use of mercenaries.

The origins of the RMA can be traced to the 1970s, when the effect of growing accuracy and lethality of munitions was observed in the wars in Vietnam and the Middle East. The so-called military reformers suggested that this implied an historic shift to the defense. The offensive maneuvers characteristic of World War II and planned in Europe for World War III were no longer possible, since tanks and aircraft were almost as vulnerable as troops had been in World War I. In particular, it was argued that this historic shift lessened the need for nuclear weapons to compensate for Soviet conventional superiority, since this could be nullified by improvements in conventional defense. The opponents of this view argued that the offense was even more important in the context of information technology, because it made possible unmanned guided offensive weapons and because of the importance of area-destruction munitions, which could destroy widely scattered defensive forces. It was the latter view that prevailed, perhaps because it left force structures undisturbed and sustained defense companies, retaining an emphasis on offensive maneuvers and delivery platforms in a more or less linear extension from the strategic bombing missions of World War II.

The consequence was what became known as "emerging technologies" in the 1980s. These were long-range strike weapons using conventional munitions that were nearly as lethal as nuclear weapons. Terms such as "deep strike," "airland battle," and the "maritime strategy" became the buzzwords of the 1980s. The idea was that the West would meet any Soviet attack by striking deep into Soviet territory. When Iraq invaded Kuwait in 1990 and the Pentagon was asked to present the military options, they were able to roll out a plan that had been prepared in the event of a southward Soviet thrust.

The Gulf War provided a model for what can be described as casualty-free war—that is to say the use of high technology either to attack an enemy directly or to support a proxy, say the KLA in Kosovo or the Northern Alliance in Afghanistan. The idea now is that this high-tech warfare can be used against "rogue states" sponsoring terrorists. The same techniques were used against Iraq in December 1998, in Yugoslavia in 1999, and now in Afghanistan. They satisfy a confluence of interests. They fulfill the needs of the scientists, engineers, and companies that provide an infrastructure for the American military effort. They allow for a continuation of the imaginary war of the Cold War period from the point of view of Americans. They do not involve American casualties, and they can be watched on television and demonstrate the determination and power of the United States government—the "spectacles" as James Der Derian has put it, that "serve to deny imperial decline."[9] It is this imaginary character from an American perspective that explains Jean Baudrillard's famous remark that the Gulf War did not happen.

The program for national missile defense (NMD) has to be understood in the same vein. Even if the system cannot work, it provides imaginary protection for the United States, allowing the United States to engage in casualty-free war without fear of retaliation. This notion is evident from the way in which Donald Rumsfeld, the U.S. defense secretary, talks about how NMD will enhance deterrence through a combination of defensive and offensive measures. The weakness of deterrence was always the problem of credibility; a problem that leads to more and more useable nuclear weapons. With casualty-free war, the credibility of U.S. action is more convincing; after all, it is said that the attack on the World Trade Center was equivalent to the use of a substrategic nuclear weapon. NMD, at least psychologically, extends the possibilities for casualty-free war.

However, from the point of view of the victims, these wars are very real and not so different from new wars. However precise the strikes, it is impossible to avoid "mistakes" or "collateral damage." It does not make civilian casualties any more palatable to be told they were not intended. Moreover, the destruction of physical infrastructure and the support for one side in the conflict, as in the case of proxies, results in many more indirect casualties. In the case of the Gulf War, direct Iraqi casualties can probably be numbered in the tens of thousands, but the destruction of physical infrastructure and the ensuing wars with the Kurds and the Shi'ites caused hundreds of thousands of further casualties and seem to have entrenched the vicious and dangerous rule of Saddam Hussein. In the current war in Afghanistan, there have probably been thousands of casualties, both civilian and military, as well as thousands of people fleeing their homes and a humanitarian disaster because aid agencies have not been able to enter the country. The help provided to the hated Northern Alliance reduces the prospects of a broad-based Afghan government that might begin a process of stabilization. Far from extending support for democratic values, casualty-free war shows that American lives are privileged over the lives of others and contributes to a perception of the United States as a global bully.

Terms like imperialism are, however, misleading. The United States is best characterized not as an imperial power but as the "last nation-state." It is the only state, in this globalized world, that still has the capacity to act unilaterally. Its behavior is determined less by imperial considerations than by concerns about its own domestic public opinion. Casualty-free war is also a form of political mobilization. It is about satisfying various domestic constituencies, not about influencing the rest of the world, even though such actions have a profound impact on the rest of the world.

NEO-MODERN MILITARISM

Neo-modern militarism refers to the evolution of classical military forces in large transition states. These are countries that are undergoing a transition from a centralized economy to a more internationally open market-oriented system and, yet, are large enough to retain a sizeable state sector. Typical examples are Russia, India, and China. They are not large enough to challenge the U.S., and they are constrained by many of the imperatives of globalization, subject to many of the pressures that are experienced by frail or failing states. They tend to adopt extreme ideologies that resemble the ideologies of the new wars—Russian or Hindu chauvinism, for example. And there are often direct links to, and even co-operation with, the shadier networks, especially in Russia. Israel should probably also be included in this category, although its capacity to retain a sizeable military sector is due less to its size than to its dependence on the United States.

These states have retained their military forces, including nuclear weapons. In the case of India, there has been a significant increase in military spending throughout the 1990s, and it could be argued that the term "arms race" could be applied to India and Pakistan, especially after the 1998 nuclear tests. Pakistan, however, could be said to be closer to the networks of the new wars with its links to militants in Kashmir and Afghanistan: in other words, somewhere between netforce and neo-modern militarism. In the case of Russia, there was a dramatic contraction of military spending after the breakup of the Soviet Union and a deep crisis in the military-industrial complex. But pressure to increase military spending has increased, and the demands of the war in Chechnya are leading to a reassessment of the relative importance of conventional versus nuclear weapons. The proposed cuts in nuclear weapons discussed between Putin and Bush will release funds for conventional improvements. China is also engaged in military expansion especially since 1998, when the military were prohibited from engaging in commercial activities. Given the reductions in Russian nuclear capabilities and the new generation of Chinese systems, China will come to look more like a competitor to Russia, especially in the nuclear field.

The type of warfare that is associated with neo-modern militarism is either limited inter-state warfare or counterinsurgency. These states envisage wars on the classic Clausewitzean model. They engage in counterinsurgency in order to defeat extremist networks as in Chechnya or Kashmir. Or they prepare for the defense of borders against other states, as in the case of the Kargil war between India and Pakistan in 1998. Unlike the United States, these states are prepared to risk casualties and, in the case of the Chechen war, Russian casualties have been extremely high. The typical tactics used against the networks are shelling from tanks, helicopters, or artillery, as well as population displacement to "clean" areas of extremists or "terrorists." The impact on civilians is thus very similar to the impact of the new wars. Yet precisely because of the growing destructiveness of all types of weapons and the consequent difficulty of overcoming defensive positions, military victory against an armed opponent is very hard to achieve. Grozny has been reduced virtually to rubble. Yet still resistance persists.

The networks have understood that they cannot take territory militarily, only through political means, and the point of the violence is to contribute to those political means. The states engaged in neo-modern militarism are still under the illusion that they can win militarily. The consequence is either self-imposed limits, as in the case of inter-state war, or exacerbation of new wars, as in the case of Kashmir, Chechnya, or Palestine, where counterinsurgency merely contributes to the politically polarizing process of fear and hate. In other words, the utility of modern military force, the ability to "compel an opponent to fulfill our will," is open to question nowadays.

PROTECTIONFORCE:
PEACEKEEPING/PEACE ENFORCEMENT

An important trend in the last decade has been the increase in peacekeeping operations. At the start of the decade, there were only eight United Nations peacekeeping operations; they involved some 10,000 troops. As of the end of 2000, there were 15 United Nations operations involving some 38,000 military troops.[10] In addition, a number of regional organizations were engaged in peace-keeping: NATO in Bosnia, Kosovo, and Macedonia; the Commonwealth of Independent States (CIS), mainly Russia, in Tajikistan, Transdniestr, Abkhazia, and South Ossetia; the Economic Community of West African States (ECOWAS) in Sierra Leone, Liberia, and Guinea.

Peacekeeping has not only increased in scale; there have been important changes in the tasks peacekeepers are asked to perform and in the way we think about peacekeeping. During the Cold War period, peacekeeping was based on the assumption that wars were of the Clausewitzean type. The job of peacekeepers was to separate the warring parties and to monitor cease-fires on the basis of agreements. Peacekeeping was sharply distinguished from peace enforcement, which was equated with war fighting, i.e. intervening in a war on one side, authorized under Chapter VII of the UN Charter.

In terms of organization, peacekeeping has more in common with the networks than with classic military forces. Peacekeeping forces are generally loose transnational coalitions. Although they usually have a clearly defined multinational command system, peacekeepers are also subject to national commands, which erodes the vertical character of the command system. Because they are often far away from the decision makers and because of the nature of their tasks, individual initiative is often more important than unquestioning obedience. Moreover, peacekeepers have to work together with a range of other agencies, international organizations like UNHCR or UNDP and also NGOs involved in humanitarian assistance or conflict resolution. A shared normative narrative based on humanitarian principles is critical in holding the networks together.

The new tasks for peacekeepers include the protection of safe havens, where civilians can find refuge, the protection of convoys delivering humanitarian assistance, disarmament, and demobilization, providing a secure environment for elections or for the return of refugees and displaced persons, or capturing war criminals. These tasks reflect the changes in the nature of the warfare. New terms like "second-generation peacekeeping," "wider peacekeeping" or "robust" peacekeeping have been used to describe these new roles. Peacekeepers nowadays operate in the context of continuing wars or insecure post-conflict situations, and they are more likely to risk casualties than were traditional peacekeepers.

A number of recent reports have emphasized that the new role of peacekeeping is, first and foremost, the protection of civilians, since they are the main targets of the new wars.[11] The new peacekeeping is indeed somewhere between traditional peacekeeping (separating sides) and peace enforcement (taking sides). I have argued that outright military victory is very, very difficult nowadays, at least if we are unwilling to contemplate mass destruction. The job of the new protectionforce is not to defeat an enemy but to protect civilians and stabilize war situations so that nonextremist tolerant politics has space to develop. The task is thus more like policing than warfare, although it involves the use of military forces. Techniques like safe havens or humanitarian corridors are ways of protecting civilians and also increasing the international presence on the ground so as to influence political outcomes.

In practice, peacekeeping has not lived up to this description. Partly this is due to lack of resources. Not nearly enough has been invested in peacekeeping and in providing appropriate training and equipment. More importantly, international lives are still privileged over the lives of the civilians they are supposed to protect. OSCE monitors left Kosovo hurriedly when the bombing of Yugoslavia began, leaving behind a terrified population who had believed, rightly or wrongly, that the orange vans of the OSCE monitors were some protection; the local OSCE staff left behind were all killed. Likewise, Dutch peacekeepers handed over the 8,000 men and boys of Srebrenica to Serb forces in July 1995 and they were all massacred. In Rwanda, UN forces were withdrawn just as the genocide of 800,000 Tutsis began, despite the impassioned plea of the Canadian UN commander, General Dallaire, to establish safe havens. There are, of course, also moments of heroism, like the Ukranian peacekeepers in Zepa or the British in Goradze, or the UN staff in East Timor who refused to evacuate their headquarters unless the people who had sought refuge there were also saved. But, as yet, these moments are insufficient to be seen to justify the commitment in resources and will that would be necessary for a serious and sustained use of peacekeeping.

Peacekeeping/peace enforcement is associated with states that could be described as postmodern[12] or globalizing.[13] These are states that have come to terms with the erosion of their autonomy (their ability to retain control over what happens in their territory) in the context of growing interconnectedness. They have thus adopted a deliberate strategy of multilateralism, of trying to influence the formation of global rules, and of participating actively in the enforcement of those rules. British Prime Minister Tony Blair attempted to articulate this position in his speech on the "Doctrine of the International Community" during the Kosovo war. "We are all internationalists now whether we like it or not," he told an audience in Chicago. "We cannot refuse to participate in global markets if we want to prosper. We cannot ignore new political ideas in other countries if we want to innovate. We cannot turn our backs on conflicts and the violation of human rights in other countries if we still want to be secure."[14]

The states that fit this category include most European states, Canada, South

Africa, Japan, as well as a number of others. Of course, most states, including the United States and Russia, engage in this type of peace operation. But it is not viewed as the main contingency for which they prepare. The new globalizing states are reorienting their military doctrines along these lines. The wars in the Balkans have had a profound impact in Europe, where concern about Balkan stability and experience in the region is shaping military thinking.

CONTROLLING WAR?

During the Cold War period, the main concern was how to prevent a war of global annihilation. Arms control was seen as one of the most important methods of prevention; it was a way of stabilizing the perception of a balance of power. A true balance of power is a war that no side can win. Because armed forces were roughly similar during the Cold War period, it was possible to estimate a surrogate balance of power based on quantitative estimates of military forces, which could be codified in arms-control treaties. This surrogate balance of power was seen as a way of preventing perceptions of imbalance, which might have tempted one or other side to start a war. In practice, of course, numbers are irrelevant since any nuclear war is likely to lead to global annihilation, but the exercise of measuring a balance of power shored up the notion of an imaginary war that could not be won.

The danger of a war of global annihilation has, thankfully, receded since the end of the Cold War. What we are now witnessing, however, is a series of real wars that cannot be won. There are no surrogate balances, except perhaps between the neo-modern military forces. The U.S. no longer has what is known in the jargon as a "peer competitor," and other types of armed forces are too varied to be compared. What I have tried to argue is that the first three types of armed forces (the networks, the new American military forces, and the neo-modern military forces) all engage in real wars with very similar consequences—indiscriminate suffering for civilians (even though the Americans claim that their greater precision and discriminateness minimizes such suffering). Nowadays, therefore, the emphasis of those who are concerned about such suffering has to be directly with the ways to control war. Limitations on weapons may be part of that wider goal, but have to be viewed from a different perspective than in the Cold War period.

Perhaps the most hopeful approach to the contemporary problem of controlling war, nowadays, is not through arms control but through the extension and application of international humanitarian law (the "laws of war") and human rights law. During the 1990s, much greater importance was accorded to humanitarian norms—the notion that the international community has a duty to prevent genocide, violations of humanitarian law (war crimes), and massive violations of human rights (crimes against humanity). Overriding state sovereignty in the case of humanitarian crises became much more widely accepted. The establishment of the Yugoslav and Rwanda Tribunals paved the way for the establishment of an International Criminal Court. The Augusto Pinochet and Ariel Sharon cases removed the principle of sovereign immunity.

Humanitarian law is not, of course, new. Its origins lie in the codification of "laws of war," especially under the auspices of the International Red Cross, in the late nineteenth century. The aim was to limit what we now call "collateral damage" or the side effects of war; above all, to prevent the indiscriminate suffering of civilians, and to ensure humane treatment for the wounded and for prisoners of war. These laws codified rules in Europe, which dated back to the Middle Ages and underlay a notion of "civilized" warfare, which was important in order to define the role of the soldier as the legitimate agent of the state, as a hero, not a criminal. (Of course, these rules were not applied outside Europe against "barbarians" or the "rude nations.")

Humanitarian law was greatly extended after World War II. The Nuremberg and Tokyo trials marked the first enforcement of war crimes and, indeed, crimes against humanity. The Genocide Convention of 1948, as well as further extension of the Geneva Conventions and the newly developing human rights law, all represented further strengthening of humanitarian law, albeit marginalized by the dominant Cold War confrontation.

What has changed in the last decades is the nature of warfare, even though some aspects were presaged in the Holocaust and the bombing of civilians in the Second World War. As argued above, violations of humanitarian law and human rights law are no longer "side effects" of war, they represent the core of the new warfare. Therefore taking seriously humanitarian law is one way of controlling the new warfare.

This is the context in which the limitation of armaments should also be understood. Recent efforts to limit or eliminate categories of weapons, like the Land Mines Convention, or the protocol to the Biological Weapons Convention, or the efforts to control small arms, are not based on the assumption of a balance between states. Rather, they are the outcome of pressure by global civil society to uphold humanitarian norms and prevent indiscriminate harm to civilians. The 1996 International Court of Justice decision about nuclear weapons, as well as several recent cases in Scotland, are based on the same line of thinking.

Taken seriously, a humanitarian approach would outlaw netforce and would restructure legitimate, i.e. state, military forces from classic war-fighting tasks to a new and extended form of protectionforce. It would outlaw WMD as well as weapons like land mines that cause indiscriminate harm. Peacekeeping and peace enforcement could be reconceptualized as humanitarian law enforcement, with appropriate equipment and training.

Such an approach would be consistent with the transformation of states along the lines of the postmodern or globalizing states. It would imply a strengthening of global rules and greater participation in the enforcement of rules. All three of the other types of warfare I have described are based on particularist assumptions about the need to protect particular communities, networks, or states, and to privilege their lives over others. There is no reason why growing interconnectedness cannot be combined with particularism and fragmentation; indeed that is the characteristic of the contemporary world. But it is no longer possible to insulate particular communities or states; even the United States is now vulnerable to transnational networks. If we are to find ways to cope with the uneven impact of globalization and to deal with the criminal and violent underside of globalization, then the main task is to construct some form of legitimate set of global rules. This is not the same as a global state; rather it is about establishing a set of global regimes underpinned by states, international institutions, and global civil society. The humanitarian regime would be at the heart of such a set of rules because of the legitimacy that derives from the assumption of human equality.

If the legitimacy of modern states derived from their ability to protect borders against external enemies and to uphold the law domestically, then the legitimacy of global governance is likely to be greatly enhanced by a humanitarian regime that takes ultimate responsibility for the protection of individuals and for upholding international law. I am not implying a single world-security organization. Rather I am talking about a collective commitment by states, international organizations, and civil society to act when individual states fail to sustain these norms and to do so within a framework of international law.

How would this approach have changed the reaction to the events of September 11? What happened on September 11 was a crime against humanity. It was interpreted, however, in the U.S. as an attack on the U.S., and a parallel has been repeatedly drawn with Pearl Harbor. Bush talks about a "war on terrorism" and has said that "you are either with us or with the terrorists." The approach of casualty-free war was adopted, using high-tech strikes and a proxy, the Northern Alliance, to destroy the state sponsoring terrorism, the Taliban, and to destroy the Al Qaeda network. (At the time of writing, some U.S. Special Forces and Marines have been deployed on the ground.) We do not know how many people have died as a result of the strikes or have fled their homes, but it undoubtedly numbers in hundreds if not thousands. The chances of stabilizing Afghanistan exist but are reduced by the dominant role played by the Northern Alliance. Most importantly, perhaps, the approach contributes to a political polarization between the West and the rest, both because of the privileging of American lives and because of the language in which the war is conducted. While the Taliban has been overthrown and, hopefully, bin Laden may be caught, there is not likely to be any clear military victory. As I have argued, the political narrative, in this case of jihad against America, is central to the functioning of the network. Casualty-free war confirms the political narrative and sets up exactly the kind of war envisaged by the Al Qaeda network.

A humanitarian approach would have defined September 11 as a crime against humanity. It would have sought United Nations authorization for any action, and it would have adopted tactics aimed at increasing trust and confidence on the ground, for example through the establishment of safe havens in the north as well as humanitarian corridors. It would have established an International Court to try terrorists. It would have adopted some of the means already adopted to put pressure on terrorist networks through squeezing financial assets, for example, as well as efforts to catch the criminals. Such an approach would also have to eschew double standards. Catching Mladic and Karadzic, the perpetrators of the Srebrenica massacre, is just as important as catching bin Laden. Human rights violations in Palestine and Chechnya are no less serious than in Kosovo or Afghanistan.

A humanitarian approach, of course, has to be part of a wider political approach. In wars in which no military victory is possible, political approaches are key. An alternative political narrative, based on the idea of global justice, is the only way to minimize the exclusive political appeal of the networks.

I am aware that all this sounds impossibly utopian. Unfortunately, the humanitarian approach may be seen in retrospect as a brief expression of the interregnum between the end of the Cold War and September 11, 2001. We are, I fear, on the brink of a global new war, something like the wars in the Balkans or the Israel–Palestine war, on a global scale with no outsiders to constrain its course. Sooner or later, the impossibility of winning such a war must become evident, and that is why we need to keep the humanitarian approach alive. Even if it cannot solve these conflicts, it can offer some hope to those caught in the middle.

11. 9/11: BEFORE, AFTER, AND IN BETWEEN

JAMES DER DERIAN

Before 9/11 and after 9/11: All social scientists must now survey international as well as domestic politics by this temporal rift. Yet, for a variety of reasons, many seem to have been stuck in a prolonged interim that thwarts scholarly inquiry. All too obviously, the sheer scale, scope, and shock of the event itself is partially to blame. Perhaps it is as well a repeat of what was heard at academic conferences after the fall of the Berlin Wall: Social scientists should not posit cause and effect from a single data point.[1] Or perhaps there is something more at work, a great deal more. After terrorist hijackers transformed three commercial jetliners into highly explosive kinetic weapons, toppled the twin towers of the World Trade Center, substantially damaged the Pentagon, killed more than three thousand people, and triggered a state of emergency—and before the dead could be fully grieved, Osama bin Laden's head brought on a platter, justice perceived as done, and information no longer considered a subsidiary of war—there was very little about 9/11 that was *safe* to say. Unless one was firmly situated in a patriotic, ideological, or religious position (which at home and abroad drew uncomfortably close), it was intellectually difficult and even politically dangerous to assess the meaning of a conflict that phase-shifted with every news cycle, from "Terror Attack" to "America Fights Back"; from a "crusade" to a "counterterror campaign"; from "the first war of the twenty-first century" to a now-familiar combination of humanitarian intervention and remote killing; from kinetic terror to bioterror; from the spectacle of war to a war of spectacles.

Under such conditions, I believe the task of the social scientist and all concerned individuals is to uncover what is *dangerous* to think and say. Or as Walter Benjamin put it best in another period between wars, "in times of terror, when everyone is something of a conspirator, everybody will be in a situation where he has to play detective."[2]

Detective work and some courage is needed because questions about the root causes or political intentions of the terrorist act have been either silenced by charges of "moral equivalency" or rendered moot by claims that the exceptional nature of the act placed it outside political discourse: explanation became identified with exoneration.[3] Reflecting the nature of the attack, as well as the chaos and confusion which followed, the conventional boundaries of the infosphere expanded during the first week to include political, historical, and ethical analysis by voices not usually heard on primetime. However, as the flow of information became practically entropic, there was a willingness (as judged by the unholy trinity of polls, pols, and programming) to accept as wisdom President Bush's early declaration that evil was to blame. From that moment, the appropriate political and intellectual focus shifted to a simple declarative with an impossible performative: to eradicate evil. Binary narratives quickly squeezed out any complex, let alone critical, analysis of what happened and why. Retribution required certainty, and certainty was a salve for the injured. Even five months after the attack, enjoying unprecedented approval ratings, President Bush would unabashedly declare in the State of the Union address that not only individual terrorists but regimes supporting terrorism "constitute an axis of evil."[4]

More sophisticated analysts, like Michael Ignatieff, also downplayed the significance of social or political inquiry by declaiming the exceptionality of the act:

> What we are up against is apocalyptic nihilism. The nihilism of their means—the indifference to human costs—takes their actions not only out of the realm of politics, but even out of the realm of war itself. The apocalyptic nature of their goals makes it absurd to believe they are making political demands at all. They are seeking the violent transformation of an irremediably sinful and unjust world. Terror does not express a politics, but a metaphysics, a desire to give ultimate meaning to time and history through ever-escalating acts of violence which culminate in a final battle between good and evil.[5]

By funneling the experience through the image of American exceptionalism, 9/11 quickly took on an *exceptional ahistoricity*. For the most part, history was only invoked—mainly in the sepia tones of the Second World War—to prepare America for the sacrifice and suffering that lay ahead. The influential conservative George Will wrote that there were now only two time zones left for the United States:

> America, whose birth was mid-wived by a war and whose history has been punctuated by many more, is the bearer of great responsibilities and the focus of myriad resentments. Which is why for America, there are only two kinds of years, the war years and the interwar years.[6]

Under such forced circumstances of being beyond experience, outside of history, and between wars, 9/11 does not easily yield to philosophical, political, or social inquiry. I believe the best the academician can do is to thickly describe, robustly interrogate, and directly challenge the authorized truths and official actions of all parties who posited a world view of absolute differences in need of final solutions. I do so here by first challenging the now common assumption that 9/11 is an exceptional event beyond history and theory, especially those theories tainted, as Edward Rothstein claimed in the *New York Times*, by "postmodernism" and "postcolonialism."[7] Second, I examine the representations, technologies, and strategies of network wars that have eluded mainstream journalism and traditional social science. I conclude by uncovering what I consider to be the main dangers that emerged from the counterterror of 9/11.

AN EXCEPTIONAL ACT?

On the question of exceptionalism, consider a few testimonials, the first from an editorial in the *New York Times:*

> If the attack against the World Trade Center proves anything it is that our offices, factories, transportation and communication networks and infrastructures are relatively vulnerable to skilled terrorists. . . . Among the rewards for our attempts to provide the leadership needed in a fragmented, crisis-prone world will be as yet unimagined terrorists and other socio-paths determined to settle scores with us.[8]

Another from a cover story of *Newsweek:*

> The explosion shook more than the building: it rattled the smug illusion that Americans were immune, somehow, to the plague of terrorism that torments so many countries.[9]

And finally, one from the London *Sunday Times:*

> He began the day as a clerk working for the Dean Witter brokerage on the 74th floor of the World Trade Center in New York and ended it as an extra in a real-life sequel to *Towering Inferno.* . . . [10]

It might surprise some to learn that these are all quotes taken from 1993, the first and much less deadly terrorist attack on the World Trade Center.[11] They are presented here as a caution against reading terrorism only in the light—the often-blinding light—of the events of September 11. Obviously the two WTC events differ in the scale of the devastation as well as the nature of the attack. 9/11 defied the public imagination of the real—not to mention, as just about every public official and media authority is loath to admit, the official imagination and preemptive capacity of the intelligence community, federal law enforcement, airport security, military, and other governmental agencies. Shock and surprise produced an immediate and nearly uniform reading of the event that was limited in official discourse to condemnation, retribution, and counterterror. But there is a professional as well as a public responsibility to place 9/11 in an historical context and interpretive field that reaches beyond the immediacy of personal tragedy and official injury. Otherwise 9/11 will be remembered not for the attack itself but for the increasing cycles of violence that follow.

If 9/11 is not wholly new, what is it? As we have seen too well, the official response was that it is a struggle of evil against good—of which, given the rhetorical excess deemed necessary by our leaders to mobilize the public to action, there have been more than a few cases in American history. As an actual practice of warfare we again received a better picture of what 9/11 is not than what it is: From the President and Secretary of Defense and on down the food chain of the national-security hierarchy, we heard that this would not be the Gulf War or Kosovo, and it most definitely would not be Vietnam or Mogadishu. And they were partially right—certainly more so than commentators from the knee-jerk factions of both the right and left who flooded the airwaves with sloppy historical analogies from World War II (Pearl Harbor and the Reichstag fire were the most prominent) and convergent conspiracy theories (the Israeli Mossad and Big Oil were pulling all the strings).

From my perspective, new and old forms of representation and violence synergized on 9/11. The neomedieval rhetoric of holy war reverberated from the minaret to the television to the Internet. A hypermodern war of simulation and surveillance was played out at flight schools, airports, and in practically every nook, cranny, and cave of Afghanistan. A remote aerial war was directed from Central Command in Tampa, Florida, 7,750 miles away from targets that were surveyed by drone aircraft like the Predator and Global Hawk, and destroyed by smart GPS-guided JDAM's (Joint Direct Attack Munitions with a circular error probability of about ten feet), CBU-87 and CBU-103 "cluster bombs" (Combined Effects Munitions containing more than 200 bomblets that have antitank, antipersonnel, as well as an incendiary capability), and dumb bombs, topped by the 15,000-pound "Daisy Cutters" (BLU-82) that explode three feet above the ground and incinerate anything within 600 yards. Special) Operations forces led an anti-Taliban coalition in a limited yet highly successful land campaign.

This strange new hybrid of conflict fully qualifies, perverse as it might sound, as a *virtuous war*.[12] Post-Vietnam, post–Cold War, and postmodern, virtuous war emerged prior to 9/11, from the battlespace of the Gulf War and the aerial campaigns of Bosnia and Kosovo in which the killing was kept, as much as it was technologically and ethically possible, virtual and virtuous. Virtuous war relies on virtual simulation, media manipulation, global surveillance, and networked warfare to deter and if need be destroy potential enemies. It draws on just war doctrine (when possible) and holy war doctrine (when necessary). Post 9/11, it now looks to be the ultimate means by which the U.S. intends to resecure its borders, maintain its hegemony, and bring a modicum of order if not justice back to international politics. The difference now is that there is an enemy with a face; in particular, 22 faces, all of them displayed on the FBI's new website of most-wanted terrorists.[13]

In the name of the holy trinity of international order—global free markets, democratic sovereign states, and limited humanitarian interventions—the U.S.

has led the way in a revolution in military affairs (RMA) which underlies virtuous war. At the heart of, as well as the muscle of, this transformation is the technical capability and ethical imperative to threaten and, if necessary, actualize violence from a distance—but again, with minimal casualties when possible.

This is not to claim that people do not die in virtuous wars, but rather that new technologies of killing skew the casualty rates, both off and on the battlefield. In the 9/11 attack, 19 terrorist hijackers killed more than 3,000 people in the United States. Overseas, by the end of January 2002, 20 American military personnel were killed in the line of duty, the majority of whom died in accidents or by friendly fire.[14] These statistics mean that more journalists *covering* the war were killed by hostile fire (10 by the end of January) than American military fighting the war.[15] The high incidence of friendly-fire deaths reflects the increased lethality of precision munitions when they are mistargeted: three members of a 5th Special Forces Group team were killed and 19 soldiers wounded after they mistakenly gave their own geo-coordinates for a satellite-guided JDAMS. It also reflects a "low risk, low yield" military strategy that some see as a lingering legacy of the "Vietnam Syndrome"—the erosion of public support if body bags come home in high numbers—which surfaced and was declared "kicked" by the first President Bush at the end of the Gulf War in 1991.[16] On the other side of virtuous war, enemy casualties are increasingly hard to come by. As the war was winding down in December, estimates of enemy combatant deaths ranged wildly, from 3,000 to 10,000. And when a lone economics professor, Marc Herold at the University of New Hampshire, assessed the number of Afghan noncombatant casualties at 3,767, a maelstrom of controversy erupted.[17]

NETWORK WARS

From the start, it was apparent that 9/11 was and would continue to be a war of networks. Whether terrorist, Internet, or primetime, most of the networks were linked by a push/pull propagation of violence, fear, and dis/mis/information. For a prolonged moment, in the first week of confusion and chaos when there was no detached point of observation, these networks seemed almost neurally attached, immersing viewers in a 24/7 cycle of tragic images of destruction and loss. A national state of emergency and trauma reached into all levels of society. It was as if the American political culture experienced a collective Freudian trauma, which could be reenacted (endlessly on cable and the Internet) but not understood at the moment of shock. This is what Michael Herr meant when he wrote about his own experience with the trauma of Vietnam: "It took the war to teach it, that you were as responsible for everything you saw as you were for everything you did.

The problem was that you didn't always know what you were seeing until later, maybe years later, that a lot of it never made it in at all, it just stayed stored there in your eyes."[18] And in a state of emergency, as in war, the first images stick. There was an initial attempt by the media to transform these images of horror into responsible discourses of reflection and action, but the blame game kicked in with a fury. Moving at the speed of the news cycle and in the rush to judgment, there was little time for deliberation, for understanding the motivations of the attackers, or for assessing the potential consequences, intended as well as unintended, of a military response.

It quickly became apparent that the war networks were not merely nodes connected by wiring of one sort of another. They conveyed, mimicked, and in some cases generated human attributes and intentions, as suggested by *Wired* founding editor Kevin Kelly, who defined a network as "organic behavior in a technological matrix." But 9/11 knocked akilter this always-problematical relationship between meat and wire. Technology-driven events outpaced organic modes of comprehension, and human actions, whether out of trauma or information overload, seemed increasingly to resemble machinic reflexes. Indeed, the first reaction by most onlookers and television reporters was to deem the event an accident. The second attack destroyed the accident thesis and as well, it seemed, our ability to cognitively map the devastating aftermath. Instead, into the void left by the collapse of the WTC towers and the absence of detached analysis, there rushed a host of metaphors, analogies, and metonyms, dominated by denial ("It's a movie"), history ("It's Pearl Harbor"), and nonspecific horror ("It's the end of the world as we have known it").

In our public culture, the media networks rather than the family, the community, or the government provide the first, and, by their very speed and pervasiveness, most powerful response to a crisis. Questions of utility, responsibility, and accountability inevitably arose, and as one would expect, the media's pull-down menu was not mapped for the twin-towered collapse of American invulnerability. Primetime networks did their best to keep up with the realtime crises.[19] But fear, white noise, and technical glitches kept intruding, creating a cognitive lag so profound between event and interpretation that I wondered if superstring theory had not been proven right, that one of the 10 other dimensions that make up the universe had suddenly intruded upon our own, formerly ordered one, exposing the chaos beneath.[20]

Indeed, after the looped footage of the collapse of the towers began to take on the feeling of déjà vu, I seriously wondered if the reality principle itself had not taken a fatal blow. Like Ignatieff, I discerned a nihilism at work, but of a different kind, of the sort vividly on display in the movie *The Matrix*. It first appears when some punky-looking customers in search of bootleg virtual reality software come to see Neo, the protagonist played by Keanu Reeves. He pulls from a shelf a green leather-bound book, the title of which is briefly identifiable as Jean Baudrillard's *Simulacra and Simulation*. When he opens the hollowed out book to retrieve the software, the first page of the last chapter appears: "On Nihilism." Clearly an homage by the two directors, the Wachowsky brothers, it all happens very quickly, too quickly to read the original words of Baudrillard, but here they are:

> Nihilism no longer wears the dark, Wagnerian, Spenglerian, fuliginous colors of the end of the century. It no longer comes from a weltanshauung of decadence nor from a metaphysical radicality born of the death of God and of all the consequences that must be taken from this death. Today's nihilism is one of transparency, this irresolution is indissolubly that of the system, and that of all the theory that still pretends to analyze it.[21]

With the toppling of the WTC, a core belief was destroyed: It could not happen here. Into this void the networks rushed, to provide transparency without depth, a simulacrum of horror, a much purer form of nihilism than imagined by moralist commentators like Ignatieff or Rothstein. In official circles, there was a concerted effort to fence off the void: The critical use of language, imagination, even humor was tightly delimited by moral sanctions and government warnings. This first strike against critical thought took the peculiar form of a semantic debate over the meaning of "coward." In the *New Yorker* and on *Politically Incorrect,* the question was raised whether it is more cowardly to commandeer a commercial airliner and pilot it into the World Trade Center, bomb Serbians from 15,000 feet, or direct a cruise-missile attack against bin Laden from several thousand miles away. The official response was swift, with yanked advertisements, talk-show condemnations, and Ari Fleischer, White House press secretary, saying people like Bill Maher of *Politically Incorrect* "should watch what they say, watch what they do."

Other protected zones of language began to take shape. When Reuters news agency questioned the abuse-into-meaningless of the term "terrorism," George Will on a Sunday morning news program retaliated by advocating a boycott of Reuters.[22] Irony and laughter were permitted in some places, not in others. At a Defense Department press conference Secretary of Defense Rumsfeld could ridicule, and effectively disarm, a reporter who dared to ask if anyone in the Department of Defense would be authorized to lie to the news media.[23] President Bush was given room to joke in a morale-boosting visit to the CIA, saying that he was "spending a lot of quality time lately" with George Tenet, the director of the CIA.[24] And then there was *New York Times* reporter Edward Rothstein, taking his opportunistic shot at postmodernists and postcolonialists, claiming that their irony and relativism is "ethically perverse" and produces a "guilty passivity."[25] Some of us were left wondering, where would that view place fervent truth-seekers and serious enemies of relativism and irony like Osama bin Laden? Terrorist foe but epistemological ally?

THE MIMETIC WAR OF IMAGES

The air war started on October 7, 2001 with a split-screen war of images: In one box, a desolate Kabul seen through a nightscope camera lens, in grainy-green pixels except for the occasional white arc of antiaircraft fire followed by the flash of an explosion; in the other, a rotating cast of characters, beginning with President Bush, followed over the course of the day and the next by Secretary of Defense Rumsfeld, Chairman of the Joint Chiefs, General Myers, and Attorney General John Ashcroft, then progressively down the media food chain of war reporters, beltway pundits, and recently retired generals. On the one side we witnessed images of embodied resolve in high resolution; on the other, nighttime shadows with nobody in sight.

Strategic and narrative binaries cropped up in President Bush's war statement, incongruously delivered from the Treaty Room of the White House: "as we strike military targets, we will also drop food"; the United States is "a friend to the Afghan people" and "an enemy of those who aid terrorists;" "the only way to pursue peace is to pursue those who threaten it." And once more, the ultimate either/or was issued: "Every nation has a choice to make. In this conflict there is no neutral ground."[26]

But the war programming was interrupted by the media-savvy bin Laden. Shortly after the air strikes began, he appeared on Qatar's Al Jazeera television network ("the Arab world's CNN") in a pretaped statement that was cannily delivered as a counter air-strike to the U.S. Kitted out in turban and battle fatigues, bin Laden presented his own bipolar view of the world: "These events have divided the world into two camps, the camp of the faithful and the camp of infidels." But if opposition constituted his worldview, it was an historical mimic battle that sanctioned the counterviolence: "America has been filled with horror from north to south and east to west, and thanks be to God what America is tasting now is only a copy of what we have tasted."[27]

Without falling into the trap of "moral equivalency," one can discern striking similarities. Secretary of Defense Rumsfeld and others have made much of the "asymmetrical" war being waged by the terrorists. And it is indeed a canny and even diabolical use of asymmetrical tactics as well as strategies when terrorists commandeer commercial aircraft and transform them into kinetic weapons of indiscriminate violence, and then deploy commercial media to counter the military strikes that follow. Yet, a fearful symmetry is also at work, at an unconscious, possibly pathological level, a war of escalating and competing and imitative oppositions, a *mimetic war of images.*

A mimetic war is a battle of imitation and representation, in which the relationship of who we are and who they are is played out along a wide spectrum of familiarity and friendliness, indifference and tolerance, estrangement and hostility. It can result in appreciation or denigration, accommodation or separation, assimilation or extermination. It draws physical boundaries between peoples, as well as metaphysical boundaries between life and the most radical other of life, death. It separates human from god. It builds the fence that makes good neighbors; it builds the wall that confines a whole people. And it sanctions just about every kind of violence.

More than a rational calculation of interests takes us to war. People go to war because of how they see, perceive, picture, imagine, and speak of others: that is, how they construct the difference of others as well as the sameness of themselves through representations. From Greek tragedy and Roman gladiatorial spectacles to futurist art and fascist rallies, the mimetic mix of image and violence has proven to be more powerful than the most rational discourse. Indeed, the medical definition of mimesis is "the appearance, often caused by hysteria, of symptoms of a disease not actually present." Before one can diagnose a cure, one must study the symptoms—or, as it was once known in medical science, practice *semiology.*

MIME-NET

It was not long before morbid symptoms began to surface from an array of terror and counterterror networks. Al Qaeda members reportedly used encrypted email to communicate; steganography to hide encoded messages in web images (including pornography); Kinko's and public library computers to send messages; banking networks called *hawala* to transfer untraceable funds; 24/7 cable networks like Al Jazeera and CNN to get the word out; and, in their preparations for 9/11, a host of other information technologies like rented cell phones, online travel agencies, and flight simulators.

In general, networks—from television primetime to Internet realtime—delivered events with an alacrity and celerity that left not only viewers but decision-makers racing to keep up. With information as the lifeblood and speed as the killer variable of networks, getting inside the decision-making as well the image-making loop of the opponent became the central strategy of network warfare. This was not lost on the U.S. national security team as it struggled after the initial attack to get ahead of the network curve. Sluggish reactions were followed by quicker preemptive actions on multiple networks. The Congress passed the "Uniting and Strengthening America by Providing Appropriate Tools Required to Intercept and Obstruct Terrorism (USA PATRIOT) Act," which allowed for "roving wiretaps" of multiple telephones, easier surveillance of email and Internet traffic, more sharing between foreign and domestic intelligence, and the divulgence of grand jury and wiretap transcripts to intelligence agencies.[28] National Security Adviser Condoleezza Rice made personal calls to heads of the television networks, asking them to prescreen and to consider editing Al Qaeda videos for possible coded messages.[29] Information about the air campaign as well as the unfolding ground interventions were heavily filtered by the Pentagon. Information flows slowed to a trickle from the White House and the Defense Department after harsh words and tough restrictions were imposed against leaks. Psychological operations were piggybacked onto humanitarian interventions by the dropping of propaganda leaflets and food packs. The Voice of America began broadcasting anti-Taliban messages in Pashto. After the 22 "Most Wanted Terrorists" were featured on the FBI's website, the popular TV program *America's Most Wanted* ran an extended program on their individual cases.

Some of the most powerful networks are often the least visible, but it was hard to keep it a secret when Hollywood was added to the mix. The entertainment industry journal *Variety* first broke the news about a meeting between White House officials and Hollywood executives. The stated intention was ominous enough, to "enlist Hollywood in the war effort":

> The White House is asking Hollywood to rally 'round the flag in a style reminiscent of the early days of World War II. Network heads and studio chiefs heard that message Wednesday in a closed-door meeting with emissaries from the Bush administration in Beverly Hills, and committed themselves to new initiatives in support of the war on terrorism. These initiatives would stress efforts to enhance the perception of America around the world, to "get out the message" on the fight against terrorism and to mobilize existing resources, such as satellites and cable, to foster better global understanding.[30]

Although some big media picked up this aspect of the story, none except *Newsweek* took note of an earlier meeting organized by the military and the University of Southern California's Institute for Creative Technology.[31] I knew about the ICT because I had covered its opening for *Wired* and *The Nation* back in 1999, when the Army ponied up $43 million to bring together the simulation talents of Hollywood, Silicon Valley, and the U.S. military.[32] Now they were gathering top talent to help coordinate a new virtual war effort:

> In a reversal of roles, government intelligence specialists have been secretly soliciting terrorist scenarios from top Hollywood filmmakers and writers. A unique ad hoc working

group convened at USC just last week at the behest of the U.S. Army. The goal was to brainstorm about possible terrorist targets and schemes in America and to offer solutions to those threats, in light of the twin assaults on the Pentagon and the World Trade Center. Among those in the working group based at USC's Institute for Creative Technology are those with obvious connections to the terrorist pic milieu, like "Die Hard" screenwriter Steven E. De Souza, TV writer David Engelbach ("MacGyver") and helmer Joseph Zito, who directed the features "Delta Force One," "Missing in Action" and "The Abduction." But the list also includes more mainstream suspense helmers like David Fincher ("Fight Club"), Spike Jonze ("Being John Malkovich"), Randal Kleiser ("Grease") and Mary Lambert ("The In Crowd") as well as feature screenwriters Paul De Meo and Danny Bilson ("The Rocketeer").[33]

It would appear that 9/11 christened a new network: the military-industrial-media-entertainment network (MIME-NET). If Vietnam was a war waged in the living rooms of America, the first and most likely the last battles of the counter-terror war are going to be waged on global networks that reach much more widely and deeply into our everyday lives.

COUNTERTERROR DANGERS

On September 11, terror came to America not by rogue state or ballistic missile or high-tech biological, chemical, and nuclear weapons of mass destruction—as presaged by the intelligence and national security experts—but by an unholy network, hijacked airliners, and the terrorist's favorite "force multiplier," prime-time, cable, and Internet weapons of mass distraction and disruption. Have we learned the right lessons since then? Or will the "evil" regimes, missiles, and high technology create more blindspots from which new threats will emerge with devastating effects? What lies ahead?

The great philosopher and ballplayer, Yogi Berra, famously said "the future isn't what it used to be."[34] The point is made all the clearer by the ambiguity of the statement: It's hard to maintain, let alone imagine, a link between a happy past and a rosy future after a disaster. My greatest concern is not so much the future as how past futures become reproduced, that is, how we seem unable to escape the feedback loops of bad intelligence, bureaucratic thinking, and failed imagination.

From my own experience, when confronted by the complexity and speed of networks, the fields of political science and international relations are not much if at all better: As disciplines of thought they are just too narrow, too slow, too . . . academic. This leaves another intellectual void, into which policymakers and military planners are always ready to rush. Currently the RMA mantra among the techno-optimists in the Pentagon is to swiftly implement "network-centric warfare." As first formulated by Vice Admiral Arthur Cebrowski (formerly president of the Naval War College and hand-picked by Defense Secretary Rumsfeld to head up the Pentagon's new Office of Force Transformation), network-centric war is fought by getting inside the decision-making loop of the adversary's network and disrupting or destroying it before it can do the same to yours. The basic idea is that people make war as they make wealth, and, in the information age, networked technology has become the enabler of both. Information and speed are now the key variables in warfare: whoever has the fastest network wins.

I interviewed Cebrowski about network war while he was still the president of the Naval War College. He came across as very smart, highly articulate, deeply religious, and quirky.[35] His comments were laced with quotes from an unusual cast of characters, like the former head of Disney's Imagineering, Bran Ferren ("The advent of interconnectivity is comparable to the advent of fire"), and Executive Editor of *Wired,* Kevin Kelly ("The first thing you need for innovation is a well-nurtured network"). In light of 9/11, one answer stood out from the rest. I asked him about the implications of network wars, where the goal is always to be faster than the opponent: Would this not squeeze out deliberation time? Did he really want machine-time to replace human-time? He replied, "As soon as you can." The goal was "to relieve humanity of a lower level decision-making process."

The shift from state-centric to network-centric modes of deterring and defeating new threats makes sense within a rational framework. However, diminishing the role of human decisions, *especially* those in which emotion plays such a significant part, might not be the best way to confront future threats of terrorism. Furthermore, after the Pentagon released the bin Laden home video in December, where dreams and theology mix with strategies of destruction and slaughter, there was little evidence of any kind of rational purchase for a network-centric deterrence to work.[36] And after witnessing that same day the revival of missile defense as the *deus ex machina* cure for American vulnerability, the consignment of "lower levels of decision-making" to networked technology seems practically suicidal.

It is clear that the allure of technological solutions reaches across cultures and often beyond rationality. Silicon and wire as well as bombs and bullets might offer short-term fixes for the immediate threats posed by terrorism. But no matter how weak the flesh, neural networks, human spirit, and political will are still needed to make the future safe again. In the rush to harden and to accelerate networks, all kinds of checks and balances are being left behind. There seems to be little concern for what organizational theorists see as the negative synergy operating in tightly coupled systems, in which unintended consequences produce cascading effects and normal accidents, in which the very complexity and supposed redundancy of the network produce unforeseen but built-in disasters.

Think Three Mile Island in a pre-1914 diplomatic-military milieu. Think Pentagon *and* Enron when Paul Virilio writes of the "integral accident":

> The proliferation of atomic weapons, freshly boosted by India, Pakistan and probably other destabilized countries on the Asian continent, is prompting the United States—the last great world power—to accelerate the famous "revolution in military affairs" by developing that emergent strategy known as "information war," which consists in using electronics as a hegemonic technology: a role it now takes over from nuclear physics. . . . It is in this context of financial instability and military uncertainty, in which it is impossible to differentiate between information and disinformation, that the question of the **integral accident** arises once again. . . . [37]

My second concern is as much political as it is theoretical: Are the social sciences intrinsically unsuited for the kind of investigation demanded by the emergence of a military-industrial-media-entertainment network? President Eisenhower in his 1961 farewell address famously warned the U.S. of the emergence of a "military-industrial complex," and of what might happen should "public policy be captured by a scientific and technological elite." Now that Silicon Valley and Hollywood have been added to the mix, the dangers have morphed and multiplied. Think *Wag the Dog* meets *The Matrix*. Think of C. Wright Mills's power elite with much better gear to reproduce reality:

> The media provide much information and news about what is happening in the world, but they do not often enable the listener or the viewer truly to connect his daily life with these larger realities. On the contrary, they distract him and obscure his chance to understand himself or his world, by fastening his attention upon artificial frenzies that are resolved within the program framework, usually by violent action or by what is called humor. . . . There is almost always the general tone of animated distraction, of suspended agitation, but it is going nowhere and it has nowhere to go.[38]

So, for the near future, virtuous war as played out by the military-industrial-media-entertainment network will be our daily bread and nightly circus. Some would see us staying there, suspended perpetually, in between wars of terror and counterterror. How to break out of the distractive, often self-prophesying circles? Are there theoretical approaches that can critically respond without falling into the trap of the interwar? One that can escape the nullity of thought which equates the desire to comprehend with a willingness to condone terrorism? The use of sloppy analogies of resistance, as well as petty infighting among critics does not give one much hope.[39] We need to acknowledge that the majority of Americans, whether out of patriotism, trauma, apathy, or reasonableness, thinks it best to leave matters in the hands of the experts. That will not change, the cycle will not be broken, until a public rather than expert assessment is made of what distinguishes new from old dangers, real from virtual effects, terror from counterterror—and whether we are then ready to live with new levels of uncertainty about those very distinctions.

Otherwise, the last word might well come from the first words I heard of the last war the U.S. fought. Circling ten years ago over Chicago O'Hare Airport, the captain came on the PA to inform us that the bombing of Iraq had just begun. In the taxi on the way to my hotel, I heard the first radio reports of stealth aircraft, smart bombs, and low casualty rates. But what stuck from that evening were the last and only words of my cab driver. In the thickest Russian accent, in a terribly war-weary voice, without the benefit of any context but the over-excitement of the radio reports, he said: "They told us we would be in Afghanistan for ten weeks. We were there for ten years."

12. IS CYBER TERROR NEXT?

DOROTHY E. DENNING

Shortly after the September 11 terrorist attack against the United States, hackers took to the Internet to voice their rage. A group called the Dispatchers announced they would destroy web servers and Internet access in Afghanistan and target nations that support terrorists. Led by "Hackah Jak," a 21-year-old security worker from Ohio, the group of 60 people worldwide defaced hundreds of websites and launched denial-of-service attacks against such targets as the Iranian Ministry of Interior, the Presidential Palace of Afghanistan, and Palestinian ISPs.[1] Another group, called Young Intelligent Hackers Against Terror (YIHAT), claimed they penetrated the systems of two Arab banks with ties to Osama bin Laden, although officials from the banks denied any security breaches had occurred. The group, whose stated mission was to stop the money sources of terrorism, issued a plea on their website for corporations to make their networks available to group members for the purpose of providing the "electronic equivalent to terrorist training camps." Later, they took down their public website, apparently in response to attacks from other hackers.[2]

One group of Muslim hackers attacking the YIHAT site said they stood by bin Laden, even as they condemned the attacks of September 11. "Osama bin Laden is a holy fighter, and whatever he says makes sense," GForce Pakistan wrote on a website it defaced. The modified web page warned that the group planned to hit major U.S. military and British websites and proclaimed "al Qaeda Alliance Online." Another GForce defacement contained similar messages along with heart-wrenching images of badly mutilated children said to have been killed by Israeli soldiers.[3] As the year 2001 drew to a close, more than 200 defacements recorded in the alldas defacement archive were attributed to GForce.[4]

The cyber attacks arising from the events of September 11 reflect a growing use of the Internet as a digital battleground. It is not at all unusual for a regional conflict to have a cyber dimension, where the battles are fought by self-appointed hackers operating under their own rules of engagement. A rash of cyber attacks have accompanied the conflict in the Mideast between Israel and the Palestinians, the conflict over Kashmir, and the Kosovo conflict, among others.

According to the *Middle East Intelligence Bulletin,* the Mideast cyberwar erupted in October 2000, shortly after the Lebanese Shi'ite Hezbollah movement abducted three Israeli soldiers.[5] Pro-Israeli hackers responded by crippling the guerrilla movement's website, which had been displaying videos of Palestinians killed in recent clashes and which had called on Palestinians to kill as many Israelis as possible. Pro-Palestinian hackers retaliated, shutting down the main Israeli government website and the Israeli Foreign Ministry website. From there the cyberwar escalated. An Israeli hacker planted the Star of David and some Hebrew text on one of Hezbollah's mirror sites, while pro-Palestinian hackers attacked additional Israeli sites, including those of the Bank of Israel and the Tel Aviv Stock Exchange. In addition to web defacements, hackers launched denial-of-service attacks against Internet service providers and other sites. Intelligence-services company iDefense reported that more than 40 hackers from 23 countries participated in the cyber protests during the period October 2000 to January 2001.[6]

iDefense also reported that two of the pro-Palestinian attackers had connections to terrorist organizations. One of these was UNITY, a Muslim extremist group with ties to Hezbollah. The hackers launched a coordinated, multiphased denial-of-service attack, first against official Israeli government sites, second against Israeli financial sites, third against Israeli ISPs, and fourth against "Zionist E-Commerce" sites. The other group, al-Muhajiroun, was said to have ties with a number of Muslim terrorist organizations as well as bin Laden. The London-based group directed their members to a web page where, at the click of a mouse, members could join an automated flooding attack against Israeli sites that were attacking Moqawama (Islamic Resistance) sites. iDefense also noted that UNITY recruited and organized a third group, Iron Guard, which conducted more technically sophisticated attacks. According to a Canadian government report, the group's call for cyber jihad was supported and promoted by al-Muhajiroun.[7]

Cyber protests have emerged in a climate where computer-network attacks have become a serious and growing threat. The Computer Emergency Response Team Coordination Center (CERT/CC), for example, reported 2,134 incidents in 1997. This number rose to 21,756 in 2000, and in 2001 it more than doubled, to 52,658.[8] Considering that many, perhaps most, incidents are never reported to CERT/CC or indeed to any third party, the numbers become even more significant. Further, each incident that is reported corresponds to an attack that can involve thousands of victims. The Code Red worm, which infected about a million servers in July and August 2001, and caused an estimated $2.6 billion in damages, was a single incident.[9]

The rise in computer-based attacks can be attributed to several factors, including the general growth of the Internet, with a corresponding increase in the number of potential attackers and targets; a never-ending supply of vulnerabilities that, once discovered, are quickly exploited; and increasingly sophisticated hacking tools that allow even those with modest skills to launch devastating attacks. The tools used to launch massive denial-of-service assaults, for example, have advanced command-and-control capabilities. The attacker runs client software to direct and coordinate the actions of server software running on potentially thousands of previously compromised "zombie" computers. Computer worms like Code Red can be used to find potential zombies and automatically install the attack software.

Although cyber attacks have caused billions of dollars in damage and affected the lives of millions, few if any can be characterized as acts of terrorism: fraud, theft, sabotage, vandalism, and extortion—yes; but terrorism—no. Their effect, while serious and not to be taken lightly, pales in comparison to the horror we witnessed on September 11.

But is cyber terrorism coming? Given that at least some hackers sympathetic to bin Laden are engaging in cyber protests, will they—or terrorists specifically trained in cyber methods—conduct future operations using nothing more than a keyboard and mouse? And if they do, will their cyber bombs target critical infrastructures or cause death and destruction comparable to that from physical weapons? Or will they use cyber terrorism as an ancillary tool to amplify the impact of a physical attack; for example, by jamming 911 services or shutting down electricity or telecommunications after blowing up a building or releasing toxic gases?

Before addressing these questions, it is important to understand what is meant by cyber terrorism. The term is generally understood to mean a computer-based attack or threat of attack intended to intimidate or coerce governments or societies in pursuit of goals that are political, religious, or ideological. The attack should be sufficiently destructive or disruptive to generate fear comparable to that from physical acts of terrorism. Attacks that lead to death or bodily injury, extended power outages, plane crashes, water contamination, or major economic losses would be examples. Depending on their impact, attacks against critical infrastructures such as for electric power, banking and finance, or emergency 911 services could be acts of cyber terrorism. Attacks that disrupt nonessential services or that are mainly a costly nuisance would not.

To assess the potential threat of cyber terrorism, two factors must be considered: first, whether there are targets that are vulnerable to attack that could lead to severe harm; and second, whether there are actors with the capability and motivation to carry out the attacks.

Looking first at vulnerabilities, several studies have shown that critical infrastructures are potentially vulnerable to cyber terrorist attack. This is not surprising, because systems are complex, making it effectively impossible to eliminate all weaknesses. New vulnerabilities are continually uncovered, and systems are configured or used in ways that make them open to attack. Even if the technology is adequately hardened, insiders, acting alone or in concert with other terrorists, may be able to exploit their access capabilities to wreak considerable harm.

Consultants and contractors are frequently in a position where they could cause grave harm. In March 2000, Japan's Metropolitan Police Department reported that a software system they had procured to track 150 police vehicles, including unmarked cars, had been developed by the Aum Shinrikyo cult, the same group that gassed the Tokyo subway in 1995, killing 12 people and injuring 6,000 more.[10] At the time of the discovery, the cult had received classified tracking data on 115 vehicles. Further, the cult had developed software for at least 80 Japanese firms and 10 government agencies. They had worked as subcontractors to other firms, making it almost impossible for the organizations to know who was developing the software. As subcontractors, the cult could have installed Trojan horses to launch or facilitate cyber terrorist attacks at a later date.

If we take as given that critical infrastructures are vulnerable to a cyber terrorist attack, then the question becomes whether there are actors with the capability and motivation to carry out such an operation. While many hackers have the knowledge, skills, and tools to attack computer systems, they may lack the motivation to cause violence or severe economic or social harm. Conversely, terrorists who are motivated to cause violence may lack the capability or interest in causing that degree of damage in cyberspace.

In August 1999, the Center for the Study of Terrorism and Irregular Warfare at the Naval Postgraduate School (NPS) in Monterey, California, issued the results of a study that assessed the prospects of terrorist organizations pursuing cyber terrorism.[11] They concluded that the barrier to entry for anything beyond annoying hacks is quite high, and that terrorists generally lack the wherewithal and human capital needed to mount a meaningful operation. Cyber terrorism, they argued, was a thing of the future, although it might be pursued as an ancillary tool.

The NPS study examined five types of terrorist groups: religious, New Age, ethno-nationalist separatist, revolutionary, and far-right extremist. Of these, only the religious groups were thought likely to seek the most damaging capability level, as it would be consistent with their indiscriminate application of violence.

In October 2000, the NPS group issued a second report following a conference that examined the decision-making process that leads substate groups engaged in armed resistance to develop new operational methods.[12] They were particularly interested in learning whether such groups would engage in cyber terrorism. In addition to academics and a member of the United Nations, the participants included a hacker and five practitioners with experience in violent substate groups. The latter included the PLO, the Liberation Tigers of Tamil Eelan (LTTE), the Basque Fatherland and Liberty-Political/Military (ETA-PM), and the Revolutionary Armed Forces of Colombia (FARC). The participants engaged in a simulation exercise based on the situation in Chechnya. Only one cyber attack was authorized during the simulation, and that was against the Russian Stock Exchange. The attack was justified on the grounds that the exchange was an elite activity and thus disrupting it would not affect most Russians. Indeed, it might appeal to the average Russian. The group ruled out mass disruptions impacting e-commerce as being too indiscriminate and risking a backlash.

The findings from the meeting were generally consistent with the earlier study. Recognizing that their conclusions were based on a small sample, they concluded that terrorists have not yet integrated information technology into their strategy and tactics; that substate groups may find cyber terror attractive as a nonlethal weapon; that significant barriers between hackers and terrorists may prevent their integration into one group; and that politically motivated terrorists had reasons to target selectively and limit the effects of their operations, although they might find themselves in a situation where a mass casualty attack was a rational choice.

The NPS group also concluded that the information and communication revolution might lessen the need for violence by making it easier for substate groups to get their message out. Unfortunately, this conclusion does not seem to be supported by recent events. Many of the people in bin Laden's network, including the suicide hijackers, have used the Internet but nevertheless engage in horrendous acts of violence. Groups that foster hate and aggression thrive on the Internet alongside those that promote tolerance and peace.

Although cyber terrorism is certainly a real possibility, for a terrorist, digital attacks have several drawbacks. Systems are complex, so controlling an attack and achieving a desired level of damage may be harder than using physical weapons. Unless people are killed or badly injured, there is also less drama and emotional appeal. In addition, terrorists may be disinclined to learn and try cyber methods given the success they have had with bombs and other physical weapons.

In assessing the threat of cyber terrorism, it is also important to look beyond the traditional terrorist groups, to those with considerable computing skills. As noted at the beginning of this essay, some of these people are aligning themselves with terrorists like bin Laden. While the vast majority of hackers may be disinclined toward violence, it would only take a few to turn cyber terrorism into reality.

Further, the next generation of terrorists will grow up in a digital world, with ever more powerful and easy-to-use hacking tools at their disposal. They might see greater potential for cyber terrorism than do the terrorists of today, and their level of knowledge and skill relating to hacking will be greater. Also, just as the September 11 suicide hijackers received flight training in American schools, terrorists could learn how to conduct cyber attacks through information-security courses offered in the United States and elsewhere.

Terrorists might also see benefits to conducting cyber attacks against critical infrastructures. Just as the physical attack against the World Trade Center severely impacted the financial and transportation sectors of the United States and elsewhere, so too might a cyber attack against critical computers supporting these sectors. The potential seriousness of such an attack is made all the more apparent by the considerable resources that the U.S. government is allocating to cyber defense of critical infrastructures and by the attention in the press. Terrorists have long targeted the infrastructure of countries, so a cyber attack may not be far fetched. The Islamic extremist Ahmed Ressam, who attempted to place a bomb in the Los Angeles airport around January 1, 2000, testified that he was trained to target "such installations as electric plants, gas plants, airports, railroads, large corporations, and military installations." He said that he chose an airport because it is "sensitive politically and economically." [13]

Cyber terrorism could also become more attractive as the real and virtual worlds become more closely coupled, with automobiles, appliances, and other devices attached to the Internet. Unless these systems are carefully secured, conducting an operation that physically harms someone may be as easy as penetrating a website is today.

Although there are no reports of Al Qaeda conducting cyber attacks against critical infrastructures or teaching methods of cyber jihad in terrorist training camps, there are some indications that cyber terrorism is at least on their radar screen. Following the September 11 attacks, bin Laden allegedly told Hadmid Mir, editor of the *Ausaf* newspaper, that "hundreds of Muslim scientists were with him and who would use their knowledge in chemistry, biology and (sic) ranging from computers to electronics against the infidels." [14]

Further, in December 2001, *Newsbytes* reported that a suspected member of Al Qaeda said that members of the terrorist network had infiltrated Microsoft and attempted to plant Trojan horses and bugs in the Windows XP operating system.[15] According to the report, Mohammad Afroze Abdul Razzak told Indian police that the terrorists had gained employment at Microsoft by posing as computer programmers. Microsoft responded by saying the claims were "bizarre and unsubstantiated and should be treated skeptically."

Regardless of whether the claim is true, the story is troubling for the simple reason that it shows that at least some terrorists are fully cognizant of the potential of cyber attacks and how such attacks can be launched with the aid of Trojan horses and insider access into the world's dominant software producer. By planting malicious code in the popular software, the terrorists could potentially steal sensitive information from Microsoft customers, including government agencies and operators of critical infrastructures, and use that information to facilitate physical or cyber acts of terror. They could sabotage data or networks, potentially causing enormous losses.

The bottom line is that hijacked vehicles, truck bombs, and biological weapons still pose a greater threat than cyber terrorism. Nevertheless, just as the events of September 11 caught us by surprise, so too could a major cyber assault. We cannot afford to shrug off the threat.

13. BLACK SEPTEMBER, INFANTILE NIHILISM, AND NATIONAL SECURITY

BRUCE CUMINGS

> I remember . . . remarking on the criminal futility of the whole thing, doctrine, action, mentality; and on the contemptible aspect of the half-crazy pose as of a brazen cheat exploiting the poignant miseries and passionate credulities of a mankind always so tragically eager for self-destruction . . . a blood-stained inanity of so fatuous a kind that it was impossible to fathom its origin by any reasonable or even unreasonable process of thought.
>
> JOSEPH CONRAD, *THE SECRET AGENT*[1]

In this manner Conrad rendered his first impressions on hearing the news that a lone anarchist had killed himself in a failed attempt to blow up London's Greenwich Observatory in 1894. It was to this old novel that I first turned after the destruction of the World Trade Center on September 11, 2001. Conrad's first impression then is my conviction now: Nothing in recent history has prepared us for such a contemptible fusion of willful mass terrorism, bloodstained earthly tragedy, and passionate, ardent conviction—the adolescent fantasy that one big bang will change the world and usher in a global "jihad," a new epoch of "Crusades," or the final solution to the eight decades of history that have passed since the Ottoman Empire collapsed. If in its catastrophic result the attack succeeded beyond the wildest dreams of its architects, it was still a species of nihilism—infantile nihilism.

In its utter recklessness and indifference to consequences, its craven anonymity, and its lack of any discernible "program" save for inchoate revenge, this was an apolitical act. What programmatic direction issues forth from the collapse of the twin towers? Casting the moneylenders from the temple? But the banks remained stable, and the stock market reopened in a week. A curse on globalization, by attacking its skyscraping symbols? Peaceful protesters and agitators had done much more in the years since Seattle to draw attention to the pretensions and inequalities of globalization than either the anarchist saboteurs in their midst, or the foolish wreckers of a pristine September day in New York. What is their next step, what is their program, what is their strategy, how will the chief terrorists know when they have achieved their goals? What would a "peace negotiation" look like with such criminals? The infernal perpetrators are dead—that is not a starting point, but the end; they accomplished a terrible but ultimately futile and self-defeating act, because they brought into being the very forces that may well put an end to two decades of mindless terrorism.

The pilots who only wanted to learn how to fly Boeing passenger planes straight, to the left, and to the right probably chose September 11 because of the ubiquity of the 9-1-1 emergency number—as in, okay, call 911 now! If so, this again expresses their puerile rage, their apolitical futility, and their brazen self-assurance: suppose God is a Hindu, not a Muslim, and instead of 70 virgins on the other side of the rainbow, they get reincarnated as the first 19 cockroaches that New Yorkers spray or squash every September 11, for eternity?

For these reasons, it seems to me that social science can have little to say about September 11, perhaps with the exception of the discipline of psychology. Later I will suggest that a certain kind of social science, grounded in history and language expertise, was not only superior to abstract models in explaining this episode and the war that followed in Afghanistan, but essential to any understanding of American relations with the Muslim world. At the time many said, Look at how the Muslims hate America: do they not have legitimate grievances? The answer is twofold: Yes, they do have legitimate grievances, and one of them is the continuing mutual terror of the Israeli–Palestinian conflict. And no, they had no particular grievances in 2001 that were different than their grievances in the past 50 years; at any point since the creation of the state of Israel it was child's play for any demagogue to stoke popular Muslim anger against the United States. The terrible violence that followed upon the collapse of President Bill Clinton's vigorous attempt to achieve a peace between Israel and Palestine may rightly be laid at the door of Ariel Sharon, Yasir Arafat, or the diplomacy by dereliction of the subsequent Bush administration, depending on one's point of view, but September 11 did nothing to advance anyone's agenda in the Middle East.

In the first of his patented and well-scripted television appearances after September 11, Osama bin Laden conjured up 80 years of humiliation, as if Palestine today, on the cusp of having the first independent state of and by Palestinians in that eight-decade period, is worse off than it was under the British mandate, that is, when it was effectively a colony; or that Saudi Arabia is led by nothing more than a contemporary version of Egypt's King Farouk or some other profligate sultan. That Saudi Arabia is corrupt and swollen with wealth that it did not earn is undeniable, but that has also been true for 60 years; the current crisis is much more likely to require some opening of that regime than to cause its demise. Osama bin Laden appeared to harbor one clear goal, to rule over Saudi Arabia and use its vast pools of oil as a weapon; one report alleged that he would like to drive oil to $166 a barrel and thereby ruin the West. Such precision from a wrecker like this! But it will never happen. This monomaniacal and homicidal lunatic came close only to ruling an utterly devastated Afghanistan in tandem with an illiterate country ignoramus[2] calling himself Mullah Omar; from the start the only question was how much havoc bin Laden could wreak before his reign of terror ended.

I have no expertise on the Middle East, but I would guess that it is the peculiar Saudi combination of Wahabi fundamentalism for the masses and hedonism for the elite that so deeply upset bin Laden, as it would a renegade son of that same elite. Like wealthy youths who joined fascist and communist movements (or the Weather Underground of the 1960s), bin Laden's taste for mass violence and his insane bravado sketches the personality of a favored and spoiled princeling, who gazes at the world through profoundly solipsistic lenses. Such a person's reach always exceeds his grasp, an attribute that sealed his fate (at least in the Afghan war detonated by September 11).

This prodigal son's posed and polished television persona likewise bespoke his self-regard, his narcissism, and his cultivation of a well-born and mannered ascetic style; through a brilliant symbolism he contrived an aesthetic that was at once compelling and chic, quickly bringing him "star" status. But the love of pixel-dot glamour betrayed a fatal modernism in this make-believe medieval cleric, not to mention his inability to grasp the postmodern truth that the televised image (or spectacle in his case), is a mere semblance of reality, a flitting chimera—here today and gone tomorrow.[3] He was television's favored face in late 2001, the follow-on to philanderer Gary Condit whose image flooded the airwaves in the summer. Soon, though, the television consumer was satiated, whether in the U.S. or in the Arab world.

For these and other reasons, I wonder if all this was a beginning—"the first war of the twenty-first century" in CNN-speak—or an ending. We have had two decades of global terrorism, roughly dating from the Iranian revolution. How much longer will it last, given that its stated goals (like the erasure of Israel or the expulsion of American power) are no more likely today than they were in 1980? How many suicidal Muslims exist with passable English and the modern abilities to manipulate credit accounts, get multiple driver's licenses and fake IDs, learn to fly jumbo jets, etc.—people who otherwise would be professionals? I cannot believe they are many. Certainly one country after another on a belt running from Indonesia to Algeria produces desperate young men by the tens of thousands, unemployable in their economies; Egypt is said to graduate 20,000 lawyers a year of whom perhaps ten per cent get jobs commensurate with their degrees. Clearly this reflects a colossal failure of development in critically important countries like Pakistan and Egypt,[4] but that is hardly anything new. It remains hard to believe that there are so many naifs willing to immolate themselves in the prime of their lives for goals that have not and cannot be attained.

A LITTLE HISTORY CAN BE A BAD THING

The terrorist attacks shocked and traumatized Americans because Americans have experienced precious few civilian casualties on their soil since the Civil War 140 years ago. World Wars I and II, the Korean War, Vietnam, and the Gulf War were all fought overseas, and the vast majority of American casualties were combatants. Fatalities in all these twentieth-century wars still fail to reach the numbing total of more than 600,000 from the Civil War (including many innocents). But now Americans have finally joined a contemporary world where civilian casualties from warfare and terrorism are among the most tragic experiences any human being can face: the death of loved ones who are also innocent. Thus the loss of life of some 3,000 unsuspecting people who happened to be working in the World Trade Center on that terrible day came as a profound shock to the American people.

After Black September a large billboard greeted Chicagoans speeding northward on the Kennedy Expressway: "Americans Will Not Forget!" read the statement in the middle, flanked on the left and right by two dates: December 7, 1941, and September 11, 2001. Pearl Harbor was one among many historical analogies used to comprehend our present crisis, even though I haven't been able to think of any ("In its desertion of every basis for comparison, the event asserts its singularity"[5]). Analogies with the Cold War are truly misplaced: Whatever one may think about the Soviet Union, it competed head-to-toe against the U.S. and offered a top-to-bottom alternative system that was at the same time modern; both powers were true believers in material progress and both were committed to a global competition between two kinds of modernism. In being so, the USSR was rational and could be deterred. It had no wish for suicide, and carefully stayed out of going to the brink with the U.S.—in Iran in 1946, Berlin in 1948, Korea in 1950, and Berlin again in 1961. The exception was the Cuban Missile Crisis, but a strong and wise American strategy of confrontation and negotiation ended that episode to the detriment of Moscow.

As Americans we witness this commonality of aspirations in a clip from CNN's Cold War documentary: The first human to descend from outer space, Yuri Gagarin, parades through Moscow in 1961 in a Zil four-door convertible with huge chrome bumpers, soaring tailfins, and wide whitewalls setting off the metallic green paint of a car that mimicked the last American four-door convertibles, still being made then by Lincoln. We cannot imagine bin Laden and his Taliban friends in such a scene; these might be the only people in the modern epoch who regret that the wheel was invented. They give new meaning to the word "antediluvian." And had it been bin Laden in 1962, he would joyfully have tugged on his end of the knotted rope that Khrushchev so memorably (and eloquently) spoke of. In short, bin Laden and his followers have not the slightest thing in common with our old enemies, whether the communists like Stalin or the national liberation figures like Ho Chi Minh. They have something in common with Saddam Hussein, but his aggression in 1990 was of the common, old-world Bismarckian variety—and it did not work.

Philosophers in the just war tradition going back to St. Augustine have long argued that self-defense is the only legitimate reason to kill other human beings, a judgment carrying the corollary that an aggressor bears an unconscionably heavy burden because he cannot know the consequences of his aggression. History is littered with testimony to this truth, and it is the truth of Pearl Harbor. It is not surprising that many Americans resorted to this analogy, since foreign attacks on the United States have occurred so rarely—essentially two big ones in two centuries, in 1812 and 1941. September 11 is clearly "a date that will live in infamy," and everyone will remember exactly where they were when they first saw or heard this news. Using a commercial airliner as a deadly missile also qualifies the attack on the Pentagon as an act of war. But these facts exhaust the analogies with Pearl Harbor.

Pearl Harbor belongs to history as garden-variety aggression: a rash and reckless attack, but one that eventually brought upon the heads of the perpetrators the gravest consequences for the future of the Japanese nation—for the first time in its long history. It was aggression, of a kind the old world had seen many times, but with a usually unremarked military efficiency: total American casualties in the Pearl raid were 2,335 naval, army, and marine personnel dead, and 1,143 wounded. Total civilians killed: sixty-eight.[6] A counterforce attack directed exclusively at military targets, it had a soldier-to-civilian kill ratio of about 34 to one. Furthermore, as Harvard's Akira Iriye has shown, Pearl Harbor followed upon an ever-intensifying U.S.–Japan cold war of many years' duration, including acts of war by the U.S. (preeminently Roosevelt's oil embargo).[7]

For all these reasons, Pearl Harbor is a bad analogy with September 11. But it is not going away. A leading liberal commentator, Bill Moyers, wrote in *The Nation* that he, too, found the comparison apt: "In response to the sneak attack on Pearl Harbor, Americans waged and won a great war, then came home to make this country more prosperous and just. It is not beyond this generation to live up to that example."[8] Flawed thinking animates the whole statement: no "great war" unfolded after September 11, the enemy was diabolical but could not remotely be compared to the might and weight of Nazi Germany or militarist Japan, millions of Americans are not fighting overseas on several fronts, and the current generation is no better or worse than the generation that won victory in World War II (except in the minds of baby-boomer commentators who took rather a long time to comprehend the immense sacrifices that their parents made in the 1940s). Still, Bill Moyers is one of America's most perspicacious commentators, which suggests the staying power of this flawed and disturbing analogy.

The September 11 attacks were utterly unexpected and unprovoked, had no rational military purpose, took an overwhelming number of innocent civilian lives, and lacked the essential relationship between violent means and political ends that, as Clausewitz taught us, must govern any act of war. They were barbarous in conception, heedless of consequences in execution, lacking a politics whether in Clausewitz's or Conrad's sense, and ultimately self-defeating of the cause they purported to champion. It goes without saying that today we cannot know the full consequences of these acts, but certainly an antiterrorist coalition was brought into being unlike anything the postwar world has seen, and which made short work of the Taliban regime. Old enemies like Russia and China joined this effort, and it became inconceivable that any great power could see its interests or prestige wrapped up in anything connected to bin Laden and Al Qaeda. His type could only rule atop an irradiated smoking ruin of modernity (probably he would like that, too), where the dark ages—or the seventh century when the Prophet Mohammed appeared (Mullah Omar fancied himself a worthy successor)—could be recreated. Otherwise bin Laden and the Taliban were the most remarkable atavisms that the modern world has ever seen.

FOREIGN POLICY AFTER SEPTEMBER 11

Black September led just about everyone to imagine that the world would never be the same—everything had changed, a caesura had opened in world history. Until three months had passed I also thought that world politics had dramatically changed: An administration that had begun with a sweeping and self-consciously assertive unilateralism in its first eight months had learned after September 11 just how many friends it had in the world, as a collegial, multilateral diplomacy quickly unfolded. NATO passed a resolution stating that the attacks on the U.S. were also attacks against NATO itself. Prime Minister Tony Blair gave new vigor to the "special relationship" between London and Washington. Various powers pledged soldiers and funds to the war in Afghanistan. It looked like the U.S. and its allies, along with Russia and China, were all committed to the common task of a global struggle against terrorism, and that a rare unity had cut across the old divisions of world politics.

Unfortunately subsequent events do not bear out this judgment. The war in Afghanistan went quickly and well, with very little allied involvement—by and large the Pentagon seemed not to want it—and soon the inherent unilateralism of the Bush administration reasserted itself. In December 2001 the U.S. announced its withdrawal from the 1972 Anti-Ballistic Missile Treaty, over Russia's opposition (and later, pained acquiescence), thus to get on with building its pet Missile Defense system, bringing great domestic pressures on Russian leader Vladimir Putin and a real threat to China's modest nuclear deterrent (which would be neutralized by Missile Defense). Powerful members of the Bush administration were intent on extending the "war on terrorism" to Iraq, which had little or no involvement with Al Qaeda and none with September 11. (All of America's allies opposed this adventure.) If in the early going it often seemed that Tony Blair was acting like a president and George Bush like a prime minister, Blair's eloquent and ringing condemnations of the terrorists did not bring him closer to the inner circle of Bush's decision-making regarding the war in Afghanistan. Likewise there was little consultation with European allies on the future of that country, except that Washington wanted the allies to shoulder the burden of peacekeeping and nation-building in postwar Afghanistan.

One is left to conclude that powerful figures in the Bush administration, like Defense Secretary Donald Rumsfeld, believe that American superiority in high-tech weaponry (demonstrated with apparent effectiveness in Afghanistan), combined with the unipolar world that resulted from the collapse of the USSR, enable the U.S. to have its cake and eat it, too—to do what it wants or what it thinks best, regardless of allied or world opinion. Rumsfeld's success in boosting the defense budget by more than 40 percent since Clinton's final year in office is testimony to his influence.[9] Secretary of State Colin Powell is an exception, but his attempt to bring new momentum to the Middle East peace process in the winter of 2001 was a complete failure, and Rumsfeld was far more prominent in defending the Bush foreign policy to the public. It remains to be seen how long the inveterate unilateralism of the Bush administration will last and what its consequences will be, particularly whether potential enemies like China and Russia will continue to grin and bear it and seek friendly relations with Washington. But it is hard to conclude that September 11 is the watershed in U.S. foreign relations that it appeared to be at the time; it seems more likely, at least from my point of view, that if the Iranian hostage crisis gave us Ronald Reagan, bin Laden has given us a more formidable Bush administration than anyone could have imagined during the 2000 election imbroglio.

THE CONTAINMENT SYSTEM

The consequences of the war in Afghanistan are difficult to gauge at this writing. When the war began, most commentary focused on the perils that other powers (Great Britain, Russia) had faced in trying to fight in or subdue Afghanistan, so when the war concluded so quickly, all too many analysts had egg on their face. It may be that a novel combination of "smart" weapons and mobile and nimble special forces combined to energize local allies (the Northern Alliance soldiers) and quickly dispatch a Taliban army that nearly all observers had thought to be formidable and resilient.[10] But it may also be that Taliban and Al Qaeda military prowess and their hold on Afghanistan were vastly exaggerated; American special forces with every high-tech accoutrement often confronted threadbare teenagers challenged by fixing a flat tire on their Toyotas, and even Al Qaeda's fight-to-the-death bravado often gave way to a pragmatic decision to live (and fight?) another day. So it isn't clear whether this war holds lessons for the new century's future conflicts or not. Certainly, though, the mainstream verdict on this victory will only bolster the claims of experts who tout an insurmountable American advantage in the effective use of military force.

In spite of this manifest victory, however, the war in Afghanistan may still have consequences that end up defeating the best intentions of the United States. A different picture emerges when we direct attention to the politically shaped containment compromises that have characterized America's wars since 1941. The likelihood is that the war in Afghanistan will lead to a permanent American commitment to try to stabilize the most unstable region in the world: the belt of populous and mostly Muslim countries stretching westward from Indonesia all the way to Algeria, and northward to Central Asia, into the former Soviet republics and the Muslim peoples of China's western reaches.

American combat troops first landed at Inch'on not in 1950, but on a warm, beautiful September day five years earlier. On another pristine September day in 2001, the eleventh day, 37,000 of them were still in South Korea. Korea is the best example in modern history of how easy it is to get into a war, and how hard it is to get out. Vietnam would have been the same, and indeed was essentially the same from the mid-1950s when Washington committed its prestige to the Saigon regime, to the mid-1970s when the war concluded with an American defeat— because the U.S. could neither sustain a stable Saigon regime nor a divided Vietnam. If it could have done so we would still be there, stuck in the aspic of another Korea (South Vietnam would have been a "NIC" until the Asian crisis of 1997, and North Vietnam would resemble North Korea).

World War II was the clearest kind of military victory, yet American troops remain on the territory of their defeated enemies, Japan and Germany, and exercise a lingering constraint on their autonomy; however many justifications come and go for that remarkable and unprecedented situation (in that the leading global power stations its forces on the territory of the second and third largest economies), the fact remains that it has persisted for 57 years and shows no signs of ending. The Gulf War came to an end when President George H. W. Bush and his advisors, preeminently Brent Skowcroft, kicked on the brakes well short of Baghdad and thus spawned the newest containment system, now a decade old, leaving upward of 9,000 U.S. troops (depending on the year) in Saudi Arabia and several new military bases there and elsewhere in the Middle East.

As 2002 dawned, the Pentagon announced a new commitment to lay down "a long-term footprint in Central Asia," as reporters put it: an air base near Bishkek, the capital of Krgyzstan, that would hold up to 3,000 troops; massive upgrading of existing military bases and facilities in Uzbekistan (e.g., the former Soviet base at Khanabad) and Pakistan (where several bases now house American forces, with next to no media access or scrutiny); creation and expansion of remnant military bases in Afghanistan; and the replacement of Marine expeditionary forces sent into Afghanistan during the war with Army regulars settling in for the long haul ("Army units tend to establish more permanent bases," reporters said with considerable understatement). The spokesman for the U.S. Central Command told reporters that in the future the U.S. will find great value "in continuing to build airfields in a variety of locations on the perimeter of Afghanistan that over time can do a variety of functions, like combat operations, medical evacuation and delivering humanitarian assistance." [11]

Other press reports detailed American plans to send some 600 troops to help combat Islamic guerrillas in the Philippines and to work together with the Indonesian military (which ruled the country for 30 years until Suharto was overthrown in 1998) in antiterrorism operations, which may inevitably embroil the U.S. in trying to maintain the precarious integrity of this far-flung island nation. [12] If the past is prelude, American forces may remain in these places for decades.

There are good social science reasons for the American inability to extricate itself from wartime entanglements, however much those commitments depart radically from anything the U.S. experienced up until 1945. Vital interests are asserted where none existed before, temporary expedients become institutional

> ican servicemen in 1993. . . . This litany points not to any lack of American courage but to a lack of political grounding that has haunted the country's foreign policy for a half-century. America's power has been technologically robust and politically fragile.

Danner found the causes for this lack of political grounding in Washington's fear of the "suspicion and impatience" of the citizenry when American power is deployed abroad, and in American politicians who are "unwilling to expend the political capital required to convince the country to act decisively when its interests are at stake."[14]

Although Danner traces this problem back to 1961, Truman and Eisenhower were no different. When the United States finally inherited the mantle of Britain's global leadership in 1947, this capped a rapid rise to world power that might have happened well before World War II, but did not happen until Franklin Roosevelt reached for preeminence after Pearl Harbor. Subsequently the U.S. became the power of last resort for just about everything, but particularly for the maintenance and good functioning of the world economy. It remains so today. Yet this hegemonic role, which statesmen like Henry Stimson and Dean Acheson understood well, was masked from the American people by a march outward characterized as defensive and unwanted: It was called containment, and that strategic cover lasted until the Cold War ended and the USSR collapsed—whereupon the American global position continued apace, unabated, with defense budgets to match.

Time and again the communist threat was invoked to get the American people to support a completely unprecedented role for their country in the world, but at least since the Gulf War (more likely since Vietnam), the justifications have worn thin. A sharp difference now exists between the American people, who can barely muster a coherent justification for why we retain such large expeditionary forces abroad,[15] and successive administrations in Washington that invent new perils and enemies from year to year: Saddam was likened to Hitler, and in 2001 China was to be our new enemy—until September 11 obliterated that foolish and dangerous notion. North Korea's economy is in collapse and it cannot feed its own people, but it remains the stated target of Missile Defense.

For the containment system to conquer a new Central Asian front will be easy in the short run; in the aftermath of such horrific attacks the American people have generally supported whatever measures the (Cold War) experienced Bush team desires, at home and abroad. In the longer run, however, a failure to roll up bin Laden's terror network, to replace the Taliban with a broad-based and self-sustaining Afghan government, and an inability to extricate American forces from becoming the policemen of Central Asia (and much of the Middle East) will tend to jeopardize all the other far-flung American security commitments.

commitments, military and bureaucratic interests proliferate, the Pentagon bean counters take over, every new appropriations season in Congress becomes an occasion for defending this or that outpost (new or old, vital or marginal)—and American power is mired in works of its own doing. Among the services, the U.S. Army finds its permanent mission in garrisoning various highly developed bases around the world; there officers confront real enemies (as in Korea) or command important posts (in Japan or Germany), and thus gain experience essential to promotion. Every Army chairman of the Joint Chiefs of Staff, for example, has served a tour of duty commanding the Eighth Army in Korea. The massive American encampment in and near Yongsan in Seoul (a base first built by the Japanese in 1894), has for decades offered a virtual country-club environment for Army folks living abroad (golf course, swimming pools, movie theaters, suburban-style homes for the officers).

In December 2000 I visited P'anmunjom once again, this time courtesy of the U.S. Army. Our hosts gave us the Army's construction of the history of the Korean War (a version that could not have changed since 1953) and a luncheon of rib-eye steak and French-fried potatoes of similar vintage, offered in a café that had a country music poster on the wall advertising Hank Williams's tour of Atlanta in 1952, a mile or two distant from North Korean positions. Most Americans know little if anything about Korea, yet the war that erupted in 1950 was the fulcrum and turning point toward a new national security state at home and permanent garrisons abroad: U.S. defense spending was pegged at $13.5 billion in June 1950, and nearly $55 billion six months later (or more than $500 billion in current dollars, a high point never reached again). The failure of the U.S. invasion of North Korea in late 1950 (termed a "roll-back" by the National Security Council) put distinct outer limits on American strategy thereafter, solidifying a bipartisan consensus that containment had to be the strategy.[13] And it is the Army that plugs the holes and maintains the containment bulwarks.

Another curiosity is that tens of thousands of troops can stay in places like Germany or Korea for decades, but 250 Marines killed in Beirut or a handful of soldiers brutalized in Somalia prompt immediate about-faces in Washington, again to the detriment of American power and credibility. The reasons for this are entirely political, and one version of this particular politics was laid out with rare concision and eloquence by Mark Danner in an important editorial:

> For at least a quarter-century American power has coexisted with American inconstancy and capriciousness. Alongside the triumphant cold war narrative we have shaped for ourselves one can easily trace another story, one of bluster and flight and uneasy forgetting: the Bay of Pigs debacle in 1961; the panicked retreat from Saigon in 1975; the humiliation at the hands of the Iranian "students" in 1979; the wholesale flight from Beirut . . . in 1984; the abandonment of Mogadishu, Somalia after the death of 18 Amer-

Anyone who would confidently chart the future today would be a fool, but the first thought that struck me after witnessing (on television) thousands of casualties resulting from an attack on the American mainland, for the first time since 1812, was that over the long haul the American people may exercise their long-standing tendency to withdraw from a world deemed recalcitrant to their ministering,[16] and present Washington with a much different and eminently more difficult dilemma than the one Mark Danner proposed: how to rally the citizens for a long twilight struggle to maintain an ill-understood American hegemony in a vastly changed world.

It has long seemed to me that we are ill fitted to be a global superpower, the power of last resort, or Madeleine Albright's "indispensable nation," because we remain backward compared to our allies in Europe and Japan. They have built a pattern of modern urban civilization that is deeply satisfying to most of the citizens who live it, because it is exciting and interesting, and buttressed by critical social safeguards for the infirm or the unemployed or the elderly—a social contract for a well functioning social market. Japan may be vegetating in the teeth of a decade-long recession, but one would never know it from the extraordinary vibrance, stability, and safety of cities like Tokyo. In Europe, particularly in Germany and France, most contemporary political leaders not only come from the generation of the 1960s, but represent much of what people were working toward then, as goals—civil rights, women's rights, collective security, a better environment, a safety net for the poor.

Successive Republican administrations since 1968 have been fighting that legacy, but the difference with Europe and Japan occurred much earlier: a fatal political departure toward the beginning of the Cold War, as Mary Kaldor has long pointed out,[17] that propelled Western Europe and the U.S. along different political paths—and the difference is still there, and may be worse than at any point since 1945. I think that only when the United States comes up to the contemporary standard of our allies in Europe and Japan, can a true coalition of nations unite and stand for the promise and the actuality of the modern, and deepen the work of extending it to the vast majority of people in the rest of the world who remain utterly outside of its promise, angrily looking in.

NATIONAL SECURITY AND THE SOCIAL SCIENCES

My last observation may strike some readers as crude, but I think the current crisis aptly illustrates the turn from actually existing reality that has activated the social sciences (and in a different way, the humanities) for at least the past two decades. I don't know what game theory or the rational choice paradigm can teach us either about the tragedy that happened on September 11, or the new war that followed it. What mix of costs and benefits, incentives and deterrents, dependent and independent variables, signals and "noise," transparencies and moral hazards, would have dissuaded the 19 suicide bombers from their task, or will predict the full consequences of the war in Afghanistan? Meanwhile the most reviled form of inquiry for self-described "cutting edge" social scientists in the past two decades, one usually caricatured as "area studies" or "ethnography" or a similar epithet, a prejudice that has led to the abject national decline of the sub-disciplines of comparative politics, political sociology, and economic history, today produces books and articles that we read with a devouring energy, because in them we have found a person who actually knows something about Afghanistan, or can read Pashto (the language of 25 million Pashtuns in Afghanistan and Pakistan). Indeed, some well grounded accounts of Afghanistan's recent history became temporary best-sellers.[18]

Meanwhile press reports in the early going had the government crying out for speakers of Arabic, Pashto, Uzbek, and other presumably esoteric languages, yet the interest is not in the intrinsic merits of studying and knowing these things, but how the knowers of the esoteric and the exotic can be used by intelligence agencies—agencies that are themselves hostage to whatever may be in the minds of the top policymakers making the key decisions as administrations come and go in Washington.[19] The most likely beneficiary of the sudden new interest in South Asia and the Middle East is the National Security Education Program, which in its requirement of government service (and preferably national security service) is a major step backward from the early Cold War years when massive Ford Foundation funding created one "area center" after another. That national program was also premised on the Cold War need for knowing the enemy, true, but it placed the intelligence and national security function where it belonged, namely, as one possible career alternative for students, with most beneficiaries becoming scholars of the "areas" and languages they studied rather than intelligence operatives. I have been critical of leaders in that early period for the compromises they made with the government and the Central Intelligence Agency, but they look like seers and geniuses in the current political atmosphere.

That agency and others like it did not look very good on September 11; indeed they were left to pick up the pieces of a catastrophic intelligence failure, worse than any since . . . well, Pearl Harbor. This reflected both the absence of intelligence officers with experience in Central Asia and the relevant languages (one authoritative source said the CIA harbors not a single employee fluent in Pashto while the National Security Agency has the grand total of *one*, meaning that Pashto intelligence intercepts were sent to the Pakistani intelligence service for translation, an agency now known to be riddled with Taliban and Al Qaeda supporters[20]), and a deeper or "structural" failure that involves the well trodden but now obsolescent paths of Cold War intelligence, a recent general decline in morale, a more longstanding risk-averse bureaucratic culture of featherbedding and back-scratching, and fears that anyone who really knows a country or region will fall victim to the sin of "going native" or "falling in love." Better to let someone who has never visited the region be the CIA's deputy chief for (what it still calls) "the Near East."[21] The intelligence failure at Pearl Harbor led to the firing of those responsible and a major Congressional investigation, but so far the primary response to the September 11 failure has been to increase the intelligence budget.

Certainly one useful and even critical role for the social sciences today would be to spell out the requirements of a national program that would simultaneously begin to create the expertise that will be needed in a twenty-first century that is beginning to look like a very long and difficult one, and that would protect the academic and intellectual integrity of the project. In this way social scientists can well serve the American people—and American democracy—in our current crisis.

14. ON WAR AND PEACE-BUILDING: UNFINISHED LEGACY OF THE 1990s

SUSAN L. WOODWARD

In the hours and days after September 11, academics and political commentators alike seemed agreed on one judgment: "The world will never be the same again." U.S. President George W. Bush was reported to have experienced a religious calling in which the event would shape the rest of his presidency. And for many who were frustrated with the indecisiveness of the 1990s, a decade spent floundering unsuccessfully to replace the Cold War with a coherent set of principles and goals ordering the international system, the U.S.–led antiterrorist campaign seemed to supply the elements that had been so decisive in 1947–50: a new global alignment of states around a singular enemy and a rhetoric promising open-ended struggle, inaugurated with a military campaign led by the world's dominant power. The opportunities were heralded in many quarters, ranging from U.S.–Russian rapprochement, a new strategic interest of the United States in multilateralism, and even possibilities for genuine "global governance."[1]

Four months into the first phase of this campaign, the shock of the attacks had given way to more sober analysis. Although there is no scholarly consensus on the causes of change in international orders,[2] many were having second thoughts, no longer convinced that the world had changed irrevocably. Moreover, those who saw the events or the U.S. response as generating structural change differed in their explanations. For example, which factors would be more influential, governmental decisions on security issues and new state alliances or business decisions and the international political economy, such as the effect on oil markets?[3] Clearly, also, issues pushed aside or under the rug by the events of September 11 would eventually resurface.[4]

One very useful measure of how much or little the world order was changing is the politics surrounding the first stage of the open-ended, antiterrorist campaign, namely, the war against Afghanistan and related peace-building efforts. As this chapter will try to show, that measure reveals a striking continuity with the recent past. The policies of the main players, in particular the United States, its NATO allies, the United Nations, the international financial institutions (IFIs), and the humanitarian, development, and human rights communities, can best be explained and understood as outcomes of the conflicts of the 1990s. They are part of an ongoing evolution in approaches to international conflict and intervention. If a new order is being built, it is grounded in those tortured conflicts in the 1990s, such as Bosnia, Somalia, and Kosovo, that frustrated so many who wanted clarity.

While the rhetoric and actions of many of the key actors in Afghanistan reflected the lessons learned from these conflicts, it is also evident that significant debates had still to be aired or resolved. Secondly, it is clear that the substantial base of accumulated new knowledge from these conflicts in both practitioner and scholarly communities was far ahead of organizational change. Adjustment and reform were on the agenda but had a long way to go. In the field of war and peace, initial signs suggest that the policy choices made by the U.S. have reinforced one trend of the 1990s, that of the militarization of peace and security, and as a result, reproduced all the lines of division and lessons that had emerged during the 1990s. And judging by the lessons that had *not* been learned in this initial phase, the issues and debates of the 1990s have been given greater force and in fluence than the new rhetoric would suggest. As for the opportunity that September 11 appeared to present, the result appears instead to have been delay in the more significant reform and innovation that appeared possible before the attacks. The extent of change that might have been must now be left to revisionist historians and counterfactual analysis.

LESSONS LEARNED

The legacy of the 1990s is seen most clearly in the histories that significant actors are bringing to their tasks—in particular, the United Nations, the United States military, and the international development and human rights communities.

In the wake of the September 11 attacks, Lakhdar Brahimi was named the United Nations Special Representative to the Secretary-General for Afghanistan (SRSG). Brahimi has more to his credit than his deep involvement with the Afghanistan conflict in the 1990s and other tough civil conflicts of the 1990s, including Haiti, Zaire, Iraq, and Cote d'Ivoire.[5] He knows the terrain. This applies equally to numerous agencies and personnel of the United Nations who have remained involved in Afghanistan throughout the sad decade, including the UN special envoy to Afghanistan, Francesc Vendrell, and the UN Resident Humanitarian Coordinator, Antonio Donini.[6] The assignment with which Brahimi's name is most associated, however, is the Panel on United Nations Peace Operations. The panel was charged in May 2000 "to undertake a thorough review of United Nations peace and security activities, and to present a clear set of specific, concrete and practical recommendations to assist the United Nations in conducting such activities better in the future."[7] It is common knowledge that the stimulus for such a review and proposed reforms of UN peace operations was the devastating criticism of the UN in Somalia, Rwanda, and Bosnia and Herzegovina and the UN's resulting loss of legitimacy during the 1990s. Brahimi chaired the panel, and its report bears his name. There was surely no one more suited to draw on the lessons of the 1990s and to bring them to bear to the task of creating a post-Taliban government for Afghanistan and designing an internationally supported transition.

It is worth noting, however, that already in 1998–99, UN officials had selected Afghanistan as the first test of its efforts to improve multilateral interventions in conflict situations with a "Strategic Framework."[8] A response to the accusations of failure in complex humanitarian emergencies[9] in the first half of the 1990s, particularly in Rwanda in 1994 but also Bosnia and Herzegovina in 1992–95 and Somalia in 1993, the framework's designers identified two problems in 1997–98 that needed remedy: the absence of a *political strategy* guiding interventions and the numerous *organizational rivalries*, conflicts, and overlaps among the various international actors in field operations. The first remedy of designing a political strategy for each intervention proved too difficult at the time, but the UN, the World Bank, and even bilateral donors increasingly emphasized the second, the necessity of better coordination to improve the effectiveness of operations. They aimed to take realistic steps toward strategy through *common programming* and *strategic coordination* of the main actors on the ground.

The distance traveled in accumulating lessons since this 1997 initiative and the Brahimi Report of 2000 is striking. How far there was yet to go, however, is revealed in the two tactical decisions taken by the Brahimi Panel: to focus on improvements that could and should be made at headquarters in New York, primarily in the Secretariat, rather than in field operations, and to focus on technical solutions to technical problems and not to deal with the political issues which many still consider primary.

Beginning immediately after September 11, Lakhdar Brahimi was actively putting into practice many of the recommendations of the Brahimi Report, such as the integrated mission task force established within weeks at the Secretariat.[10] His warnings, as with those of the Secretary-General, about the need for speed,[11] about matching what the UN can accomplish to the resources member states are willing to provide, and, above all, a willingness to "say no" to the Security Council if a mandate cannot be implemented, telling the council "what it needs to know, not what it wants to hear" and requiring "clarity,"[12] all come directly from the Report.

The insistence by Brahimi and other UN officials that they would not begin a UN peace-building operation until a sustainable cease-fire had obtained and that security would have to be provided by others, moreover, was a lesson drawn directly from the perceived failure in Bosnia and Herzegovina in 1992–95. Similarly, Brahimi's firm declaration that the UN will not make Afghanistan a protectorate, filling the vacuum of state institutions that currently prevails there, and that it will limit its mission to two years, reflects the lessons of UN missions in Kosovo (UNMIK) and East Timor (UNTAET). Some commentators see this emphasis on making the peace-building effort in Afghanistan as much as possible an Afghan process as a reversal of the 1990s trend toward ever more assertive international interventions. In fact, it is a result of lessons drawn from that trend about the long-term ineffectiveness of such assertiveness. It is also an opportunity to demonstrate whether the 1990s rhetoric coming from development agencies and international organizations concerning the necessity for "local ownership" can be realized.

Many of these lessons were operating as well in Brahimi's push to get a post-Taliban Afghan administration in place as soon as possible, culminating in the UN Talks on Afghanistan held in Bonn from November 29 to December 5, 2001, with representatives of non-Taliban Afghan factions and groups. Chaired by Brahimi, and held at the invitation of the German government, the talks were based on the lessons of all UN peace-building missions in the 1990s that "politics must come first," and an effective state is key to the success of peace-building. Perhaps reflecting most clearly the ongoing disappointment with the results of the Dayton agreement and its implementation in Bosnia and Herzegovina, with its lack of local legitimacy and the failure to reintegrate governmental and military institutions, the UN negotiators chose to build into this political agreement from the start an Afghan-dominated political process and a government structure that gives priority to national unity.

Thus, an "interim administration" was set up at Bonn to govern for six months, followed by a transitional government selected by an Afghan tradition, a *loya jirga* (a traditional parliament, or council of elders), which would govern for 18 months and be responsible for establishing a constitutional commission that would design the new Afghan state. Only after this second, constitutional *loya jirga* produced a constitution would elections be held, reflecting an additional lesson of peace-building in the 1990s that holding elections rapidly after war and without the necessary institutional context does not foster peace and democracy. The Bonn process gives to the international community an "assistance role" only.

Most important in that assistance was yet another lesson: essential to peace is a security presence by neutral third parties deployed immediately and rapidly following conflict.[13] Approval was sought and obtained at Bonn from members of the new interim administration for the International Security Assistance Force (ISAF). It would be authorized by the UN Security Council but not mounted by the UN, conceding (after Kosovo) the necessary legitimating role of the UN while avoiding the constraints entailed in a UN peacekeeping force. The British government, which agreed to command the force, committed to have lead elements in Kabul by the day that the interim administration was inducted, December 22, 2001.[14] Equally important, according to the Bonn agreement, immediately after the official transfer of power, priority should be given to the integration of all armed groups in the country (mujahedeen, Afghan armed forces, and other armed formations) into a single Afghan security force with full command and control by the Interim Authority, to be reorganized rapidly into a new Afghan army.[15]

There is also evidence of the hard lessons learned in Somalia, Bosnia and Herzegovina, and Kosovo from the debilitating effects of conflict between the United Nations and the United States. Brahimi's approach was to protect the legitimacy of the political process by insisting successfully on UN leadership, made possible by the quick action of the Security Council, countering U.S. preparations for a meeting in Turkey and a U.S.–rather than UN–composed invitation list. At the same time he conceded to another lesson, that a constructive role by the U.S. was also critical to success, and actively sought full U.S. support behind his efforts.

Preparations for the Bonn talks and their implementation drew on internal UN lessons from the 1990s, such as incorporating academic expertise on the country in question into the SRSG's team and close coordination within the Secretariat in New York through the creation of a separate UN office for Afghanistan to which heads of all agencies with responsibilities in the United Nations Mission for Assistance to Afghanistan (UNAMA) would report. In contrast to the complex organizational structure in the Kosovo and East Timor missions based on four pillars, each headed by an autonomous agency, this UN office would be organized into only two pillars, one political and one for humanitarian and development assistance. The second pillar aims to provide an organizational response to the much discussed *gap* between relief and development that occurs in the first phase of peace. From the interdepartmental mission task force established in late September to the Special Envoy's office, the entire UN organizational response was increasingly being seen as a test of the Brahimi Report.

The second major actor whose behavior reflects lessons learned during the 1990s is the United States military. Institutionally best organized to think in terms of lessons through its system of "after-action" analyses, the U.S. armed forces have, in fact, been adapting both doctrine and operations in response to the nonconventional wars of the 1990s. One can read clearly in current policy not only the legacy of Vietnam about which so many speak, but more recently the experiences of the Persian Gulf War, Somalia, Haiti, Bosnia and Herzegovina, and Kosovo. Many interpret the post-Vietnam fear of "quagmire" as a reluctance to become engaged in "somebody else's war in a far away place," including the apocryphal defense against engagement in Bosnia in 1992 attributed to then–Chairman of the Joint Chiefs of Staff, Colin Powell, that "we don't do mountains." In fact, "quagmire" for Vietnam-era officers like Secretary of State Powell has a different meaning: sending the military to do a job where the political goal and direction were not clear and, above all, without the necessary political support at home. Although the Powell Doctrine on the need for "overwhelming force" is said to have been the reason for success in the Gulf War as well as the criterion used in U.S. operations in Bosnia and Yugoslavia, far more important in all three cases was the effort spent on creating and maintaining the international coalition behind the operation and the political support of the American public. The same priority governed, and still governs, the actions of Secretary Powell and President Bush beginning on September 12. By January the problem appeared instead to be how to manage conflicts between the need to maintain international support and that of the public. Powell's concern that military success requires leadership, but with allies whom you consult and keep regularly informed, seemed increasingly in conflict with the rhetoric and implications of the Bush doctrine (the "axis of evil" in the State of the Union address), apparently crafted for domestic consumption.[16]

The view that a radical break in world order is occurring as a result of September 11 tends, in fact, to come from a focus on the U.S. Is its post–Cold War hegemonic role to be tempered by a greater interest in multilateralism? Does the war against the Taliban and Al Qaeda represent a new kind of war and a new kind of American military? What would be the consequences of both? Although journalists have been quick to declare newness on the part of the U.S. military,[17] the imprint of U.S. military interventions in Iraq in 1991 and particularly in Bosnia in 1995 and Yugoslavia (Serbia, Montenegro, and Kosovo) in 1999 are in full view. All three cases have acted as a testing ground for the argument, hotly disputed by military strategists, that a war can be won from the air so as to take advantage of American superiority in military technology and to minimize the risk to the lives of American soldiers. In all three cases, but especially in Bosnia and Kosovo, the ground component many still insist is necessary to win *militarily* was provided by local troops and by small teams of highly trained special operations forces to advise and supply local forces and to guide bombers to their targets.

This has been the strategy in Afghanistan.[18] Also not new are the crucial roles played by intelligence (mainly obtained from the air but relying also on the special operations teams and intelligence operatives) and information warfare.[19] Heightened awareness of the importance of public relations to a bombing campaign characterized the Gulf War as well as Bosnia, although it is most noticeable in the Kosovo case, and now commonly includes simultaneous air drops of food packs, attention to the mass media campaign at all levels in the chain of command, and a repetitive "line" aiming to distinguish between victims and enemy.

The difference between those operations and Afghanistan lie in the technical improvements in the equipment and precision with which the Pentagon attempts to execute the same strategy. This includes greater sensitivity to public opinion since Kosovo about minimizing "collateral damage," although not so great as to reduce civilian casualties or to end the wide use of cluster bombs; the increasingly standard-issue use of new communications equipment such as night-vision goggles, laptop computers and electronic mail, computerized cameras, satellite telephones and radios, and the satellite-guided Global Positioning System; and the further development and use of precision-guided weapons and unmanned aerial surveillance vehicles (UAVs) such as the Predator.[20]

The mark of Kosovo as a testing ground for U.S. military operations demonstrates the evolutionary character of American military strategy and operations in the course of the 1990s, at the beginning of which any action other than conventional warfare was classified as "operations other than war (OOTWAs)." Its effect on the *political* component of warfare, however, has been striking. Repeated denials that U.S. bombers had attacked the warehouses in Kabul (twice) of the International Committee of the Red Cross, the UN mine action center, and Afghan villages—so reminiscent of Operation Allied Force against Yugoslavia—suggest that the Pentagon learned in the Yugoslav case that this tactic would work. The early public debate, particularly among members of Congress, over whether ground combat troops would have to be sent if the war was to be won, likewise echoed the Yugoslav operation.[21] But the administration had learned that one should never signal reluctance to use conventional forces, whatever one's intentions. Thus, the small units of special operations forces and Marines deployed from the marine expeditionary units (MEUs) were given publicity, to imply American willingness to put combat soldiers on the ground and to fight. Similarly, the development of forward military bases around such operations is now exploited for its psychological effect as well as logistical purpose.[22]

Most important in political lessons drawn appears to have been the clear U.S. decision that there would be no delays or complications in waging the military battle due to quarrels over the legal basis for the use of force internationally, as occurred between October 1998 and March 1999 in the Kosovo case. Alongside its pursuit of a global coalition, the U.S. declared immediately and persistently that the war was a case of self-defense and American national security, governed by Article 51 of the United Nations Charter. Although the U.S. sought and received unanimous support from the UN Security Council, it had no intention of allowing any UN resolution to constrain U.S. military conduct of the war, nor under any circumstances even to allow core members of the coalition to influence military operations. Although the Bush administration appeared to welcome some British military participation in the war and the active diplomatic and rhetorical support in building and maintaining the international coalition from Prime Minister Tony Blair, the balance was fundamentally different from the Yugoslav operation. The U.S. would define the policy, craft the rhetoric, and take all military decisions on its own.

In distinguishing between coalition politics and coalition warfare, moreover, the U.S. was reinforcing the position that had caused such controversy over the wars in Croatia, Somalia, Bosnia, and Kosovo, namely, distinguishing what military operations the U.S. would and would not do and, as a result, shaping the path and outcome of international intervention in each case. The focus of tension in the Afghan case first occurred over the dire security situation in Afghanistan for humanitarian workers during October–November 2001, and insistence by British development and foreign office officials and international humanitarian organizations on deploying troops to areas cleared of Taliban, at least, to protect the delivery of food and shelter to Afghan civilians. Opposition by American military officials to any international security presence while the U.S. was waging the war continued until the Bonn agreement, and it was then only allowed to deploy to the Afghanistan capital, Kabul, for a political purpose: to prevent the Northern Alliance from dictating the outcome of a post-Taliban settlement by capturing the capital.

U.S. insistence on the unity of military command, under U.S. leadership, and the separation of military and peacekeeping activities perpetuates the core UN dilemma of the 1990s—between deploying missions on terms that violate the conditions of success, namely the integration of civilian and military activities and a single command structure under civilian leadership, or foregoing U.S. participation and the resources that are also necessary for success. The effects were predictable, threatening the key lesson of the Brahimi Report on peacekeeping operations—that mandate, mission, and resources must be matched—and reviving European sensitivity about the growing gap in military capabilities between the U.S. and Europe and the division of labor being dictated by Washington.[23] After a prolonged debate about command and control, the British and the UN agreed to the U.S. position, subordinating the ISAF to the chain of command under General Tommy Franks and U.S. Central Command in Tampa, Florida, and thus the peace-building activities to the priorities of continuing the war.[24] But the design of the ISAF also reflects other lessons that European allies have drawn from the 1990s. Thus, the British were willing to lead the force but only to get it jump started for the first three months. France insisted on a six-month limit to its first mandate. All countries willing to contribute troops refused a traditional UN mission in favor of a "coalition of the willing" authorized by the UN, and the mandate gave the force as robust rules of engagement as possible under the UN Charter. It is no longer the U.S. army only that worries about "mission creep," the tendency for such operations to broaden in scope and duration once they are deployed, but also the British and their European allies.

One of the clearest innovations of the 1990s was the effort by many actors, governments included, to redefine the concept of security after the cold war, such as to put greater emphasis on human security than state security, to begin a dialogue between the defense and development communities over the relation between security and development, and to give greater attention to the need in post-conflict settings for civilian security by the police and courts rather than the traditional attention to armies and hard security. This development had substantial influence on the Brahimi Panel and its recommendations, which called for a "doctrinal shift" in peace operations[25] to recognize that postwar security is a matter for policing far more than for the military. Discussions in the fall of 2001 over a postwar policy for Afghanistan suggested that this battle of the peace operations in Bosnia, Kosovo, and perhaps Haiti, had been won, as planning for an international security presence gave priority to paramilitary police forces (gendarmerie, carabinieri, civil guard) trained for this purpose, while saving soldiers to secure strategic objects such as airports for humanitarian deliveries. The effect of the U.S. military position, however, suggests a substantial retreat. The antiterrorist campaign, beginning with Afghanistan as sanctuary to Osama bin Laden and Al Qaeda, and continuing in the Philippines, Indonesia, and in the debate over Iraq, has been a military campaign, while those suggesting a legal course through domestic or international courts found military criteria applied. The effect of the debate over command and control and American preferences was to prevent the preparation necessary to mobilize the paramilitary, police units that even the U.S. military favored. Those who saw the underlying conditions for continued terrorism in the development distortions and the increasing global inequalities over the 1980s and 1990s were told that increases in U.S. defense spending prevented any increase in U.S. foreign aid for development.[26] And despite Brahimi's success in getting U.S. support behind the political process, it remained unwilling to participate in any peacekeeping force, whether UN or coalition-of-the-willing, despite the clear lessons from Bosnia-Herzegovina in the contrast between UNPROFOR in 1992–95 and the NATO-led IFOR/SFOR after 1996 (the former without U.S. participation in peacekeeping, the latter with). Rebuffing even an explicit request from Interim Prime Minister Hamid Karzai on January 28, 2002, U.S. President Bush repeated this long-held position, offering U.S. logistical support to ISAF and training for the new Afghan army (leaving the police to Germany) but no U.S. troops. Multilateralism, in sum, is both essential to such operations and has very clearly defined limits for the U.S.

A third, less public but no less important actor in this evolving drama is the bilateral and multilateral development community, above all, the World Bank. Discovering in the course of the 1990s that a majority of countries in arrears to the Bank were countries in conflict[27] and under mounting external criticism for what appeared to be a connection between state failure and violent conflict, on the one hand, and development assistance and economic reform packages from the international financial institutions, on the other, the Bank began its own adjustments. In 1996, a new president of the World Bank, James Wolfensohn, created a Post-Conflict Unit, and in April 1997, it published a *Framework for World Bank Involvement in Post-Conflict Countries.* Also in 1996, the Operations Evaluation Department was tasked to review its involvement in post-conflict cases (18 countries with 157 Bank-supported operations representing $6.2 billion in lending at the time[28]) and to draw lessons for future policy. The Bank became active in peace negotiations in Guatemala and Bosnia-Herzegovina to coordinate postwar reconstruction with peace processes better, and insisted on greater lead time (preferably two years) to prepare reconstruction plans. By 1997–99, substantial policy initiatives and new mechanisms for "post-conflict" operations had developed as well at the International Monetary Fund (IMF), the United Nations Development Programme (UNDP), the Development Assistance Committee (DAC) of the Organization for Economic Cooperation and Development (OECD), and many bilateral development agencies such as the United States Agency for International Development (USAID), the British Department for International Development (DFID), and the development agencies of Canada (CIDA) and Sweden (SIDA).[29] Most of the improvements, like those of the U.S. military, focused on operational techniques, particularly efforts to improve the delivery of aid—disbursing it, for example, faster, more efficiently, with greater flexibility and transparency, and with better coordination among donors. And despite greater use of both internal and external evaluations for each operation to gather lessons learned, the actual measures of evaluation are also technical, such as performance criteria for the delivery of money or the completion of economic projects and programs. They do not assess their contribution to, or conflict with peace-building, as critics charge.[30]

Nonetheless, by the late 1990s, the experience of the World Bank in specific missions—particularly the relatively "rich" cases of Bosnia and Herzegovina and of West Bank/Gaza (Palestine)—had created precedents for new missions, such as special trust funds for demobilization, de-mining, budgetary and recurrent expenditures, and a post-conflict project fund. In 1999, the World Bank assigned to its Post-Conflict Unit the task of preparing quarterly monitoring reports on countries and regions affected by conflict, and set out procedures for more systematic attention in performance reviews and operations evaluations to conflict/post-conflict concerns.[31] By 2000, the World Bank required Watching Briefs for countries in conflict or in danger of conflict, including Afghanistan, and its classic infrastructure-based approach was under review in light of the lessons of the 1990s that it had neglected to consider the importance for reconstruction of human and social capital, gender relations, and institutions.[32]

In the case of Afghanistan, moreover, UN special envoy Francesc Vendrell had already requested in 2000 that the Bank begin planning for reconstruction, resulting in an initial plan by early 2001. The identified need for a specific resource mobilization mechanism for post-conflict recovery of a combined developmental and humanitarian nature was being addressed in the organization of pillar two in Brahimi's office (a Canadian with substantial experience in Afghanistan, Nigel Fisher, was chosen as its head). The general lesson drawn by the World Bank and the bilateral developmental agencies in regard to peace-building, that speed was essential, was shaping the flurry of activities beginning in October 2001 to design assistance strategies[33] and mobilize donors. An international conference on financing the rebuilding of Afghanistan was convened in Washington by the U.S. and Japan in November 2001, followed by one in Brussels in December, and a donors' pledging conference in Tokyo, in January 2002.

Finally, a measure of the irreversible changes that took place in the 1990s is the prominent role of the human rights community. Their organizational strength and public relations skills, developed during the 1990s, are everywhere in evidence following September 11. Reflecting a trend that took a qualitative leap in the Guatemalan peace process and the establishment of international criminal tribunals for former Yugoslavia and Rwanda, the human rights component of the Bonn Agreement is the one independent authority granted the United Nations in assisting the interim Afghan authorities: its "right to investigate human rights violations and, where necessary, recommend collective action."[34] The community asserted a highly public role at the Tokyo donors' conference in emphasizing the necessity of abiding by human rights standards as a condition for the disbursement of aid pledged.[35] It even succeeded in holding the U.S. government accountable to the Geneva Conventions in regard to the treatment of Afghan and Al Qaeda prisoners. Few members of the international public can claim ignorance of the laws of war after this highly public pressure campaign in January–February 2002.

LESSONS NOT LEARNED

For all the lessons that have been learned during the 1990s, there are as many or more that have not. Whether the order being shaped by current events results in real change will depend far more on the latter. This can be seen particularly by comparison with the interventions in former Yugoslavia—above all Bosnia-Herzegovina, Kosovo, and Macedonia—which have had such great influence over the thinking, habits, instincts, and actions of key actors now engaged on Afghanistan. Moreover, the many similarities between the Balkans and Afghanistan, despite the fundamentally different policy objective of the international interventions in the two and the different role of state borders, make the unfinished business of these unlearned lessons even more significant.[36] Five lessons stand out.

The first lesson is widely recognized, and widely ignored. Indeed, a prominent place is given in the Brahimi Report to conflict prevention. The wars in Bosnia-Herzegovina, Kosovo, and Macedonia, like the disintegration of former Yugoslavia itself and the wars that resulted, were not inevitable; they could have been prevented. This lesson is so clear in all of the wars of the 1990s that the Carnegie Foundation President David Hamburg created in May 1994 a special commission, the Carnegie Commission on Preventing Deadly Conflict, to raise awareness of this fact and put prevention on the international agenda.[37] Yet the chain of events from the U.S. arming and training of Afghan and Pakistani mujahedeen to fight the Soviets in Afghanistan, to the Taliban and Al Qaeda and its international network, including fighters sent to Bosnia-Herzegovina, Somalia, Chechnya, and Central Asia, is direct. The U.S. government's "lift and strike" policy (lift the arms embargo and bomb Serb positions) that used covert operations to arm the Bosnians and then the Kosovo Albanians, was an international copy of the original Afghan policy (designed in both cases by the same person, now President Bush's special envoy for Afghanistan). One consequence in both instances was to spread the instruments of war (arms, trained soldiers, military equipment) and trafficking networks far beyond their initial geographical focus (such as from Afghanistan to Bosnia and from Bosnia to Kosovo) and to undermine the assumptions as well as the practice of a Western policy of containment.

By the mid-1990s, the U.S. government was spending millions for research on "early warning."[38] Those who argue on the basis of actual outcomes that the problem is not early warning, but early action, have had little effect. Similarly, the intelligence failure of September 11 reveals a comprehensible, rational pattern of attacks beginning in 1993, and periodic warnings from the director of the Central Intelligence Agency (CIA) and other U.S. officials that terrorism against the United States was its primary security threat.[39] The CIA had already begun in 1997 under Director George Tenet to revive its earlier networks in Afghanistan and create a ground presence.

A second lesson from those earlier cases is that the logic of war wins out every time over other concurrent policies, particularly diplomatic negotiations and humanitarian goals. The evolution from a military strike of revenge demanded by an outraged U.S. public, to a war against Osama bin Laden, then to a war against the Taliban, and then to build a new state in Afghanistan and the security and economic bases of its survival, is a pattern we have seen before. The bombing of Yugoslavia in spring 1999 was also driven by rising anger at a particular individual, Slobodan Milosevic, and by a perceived pressure from public opinion "to do something." When the bombing campaign did not produce nearly instant success, as U.S. and UK policy makers apparently expected, the goals (and legitimating rhetoric) of the operation began to change in mid-course. By the end, little damage had been done to the Serbian security forces, and there was an international protectorate for Kosovo under UN mandate including a NATO-led security force (including U.S. soldiers) with no defined end date. In the case of Afghanistan, the goal of capturing Osama bin Laden and doing irreparable damage to Al Qaeda gave way to a change of government in Afghanistan and a long-term commitment to its reconstruction and stabilization. In both cases, the U.S. military appears to have underestimated the enemy's will and ability to resist such that tactics, timing, and even goals had to be adjusted rapidly once the air war began.[40]

In the Balkans, the effort to combine three objectives simultaneously—a humanitarian operation, a war (dominated by air power and intelligence, in particular), and political negotiations—was continually frustrated by this simple lesson, that the logic of war dominates all other objectives. The war creates more refugees and internally displaced persons, makes aid workers hostages or forces them to flee the country entirely, and creates conflicts over communication and transportation routes between the military and humanitarian operations, which hinder both. The security situation dramatically worsened for humanitarian operations in Afghanistan, as in Kosovo, and even when UN workers began to risk return, strict rules for their security had to be imposed by the UN that would

limit significantly the size of the postwar mission because of the additional resources required. Hundreds of thousands of Afghans fled their homes to escape
the bombing. Not only did banditry and lawlessness on the roads and in the cities
increase for Afghans as well as humanitarian workers, but whole new waves of
displaced persons and refugees were being created as populations resettled by
the Taliban were dispossessed by persons who took advantage of their new dominance to reclaim their land by force (repeating an old pattern of periodic re-
versals between winners and losers in the contest over land, and its resulting
resentments).

Similarly, the American strategy of relying on local armies for the ground
component of the military campaign is directly in conflict with the political goals
of diplomatic negotiations for a postwar state.[41] Those troops, for example, the
KLA in Kosovo or the Northern Alliance, gain overwhelming advantage in any
postwar settlement, from the terms of negotiations to the extent to which a
diplomatic agreement can prevail over the political and economic reality created
by war. Part of the military campaign itself becomes driven by the locals' fight for
such advantage and bargaining leverage. The pace of negotiations is inevitably
slower than that of war, and no warlord with any real possibility on the ground
will negotiate sincerely while it is in play. Control over territory trumps all normative theories about the best political arrangements to achieve postwar reconciliation and stable government.

Thus, at the same time that the Bonn talks aimed at making a post-Taliban
government representative of the entire country and signaling the path toward
peace, the U.S. military was arming and supporting certain Afghan warlords to
achieve their war aims, including in some cases providing money and supplies to
direct rivals of the interim leaders.[42] Brahimi's attempt to create a neutral, technocratic administration that could win local legitimacy through competence
and dissociation from the war and insecurity had to be compromised in order to
buy support from key warlords, such as General Dostum, with ministerial posts.
The increased likelihood of "spoilers" in the peace process in numerous regions
in the country was already being demonstrated within weeks after Bonn in new
fighting between warlords who refused to concede to Bonn appointees, and in
deadly rivalries within the new administration.[43] In the case of Kosovo, former
KLA leaders have been able to prevent the formation of a postwar government
despite elections, and political assassinations occur regularly. In Bosnia and
Herzegovina, six years after a peace agreement, the lack of economic reform and
growth is attributed to the stranglehold over key economic assets, such as factories, power plants, mines, and telecommunications, which wartime parties
grabbed with force at the end of the war for personal and party coffers. In Af-

ghanistan, the race to use newly acquired weapons and ammunition to seize spoils of war was returning the country to the levels of insecurity and chaos of competing warlords in the 1990s that paved the way for Taliban rule. And it was making particularly difficult the delivery of humanitarian assistance and the start of economic activities. Nevertheless, the many UN and Afghan officials who began to urge in late January 2002 that the mandate of the ISAF be extended in duration, size, and geographical reach (beyond Kabul) to deal with the dire security conditions faced the greatest opposition from U.S. military officials. According to U.S. Deputy Assistant Secretary of Defense for Peacekeeping and Humanitarian Assistance Joseph Collins, "Our first priority is to insure non-interference in the war." [44]

A third lesson regards economic assistance and strategy. The extent to which Afghanistan has been the recipient of numerous efforts at humanitarian relief, development assistance, and peace-building over the last 30 years makes it a particularly interesting test of whether the humanitarian and development community has learned the lessons of the 1990s, as discussed above. [45] Certainly many practitioners and experts alike appeared eager to use the Afghan case as an opportunity to learn from past mistakes. [46] Moreover, the talk at the donors' pledging conference held in Tokyo in January 2002 pointed explicitly to the need to avoid the errors of recent operations such as East Timor, Kosovo, and Bosnia and Herzegovina. The multilateral donors (in this case the World Bank, the UN Development Programme, and the Asian Development Bank) emphasized donor coordination, such as sharing leadership, creating a common trust fund for government salaries and recurrent expenditures, and crafting a common strategy document to avoid competition between alternative approaches to economic reconstruction. UN officials, in particular, stressed the importance of an economic strategy designed to meet the needs of peace, replacing the conflict between IFI-led technocratic approaches to development and the tasks of the peace mission that had plagued peace-building in the past. Organizers worked hard to obtain multiyear pledges, despite countries' bureaucratic obstacles, so as to signal genuine international commitment to Afghans and to acknowledge that peace-building is a long-term process, not one that can be resourced a year at a time. There was also at least rhetorical recognition of the need to set priorities on security (identified as community policing and de-mining), agriculture (getting crops in the ground by spring), immediate employment (through public works projects), and to get children off the streets and into school by March 2002.

Behind the rhetoric, however, the plague of donor competition hints far more at business as usual. Acrimonious competition over who would take the lead in the reconstruction effort and who would be included in this group, already apparent during the fall of 2001, had become institutionalized by the time of the Tokyo conference. Long-time donors to Afghanistan, including members of the Afghan Support Group, such as Norway, Germany, other Scandinavian countries, and the Netherlands, are willing to channel their efforts through the United Nations, while members of the Steering Group for Reconstruction of Afghanistan—created after the war began among Japan, the U.S., Saudi Arabia, and the European Commission—insist on bilateral programs to retain control over their funds while channeling the necessary multilateral efforts through the World Bank. As a result there is not one Trust Fund but two: one for budgetary support (including government salaries), set up as an emergency in December by the UN, but poorly funded despite long-term operating needs;[47] and one far better endowed for the long-term economic development program under the World Bank. Another result is the insistence of those in the latter group on bilateral programs that focus on national economic interests and visible (sometimes called "photogenic," "vanity" infrastructure[48]) projects for home consumption rather than on what the country might truly need.[49] In place of a common approach or even a strategic coordination mechanism, references to donor coordination at Tokyo were not transparent and appear to remain confined to sectoral working groups, as in Bosnia and Herzegovina, as if the consensus about sustainable development and integrated approaches had not affected the tradition and organization of development aid according to sectors. The organizational innovation to combine relief and development under one office was not reflected in programs or planning, where the gap remains. Instead of a reconstruction program designed to support the peace-building process and crucial first step of creating a functioning government and administration, the principle of conditionality (setting conditions for aid in the old manner) dominated donors' speeches. For example, aid would be withdrawn "if the country did not make progress towards democracy," was "conditional on all the country's warlords and ethnic groups contributing" to the power-sharing deal reached at Bonn, was "contingent on cost efficiency," and would "work as a weapon against Mr. Karzai's enemies."[50]

Although the first stages of economic assistance and strategy thus suggest that little has changed in the activities and approaches to post-conflict reconstruction of the major donors, one debate of the 1990s emerged in two clearly distinct, opposing schools of thought. One, victorious at Tokyo, emphasized the key importance of speed—to provide a peace dividend with quick impact projects and public works for the population so that they did not return to war and violence, and to fill the gap left after relief ceases and before longer-gestating development projects kick in.[51] The other school of thought, more common among Afghan experts and scholars of peace-building experience, emphasizes that "politics must come first" and that aid programs that move too far ahead of the political process ignore the lessons of all successful transitions, whether from war to peace or from authoritarian rule to markets and democracy. The fatal flaw of current post-conflict reconstruction strategies, this school argues, is their unacknowledged dependence on a functioning government and functioning financial and legal institutions—to absorb the aid delivered, adopt the necessary policies, and implement those decisions.[52] Such governments and administrations do not exist under conditions of war and severe war damage—human capital is the scarcest commodity after wartime, but the Afghan case may well be the worst. They take time to create, and they do not emerge spontaneously.

In fact, donors themselves find it difficult to work without sovereign counterparts and functioning governments. In Afghanistan, where so large a proportion of economic activity is done illegally—surreptitious, smuggled, or criminal—and what financial infrastructure there is for trade and commerce (such as functioning banks) is in Pakistan, the problem is acute. Even quick-impact projects to provide early employment, agricultural revival, and basic social services that are essential to sustaining the peace depend first on a government that can provide these services, restore social trust, enforce the law, and protect human rights. Yet, despite their now-common reference to the decisive role of institutions in economic reform and development, donors still appear to assume that a political agreement will produce such a government. They thus supported the priority placed by Lakhdar Brahimi on getting an interim Afghan administration agreed upon and in place rapidly, but then rushed in to fill a vacuum they perceived on reconstruction even before the Bonn talks had begun. In addition to preempting the organizational lessons that Brahimi carefully put in place (see discussion above) and running ahead on their own path, donors thus only gave lip service to the importance of local ownership and government institutions as they assessed needs and set policy priorities without any serious input from Afghan authorities or civil society. Speed, in their view, took priority. By the time the transitional government is selected by the *loya jirga* in June 2002, the principles of the reconstruction program will have been set.

Instead the Tokyo conference created an *implementation* committee in which some members of the interim administration would sit alongside representatives of the international financial institutions,[53] calling on the interim authorities to create a national consensus behind the donors' program. While emphasizing speed, donors also refer to the need for caution, given the fragility of the interim authority, and they acknowledged that the government would have a real problem in absorbing the large amounts of aid pledged at Tokyo, as if these two difficulties were not normal under these conditions and had to be addressed. Indeed, under the principle of conditionality, donors demanded that the new authorities meet conditions for aid which they did not have the capacity yet to do and which Afghans themselves might not have considered priorities.

The disconnect between lessons learned and the current aid plans is particularly striking in the field of security. Universally accorded top priority, it appears to remain outside the donors' scope. Limited resources are as responsible as short-term U.S. military objections for the narrow commitment to security in Kabul alone. The focus instead on training an eventual Afghan army and police will neither fill the immediate security gap nor is the funding yet pledged. Yet basic trade and commerce, and the beginnings of economic revival, cannot occur without restored security on the roads, just as the intense international spotlight, including at Tokyo, on women's rights is of little use without first providing security for women.[54]

A fourth lesson concerns the political bases for creating the stable, effective, and legitimate government that the above discussion identifies as critical. On the one hand, it is generally assumed and routinely stated that the political deal at Bonn had to be based on the principle of power sharing among leaders of groups identified in ethnic, religious, and tribal terms. On the other hand, an integral part of the debate on economic assistance, paralleling the division on economic strategy, is a debate on the structure of the post-Taliban government.[55] Should the reconstruction program be based on recognition of the warlords and tribal loyalties as the existing power structure in the country, with the corresponding need for a federalized political structure that gives autonomy to these regional commanders? Or should it insist on building Afghan national institutions, judiciously balanced between central and local authorities? Outside commentators tend to argue the first on the grounds that working with warlords is the more realistic approach, given current conditions, because the alternative would require more resources than the international community is willing to spend. Afghan experts are adamant on the second, that Afghans themselves want a national government based on the legacy of the 1960s and 1970s and that the first camp misrepresents both reality and the key element of popular legitimacy. In Paula Newberg's version, those in the first camp "overestimate the power of the warlords" and "make flawed assumptions about Afghans' loyalties and dangerously underestimate the potential for a centralized, cohesive Afghan state and nation to develop."[56] Not only are Afghans "fearful of a new phase of warlordism supported by the U.S.," according to Ashraf Ghani, but "Afghan nationalism is strong" and "only a nationalist state would have the capacity and commitment to break and destroy the networks of terror."[57] There are also alternatives to warlord leadership. Ghani identifies the substantial capacity of Afghan professionals who have fled the country but would return, while Barnett Rubin emphasizes the substantial capacity at the local level. Further, the most prominent current warlords were not in the country until they were invited back by Ahmed Shah Massoud, the Northern Alliance commander assassinated on September 9, 2001. They returned in 2000–2001 under very strict controls over supplies—a system of control that only broke down under the U.S. war plan during November 2001.

This debate reflects in part the second unlearned lesson cited above, that the logic of war tends to overwhelm local conditions. But it also reveals lessons that are being drawn from the 1990s, in particular the best way to deal with potential "spoilers" to a peace process. In nearly all cases of peace agreements to end civil wars, from Cambodia and Angola to Bosnia and Herzegovina and Kosovo, there is an unresolved debate about whether it is better to bring potential spoilers "into the tent" or to isolate them. The danger of spoilers is inversely proportional to the resources that international actors are willing to spend on disarmament and demobilization. If groups are left with guns and view the peace agreement as disadvantageous, they can choose to go back to war. Short of war, if they control substantial territory and roads, humanitarian deliveries and economic activity will depend on their cooperation. In instances such as Bosnia and Herzegovina or Kosovo, there is an additional difficulty in creating a state and national identity appropriate to this new state and its borders where there had not been one before.

The debates over Bosnia and Herzegovina, however, suggest that the political preferences of outsiders frequently cloud the conclusions they draw about more effective implementation strategy. Was the extreme decentralization of the Dayton Accord necessary to end the war and buy the support of potential spoilers? Was the accommodation of the international mission to the realities on the ground necessary to help implement that accord, or a major failing which strengthened warlords? Was the increasingly assertive intervention to impose a common state and institutions against local resistance likely to succeed or not?

Thus, the debate about Afghanistan revolves more around which lessons from elsewhere are appropriate to the Afghan context than about which are inherently correct. In what way are the warlords potential spoilers? What are the most effective tactics toward them, and which measures of confidence-building, such as political inclusion, are necessary? According to Afghan experts, the Bonn agreement was made among victors only, there is no need to invent the idea of an Afghan national state, and the winners are so beholden to the U.S.–led war against the Taliban that international actors have unusual leverage to support a process that would create a legitimate and effective state.

The diplomatic emphasis on a political deal—power sharing—among leaders as the basis for a postwar government also contains serious flaws. Although the Bonn agreement created a political process aimed at getting beyond an interim, emergency deal to an increasingly local process that would be seen as legitimate, the policies of the aid community in requiring implementation of that agreement *as a condition* for aid defy the lessons of Bosnia and Kosovo. Likewise, the proposals that aid be channeled through warlords, rather than aimed at the creation of effective national institutions at the central, provincial, and district level, work directly against Brahimi's suggestions.

Power sharing is now the dominant method favored by diplomats and many scholars for war termination, but its success in generating a functioning government and sustainable peace is thin indeed. The concept of power sharing is based on a concept in the literature of political science called consociationalism to explain the stability of democracy in ethnically or religiously divided societies. By a technique of elite cartel, politics occur among political leaders who represent each ethnic or religious group and, it is assumed, group interests, and who make decisions by consensus.[58] The case that gave rise to the concept, however, was the Netherlands, a stable, wealthy country for centuries, while one of the earliest examples that was said to fit, Lebanon, was quietly removed from the list when the country disintegrated into civil war. A second contribution to the principle of power sharing came with the literature on democratic transitions in Latin America and southern Europe in the 1970s and 1980s, in which it was argued that a successful mechanism for the transition from authoritarian to democratic rule had been elite "pacts"—agreements made behind closed doors among representatives of the country's main political parties. This argument is disputed as an explanation for successful transitions and as applicable to other cases, but its circumstances are even more unrelated to those subject to diplomatic negotiations. In the cases of elite pacts, governmental administration continues to function throughout the pacting process, and there is no war. Neither version of the power-sharing arrangement, moreover, is democratic, in the current sense implied by donors' emphasis on civil society, nongovernmental organizations, and "bottom up," community participation in peace-building.

Where the choice for negotiating parties, moreover, is to give up control over an armed group, materiel, and territory in exchange for a government ministry, when no government yet exists and it is unclear that others will also disarm, power sharing is unlikely to be persuasive. Even where such agreements do emerge, power sharing becomes a method of sharing the spoils (such as economic aid) and perpetuating the war economy. Secondly, power sharing requires negotiators to identify the relevant groups to be represented rather than leaving it to an open political process. Third, because power-sharing agreements are based on group representation by single leaders, they give external legitimacy to a monopoly of those leaders over representation of their ethnic, religious, or tribal group to the exclusion of rivals and, therefore, institutionalized competition (that is, democracy) within the group. Its effect is to lock in gains from war and control over arms against alternative principles and traditions of representation. The difficulty of reversing this institutionalization of war gains is particularly noticeable in the cases of Bosnia and Herzegovina and Kosovo. "The challenge for peace-building in Afghanistan," write a team of Norwegian experts, "is to demilitarize the political process, not invite its militarization as federalism might do." [59] Finally, the power sharing principle assumes that the problem to be solved politically is ethnic and tribal conflict, whereas it is often the case that local identities are highly contingent on temporary power balances, shifting for personal advantage under conditions of severe risk and insecurity. As Rubin and his colleagues wrote about Afghanistan in June 2001, "The origin of the war is not ethnic, and the solution will not be ethnic, but the conduct of the war is ethnic, which has had corrosive effects on the potential for national reconstruction." [60]

The focus on a power-sharing agreement, in fact, is most likely to occur when a country is enmeshed in a regional dynamic in which neighbors have strong and assertive interests. Weak buffer states, either in the interstices of imperial and major power alliances or in a regional security complex, such as Bosnia-Herzegovina, Macedonia, Somalia, and Afghanistan, are most likely to have power-sharing agreements imposed by outsiders as a way of satisfying the interests of neighbors. Their outcome is more often, as currently seen in Bosnia-Somalia, a de facto partitioning of the country's territory among regional spheres of influence and a resulting partitioning of the state itself. In the case of Bosnia-Herzegovina, the result has been political stalemate since its peace agreement of November 1995 and a continuation of local conditions that are favorable to illegal trafficking, organized crime, and terrorist networks.

This raises the fifth and last lesson, the regional dimension of the conflict. This is, perhaps, the most important of the unfinished legacy of the 1990s because it emerges in each case of the decade, but appears to be the most difficult to address. Most internal conflicts of the kind that bred the Taliban are not actually internal. As the Brahimi Report emphasizes, they are "transnational," or as Rubin and his colleagues elaborate for Afghanistan, its "conflict forms the core of a regional conflict formation." [61] Military campaigns, political negotiations, and economic reconstruction that ignore the regional embeddedness of such cases cannot succeed.[62] Cease-fires may even be locally stable, as long as international military and police forces remain on the ground to enforce them, but their most common outcome is spillover into some other part of its region. Most of the African conflicts (East, West, and Central) fit this scenario, as do the cases of Bosnia-Herzegovina (to Kosovo) and Kosovo (to Macedonia) and the entire Caucasus region. As Rubin and his colleagues characterized Afghanistan several months before September 11, "The war is not a civil war but a transnational one. The transnational links are too deep to be untangled and will have to be transformed. . . . A more desirable policy goal [than 'peace'] would be reconstructing the country as part of the interstate and economic structure of an entire region." [63]

Although peace-building is necessarily state-building, there is little if any attention to the external aspects of stable states—that states are not only domestic political systems but, by definition, elements of a system of states. Cross-border relations are as crucial to their identity and stability as are the construction of effective governmental institutions. Although Afghanistan has a distinct advantage over the other cases cited in the Balkans, Caucasus, and much of Africa in that its national borders and identity are not challenged from within and, for the most part, from without, it nonetheless has delicate relations with neighbors over border security. The spillover mechanism, as seen in the Balkans for example, does not follow the natural analogy of floods and wild fires but a psychological process whereby neighbors are also locked into regional contexts in which the security of their border with Afghanistan affects their relations with other neighbors, as in the clear cases of Pakistan and Iran. The effect of the war against the Taliban on Pakistani foreign policy and security, translated, by this mechanism, directly into increased hostilities over Kashmir between Pakistan and India, threatening both nuclear confrontation and American policy toward the Taliban. The prevalence of transborder communities is a separate, but equally important mechanism in all these cases, such as the role of the Pashtun population in Afghanistan and Pakistan. Much of the areas currently in conflict are also located at the centers of region-wide transportation networks in which regional trade regimes, whether based on smuggling and diaspora or criminal networks, or on legal trade, define their economies and prospects for economic growth.

Here, too, knowledge is ahead of practice. Discussion among development actors emphasizes the crucial role of a regional market and a regional transportation network to Afghan development. Afghan experts stress the need to reduce the incentives to smuggling in the regional network from Afghanistan through Pakistan and Dubai and on to Europe and to make it possible for traders to operate legally. But with the partial exception of refugee agencies, the relief and reconstruction programs focus on Afghanistan alone rather than a regional framework. As for policies toward Afghanistan's numerous neighbors, perhaps best illustrated by the U.S.–Iran tensions, little has changed in the great game of larger geopolitical interests of the major powers toward specific countries.

UNFINISHED LEGACY

The prediction of global change after September 11 was based on two kinds of reactions: for some, the demonstration effect of so striking a reversal in world power between the invulnerable strong and the vulnerable weak; while for others, the opportunity raised by the American response for creating a new world order after the floundering 1990s. Phase One of the antiterrorist campaign reveals a striking continuity of actors, issues, and disputes of the 1990s on both accounts. It continues the type of military engagement which U.S. forces actually faced during the 1990s, as opposed to the type guiding U.S. strategic planning, training, and weaponry—namely, failing states, humanitarian emergencies, and profound power asymmetries.[64] As for the opportunity for a different world order, even the hopes raised by the new global assertiveness of the Bush administration echoed both the debate over Bosnia and Herzegovina in the mid-1990s and the confirming consensus once the U.S. did engage directly in 1995 that American leadership and intervention were necessary to global peace and security.

At the same time, the opportunity to learn from the 1990s appears to have been missed. Substantial moves to redefine security in the post–Cold War period toward human security appear to have bowed to the antiterrorist campaign. The momentum on conflict prevention has also appeared to stall. Although the attack came from non-state actors in a global, transnational network, the response reasserted the primacy of sovereignty and states, as is evident in the U.S. war on the government of Afghanistan; the global campaigns of UN Security Council Resolutions after September 11 that hold states responsible for fighting terrorism and its financial resources;[65] greater cooperation among state intelligence agencies; and the first steps of the second phase of the campaign in military assistance to the Philippines, Georgia, and Yemen and perhaps against Iraq, Somalia, and Indonesia. And there is no greater attention to the regional dimension of such conflicts and their ability to spread despite its recognized role.

There has also been a notable reversion to the organizational rivalries of the 1990s, despite the lesson learned then on the need for strategic and programmatic coordination. The divergence between the U.S.–led path and that begun by United Nations Special Representative Brahimi is particularly clear. Although the early days of the campaign seemed to coincide with a reinvigorated UN and particularly its reforms on peacekeeping operations (symbolized in some ways by the decision of the Nobel Committee to award Secretary-General Kofi Annan and the organization the Peace Prize on December 10, 2001), complaints about UN bureaucracy, rigidity, and timidity were already resurfacing in early 2002. Rivalries and disputes between departments of government, especially defense and foreign affairs, between emergency relief and development agencies, among Western allies, and among major development donors also repeated those of the 1990s. Donors and peace-builders have not moved much closer to being able to create a political strategy for effective intervention or to putting resources and creativity behind state-building—despite Brahimi's efforts. Disputes over assistance strategy for Afghanistan suggest that organizational interests take priority over lessons learned for more effective action. Even the arguably new element of the U.S.–led response—the crafting of a post–Cold War ideology and rhetoric in support of American leadership—was put in service of a conventional policy. Not surprisingly, the decision to unleash an American military campaign against the political leadership of a failing state embedded in a regional conflict formation exposed the same fault lines in the Western alliance that had hamstrung policy toward Bosnia and shaped the lessons which all had taken into Kosovo.

The war does seem to have opened a new geostrategic front for Western powers in Central Asia. The closer alliance with Russia reinforces that move. The CIA has reversed a pattern in the 1990s in which covert operations were politically unacceptable, moving since 1997 to create what is currently "the largest on-ground military presence since Vietnam" and a substantially enlarged counterterrorism center.[66] The campaign provided further justification for the U.S. to leave more of the Balkan operations to Europeans, and the role of NATO as a collective security and defense organization appears in eclipse.[67] But because there is little new in the policy response, even to the extent of appearing to ignore those lessons that are known and thus could have been learned from the 1990s, the change suggests this is a geographic shift only, not one that provides an escape to new principles and order.

There are a number of possible explanations for this striking disconnect between knowledge and practice in the response to September 11. An institutionalist explanation might point to the remarkable resilience of the institutions and principles built (under American leadership) during the Cold War.[68] The first response by NATO allies within days of the attack to invoke Article V for the first time in the organization's history could be explained this way. Growing disenchantment and public criticism from those same allies over the apparently unchecked unilateralism of U.S. rhetoric and policy as the campaign and the next phase took shape suggests otherwise, however. The extent to which the world of humanitarian relief and development assistance has become institutionalized might point to this interpretation for these actors, but it would not explain the contrast between parts of the UN bureaucracy which appeared ready and able, under Brahimi, to bring practices in line with lessons their own studies urged and other actors, such as the multilateral development agencies, which were not.

An explanation that focuses on the role of ideas and ideology in foreign policy might point to the security doctrine of a conservative Republican administration and the bureaucratic influence it hands to the Pentagon over the State Department.[69] But the differences in this regard between the Bush administration and the preceding Clinton administration are not particularly great. A bureaucratic explanation would argue that organizational interests pose obstacles to innovation, particularly in crises, despite the commonsense view that the opposite should occur. One version would focus on the tendency toward habitual behavior in response to crises. The need for a rapid response by large-scale organizations and for reducing uncertainty under high risk encourages individuals to reach for what they know and trust. Another version would focus on bureaucratic behavior, which is oriented to maximizing a bureau's budget.[70] Because crises tend to unlock extraordinary resources, the enticement to competition and rivalry among eligible agencies over funds outweighs forces in favor of innovation. Finally, a political economy explanation might point to the way that the crisis reinforced the existing power of key economic interests, particularly in the U.S., such as oil producers or defense contractors.

Whatever the explanation, the choice of a U.S. military response reinforced one strand of lessons drawn during the 1990s that urged greater militarization of peace and security. Calls had mounted over the decade for more robust rules of engagement in peace operations, and the military equipment needed for such robustness, for greater cooperation between militaries and humanitarian and development organizations, and for peace enforcement in place of peacekeeping. Thus there were ever more frequent calls for the use of force and well-equipped militaries as a first or early option, not a last resort. Issues of prevention, security, and intervention came to be narrowed to the use of force, and thus those willing to provide it. Would the U.S. contribute its forces to help prevent war or genocide (for example, as an interposition force in Croatia or Rwanda), to prevent war's spread (for example, from Croatia to Bosnia-Herzegovina, from Kosovo to Macedonia, or from Rwanda to Zaire/Congo), or to implement peace agreements that would stop wars (for example, the many peace plans negotiated for Bosnia and Herzegovina before the Dayton Accord, or the many African instances during the decade)? If the U.S. would not, who would? If it were the United Nations, would the lessons learned from the 1990s about the resources needed, such as a robust mandate of peace enforcement or the crucial role of neutral third parties in providing security in the first stages of peace-building, be provided? The primary lesson of the Brahimi Report, that mission, mandate, and resources must match and that if they do not, the Secretary-General should say "no," is based on this (negative) experience. So too are the fault lines dividing the U.S. and its European allies on matters of defense and international security and the failure to apply known lessons on security and aid to the Afghan theater. The lesson of the 1990s is that the U.S. choice regarding the use of force appears to govern the choices made by others, including peace-building strategy.

If the lessons of the 1990s are a guide to the future, the result will thus be to continue the frustrations of the 1990s. But if the initial objectives of the military campaign in Afghanistan are not met, and if forthcoming resources cannot provide sufficient security for Afghan state-building, the opportunity to crystallize debates over lessons learned and to take new approaches to peace and security may yet reemerge. The more likely outcome is to require another exercise in containment, to hide the lack of success with yet another American military deployment. Korea specialist Bruce Cumings suggests in these pages that the U.S. appears to have committed itself, perhaps inadvertently, to another unending engagement in Central Asia, as it did in Japan, Germany, Korea, and Saudi Arabia.[71] If opposition to the latter did indeed motivate those who planned and executed the September 11 attacks, then even the hopes for a new world order will have been eclipsed by the logic of war.

PART IV

TERRORISM AND DEMOCRATIC VIRTUES

15. UNHOLY WARS.
RECLAIMING DEMOCRATIC VIRTUES
AFTER SEPTEMBER 11

SEYLA BENHABIB

1.

It has become clear since September 11 that we are faced with a new form of struggle that threatens to dissolve the boundaries of the political in liberal democracies.[1] The terror network of Al Qaeda and its various branches in Egypt, Pakistan, Malaysia, Indonesia, Algeria, the Philippines, and among Islamist groups in Western Europe, is wider, more entrenched and sophisticated than it was believed to be. The attacks unleashed by these groups (and their potential sympathizers in the United States and Europe among neo-Nazis and white supremacists), especially the continuing threat to use biological and chemical weapons against civilian populations, signal a new political and military phenomenon which challenges the framework of state-centric politics.

Historians always warn us that the unprecedented will turn out to have forerunners somewhere, and that what seems new today will appear old when considered against the background of a longer time span. Nevertheless to "think the new" in politics is the vocation of the intellectual. This is a task at which luminaries like Susan Sontag, Fredric Jameson, and Slavoj Zizek—who, in the immediate aftermath of September 11,[2] seized the opportunity to recycle worn-out 1960s clichés about Western imperialism and hegemony—have failed us. These events cannot be understood through the lens of an anti-imperialist struggle by the "wretched of the earth" against the economic and political power of the hegemonic West. Neglecting the internal dynamics and struggles within the Islamic world, and the history of regional conflicts in Afghanistan, Pakistan, India, and Kashmir, these analyses assured us that we could continue to grasp the world through our old categories, and that by blaming the policies and actions of Western governments, we could immunize ourselves against the enmity and hatred directed toward one as a member of Western societies. Such views help us neither to grasp the unprecedented nature of the events unfolding since September 11, 2001 nor to appreciate the internal dynamics within the Arab Muslim world which have given rise to them.

The line between *military* and *civilian targets,* between military and civilian populations, had already been erased during the aerial bombings of World War II. This is not what is new since September 11. The bombing of London by the Nazis, and of Dresden, Hiroshima and Nagasaki by the Allies dramatically crossed the line which separated military and civilian targets in modern warfare.

In the 1950s, the Algerian War marked a new variation in this process of the erasure of the line between the front and the home, the soldier and the civilian. The Algerian Resistance against the French aimed at destroying the *normalcy of everyday life* for the civilians of the occupying population. By blowing up the French residents of Algeria in cafes, markets, and train stations, the Resistance not only reminded them that they were the enemy but that there could be no "normal life" under conditions of colonial occupation. Since that time, this kind of terror—which fights against the superior military and technical weapons of a mightier enemy by tearing apart the fabric of everyday life through interrupting normal routines by rendering every bus and railroad station, each street corner or gathering place into a potential target—has become one of the favorite "weapons of the weak." The strategy of this kind of struggle is to make life so un-livable for the enemy civilians that they concede defeat even if they enjoy superior military power. The Palestinian *intifada*, at least in part, follows the Algerian model: By creating conditions of continuous fear, insecurity, and violence in the land of Palestine, it aims at destroying the resolve of the Israeli civilian population to continue a normal life.[3] In recent years, however, infiltrators from Islamist groups like Hamas and Hezbollah into the ranks of the Palestinians, and the widespread practice of "suicide bombings," are changing the nature of the *intifada* as well.

The bombing of the World Trade Center and the Pentagon is unlike both the total war waged in the struggle against fascism and the terrorism against the occupier initiated by the Algerians. These attacks, perpetrated against a civilian population in its own land, and against a country in no state of declared hostility with the attackers, not only defy all categories of international law but reduce politics to apocalyptic symbols. Until Osama bin Laden released his terse video celebrating September 11, his deed had no political name: In whose name or for whom were they acting? What political demands were they voicing? The brief references to the stationing of U.S. troops in Saudi Arabia, to U.S. sanctions against Iraq, and to the U.S. support of Israel were shrouded in the language of "jihad" (holy war) and obfuscated by allusions to the lost glory of Islam in the thirteenth century through the loss of "al Andalus"—of Spain—to the Christians. While it is conceivable that Palestinian terror could end one day if Israel withdrew from the occupied West Bank, released Palestinian prisoners of war, found a settlement for the refugees, and somehow resolved the question of

Jerusalem, it is unclear what, if anything, could end the *jihad* of the Osama bin Laden network against the U.S. and its allies. Theirs is a war of "holy" vengeance, a war designed to humiliate the mighty "Satan" in New York and Washington by turning the weapons of the most developed technology against the society which created them.

The result is a sublime combination of high-tech wizardry and moral and political atavism, which some have named "jihad-on-line." But this unholy politics threatens to undo the moral and political distinctions that ought to govern our lives, distinctions as between enemy, friend, and bystander; guilt, complicity, and responsibility; conflict, combat, and war. We have to live by them even if others do not.

One of the most commonly heard contentions in the aftermath of September 11 was that even if the terrorist attacks upon the World Trade Center and Washington equaled war in the civilian and property damages they inflicted, the deliberateness and precision with which they were executed, and the brazenness with which they violated customary moral, legal, and international norms, the U.S. Congress could not actually declare "war," not because the perpetrators were as yet unknown, but because a state can declare war only against another state. The idea that a democratic nation-state would declare war upon a global network of loosely organized sympathizers of a religious-cum-civilizational cause strained all categories of international law with which the world has lived since 1945, and in which nation-states are the principal recognized actors. For this reason, military action in Afghanistan was not preceded by a declaration of war; rather Congress authorized the President to do whatever is necessary to fight the global terror network and to bring the perpetrators to justice, but it declared war neither upon the Taliban (whom most nations did not recognize as a legitimate regime) nor upon the Afghani people. It is as if the territory, the terrain of Afghanistan, was our enemy, in that this terrain offered a sanctuary and an operational base for one of the great fugitives of our time—Osama bin Laden. Ironically, the people of Afghanistan had themselves fallen "captive" or "prisoner" to one who operated on their territory, and to whom the Taliban had granted refuge. Afghanistan is a decaying or failed nation-state, and this very condition of decay permits us to understand all the more vividly the principles of national sovereignty which have governed international relations since the Second World War.

Recall here Max Weber's classically modernist definition of the state as "the legitimate monopoly over the use of violence within a recognized and bounded territory."[4] Modern statehood is based upon the coupling together of the principles of *territoriality, administrative* and *military monopoly,* including the use of violence, and the *legitimacy* to do so. When states decay, dissolve, or secede, these three principles fall asunder. Their territory can become a staging ground for operations not only of guerrilla warfare, but of drug smuggling, weapons production, contraband, and other illegal activities; administrative and military competence is overtaken by units at the substate level such as warlords, commandos, traditional chieftains, or religious leaders; and legitimacy loses its representational quality in that there is no longer a unified people to whose will it either refers or defers—legitimacy either flows from the barrel of a gun or from other sources of supra- and subnational ideological worldviews, be these race, religion, or civilization based.

The decaying and weak nation-states of the contemporary world bear similarities as well as differences to the totalitarian regimes of the mid–twentieth century. The breakdown of the rule of law; the destruction of representative and democratic institutions; the pervasiveness of violence, and the universalization of fear are features of both state forms. The totalitarian regimes of the mid–twentieth century, however, although at times they mobilized "the movement" against the state bureaucracy, by and large strengthened and rebuilt the state by rendering it subservient to their ideologies. But the postmodern/quasi-feudal states of the present, like Afghanistan, Chechnya, Bosnia, and Rwanda, emerge as a result not of the strengthening but of the destruction of the territorial and administrative unity of the state in the name of subunities, which are then globally networked. As Hannah Arendt has shown us, totalitarian movements also had globalizing ambitions in that they touted supranational ideologies like pan-Germanism and pan-Slavism.[5] Yet the global ideologies of today's terror movements are both larger and smaller in range. Instead of the ideology of linguistic or cultural unity, today we are facing ideologies aimed at tribes, ethnicities, or at a vision of a community of believers that transcends them all, namely the *Islamic umma of the faithful.* The new unit of totalitarianism is the terrorist cell, not the party or the movement; the goal of this new form of war is not just the destruction of the enemy but the extinction of a way of life. *The emergence of non-state agents capable of waging destruction at a level hitherto thought to be only the province of states and the emergence of a supranational ideological vision with an undefinable moral and political content, which can hardly be satisfied by ordinary political tactics and negotiations, are the unprecedented aspects of our current condition.*

This remark should not be taken to suggest that I attribute an overarching rationality or normativity to the state use of violence. State terrorism can also be brutal, unjust, and merciless—recall the war of the Yugoslav state against the Bosnians and the Kosovar Albanians. The point I am emphasizing, however, is that in liberal democracies the monopoly which the state claims over the use of the means of violence is always in principle, if not in fact, subject to the rule of law and to democratic legitimation by the citizenry. These internal constraints upon the legitimate use of violence are then carried into the international arena, where sovereign states bind themselves to limit their use of violence by entering into pacts and associations, signing treaties, etc.

The end of the bipolar world of the Cold War has brought with it not just multiplurality but a global society in which non-state actors have emerged as players possessing means of violence but who are not subject to usual constraints of international law and treaties. All treaties which have hitherto governed the non-use and proliferation of biological, chemical, and nuclear weapons are threatened with irrelevance, since those who will deploy them have never been their signatories. Furthermore, not being recognized as legitimate political entities, these groups have no responsibility and accountability toward the populations in whose midst they act and which harbor them. Suppose Al Qaeda possesses scud missiles with nuclear warheads, which they may have obtained from Iraq or from the Russian Mafia or other weapons smugglers. What would prevent them from firing these missiles against population centers in Afghanistan, Pakistan, India, or Israel if this would serve some purpose? Since they are accountable to no one, the collateral damage which they may cause even to their own allies and sympathizers is of no concern to them. Whereas terrorist groups like the Basque ETA and the IRA still have to be governed by some sense of proportion in the damage they inflict and the violence they engage in (in order not to lose all sympathy for their cause in world public opinion), these new terror networks are not motivated by foreseeable political goals analogous to the independence of the Basque land from Spain and France, or the removal of the Irish Catholic population from Northern Ireland and unity with UK Protestants, and such. Nor are these groups fighting for hearts and minds in the West by seeking the conversion of the population to Islam and to Islamic ways of life. "Jihad," which can also mean the struggle of the soul with itself to lead the virtuous life as dictated by the Qur'an,[6] when it was practiced by Islamic armies in the centuries after the death of Mohammad (632 AD), aimed at the conquest of the land of the "infidels" in order to force their conversion to Islam. People of all races, colors, ethnicities, and tongues could convert to Islam and become "good Muslims." It is this option of conversion which has made Islam into the biggest Abrahamanic religion of the world, and ironically, it is the very absence of this conversion mission that is striking in the new jihad.

The new jihad is not only apocalyptic; it is nihilistic. Osama bin Laden's statement that his men love death as much as the Americans love life is an expression of superb nihilism. The eroticization of death, as evidenced on the one hand by the frequently heard vulgarisms about *huris,* the dark-eyed virgins who are to meet the warriors in the afterlife, but on the other hand and more importantly, by the destruction of one's own body in an act of supreme violence which dismembers and pulverizes it, is remarkable. Human beings have died throughout the centuries for causes they believed in, to save their loved ones, to protect their country or their principles, to exercise solidarity, and the like. But the emergence of "suicide bombings" among Islamist groups on a mass scale is astonishing. As many Qur'anic scholars have pointed out, there is no theological justification for this: It is one thing to die in war and yet another to make the destruction of one's body along with those of others the supreme weapon. In order to quell such waves of suicide bombings, the Israeli authorities resorted to an atavistic practice: They made it publicly known that they would bury the remains of suicide bombers in shrouds of pigs' skin (an animal that is considered *haram*—taboo— by Jews and Muslims alike) in order to prevent their ascent into heaven in accordance with Islamic faith. It is of course hard to know whether men of the sophistication and worldliness of Muhammad Atta and others who have lived in the capitals of Europe and the West and who have attended universities as well as bars, movie houses, and brothels, believe in the afterlife. Not only is it clear that the very strict version of Islam—Wahabism—which Osama bin Laden follows, is not shared by all even within his own group, but the Egyptian Brotherhood which was the original organization for many Islamist philosophies in the 1950s had its own version of things, as do members of the Algerian terror network. These networks of young militants who trot the globe from Bosnia to Afghanistan, from Paris to Indonesia, and back to Baghdad, Hamburg, or New York, are like Islamic soldiers of fortune, not in search of riches, but in search of an elusive and decisive encounter with death. In this regard they bear more resemblance to chiliastic sects among all world religions than to the Muslim armies of the Umayyad, the Abassids, or the Ottomans. While using friendly Muslim governments and their hospitality for their own purposes, these groups pose a clear threat to any established form of authority—which may have been one reason why the Saudis renounced Osama bin Laden's citizenship and rendered him an international fugitive.

As in the past century, faced with a novel form of totalitarianism, democracies confront unique challenges. The presence of an enemy who is neither a military adversary nor a representative agent of a known state creates confusion as to whether it is the police and other law enforcement agencies or the military who should take the lead in the investigation and the struggle—the lines between acts of crime and acts of war get blurred. The concept of an "internal enemy," which is now being promoted against "suspect groups" through surveillance, wiretapping, and stricter immigration controls, is not one that democracies can live with. The category of the terrorist as an "internal enemy," as one who is among us, even if not one of us, strains the democratic community by revealing that the rule of law is not all-inclusive and that violence lurks at the edges of everyday normalcy. Our thinking about foreigners, refugees, and asylees becomes colored by the image of others as potential enemies; the "other" becomes the criminal. We may be at a point in history when indeed the state-centric system is waning: global terrorism and the formation of a global economy and civil society are part of the same maelstrom. Yet our laws as well as institutions, practices as well as alliances, are governed by state-centric terms which presuppose the unity of territoriality, the monopoly over the use of the means of violence, and the attainment of legitimacy through representative institutions.

The normative strain on state-centric categories is evidenced by the recent blunders and legal embarrassments of the Bush administration in the issue of the status of the captured Al Qaeda and Taliban soldiers, who have been quartered in Guantánamo Bay, Cuba. Since Guantánamo Bay is a military base and not part of the territorial U.S., it is constitutionally a no-man's-land. It serves as an extraterritorial and extralegal space in which "the unwanted business" of various administrations, like the locking up of Haitian refugees under the Clinton administration, can be carried out. Furthermore, faced with the outcry of world public opinion and particularly of European allies, the treatment of the captured prisoners was subject to increased scrutiny. Without clarifying the extralegal status of Guantánamo Bay, Attorney General Ashcroft and President Bush introduced a distinction between "legal combatants," i.e. prisoners of war who would fall under the protection of the Geneva Conventions, and "illegal combatants," whose rights would not be so protected. President Bush appealed to the distinction introduced during the Vietnam War era between South Vietnamese army members and civilians who were considered prisoners of war, and the Vietcong who were not, as precedent. Yet the juridical tenability of these distinctions in light of customary international law as well as the Geneva Conventions remains a matter of contention.

More significantly, the USA PATRIOT Act, which was passed by Congress on October 25, 2001, proceeds, as Ronald Dworkin has pointed out, from a "breathtakingly vague and broad definition of terrorism and of aiding terrorism,"[7] and relaxes rules that protect people suspected of crime from unfair investigation and prosecution. There are close to 600 detainees of Middle Eastern origin in U.S. prisons who have been denied counsel and even visiting rights with their families. In numerous cases, their crime seems to be no more than infractions of immigration laws like overstaying their visas. While we cannot deny the legitimate security concerns of the U.S., the emergence of a "security state" and the speedy violation of the extension of constitutional protections to "illegal aliens and combatants" is worrisome for the future. History teaches us that the "chickens come home to roost," and that violations of the rights of others sooner or later affect our civil liberties as well.

Of course, (and this cannot be said clearly and loudly enough by the citizens of Western democracies), a radical revision of U.S. and NATO policy vis-à-vis the Arab world and south-Central Asia is needed. The U.S. and its allies have to stop propping up military dictatorships and religious conservatives in these areas in order simply to secure oil supplies. Democratic movements within the burgeoning civil societies of countries like Egypt, Turkey, Jordan, and the new Iran must be supported. A general UN conference must be convened to deal with the rights of nations, ethnicities, and other minorities without states in this region, like the Kurds in Turkey, Iraq, and Iran; the Shi'ites in Iraq and the Baha' is as well as the Azeris in Iran. Efforts analogous to the Marshall Plan in postwar Europe or the Soros Foundation in Eastern Europe must be developed and furthered for entire regions. But even if all these initiatives are undertaken, I believe that a more daunting cultural struggle and civilizational malaise is unfolding before our eyes.

2.

The events of September 11 at first seemed to offer a belated confirmation of Samuel Huntington's famous thesis of the clash of civilizations. Huntington wrote: "It is my hypothesis that the fundamental source of conflict in this new world will not be primarily ideological or primarily economic. The great divisions among humankind and the dominating source of conflict will be cultural. Nation-states will remain the most powerful actors in world affairs, but the principal conflicts of global politics will occur between nations and groups of different civilizations. The fault lines between civilizations will be the battle lines of the future."[8] Proceeding from a holistic understanding of cultures and civilizations—terms which he at times conflated and others distinguished— Huntington was unable to differentiate one "civilization" clearly from another, with the consequence that, apart from the vague juxtaposition of "the West and the rest," he could not specify how many civilizations there are.[9] Edward Said pointed out that Huntington made civilizations and identities into "shutdown, sealed-off entities that have been purged of the myriad currents and countercurrents that animate human history, and over centuries have made it possible for that history not only to contain wars of religion and imperial conquest but also to be one of exchange, cross-fertilization, and sharing." [10]

It is precisely this history of cross-fertilization—exchange as well as confrontation—between Islamic culture and the West to which we must pay increasing attention. One of the principal thinkers of the Islamist[11] movement, Sayyid Qutb, an Egyptian who studied philosophy in France and briefly visited the United States, developed a civilizational critique of the West for its corruption, coldness, heartlessness, and individualism. His critique resonates with themes from the works of Nietzsche as well as Heidegger, from Adorno and Horkheimer as well as contemporary communitarians.[12] Describing the current condition of the West as one of "jahiliyya," a lack of knowledge, ignorance, the Islamists advocate a return to Qur'anic law—the *shari'a*—and Muslim precepts to fight the corruption of the Western way of life. To combat the condition of *jahiliyya,* it is necessary to rebel and establish a countercommunity (*jama'a*) and spread it through *jihad.*[13] Very often, the Islamists' struggle against *jahiliyya* took the form of a struggle against established authorities in their own countries and their "corrupt," Westernizing policies.

This clash within Islamic countries between Islamist religious forces and modernizers like Kemal Ataturk in Turkey, Habib Burgiba in Tunisia, Gemal Abdel Nasser, Anwar Sadat, and Hosni Mubarek in Egypt, the deposed Reza Shah Pahlavi in Iran, and even Saddam Hussein in Iraq, is old, deep, and powerful. The modernizers in these countries have usually come from military rather than civilian backgrounds, and by transforming one of the few intact institutions of the old regime—namely the military bureaucracy—into an instrument of political power and hegemony, they have consolidated their authority, often with limited popular support and scanty democratic institutions. All over the Islamic Arab world this *military modernization* paradigm, in which Syria and Iraq had participated through the Ba'ath regimes in the 1970s, has lost ground. The defeat of the Egyptian armies by Israel during the Six-Day War, the Israeli occupation of the Golan Heights and the West Bank, are reminders to the military elite of these countries, less of the plight of the Palestinians, whom they have massacred and oppressed when it suited their interests (remember Black September in Jordan in 1970, in which Palestinians were killed by the thousands; or the persecution of the Palestinians by the Saudis because of their support for Saddam Hussein during the Gulf War), but of the failure of their own truncated projects of modernization. Israel is a thorn in the side of these regimes, whose very presence is a bleeding reminder of their own failure to modernize in military, technological, and economic terms.

The revival of Islamist movements is best understood in the light of the failure of most of these societies to succeed in combining a prosperous economy, *with* political democracy, and a Muslim identity.[14] Islamism emerges as a plausible civilizational project, not just against the West, but in the first place against the failure of Westernizing elites who have only managed to import a truncated modernity into their own societies. Some of these modernizing elites had considered themselves "socialists" of sorts. The Ba'ath regimes in Syria and Iraq, and even the kind of pan-Arabism envisaged by Nasser in the early 1960s, advocated strong redistributionist economic measures, built up huge public sectors (in state-owned utilities, for example), and practiced what could be called "statist modernization" from above. The demise of the Soviet Union has left these states with no patrons. Need we remind ourselves that the mobilization of the Islamist *mujahedeen* in Afghanistan began against the Soviet invasion of the country in 1973—an invasion the Soviets engaged in to support their own backers, the leftist *fedayyeen?*

The collapse of really existing socialisms, and the failure of state-guided modernization from above has created an enormous vacuum in the ideological life of these societies. And into this vacuum have rushed Islamist fundamentalists. Osama bin Laden is the most spectacular member of a long chain of critics in the Islamic world, who, more often than not, have transformed their local struggles against their own corrupt and authoritarian regimes (Nasser banned the Islamist Muslim Brotherhood and hung some of their leaders) toward the outside, toward the external enemy.

3.

I want to end with Max Weber's question: Which directions do religious rejections of the world take, and why?[15] There is a fundamental conflict between secular, capitalist modernity, driven by profit, self-interest, and individualism, and the ethical world views of the world's religions. The religious world views preach various forms of abstinence, renunciation of riches, the pursuit of virtue in the path of God, the exercise of solidarity among members of the faith, and the disciplining of everyday life to do the work of the Lord. What is it, Weber asked, that enables some religious interpretations of the world to make their peace with the new world of modernity? For Weber the Protestant ethic exhibited its "elective affinity" to capitalism by transforming the abstinent and methodical pursuit of one's vocation in the service of God into the methodical, predictable, disciplined pursuit of work and profit in this world. This process took several centuries and not all early modern Christians accepted its logic: Millenarian movements who rejected the capitalist control of everyday life for the sake of disciplined labor and profit accompanied the rise of Western modernity.

The Protestant—and more narrowly Calvinist—transformation of religious salvation into an earthly vocation of hard work in the service of an unpredictable God is one among the many paths that the religious accommodation with the world can take. It is also possible to split the religious and mundane spheres in such a way that one altogether withdraws from engagement with the world; the religious abnegation of the world remains an option. A third option—besides engagement or withdrawal—is to *compartmentalize* by separating the spheres of life which come under the ethical dictates of religion from those like the public spheres of the economy which do not. Throughout the Islamic world, such a strict separation of religious observance (in the domain of family life and everyday practices of prayer, cleanliness, food, and sexuality) from the sphere of the economy in the "bazaar" (the marketplace) was practiced. This separation of the *home* from the *market* was made possible by the practice of Islamic tolerance toward the other Abrahamanic religions, like Judaism and Christianity. The Ottomans adopted this "separate spheres" model, and permitted the wide array of ethnic groups and peoples whom they dominated to govern themselves in their own communal affairs according to their own religious and customary traditions (the so-called *millet* system). Global modernization is destroying the fragile balance between these separate spheres; this may explain in turn the obsessive preoccupation with controlling female sexuality which all Islamist groups exhibit.

Technical modernization, which brings along with it the gadgets of modernity like computers, videos, DVDs, cell phones, satellite dishes, is no threat to the Islamists.[16] In fact, there is a ruthless exploitation of this new media to convey one's message to one's believers. Neither is finance capitalism as such problematic from an Islamic perspective. Attempts exist all over the Muslim world to reconcile the *shari'a* with modern financial institutions. Whether it is the *hawala* method of money transfers which bypass modern banks and rely on personalized contacts among money lenders, or the practice of the obligation of the rich to the poor by sharing 5 percent of one's wealth, as dictated in the Qur'an (a practice that is partially behind the founding of the *madrasas*—institutions of religious learning—for the orphan children of war in Afghanistan by wealthy individuals all over the Islamic world), institutional innovations such as to make Islam compatible with global capitalism are taking place. The threat to the separate spheres model is primarily a threat to family and personal life.

Global capitalism is bringing images of sexual freedom and decadence, female emancipation, and equality among the sexes into the homes of patriarchal and authoritarian Muslim communities. It is Hollywood which is identified as America, and not the Constitution or the Supreme Court, or the legacy of Puritanism and town meetings. The fast-circulating images of sexual liberty and decadence, physical destruction, and violence, sell very well globally because their message is blunt and can be extricated from local cultural nuance. The threat felt by these groups in the face of Hollywood's images of decadence needs to be contrasted with their equally cynical recycling of such images through the mimicry of violence and destruction. More than one commentator has pointed out how "cinematographic" the images of the airplanes full of passengers flying into the twin towers of the World Trade Center were.

In a global world, it is not only images that travel; individuals all over the Islamic world are part of a large diaspora of migration to the West. Sizeable Muslim communities exist in every large European and North American capital. These migrant communities attempt to practice the separate-life-spheres model in their new homes. But the children of Muslim migrants are caught between worlds, between educational institutions and the influence of mass culture, on the one hand, and the authoritarian and patriarchal family structures from which they emerge on the other. There is a continuous renegotiation of clashing moral codes and value orientations in the minds of this younger generation, and particularly of women. If we want to understand why so many educated, relatively well-off Muslim males from cities like Hamburg, London, and Paris would participate in the actions of September 11, we have to understand the psychology of Muslim immigrants in their encounters with secular liberal democracies of the West. Given the failure of their own home-grown versions of modernity like Nasserism and the Ba'ath movement, given the profound assault on their identity as Muslims which the global entertainment industry brings, and given the profound discrimination and contempt which they experience in their host societies as new immigrants who are perceived to have "backward" morals and ways of life, many young Muslims today turn to Islamism and fundamentalism. Commenting on "*l'affaire de foulard,*" (the veil affair) in France, in which some female students took to wearing traditional veils—less as a sign of submission to religious patriarchy than as an emblem of difference and defiance of homogenizing French republican traditions—the French sociologists Gaspard and Khosrokhavar capture this set of complex symbolic negotiations as follows: "[The veil] mirrors in the eyes of the parents and the grandparents the illusions of continuity whereas it is a factor of discontinuity; it makes possible the transition to otherness (modernity), under the pretext of identity (tradition); it creates the sentiment of identity with the society of origin whereas its meaning is inscribed within the dynamic of relations with the receiving society; . . . it is the vehicle of the passage to modernity within a promiscuity which confounds traditional distinctions, of an access to the public sphere which was forbidden to traditional women as a space of action and the constitution of individual autonomy. . . ." [17]

We can intervene in this process of complex cultural negotiations as dialogue partners in a global civilization only insofar as we make an effort to understand the struggles of others whose idioms and terms may be unfamiliar to us but which, by the same token, are also not so different from similar struggles at other times in our own cultures; through acts of strong hermeneutical generosity, we can still extend our moral imagination to view the world through the other's eyes. [18] While I believe that at this stage of the conflict the use of force against the Osama bin Laden network is inevitable and justified, the real political task ahead is to engage in a dialogue with the hearts and minds of millions of Muslims around this globe—beyond vengeance and without apocalyptic expectations. Democracies cannot fight holy wars. Reason, compassion, respect for the dignity of human life, the search for justice, and the desire for reconciliation are the democratic virtues which are now pitted against acts of apocalyptic hatred and vengeance.

16. TERRORISM AND THE ASSAULT ON POLITICS

PETER ALEXANDER MEYERS

Στην Ευθυμια, εναντια στο φοβο

1.

You may have followed with curiosity and trepidation the outpouring of words after September 11. You may have been glad for the information and analysis. Heartened by the many debates set in motion. Still, if you are like me, you may feel dispirited that our talking has been so directly shaped by the event.[1]

How odd to even say this! Of course we must take seriously the event of September 11. We must speak it, understand it. Nevertheless, *our primary concern cannot be to protect ourselves against an act already committed.* To focus too much on September 11, Al Qaeda, or "the present threat" is to enter the logic of terrorism. That is what disturbs me. Will we allow the terrorist to impose an agenda of death on the living, an agenda of one obsessive moment on the passage of time?

Yet, speak we must. Aiming to escape from this trap, I have written of things that seem far from the matter at hand. I bear down on *politics,* not terrorism. I try to make clear not the attackers but what they attacked; not what we lost, but what we must defend. This version of politics is then contrasted with a more familiar one. All this matters for how we understand democracy. Finally, having chosen and prepared the ground on which I want to fight, I confront the terrorist act itself. My purpose is to show how its consequences depend more on us than on "them." After September 11, we must renew and broaden our practice of politics rather than allow the terrorist moment to contribute to its further degradation. If I succeed in clarifying something of what is at stake in this alternative view of politics, you will agree that from start to finish these considerations belong to the space left—or the space created—at the lower end of Manhattan.

The World Trade Center and the Pentagon were attacked on one day, September 11, 2001. On that day, a passionate desire for *e pluribus unum,* unity grounded in "truth" and "moral certainty," called for little justification. Months later, with war waged, institutions transformed, new laws in place, and with profound changes in everyday life well under way, hyperbolic talk about "certainty" and "good vs. evil" must be interrogated. Such talk does not derive entirely from that one terrible day. Whatever caused the event, whatever it portends, American public culture was well prepared to host those who would transform political and moral questions into self-assured empirical assertions about what we must do and why. Indeed, many old contests—from the Cold War to the "Culture Wars"—circle around the new topic of September 11, fanning its flames.

My main purpose in this essay is to argue that the acts of September 11 were an assault on politics itself and that a citizen's most important response—to those attacks and to subsequent ones—is to defend politics. The question under consideration here is *what* exactly must we defend? For I do not mean by "politics" merely the public roles played by leaders or citizens; nor do I refer to the Constitution or to the institutions of government. I invite you to see that a broader, alternative, and more sure understanding of politics begins with the inescapable truth of human implication in language.

"Man is by nature a political animal," wrote Aristotle in the *Politics,* and we "alone of the animals possess speech."[2] Dogs and chickens can howl or squawk with pain or pleasure; they have a *voice* (*phônê*). It is the miracle of human *speech* (*logos*) that only we can indicate to each other what is "advantageous and what is harmful, what is just and unjust."[3] The people of Homer were convinced that to live without politics one would have to be less or more than human, either a beast or a god.[4] What distinguishes beasts and gods is their tendency to "go it alone," to opt for unilateralism, with its inherent descent toward violence. Human beings have the alternative of politics, and we are often compelled by desire or constrained by circumstances to deploy it. People rely on violence when—for whatever reason—they are desperate or hubristic.[5]

The claim that "man is by nature a political animal" (*hoti ho anthrôpos phusei politikon zôion*) is more complicated than it seems. First, the word "man" (*anthrôpos*) refers to human beings in the plural and not to one human being. This plurality is underscored by the fact that, by definition, the city (*polis*) in which "man" must live contains more than one person. "By nature" (*phusei*), therefore, does not mean that there is "some authentic political substance" that "belongs to our essence." *One* man, rather, "is apolitical." "Politics exists in the in-between" of *plural* men "and is established in relation."[6] We do have natural capacities—like speech—and, because human beings cannot "go it alone" under normal circumstances, we are pressed by our nature to use language to constitute political relationships. *But neither the emergence nor the durability of politics is guaranteed.* If Aristotle meant to say that politics is guaranteed by nature the way gravity is guaranteed by nature, he was wrong. Once we begin to live together there are two basic possibilities for coordinating our activities in the face of novel circum-

stances: Either the needs and desires of some are imposed on the others with violence, or differences are negotiated through language. It is precisely the chance
provided by language to escape from "civil warre" that makes politics distinct,
something which happens in-between people and not imposed by one on another. Thus, the first thing to say in defining politics is that it is not violence. The
two are antithetical.

Yet, experience tells us that violence and politics often go hand in hand. And
it is unquestionably true that politics is often engendered from acts of violence,
or leads to them. But the relation between violence and politics is neither simple nor direct. It demands much closer scrutiny than we ordinarily give to it.
Even when politics emerges from "civil warre," it is a consequence which an-
nuls its cause. The ancient violence of founding does not reside forever after in
the constitution.[7] Violence is an act, not a substance; it cannot be stored by
governments or sovereigns for later use. Likewise, when politics *gives issue to
combat,* that is a sign of its failure.[8]

Not everything, not every moment of life, is political. Nonetheless any other
fact of human existence can become implicated in politics. Of course, violence is
one of these facts. Logically speaking, a clear distinction between violence and
politics is a precondition for the implication of the former in the latter. For this
reason, the contemporary tendency to be overly capacious in using the word "violence" has become a source of confusion. It tends to defeat its own purpose. The
advocate of social justice who points to verbal violence, symbolic violence, the
inherent violence of institutions, etc., can be all too facilely rebuffed: If violence is
everywhere, where is the alternative? Likewise, if everything were political, politics would have no meaning, offer no recourse. With an often well-intentioned
but ill-conceived imprecision concerning violence, politics loses the specific difference which brings it into being.

If politics is *not violence,* what else is it? This is an important question if we are
to understand how citizens can defend politics after September 11. For simplistic
nonviolence is no better a response to terrorism than simple violence. Three additional conditions characterize politics in the sense I want to advance here. Each
of them is tightly bound up with our use of language.

The first condition of politics is the *plurality* of human beings I mentioned
just above. Plurality is not the same thing as the related idea of *difference.* Difference is a logical or philosophical notion rather than a political one. It refers primarily to qualities which, for one reason or another, inhere in individual people.
I am different from *you* because I am short and you are tall, because I wear blue
shirts and you wear brown ones, etc. *Plurality* takes this into account, but goes a
step further. Plurality is an attribute of the *we:* It constitutes a kind of space

in-between people, a space which results from but which is not reducible to such differences. Clever and sometimes revealing verbal games can be played by bouncing between identity and difference.[9] But plurality is destroyed by identity.[10] This is what sets politics apart from other types of associations—families, lovers—in which similarities are most important. Qualities shared in common bring people together, identifying them as *a* family or *a* couple. At least in the idealized form of these relationships, the in-between space which politics requires disappears. Negotiation becomes undesirable or unnecessary.[11] In contrast with politics, love has this extreme proximity in common with violence.

A second condition of politics is the inescapable fact that diverse people living together not only remain at some distance from each other, but are also connected without losing their distinctiveness.[12] This "connectedness" is what sociologists since Rousseau have called *le lien social.* In one word, it is *dependence.*[13] The many uses of this single word[14] show how this basic fact runs through various aspects of experience. Viewed subjectively, which is to say as it is lived by individual people, dependence consists in a number of conditions which change the character of action.[15] Viewed objectively, dependence is *social space,* or the in-between of plurality.

The "connectedness" that dependence represents is a fact of our nature. It is created by a sort of mitosis: As we go about our habitual practices, new connections split off from old ones, as when the person I see time and again at the market automatically smiles at me on the subway, or when the person I telephone repeatedly for administrative reasons tells me spontaneously about the house she is buying in Brooklyn. These new connections are piggy-backed on preexisting dispositions.

Beyond this patterning, both building from it and eventually reshaping it, human beings are constantly taking aim at some goal and acting in that direction. To do so, we must start from where we are. From the start we are not in control, and connections to things and other people assume the character of dependence as we try to make something of them. Dependence, whatever its shape and scope and direction, almost always emerges as an *unintended consequence of action.*[16] Only in the rarest of cases does someone *want* to become dependent. It just happens in the course of going about our various projects. In the process, connectedness takes on a significance, even a "life" and reality of its own, which was not written into anyone's plan and is inextricable from the world in which we live.

The general problem to which politics responds—the problem of power—is characterized by a systematic creation of moments which can be opportunistically exploited because, as unintended consequences of action, they are not "owned" by anyone and no one is responsible for them but, as dependence, they constitute real benefits or burdens for people.[17] To see how politics here and there emerges from dependence is to understand with modern sociological precision Aristotle's *anthrôpos phusei politikon zôion*.

Plurality and dependence combine with the rejection of violence to create a certain kind of space, with a certain kind of structure. This is the set of conditions within which the human capacity for speech constitutes politics. I put it this way because, once again, not everything is political. Certainly, not all speech is political. Politics emerges from and decays back into other aspects of the human experience. The specificity of politics, what makes it in fact a viable alternative to violence, is the way that speech changes this *certain kind of space in-between* human beings. This space exists in general as plurality and dependence.[18] But politics is always about particulars, and this brings us to the third condition which characterizes politics in the broad sense. What specifically reconfigures this space *as political* is the introduction of a third party (judge, ally, tie-breaker, voter, principle of "reality" or "justice," etc.) into a contest between two others. This "third" is, in one word, the *public*. The act of implicating a public, or *publicizing*, changes the balance of forces or interests between the two parties already in contest or dispute. This is what opens the situation to the innovations required for a resolution without the recourse to violence or love. Because the "third" does not yet share, or does not yet see that he shares, the material interests in dispute, this process of implication can only take place through language.[19]

2.

If these fundamental conditions of politics seem too minimal, it is because until rather recently we (citizens and political scientists alike) have identified politics with control of the Modern State. By the "Modern State" I mean roughly the ensemble of administrative, legal, military, and financial institutions which are formed in the relationship of legitimate sovereignty over citizens and in a relationship of antagonism with other States. The spirit, if not the letter, of this conception of politics was famously advanced by Max Weber in a speech at the University of Munich in 1918:

> What do we understand by politics? . . . the leadership, or the influence of the leadership of a political association [*Verband*], hence today, of a State. But what . . . from the sociological point of view . . . is a "State?" . . . Ultimately, one can define the modern State sociologically only in terms of the specific *means* peculiar to it, as to every political association, namely, the use of physical violence [*Gewaltsamkeit*]. . . . Of course, force [*Gewaltsamkeit*] is certainly not the normal or the only means of the State—nobody says that—but force [*Gewaltsamkeit*] is a means specific to the State. Today the relation between the State and violence [*Gewaltsamkeit*] is an especially intimate one . . . we have to say that a State is a human community [*Gemeinschaft*] that (successfully) claims the *monopoly of legitimate use of physical force* [*Gewaltsamkeit*] within a given territory."[20]

This view of politics long predates Weber. It appears in another guise in the "Social Contract" tradition found in political thinkers like Hobbes, Locke, and Rousseau and then later in John Rawls. In Hobbes' classic version, the extraordinary book *Leviathan*, fear-filled people caught in the deadly unchecked violence of a "war of all against all" make a contract to give absolute power over themselves to a sovereign so as to then live in peace. With the advent of this commonwealth, the majority of citizens speak only at the Sovereign's pleasure. This, I want to suggest, is not a political theory, but an *anti*political one.

Weber's now-commonplace description of the State contains the same contradiction. Politics begins in the alternative between speech and violence, in choosing the former over the latter. Contrary to what Weber explicitly says, however, to identify the State with violence[21] (even with "legitimate" violence) is to *exclude* it from politics. Mark my words: I am not saying that States do not *really* exist. Likewise, it would be ridiculous to think that the State is irrelevant *for* politics. The all-too-common idea of a modern society without a State is an infantile fantasy. My point here is that the same State which creates conditions for public debate or elections may also withhold information important for the deliberation of citizens;[22] the same State which breaks down overweening corporate power may also hand over to its cronies the licentious exploitation of broadcast frequencies or natural preserves filled with oil. In short, the State may foster politics or it may be an instrument of *depoliticization*.

The general goal in the field of politics is to maintain a peaceful order, viz. to live together and negotiate the problems of power which arise every day. This may or may not involve, as Machiavelli told the Prince, the maintenance of *il suo stato*. Standard ways that modern political theory has linked politics to the State ("sovereignty," "legitimacy," "representation") are no longer sufficient for citizens who, in times of crisis and in defense of politics, ask *How exactly are the practices and institutions which compose the State implicated in a larger field of politics?*

The idea that politics is more bound up with administrative control than with self-government is hardly foreign to the American scene. Reading Alexander Pope's famous lines, "For forms of government let fools contest, That which is best administered is best,"[23] John Adams could write in 1776 that Pope "flattered tyrants too much" and that "nothing can be more fallacious than this."[24] But a decade later, Alexander Hamilton approved heartily this sentiment.[25] This was not a passing fancy. However much Madison may have insisted that politics is *for* the people,[26] the winning Federalists thought it would be better if it were not *by* them.[27] Not surprisingly, the focus on administration corresponded to an identification of politics with executive power.[28] After Benjamin Franklin predicted that "the executive will be always increasing here, as elsewhere, till it ends in a monarchy,"[29] Hamilton made sure to argue point-by-point the difference between a president and a king.[30] He, and his intellectual progeny, would nonetheless have found little unpleasant or surprising in the eventual appearance of an "imperial presidency" or a "national security State."

Of course, this has not been the only view of politics in America. But it has been a dominant one. Why it proved so durable is a long and complicated story. What may be said briefly here is that it was self-defeating. To see what I mean, consider the following strange coincidence of events. Disenfranchised Americans struggled to gain the coveted rights of citizenship from the Founding up to the end of World War I. In the same period, voting day became the most important political moment in the life of citizens. Yet, what those elected to manage the State actually did as administrators seemed less and less relevant to everyday life in the *polis*.[31] With the right to vote won, the rate of participation in elections dropped precipitously. Today, about half of citizens eligible to vote find this right no longer worth exercising. Some observers count this as a withdrawal from politics, the "privilege" of a liberal society. I suspect that it is rather a popular recognition of the false identification of politics with the State. Why? Because it has been followed by a migration of political activity into sites, practices, and institutions of many other kinds.[32] A tradition of thought in full renewal today groups these non-State activities and associations under the phrase *civil society*.[33]

The distinction between *civil society* and the State took form in the writings of Hegel and Marx as they adapted it from thinkers of the Scottish Enlightenment. Inquiry into "civil society" arrived on the heels of strict Mercantilist controls and was shaped by the nineteenth-century experience of increasing and increasingly unregulated competitive market activity. As a consequence, civil society was easily understood as essentially economic.[34] Within a century-old tradition of *political economy*, emphasis on the analysis of market practices (however widely framed by Marx and others) contributed to the unfortunate sharpening of the distinction between politics and economics.[35] This reinforced the idea that whatever society was, it was not political. It, in turn, strengthened the connection between politics and the State.

Against this tide, others continued to remark on *the political quality of society*. Alexis de Tocqueville's *Democracy in America* (1835–40) set the standard. Tocqueville deployed observations on the wide social dispersion of political practices in Jacksonian America to jar a French political imagination dulled by absolutist *présupposés*, persistent cultural residues of the *ancien régime*. The reception of Tocqueville's book in America suggests the changing fortunes of this alternative view. At least six different American editions were published before the Civil War and then, except for a brief reappearance around 1900, the book exited the scene until after World War II. It is indicative that the standard twentieth-century text, the *History of Political Theory* (George Sabine; 1937), does not mention Tocqueville once; nor do sophisticated attempts to break the grip of the concept of the State on political science, like the work of Easton or MacIver.[36] Sheldon S. Wolin gave him just four diffuse sentences in the 528 pages of his famous *Politics and Vision* (1960). That this same Professor Wolin published 680 pages on Tocqueville in 2001 is emblematic of his meteoric reappearance in political thinking following a major new translation in the mid-1960s, a steady flow of new editions, and another translation in 2000. Indeed, today it is difficult to avoid hearing the name of Tocqueville everywhere.

The interest in Tocqueville represents the resurgence of politics within civil society. But what explains it? It is possible to respond to this question in very basic terms. There are exigencies which derive from the plurality of everyday life, and they have reasserted themselves. While the State is unparalleled as a structure for making and executing public decisions, or as an instrument for agglomerating resources for public use, no State could completely satisfy every human need for political association. It is not an institution adept at the everyday displacement of violence by dialogue. Police may set the outside limits of this process, they may help reduce crime, but nothing is a substitute for community engagement in policing.[37] Likewise, even a transnational extension of our dependence and communicative capacities does not trump the fact that politics emerges *in some place* where people *live together* (in the most banal sense of these words). Thus, the idea of a *national* political discussion is almost a contradiction in terms. I propose that the revival of a political understanding of civil society has been powerfully motivated by the necessary failures of unilateral State action.[38]

Our identification of politics with the State is a weird and inverting lens. We have often seen the repatriation of politics within society as *antipolitics*. Even social activists have been convinced that they must avoid "politicizing" issues to treat them effectively. This peculiar situation became apparent when viewed from a distance. Political scientists had to look outside their discipline to discover the political moment sociologists had found in "micro-politics" or "new social movements."[39] More generally, Americans had to look beyond our national borders to discover—against all we had been taught—that civic struggles could bring down seemingly uncrackable totalitarian States.[40]

At home, the disdain for politics has grown with the defeat of expectations that were false to begin with. Politics is about *living together,* which is to say engagements between citizens. This is a disorderly business, and no State could ever have imposed thorough-going order on it. Ordered or not, civil society does have motive forces: they are need, desire, habit, chance, and dozens of others. These motive forces and their consequences become susceptible to political orientation when they pass through the medium of everyday language. The pretense of the state was to impose the technical logic of means-oriented rationality on something vastly more complex; this had to fail. When it did, this failure appeared on the scene as the corruption of politics itself.

The extent to which interested or antidemocratic parties instilled us with false expectations aimed to exclude politics from everyday life should not be underestimated. And certainly a political system based on majority rule but in which winners buy elections and "elections" are decided by judicial fiat is *on its own terms* corrupt. But another kind of corruption is less visible and more pernicious. In the long run, a misunderstanding of the very nature of politics has undermined citizens' capacities and dispositions for citizenship in the most basic sense. The reversal which sequesters politics in the State, and thus hides politics from those who must *do it,* has inclined citizens to see even *necessary* State actions as instances of corruption. Is it any surprise that Americans are ready to consign this kind of "politics" to the garbage pail and go about living their lives?

3.

But life is interrupted. Insecurity strikes like a missile. The ancient political question haunts us: How shall *we* live, today?

You will not be surprised if I say that our best option is democracy, the regime which makes most of the specifically human capacity to use language to displace violence in our everyday living together.[41] It is an answer nonetheless fraught with missteps and contradictions.

If democracy is the best instance of politics, and politics is the exclusion of violence, why then do democracies produce so much violence? Although decidedly antidemocratic regimes like the Nazis or the Khmer Rouge were overwhelmingly violent, history also confirms a special kind of entanglement of democracy with violence.[42] Here we need to be precise: Even if it were true that democracy is *founded* on violence, that would not explain its *production* of violence. Nor, I am convinced, does democracy *release* a violence already boiling within the mass of humanity. Democracy's entanglement with violence is, rather, a secondary and unintended consequence of the extraordinary complexity of self-government, with its refusal to place everything in the hands of a small group of kings or commanders—be they the rich, the virtuous, or the experts. An insistent reliance on speech over violence is as necessary for democrats as the web for the spider; it is likewise a construct of astonishing fragility. The frequency of violence points not to democracy's hidden essence, but to how easily and often it fails.[43]

The simplest logic is required to see that when politics in general disappears, democracy in particular will go down with it. Ancient thinkers understood that democracy could destroy itself if, following imperial ambition, it slipped into despotism. It is a relatively recent insight, however, that other factors might destroy democracy indirectly, eroding the ground of politics out from under our feet. We now know that even Aristotle's *zoon politikon* must constantly be on guard to spin out his history in accordance with his nature. Failure to accept this will leave democrats grasping to understand what is happening to them.

If you learned your Hobbes, you may still read him with profit, but you must read him backwards. If the "war of all against all" comes, it comes *after* the social contract has failed to live up to its promise, after citizens have lost their political capacities and politics has come apart at the seams. And if violence and "civil warre" are avoided, it is because what Hobbes sought to place under the sovereign's sway in the commonwealth—all the disorderly associative tendencies and spontaneous talking of citizens living their lives—cannot be suppressed. Politics is not guaranteed but only made possible by our nature; it can wither and die just as much as it can be made to flourish.

The question is, how? To decipher what is happening to democracy—growth or decay—from *within* democracy is enormously difficult. A crisis like September 11 provides, perversely, an opportunity. It makes visible what was taken for granted, allows us a moment to see more clearly who we are and where we are going.

Of all that distinguishes the original democracy of the Athenians from our own efforts, the American founders rightly focused on differences of size and complexity: Athens was a city, America is a nation; Athenian citizens had Athenian progenitors, ours have come from every corner of the earth, bearing with them a bewildering plurality of persuasions. Whatever its form, the democratic *regime of speech* seems almost to require a commitment to equality. Everyone can talk, and, surely, everyone has something to say. The Athenians institutionalized this equality in the principle that a citizen must rule and be ruled in turn. However, they tried to reduce the disorderly consequences of equality by strictly limiting the application of this principle. Women, slaves, foreign workers—the majority of *people*—were excluded from the number of *citizens,* and inequality prevailed in ancient times. Democracy was reborn in the nineteenth century when democrats began to take more seriously the principle of equality. They turned it against slavery in the fields and in the kitchen.[44] Thus, distinctively modern versions of democracy have combined an enlarged understanding of equality with the attractions of freedom.[45]

One feature of our unusual historical moment is that the sudden and almost total crisis of communism as a form of government all but banished the classical strategy of thinking politics by comparing regimes.[46] Failing precedents and lacking tools for interpretation, it has been easy to forget that the love of democracy is little more than 100 years old. In the "age of democratic revolutions" few people were democrats.[47] History and our history books have taught us that *freedom* is the answer to the questions: what draws people to democracy? and why would they lay down their lives for it? Yet, no one lives, and almost no one really expects to live, entirely unbound. The slightest experience shows that ties to others are as often the solution to as they are the cause of our problems. Thus, it seems to me that the attraction to democracy is even deeper, more visceral.[48] Faced with the vicissitudes of life, our natural reaction is not to *seek freedom,* but to *speak out.* Democracy excites us because it offers practical possibilities for living as we must, using language to exploit our dependence on others, and constantly negotiating the boundaries of diversity rather than simply escaping from or transgressing them. This politics does not start from freedom, but pursues it; this speech is not *merely words,* but the activity of politics. Freedom depends on politics and politics depends on speech. The public conditions of speech, therefore, are the absolute center of democracy.[49] It is not by chance that as the love of democracy grew, public speech regained its place in political life as the first practice of liberty.

Again, the twists and turns of our history! The emergence of a public sphere centered by the act of *speaking out* was conjoined with the identification of politics and the State.[50] The offspring of this marriage was the extraordinary judicial elaboration of First Amendment rights which began around World War I and which eventually produced a "rights revolution." For all the enormous political value this represents *for* citizens, the *right* to speak is nevertheless part of a juridical—not a political—relationship between the State and the citizen. It does not, by far, manifest all that is political in public speech. Nor does it show why the desire to *speak out* operates through the claims of liberty, and why this is crucial for democracy.

In tandem with the revived *politics of civil society,* many minds have been bent to inquire into the conditions necessary for public speech and the consequences it produces for the practice of democracy in our present historical circumstances. Many questions have been broached—from deep theoretical speculation to gritty inquiry into town meetings and the use of "new media." There are many *private* values of speech—like self-expression—but they are not essential here. Since the Enlightenment, the *social* value of free public speech has been widely asserted in four main ways. The first concerns the modern economy. With a highly developed division of tasks and complicated structures for deal-making and transactions, unrestricted public speech is said to be the best way to make sure everyone has the same information; this diffusion of information facilitates the operation of markets and relatively rapid correction of market failures.[51] The second justification for free public speech is that, by bringing the errors of individuals under the critical scrutiny of other people with different experience, it leads us toward truth and to hold truth with the conviction necessary to act on it. The third justification asserts that public speech makes individual experiences accessible to others, and thus feeds the creativity necessary to solve manifold social problems. Individual imagination is never up to this practical task. Finally, public speech establishes a basis of legitimacy for social action by gaining, in some form or another, a consent that can be verified by third parties in case of a dispute.[52]

Yet, the specifically *political* value of public speech is still in the process of elaboration. Some reasons for it were discussed above. I will add here only this: Liberty and democracy are not the same thing. Liberty is a consequence of politics, democracy one of its forms. Even Adam Smith, advocate of a "system of natural liberty," did not imagine liberty as a "state of nature" or as life without political associations, including the State. If public speech were justified, its value asserted and defended, only on grounds of liberty, the active promulgation of it would remain a mystery, and its practice would die out. People would simply act so as to avoid as many constraints as possible. Yet, those who love liberty have often taken positive action to defend politics. That is why, for example, so many institutions and practices which characterize modern democratic life involve disposing citizens to speak, educating that capacity, and creating wherever possible circumstances for its exercise. The democratic citizen is apprenticed in schools, libraries, town meetings, museums, civic associations, talk shows, and the like. We are apprenticed to the public sphere. So, it might be said that the *political* value of public speech is simply *that it is our only way to live together every day without violence.*

Love of country in a modern democracy has no higher form than defense of the present and future public sphere. This ground is gained with difficulty and must be held. Our Constitution is no "machine that . . . goes of itself," and not even the noble rights it provides are sufficient to defend democracy as a political way of life.[53] That takes vigorous exercise of public speech. Whoever sets dissent against patriotism is a seditious scoundrel . . . or a fool.

4.

Others in this volume examine the terrorist, and the worlds from which he springs. I will now focus on *the act of terrorism* to ascertain its meaning for the

democratic citizen as a *zoon politikon*. Our first measure in this must be its consequence for the public sphere. By this measure, terrorism produces two kinds of
disorder. One is evident, the other hidden. The first is the spectacle itself. The
chaos on the ground seems, paradoxically, to affirm a kind of orderliness of the
public sphere. A terrorist act monopolizes in one instant all the means of mass
communication. Images of death and destruction are everywhere, yet the public
sphere itself explodes with life. The act concentrates us. All faces turn to the news,
all talk to the event. Suddenly, each citizen is animated by the tight spring of one
precise fear. Our curiosity is pointed in one direction. Two planes destroy the
World Trade Center in Manhattan: the diffusion of this localized act into everyday life around the nation and around the globe seems to affirm—in some horribly inverted way—the vitality of the press, the media, the nation. Exactly that
same obsessive broadcast of the news which brings us to the terrorists' terror constitutes its apparent remedy: our newly pointed knowledge and angry unified
resolve.

This new or renewed sense of unity or purpose—gleefully announced by "social capital" advocates like Robert Putnam[54]—hides a second and more enduring
disorder of terrorism's making. It is hidden behind a mistaken equation: The
commotion of commentators and self-inflated monologuists is not the same
thing as the real public sphere they are supposed to serve. *To speak* is not the same
thing as *to be spoken to*. To be spoken to is not the same as *listening*, something
that is itself prerequisite to the transformative possibility of *good public speech*.[55]
The media—simply by "doing their job," whether in good faith or with the lust
for profit—abet the terrorists.[56] They must bring us the news. Terrorism, well
represented, harps on astonishment, that first of all our passions. Astonishment
is a suspension of time, of judgment, of action, and of words.[57] Terrorism constitutes an image, and this instrument removes the words from the mouths of citizens. It reduces us to speechless shock. The bestial act imposes a consensus of
brutes in which the animal *voice* of anguish and the godlike presumptuousness of
unchecked power submerge the all-too-fragile democratic practices of political
speech.[58]

President Bush echoed the sentiments of many in declaring that we will not
let enemies use our system against us.[59] This noble sentiment screams with an ignorance of politics and the hubris of State power.[60] *Appropriations of the unintended consequences of other people's actions are the absolute center of modern
politics.*[61] Any political engagement mobilizes the dependence shared by the parties engaged; to make something public is to make it available, common. Only
unilateral violence can hope to exclude this possibility (and even that sometimes

fails). Following September 11, therefore, if anything resists this kind of appropriation it will be the very act of the terrorists, not "our system."

Like a virus, terrorism launched into the "system" can wreak extensive havoc without further inputs. The extent of its malicious accomplishment is a function of how it exploits the organism into which it is inserted. Osama bin Laden recognized political laws of gravity. Seize unintended consequences of action, use "their" technology and transport system to bring down a pair of mighty buildings; count on the subsequent American reaction to accomplish the rest. He predicted that the act would create ripples in the larger context of American political culture, and thus produce crises both economic and political.

In fact, exactly what Osama bin Laden has used against us is our public sphere. The American public sphere today is a complex balance of certain kinds of rights, historically specific degrees of technical mediatisation, a particular range of citizen capacities and dispositions, structures of administrative practices, modes of control over fungible resources, etc. Also weighing in the scales are such notoriously difficult-to-measure characteristics as trust, belief, and "open-ness," which is to say the willingness to limit aspirations to "mastery" and allow "drift" to be part of the order in which we live together everyday. It is an imperfect *order;* it has fragile boundaries within and without. *To be an order* is a matter of balance, and thus the public sphere contains inherent possibilities for imbalance. Time, not control or structure, is the essential element in the maintenance of balance. This is because the public sphere is an order of life, of living, and thus of change and transformation; balance, and imbalances, arise in the course of events; what matters most in maintaining order is that the rhythm of publicizing and public response more or less corresponds to the time or urgency of needs. When these two trains run at different speeds, we are in trouble.

In other words, Osama bin Laden knew the commonplace: that Americans live within a tense and shifting balance of liberty and security; that an attack like this one increases the demand for security; that this, in turn, will increase the demand for liberty; that liberty, once endangered, cannot defend itself (*bellum omnium contra omnes*) and that an unsatisfied demand for liberty increases the pressure on civil and political rights. Rights are created and sustained by the State. This constitutes one of the central paradoxes of modern politics: the State must respond to contradictory demands for *both* liberty *and* security. In the longer-run of American history the balance has been sufficient to maintain stability. That is, even if for some people the balance has not been satisfactory, the whole system has not been terminally disturbed. But in times of crisis, contradictory demands overflow their usual proportions. Every case is a short-term problem; even landmark cases only become decisive because the system's balance subsequently changes for many reasons that did not adhere at the time they occurred. What pushes a situation over into crisis is the replacement of a relatively small number of short-term problems by a larger number of short-term problems. Terrorism disorders the "system" by imposing at once, in a hundred different ways, and for thousands of different people, the question "what are we going to do today?" to be both safe and free.[62] This question is not posed for the victims, but for everyone else. It is not spoken with the foreign accent of the terrorist, but in the familiar tones of the policeman, the neighbor, the judge, the co-worker, or the President.

And that, dear Reader, is the problem. What is wrong with this picture is that there is no general or abstract "trade-off" between liberty and security. This "trade-off" exists only under certain circumstances. The opposite of liberty is not security but *despotism.* The real tension which characterizes the extraordinary balancing act of any successful democracy is between a political culture favoring liberty and one favoring tyrants or plutocrats. And this political culture is a matter of what we do with and to ourselves. Terrorists have no say in it.

Unchecked self-assertions by the Bush administration increasingly side-step the Constitutional balance of powers. They fit into the pattern of an "imperial presidency" for which the "war on terrorism"—wherever it is being fought—has become a domestic political opportunity. This opportunity is increased by the indistinctness of the war: The enemy is invisible, has no specific territory that can be overrun, and has assets which are hard to identify or seize. The enemy may be *right here* as much as *over there.* This makes possible—even "necessary"—the conduct of a war without limits, domestic or foreign. Unlimited war facilitates an executive branch that aims to act like a rapacious business corporation, drawing every kind of resource and activity under its control.

September 11 has spurred renewed efforts to analyze the present and future condition of our polity. An intense debate has been engaged over questions of civil rights and the police powers of the State. Thus the righteous uproar over the "USA PATRIOT Act."[63] Thus the clamor against President Bush's far-reaching order of November 13, 2001, which brings anyone he deems a terrorist under the jurisdiction of military commissions ultimately controlled by himself and the Secretary of Defense. The crucial problems with such innovations is clear: the State is multiplying the types and scope of police powers in apparent contradiction to protections provided by Constitutional rights; likewise, the executive branch is encroaching on judicial power and independence. A disturbing number of these encroachments clearly violate established practices of the rule of law.

This chain of consequences—usurpations of power and reactions against them—is nearly "hard-wired" into our political culture. It was anticipated by Osama bin Laden and is now being enacted by those who occupy the executive branch. Admirable resistance to this process has focused on the defense of civil rights. An astonishing number of people, crossing a wide spectrum of political positions, agree with Nancy Chang of the Center for Constitutional Rights in New York City:

> . . . We can have peace and security without a constriction of the Bill of Rights . . . the worst thing that could happen as a result of the tragedy that has befallen our nation would be to sacrifice freedom, civil rights and civil liberties in the name of national security and the war against terrorism. If in our legitimate desire for security we surrender basic freedoms, then the terrorists win.[64]

The American Civil Liberties Union (ACLU) and the conservative Eagle Forum are saying the same thing.[65] William Safire and the editors of *The Nation* are holding up the same flag. There, too, is the National Rifle Association. We are all there. This is right. It is just.

This is exactly what worries me. When it comes to real questions with real stakes, all these strange bedfellows do not agree in the least. They are often bitter adversaries. "Bipartisanship" and "consensus" are tactics of *antipolitics*. Agreement is not the foundation of politics, but something that appears when there is no longer an issue and politics has lost its reason. This consensus is an evasion of politics. It is not even a gathering around the questions as posed—*what does liberty mean? how shall we balance it with security?*

Shared in this consensus, rather, is exactly the conception of politics that my argument in the first part of this essay was meant to bring into question. A politics centered by civil rights is a politics of the State. Right now, there is indisputable good sense in this conception: The Constitution grants rights not only to protect individuals but to create a public sphere in which those who claim their rights may be judged and their claims redeemed by their fellow citizens.

However, the failure, the unraveling thread of this way of thinking is this: The exercise of a right does not create it. In logic and in history, something else comes before. That something is *power*, the burden from which we are relieved by our rights. The progenitor of that power is politics.

Each right is part of a whole political culture. That is what makes it operative. A right is a momentary defense within the construction of problems which arise and are settled in the long course of time. A right *identifies* the person to whom it applies and marks him as an "object" for judgment.[66] By contrast, politics is relational; it concerns the ongoing negotiations and adjustments between plural persons. Rights are forms for the investment of meaning; politics is a way of structuring a space of relationship.[67]

While politics has features which are negative (it is not-violence) and positive (it deploys speech in three-way relationships to alter the social space of plurality and dependence), rights are wholly negative or defensive. When right is mistaken for politics, the positive function of the latter all too easily becomes an attribute of the former. A right becomes an entitlement. Entitlements are positive benefits rather than protections. That is, they are applications of power rather than protections from it. Entitlements are gained without the action or the responsibility of either the one who grants them or the one who receives them.[68] Political questions cannot long be settled in this fashion because (to paraphrase Benjamin Franklin) unchecked powers will always increase until they end in despotism.

This is a reigning confusion in America. Since World War II, recourse to rights has increasingly become a reflex of Americans. More and more of our political life is conducted through the instrument of rights. With every satisfied claim to a right, another dozen appear on the horizon; there seems to be an inexorable logic of expansion. Yet, from what power do these new rights protect us? How is this power constituted? Is this growth the flip-side of the contemporaneous release of executive power from its traditional balancing constraints? Has the systematic defense against despotism shifted away from a counterbalance between branches of government? Can we really expect *individual citizens* to counterbalance the power of the State when, paradoxically, all that protects them *is that State?* Is this power producing, and in turn fed by, everyday uses of rights claims by citizens against one another?[69]

This upward spiraling circle of an executive assertion of power and a citizen claim of right may help to explain an otherwise surprising phenomenon: the coincidence of the "rights revolution" with an increase in "antipolitics." Indeed, there is a sense in which the turn to rights as a solution to all the problems of civil society should be counted as a rejection of politics, a hiding behind the limited and misleading identification of politics with the State.[70]

Above, I distinguished between two conceptions of politics. *This difference is itself important for politics.* The predominant view centers on the relationship between the citizen and the State. The other concerns the everyday fact of living together which comprises a wide range of experiences citizens have with other citizens. Rights *seem like they fit into the second, but in fact they are part of the first.* This is because rights do not exist without the State: the State *is* both the power against which rights are held and the guarantor of those rights . . . against itself. In the United States, part of this paradox is resolved by the institutionalized separation of powers or functions within the State. Judges, for example, can block or reverse police actions; presidents can be impeached. Nothing, however, guarantees that the balance will hold. The resistance to tyranny can only come from politics. Those who benefit from de-politicizing conflicts, and thus work in favor of it, are aided by many of our most cherished beliefs, which include, as we have seen, the misleading idea that our problem after September 11 is how to trade liberty for security, or vice versa.

Do not get me wrong. The debate over police and judicial powers is profoundly important. But not because justice and rights come first. Rather, resistance to these new powers is important because actions taken by the executive branch since September 11 *tend to subvert the very possibility of politics.* Every time fundamental rights are attacked, the future of politics grows dimmer.

Yet, this is the conundrum: We may be in a situation where what we *inescapably have to do,* which is to preserve Constitutional protections, is itself part of a long-run problem. The logic is something like this: The attack comes, and the crisis is *now;* reason and fear tell us to forget the long-run and fight today's fight; obstacles must be removed, and this takes power; rights are themselves such obstacles, so they are set aside "for now" in favor of quick and decisive executive power; liberty-loving people object to this, but can only do so by exaggerating their defense of basic rights; even those who were perhaps fruitfully engaged in the politics of civil society have their political energies shifted back to the State-centered paradigm; but (as I have argued above) this shift is a kind of *antipolitics;* thus, under conditions of crisis an intention to protect democracy diminishes politics; democracy without politics is impossible.

In politics between citizens, what is it that counts more than rights and the State? What is it, in practice, that may be endangered by an exaggerated emphasis on rights? Everything that forms the citizen; everything that creates in us dispositions to speech over violence or capacities for speaking; everything that facilitates the act of publicizing and the deliberation and negotiation which follow from it; everything that preserves the *living* plurality of our company; everything that promotes recognition of our dependence on each other and prompts responsibility-taking, or forgiveness, for our inevitable transgressions of it. In sum, the long-run of politics resides in the character and art of the democratic citizen, in our everyday capabilities to create and to maintain the kind of political space which makes dialogue and negotiation, and thus simply living together everyday, a possibility.

And still, events, *and reactions to events,* continue to press us back to the short-run. It was inevitable that words would fail. A violent reaction—bestial or god-like, depending on where you stand—had to come on the heels of the terrorists' explosive act. Their violence arrested our words. It damaged the organ of our common sense—language. It snapped us into the present, locked us out from the storehouse of experience, the archive of history—language. Utterly entangled in life, language is not just for today, but for tomorrow as well. Thus, as the terrorist saps our words he attacks the future. The terrorist would reduce our dispositions in favor of speech and our capacities for it. He would corral us into a speechless unanimity. But in unanimity there is no future.

17. THE THREAT TO PATRIOTISM

RONALD DWORKIN

1.

What has Al Qaeda done to our Constitution, and to our national standards of fairness and decency? Since September 11, the government has enacted legislation, adopted policies, and threatened procedures that are not consistent with our established laws and values and would have been unthinkable before.[1]

On October 25, 2001, Congress passed the "USA PATRIOT Act" with only one dissenting vote in the Senate and 66 in the House. That statute sets out a new, breathtakingly vague and broad definition of terrorism and of aiding terrorists: Someone may be guilty of aiding terrorism, for example, if he collects money for or even contributes to a charity which supports the general aims of any organization abroad—the IRA, for example, or foreign antiabortion groups, or, in the days of apartheid, the African National Congress—that uses violence among other means in an effort to oppose American policy or interests. If the attorney general declares that he has "reasonable grounds" for suspecting any alien of terrorism or aiding terrorism in the broad sense that is defined, then he may detain that alien for seven days with no charge. If the alien is then charged with any, even a wholly unrelated, crime, and the attorney general finds that "the release of the alien will threaten the national security of the United States or the safety of the community or any person," he may be detained for six months, and then for additional six-month periods so long as the attorney general continues to declare that his release would threaten national security or anyone's safety.[2]

The Justice Department has now detained several hundred aliens, some of them in solitary confinement for 23 hours a day. None of them has been convicted of anything at all, and many of them have been charged with only minor immigration offenses that would not by themselves remotely justify detention.[3] It has refused repeated efforts on the part of journalists, the ACLU, and other groups even to identify these detainees.[4] So our country now jails large numbers of people, secretly, not for what they have done, nor even with case-by-case evidence that it would be dangerous to leave them at liberty, but only because they fall within a vaguely defined class, of which some members might pose danger.

The USA Patriot Act relaxes many of the other rules that protect people sus-pected of crime from unfair investigation and prosecution. It greatly expands the government's power to conduct searches of the premises and property of citizens and aliens alike without informing them. Such secret searches were formerly per-mitted, pursuant to a special warrant for that purpose, only if the primary pur-pose of the search was to collect information about a foreign nation's activities in this country. Now they are permitted if the primary purpose is to collect evidence of a crime that can be used in a prosecution, so long as intelligence-gathering is a subsidiary purpose, as it can always be said to be when a suspected terrorist's property is searched. So no one may now be confident that his premises have not been searched by the government without his knowledge.[5]

The Justice Department has also, without any congressional approval at all, unilaterally altered other important safeguards against injustice, including, for instance, the right of someone suspected or accused of a crime to consult in pri-vate a lawyer of his own choosing. On October 31, the department announced that it had the authority to "monitor" conversations between detainees and the lawyers they consulted to plan their defense whenever, according to the attorney general, "there is a substantial risk" that such conversations could facilitate ter-rorism by passing on information or instructions.

The order does provide that the detainee and lawyer must be advised that their conversation will be overheard (except when a judge permits secret moni-toring) and that the monitoring must be conducted by a special team from within the Justice Department whose members are directed not to divulge to those actually prosecuting the detainee any part of the conversation that would be covered by the traditional lawyer–client privilege. But monitoring, even with these qualifications, seriously undermines people's constitutionally guaranteed right to counsel of their choice when they are accused of a crime: Only the most trusting prisoner will be willing to discuss defense strategy candidly with his law-yer if he knows that agents from the organization that is trying to convict him are listening.

On November 13, in the most dramatic declaration so far, President Bush an-nounced that any non–U.S. citizen that he declared a suspected terrorist—aliens resident in the United States for many years as well as soldiers captured in com-bat in Afghanistan—might be tried, at his sole discretion, by a military tribunal rather than in an ordinary criminal court. Such tribunals might be secret, and would be governed by special rules laid down by the secretary of defense, includ-ing provisions for the "qualifications" and "conduct" of lawyers representing the accused; the ordinary rules of evidence would not apply; the tribunal might de-clare a defendant's guilt even though not satisfied of his guilt beyond a reasonable doubt; its verdict, including any death penalties it might order, could be taken by a two-thirds vote of its members; and that verdict might be reviewed only by the President, or the secretary of defense if the President so designates. This is the kind of "trial" we associate with the most lawless of totalitarian dictatorships. If any American were tried by a foreign government in that way, even for a minor offense, let alone a capital crime, we would denounce that government as itself criminal.

Bush's military tribunal plan, as originally announced, provoked more criticism than any other part of the government's new hard-line criminal justice rules, not only from liberal commentators and organizations, including the *New York Times,* but also from some conservatives, such as the columnist William Safire and Republican Representative Bob Barr of Georgia. Our ordinary federal courts, they said, have shown themselves fully capable of trying terrorists in the past, and could do so again. Trying aliens in secret military tribunals would outrage public opinion in the Muslim world and undermine our claims that we were seeking justice, not intimidation or revenge. Moreover, foreign democracies would be much less likely to extradite suspected terrorists to this country, or even to share information that might be used in prosecuting terrorists, if they considered our methods of trying them unfair or unsafe. (Indeed, as Aryeh Neier wrote recently in the *New York Review of Books,* Baltazar Garzón, a prominent Spanish judge, has said that the European Convention on Human Rights, which almost all European nations have joined, would prohibit extraditing any suspects to a nation that used such tribunals as criminal courts.[6])

On December 28, the *New York Times* reported that in response to these criticisms the government is considering revisions to the military tribunal scheme that would provide for a presumption of innocence; impose a beyond-reasonable-doubt standard for conviction; guarantee the right to counsel of one's choice; require a unanimous decision imposing the death penalty; and provide for some form of appellate review.[7] No such revisions have yet been announced, but it is significant that the Justice Department has decided to try Zacarias Moussaoui, probably the most important prisoner it has detained so far, in an ordinary federal court in Alexandria, Virginia, rather than in a special tribunal. (Moussaoui was arrested last August after suspicious behavior in a flight school, where he wanted instruction in flying but not in taking off or landing. It is widely suspected that Moussaoui would have been among the hijackers on September 11 if he had not been arrested earlier.)

Still, the government apparently intends to use special tribunals of some sort to try, for as yet undesignated offenses, a large group of people captured in Afghanistan and flown to a detention center at the American military base on

Guantánamo Bay in Cuba, where prisoners are kept in small, low cages whose chain-link walls expose them to the weather, and are provided with an inch-thick mat and a bucket for a toilet. According to press reports, the prisoners so far transported to Cuba wore blacked-out goggles during the long trip, and their beards, which many of them regard as required by their religion, were shaved (allegedly to protect against lice). The prisoners presumably include Afghan soldiers fighting under the direction of the Taliban, which was the effective government of their country, and they would seem plainly entitled, as prisoners of war, to the provisions of the Geneva Conventions, one of which states that if there is doubt whether or not a person is entitled to be treated as a prisoner of war, the issue must be decided by a competent tribunal. Though Bush initially declared that the detainees were not deserving of the protections of the Geneva Conventions, and Attorney General John Ashcroft and Secretary of Defense Donald Rumsfeld agreed, Secretary of State Powell asked the President to reconsider that decision, among other reasons, in order to protect American soldiers taken captive in the future. Bush has now agreed to reconsider it. But he also prejudged the decision of any tribunals that might be organized: He said that the detainees were all "killers" who would not be granted the status of prisoners of war. His statement does not encourage hope that the decisions of the tribunals would be independent and fair.[8]

The government's dubious laws, practices, and proposals have provoked surprisingly little protest in America. Even some groups that traditionally champion civil rights have, with surprisingly few reservations, supported the government's hard line.[9] Polls suggest that nearly 60 percent of the public approves even the use of military tribunals.[10] We should not be surprised at any of this. September 11 was horrifying: It proved that our enemies are vicious, powerful, and imaginative, and that they have well-trained and suicidal fanatics at their disposal. People's respect for human and civil rights is very often fragile when they are frightened, and Americans are very frightened. The country has done even worse by those rights in the past, moreover. It suspended the most basic civil rights in the Civil War, punished people for criticizing the military draft in World War I, interned Japanese-American citizens in detention camps in World War II, and after that war encouraged a Red Scare that destroyed the lives of many of its citizens because their political opinions were unpopular. Much of this was unconstitutional, but the Supreme Court tolerated almost all of it.

We are ashamed now of what we did then: we count the Court's past tolerance of antisedition laws, internments, and McCarthyism as among the worst stains on its record. That shame comes easier now, of course, because we no longer fear the Kaiser, or kamikazes, or Stalin. It may be a long time before we stop fearing international or domestic terrorism, however, and we must therefore be particularly careful now. What we lose now, in our commitment to civil rights and fair play, may be much harder later to regain.

True, it is politically difficult for elected officials to criticize or oppose hugely popular government policies. John Ashcroft has already told us that those who oppose his policies are giving aid and comfort to the terrorists. But this intimidation makes it all the more important to scrutinize the arguments that have been put forward to justify such a major retreat from our traditional concern for fair play and for the rights of anyone accused of serious crime.

2.

Some of the arguments are transparently weak. It is often said, for example, that terrorists do not deserve the traditional protections we afford other suspects, because terrorists do not respect freedom themselves. Defending his military tribunal scheme before a group of applauding prosecutors, President Bush declared that "non-U.S. citizens who plan and/or commit mass murder are more than criminal suspects. They are unlawful combatants who seek to destroy our country and our way of life."[11] Professor Laurence Tribe of Harvard Law School said something remarkably similar. Though he opposed the military tribunal plan as originally conceived, he did not oppose a revised and improved version of the plan, noting that American soldiers accused of crime are subject to courts-martial, not ordinary criminal trials. "Why should members of Al Qaeda and those who aid them enjoy a constitutional right to a theoretically purer form of justice than our own soldiers?" he asked.[12]

But the President's order calls for a military trial when he determines only that "there is reason to believe" that someone is a member of Al Qaeda, or has engaged in or conspired to commit acts of international terrorism, or has harbored or aided such people. Almost the entire point of any criminal trial—civilian or military—is to decide whether those who are accused of crimes are actually guilty of them, and it is particularly worrying that the President, who would have the right to review verdicts and final decisions under the military tribunal arrangements he proposed, claims that his suspicion is tantamount to guilt. In view of the numbers involved, there is an evident danger that some innocent people who would have been acquitted under the stricter rules of an ordinary American criminal trial will in fact be convicted and punished, perhaps with death, in military trials. It seems even more likely that many of the hundreds of aliens now being detained month after month, in secret and on trivial charges, are not terrorists, do not aid terrorists, and would pose no danger to the community if they were released. Of any proposed set of procedures, we must ask not whether the guilty deserve more protection than those procedures afford, but whether the innocent do.

A second argument insists that the administration's new measures are justified because they mainly target aliens, and aliens have either no rights under our constitutional system or, at least, fewer rights than citizens do. The Fifth Amendment's Due Process Clause declares, however, that no *person's* life or liberty may be taken without due process of law, and the Supreme Court has several times held that aliens within the United States are in principle entitled to the same due process as citizens. Foreigners seeking to emigrate to the United States, it is true, have no rights to any form of hearing or other process in considering their applications. But, as Justice Breyer said in *Zadvydas* v. *Davis*,[13] an important case the Court decided last June, "once an alien enters the country, the legal circumstance changes, for the Due Process Clause applies to all 'persons' within the United States, including aliens, whether their presence here is lawful, unlawful, temporary, or permanent."

In the *Zadvydas* case, the Court held, by a five to four majority, that it would violate the Due Process Clause for Congress to permit the Immigration and Naturalization Service indefinitely to detain immigrants who had been ordered deported but whom no other country would admit. Presciently, Breyer added that the Court was not considering "terrorism or other special circumstances where special arguments might be made for forms of preventive detention and for heightened deference to the judgments of the political branches with respect to matters of national security." But he presumably meant no more than what he said: that the Court was not deciding, either way, whether aliens who had been ordered deported, but no other country was willing to accept, could be detained indefinitely when the government alleged this to be necessary for national security.

Certainly nothing in his statement, or in any other Supreme Court decision, holds that lawfully resident aliens may be tried for crimes allegedly committed in this country in special military tribunals without the normal rules of evidence, or that they may be denied the benefit of private conversations with a lawyer, or that they may have their homes searched without their knowledge when the search is a fishing expedition to discover evidence that may be used in charging them with some crime or other.

Proponents of trying aliens in special military tribunals cite as a precedent the so-called "Saboteurs Case"—*Ex Parte Quirin*—which the Supreme Court decided on July 31, 1942.[14] In that case, eight German soldiers, all of whom had lived for substantial periods in America and returned to Germany before the war, landed from submarines on the Long Island and Florida coasts with explosives and instructions to "demoralize" this country by blowing up munitions factories and civilian crowds. Though the FBI claimed credit for intercepting them, and President Roosevelt gave J. Edgar Hoover a medal for his vigilance, the saboteurs were in fact discovered only when one of them, who had landed with the intention of divulging the plot, reported it to the police.

Roosevelt insisted that the Germans be tried in a secret military tribunal; in retrospect, at least, it seems plain that secrecy served only to protect the FBI's false account and thus assure the nation that its borders were secure. Lawyers appointed to represent the Germans appealed the order to try them before a military tribunal. The Supreme Court heard arguments and decided the case in great haste: The Justices ruled that it was not improper to try the defendants in military tribunals, but they did so without any justifying opinion, which they promised to supply later. The saboteurs were quickly tried in secret, and six of them were executed on August 8, 1942. (Roosevelt commuted two of the sentences, including that of the German who revealed the plot.)

The defendants argued to the Supreme Court that they were entitled to the Constitution's guarantees of due process and trial by jury, and so should have been tried in ordinary courts, not by special military tribunals. When the Court finally published its opinion, more than two months after the executions, it replied, unanimously, that the constitutional guarantees were not intended to supplant the nation's laws of war, which before the Constitution was adopted permitted military tribunals to try enemy combatants accused of unlawful acts of war (the Court cited the conviction of British Major John André for spying during the Revolutionary War).

The government should be embarrassed to appeal to the *Quirin* decision as justification for its treatment of aliens now, because that decision, like the Court's 1944 decision permitting the detention of Japanese-Americans,[15] is widely regarded as overly deferential to the executive and, in a crucial part, wrong. (Justice Frankfurter, in a bizarre and embarrassing memorandum to his fellow justices, had pleaded with them to ignore legal niceties and do what Roosevelt asked as part of the war effort.[16]) The case is a useful reminder of how shortsighted and, in the long run, self-defeating the appeal to judges to show unity with the executive often is.

In any case, the military trials condoned in the *Quirin* case can be distinguished from those that President Bush's order contemplates. Chief Justice Stone's opinion for the Court in the 1942 case emphasized that Congress had declared war on Germany, which was therefore an enemy power, that the defendants did not deny that they were acting on behalf of that enemy power, and that they were therefore unlawful combatants. Congress has not declared war on Afghanistan or the Taliban or even Al Qaeda, and the President's order is therefore a decision of the executive branch acting alone, rather than with legislative concurrence.[17] Even if Congress had authorized the order in some way, the Court's *Quirin* decision, which assumed that the defendants were acting on behalf of an enemy nation, would not automatically apply to the much broader class of suspects the President has designated.

It is true that the line between a conventional enemy power and an international terrorist group is fuzzy, and that the old rules of war need to be revised. Perhaps our law should treat some aliens who cross our boundaries planning terrorism as if they were soldiers committing unlawful acts of war on behalf of an organized enemy. But we could not plausibly treat everyone to whom the President's order applies in that way. Basque separatists, IRA splinter groups, Colombian drug lords, and foreign Mafia chieftains no doubt act in ways harmful to American interests and may be subject to arrest. But we would not be justified in labeling them as unlawful combatants in a war and then shooting them as spies because they were not wearing uniforms.

The most powerful argument in favor of the administration's new measures, however, is very different, and it has undoubted force. What any nation can afford to provide, by way of protection for accused criminals, must at least partly depend on the consequences such protections would have for its own security. The terrorist threat to our security is very great, and perhaps unprecedented, and we cannot be as scrupulous in our concern for the rights of suspected terrorists as we are for the rights of people suspected of less dangerous crimes. As Justice Jackson put it in a now-often-quoted remark, we cannot allow our Constitution and our shared sense of decency to become a suicide pact. Professor Tribe put the point this way: It may be right, in more normal times, to allow a hundred guilty defendants to go free rather than convict one innocent one, but we must reconsider that arithmetic when one of the guilty may blow up the rest of Manhattan.[18]

We must, however, take care to distinguish two conclusions that might be thought to follow from these arguments. We might think, first, that the requirements of fairness are fully satisfied, in the case of suspected terrorists, by laxer standards of criminal justice which run an increased risk of convicting innocent people. Or we might think something very different: that even though laxer standards would be unfair, we must nevertheless adopt them to protect ourselves from disaster. If we accepted the first conclusion, we would think ourselves justified in setting lower standards of protection for anyone suspected of terrorism, and we would see no reason to attempt to mitigate the heightened risk for innocent suspects by adopting substitute protections. If we accept only the second conclusion, however, and concede that we are treating some people unfairly, we should demand a much more discriminating approach. We should insist that government show that unfair treatment is necessary, not for some widely defined category of persons, but, so far as this is practicable, for individual suspects or detainees, one by one. We should also try to mitigate the unfairness in every practicable way when we deem that unfairness necessary. When we treat individual people unfairly for our own safety, we owe them as much individual consideration and accommodation as is consistent with that safety.

Much of the rhetoric defending the administration's new measures seems aimed at justifying lower standards for all suspected terrorists as being fair. We are told that fairness to criminal suspects requires only that we strike an appropriate trade-off or balance between two values—freedom and security—each of which, unfortunately, can sometimes be served only at the cost of the other. Because terrorism is a horrific threat to security, we are, it is said, justified in striking the balance differently for that crime; and it is therefore not unfair to subject suspected terrorists to a higher risk of unjust conviction.

The scope of the new policies seems to assume that conclusion. They presuppose that the undoubted dangers of international terrorism permit a degraded standard of protection for anyone who might be thought connected to terrorism—a standard that allows mass preventive detention, general invasions of the right to counsel, indifference toward privacy, and contempt for the Geneva Conventions. Even the administration's few critics seem to accept the idea that fairness is a matter of balancing risk and rights. Senator Russ Feingold of Wisconsin, the single senator who voted against the USA Patriot Act, conceded the need for a new balance between security and freedom in the face of the terrorist danger. He claimed only that that act got the new balance wrong.

In fact, however, the familiar metaphors of "trade-off" and "balance" are deeply misleading, because they suggest a false description of the decision that the nation must make. They suggest that "we"—Americans in general—must decide what mixture of security and personal freedom we want for ourselves, in much the same way as we decide how elaborate a network of intercity roads we want once we know how much such roads cost and what their impact on the countryside might be. If that really were our choice, it would be an easy one to make. None of the administration's decisions and proposals will affect more than a tiny number of American citizens: almost none of us will be indefinitely detained for minor violations or offenses, or have our houses searched without our knowledge, or find ourselves brought before military tribunals on grave charges carrying the death penalty. Most of us pay almost nothing in personal freedom when such measures are used against those the President suspects of terrorism.

The issues we actually face are very different, however, and the balancing metaphor obscures those issues. We must decide not where our interest lies on balance, but what justice requires, even at the expense of our interests, out of fairness to other people—those resident and foreign aliens who might very well be ensnared in the less protective and more dangerous legal system the administration is constructing for them. We cannot answer that question by simply comparing the costs and benefits to any person or group.

Nor can we answer it, as the balancing metaphor also suggests we can, by composing a sliding scale that shows how individual rights we grant accused criminals are diminished in proportion to the danger the crime of which they are accused poses to our security. It is true that the rights we have traditionally recognized impair our security to some degree. We might well be a safer society if we allowed our police to lock up people they thought likely to commit crimes in the future, or to presume guilt rather than innocence, or to monitor conversations between an accused and his lawyer. But our criminal justice system has not evolved through calculations of precisely how much risk we are willing to run in order to give any particular class of accused criminals a certain degree of protection against unjust conviction: we do not give accused murderers, for example, less protection than accused embezzlers or jaywalkers.

The traditional rights of an accused have developed piecemeal over time, and can only be explained historically, at least in detail. They have roots in the English common law and were shaped and developed, step by step, in discrete expansions, modifications, and contractions, largely in decisions of the Supreme Court interpreting the abstract language of the Constitution, such as the requirement of "due process" of law. Some of the most important of the rights now enforced were recognized only within the last 50 years. Much of what we take to be indispensable—jury trials and the complete separation of judicial from prosecutorial functions, for example—are not features of the criminal system of other democracies whose fairness is not in doubt; they have other features our system lacks, however—conspicuously, a ban on death as a punishment—so that the fairness of two systems can only be compared as a whole, and inexactly.

Nevertheless, the rights that we have evolved in that way are those that we now, as a nation, deem the minimum that we owe to anyone who is accused of a serious crime and pursued and tried within our system of criminal justice. Fairness requires, as a matter of equal concern for anyone who might be innocent, that we extend those rights to everyone brought into that system.[19] Whenever we deny to one class of suspects rights that we treat as essential for others, we act unfairly, particularly when that class is politically vulnerable, as of course aliens are, or is identifiable racially or by religious or ethnic distinction. It makes no sense to say that people accused of more serious crimes are entitled to less protection for that reason. If they are innocent, the injustice of convicting and punishing them is at least as great as the injustice in convicting some other innocent person for a less serious crime. So we must reject the balancing argument—it is confused and false. If we believe that in our present circumstances we must subject some people to special risks of grave injustice, then we must have the candor to admit that what we do to them is unjust.

Do we really face such extreme danger from terrorism that we must act unjustly? That is a difficult question. We cannot yet accurately gauge the actual power of the linked groups of terrorist organizations and cells that apparently aim to kill as many Americans as possible. Indeed we scarcely know the identities and locations of many of these groups. The September attack was made more feasible by our own failures, and we could do much to correct those failures without sacrificing traditional rights. The FBI and other agencies failed to notice or investigate important warning signals, and there were unpardonable defects in airport security that we have apparently still not repaired, for the shameful reason that employing competent airport security personnel is expensive. It is unclear, moreover, how far the administration's various new measures, including military trials, would actually help to prevent future attacks.

But Al Qaeda killed, by latest reckoning, approximately 3,000 people in minutes on September 11, which is a quarter of the number of murders in the entire country in 1999. If they or some other terrorist organization has or gains access to nuclear, chemical, or biological weapons and the means to use them, then the threat to us would be truly enormous. It would justify unusual and, in themselves, unfair measures if the government thought that these would substantially reduce the risk of catastrophe. Even then, however, it would be imperative to permit only the smallest curtailment of traditional rights that could reasonably be thought necessary, and to attempt to mitigate the unfairness of these measures so far as safety allows. In several respects, the administration's new criminal justice policies fail that test.

First, as I have emphasized, the new policies define those who may be treated unfairly very broadly, instead of insisting on a more discriminating test of the actual danger a suspect poses. Ali al-Maqtari, for example, a Muslim visitor, was arrested on September 15, and jailed under harsh conditions for eight weeks. Apparently he was arrested because his wife wore an Arab headdress, because he and his wife spoke a foreign language to each other—French—and because they had box-cutters with them, which he used in his job in a market and she in the shipping room of a nursery.[20]

Second, the new measures provide that in each case the determination that some special danger requires bypassing traditional rights, and running a higher risk of injustice, is to be made by the executive branch alone—by the President, or by the attorney general or some other official who is subject to the President's direction. True, detainees can challenge certain of these rulings in court, through the limited form of habeas corpus proceeding that the Patriot Act allows, for example. But detainees may be unaware of their rights, or have difficulty finding effective counsel,[21] and it would seem obviously fairer to require a further independent judicial check on those decisions: to require, for example, that no suspect be detained for extended periods without trial unless the government has convinced a judge—in a private hearing in chambers, if necessary—that security would be jeopardized by releasing him, and that no conversations between a prisoner and his lawyer be monitored unless not only the attorney general but an independent judge has been satisfied that allowing such conversations to be private would jeopardize the lives of others.[22]

Assigning judges such roles would presumably not itself threaten national security—federal judges are as responsible and loyal as any other officials—and it would make it more likely that the special powers were exercised only when genuinely necessary. It may be that judges will be excessively deferential to the government in such proceedings. But that is no reason for not giving them the power to intervene when they believe that the government's position is indefensible.

Finally, the government apparently intends to seek the death penalty in its prosecution of some of those it accuses of terrorism. But if it chooses to try them under conditions that run an increased risk of convicting the innocent—before special military tribunals in which they would have fewer rights than in ordinary criminal courts, for example—then it seems irresponsible to ask for death as a punishment, because that penalty is unnecessary for safety and magnifies the horror of an unjust conviction. We may need to incarcerate suspected terrorists to avoid great danger, but we do not need to kill them.

Our government has already gone too far, then, in displacing the constitutional and legal rights that we have evolved as our own national standard of fair play in the criminal process. Of course we are frightened of the power of suicidal terrorists to kill again, perhaps on an even more massive scale. But what our enemies mainly hope to achieve through their terror is the destruction of the values they hate and we cherish. We must protect those values as well as we can, even as we fight the terrorists. That is difficult: it requires discrimination, imagination, and candor. But it is what patriotism now demands.

18. GUARDING THE GATES

ARISTIDE R. ZOLBERG

The events of September 11 accentuated a fundamental challenge for United States immigration policy. The imperatives of globalization, which are at the center of America's external economic policies, had been prompting the United States to facilitate the entry of foreign nationals. But the attacks of September 11 provoked an abrupt reversal of course. In response to the imperatives of national security, there were immediate calls for draconian measures to police the country's territorial borders. These conflicting imperatives arise from the peculiar structure of the contemporary world system, which is characterized by steadily more important transnational economic and cultural processes, but a still largely "Westphalian" political framework—founded on territorially based sovereign states, with a putative monopoly on the use of organized violence. Whereas globalization, as well as commitment to civil liberties, fosters an expansion of the international movement of persons, extending across all social strata and poor as well as affluent countries, national security calls for the imposition of restrictive controls that impede movement.

Further complicated by the proliferation of non-state actors with a significant capacity for violence, this configuration presents the United States with a dilemma. As one experienced analyst has commented, "building a Fortress America will not work. It will be incredibly expensive, disrupt commerce, and infringe civil liberties."[1] However, as the spokesman for an anti-immigrant organization pointed out early on, "it seems clear that the 19 terrorists of September 11 were all foreign citizens and entered the United States legally, as tourists, business travelers, or students. This was also true of the perpetrators of previous terrorist acts. . . . While it is absolutely essential that we not scapegoat immigrants, especially Muslim immigrants, we also must not overlook the most obvious fact: the current terrorist threat to the United States comes almost exclusively from individuals who arrive from abroad."[2] It thus appears unavoidable that these conflicting impulses be addressed.

On the eve of the events, immigration issues had largely receded from the political arena, as the policies elaborated from the mid-1980s onward appeared quite stable. Overall, immigration is largely driven by persistent economic necessity in developing countries that are linked to the United States by way of family networks, with Mexico and China currently as the leading sources. Following the exhaustion of the refugee flow from Southeast Asia and the resolution of political crises in Central America, the United States reduced its annual quota of refugees admitted for resettlement, while concurrently deterring asylum-seekers by toughening qualification requirements. In the face of charges that ongoing policy fostered heavy welfare costs, admission requirements were raised in 1996 and legal immigrants denied federal transfer payments—a policy that shifted the burden to states and localities, and was subsequently softened at their behest. Concurrently, in the face of growing labor demand in the boom years, particularly from politically weighty sectors such as the information industry, additional admissions were provided for more skilled immigrants, as well as temporary worker programs. Overall, following three years of extraordinarily high inflows attributable to the legalization program of 1986, admissions in the 1990s stabilized to an average of about 760,000 a year. However, the immigration system also includes a substantial illegal—but in effect tolerated—segment, made up of illegal border crossers and overstayers. Supplying low-skilled, inexpensive labor to a variety of sectors from agriculture to retail, this pool doubled in size in the 1990s to reach 8.7 million in 2000—about 2.5 percent of the total U.S. population—increasingly more male and Mexican. Together, legal and illegal immigration made for an average intake of 1.2 million a year in the 1990s, an historical record with regard to both numbers and diversity.[3] As a result, the United States is once again a "nation of immigrants," with an estimated 31.1 million foreign residents as of March 2000, constituting about 11 percent of the population—an approximate doubling since 1960, when the proportion reached its lowest level since Tocqueville visited a country he characterized as "Anglo-American."[4]

Although the high levels of legal and especially illegal immigration evoked mixed reactions among the general public, as recorded in opinion polls, on the eve of the events there was little or no restrictionist fervor in Congress. Throughout the 1990s, the Clinton administration assuaged perennial demands for greater control over illegal immigration by doubling the size of the U.S. Border Patrol and building showcase walls in Texas and California, but as one shrewd assessment puts it, this was "less about achieving the stated instrumental goal of deterring illegal border crossers and more about politically recrafting the image of the border and symbolically reaffirming the state's territorial authority."[5] While Republicans traditionally favored labor immigration, notably in the form of "guest worker" programs for agriculture, they simultaneously leaned toward restrictionism on cultural grounds; however, from the very outset of his presidential campaign, George W. Bush firmly opposed the anti-Hispanic leanings that had recently cost his party dearly in California.[6] Concurrently, south of the border, "free market" candidate Vicente Fox called for a new immigration relationship with the United States, involving possibly an enlargement of the annual quota, as well as a temporary workers program of some sort. Seriously taken up by Washington, Fox's proposals prompted the formation of a binational planning team and were brought to public attention in the course of his state visit just days before the attack, evoking a warm response from his American counterpart.

Lying in wait for opportunities, anti-immigration advocates quickly turned the 9/11 attack into a demonstration of the soundness of their cause. The spokesman cited earlier concluded by pointing out to the Senate, "Thus, our immigration policy, including temporary and permanent visas issuance, border control, and efforts to deal with illegal immigration are all critical to reducing the chance of an attack in the future." In a more extreme vein, Patrick Buchanan urged an immediate moratorium on all immigration, an expansion of the Border Patrol to a force of 20,000, a radical reduction of visas issued to nationals of states that harbor terrorists, and the expedited deportation of "the eight-to-11 million illegal aliens, beginning with those from rogue nations." Moreover, "President Bush's amnesty proposal"—a provocatively selective reference to the ongoing negotiations between the United States and Mexico—"should be quietly interred."[7] The tragedy undoubtedly helped propel Buchanan's latest dose of vitriol, *The Death of the West*, which purports to demonstrate "How dying populations and immigrant invasions imperil our country and civilization," onto the *New York Times* best-seller list in early 2002.[8]

Overall, however, reactions were more mixed. In the absence of a timely survey of public opinion focused on the subject, it is obviously impossible to ascertain how the events affected general American attitudes toward immigration and immigrants. On an impressionistic level, in the immediate aftermath there was a spate of scattered aggressions against people who were seen as resembling the terrorists or believed to sympathize with them, occasionally with tragic consequences; but there were also reports of Americans going out of their way to reassure their immigrant neighbors and acquaintances, with no way of assessing the balance between the two kinds of incidents.

In contrast with previous surges of securitarian nationalism provoked by international conflicts, most notoriously in the wake of Pearl Harbor, when the U.S. government treated all ethnic Japanese as suspects, including American citizens, governmental responses were restrained. Not only were there no wholesale denunciations of particular groups, but instead, the President pointedly visited a mosque and the mayor of New York explicitly admonished the city's residents not to seek revenge on Arabs or Muslims. Again in contrast with the past, while the events stimulated considerable talk of the need to modify American immigration policy, in practice the proposed changes were almost entirely circumscribed to matters of "border control," and there were no widespread calls to reduce immigration. Senator Edward M. Kennedy, chairman of the Senate Judiciary Committee's Subcommittee on Immigration, insisted that "Immigrants are not the problem, terrorists are the problem," and President Bush declared in the same vein, "We welcome legal immigrants but we don't welcome people who come to hurt Americans."[9]

However, the President then went on to announce immediate measures to enhance security by tightening admission procedures as well as to search for the enemy within, which led to the targeting of Muslims and Middle Easterners for interrogation and, in many cases, their incarceration and subsequent deportation. Moreover, the administration asked for a much-enlarged arsenal of legal weapons to fight terrorism, which included an array of measures targeting the alien population as well as a comprehensive system of border control. As will be seen, despite some demurrers from civil liberty organizations, the administration's proposals evoked broad bipartisan support and it speedily obtained most of what it sought.

The following week, the President named a Foreign Terrorist Tracking Task Force to recommend specific changes in laws and admission procedures, including those covering student visas, in order to deter would-be terrorists from entering. Concurrently, bipartisan proposals got under way in Congress to give the State Department and the Immigration and Naturalization Service (INS) electronic access to FBI and CIA "lookout lists" of potential criminals and terrorists, as well as to establish sophisticated identification technology at all ports of entry. This would, in turn, require tightening identification requirements for visa applicants by subjecting them to biometrics such as fingerprints. There was also considerable talk of creating a centralized system for keeping track of the whereabouts and activities of alien residents and visitors, including students. Perennially criticized by both the anti- and pro-immigration camps for its mismanagement of the border, the INS came under acute fire and appeared to be not much longer for this world.

The heightened prominence of "border control" in American policy discourse highlights the fact that immigration, properly speaking, constitutes a subcategory of a more comprehensive and much vaster phenomenon, the movement of people across international borders. Yet while the study of international *migration* is a well-established field within the social sciences, international *movement* has evoked little analytic interest. The distinction is not merely a matter of legal regulation but reflects tangible social realities involving duration of the stay in the foreign country and the activities carried out during that period. It is reflected in census enumerations, which do not count visitors as "residents," and consequently in demographic analyses, which do not consider them as "population." Whereas all international migrants start out as border crossers, most border crossers do not become migrants but remain visitors. The events of 9/11 provide a case in point: not a single one of the known hijackers, nor any of the other suspects subsequently identified, qualified as an "immigrant," in the sense of someone who was legally admitted to the United States for permanent settlement or had lived there illegally for an extended period. As it happens, they had all entered the country legally as duly authorized visitors, although some subsequently overstayed the allowed period and hence had become "illegal aliens" by the time they committed their crimes.

Border control has long been recognized, in theory as well as in practice, as a vital operational feature of the Westphalian state system. As Emerich de Vattel reasoned in his foundational mid–eighteenth century treatise of international law, control of the entry of foreigners into the realm is a sine qua non of sovereignty since, in its absence, hostile armies could just walk in. In the intervening centuries, the vast expansion of travel and the proliferation of regulations pertaining to movement gave rise to elaborate institutions involving physical barriers and designated administrative checkpoints, coupled with standardized official documents identifying the nationality—more precisely expressed by the German version of the term, "state belongingness"—of the border crossers.[10] Successive revolutions in transportation, which radically lowered the cost of travel and rendered it accessible worldwide, together with the rise of international tensions at the turn of the twentieth century, rendered *refoulement* at the border increasingly inconvenient and risky. Thus was prompted the institutionalization of "remote control," i.e. the requirement of obtaining permission to enter before embarking on the journey, by way of a visa entered in the passport by an official of the state of destination.[11] The generalization of what amounts to a projection of national borders into the world at large was vastly facilitated by the advent of air travel and has become a routine procedure in international airports worldwide. Harnessed to its implementation, transportation companies function, in effect, as ancillary border police.

A vast increase in international migration in the final decades of the twentieth century, attributable to generic world inequality, enhanced accessibility of long-distance transportation, the proliferation of human transnational networks, as well as to a loosening of controls on exit in the ex-colonial and ex-communist worlds, precipitated widespread calls throughout the world of affluent societies for the modernization and tightening of traditional border controls. In response, the United States enacted the Illegal Immigration Reform and Immigrant Responsibility Act of 1996 (IIRIRA), which mandates the elaboration by the federal government of an "Integrated Entry and Exit Data System." From this perspective, it is evident that the 9/11 attack merely had the effect of raising the priority of border control somewhat higher on the policymakers' agenda.

Under contemporary conditions, border control entails a staggering task. In a given year, the INS inspects some 450 million persons entering by land and another 100 million entering by air or by sea, amounting altogether to approximately twice the entire population of the United States.[12] Leaving aside returning U.S. citizens and foreign daily commuters with multi-entry passes—for example, Canadian nurses in Detroit-area hospitals and Mexican factory hands in El Paso—the number of foreign entrants is in the neighborhood of 60 million. In 2001, the United States issued seven million new visas to foreign nationals, of which some 800,000 were awarded to immigrants proper, about 600,000 to students, and most of the remainder to tourists or business visitors. About half of all documented entries consist of visitors covered by the Visa Waiver Program, currently including 29 countries—among them all of Western Europe and Canada—whose nationals are considered unlikely to overstay or to engage in criminal activity.

These considerations help place the security challenge in perspective. Overall, approximately one of every 500,000 visas awarded in the two-year period preceding 9/11 went to a hijacker or one of their suspected associates. More precisely, some 120,000 visas were issued to Saudi nationals, of which 15 went to future hijackers—approximately one per 8,000, or .01 percent. The one suspect in detention in the U.S. on charges related to the 9/11 affair is a Morocco-born individual who had acquired French nationality, and hence was admitted without a visa, making for an infinitesimal ratio of dangerous individuals among the millions of entrants who were visa-exempt.

The difficulty of redesigning border control to provide greater security is exacerbated by the division of the task between two disparate segments of the American state, leading to protracted turf wars. Since visas must be awarded abroad, the function naturally devolves to the Department of State, which elaborated a bureaucracy for that purpose in the 1920s. However, control of entry at the border proper falls within the sphere of domestic policing, conducted by the INS. Consular officers who issue visas have very limited information about applicants, other than what the latter provide. Although in recent years the consulates gained access to an INS database of 5.7 million individuals with past immigration problems, this does not cover first-time applicants. The FBI has refused to open its own database to the INS or to the Department of State; but even if this were to change, it would prove of little assistance in detecting foreign terrorists, since they are unlikely to have accumulated criminal records in the United States. Moreover, neither of the agencies that regulate admissions has access to data from intelligence agencies that monitor threats emanating from the outside world.

The first legislative measure explicitly designed to offset the vulnerability exposed by the attack was the "Uniting and Strengthening America by Providing Appropriate Tools Required to Intercept and Obstruct Terrorism Act of 2001," an unwieldy title elaborated to produce the bombastic acronym, USA PATRIOT Act. Signed by President Bush on October 26, it was initiated by Attorney General John Ashcroft one week after the attack in the form of a "Mobilization Against Terrorism Act" (MATA), which allowed for the deportation, without a hearing or presentation of evidence, of any alien whom the Attorney General had "reason to believe" would "commit, further, or facilitate" acts of terrorism.[13] While the proposal was being circulated, Ashcroft established interim regulations that mandated detention for any alien certified as a terrorist, even if the individual were granted relief from deportation. The Lawyers' Committee for Human Rights warned that this would constitute a major change in immigration law. Although both Democratic and Republican congressional leaders generally supported the proposals, there was concern about the limits placed on judicial review of detention and deportation, as well as about the loose standard for detention.

Indefinite detention subsequently emerged as the central issue in both houses. On October 3, the House Judiciary Committee unanimously approved (36 to 0) a compromise "PATRIOT" bill, which restricted indefinite detention and provided compensation for victims of 9/11 and their families. But the Senate version of the bill did not impose restrictions on indefinite detention. The Bush administration immediately began lobbying on behalf of the Senate version and persuaded Congress to negotiate a compromise. In the end, the Senate version largely prevailed, albeit with the inclusion of a six-month review of the detention of certified terrorists. Speaking on behalf of a broad coalition of humanitarian, religious, human rights and civil liberties organizations, the American Civil Liberties Union urged Congress to reject the measure altogether, charging that it was "based upon a false dichotomy: that safety must come at the expense of civil liberties." Nevertheless, the reconciled version was overwhelmingly approved, by 357 to 66 in the House and 98 to 1 in the Senate.

Albeit beginning with an "expression of the sense of Congress" condemning discrimination against Arab and Muslim Americans, the new act expands the definition of terrorism, which was already grounds for denying admission and for deportation, to include use of any "weapon or dangerous device" with the intent to endanger persons or cause damage to property. It gives law-enforcement agencies broader powers to pursue terrorists through search warrants and eavesdropping and provides for the possibility of holding aliens without charges for up to six months, with the possibility of renewal, subject to a review that puts the burden of proof on the government to demonstrate that the alien's release will threaten national security, or the safety of the community, or any person.[14] Judicial review is limited to habeas corpus review. With regard to border control, "USA PATRIOT" authorizes a tripling of the number of Border Patrol personnel, customs personnel, and immigration inspectors along the northern border, as well as improvement in monitoring technology. It also grants INS and State Department personnel access to FBI files for the purpose of checking the criminal history of visa applicants. Most importantly, it sets a two-year deadline for full implementation of the "Integrated Entry and Exit Data System" called for in 1996.

While the process of elaborating new instruments of control got under way, immediate efforts to achieve greater security focused more narrowly on nationals of Arab and Muslim countries. On November 9, the State Department announced it would subject male visa applicants aged 16 to 45 from 26 nations in the Middle East, South Asia, Southeast Asia, and Africa, to special scrutiny. Reflecting the administration's determination to avoid closing the door more generally, this decision was criticized by advocates of tighter immigration on the holier-than-thou grounds that "There should be a consensus in the United States that we don't want an ethnic- or religious-based immigration system."[15] Concurrently, the State Department accelerated its pending review of six of the 29 countries whose citizens are exempt from visas, Argentina, Belgium, Italy, Portugal, Slovenia, and Uruguay, on the grounds that these countries have problems ranging from economic crises to passport fraud and theft.[16]

Student visas were singled out for special concern in the light of reports that most the terrorists were "intellectuals," and of the by-now-notorious fact that such visas can be obtained by registering in a wide range of institutions, including proprietary schools that teach flying or English (whose use in obtaining a visa is widely advertised in the New York subway), and that at least one of the terrorists never registered at the school that certified him as a student. Despite early talk of suspending student visas altogether for an extended period of time, subsequent proposals were much more limited; however, institutions that certify foreign students will henceforth be required to report on their attendance. This requirement does not entail new regulations, because most education visas require students to sign a waiver permitting their educational institutions to provide to immigration officials the particulars of their course of study and their whereabouts. But years ago the government asked administrators "to stop sending this information to Washington . . . because the INS could not scale the mountain of paperwork." In the wake of 9/11, however, 220 institutions reported having been contacted by FBI and INS agents to collect information about students from Middle Eastern countries.[17] In late November, Senator Dianne Feinstein and three colleagues introduced a comprehensive visa-reform bill that would close "loopholes" for student and other temporary visas by imposing tight notification and reporting requirements; however, difficulties in implementing even existing controls made it unlikely that the situation would substantially change in the near future.[18]

As noted earlier, however, even if more effective visa screening procedures were to be successfully implemented, this would not resolve border leakage. The order of magnitude of the problem can be inferred from the fact that in 2000, the Border Patrol arrested roughly one million people trying to sneak into the United States from Mexico, and 12,000 from Canada, including among the latter 254 persons from 16 Middle Eastern countries. That same year, U.S. agents also detained or turned back some 4,000 people at Canadian checkpoints alone. Estimates of the number of undocumented entries range very widely, but a reasonable suggestion is that, together with equally undocumented exits, they result in a net inflow of about 200,000 illegal aliens a year. In the light of 9/11, the Census Bureau's estimates of the illegal population, released in late October, made for screaming headlines.[19] Although a subsequent breakdown by nationality indicated that half of them originated in North and Central America, with Mexico alone providing 44 percent, many headlines chose to emphasize that "115,000 Middle Eastern Immigrants Are in the U.S. Illegally."[20]

While unauthorized entry from the south is an old story, initial announcements—subsequently disconfirmed—that several of the hijackers entered surreptitiously across the Canadian border came as an especially frightening revelation, as that line hardly figures in American consciousness as an international divide: albeit twice as long as its Mexican counterpart, with 115 official entry points as against 41, the Canadian border is guarded by only 334 agents, as against some 9,000 in the south.[21] There is little illegal penetration into Canada itself, since its geographical configuration makes it nearly impossible to enter by land (except from the U.S. side). But Canada maintains a generous visitor policy, much like the United States, and in contrast with U.S. practice since 1996, does not detain asylum seekers, of whom some 10,000 disappear every year. Initial moves by the United States to tighten the border with existing federal personnel wreaked havoc with the regional economy, which depends on the comings and goings of hundreds of thousands of daily commuters and shoppers. To enhance security without creating unacceptable delays, the Michigan National

Guard was assigned to patrol the U.S.–Canadian border on the Detroit side of the Ambassador Bridge.

In its quest for a more permanent solution, the United States faces a choice between two approaches: either to elaborate a draconian apparatus of physical and administrative barriers along the longest stretch of relatively open international boundary in the entire world, or to incorporate the two countries into a jointly managed "security perimeter." The first alternative not only runs counter to a long tradition of trust and friendship, but is likely to be strongly opposed by powerful economic interests on both sides. However, the "joint security perimeter," which is welcomed by the Canadian security establishment including its present Minister of Immigration, raises the hackles of nationalists, notably Prime Minister Jean Chrétien, as yet another infringement on Canadian sovereignty. Nevertheless, there is little doubt that if security concerns persist, as they are likely to do, the two countries will elaborate a North American counterpart of the European "Schengen" system, which originated as an undertaking by the northern tier of European Union members plus Switzerland against the "leaky" Mediterranean south. It is noteworthy that in the wake of 9/11, the Canadian government itself fast-tracked legislation to tighten security at points of entry, and it was reported that the courts would authorize racial profiling for this purpose.[22]

Although none of the identified terrorists is thought to have entered by way of the southern border, this is hardly comforting. For example, prosecution documents filed in a Federal conspiracy trial in El Paso in October 2001 provide evidence of the smuggling of 132 Middle Easterners into the United States from 1996 to 1998 by an organization headed by an Iraqi-born naturalized Mexican. The documents further indicate that as many as 1,000 of them were brought in since the organization was launched in 1980.[23] Overall, U.S. policy might be characterized as one of "draconian laxity," involving routine enforcement known by all to be ineffective, punctuated by intermittent highly visible demonstrations of effective control of a circumscribed sector. This peculiar mix has been fostered by the protracted face-off between an economically grounded laissez faire alliance that encompasses a wide range of American employers—down to individual households eager to hire gardeners—as well as the Mexican state and Mexican workers, arrayed against a politically grounded regulatory camp driven by the identitarian concerns of non-Hispanic whites, championed by the California Republican party. One of the most surprising developments of the 2000 presidential campaign was the determination of George W. Bush to move away from his party's traditional position on this matter. Consequently, despite evidence of a worsening economic downturn, on the very eve of the attacks, the United States and Mexico were engaged in unprecedented high-level bilateral negotiations toward an innovative immigration program.

Choices with regard to the southern border are similar to those facing the United States in the north. In the wake of 9/11, negotiations over immigration reform were variously announced to be "dead in the water" or "on the back burner"; however, in early November it was announced that they would resume at the end of the month. In addition, President Vicente Fox proposed the inclusion of Mexico along with Canada into a security perimeter that covers all NAFTA territory, and his national-security official subsequently traveled to Washington prior to the discussions on immigration to meet with Homeland Security Chief Tom Ridge on this matter. Former INS Commissioner Doris Meissner has suggested that while the creation of a "North American safety perimeter" is "the best answer to the difficulty of defending thousands of miles of remote territory," this will take considerable time. In the short term, she suggests differential priorities: on the Mexican side, steps to weaken migrant-trafficking organizations that facilitate illicit entry by third-country nationals; on the Canadian side, broad information sharing extending to intelligence, as well as accelerating strategies and technologies for joint border enforcement.[24]

Beyond discussions of border control, the events also triggered proposals to make the United States more secure against the enemy within, by subjecting foreign residents to systematic verification. This would be no easy undertaking, given a target population that amounts to 11 percent of the total, not including millions of temporary visitors. Given the apparent source of the aggression, for many Americans the distinction that matters most is between putatively safe immigrants and dangerous ones, identified as "Arabs" or "Muslims," or "Middle Easterners" more diffusely—including South Asians. It should be noted that "Arabs" and "Muslims" overlap only in part: Until recently, the U.S. population of Arab origin was overwhelmingly Christian, as illustrated by former White House Chief of Staff John Sununu and current Energy Secretary Spencer Abraham, as well as the scholar and public intellectual Edward Said.

The size of these groups has itself become an object of controversy. In keeping with the common practice of inflating numbers for purposes of ethnic representation, the Arab-American Institute claims that persons of Arabic ancestry total over three million; but ancestry responses on a recent census survey indicate just over one million, of whom the largest groups are Lebanese, Egyptian, and Syrian.[25] Since Islam is a religion and not a nationality or an ethnicity, "Muslim" does not figure among the origin categories recorded by the census, any more than does "Jew." But an April 2001 report issued by the Council on American-Islamic Relations in Washington, D.C., stated that two million people are associated with a mosque, and estimated on that basis a total Muslim population of six to seven million, of whom 33 percent are South Asian, 30 percent African-American, and 25 percent Arab.[26] However, the American Jewish Committee expressed concern that these statistics indicated that Muslims outnumbered Jews, and that "it would buttress calls for a redefinition of America's heritage as 'Judeo-Christian-Muslim,' a stated goal of some Muslim leaders." It then commissioned a report of its own, which criticized the Mosque Report for unsound methodology and concluded that there are at most 2.8 million Muslims in the United States.[27]

Interpretations of the current conflict as a confrontation between a purified Islam and a decadent Judeo-Christianity that corrupts Muslims creates an uncomfortable dilemma for some American Muslims, as the special relationship between the United States and Israel has long done for most Arab-Americans. In the present climate, opinions that deviate from the accepted range might be construed as tacit or even active support for terrorist undertakings. For example, Sheik Muhammad Gemeaha, imam of the Islamic Cultural Center of New York's main mosque, characterized the attacks as a Zionist plot. He left for his Egyptian home two weeks after the attack, reportedly because his family was threatened.[28]

In any event, despite repeated injunctions by President Bush and other elected officials to avoid blaming groups wholesale, security measures taken by U.S. agents self-evidently entailed ethnic profiling. Under pressure from the press and civil liberties groups, Justice Department officials revealed in early November that they had detained 1,147 people in connection with the attacks, over half of whom had been released at that point. Some were identified on the basis of circumstantial links with the attack, but many "were picked up based on tips or were people of Middle Eastern or South Asian descent who had been stopped for traffic violations of for acting suspiciously."[29] The total included 235 people detained for immigration violations, mostly Arab or Muslim men, of whom 185 were still in custody. One tragic case involved a 55-year-old Pakistani overstayer, dismissed by the FBI as of no interest, who died of coronary disease while in jail awaiting deportation.[30]

On November 13, the Justice Department announced it would further pick up and question some 5,000 Middle Eastern men aged 18 to 33 who entered the country legally on student, visitor, or business visas since January 1, 2000. Although officials said the interviews were intended to be voluntary and the people sought were not considered suspects, the move was sharply criticized by civil liberties organizations as a "dragnet approach that is likely to magnify concerns of racial and ethnic profiling."[31] In the face of mixed reactions by local police forces and halting implementation, the December 4 deadline was extended until the

10th; but subsequent reports indicated further lagging.[32] Although throughout the proceedings, the Justice Department resisted providing public information on its actions and their results, there were some indications that established procedural guarantees began to enter into play. For example, on December 19, a Philadelphia federal appeals court ruled that the government's mandatory detention policy was unconstitutional and that each detainee was entitled to an individualized bond hearing. Civil rights organizations increasingly entered into the fray as well.[33] Although the roundup resulted in the incarceration of many Middle Easterners for violations of immigration regulations—mostly by way of overstaying, which was likely to lead to their deportation—there were no indications that it produced any suspects related to the 9/11 events. In January, the Justice Department announced a new effort to find and deport people who have ignored deportation orders, to begin with the tracking down of several thousand men from Muslim and Middle Eastern countries.

Last but not least, the attacks have also triggered a spate of proposals to subject foreigners to some sort of mandatory identity documentation. Somewhat paradoxically, in the American situation the absence of such documents for the general population is repeatedly hailed as an indication of the regime's superiority over many of its European counterparts in the sphere of individual liberty. Thus the imposition of such a requirement on aliens is especially invidious. Moreover, how is an agent, setting out to verify identity and status, to know whether the person in question is a U.S. citizen or a foreign national? Since "aliens" as a whole are not phenotypically distinct from "Americans," we can anticipate the grossest sort of ethnic profiling, which would inevitably lead to numerous "mistakes," provoking outraged reactions on the part of citizens, and hence negative political feedback.

The alternative would be to institute a universal state-issued identity document. While this is accepted as routine in a number of European democracies, and even viewed as a positive good from a civil liberties perspective because it provides some degree of protection against arbitrary police behavior, within the American context it would be perceived to alter profoundly the established balance between freedom and control. Issuance of such a document by the federal government would be absolutely unacceptable to conservatives and viewed with considerable suspicion by the mainstream. In practice, the nearest thing already in existence to such a document is the state-issued driver's license, which might be expanded to nondrivers; however, this is based on proof of legal residence, often loosely established, rather than on citizenship, and would require the establishment of countrywide uniform standards. Yet despite the normative and political difficulties involved, it is likely that some form of reliable biometricallybased identification will emerge in practice, probably on a voluntary basis, to speed up processing through the country's proliferating public and private security checkpoints.

In conclusion, the attack on the United States confirms what had already been evident from less spectacular manifestations of international terrorism: the growing importance of non-state actors in the contemporary world system. Nevertheless, American responses are being cast primarily within a classically Westphalian framework: calls for a crash program to enhance each state's capacity to police its territorial borders, to identify and neutralize foreign-origin enemies within, and to improve intelligence abroad. Not only does the elaboration of obstacles to international movement clash with the objectives of economic globalization, but globalization in turn provides negative feedback for national security, since it brings about greater population diversity so that, whoever the dangerous group turns out to be, the targeted society is likely to have such people in its midst. Evidence of vulnerability to such attacks enhances the value of protection while downgrading the social costs heightened protection imposes, notably on residents who share an ethnic origin with the putative terrorists or are thought to resemble them. Moreover, interpretations of the conflict as an essentially cultural one, opposing Islamic fundamentalism to Western civilization, foster suspicion of Muslims of any kind, much as in the initial years of the Cold War, interpretations of the conflict as an ideological one led many to impugn the loyalty of every left-winger.

Nevertheless, a murderous attack *did* take place, and it is hardly unique; nor is the United States the only target. Moreover, while the military response it provoked disrupted the source network, it is evident that other such networks already exist and that others are likely to come into being. Although over the long term, terrorism is subject to reduction by structural change, and containment of particular manifestations can be achieved by local intervention, overall, the danger will persist for the indefinite future. Under the circumstances, the Westphalian approach still has a lot going for it, despite its archaic character, but it must be updated in the light of contemporary conditions. Effective protection is not only desirable in itself, but its reality will reduce the appeal of blunt and counterproductive solutions, such as those proposed by Buchanan.

To be fully effective, security must not be focused on geographical borders or on the home territory, but projected outward. If there is to be a crash program, it should be directed at the improvement of America's capacity to identify dangerous operations in the making abroad. Contrary to the tendency of going it alone, the development of the appropriate intelligence capability requires cooperation with friendly states that have greater experience in the sphere under consideration. Such intelligence is in turn a prerequisite for the implementation of a more effective screening system for foreign visitors, which is fully possible under existing law. Much can be done to overcome turf wars and to improve the accessibility of relevant information. Beyond this, rather than the border patrol, which has been the major beneficiary of recent investment in border control, priority should be given to consular staffing. As Doris Meissner has pointed out, "Consular work—more a rite of passage than a job requiring substantive expertise—does not enjoy high standing in the hierarchy of responsibilities for U.S. diplomats. Expert senior officers are in short supply and are spread too thin. This model is not tolerable in the face of terrorism. Instead, visa work must be treated as a career specialty. . . . If this work is not suited to Foreign Service careers and rewards, it should be done by a new civil service cadre dedicated to this mission. . . ."[34] In the same vein, more can be done to provide advance passenger information so as to improve the security of flights without jeopardizing processing speed.

While vigilance is called for internally as well, nothing has emerged so far to suggest that extraordinary measures are required for this purpose. For the time being, the more urgent internal security task is to provide adequate protection to minorities victimized by the diffuse anger of the uninformed and insure that in their encounters with American law they are accorded the full benefit of the procedural rights that constitute one of the major foundations of democracy. Immigrants who feel welcome rarely set out to destroy their new home.

PART V

COMPETING NARRATIVES

19. THE POLITICAL PSYCHOLOGY OF COMPETING NARRATIVES: SEPTEMBER 11 AND BEYOND

MARC HOWARD ROSS[1]

INTRODUCTION

Many Americans are deeply troubled by the often tepid reactions from the Muslim world to the September 11 attacks, and by the images of street protests they saw in Muslim countries against U.S. military actions in Afghanistan. These reactions have led to a spate of stories in the popular press and television asking, "Why do they hate us?" and for some these stories demonstrate the existence of a clearly defined enemy who, because they have not signaled that they were with us, must be against us. Is this the clash of civilizations that Harvard political scientist Samuel Huntington described almost a decade ago, pitting Islam against the West?[2] Huntington's scenario, I argue, leads us to overemphasize objective cultural differences as a cause of conflict between people from different cultures. Instead, this chapter argues that it is more useful to focus on the social and psychological processes by which subjective differences between cultures produce clashing frameworks for action that are at the core of the current conflict.

As a political psychologist I have been particularly interested in how people make sense of complex, emotionally powerful events and why different, seemingly contradictory, accounts of what seems to be the same event so frequently coexist. These different accounts are often referred to as narratives. In focusing on narratives I am not dismissing the importance of the structural features of the contemporary international system or of the competing interests of different actors. Rather, they are not my focus in this article. Narratives matter for at least three different reasons.[3] First, a narrative's metaphors and images can tell us a great deal about how individuals and groups understand the social and political worlds in which they live, and explain the conflicts in which they are involved.[4] Second, they can reveal deep fears, perceived threats, and past grievances that drive a conflict. Third, narratives are important because they privilege certain actions over others. For example, defining the September 11 attacks as an act of war, which was central to the Bush administration's narrative, provided support for different kinds of responses than defining them as a criminal act would have done. Similarly, the United States first announced that captured Taliban and Al

Qaeda are "unlawful combatants," and not prisoners of war entitled to be treated in accord with the Geneva Conventions, although as of early February 2002, this issue was still being debated within and outside the Bush administration.

Narratives can be analyzed in several ways. Of great significance to an analysis is what a narrative includes and excludes. Often opposing parties' narratives do not directly contradict each other. Rather, opponents draw on distinct metaphors, emphasize different actions, cite clashing motivations, and communicate opposing affect to such an extent that it is sometimes hard for a naïve observer to recognize that the narratives protagonists offer are describing the same conflict. On the surface level, narratives are stories about the unfolding of events. At a deeper level, they reveal something about the motivations and reactions of the parties, sometimes explicitly and sometimes indirectly. In addition, narratives make emotionally significant connections across time periods through the culturally significant images and metaphors they invoke. Analysis of narratives from these various perspectives helps us understand what is driving parties in a conflict; furthermore, we can use this understanding as part of the process of developing constructive solutions.

This article has four sections. In the first I discuss the key features of psychocultural narratives and their origin in deeply rooted cultural worldviews and group identity. Second, I discuss narratives concerning September 11 and its aftermath, arguing that alternative narratives exist not only between the U.S. and Muslim worlds, but within each of these as well. Third, I explore the multiple, but not mutually exclusive, roles narratives play in intense conflicts: as causes, reflectors, and exacerbaters of conflict and its escalation. As causes, narratives serve as gatekeepers ruling in or out options for groups, decision-makers, and politicians. As reflectors, narratives reveal how protagonists understand a conflict and their own underlying motivations, as well as those of their opponents. As exacerbaters, narratives provide in-group support and solidarity that promote negative images of an enemy, escalatory actions, and offer little room for accommodation. In this section I also examine how narratives can be significant in developing constructive solutions that move a conflict toward settlement. Finally, I consider implications from the analysis for U.S. relations with the Muslim world. I emphasize not only that good settlements must meet the real interests of the protagonists, but also that they must be framed to address the emotional fears and threats that drove the conflict in the first place. Central to this process is the development of new narratives, ones which do not directly challenge older ones, but which reframe them in more inclusive terms that deemphasize the emotional significance of differences between groups and identify shared goals and experiences.

PSYCHOCULTURAL NARRATIVES

First let me say something about what a psychocultural[5] narrative is and how this concept can help us understand and manage conflict. Narratives are explanations for events—large and small—in the form of short, commonsense accounts (stories) that often seem simple. However, the powerful images they contain and the judgments they make about the motivations and actions of one's own group, and opponents, are emotionally powerful. Narratives are not always internally consistent. For example, group narratives often alternate between portraying one's own group as especially strong and as especially vulnerable—and the same holds for the portrayal of the opponent.[6] Narratives meet a number of needs and are especially relevant for groups and individuals caught in situations of high uncertainty and high stress. When people are most disoriented, such as during the period following September 11, they struggle to make sense of events; shared narratives that are reinforced within groups help them find reassurance and cope with high anxiety. Opposing groups with divergent beliefs and experiences develop and maintain different narratives of the same event. All cultural traditions have access to multiple preexisting narratives that provide support for diverse actions in times of apprehension, as we can see in the many citations from the Quran and the Bible used to justify responses to September 11.[7] Narratives, therefore, are not made from whole cloth, but are grounded in selectively remembered and interpreted experiences and projections from them that resonate with a large number of people.

Narratives are rooted in shared culture and worldviews. Culture is usefully understood as "an historically transmitted pattern of meaning embodied in symbols, a system of inherited conceptions expressed in symbolic forms by means of which men [sic] communicate, perpetuate, and develop their knowledge about and attitudes towards life."[8] This definition of culture emphasizes public, shared meanings. Behaviors, institutions, and social structure are understood not as culture itself but as culturally constituted phenomena.[9] Culture from this perspective is a worldview that includes both cognitive and affective beliefs about social reality and assumptions about when, where, and how people in one's culture and those in other cultures are likely to act in particular circumstances.[10] It is politically relevant that these shared understandings occur among people who also have a common (and almost invariably named) identity that signals distinctions between the group and outsiders. In sum, culture is a framework for interpreting the world that marks "a distinctive way of life" characterized in the subjective we-feelings among group members, and expressed though specific behaviors including customs and rituals—both sacred and profane—that mark the daily, yearly, and life cycle rhythms connecting people across time and space. Cultures and cultural differences do not themselves cause conflict. People are the cause; and it is important to understand how leaders and groups use culture and the deep feelings it evokes in mobilization.

Shared worldviews provide the deeply emotive images and references that are the building blocks of psychocultural narratives, and in recent years, scholars have analyzed the dynamics of narrative development from a variety of theoretical perspectives.[11] A key point these scholars make is that narratives invoke the past in response to contemporary needs for meaning and control over ambiguous and stressful situations. Narratives are normative accounts with heroes and villains and lessons about how life should be lived. They offer in-group versions of the past, including the origin and development of the group, and they invoke past threats, conflicts with enemies, and laud group survival. In some cases, there is a conscious effort to develop a narrative with an eye toward future political goals, as was the case in Israel during the Zionist period, and in South Africa among Afrikaners following the Boer War.[12] In most situations, however, world views and the narratives to which they give rise look much more like patchwork quilts sewn together over a long time period.

In bitter conflicts, among the strongest feelings people have are fears about attacks on their identity. Usually these fears result from perceived denigration and humiliation, evoked from past losses and linked to present dangers. In violent conflicts, the fears also include concern for physical security and fears of extinction of the self, family, and the group and its culture, including its sacred icons and sites.[13] All groups exert conformity pressures on their members, and these are greatest in high-stress conflict situations. In times of uncertainty, narratives connect individual and group identity, heightening in-group solidarity and a sense of linked fate that inhibits social and political dissent. As part of this dynamic, disagreement quickly becomes disloyalty, and often those holding dissenting views are careful not to express them publicly, and sometimes even in private.

Within communities, high conformity pressures increase acceptance of the dominant elements in a narrative.[14] Political leaders intuitively know that building consensus using the key elements in a narrative can be crucial to mustering support for their actions, which are presented as "naturally" following from shared understandings. In short, we can view securing active consensus on narratives as public opinion formation that is both an effort by individuals to reduce their own anxiety, and a strategy on the part of leaders to mobilize public support. A good indicator of this is greater homogeneity of publicly expressed opinions and public acceptance of key parts of the dominant narrative for whatever conflict is current. For example, prior to the outbreak of the Gulf War in January 1991, American public opinion as expressed in surveys, newspaper editorials, and in Congress was quite divided on the question of the war with Iraq. Once the fighting began, however, public support for military action increased dramatically in a very short period of time.[15] Few surveys, however, clearly answer the question of the degree to which people actually change their attitudes toward what they perceive as the dominant view in their society, versus the extent to which they engage in what Timur Kuran calls preference falsification to avoid ostracism or even persecution.[16]

There are times when group consensus around a narrative increases, but there are many others when within-group differences are highly significant. Often our language implies that opposing parties in a conflict are internally unified, while in most long-term significant conflicts, we should recognize that there is considerable diversity *within* each community that reflects significant debates and disagreements. In Northern Ireland and the Middle East, for example, for a long time there have been strikingly different narratives *within* both the majority and minority communities over the use of violence and the conditions under which peace is possible. These disagreements reflect deep differences in the fears the conflict evokes and contrasting motives attributed to the other side. On the one hand, there is a view of the other community as capable of living in relative peace and harmony with one's own group, while on the other, any move toward peace is viewed with suspicion, heightens insecurity, and is viewed as a potential first step toward even greater demands. These competing interpretations sometimes reflect in-group differences in interests, but the emphasis here is on their very divergent emotional messages.

Narratives exist at different levels of specificity. Some focus on general questions such as the origin of the group, while others are built around particular events such as a single battle or the fate of a past leader. Narratives rely on timeless images and metaphors. This "time collapse" evokes the emotional rather than the chronological immediacy of the past.[17] For example, Zerubavel shows how early–twentieth century Zionists stressed parallels between ancient Israel of the first and second temple periods while variously ignoring or denigrating the almost 2,000 years of Jewish exile.[18] Resistance and revolt were emphasized in school texts and new holidays, and the myths and rituals surrounding them were developed and widely celebrated. Battles such as Masada became enshrined as celebrating revolt although they ended in mass death. Celebrations of Chanukah emphasized the Macabee revolt against Syrian rule and downplayed the "miracle" of one day's oil burning for eight days, the central lesson of the story during the Exile period. Zerubavel argues that following the Nazi Holocaust, the lesson of "Never Again" further reinforced the meaning of ancient revolts of Bar Kokhba and Masada for contemporary Zionists.

Narratives are central to understanding "who is a people" and to articulating what in their "imagined past" is shared. These narratives articulate an ethnic conception of the nation that emphasizes one's community of birth and shared culture.[19] Harkening back to historical events, such as battles, is one common way in which a shared community of experiences is communicated. Serbs emphasize the defeat of Prince Lazar in Kosovo in 1389, Quebequers continue to mark the English victory over the French on the Plains of Abraham in 1759, and some French still recount that it was the English who burned Joan of Arc. All of these references presume a people and identity with a direct link to the present that, in fact, is built more to meet contemporary needs than a reflection of historical reality.[20]

The Israeli case is especially interesting since Zionism's call to bring together Jews from all parts of the world meant that people arrived in Israel with little in common other than their religious identity, which itself has been hotly debated and fought about at times.[21] The development of a common language, shared institutions, and a national narrative became a central part of the task of acquiring "a land without people for a people without a land." Note that this phrase reflected and reinforced a narrative which presumed that Palestine had been empty for 2,000 years, and that the Arabs living there were mere visitors.[22] In no way am I suggesting that the "imagined community"[23] is transformed into a real community making claims to a state only through cultural dynamics and their narratives. I am arguing, however, that they are an integral, and often ignored, part of this political process.[24]

There is no simple relationship between culture and narratives. The very generality of culture means that it can give rise to multiple narratives to cope with the same event or series of events. Edward Linenthal illustrates this idea particularly well in his examination of how Oklahoma City residents, in particular, and Americans more generally, came to understand the 1995 bombing of the Alfred P. Murrah Federal Building, which killed 168 people.[25] He describes three different, but not necessarily incompatible, narratives to explain the attack and responses to it. The progressive narrative emphasizes renewal and recovery as people struggled to rebuild the city and their lives. The redemptive narrative put the horrific events in a religious context, emphasizing the struggle between good and evil and ultimate redemption. The toxic narrative stresses the ongoing disruption and insecurity in many lives after the bombing and the losses that cannot be restored.[26] Linenthal's analysis shows how each of these narratives is deeply rooted in American culture. They exist side by side, he argues, and many survivors and family members of victims could readily identity how all three reflected their own experiences and emotions at different times.

While a key feature of narratives is to explain the past, we must always recognize that the meaning of the past is also contested and periodically redefined. In recent years, American historians and educators have had bitter disagreements over what should be taught in social studies and history courses.[27] Conflicts over the control of historical narratives are fought out in decisions about museum presentations and battlefields and other memorials.[28] Contemporary conflict over the past is intense because it has implications for group identity in the present. Sometimes this conflict is played out in dramatic fashion, as it has been at the Little Bighorn battlefield site in Montana. Linenthal argues that the issue was not only the presentation of the battle between General George Custer's cavalry forces and the Sioux and Cheyenne warriors in June 1876, but the larger question of the relationship between expanding American society and the native peoples living in the west.[29] For many years, veneration of Custer and his troops as martyrs emphasized the American civilizing mission, in contrast to the degrading, colonizing experience central to the Native American narrative. For whites, the massacre was a testimony to the need for conquest and control over native peoples, and Linenthal describes it as "a model for the transformation of . . . defeats into moral victories,"[30] not unlike Israeli interpretations of Masada.[31] For Native Americans, in contrast, the battle signifies effective resistance against white oppression. The 1970s saw bitter conflict over the presentations at the battlefield site—including its name—and irreconcilable demands of the Custerphiles and the Custerphobes. Efforts by the National Park Service to recognize the accounts of both sides satisfied few in either camp. For example, the proposal to include a quote from Sioux medicine man Black Elk in the visitors center was seen by hardliner Custerphiles "as a form of pollution of the sacred ground,"[32] while Native Americans demanded more explicit acknowledgment of Custer as the symbol of their mistreatment by the U.S. government.[33]

Powerful narratives are more than verbal accounts filled with richly evocative images. They invariably invoke sacred objects, sites, and rituals that reinforce the emotional connections among members of a group. Physical objects and sites are linked to narratives and group identity through rituals that enhance a narrative's emotional significance and explain its persistence over time. Many examples of this connection abound in group holidays and rituals that assert relationships between the present and past through sacred objects, holy sites, special foods, and prayers. Zerubavel describes the development of Masada in the Zionist period as a pilgrimage site for Israeli youth, and the powerful emotional role it came to play for them.[34] The creation of, and visits to, the Vietnam War Memorial in

Washington helped Americans to move past their pro- and antiwar positions of the 1960s and 1970s and to develop a new, more inclusive account of the period. It is not so much that past disagreements over the war changed, but that they became less salient in comparison with the recognition of the large-scale loss and suffering for families and communities that resulted from bringing people together at the site where they shared common emotions.

Flags, memorial sites, inaugural ceremonies, sacred holidays, and state funerals are ritual objects and events that reinforce in-group identity and the emotional power of the group's narratives;[35] they can also be sources of intense conflict.[36] In recent years in the American South there has been bitter disagreement over whether the Confederate battle flag should be hung over state capitols or appear as part of state flags and how, where, and whether Confederate memorials should be presented.[37] In New York, a few months after September 11, there was deep disagreement in reactions to a statue produced to memorialize firefighters' efforts at the WTC site because it included a white, Hispanic, and black firefighter even though the men in the photo on which it was based were all white.[38] Despite the sincere intentions of the funder and artist, the competing needs were so intense that an alternative memorial will be designed.[39]

ALTERNATIVE/COMPETING NARRATIVES AND SEPTEMBER 11

Hostile narratives did not directly cause the September 11 attacks on the World Trade Center; nor are they the simple cause of the U.S. military responses in Afghanistan and elsewhere. They did, however, contribute to the dynamics in which both of these actions took place. Narratives, therefore, are important in understanding the roots of the conflict, the reactions of many of the protagonists, U.S. and other responses to the attacks, and the future actions that are, or are not, contemplated. In brief synopsis, Al Qaeda framed the U.S. as a mortal enemy, and the conflict with it as a *jihad* in which civilians and governmental officials are not distinguished, thus justifying the dramatic and brutal attacks and ruling out any kind of dialogue or political accommodation with either the U.S. or American allies in the region. Similarly, the American declaration of a "war on terrorism" produced an emphasis on military and diplomatic action and significant symbolic efforts to distinguish between the vast majority of Muslims and Al Qaeda's brand of fundamentalism and use of religion for political purposes.

In thinking about the major protagonists' narratives, consider how they offer an explanation for events and prioritize possible responses.[40] Furthermore, consider how the legitimation of one narrative over another provides support for those who cite key parts of the narrative as a justification for their own actions. For example, American and British insistence that rooting out terrorism meant a "zero-tolerance" policy allowed other states, such as Israel and India, to engage in actions against targets that would not have been as likely six months earlier. In the U.S., the widespread public support for strong actions against terrorists led the government to (1) initially define captured Taliban and Al Qaeda as unlawful combatants not falling under the Geneva Conventions' regulations for treatment of prisoners of war, (2) carry out long-term domestic detention of suspected terrorists and those who might have some knowledge of them or their activities, and (3) decide to use military tribunals to try non-American terrorists.

There are many different narratives we can identify involving September 11. To further explore the significance of narratives, consider the following two accounts, the first of which resonates for most of the American public and the second of which baffles many Americans:

> Two huge commercial jetliners smash into the twin towers of the World Trade Center. Soon after, the buildings collapse. Fires rage for weeks; eyewitnesses tell of the horrors they saw or experienced. Thousands die as the public learns that terrorists willing to commit suicide hijacked four planes and turned them into weapons of mass destruction in the name of their political/religious beliefs. This is an evil act and an act of war—a sneak attack like Pearl Harbor. It is perhaps a new kind of war, but a war nonetheless and the only response to being attacked is to attack back, both to punish those responsible for the carnage and to prevent future attacks. Defending civilization against terrorism requires hunting down the supporters and perpetrators of terror and the regimes that support them.

For many the truth of this narrative is self-evident. Anyone denying or even questioning it is either an enemy or delusional (or both). The link between the events themselves and the conclusions is seamless to those who accept it. But a different narrative also exists:

> Two huge commercial jetliners smash into the twin towers of the World Trade Center. Soon after, the buildings collapse. Fires rage for weeks; eyewitnesses tell of the horrors they saw or experienced. Thousands die as the public learns that terrorists willing to commit suicide hijacked four planes and turned them into weapons of mass destruction in the name of their political/religious beliefs. This may have been an evil act, but now the suffering Americans know what it is like to live in physical terror. It is an experience Palestinians and Iraqis and others in the Middle East have known for years. This will lead, once again, to attacks on Muslims—this time in Afghanistan, and perhaps in other countries. Once again, innocent civilians will bear the brunt of the suffering from the attacks from the Western powers while corrupt regimes give tacit support to the U.S. As bombs fall from 30,000 feet and civilians die, new refugees will be created in a land that has already suffered from more than 20 years of ongoing war.

These two narratives start in the same place, but then head in different directions that evoke far different images. Where the first emphasizes the reassurance that a strong, military response can offer, the second expresses fears that this strong response will quickly become a vengeful attack on a vulnerable religious community. Whereas the first invokes images of justice, the second predicts uncontrolled revenge and more of the injustice that has characterized the relationship between the West and Islam at least since the First Crusade. The second narrative asks, if Americans claim that justice is so important, why have Palestinians been neglected for so long and subjected to frequent attacks using American-made sophisticated weapons? Why are Iraqi children unable to meet their basic nutritional needs while its leaders live in palaces? In short, the second narrative expresses the deepest vulnerabilities, humiliation, rage at both the West and the leaders of Muslim countries, and fears of annihilation.

The second narrative is connected to the anger and resentment against the U.S. in many parts of the Islamic world, but it doesn't mean that all Muslims agree with it or hate the U.S. The power of the narrative is its plausibility, meaning that it resonates with how many Muslims understand historical conflicts with the Christian world as well as more recent events in their own lifetimes. At least four events are especially relevant here: (1) American support for the Shah of Iran and opposition to the Iranian revolution; (2) unconditional support for Israel despite its government's refusal to take significant steps towards the achievement of a Palestinian state; (3) the Gulf War, which was justified in the West in terms of turning back Iraqi aggression but which was widely understood by Muslims as propping up autocratic, unpopular, and corrupt regimes upon whom American oil supplies depended; and (4) threats to Islamic holy sites in Saudi Arabia and Jerusalem resulting from not only American presence in the region but the more diffuse forces of modernization and globalization which threaten Muslim cultures. A psychocultural analysis of these particular events focuses on the emotional intensity and the deep fears and humiliations they invoke through their connections to past experiences. Emotional intensity is not explained simply in terms of the substantive issues at stake in each of these situations, but also by the deeper existential experiences that are involved.

One could view the two narratives as further evidence that the world can be neatly dichotomized—those who are for us and those who are against us—and deduce therefore that escalating conflict is inevitable, as Huntington's "clash of civilizations" thesis would suggest.[41] It is also possible to attribute the attitudes and behaviors of those involved solely to their culture and religion. However, to do either would be a serious oversimplification, with policy consequences that are likely to exacerbate, rather than ease, future problems. Instead, the complexity and ambiguity of the narratives themselves, as well as the experiences underlying them, offer insights for future American policy and for bridging what might appear to be two completely incompatible worldviews.

It is interesting to examine the attribution of responsibility in the two narratives. They both reflect the idea that states are not the only relevant international actors today. However, the two narratives understand this shift in somewhat different ways: the first one in its identification of multinational terrorist networks and the second in its invoking of forces such as globalization, capitalism, and secularism. However, there is also significant ambivalence about this new reality and almost a yearning for a system in which states are the dominant actors, since they are much easier to blame when things go wrong than abstract forces such as globalization, or vague entities such as terrorist networks. As a result, despite all the talk about global networks in the aftermath of September 11 and references to "the street" as opposed to the state, Neil Smith is probably correct when he argues that post–September 11 discourse quickly returned to a national one, emphasizing state actors.[42] Within the U.S., the focus on homeland security and the policy focus on attacking those "states who harbor terrorists" are consistent with this state-centric emphasis.

By setting different action priorities, the two narratives reveal important between-group differences. However, there are within-group differences as well, some of which reflect underlying competing interests. Narratives in Muslim countries such as Pakistan, Saudi Arabia and Egypt differentiated between their long-term wariness of Western treatment of Islam and their condemnation of the attacks. More generally, many Muslims are struggling with the question of how to balance, on the one hand, their disgust at the attacks and, on the other hand, their equally strong rejection of American policies which support corrupt, authoritarian regimes in the region, and their opposition to high-tech military action which threatens Muslim civilian populations. Likewise many Americans found themselves searching to articulate a narrative of September 11 that recognizes the horrific and inexcusable nature of the WTC attacks, but also acknowledges the injustices of previous Western actions against Islamic peoples and the risks of emphasizing only a military response, of permitting a loss of civil liberties, and of turning attention away from domestic issues and social priorities. Listening to politicians and reading the American press clearly shows that even five months after September 11, there is more consensus on some parts of the narrative than others, just as Linenthal found in Oklahoma City.[43] Finally, it is worth pointing out that the two narratives have important points of agreement (the horror of the WTC attacks) and other areas where there are differences of focus (past injustices) but not explicit disagreements. Recognizing the diversity of opinions and complexity of feelings within each side can sometimes be a step toward identifying common concerns or to articulating areas for possible future cooperation.

NARRATIVES AS CAUSES, REFLECTORS, AND EXACERBATERS OF CONFLICT AND CONFLICT RESOLUTION

Narratives play a causal role in the conflict process when they frame cognitions and emotions that structure and limit the actions individuals and groups consider as plausible. In this process, narratives shape what constitutes evidence and how it is to be used. When narratives portray no possible common ground between opponents, there will be no search for alternatives to fighting. Thus there will be political pressures for leaders to pursue certain kinds of action, while other options will have already been eliminated. From this perspective, narratives do not force parties to take a particular action, if for example they lack the capabilities or support, but narratives may be crucial in limiting the range of choices that are considered. A good example of this is found in Finley, Holsti, and Fagen's analysis of U.S. Secretary of State John Foster Dulles's interpretation of the behavior of the Soviet Union leadership and their motivation in the 1950s.[44] They argue that even when Khruschev provided signals of a major shift in Soviet policy after Stalin's death, Dulles continued to read these only as signs of weakness, and not as possible evidence of a change of motivations and behaviors from the new leadership. In analyzing September 11 and responses to it, the narratives dominating each party's thinking shaped the actions they considered and eventually undertook.

Narratives are also reflectors of deeper worldviews and assumptions the parties make about each other. These reflections of "the real world" provide significant cues to ingroup members and can make it clear that dissenting from a societal consensus is risky. For example, following September 11, Americans quickly moved to a strong consensus that Osama bin Laden and his supporters were responsible for the terrorist attacks. Those trying to articulate other possibilities were likely to find themselves labeled as "naïve," "in denial," or "conspiracy theorists." Elsewhere in the world, other accounts emerged and received support, and evidence the United States and Britain presented was either questioned or seen as inadequate. In many Muslim countries the story circulated for months in the press and streets that Israel had orchestrated the attacks to turn the U.S. against Islamic states and had managed to secretly notify all Jews working in and around the WTC to stay home that morning. Within the U.S., the consensus rapidly developed for a strong military response in Afghanistan, even if no Afghans had been directly involved in the attacks. Others, including those who condemned the attacks, were skeptical that military action would be effective in rooting out terrorism even if it weakened or destroyed the Taliban regime and Al Qaeda forces in Afghanistan.

Narratives as reflectors are important for those trying to make sense of a conflict and for those who make decisions about how to move a conflict toward a constructive outcome. Political psychologist Vamik Volkan writes about "emotional hot spots" that are part of all intense conflicts. When narratives bring them to the surface, this not only promotes understanding of the deeper roots of complex conflicts,[45] but it also identifies barriers to change and points toward opportunities for strategic intervention. This argument emphasizes that unless the central fears and concerns of each party are addressed, settlement efforts are not likely to be successful. In many situations, one side in a conflict has an incomplete, or even inaccurate, understanding of what opponents need and how they frame the situation,[46] as was the case with Dulles mentioned above. Herbert Kelman argues that one of the significant benefits of the Israeli–Palestinian problem-solving workshops he has organized for 30 years is that key people on each side acquired a more realistic sense of what the other side was thinking and what they needed. As a result, new understandings developed, new language and metaphors came into use, and each understood much more fully and realistically what a peace process and eventual settlement might look like.[47] The narratives participants provided in his workshops often surprised those on the other side, reflecting deep fears central to each group that needed to be understood for movement toward peace talks to occur. Sparks and others describe a similar learning experience in the peace process involving the African National Congress (ANC) and white South African government in the 1980s, prior to Nelson Mandela's release from prison and the legalization of the ANC in 1990.[48] Meeting in a variety of places, often outside South Africa, each side developed a clearer picture of the other's positions and needs and concluded that negotiations could be fruitful.

As exacerbaters of conflict, narratives emphasize differences among the parties and support continuing hostility and escalating responses. The dominant American narrative of the war on terrorism against Al Qaeda and the Taliban left no room for negotiation. In fact, at times this led to significant tension with some Afghan factions for whom negotiations, allegiances, and amnesty were strategic, not moral, decisions. Other countries used the American narrative to serve their own goals. Israeli Prime Minister Ariel Sharon declared that Yasir Arafat was the Israeli bin Laden and launched intense military raids in the West Bank and Gaza (including an increase in targeted assassinations), saying he was responding appropriately to the terrorist threats. Likewise, following an attack on the Indian parliament in December 2001, India fully mobilized its armed forces and demanded strong Pakistani action against Islamic groups and leaders it labeled terrorist. Other countries, such as Uzbekistan and the Philippines, also sought U.S. support against opposition groups in the name of the war on terrorism, an appeal the U.S. has a hard time refusing given its own post–September 11 rhetoric. Finally, some like Russia and China endorsed the American position and then used it to move against internal opponents.

As causes, reflectors, and exacerbaters of conflict, narratives play an active role in the dynamics of escalation. We can examine tipping points in conflicts, asking when previously rejected beliefs and behaviors come to be viewed as acceptable and even desirable. In his analysis of such tipping points, Laitin focuses on language adoption, but his analysis is framed more generally and is thus relevant to understanding public opinion and the actions conflicting parties consider.[49] Public opinion is both a constraint on, and promoter of, the actions leaders consider, and can shift quickly in support of actions taken if they are perceived likely to be effective. In the period following September 11, there was a rapid movement toward public consensus on the attribution of responsibility and the appropriateness of military and diplomatic actions. That this consensus was formed across many divergent groups, ranging from small ethnic communities to large countries, shows how quickly opinions can shift when tipping points are reached.[50]

The preceding analysis emphasizes the role narratives can play in the escalation of conflict. However, it is important to recognize their potential in de-escalation as well. This role is illustrated dramatically in the period following World War II, as new relationships among former enemies were built in Europe and between the U.S. and Japan. But narratives are also at play in more slowly changing relationships, such as the U.S. and China since 1972, or the U.S.–Russian relations in the second half of the 1980s. Evolving narratives also play a role in peace processes in long-term conflicts, such as South Africa, Northern Ireland, and the Middle East, as groups on all sides come to believe that movement toward a settlement is possible, even with those who were previously viewed as "beyond the pale." In these situations, there is a significant shift in how each side describes the other (sometimes including the name by which they are called) and the gradual emergence of images of the benefits peaceful coexistence could bring. When the narratives begin to include more nuanced views of the other side, people can envision a future apart from the intense conflicts, and political leaders have newly opened space to move the peace process forward.[51] This occurred most dramatically in South Africa, but in Northern Ireland and the Middle East (prior to September 2000) the same shifts of public opinion and discourse have also been present.

Narratives that promote peace processes arise when there are explicit connections made between culturally available references and events on the ground. These connections are seen in changes in language—for example, when Israelis began to talk about the establishment of an independent Palestinian state and met publicly with the PLO leaders, or when white South Africa foresaw the inevitability of majority rule and began to facilitate its implementation. Changing the narrative frame can also facilitate de-escalation when it helps people caught in conflict to envision alternatives to ongoing confrontation. To do this, each side must take on the perspective of the other, and learn that there is someone to talk to on the other side and something to talk about.[52]

Because narratives are about images and emotions, not just cognitions, we must examine the symbols and rituals associated with them. Some of these are very dramatic gestures, such as the example of Egyptian President Anwar Sadat's 1977 trip to Jerusalem and his address to the Israeli Knesset, or Nelson Mandela donning a Springboks jersey.[53] Powerful narratives often involve behaviors such as ritual reenactments of historical events, the construction of memorials, or the development of sacred holidays when the narratives are retold and passed to succeeding generations.[54] When rituals are opened to include previously disputing groups, they can serve to support new narratives of coexistence and even reconciliation. In Northern Ireland, for example, a Protestant cultural organization in Derry (the region's second-largest city) recently recast its annual celebratory parade in the context of a more inclusive city festival, which is open to Catholics as well as Protestants.[55] One strategy Volkan has adopted is visiting "hotspots"—actual locations where deep differences are evoked. In Estonia, for example, Estonians and Russians met at the site of a former Soviet nuclear submarine base, and the Estonians expressed how the Russian use of the base was humiliating to them.[56]

NARRATIVES AND U.S. RELATIONS WITH THE MUSLIM WORLD IN THE AFTERMATH OF SEPTEMBER 11

Narratives can and do change, but not necessarily when they are confronted directly. Simply telling people that their story of events is wrong is rarely successful, because there is often great emotional attachment to an account, which is defended from such frontal assaults. It is the images and organization of narratives that give them their power, not the facts. A strategy to develop more inclusive narratives in the West (especially in the U.S.) and the Muslim world needs to be part of an effort to address the causes of the terrorist attacks and the support they received. To do this, new experiences and emotional connections need to be introduced that alter the salience of elements in the existing exclusive narratives, and invite new and/or revised linkages among their key elements. Developing these narratives could have significant implications for future American policy toward the Muslim world in general and the Arab world in particular. Given the hypothesis that narratives are produced interactively, and that change in one group's perceptions of the opponent can alter its own narrative, there are constructive steps that can be taken to help resolve the current conflict.

Here I focus on what the U.S. can do differently in its interaction with the Muslim world. This emphasis does not mean that it is only the U.S. that needs to rethink the situation and alter its behaviors. There is a more complex system at work here, in which many state and non-state actors have colluded to create and maintain the current situation. Muslim regimes have been reluctant at best, and often completely unwilling, to address expanding participation and political voice, the distribution of social benefits, severe inequality, and sustainable local development. How these issues are best addressed is not easy for an outsider to say and certainly will need to reflect the different realities in individual states. The same kinds of issues I raise here concerning American behavior can usefully be raised about the Arab world, and a vigorous discussion along these lines is needed if the current situation is to change.

• *Better listening and learning.* The U.S. needs to better understand the roots of anger, and even rage, directed toward it from parts of the Muslim world. It is easy to point the finger at demagogic figures, such as Saddam Hussein, Osama bin Laden, or the Taliban, but the question should focus not just on the hate and propaganda they are spreading but also on why their audience seems so receptive. It is far easier to understand the motives of sellers than buyers. However, it is necessary to understand the deeply rooted vulnerabilities, fears, and humiliations so many Muslims feel in regard to the West in general—and the U.S. in particular—and to recognize the importance of past experiences and perceptions in current reactions. The goal is not to challenge the specific beliefs people hold, but to understand much more fully why they feel as they do. What is it in their experiences that lead to strong feelings around past events, and what connects them to the present?

• *Acknowledgment.* There is a long and bitter history of relations between the Christian and Muslim worlds, and the Muslims still have vivid, bitter cultural memories of the massacres and desecration of their holy sites during the Crusades, the expulsions from Spain and Portugal in the late fifteenth century, and European colonization in the nineteenth and twentieth centuries. Pope John Paul II's visit to a mosque in Damascus in 2001 (the first ever by a pope) was a small effort to acknowledge this past. It might easily be contrasted with President Bush's reference to the war against terrorism as a Crusade in the first days after September 11. Acknowledgment can be both verbal and symbolic. It involves empathy without necessarily communicating apology or agreement. What are acknowledged are the deep feelings and threats a group feels. This can be painful for all sides, but it can result in a lowered intensity of feelings or even, when accompanied by meaningful actions, the rearrangement of connection among elements in a narrative.

• *New policies, actions and labels.* The U.S. administration has worked hard to define its response as an attack on terrorists and their supporters, not one against the Muslim world. It is not yet clear how successful this definition has been in countries such as Pakistan, Egypt, Saudi Arabia, or Iran, given the deep distrust of the U.S. Actions are needed which communicate this message more fully. It is also important that the U.S. make a major effort toward a just settlement of the Israeli–Palestinian conflict and change its policy toward Iraq, which is ineffective in achieving its key goals, and also puts the U.S. in a completely untenable humanitarian position. Probably the most difficult challenge will be to stop turning a blind eye to oppressive, corrupt regimes just because they happen to be aligned with the U.S. or supply needed resources. Making social justice and democratization in the region a high priority is long overdue, and the U.S. has to recognize that some of the strongest voices for democratization and egalitarian development are sometimes Islamic. If the U.S. continues to support regimes throughout the region which suppress all dissent, especially when that dissent speaks with an Islamic voice, the U.S. will continue to be the target of increased anger that arises from hopelessness and gives rise to extremist and terrorist groups.

A single common narrative that is widely accepted by both Muslims and Americans will not emerge from, nor be the goal of, such a process. It would be naïve to think that differences in culture, historical experiences, and political disagreement could be bridged so easily. It ignores the reality that on both sides significant change will have to focus on behaviors and not just what is said. In addition, when there are strong differences in how two parties see the world, it is important that these differences be acknowledged and explored and not just swept under the rug. Since September 11, the American media and many groups in American society have made a sincere effort to better understand the controversial role the U.S. has played in the Muslim world in recent decades. Many Americans better understand the complexity and diversity of Islam, the frustrations many Muslims feel, and the absence of democratic institutions and practices in some of the strongest U.S. allies in the Muslim world.

Rather than one joint narrative, the goal should be that the several narratives become less polarized, hostile, and distrustful. Perhaps they should have more common elements, but more importantly, they should have a more nuanced language and one that suggests, or at least permits, strategies for interaction and mutual adjustment. It may be that these can be built only through the participation of additional voices, such as those in Central Asia, Muslims in the U.S., and others who have been relatively unheard to date. First steps from the U.S., as the strongest power, surely are needed as part of this process.

When asked at a press conference on October 11, 2001 why people in the Muslim world hate the U.S., George Bush expressed amazement and replied, "That's because they don't know us." Some might respond that "they know us all too well." The answer I have offered here does not deny that knowing, and communicating with, an opponent can sometimes improve a relationship, but says that often this is not enough. Rather, this analysis draws attention to the role that structural relationships, specific policies, and deep emotions play in complicated, deep conflicts. In no way is it a justification for the horrible acts perpetrated on innocent people on September 11; my effort at explanation is aimed at understanding some of the underlying dynamics at work to make such future actions less likely. The U.S. military action may well achieve a number of its immediate goals. However, only when the deepest fears of each side are diminished, and the narratives of all parties become more complex and nuanced, will events such as September 11 become less likely. Where the clash of civilizations argument (offered by both Huntington and bin Laden) presents the conflict between Islam and the West as inevitable and enduring, the perspective here suggests that despite the deeply rooted historical nature of this conflict, there is much that can be done in the coming years to transform the conflict in more constructive directions and to lower its salience and intensity.

20. ORDINARY FEELINGS, EXTRAORDINARY EVENTS: MORAL COMPLEXITY IN 9/11

RAJEEV BHARGAVA

1.

In India, as elsewhere, every person understood that cry for help, the horror and fear writ large on terror-stricken faces, the trauma in the choked voices of people who saw it happen, the hopeless struggle to control an imminent breakdown in public, the unspeakable grief. For one moment, the pain and suffering of others became our own. In a flash, everyone recognized what is plain but easily forgotten: that inscribed in our personal selves is not just our separateness from others but also sameness with them; that despite all socially constructed differences of language, culture, religion, nationality, perhaps even race, caste and gender, and over and above every culturally specific collective identity, we share something in common. Amidst terror, acute vulnerability, and unbearable sorrow, it was not America alone that rediscovered its lost solidarity but, across the globe, almost everyone who heard, saw, or read about these cataclysmic events seemed to reclaim a common humanity.

As we empathized with those who escaped or witnessed death and relived the traumatic experience of those who lost their lives, we knew of a grave, irreparable wrong done to individuals, killed, wounded, or traumatized by the sudden loss of family and friends. These individuals were not just subjected to physical hurt or mental trauma, they were recipients and carriers of a message embodied in that heinous act: from now on they must live with a dreadful sense of their own vulnerability. This message was transmitted first to other individuals in New York and Washington, then quickly to citizens throughout the democratic world. The catastrophe on the east coast has deepened the sense of insecurity of every individual on this planet.

However, this was not the entire text of messages sent by the perpetrators. The rest is revealed when we focus on our collective identities, or rather on the irreducibly collective dimensions of the tragedy that unfolded on that terrible, terrible Tuesday. Unlike the first, which allows a plain and simple good to be distinguished from unambiguous evil, these messages were disturbingly ambivalent, morally fuzzy, and less likely to sift good from evil, more likely to divide rather than unite people across the world. One such message, which the poor, the powerless, and the culturally marginalized would always like to have communicated to the rich, the powerful, and the culturally dominant—although not in this beastly manner—is this: We have grasped that any injustice done to us is erased before it is seen or spoken about, that in the current international social order, we count for very little; our ways of life are hopelessly marginalized, our lives utterly valueless. Even middle-class Indians with cosmopolitan aspirations became painfully aware of this when a country-wide list of missing or dead persons was flashed on an international news channel: hundreds of Britons, scores of Japanese, some Germans, three Australians, two Italians, one Swede. A few buttons away, a South Asian channel listed names of several hundred missing or dead Indians, while another flashed the names of thousands with messages of their safety to relatives back home.

Hard as it was to acknowledge it in the immediate aftermath of September 11, it must be admitted that the attacks on New York and Washington were also meant to lower the collective self-esteem of Americans, to rupture their pride. Not all intentional wrongdoing is physically injurious to the victim, but every intentionally generated physical suffering is invariably accompanied by intangible wounds. The attack on September 11 did not merely demolish concrete buildings and individual people. It tried to destroy the American measure of its own self-worth, to diminish the self-esteem of Americans. Quite separate from the immorality of physical suffering caused, is not this attempt itself morally condemnable? Yes, if the act further lowered the self-worth of a people already devoid of it. But this is hardly relevant in the case of America, where sections of the ruling elite ensure that its collective self-worth borders on supreme arrogance, always over the top. Does not the Pentagon symbolize this false collective pride? Amidst this carnage, then, is the sobering thought that occurs more naturally to poor people of powerless countries: that occasionally even the mighty can be humbled. In such societies, the genuine anguish of people at disasters faced by the rich is mixed up with an unspeakable emotion which, on such apocalyptic occasions, people experience only in private or talk about only in whispers.

The whispers, the hushed tone in which people had spoken about uncomfortable feelings, did not last too long after September 11. Soon, several left-oriented intellectuals, the world over, vociferously appealed to ordinary Americans to explore the deeper reasons that underlie terrorism, pointing toward America's dubious foreign policy that has caused millions to suffer in Vietnam, Chile, Palestine, Iraq, and Sudan, to name just a few countries. Madeleine Albright's infamous remark justifying the suffering and death of Iraqi children ricocheted from newspaper reports to television channels. Americans were coaxed to reexamine what their leaders do in their name. American ignorance and innocence were ridiculed: If only ordinary Americans cared to look at what was really going on alongside the American way of life and the rhetoric of freedom, they would begin to understand what happened on September 11 and why many ordinary people in the non-Western world were overcome with the feeling that it was more or less what America deserved; "damnable yet understandable payback, rooted in injustice, reaping what the empire has sowed." [1]

2.

Naturally, American intellectuals reacted with horror and disdain for such "ideological excuses for terrorism." They asked if a grave wrong committed today can be justified by a wrong committed in the past, in a different context and time? Could America never do anything right and Americans never be allowed to be victims? Do not Americans have feelings like others, ordinary feelings like ordinary people elsewhere? Should not these feelings be properly understood? Surely, there has to be a deep-rooted anti-American prejudice in most such intellectual responses from the non-Western world. They could respectfully listen to reasoned political opposition to American foreign policy but not accept the pathetic ideological reflex that was characteristic of these anti-American responses. [2]

It is hard to deny the presence of prejudice, rhetoric, and the sledge hammer of ideology in current critiques of America. And it is even harder to accept the view of the skeptic that denies the very distinction between rhetoric and argument, between ideology and reasoned political theory. It is true, of course, that both reasoned political argument and ideology seek to win over others, but they do so in dramatically opposite ways. One, steadfastly committed to transparency, provides every conceivable reason for its principles and value-based conclusions; the other short-circuits moral values, reduces principles to formulae, almost always privileges the use of rhetoric over reason, and permits half-truths, even lies.

Yet, for all the validity and usefulness of the distinction between reasoned political argument and ideology, we must try not to seal them off altogether or wholly overlook what they have in common. [3] For a start, the world of the political theorist is not entirely devoid of rhetoric and emotion, nor is the universe of the ideologist completely lacking in reflexiveness, internal coherence, or rational thought. Likewise, no matter how well justified, a rationally defended belief system still contains an element of extra-rational preference and some prejudice. For all the justified complaints against ideology, should we not acknowledge, in the end, the grain of truth it might contain about us and our world? No matter how exasperating its form and how crude its technique, should we not address its content? Anyhow, ideologies are shaped by their practical function, by the inherent logic of what they are meant to deliver, i.e. a broad conceptual map of the social and political world without which a political agent cannot think, decide, or act. Ideologies are necessarily gestural, uncertain steps in the dark that may lead to invaluable and indispensable insights about the social and political world. Surely, it must be admitted that reasoned political argument is not always necessary for this purpose, and never sufficient. Reason may fine-tune some ideologies or help defeat others, but it cannot replace them. Alas, even those of us who loathe the form of ideology must closely attend to its content. The ideology of anti-Americanism must not be dismissed as prejudice standing against enlightened reason.

However, what appears to have invaded the public sphere well before, and certainly after, the air strikes is galaxies away from not only the careful, issue-based, reasoned opposition to U.S. foreign policy but also from the ideology of anti-Americanism. Far beneath the anti-Americanism of the ideologue lies a magma of impression, emotion, and confused thought of ordinary people that just a while ago was self-directed and is now suddenly targeted at the other. It is this chaotic, sweltering cesspool that non-Western intellectuals are trying to hold in their hands and then carry into the international public domain. It is quite wrong to call this ideology. Such mixtures of impressions and feelings, having settled slowly over the years, independent of our will, suddenly and unexpectedly reveal themselves under the impact of cataclysmic events. They are not content-less, however. Often, they are beliefs masquerading as feelings, the common man's interpretation of larger social and political situations based on directly felt experience and the itsy-bitsy information filtering through to him, the ordinary person's very own causal account of her suffering, produced in her view by a chain of oppression that resides in her home but originates and begins its devious journey from somewhere in America. The cognitive content of these feelings is this: the world is governed by two sets of international laws, one exclusive to America and its allies (rich, Western, white), and the other for the rest of the poor, non-Western world. A single American life is worth more than a thousand others. (The collective dimension mentioned above.) Is it such a remarkable fact that struggling, harried people, breathing a trifle freely for the first time, sometimes in an incipient egalitarian society, wish not to take any personal responsibility for their own enduring woes, that they overreact with anger, blame, and schadenfreude? Surely not any more remarkable than to discover that people with excessive wealth and power are generally insensitive to those without it, that they do not even notice their existence.

3.

Non-Western intellectuals are trying to open a chink for people in America in order to give them a glimpse of these convoluted feelings. This is frequently done not in the language of reasoned political theory but in a somewhat defective, insensitive, shockingly brazen form that, alas, is yet another import from the West. Most Americans, reacting adversely and perhaps hastily to expressions of anti-American feelings, are unable to catch what is going on here. This inability is linked, no doubt, to that peculiar narrowness of vision which accompanies power and wealth. Many Americans fail even to see the problem under discussion. Some do, but then quickly wish it away by telling themselves that it is so huge and intractable that nothing can solve it. A tiny group of American intellectuals is willing to acknowledge the problem, can even see the need to do something about it, but cannot bring itself to identify the causal connection between the conduct of their government and business corporations and the abysmal condition of the poor. They cannot grasp that the global political and economic order is deeply structured in a manner that benefits the rich in the developed world and severely harms the global poor.

Of course, not all American intellectuals are myopic or insensitive. The best among them recognize that most rich countries are particularly protectionist about precisely those sectors in which developing countries provide tough competition. For instance, they can see that the technical and intellectual preconditions of a more equitable trade are nonexistent in most poor countries, that few poor countries can afford to bring their cases to the WTO or even have missions at the headquarters in Geneva, and that factors such as these have a gigantic impact on employment, income, tax revenues, and economic well-being in the developing world.[4] Such intellectuals also know that CIA funds were committed toward organizing the Muslims of the world into a global jihad against communism and that American assistance to the Afghan Islamists ran into billions of dollars. They are not unaware of the nefarious activities of their government in Chile, Nicaragua, Guatemala, Haiti, and a host of other countries. They support reasoned international opposition to their government's unjust policies. But even the most celebrated of these intellectuals were puzzled, disturbed, and enraged when confronted with the morally ambivalent statements of non-American left-liberal intellectuals that, in the same breath and the same narrative, condemned both the terrorist and his enemy, and sympathized with both those facing continuing oppression and the most recent, unexpected sufferers at the hands of the terrorist. What they want instead is outright condemnation, without pause, qualification, equivocation or, somewhat curiously, even understanding. At the very least, they wish to postpone understanding in the belief that any attempt to understand the act now is to condone it. Surely, they would say, a situation and time such as this demands simple and elementary, not complex morality.

Take Michael Walzer's typically incisive piece in the *American Prospect*.[5] He writes "As Americans we have our own brutalities to answer for—as well as the brutalities of other states that we have armed and funded. None of this . . . makes Terrorism morally understandable. Maybe psychologists have something to say on behalf of understanding." There is much in this piece which I admire and with which I agree. But I wish to draw the attention of the reader to something in it which is quietly discomforting.

Walzer correctly notes that an act of terror, though chosen collectively and strategically, is so unambiguously evil that even its perpetrators cannot morally justify it. However, for many left-liberal intellectuals, the disavowal of moral justification of terror stops well short of its condemnation. Indeed, Walzer claims, a whole politics of ideological apology has been spawned in the West since September 11. Foremost among these excuses for terror is that it is used as the very last resort. The image presented is of an oppressed and embittered people "who must be terrorists or nothing at all" because they have "tried every form of legitimate political action, failed everywhere, until no alternative remains but the evil of terrorism." For Walzer, far from attempting and exhausting every political action and then having run out of options, terrorists typically choose terror as the first option.

Walzer is right about terrorists; terror is indeed their first option. Quite simply, the description that "they (the oppressed) have tried all political possibilities and failed" does not apply to them. But it does fit a category of agents not mentioned by Walzer. A group of moderates, oppressed but not embittered, exist who have tried every conceivable form of legitimate political action, exhausted all options, and failed, but who have refused all along any form of violence, most of all terror. Unfortunately, the political space left vacant by their persistent failure and subsequent retreat is swiftly occupied by an impatient, embittered, almost-lunatic fringe, predisposed to deploy terror and previously sidelined, for that very reason, by the moderates. The extremists, particularly the terrorists among them, gain squarely at the expense of the moderates.

What causes the failure of the moderates? What mechanism brings this about? First, the obdurate indifference of the state to the peaceful, legitimate demands of the moderates. The state, "the enemy of the terrorist," hears the voice only of unreason: shrill polemic and deafening, hysterical psychobabble. Moderates who have "learnt the art of repetition, who do the same thing over and over again" are left unheard, unattended, and eventually unsung. Shown to be ineffective by an unresponsive state, and drowned by the fervent hyperbole of the extremists, they gradually lose legitimacy in the eyes of their own supporters, the ordinary people. The matter does not end here. Despite contrary appearances, the state is always an active player in the game, ignoring moderates, often responding quickly to extremism and almost always creating conditions conducive to unreason. In a sense, the state colludes with terrorists to defeat moderates because deep down it knows that its own interests do not match the real interests of ordinary people and that only moderates, who properly reflect these interests, pose a real threat to its existence. The plain truth is that the terrorist is a minor player in the larger struggle of the moderates (and the people they represent) and the unjust state they confront.

Every struggle between the oppressors and the oppressed operates on at least two levels: the hard-nosed, forceful battle over brute power, and the even more significant one over moral legitimacy. People fight oppressive situations because these situations are morally reprehensible. But some ways of fighting oppression not only fail to alter this inherent immorality of the situation of the oppressed but induce further moral regression. These methods, at least temporarily, change the moral relations between the oppressor and the oppressed. By awarding moral advantage to the oppressors, a morally reprehensible act by the oppressed actually helps the long-term interests of the oppressor. This is how acts of terror perpetuate the injustice they allegedly fight. When people are seen to be represented by terrorists rather than by moderates, they are virtually identified with them—seen to be terrorists themselves—and, from then on, their cause no longer enjoys the wider legitimacy it once possessed. Therefore, it is always in the interest of oppressor states to infect moderates with terrorism, to act in ways that increase the probability of an extremist victory over moderation.

How accurate then is Walzer's picture of the ground a reality? In my reckoning, only partly. For Walzer, there exist two active combatants in the struggle, the terrorists and their enemy, typically the state.[6] But, as we have seen, what is witnessed on the ground is a tripartite struggle between three deeply implicated political agents: moderates, extremists, and the oppressor state/states. The success of one directly affects the chances of success of others. When moderates begin to run out of options, the extremists come marching in. When extremists step in, the oppressor state appears ever more reasonable and gains moral ground. When the state remains unresponsive, it ensures the future success of extremism. And so on. What, then, in his small but significant piece, Walzer does not fully appreciate is that the oppressed is not one agent but many. There are different types of agents fighting for the same cause. Which is why it is possible to at once condemn the terrorist but support other agents against oppression. It is possible to condemn terrorism and, without giving excuses for it, to try and understand its underlying causes. It is even possible to find something morally worthwhile in a cause which terrorists undermine by their endorsement. The moral justification of our claims against oppression disappear neither when terrorists hijack them nor when terrorists are defeated. What looks like an ideological excuse for terrorism may really be a moral justification of the struggle of the marginalized moderates against unjust practices of their own states and against the support frequently extended to their states by Western powers.

4.

Victims of September 11 reacted with quiet dignity in the face of overwhelming grief, not uncommon in people benumbed by the horror that has recently visited them. But soon there was extreme moral revulsion also and perhaps an understandable expression of the need for vengeance. Even as some people unfairly, preposterously become the victims of this newest hatred, there were calls for revenge. How are these feelings to be assessed?

Can anything at all be wrong with hating ruthless strategists who achieve their political goals by the indiscriminate slaughter of innocent civilians, by random acts of violence designed to terrorize ordinary people? How can it be wrong for a woman to hate the rapist who has permanently scarred her or for victims to hate the organizers of mobs that lynched them? At issue here is not the feeling of *ressentiment*, an intense desire to hurt others in order solely to gain comparative advantage for oneself. Of course, malicious hatred is morally obnoxious. But people overcome by hatred toward the perpetrators of the carnage on September 11 were not driven by malice or spite. Hating the wrongdoer is not morally inappropriate. And if so, it must be morally permissible to desire to hurt the wrongdoer. There must be some room in our moral topography for what the philosopher Jeffrie Murphy calls retributive hatred.[7] It is extremely abnormal if self-respecting persons do not experience righteous anger, even hatred, toward those who have wronged them.

Yet, it is not always wise or morally appropriate for victims to act on these feelings. It is imprudent because retaliatory action sparks off escalating cycles of revenge and reciprocal violence, certain to plunge the entire world into greater suffering, pain, vulnerability, and insecurity. Besides, the same motive of revenge is known to unleash even greater tragedies. How do we make sure that today's victims do not become tomorrow's perpetrators of much worse? Can they be prevented from committing horrific excesses? What if the original motive of revenge unravels an unappeasable thirst for violence? If the lessons of history teach us anything at all, it is that barbaric acts of one group solicit equally barbaric acts from others. No matter on whom the first blow was struck, if our aim is to terminate barbarism, then it must be stalled now, suddenly, and abruptly. In the shifting sands of the complex ethic at work here, the entire moral advantage rests with victims of the immediate crime, and if the vision that generally motivates them is to come to good eventually, it is best, all things considered, to forgo the temptation to act on retributive hatred and feelings of vengeance.

To restrain vengeful motives is wise for another reason. When the mighty retaliate, they do not usually do so to grant equal status to offenders. It is rather more likely that, by a massive display of strength, the offenders are shoved further back in their less-than-equal place. The not-so-hidden text of such retaliation is to teach an abject lesson to all: Never again dare the supremacy of the powerful. Therefore, it never surprises anyone when a disproportionate and symbolic show of force to maim and crush the enemy flows from the very same motive of vengeance. It is true, of course, that some acts of revenge are the wellspring of equality and refute claims of supremacy by wrongdoers. However, the spectacular show of violence on September 11 and in the days to come was always going to reveal a different logic of alternating claims to superiority.

But is it not true that a specific, brief, well-targeted use of force can sometimes end current wrongdoing as well as prevent future acts of grave wrongdoing? Indeed, has not the defeat of the Taliban proved precisely that and therefore justified the use of force? Things may not be as clear-cut as that. For a start, estimates of casualties in Afghanistan are well above the number tragically killed on September 11.[8] We may not have witnessed on our television sets ghost towns with terror-stricken faces, choked voices, desperately crying for more help, but we need no imagination to sense the scale of the continuing problem in Afghanistan. Besides, it is still too premature to judge whether the Taliban has really been defeated. True, a Taliban-led government has fallen, but its forces have simply melted away into the rural areas; they have not disarmed and demilitarized. The Taliban militia may have become inactive but has not lost the capacity to reassert itself. Nor have the members of Al Qaeda been captured. They too have simply dispersed. Indeed warlordism and disorder may have grown even further. As for those orphaned in this recent war, only time will tell how they will behave a few years from now. As is well known, much of the Taliban was constituted by children orphaned and brutalized by the civil war and fueled by their hopelessness, discontent, and anger. With the Bush administration openly nurturing a desire to extend the war to other areas, and with the Afghan issue itself far from settled, who can say with confidence that the world has come out of the vicious cycle of revenge?

September 11 should have become a watershed event that began the serious questioning of this warped logic and set new standards of international retributive justice, not revenge. This, as we all know, has not happened. Instead, American action in Afghanistan continues the ugly tradition of unilateral state action to punish other "deviant" states. American might should have been restrained, perpetrators brought to book in an international court of justice and tried for crimes against humanity. This would have just been a beginning.

A larger process of reconciliation should then have been set in motion, by first decoding messages of marginalized collectives hidden under the gruesome rubble of Tuesday's destruction and then placing them for discussion by moderates from all over the world. Only by properly understanding the social, cultural, and spiritual basis of self-respect in our troubled times could we ever have begun to address the problems violently thrown at us on September 11. Reconciliation between cultures, between peoples, is not impossible, and mutual understanding, though difficult, is a crucial first step toward it. To begin understanding one another, we need global forums where, without fear of permanently offending each other, people can express themselves freely. I believe left-liberal intellectuals, though somewhat divided these days into pro- and anti-American camps, have a pivotal role in establishing such forums.

I have been pleading with American intellectuals that they should attend to the content of feelings, not obsessively demand that they be expressed in their preferred form and to not confuse the moral articulation of the just demands of moderates with an ideological apology for terrorism. But my non-American intellectual friends should introspect too.[9] Insensitivity and ignorance are not unique American faults. Much of the Indian elite is shockingly insensitive to the appalling conditions under which their fellow citizens live and alarmingly ignorant of the horrors in large parts of Africa. How can we then expect the even more wealthy, powerful, and privileged to be any different? Humans everywhere in the world tend to build a wall around themselves, and the more comfortable they are within these walls the less likely they are to notice those outside such walls. Perhaps this is a time for all of us to look within and catch this ugly, decidedly uncomfortable truth about ourselves. Only then will all of us properly face up to the ambivalence and internal conflict that always accompanies a morally complex event such as September 11. Perhaps, only then will mutual understanding begin.

5.

I have spoken of two dimensions to the message hidden in the mangled remains of the destruction of September 11. The moral horror of the individual dimension of the carnage was unambiguous and overwhelming. But as we examined its collective dimension, a less clear, more confusing moral picture emerged. How, on balance, after putting together these two dimensions, were we to evaluate this complicated moral terrain? The answer had to be swift and unwavering. The focus in the immediate aftermath of the tragedy had to remain on the individual and the humanitarian. To have shifted our ethical compass in the direction of the collective would have weakened the moral claims of the suffering and the dead. And that would plainly have been wrong. Nor would it have been enough to have made merely a passing reference to the tragedy of individuals, a grudging concession before considering the weightier political crimes of a neo-imperial state. Then, as always in such situations, the moral claims of individuals are supreme. If so, to have aggressively emphasized the collective dimension of the tragedy at that inopportune time was horribly indecent. But equally, to continue to screen off the collective dimension, to keep ignoring what ordinary people in the non-Western world feel, would obscure from view that this new tragedy is part of a chain of tragedies. It would also prevent us from understanding how all such tragedies, always lived individually, can be prevented in the future; surely, this would only perpetuate another already existing moral wrong.

21. CLOSE ENCOUNTERS: ISLAM, MODERNITY, AND VIOLENCE

NILÜFER GÖLE[1]

1. THE TERRORIST MOMENT

I was driving down the hill on the campus of Bosphorus University with Uğur, a Ph.D. student of mine working on Islamic coffee houses in Istanbul. We were discussing the new forms of Islamic appearances in secular public spaces, when my cellular rang. It was my niece Zeynep, working in international banking (plugged in constantly to the Internet and to information networks), who informed me of the catastrophe. At that very moment only one of the twin towers of the World Trade Center along with the Pentagon was hit. I rushed home to watch the television and found myself witnessing the second attack. I was sitting stunned for hours in front of the screen, zapping between CNN, Turkish and French channels, and trying to find words that would give meaning to the images. The scope of destruction and the incessant repetition of images were creating a hypnotizing effect. Images were acquiring a sort of autonomy in the mind working their way through senses and emotions rather than being processed by words and rationality. It took me several days to shake off this state of apathy and contact my friends living in the States.

To my surprise, they all gave very detailed, precise, and personalized accounts of the moment. As I am doing myself right now. How they learned about the attack, where they were, and what exactly they were doing at that very moment, how they reacted emotionally and worried about their close ones, were meticulously described in their emails.

A colleague witnessed the catastrophe real close. He was changing planes in Washington when the plane hit the Pentagon, had to leave the airport, and took the first train allowed to leave town. ". . . I was worried about S. because he was in New York and I couldn't reach him by phone. . . . Meanwhile, S. heard the first Trade Center blast when he was in the shower. Thinking it was a car wreck, he went to the window and looked out. I'm attaching the photo he took from our living room window, hoping your software can open photos."

Indeed photos, sent around the world digitally, were hinting at the visual experience of the moment, as a "snapshot." Maybe for the first time in history a terrorist event was being witnessed live, in real time, as an ocular experience and by so many people. September 11 was experienced personally, visually, simultaneously, and globally by those situated in different locations and publics. The terrorist moment took place in a global public space. The personal stories of those who were in the vicinity of the World Trade Center were particularly intense. But all, from different parts of the world, in different cities, in Cairo, Montreal, New Delhi, Barcelona and from different publics, Muslim or Western, expressed a personal need to locate themselves and give a personal account of the circumstances under which they first heard about the terrorist attack and how they reacted to it.

The media, the newspapers, the Internet, most conversations, all moved and circulated information, stories, ideas, and pictures among different publics. Through repetitive images and the circulation of anecdotes, the moment was recorded and engraved in our collective memory. As in the case of an earthquake, the loss of a loved one, a fracture occurred; a fracture which took command of the memory. A sense of before and after developed as in the case of a tragic date. Narrating meant recapitulating retrospectively and over and over again the factual details from a personal angle; as if memorizing the moment could help to comprehend the tragic event.

September 11 now became 9/11, a date, a history-making moment, or rather a history-vanishing moment. Either way, we witnessed how the personal and the historical were intrinsically connected. History with a capital *H* was written with a collectivity of personal narrations from different locations. We had the impression of entering into History through a personal gateway. The terrorist instance turned into a calendar day, a historic moment. By the way, in Arabic, in Turkish, and in Persian the same word, "tarih," stands both for a date and history.

September 11 took place in a concentrated yet relatively short temporality, peculiar to an act of terrorism. Yet within the moment of terror were condensed different temporalities, ages of history. Terrorism on September 11 and the U.S. counterattack on the Taliban opened up the Pandora's box of a collective unconscious evoking the Crusades and drawing upon categories of distinction between the "civilized" and the "barbarians." Layers of history and memory were compressed and juxtaposed without chronological order in that moment: The hijackers viewed their action in reference to the history of Islam in the seventh century (especially the ten-year period between 622, the year of the Prophet's flight from Mecca, and 632, the year of his death) during which battles of the Prophet built the Islamic society against the infidels.[2] Whereas for the Western publics, the act evoked the shadows of very different historical moments, ranging from the Persian invasion of Athens, the Turks attacking Vienna, the assassination of John F. Kennedy in 1963, to the recent bomb attack at the World Trade Center in 1993.

2. VISUALIZING VIOLENCE

Different realities and distant temporalities are brought together by these collages that fix the history of September 11: history understood both as an image and the narrative attached to it.[3] On September 11 the instant as fracture and the image as violence imposed themselves on the mind. Since then we have been trying to find appropriate words, sort out a narrative that will accompany them.

Terror as usual was faceless, but also voiceless. Likewise New York; mutilated and muted. Silence accompanied the catastrophe. Absence of demands on the part of the perpetrators, absence of meaningful narratives on the part of the spectators. We were reduced to being passive spectators; it was like watching a silent movie on the apocalypse. Those who could see the World Trade Center, watched in silence behind their double windows; others watched in real time in front of their television screens. Terrorism burst onto the stage of history, but the spectators were reduced to silence and to impotence, their capacity to act and to intervene were blocked, their subjective will to act was annihilated. The only heroic action was that of the firemen and police—who dramatically turned into involuntary martyrs.

During the attacks, the senses were heightened as in the case of a war, and through the media, the visual sense was traumatized. The attacks—blending terrorism, catastrophe, and war in one single stroke—spread through ocular violence.

Building a narrative, that is, attaching a meaning to September 11, should hence start from the temporality of the instant and the image, and not from the long-term causes nor from textual interpretations. In other words instead of enumerating economic, political causes or religious interpretations that have preceded the act, and advancing ethical arguments for the future, we first need to fix the image, give a pause, free it from the past and future time horizons, suspend it in the present, and expand it in search of new details and perspectives. We can visualize September 11 as a "snapshot" (note that the vocabulary meaning evokes violence: both a break and an explosion), as an *instantané* (in French) or as an *Augenblick* (in German) to link temporality and image, to capture both the suddenness of the moment and the intensity of the visual. The act of terror in this perspective appears as a *Momentbild,* as a momentary image that bears significance beyond that moment.[4] Once we frame the picture, then we can change the scales, shift from the micro to the macro,[5] move back and forth between the particular instance of the event and the structural long-term processes, and turn thereby the synchronic temporality of the picture into a moving picture, that is a movie (in my view on Islam and modernity) with historical agency and depth.

Understanding September 11 requires building a narrative starting from the terrorist moment as an instance, an exemplary incident which, in one moment, makes appear different temporalities and a range of issues hitherto suppressed in one instant.

Furthermore, there were two instances, two "snapshots," not one. It is only when the second tower was hit that in our minds the possibility of an accident ended, terrorism revealed itself, and bin Laden's name and Islam were associated.

It is at that moment that I found myself saying that this could not be the work of Islamists. First, the scale of terrorism, with four hijacked planes attempting to hit four targets simultaneously, seemed to me almost too big, American size, to be imagined by Muslims. Secondly, long-time meticulous preparation in silence and technological expertise were not typical of Islamic activism. I had the conviction with many others that Muslims could not have cooperated and executed such a large-scale technical action to perfection. In the first hours, Agence France Press mentioned the name of a Japanese terrorist group; with the Kamikaze tradition, technical mastery, and the Hiroshima vengeance, a plausible rumor, it seemed to me. After all, in the case of the Oklahoma attack (1995) we were misled; the terrorists were not Islamists but white-supremacist American groups. Well, this was obviously wishful thinking on my part. There is no neutral public, and I was thinking and speaking as a member of the most concerned public; Muslim, Middle-Eastern, and a sociologist on Islam. In my work, I have been trying to highlight modes of intersection between Islam and modernity, rather than adopting the perspective of a "clash" between the two. Islamic terrorism meant a triple defeat for me; religious, intellectual, and personal. However, my initial refusal to believe that Islamist actors were responsible for September 11 went beyond my wish to repress this embarrassing and painful reality. My arguments on the incapacity of Muslims to undertake such a large-scale high-tech attack expressed as well a hidden contempt (self-contempt?) for Muslims—a contempt that this very attack meant to reverse and invalidate, as I would realize later.

3. A NEW MAPPING OF THE ISLAMIC SOCIAL IMAGINARY

The terrorists were trained and acquired engineering and technical expertise in the United States and in Germany, effortlessly emulated the common lives of Western suburbia, performed in full recognition of the supremacy of the media, and were tuned in to the forces of (anti)globalization. The attack was an attack from within. The terrorists themselves were a product of the modern world, using modern arms, attacking modern targets. Islam was not turning against some kind of external, colonial, or occupant force of modernity. In an ironical sense, Islam was never so close to Modernity, both in metaphorical and in literal sense; so close as to collide and mutually annihilate, just like the double crush/crash of the planes and the twin towers tragically symbolized.

The attacks of September 11 were condemned by many publics (including Muslim ones), but silently or even overtly endorsed by many others (and not only by Muslim ones). The reasons for this tacit consent were mainly enumerated in geopolitical or economic terms.[6] The division and yet the proximity between the rich and the poor; a world speaking the language of human rights, while many suffered under authoritarian regimes; those oriented toward success versus those without future; a world of citizenship versus a world of corruption; a world of libidinal consumption versus territories of famine—certainly there is a perturbing gap that fuels emotions of resentment, injustice, and revenge. But enumerating long-term structural causes is not sufficient to decode terrorism. It certainly helps us to understand the historical and political stage on which the terrorist act is played out, but at the same time such arguments exteriorize and objectify the reasons of terrorism and thereby omit its intrinsic motifs and trivialize the connections with Islam. Especially when such a historical-causal understanding of the phenomenon is coupled with the liberal inclination not to reduce Islam as a universal religion to a particular act of terrorism, the importance of the event itself fades away. The terrorist instance becomes secondary in view of the long-term past causes, on the one hand, and the ethical concerns for the future, on the other. Such self-critical Western analysis unintentionally ends up reducing terrorism to an epiphenomenon. Arguments such as "bin Laden is a product of American politics" attribute full agency to the Western powers, whereas Muslims appear just as victims. Certainly, holding on to the view of a Western-centered and manipulated world, however unconsciously, has a soothing and reassuring function. Yet the attacks of September 11 attempted, even if only for a day, to reverse the roles, revealed the vulnerability of the Western powers, and turned Americans to victims. Although the war on the territory of Afghanistan aimed to restore the power relations and ended up creating new victims, the reasons for the tacit approval of the terrorists' act should be sought in the direction of this displacement of power relations between the West and Muslims. September 11 undoubtedly provoked shame among Muslims, but also a hidden feeling of pride and empowerment. However, this unacknowledged disposition does not mean the endorsement of Islamist radicalism, let alone bin Ladenist terrorism. But it contributes to the elaboration of a collective Islamic imaginary.

In the aftermath of September 11, the new mapping of an Islamic collective imaginary which was already taking place independently of national differences, religious-confessional divisions, or popular tradition, became more apparent. The Islamic revolution in Iran in 1979, the assassination of Anwar Sadat in 1981, Khomeini's *fatwa* against Salman Rushdie in 1989, the destruction of the Buddha statues in Afghanistan by the Taliban in 2001, the attacks on American on September 11, 2001 are among the "Sign Posts"[7] in the making of an Islamic collective imaginary which transcends the national frontiers and religious distinctions between Sunni and Shi'te Islam. It extends the territory of Islam, conquering (as in the case of "futuhat") not new territories, but the social imaginaries both in Muslim-majority and Muslim-minority situations. Each offensive constitutes a political (or rather a "meta-political"[8]) icon and has a religious reverberation. Application of *shari'a* (Islamic revolution), call for *jihad* (September 11), but also blasphemy (*The Satanic Verses*), idolatry (the Buddha statues), and usury (Western banking) reactivate and penetrate, by adherence as well as by resistance into Muslim consciousness. The religious lexicon is used and misused to give meaning to these practices as well as to resurrect a collective Islamic repertoire. Religious idiom and the antagonism with the icons of Western culture provide a sense of collective empowerment and the elaboration of Muslim self-definitions. In a modern world speaking the language of emancipation, tolerance, and liberalism, blasphemy, idolatry, and *jihad* appear as a religious reminders of limits, prohibitions, and duties for Muslims.

These micro-acts, seemingly isolated in time and space, express both an antagonistic engagement with the West and the reinforcement of an Islamic community, *umma*, guided by moral values of Islam. The centrality of moral values shapes the relations between religion and politics as well as individual and society in Islam. "The virtuous Muslim is thus seen not as an autonomous individual who assents to a set of universalizable maxims but as an individual inhabiting the moral space shared by all who are together bound to God (the *umma*)."[9] Complex notions of both *jihad* (religious war)[10] and *shari'a* (religious norms and laws derived from Qur'an and the Sunnah—words and deeds of the Prophet), as manifestations of religious obedience to God, illustrates the close linkages between the interiorization of religious morality and the community (*umma*) as a religious-political space. Neither *jihad* nor *shari'a* are confined exclusively to the realm of *ulema*, politics and the state. *Shari'a* is the foundation of an Islamic way of life. It governs every aspect of life from matters pertaining to ritual purity to questions related to interest-free banking and jurisprudence. Islamic religion is more about how one lives than what one believes. And the veiling of women as the most powerful meta-political icon contributes to the daily performance of Islamic morality, to the disciplining of self, body, and space in counterdistinction with the Western conceptions of the emancipatory self. The different manifestations of the veiling issue in different contexts, ranging from state enforcement (as in Iran), community pressure (as in the Egyptian case) to individual choice (as in Turkey), illustrate well the difficulty of differentiation between individual, community, and state enforcement in regard to religious issues.

The call for *jihad* entails both the meaning of making an effort on the path of God, ranging from a warrior military sense to a more moral version, encompassing individual interiorized effort, and community improvement. Martyrdom is associated with the warrior interpretation of *jihad* and the devotion to community's defense. However the suicide-attacks on September 11 inject a novel notion of martyrdom into the Muslim imaginary: There is no defense of any communal purpose, but a status to be achieved by the individual warrior and performed as a pure act of worship to please God, irrespective of God's specific command. Consequently martyrdom ends up blending into a new kind of nihilism.[11] Martyrs themselves are uprooted as well; they are recruited from different regions and countries, illustrating both the global and de-territorialized feature of the Islamist action.[12]

4. TWINS AND MIMETISM

The targets on September 11 were the Pentagon in Washington and the World Trade Center in New York. Both targets represent the international, outward-looking face of America, both military and economic. But in the last decades, financial capitalism rather than military domination stood for the expansionist power of the United States. No wonder that it is the collapse of the twin towers, the temple for financial capitalism, which came to be the pictogram of September 11. It was not just the human lives lost or bodies that disappeared which shocked the public, but the images of the planes crushing one after another into the towers, the fire, silhouettes of human bodies jumping out of the buildings, and the collapse of the towers that caused a deep trauma for our visual and ethical memory.

The airplane and the skyscraper, respectively the arms and the target of the terrorists, were the two major technological symbols of the industrial era and therefore a little bit outdated in the digital/communication era. Both represented and facilitated human mobility, the sense of exploration, and the possibility for urban concentration. In today's information age, neither the planes nor the skyscrapers were subject to major innovations; we have reached the limits of speed and height: Or rather they have become so common, so familiar that they could no longer be seen—until September 11, the day when both the airplanes and the skyscrapers turned into unfriendly, hostile sites for all.

The twin towers, when they were dedicated in 1973, were presented (and heavily criticized) as the hallmark of modern architecture, as the first buildings of the twenty-first century. The matrix of steel and glass invoked the modern aesthetic of transparency and solidity. They expressed the engineers' genius and their arrogance for overcoming natural limits. For the architect of the twin towers, Minoru Yamasaki, there was almost no limit of height: "It does not matter how high you go . . . what really matters in Manhattan is the scale near the ground." [13] As the tallest buildings, the twins imposed themselves as an (phallic) architectural icon in the New York skyline.

The twin towers no longer tell the world: "Divided we stand." Eric Darton, writing their biography in 1999, proposed to, almost prophetically, unbuild the towers from the landscape, that is, to make New York's World Trade Center symbolically disappear from our perspective in order to get to know its history of construction, story by story. Indeed, what do the twin towers really stand for? What did the terrorists actually make disappear as an icon?

That night, after the collapse of the twin towers, I did not want to go to sleep. Not fear of insomnia, but fear of the next day. The next day was not promising to be a better day. I was anxious of awaking in a world which did not bear any promise for the future. The terrorists have attacked the linkage between a new and a better day; have attacked the faith in work and progress, and foremost they have shattered the innocent pleasures of the routine of daily work.

One knows that the twin towers were office buildings, yet their architectural design made it nearly impossible to imagine that they were full of people, observed Eric Darton. The design of the World Trade Center did not give any indication of the purpose of the buildings. To the human eye, "trade towers disappeared as sites of human habitation." [14] In a similar but tragic way, the terrorist attack on the September 11 made the bodies disappear both materially and visually. The buildings were crumpling under our gaze, but the death of so many thousands was not visible to the eye, remaining just an abstract figure. The media self-censorship caused either by respect for human dignity or for the invincibility of the "sole remaining" superpower was responsible for not showing human agony. We still had to realize that bodies had simply vanished and incinerated under steel, glass, and fire and that families of victims yearned for their loved-ones' bodies for mourning. The disappearance of the bodies was counter-balanced by the daily publication of victims' biographical profiles in the newspapers. [15]

Darton, writing before September 11, points out that there is a kindred spirit linking the apparently polar realms of skyscraper builder and the skyscraper terrorist: "To attempt creation or destruction on such an immense scale requires both bombers and master builders to view living processes in general, and social life in particular, with a high degree of abstraction. Both must undertake a radical distancing of themselves from the flesh and blood experience of mundane existence 'on the ground.'" Darton quotes Gaston Bachelard who, in the *Poetics of Space*, speaks of distancing oneself from the flesh and blood experience of ground life to manufacture a daydream, a reverie, separated from the restless world. The daydream world offers up the impression of domination at little cost.[16] September 11 entails a radical distancing from flesh and blood existence of ground life (by the very arms and targets, namely plane and high-rise buildings, it raises itself well above the ground-level). It manufactures a science-fictional dimension separated from the real world both for the suicide-attackers themselves and for the victims, as well as the victimized eyewitnesses. It shares a mimetic desire of domination with the skyscraper builder.

The profile of some of the victims and the terrorists have similarities: same thirty-something generation, high-tech education (the life stories of the victims suggest that those at the World Trade Center were on average less specialized in high-tech and financial skills than one thinks). Yet the centrality of work in the lives of the victims and the absence of a work-oriented life for these Muslim terrorists separated their experiences. The terrorist accomplishment (meaning also work) is mimetic in reverse; it invalidated the work of others, a work day was made to be worthless. September 11 attacked the innocent belief in and the optimism for the future anchored in the daily routine of work as an organizing category of our modern personality and lives.

In this contemporary myth of the Tower of Babel, the hubris of the builders who defied space competed with the hubris of those who despised the vanity of the human condition and waived the threat of a sacred punishment. Industrial arrogance inspired by construction, science, and work, and terrorist arrogance sanctioned by destruction, religion, and death clashed.

On September 11, two towers were attacked by the two planes. Twin attacks against the twin towers.

5. FEARING SAMENESS AND QUEST FOR PURITY

The phobia for twins in traditional societies is common knowledge. Twins are feared and considered a punishment; physical resemblance is judged enigmatic because the disappearance of differences creates a problem of classification. The impurity of the sameness is feared to be contagious. And like all impurities, it attracts violence.[17] The relation between sexuality and violence is part of the common heritage of different religions. The twins, just like women and menstruation, are considered to be impure.[18]

The fear of impurity is revealed in the notes by the mastermind of the attacks, Mohammed Atta, that were left behind in the car that he used. A handwritten document in Arabic depicts in detail the religious prescription and the practical precautions to follow for achieving the unity of body and spirit and for succeeding at his last mission. The text specifies that the plan should be examined; that the suitcase, the clothes, the knife, the tickets, the passport should be checked; that the clothes should be tightened as the righteous predecessors have done in preparation for a battle; that a ritual washing should take place; that excess hair should be shaved from the body, and perfume applied to it in order to purify the body and the spirit.[19] The testimony of Mohammed Atta expresses overtly the fanatical fear of impurity from contamination by women and sexuality: "The one who will wash my body should wear gloves so that my genital parts should not be touched." It adds: "I don't want pregnant women or a person who is not clean to come and say goodbye to me because I don't approve of it. . . . I don't want any women to go to my funeral or later to my grave."

The phobia for women and twins mirrors the reaction engendered by proximity with that which is impure and with sameness. Sameness creates a problem for the contemporary Muslim world (read Muslim men). Modern society is a society of uniformization and homogenization of experience; it is worked out by the principle of equality. Equality has an unintentional consequence of creating (twin-like) "sameness." The aspiration for an egalitarian and democratic life has as its consequence the disappearance of hierarchies and frontiers between men and women, the old and the young, and between the cultural and the natural. The religious certainty anchored in the territory of nature (geographical, biological, and corporal) is shattered by industrial, medical, and genetic inventions. Women are at the center of these transformations; both in relation to cultural values and to bodily experiences. As women reconstruct their identity in regard to cultural criticism and gender consciousness, the differences between the cultural and the natural, the private and the public, the feminine and the masculine are blurred. The interchangeability of roles, clothes, and spaces between sexes become ordinary practices. The values of the modern world cherish borrowings, and the multiplicity of identities. Modernity has an inescapable, inevitable dimension; it spreads out globally, it becomes a model of reference by seduction, contamination, multiplication, and cloning. The twin posture of the towers, according to some critics, exemplified a coercive, antidemocratic and pernicious form of late capitalist extreme repetition, "the threat of insane multiplication."[20] There exists one "World Trade Center" building in every big city of the world.

And the Muslim world is far from making an exception. In Kuala Lumpur, Malaysia exists a replica of the twin towers.

The closeness between the Muslim world and modernity, like the intimacy between men and women, is a nodal point around which tensions are built. It is not the "choc" of difference and distance, but on the contrary, the closeness and intimacy which are at the origin of these tensions. Islam, especially that of the Middle East by its closeness to and ties with Europe—by means of geography, monotheism, voluntary modernization, colonization, and immigration—reveals most dramatically the problem of "small difference" and fear of sameness. Islamism is a collective and conflictual expression of this involuntary yet intimate encounter with modernity.

Contemporary Islamism is based on a double movement and tension: antagonistic posture with modernity and de-traditionalization of religion. Radical Islamism does not subscribe to the traditional interpretations of religion; Islamist discourse is simplistic, anachronistic, cut off from its referential context of the Qur'an. Islamism operates as a sort of ideological amalgam between different schools of Islam, national cultures, and popular customs. The authority of the religious hierarchy (*ulema*) for interpreting religious texts and jurisprudence is disregarded and faces erosion because of the democratization-cum-vulgarization of religious idiom. Laypersons who speak the language of Islam without institutional authority of religious schools and knowledge find legitimacy in their activism. Activism and terrorism provide, or rather impose, a new source of legitimacy for Islamic idiom. Who will decide what is licit and illicit in Islam? Who has the authority over the interpretation of religious texts? Who can give a *fatwa* and declare a *jihad?* These questions all become very problematic as Islam is de-traditionalized in the hands of Islamism in particular, and in the face of the modern secular world in general.

The marriage between the Taliban movement and bin Laden seems a mis-fit when one considers the distance of the first and the familiarity of the second in regard to the modern world. But the quest for Islamic purity implies separation both from women and modernity. The question of women is pivotal for the antagonistic engagement of Islamists with modernity. The Taliban movement is the most fanatic expression of the phobia of women, and the most radical attempt of seclusion of women in their bodies, in the interior space of the home. One cannot forbid modernity without forbidding women. "The Forbidden Modern"[21] implies this intrinsic relation between modernity and women. In the backstage of September 11, the seclusion of women is carried out, while the engineer-hijackers occupied the front stage.

Islamic veiling is a reminder of difference; a curtain, a boundary-maintenance between men and women, between interior and public exterior spaces, Islam and modernity. But at the same time, Islamic women make their way into spaces of modernity, acquire public visibility and socialize with men. They become active members of a political movement, participate in public life, have access to higher education, pursue professional careers. This paradox constitutes the central knot in view of the orientation of Islamism in general and of women in particular. Islamist engineers and veiled women reveal the tensions between rationality and faith, veiling and public visibility.[22] The recognition of this tension opens up a realm of self-reflexivity and creative conflictuality. The denial leads to ideological dogmatism and destructive antagonism.

The central question addressed to Islamists in particular and to the Muslim world in general is to know the ways in which they can come to terms with their own experience of modernity. Because modernity is more and more an intrinsic value and lived practice. September 11 was meant to express a radical antimodernity, but by the same token its actors have confessed to their being close to modernity. The "neo-martyrs,"[23] the de-traditionalized actors of the Muslim world, in destroying the most troublesome symbols of modernity, the twin towers, have destroyed their own twins. They have mutilated themselves, as they have mutilated their women. They have pushed Muslims to mourn their own modernity.

In other terms, Islamism expresses the ambivalence between being both "Muslim and Modern," or rather expresses a double negation, being "neither Muslim nor Modern," and thereby intensifies the unresolved tension between Islam and modernity. September 11 put a cathartic and tragic end to this tension. The fear of the sameness of modernity led them to search for purity through a destructive performance and to exorcize the modern in themselves.

6. APPEARANCE THROUGH DISAPPEARANCE: ISLAM ERUPTING IN PUBLIC

On September 11, the vulnerability of the United States was revealed. Thus the Americans tragically joined the rest of the world.[24] The city of New York was just like any city in the world, chaotic, crowded, and in ruins: "Lower Manhattan was like a city after an earthquake . . . Wall Street executives were wandering like the homeless. Streets like Kinshasa. Rubble like Beirut or the West Bank."[25] The premodern Taliban movement enters the stage of modern history with bin Laden-engineered terrorism. The United States and Afghanistan, one highly controlled and protected and the other totally abandoned to terrorism, meet one another in the same cycle and the coeval time of a globalized world. Globalization was furthermore accelerated as the most distanced in time, place, and civilization were brought together, and not always without anxiety nor confrontation. In particular the juxtaposition of images from New York and Kabul, and furthermore those of George W. Bush and Osama bin Laden, created a kind of surreal yet an embarrassing collage.[26]

September 11 had an unintended consequence, namely the appearance of Islam on the global stage. Since then, Islam is more than ever present in the transnational public sphere. "Islam" is teleported to the center of the collective imaginary. Islam, until then identified as a political issue and confined to the Middle East and to Europe, made its entry into the American consciousness. The mosque gained public recognition with the visit of President Bush. Hitherto unknown Qatar television channel Al Jazeera acquired global visibility.

I heard myself egoistically saying that I was going to lose the only relatively neutral public, namely the American public, for the reception of my work on Islam. Islam making its entry in the American public consciousness will most probably mean extension and multiplication of stereotype images and prejudiced arguments—leading to yet another missed opportunity for a dialogical relation between Islam and the West.

Islam, until now absent from globalization, becomes its active agent. Ironically, the interest in knowing and taming Islam increases the exchanges among different national publics and accelerates the creation of a transnational public sphere. Either interconnectivity between different national publics are intensified or new ones are launched. The French newspaper *Le Monde* published for the first time articles in English from the *New York Times;* the Turkish daily *Radikal* systematically published in translation selected articles of opinion-leaders and intellectuals from all over the world. Some of the experts or spokespersons of Islam circulate constantly among different national publics and television programs. Western languages are now familiar with the Islamic idiom (*jihad, fatwa* are used in daily language); the books on Islam enter into the mainstream market. Islam has become an active agent in the circulation of ideas, commodities, and people. Debating Islam enforces the expansion of the global frontiers of the public, media and market.

On the one hand, the martyrdom which aimed at purity ends up, albeit unintentionally, mixing and breeding Islam into the modern consciousness. On the other hand, the presence of Islam on the front stage of history defies and deconstructs the monocivilizational definitions of modernity.

Indeed, Islam and Modernity have never come so close.

22. AMERICA AND THE WORLD: THE TWIN TOWERS AS METAPHOR

IMMANUEL WALLERSTEIN[1]

1. AMERICA THE BEAUTIFUL

O beautiful for patriot dream/That sees beyond the years/Thine alabaster cities gleam/Undimmed by human tears!/America! America!/God shed his grace on thee/And crown thy good with brotherhood/From sea to shining sea!

"AMERICA THE BEAUTIFUL"

On October 24, 1990, I was invited to give the opening lecture of the Distinguished Speakers Series in celebration of the bicentennial of the University of Vermont. I entitled that lecture: "America and the World: Today, Yesterday, and Tomorrow."[2] In that talk, I discussed God's blessings to America: in the present, prosperity; in the past, liberty; in the future, equality. Somehow God had not distributed these blessings to everyone everywhere. I noted that Americans were very conscious of this unequal distribution of God's grace. I said that the United States had always defined itself, had always measured its blessings, by the yardstick of the world. We are better; we were better; we shall be better. Perhaps blessings that are universal are not considered true blessings. Perhaps we impose upon God the requirement that She save only a minority.

Today, we live in the shadow of an event that has shaken most of us, the destruction of the twin towers on September 11, 2001 by a group of individuals so dedicated to their ideology and their moral fury at the United States that they conspired for years to find ways to deal a deadly geopolitical blow to America and those they deemed its supporters around the world, and they did this in a way that required sacrificing their own lives. Most Americans have reacted to the events with deep anger, with patriotic resolve, and yet with considerable and persistent puzzlement. Puzzlement about two things: why did this happen? and how could it happen? And the puzzlement has been laced with a good deal of uncertainty: what must be done, what can be done, in order that such an event will not, could not, happen again?

As I look back on what I said 11 years ago, I do not wish to change anything I said then. But I do feel a bit of unease about the stance from which I spoke. I wrote as though I were an ethnographer from elsewhere, from Mars perhaps, trying to understand this curious species, *humanus americanus.* Today, I think that is not good enough. I am to be sure a human being, and concerned with the fate of humanity. But I am also an American citizen. I was born here. I have lived here most of my life. And I share full responsibility, along with everyone else in my position, for what has happened here and what will happen here. I have a moral obligation to view America from inside.

So, I wish to look at America and the world a second time. But this time I do not want to see how Americans see themselves through the prism of the world, but rather how Americans have seen the world, and how Americans might wish to see the world from here on in. And I am very aware that here I tread on contentious ground.

It is a rare president of the United States, in the twentieth century at least, who has not at some point made the statement that the United States is the greatest country in the world. I'm not sure our omnipresent public-opinion polling agencies have ever put the question directly to the American public, but I suspect that the percentage of the U.S. population that would agree with such a statement is very large indeed. I ask you to reflect on how such a statement sounds, not merely to persons from poor countries with cultures that are very different from ours, but to our close friends and allies—to Canadians, to the English, and of course to the French. Does Tony Blair think the United States is the greatest country in the world, greater than Great Britain? Would he dare think that? Does Pope John Paul II think it? Who, besides Americans and those who wish to migrate to the United States, believes this?

Nationalism is of course not a phenomenon limited to people in the United States. The citizens of almost every country are patriotic and often chauvinistic. Americans are aware of that, no doubt. But they nonetheless tend to note the fact that many people across the world wish to emigrate to the United States, and that no other locus of immigration seems to be quite as popular, and they take this as confirmation of their belief in American superior virtue as a nation.

But in what do we consider that our superior virtue consists? I think that Americans tend to believe that others have *less* of many things than we have, and the fact that we have more is a sign of grace. I shall thus try to elaborate the many arenas in which this concept of "less-ness" may be thought to exist. I shall start with the one arena about which most Americans seem to be quite sure. Other countries are less modern, meaning by modernity the level of technological development. The United States has the most advanced technology in the world. This technology is located in the gadgets found in our homes across the country, in the networks of communications and transport, in the infrastructure of the country, in the instruments of space exploration, and of course in the military hardware that is available to our armed forces. As a result of this accumulation of technology, Americans consider that life in the U.S. is more comfortable, that our production competes more successfully in the world market, and that therefore we are certain to win the wars into which others may drag us.

Americans also consider their society to be more efficient. Things run more smoothly—at the workplace, in the public arena, in social relations, in our dealings with bureaucracies. However great our complaints about any of these practices, we seem to find, when we wander elsewhere, that others manage things less well. Others do not seem to have American get-up-and-go. They are less inventive about finding solutions to problems, major and minor. They are too mired in traditional and/or formal ways. And this holds the others back, while America forges ahead. We are very ready, therefore, to offer friendly advice to all and sundry—to Nigerians, to Japanese, to Italians—about how they could do things better. The emulation of American ways by others is considered a big plus when Americans assess what is going on in other countries. Daniel Boone plus the Peace Corps comprise the bases of an evaluation of comparative political economy.

But of course most Americans would deny that the less-ness of others is merely material. It is spiritual as well. Or if the term spiritual seems to exclude the secular humanists, it is cultural as well. Our presidents tell us, and our patriotic songs remind us, that we are the land of liberty. Others are less free than we are. The Statue of Liberty stretches out its hand to all those "huddled masses yearning to breathe free."

Our density of freedom is visualized in so many ways. Which other country has the Bill of Rights? Where else is freedom of the press, of religion, of speech so honored? Where else are immigrants so integrated into the political system? Can one name another country in which someone arriving here as a teenager, and still speaking English to this day with a thick German accent, could become the Secretary of State, the chief representative of Americans to the rest of the world? Is there any other country where social mobility, for those with merit, is so rapid? And which country can match us in the degree to which we are democratic? Democratic not merely in the continuing openness of our political structures, the centrality of a two-party system, but also in our quotidian mores? Is the United States not the country which excels in maintaining the principle of "first come, first served" in the practices of daily life, this as opposed to a system in which those who have privilege get preference? And these democratic mores, in the public arena and in social life, date back at least 200, if not almost 400 years.

From melting pot to multiculturality, we have prided ourselves on the incredible ethnic mix of real American life—in our restaurants, in our universities, in our political leadership. Yes, we have had our faults, but we have done more than any other country to try to overcome them. Have we not taken the lead in the last decades in tearing down barriers of gender and race, in the constantly renewed search for the perfect meritocracy? Even our movements of protest give us cause for pride. Where else are they so persistent, so diverse, so legitimate?

And in the one arena where, up to 1945, we tended to admit that we were not the avant-garde of the world, the arena of high culture, has that not now all changed? Is New York not today the world center of art, of theater, of music performance, of dance, of opera? Our cinema is so superior that the French government must resort to protectionist measures to keep French audiences from seeing still more of it.

We can put this all together in a phrase that Americans have not used much, at least until September 11, but which we largely think in our hearts: We are more civilized than the rest of the world, the Old World as we used to say with a token of disdain. We represent the highest aspirations of everyone, not merely Americans. We are the leader of the free world, because we are the freest country in the world, and others look to us for leadership, for holding high the banner of freedom, of civilization.

I have meant none of this ironically. I am deeply persuaded that this image of the less-ness of the rest of the world is profoundly ingrained in the American psyche, however many there may be who will be embarrassed by my presentation, and insist that they are not part of such a consensus, that they are (shall we say?) more cosmopolitan in their views. And it is in this sense, first of all, that the twin towers are a perfect metaphor. They signaled unlimited aspirations; they signaled technological achievement; they signaled a beacon to the world.

2. ATTACK ON AMERICA

What the United States tastes today is a very small thing compared to what we have tasted for tens of years. Our nation has been tasting this humiliation and contempt for more than 80 years. . . . But if the sword falls on the United States, after 80 years, hypocrisy raises its ugly head lamenting the deaths of these killers who tampered with the blood, honor and holy places of the Muslims. The least that one can describe these people is that they are morally depraved.

OSAMA BIN LADEN
OCTOBER 7, 2001

Osama bin Laden does not think that America is beautiful. He thinks Americans are morally depraved. Now, of course, there are some Americans who also think that most Americans are morally depraved. We hear this theme from what might be called the cultural right in the United States. But while the critiques of the U.S. cultural right and those of Osama bin Laden overlap insofar as they deal with everyday mores, bin Laden's fundamental denunciation concerns what he calls U.S. hypocrisy in the world arena. And when it comes to America in the world arena, there are very few Americans who would agree with that characterization, and even those who might say something similar would want to nuance this view in ways that bin Laden would find irrelevant and unacceptable.

This was one of the two great shocks of September 11 for Americans. There were persons in the world who denied any good faith at all to American actions and motives in the world arena. How was it possible that persons who had less of everything worth having doubt that those who had more of everything had earned it by their merit? The moral effrontery of bin Laden amazed Americans and they found it galling.

To be sure, bin Laden is scarcely the first person to make this kind of verbal attack, but he was the first person who has been able to translate that verbal attack into a physical attack on U.S. soil, one that caught America by surprise and, momentarily at least, helpless. Until that happened, Americans could afford to ignore the verbal attacks so rampant in the world as the babblings of fools. But fools had now become villains. Furthermore, the villains had been initially successful, and this was the second great shock. We were supposed to be in a position to be able to ignore such criticisms because we were essentially invulnerable, and we have now discovered that we are not.

It has been frequently said that the world will never be the same again after September 11. I think this is silly hyperbole. But it is true that the American psyche may never be the same again. For once the unthinkable happens, it becomes thinkable. And a direct assault on mainland America by a scattered band of individuals had always been unthinkable. Now we have had to establish an Office of Homeland Security. Now we have the Pentagon discussing whether they should establish what they call an area command, a military structure hitherto limited to the areas outside the U.S. covering all the rest of the world, that would cover the United States itself.

Above all we now have "terrorists" in our vocabulary. In the 1950s, the term "Communists" received expansive employ. It covered not only persons who were members of Communist parties, not only those who thought of themselves or were thought of by others as "fellow travelers," but even those who lacked sufficient "enthusiasm" for the development of a hydrogen bomb. This was, after all, the specific charge that led the U.S. Atomic Energy Commission in 1953 to suspend the security clearance of J. Robert Oppenheimer, the very person who was known as, and had hitherto been honored as, the "father of the atomic bomb."

The term "terrorism" has now obtained the same expansive meaning. In November 2001, I watched a television program, *Law and Order*. The plot for this particular episode revolved around the burning down of a building in the process of construction. The background to this was that the contractor had received the land from the city, land which had previously been a neighborhood garden, tended to by the community. There was opposition to this construction in the community. A group of young persons identified as "environmental activists" decided to burn down the building in protest. The complication was that, by accident, someone was in the building unbeknownst to them, and died in the fire. In the end, the arsonists are caught and convicted. The interesting point of this banal story is that, throughout the program, the arsonists are repeatedly referred to as "terrorists." By any definition of terrorist, it is a stretch to use the term in this case. But no matter! It was so used, and it will continue to be so used.

We are the land of liberty, but today we hear voices—in the government, in the press, in the population at large—that we have accorded too much liberty, especially to noncitizens, and that "terrorists" have taken advantage of our liberty. Therefore, it is said, the privileges of liberty must give way to procedures that meet our requirements for security. For example, we apparently worry that if we catch "terrorists" and put them on trial, they may then have a public forum, they may not be convicted, or if convicted they may not receive the death penalty. So, in order to ensure that none of these things happen, we are creating military courts to be convened by the president, with rules to be established by him alone, with no right of appeal to anyone, courts that will operate in total secrecy, and are able to proceed rapidly to a conclusion—presumably to a death penalty, probably also carried out in secret. At the close of such trials, all we may be allowed to know is the name of the person so condemned. Or perhaps not even that. And in our land of liberty, this is being widely applauded, and at most halfheartedly opposed by a brave minority.

We consider, we have stated publicly, that the attack on America is an attack on our values and on civilization itself. We find such an attack unconscionable. We are determined to win the worldwide war against terrorism—against terrorists *and all those who give them shelter and support*. We are determined to show that, despite this attack, we are and remain the greatest country in the world. In order to prove this, we are not being adjured by our President to make individual sacrifices, not even the small sacrifice of paying more taxes, but rather to carry on our lives as normal. We are, however, expected to applaud without reservation whatever our government and our armed forces will do, even if this is not normal.

The extent of this requirement of "no reservations" may be seen in the widespread denunciation of those who try to "explain" why the events of September 11 occurred. Explanation is considered justification and virtual endorsement of terror. The American Council of Trustees and Alumni (ACTA), an organization whose founders are Lynne Cheney and Senator Joseph Lieberman, issued a pamphlet in November 2001, entitled "Defending Civilization: How Our Universities Are Failing America and What Can Be Done About It."[3] It is a short pamphlet, which makes its points with remarkable pithiness. It says that "college and university faculty are the weak link in America's response to the attack." It continues with this analysis:

> Rarely did professors publicly mention heroism, rarely did they discuss the differences between good and evil, the nature of Western political order or the virtue of a free society. Their public messages were short on patriotism and long on self-flagellation. Indeed, the message of much of academe was: BLAME AMERICA FIRST!

The pamphlet devotes most of its space to an appendix of 117 quotations which the authors feel illustrate their point. These quotations include statements not merely of such persons as Noam Chomsky and Jesse Jackson but of less-usual targets of such denunciations: the dean of the Woodrow Wilson School at Princeton, a former Deputy Secretary of State. In short, the authors of the pamphlet were aiming wide.

It is clear at this point that, even if the events of September 11 will not alter the basic geopolitical realities of the contemporary world, they may have a lasting impact on American political structures. How much of an impact remains to be seen. It does seem, however, that the puzzlement of Americans of which I spoke—why did this happen? and how could it happen?—is a puzzle to which we are not being encouraged to respond, at least not yet.

The twin towers are also a metaphor for the attack on America. They were built with great engineering skill. They were supposed to be impervious to every conceivable kind of accidental or deliberate destruction. Yet, apparently, no one had ever considered that two planes filled with jet fuel might deliberately crash into the towers and hit the buildings at precisely the point, 20 percent down from the top, that would maximize destruction. Nor had anyone anticipated that the buildings could collapse slowly, overwhelmingly, and in everyone's view, bringing down other buildings in their wake. No one ever expected that the fires such a collapse ignited would continue to burn for months afterward. The U.S. may be able to avenge the attack, but it cannot undo it. Technology turns out to be less than perfect as a protective shield.

3. AMERICA AND WORLD POWER

Anti-Catholicism, as it evolved [in Great Britain in the eighteenth century], usually served a dialectical function, drawing attention to the supposed despotism, superstition, military oppressiveness and material poverty of Catholic regimes so as to throw into greater relief supposed Anglo-British freedoms, naval supremacy, and agrarian and commercial prosperity, and consequently superior mode of empire.

LINDA COLLEY[4]

I start with this quote from Linda Colley to remind us that the United States is not the first hegemonic power in the history of the modern world-system, but rather the third, and that hegemony has its cultural rules as well as its vulnerabilities. One of the cultural rules is that the denigration of others is indispensable to sustaining the internal self-assurance that makes possible the effective exercise of world power.

There is nothing so blinding as success. And the United States has had its fair share of success in the past 200 years. Success has the vicious consequence that it seems to breed almost inevitably the conviction that it will necessarily continue. Success is a poor guide to wise policy. Failure at least often leads to reflection; success seldom does.

Fifty years ago, U.S. hegemony in the world-system was based on a combination of productive efficiency (outstripping by far any rivals), a world political agenda that was warmly endorsed by its allies in Europe and Asia, and military superiority. Today, the productive efficiency of U.S. enterprises faces very extensive competition, competition first of all coming from the enterprises of its closest allies. As a result, the world political agenda of the United States is no longer so warmly endorsed and is often clearly contested even by its allies, especially given the disappearance of the Soviet Union. What remains for the moment is military superiority.

It is worth thinking about the objectives of U.S. foreign policy, as pursued for the last 50 years by successive U.S. governments. Obviously, the U.S. has been concerned with threats posed by governments it considered hostile or at least inimical to U.S. interests. There is nothing wrong or exceptional about this. This is true of the foreign policy of any state in the modern world-system, especially any powerful state. The question is how the U.S. thought it could deal with such threats.

In the 1950s and 1960s, the U.S. seemed to be so strong that it could arrange, without too much difficulty and with a minimal use of force, that governments it did not like either could be neutralized (we called that containment) or, in the case of weaker governments, could be overthrown by internal forces supported covertly by the U.S. government, assisted occasionally by a little old-fashioned gunship diplomacy.

Neutralization was the tactic employed vis-à-vis the Communist world. The U.S. did not seek to overthrow the Soviet Union or any of its satellite regimes in east and central Europe. Basically, it did not seek this because it was not in a military position to carry this out against the expected resistance by the government of the USSR. Instead, the U.S. government entered into a tacit accord with the USSR that it would not even try to do this, in return for a pledge by the Soviet Union that it would not try to expand its zone. We refer to this in code as the Yalta Agreement. If one doubts the reality of this agreement, just review U.S. foreign policy vis-à-vis the German Democratic Republic in 1953, Hungary in 1956, Czechoslovakia in 1968, and Poland in 1981.

The accord was not, however, intended to apply to East Asia, where Soviet troops were absent, thanks primarily to the insistence of the Communist regimes in China and North Korea. So the U.S. did in fact try to overthrow these regimes as well as that in Vietnam. It did not, however, succeed. And these failed attempts left a serious scar on American public opinion.

The United States, however, was able to enforce its will in the rest of the world, and did so without compunction. Think of Iran in 1953, Guatemala in 1954, Lebanon in 1956, the Dominican Republic in 1965, and Chile in 1973. The coup in Chile by General Pinochet against the freely elected government of Salvador Allende, with the active support of the U.S. government, occurred on September 11. I do not know whether or not Osama bin Laden or his followers were aware of this coincidence of dates, but it is nonetheless a symbolic coincidence that many, especially in Latin America, will notice. It also points to a further metaphor of the twin towers. The twin towers were a marvelous technological achievement. But technological achievements can and will be copied. The Malaysians have already copied the twin towers architecturally, and a bigger skyscraper is being built right now in Shanghai. Symbols too can be copied. Now we have two September 11 anniversaries, on which victims mourn.

In the 1970s, U.S. foreign policy methods changed, had to change. Chile was the last major instance in which the U.S. was able so cavalierly to arrange other governments to its preferences. (I do not count the cases of either Grenada or Panama, which were very small countries with no serious mode of military defense.) What had caused this change was the end of U.S. economic dominance of the world-economy, combined with the military defeat of the United States in Vietnam. Geopolitical reality had changed. The U.S. government could no longer concentrate on maintaining, even less on expanding, its power; instead its prime goal became preventing a too-rapid erosion of its power—both in the world-economy and in the military arena.

In the world-economy, the U.S. faced not only the hot breath of its competitors in Western Europe and Japan, but the seeming success of "developmentalist" policies in large parts of the rest of the world, policies that had been designed expressly to constrain the ability of countries in the core zone to accumulate capital at what was seen to be the expense of countries in the periphery. We should remember that the 1970s was declared by the United Nations to be the "decade of development." In the 1970s, there was much talk of creating a "new international economic order," and in UNESCO of creating a "new international information order." The 1970s was the time of the two famous OPEC oil-price rises, which sent waves of panic into the American public.

The U.S. position on all these thrusts was either ambiguous discomfort or outright opposition. Globally, a counterthrust was launched. It involved the aggressive assertion of neoliberalism and the so-called Washington Consensus, the transformation of GATT into the World Trade Organization, the Davos meetings, and the spreading of the concept of globalization with its corollary, TINA ("there is no alternative"). Combined, all these efforts amounted to a dismantlement of the "developmentalist" policies throughout the world, and of course particularly in the peripheral zones of the world-economy. In the short run, that is in the 1980s and 1990s, this counteroffensive led by the U.S. government seemed to succeed.

These policies on the front of the world-economy were matched by a persistent world military policy which might be summarized as the "antiproliferation" policy. When the United States successfully made the first atomic bombs in 1945, it was determined to maintain a monopoly on such very powerful weapons. It was willing to share this monopoly with its faithful junior partner, Great Britain, but that was it. Of course, as we know, the other "great powers" simply ignored this claim. First the Soviet Union, then France, then China achieved nuclear capacity. So then did India and later Pakistan. So did South Africa, whose apartheid government, however, admitted this only as it was leaving power and was careful to dismantle this capacity before it turned over power to the successor, more democratic, government of the Black African majority. And so did Israel, although it has always denied this publicly. Then there are the almost-nuclear powers, if indeed they are still in the almost category—North Korea, Iran, Iraq (whose facilities Israel bombed in the 1980s in order to keep it in the "almost" category), Libya, and maybe Argentina. And there are in addition the former Soviet countries which inherited this capacity—Ukraine, Belorussia, and Kazakhstan. To this must be added the other lethal technologies—biological and chemical warfare.

These are so much easier to create, store, and employ, that we are not sure how many countries have some capacity, even a considerable capacity, in these fields.

The United States has had a simple, straightforward policy. By hook or by crook, by force or by bribery, it wishes to deny everybody access to these weapons. It has obviously not been successful, but its efforts over the past years have at least slowed down the process of proliferation. There is a further catch in U.S. policy. Insofar as it tries to employ international agreements to limit proliferation, it simultaneously tries not itself to be bound by such constraints, or to be minimally bound. The U.S. government has made it clear that it will renounce any such restraints whenever it deems it necessary to do so, while loudly condemning any other government that seeks to do the same.

As a policy, nonproliferation seems doomed to failure, not only in the long run but even in the middle run. The best that the U.S. will be able to do in the next 25 years is to slow the process down somewhat. But there is also a moral/political question here. The United States trusts itself, but trusts no one else. The U.S. government wishes to inspect North Korean locations to see if it is violating these norms. It has not offered the UN or anyone else the right to inspect U.S. locations. The U.S. trusts itself to use such weapons wisely, and in the defense of liberty (a concept seemingly identical with U.S. national interests). It assumes that anyone else might intend to use such weapons against liberty (a concept seemingly identical here, too, with U.S. national interests).

Personally, I do not trust any government to use such weapons wisely. I would be happy to see them all banned, but do not believe this is truly enforceable in the contemporary interstate system. So personally I abstain from moralizing on this issue. Moralizing opens one to the charge of hypocrisy. And while a cynical neo-realist (a category that probably includes me) would say that all governments are hypocritical, moralizing jars badly if one wishes to attract support in other countries on the basis of one's comparative virtue.

4. AMERICA: IDEALS VERSUS PRIVILEGE

To suggest that the universal civilization is in place already is to be willfully blind to the present reality and, even worse, to trivialize the goal and hinder the materialization of a genuine universality in the future.

CHINUA ACHEBE[5]

[T]he opposition between globalization and local traditions is false: globalization directly resuscitates local traditions, it literally thrives on them, which is why the opposite of globalization is not local traditions, but *universality*.

SLAVOJ ZIZEK[6]

The story of U.S. and world power can be resumed quite simply at this moment. I do not believe that America and Americans are the cause of all the world's miseries and injustices. I do believe they are their prime beneficiaries. And this is the fundamental problem of the U.S. as a nation located in a world of nations.

Americans, especially American politicians and publicists, like to speak about our ideals. An advertisement for the "bestselling" book of Chris Matthews, *Now, Let Me Tell You What I Really Think,* offers this excerpt: "When you think about it, we Americans are different. That word 'freedom' isn't just in our documents; it's in our cowboy souls."[7] "Cowboy souls"—I could not have said it better. Our ideals are perhaps special. But the same people who remind us of that do not like to talk about our privileges, which are also perhaps special. Indeed, they denounce those who do talk of them. But the ideals and the privileges go together. They may seem to be in conflict, but they presuppose each other.

I am not someone who denigrates American ideals. I find them quite wonderful, even refreshing. I cherish them, I invoke them, I further them. Take for example the First Amendment to the U.S. Constitution—something correctly remembered at all the appropriate ceremonies as incarnating American ideals. Let us, however, recall two things about the First Amendment. It was not in the original Constitution, which means it wasn't considered a founding principle. And public opinion polls have often shown that a majority of the American public would change, diminish, or even eliminate these guarantees, in whole or in part, even in so-called ordinary times. When we are in a "war" such as the "war on terrorism," then neither the U.S. government nor the U.S. public can be counted on to defend these ideals, and not even the Supreme Court can be relied upon to hold fast to them in an "emergency." Such defense is left largely to an often timid organization with at best minority support in public opinion, the American Civil Liberties Union, membership in which is often cited as a reason not to vote for someone in a general election. So, I am in favor of freedom of speech and freedom of religion and all the other freedoms, but sometimes I must wonder if America is.

The reason of course is not that there is absent a Voltairean streak in the American public, but that sometimes we fear that our privileges are in danger of erosion or disappearance. And, in such cases, most people place privilege ahead of ideals. Once again, Americans are not unusual in this regard. They simply are more powerful and have more privileges. Americans are freer to have the ideals because they are freer to ignore them. They have the power to override their cowboy souls.

The question before Americans is really the following: If American hegemony is in slow decline, and I believe it unquestionably is, will we lose the ideals because we will have less power to override them? Will our cowboy souls erect barbed wire around our national ranch in order to guard our privileges in danger of decline, as though they could not escape through the barbed wire? Let me suggest here another metaphor that comes from the twin towers. Towers that are destroyed can be rebuilt. But will we rebuild them in the same way—with the same assurance that we are reaching for the stars and doing it right, with the same certainty that they will be seen as a beacon to the world? Or will we rebuild in other ways, after careful reflection about what we really need and what is really possible for us, and really desirable for us?

And who is the "us"? If one follows the statements of Attorney General Ashcroft, seconded by many others in the U.S. government, in the press, and among the public in general, the "us" is no longer everyone in the U.S., not even everyone legally resident in the U.S., but only U.S. citizens. And we may wonder if the "us" may not be further narrowed in the near future. As Zizek points out, globalization is not the opposite of localism, it thrives on localism, especially the localism of the powerful. The "us" is by no stretch of the imagination *homo sapiens sapiens*. Is *homo* then so *sapiens*?

5. AMERICA: FROM CERTAINTY TO UNCERTAINTY

Darwin's revolution should be epitomized as the substitution of variation for essence as the central category of natural reality. . . . What can be more discombobulating than a full inversion, or "grand flip," in our concept of reality: in Plato's world, variation is accidental, while essences record a higher reality; in Darwin's reversal, we value variation as a defining (and concrete earthly) reality, while averages (our closest operational approach to "essences") become mental abstractions.

STEPHEN JAY GOULD[8]

Nature is indeed related to the creation of unpredictable novelty, where the possible is richer than the real.

ILYA PRIGOGINE[9]

President Bush has been offering the American people certainty about their future. This is the one thing totally beyond his power to offer. The future of the United States, the future of the world, in the short run, but even more in the medium run, is absolutely uncertain. Certainty may seem desirable if one reflects on one's privileges. It seems less desirable if one thinks that the privileges are doomed to decline, even disappear. And if it were certain that the Osama bin Ladens of this world, in all camps, were to prevail, who would cherish that certainty?

I return to the question I raised before as one of the puzzles that Americans are feeling right now: what must be done, what can be done, that an event like that of September 11 will not, could not, happen again? We are being offered the answer that the exercise of overwhelming force by the U.S. government, military force primarily, will guarantee this. Our leaders are prudent enough to remind us that this will take some time, but they do not hesitate to make medium-run assurances. For the moment, it seems that the American people are willing to test this hypothesis. If the U.S. government is receiving criticism at this moment, it is coming mostly from those who believe its expression of military power is far too timid. There are important groups who are pressing the U.S. government to go much further—to operate militarily against Iraq, and some would add Iran, Syria, Sudan, Palestine, North Korea. Why not Cuba next? There are some who are even saying that reluctant generals should be retired to make way for younger, more vigorous warriors. There are those who believe that it is their role to precipitate Armageddon.

There are two ways one can argue against this. One is that the United States could not win such a worldwide military conflagration. A second is that the United States would not wish to bear the moral consequences, first of all for itself, of trying to do so. Fortunately, one does not have to choose between realism and idealism. It is not belittling of our moral values that they are seconded by elementary common sense.

After the Civil War, the United States spent some 80 years pursuing its manifest destiny. It was not sure, all that time, whether it wished to be an isolationist or an imperial power. And when, in 1945, it had finally achieved hegemony in the world-system, when it had (in Shakespeare's choice) not only achieved greatness but had greatness thrust upon it, the American people were not fully prepared for the role they now had to play. We spent 30 years learning how to "assume our responsibilities" in the world. And just when we had learned this reasonably well, our hegemony passed its peak.

We have spent the last 30 years insisting very loudly that we are still hegemonic and that everyone needs to continue to acknowledge it. If one is truly hegemonic, one does not need to make such a request. We have wasted the past 30 years. What the United States needs now to do is to learn how to live with the new reality—that it no longer has the power to decide unilaterally what is good for everyone. It may not even be in a position to decide unilaterally what is good for itself. It has to come to terms with the world. It is not Osama bin Laden with whom we must conduct a dialogue. We must start with our near friends and allies—with Canada and Mexico, with Europe, with Japan. And once we have trained ourselves to hear them and to believe that they too have ideals and interests, that they too have ideas and hopes and aspirations, then and only then perhaps shall we be ready to dialogue with the rest of the world, that is, with the majority of the world.

This dialogue, once we begin to enter into it, will not be easy, and may not even be pleasant. For they shall ask us to renounce some privileges. They will ask us to fulfill our ideals. They will ask us to learn. Fifty years ago, the great African poet/politician, Léopold-Sédar Senghor, called on the world to come to the "*rendez-vous du donner et du recevoir.*" Americans know what they have to give in such a rendezvous. But are they aware of something they wish to receive?

We are being called upon these days to return to spiritual values, as though we had ever observed these values. But what are these values? Let me remind you. In the Christian tradition (*Matthew* 19:24), it is said: "It is easier for a camel to pass through the eye of a needle than for a rich man to enter the kingdom of God." And in the Jewish tradition, Hillel tells us: "Do unto others as you would have them do unto you." And in the Muslim tradition, the Koran (52.36) tells us: "Or did they create the heavens and the earth? Nay! They have no certainty." Are these our values?

There is of course no single American tradition or single American set of values. There are, and always have been, many Americas. We each of us remember and appeal to the Americas we prefer. The America of slavery and racism is a deep American tradition, and still very much with us. The America of frontier individualism and gunslinging desperados is an American tradition, and still very much with us. The America of robber barons and their philanthropic children is an American tradition, and still very much with us. And the America of the Wobblies and the Haymarket riots, an event celebrated throughout the world except in America, is an American tradition, and still very much with us.

Sojourner Truth, telling the National Women's Congress in 1851, "Ain't I a woman?" is an American tradition. But so were those late–nineteenth century suffragists who argued for votes on the grounds that it would balance the votes of Blacks and immigrants. The America that welcomes immigrants and the America that rejects them are both American traditions. The America that unites in patriotic resolve and the America that resists militarist engagements are both American traditions. The America of equality and of inequality are both American traditions. There is no essence there. There is no there there. As Gould reminds us, it is variation, not essence, that is the core of reality. And the question is whether the variation amongst us will diminish, increase, or remain the same. It seems to me exceptionally high at the moment.

Osama bin Laden will soon be forgotten, but the kind of political violence we call terrorism will remain very much with us in the 30 to 50 years to come. Terrorism is, to be sure, a very ineffective way to change the world. It is counterproductive and leads to counterforce, which can often wipe out the immediate set of actors. But it will nonetheless continue to occur. An America that continues to relate to the world by a unilateral assertion that it represents civilization, whether it does so in the form of isolationist withdrawal or in that of active interventionism, cannot live in peace with the world, and therefore will not live in peace with itself. What we do to the world, we do to ourselves. Can the land of liberty and privilege, even amidst its decline, learn to be a land that treats everyone everywhere as equals? And can we deal as equal to equal in the world-system if we do not deal as equal to equal within our own frontiers?

What shall we choose to do now? I can have my preferences but I cannot, you cannot, predict what we shall do. Indeed, it is our good fortune that we cannot be certain of any of these projected futures. That reserves for us moral choice. That reserves for us the possible that is richer than the real. That reserves for us unpredictable novelty. We have entered a terrible era, an era of conflicts and evils we find it difficult to imagine but, sadly, one to which we can rapidly become accustomed. It is easy to allow our sensitivities to be hardened in the struggle to survive. It is far harder to save our cowboy souls. But at the end of the process lies the possibility, which is far from the certainty, of a more substantively rational world, of a more egalitarian world, of a more democratic world—of a universality that results from giving and receiving, a universality that is the opposite of globalization.

The last metaphor that is attached to the twin towers is that these structures were, are, and will be a choice. We chose to build them. We are deciding whether or not to rebuild them. The factors that enter into these choices were and are and will be very, very many. We are rebuilding America. The world is rebuilding the world. The factors that enter into these choices are and will be very, very many. Can we maintain our moral bearing amidst the uncertainty that the world we have made heretofore is only one of thousands of alternative worlds we might have created, and the world that we shall be making in the 30 to 50 years to come may or may not be better, may or may not reduce the contradiction between our ideals and our privileges? *In-sha 'a-llah.*

23. VIOLENCE AND HOME: AFGHAN WOMEN'S EXPERIENCE OF DISPLACEMENT

SABA GUL KHATTAK[1]

INTRODUCTION

September 11 and its repercussions took everyone by surprise—most of all poor Afghans who had to flee their homes in the midst of U.S. bombing of Afghanistan. Even though many crossed over into Pakistan, they continued to feel the tremors in Quetta and Peshawar and along the Pak-Afghan border. The severity of U.S. bombing is indicated by the fact that over the course of one month, it used more than half a million tons worth of bombs; this converts to twenty kilos for every man, woman, and child in the country.[2]

Why did the richest and the most militarily powerful country in the world bomb the poorest and most devastated country of the world? How do we analyze the U.S. bombing of Afghanistan? Was this bombing a ceremonial reaffirmation of power? Was it about avenging the September 11 hijackings, the subsequent destruction and damage of the WTC and the Pentagon respectively, and the death of thousands of innocent people? Was it about the display and exhibition of U.S. armaments for international buyers? Was it about ensuring oil supply lines and warm water ports a la Carter Doctrine? Was it primarily about ridding the world of terrorism and terrorists? Was it about restoring peace and eventually democracy in Afghanistan? Was it, in addition to all this, about liberating Afghan women from the oppression of the Taliban (though not a patriarchal culture that kept them back, whether in Afghanistan or in refugee camps in Pakistan and Iran)? Was it about the American resolve not to live in fear? Or, was it about getting Osama bin Laden, dead or alive?

Why are the answers to this issue important? Why must we establish the primacy of one answer and, through that hierarchy, talk about U.S. goals and priorities? Probably because we feel an urgent need to make sense of international politics. But to make sense of the madness, we cannot restrict ourselves to mainstream understandings, whether they spring from conservative, centrist, liberal, progressive, or left-oriented perspectives.

In the present context, to attempt to understand the American bombing of Afghanistan, we need to look at the issue from the Afghan perspective, and within that perspective through the lens of gender. For the Afghans, the bombing and its motivation are not connected with the shock that the U.S. and some others around the world experienced on September 11. For the Afghans, the bombing represents yet another wave of violence in a 21-year history of relentless conflict. It has, once again, driven them out of their homes and their country, making them insecure refugees or IDPs (internally displaced persons) because no country will allow them in. For a majority of poor Afghan women, the WTC and the Pentagon were and continue to be unknown entities, and September 11 makes no sense, as the calendars they follow are based on memory or the lunar cycle. Hence the events and the dates are as remote from their lives as Mars. Their systems of reference and signifiers are different.

INTERNATIONAL POLITICS, CONFLICT, WOMEN, AND HOME

This chapter discusses the constant disruptions in the uniform meanings of home for Afghan women refugees due to the direct impact of war upon their lives. To begin, we look at the different ideas that are contained within and underlie the concept of home. In this regard, we take home to be more than the binary division of public and private, though these concepts are at the root of the idea since home serves to include as well as exclude, more or less like a state or a nation.

The constitution of private and public space is fundamentally an ideological divide that keeps shifting in accordance with changes in economic and social realities. The public/private divide is also a gendered divide as men are associated with the public spheres of politics and work and women are associated with the private sphere of home and family. The state is identified with the public sphere but its incursions extend into the private sphere as it legislates for the protection of the latter. There is a definitional shift when one looks at the state in the context of international relations. The state as an entity among a polity of nations identifies itself with the home/the private sphere when it comes to issues concerned with internal policies. This is why it is possible to talk about domestic policy. However, the connection between the home (in its actual form) and the state in the context of violent conflict remains unseen. While a declaration of war is viewed as an attack upon the greater home (the state), the attack on actual homes in the context of armed conflict is rarely taken into consideration and infrequently emerges as an issue of concern.

One associates wars with battlefields and with men, whether they ride horses, tanks, jeeps or helicopters and planes. Wars are associated with wide-open spaces—public spaces—not with homes. Homes are associated with women and with the family, hence they belong to the private sphere. International law regarding war and armed conflict reinforces such dichotomies by drawing a distinction between combatants (soldiers) and noncombatants (civilians), and going into great detail about the areas that can be attacked or bombed—such as airfields—and areas that are outside the purview of war—such as homes and communities. Many of these laws have been ineffective and widely challenged by women's groups and victims of wars over the last decade, and before that by warring parties contesting the definition of combatant and noncombatant due to the involvement of entire populations in war efforts. The former case has been taken up by feminists and like-minded groups who insist that sexual violence must be recognized as an instrument of war and were recently successful in having rape declared a war crime.

The recognition of rape as a war crime admits the fact that women constitute an integral part of war not only because women are women but also because their bodies and beings have representational and symbolic value. Although rape and other forms of corporeal punishment and humiliation leave deep scars and therefore are of immediate concern, the destruction of homes and villages is also debilitating and is also used as an instrument of war to spread fear and intimidation. The tendency of marauding armies in the past to murder, loot, and burn that which they could not carry with them resulted in the destruction of entire villages and communities. While this has been widely documented, very few people have looked at the issues that emerge out of these acts of violence.

The destruction of home and community has implications that go beyond the physical being of these places. These range from ideas of self, of identity, creativity, personal efficacy, interpersonal relations and one's worldview. Some of these issues have been addressed and analyzed by anthropologists in the context of recent conflicts. However, these accounts are generally restricted to documenting and observing changes in human relations in the context of individual violence such as murder, rape, and ritualistic violence. One seldom comes across accounts that make the connection between the violence of war and conflict in conjunction with the dislocation of people from their homes. This kind of violence is rarely discussed.[3]

The women's movement, spearheaded by feminists in the 1960s and 1970s, looked upon the home with suspicion as they exposed its myth as a nurturing, sacred space and drew attention to the brutality and oppression women face when they question family values and challenge male authority.[4] The home, because it is the symbol of the private sphere, assured of privacy by the state due to the social contract, is guarded by patriarchal traditions as a space that cannot be questioned. One result is that violence (predominantly perpetrated by men) can continue to go unquestioned so long as it does not result in murder. On some occasions even murder is condoned in the name of tradition or narrowly enforced morality. It was thus an important step forward for feminists to focus on the abusive aspect of the home—an aspect long accepted and seldom addressed to the advantage and protection of women.

Bringing domestic violence out of its centuries-old closet is a critical contribution. But here we focus on the home as a positive locus of identity for women rather than adhering to the feminist position considering home to be primarily the first site of oppression for women.[5] This is not to deny the validity of the feminist position but to limit the parameters for the present analyses in the context of displacement. However crucial such a focus is for understanding women's multiple oppressions, it serves to take attention away from other equally important connections that revolve around the home in the context of violent conflict. In this regard, it is important to view the relationship from other angles also if we are to understand the complexity of women's experiences and the shaping of their relationship with home by war and conflict, especially when homes are targeted. In this context, home as the site for domestic violence becomes one aspect among others of women's complex experiences.

AFGHAN WOMEN'S EXPERIENCE OF INSECURITY

Many of the observations in this chapter depend upon a collection of 50 plus qualitative in-depth interviews with Afghan refugee women that were conducted over a period of two years between 2000 and 2002.[6] The purpose was to investigate the gendered effects of conflict upon women. The interviews were conducted in Pashto and Dari, and these were later transcribed and translated. We do not disclose the names of the respondents for reasons of their personal security.

There are several ways in which one can discuss the concept of home in the context of Afghan women refugees' lives. First, one can discuss it in the context of the most recent exodus of Afghans (mostly women and children) fleeing American bombing of Taliban-held cities starting October 7, 2001. This was preceded by an exodus of Afghans uprooted by drought and near-famine situations. As the actors at the political helm of affairs changed, so did the refugees and their experience.

To go back to the beginning, one can talk about the initial phase of the conflict between the former USSR army and what may be generically termed the Afghan resistance from 1979 to 1992. This conflict affected especially the lives of rural women, as the source of resistance came from the more conservative sections of the population rather than the educated elite of Kabul. The second phase of the conflict began when the *Mujahedeen*[7] took over between 1992 and 1996. This phase affected urban professional classes and resulted in their dislocation. This was also the beginning of the "ethnic-ization" and "sectarian-ization" of the conflict. The third phase of the conflict, with the coming of the *Taliban* in 1996, affected all women, irrespective of class, sect, or ethnicity.[8]

All of these phases of conflict have produced different types of refugees; additionally, there are many who repatriated and then returned to Pakistan as the violence and war did not subside. Although there have been different effects of the conflict upon the homes and lives of these different categories of women and refugees in general, there are some narratives that are common to all women. Over the course of the conflict, as bombs and rockets fell upon houses, people were forced to flee their homes as villages and cities became sites of fighting and terror. According to Trinh T. Minh-ha, the story of refugees "exposes power politics in its most primitive form . . . the ruthlessness of major powers, the brutality of nation states, the avarice and prejudice of people."[9] The story of Afghan refugees contains tales of terror unleashed by major powers, neighboring states, as well as their own people. Their experiences cannot be grouped under neat categories associated with exile, migration, or refugeehood. Indeed, their experience should be analyzed in all these contexts as well as others, and at several levels. At the most basic level, it does not matter whether the bombs are manufactured in the U.S.A. or the former USSR. What matters to the people is what the bombs do to them when they are dropped. As one Afghan woman in Pakistan, a recent refugee from the bombing, explained, "*Jung sho—Kabul taa raalo*" (fighting erupted and it reached Kabul), or as another woman put it in an understated way, "the circumstances became unbearable," meaning the bombing was horrendous. For the women then, what mattered was that they had to flee their homes in order to be secure.

For many of the poor displaced women and their children, the removal of the Taliban and the killing and looting carried out by the Northern Alliance is not tantamount to liberation, nor does the promise of democracy hold meaning. The players in the conflict are irrelevant—much more so for women than men, who have some sensitivity to whose bombs are raining down, although many have learned to distance themselves from the warring factions. What women underscore is their need for peace (*qaraar—araami*). One respondent, when asked if her son will wage/continue the *jihad* (holy war), promptly emphasized that he will only work to establish peace. This is a contrast to the mother of 20 years ago who was willing to sacrifice her son's life for the war. But while the yearning for peace is increasingly voiced by Afghani women, very few have creative ideas about how to achieve it. One senses in the interviews that the immediacy and intensity of the violence they have undergone requires a time to heal before they can create narratives of their collective experience and visions of peace and reconstruction.

HOME AND THE AFGHAN REFUGEE WOMEN EXPERIENCE

Leaving the home behind is not only about acquiring security, it is also about leaving behind a sense of identity, a culture, a personal and collective history. Indeed, the word "home" has several connotations for women, and thus both the making of and the abandonment of the home are important.

Afghan women find it hard to grapple with the sense of danger and threat they now associate with home as a result of the 21-year conflict. Instead of being a safe haven, home and homeland now also represent places of peril. Displacement from home and country evokes a deep sense of loss and resentment as well as despondence. Simultaneously, there are constant attempts and thoughts of going back. These are accompanied by various recollections and depictions of home representing peace and plenty—an important coping mechanism as there is hope that this memory can one day in the future be revitalized. We thus find that there are several interpretations and representations of home—some of which are conflicting and paradoxical—that coexist in Afghan women's discourse of home and displacement.

Starting from the broader parameters of a conception of home, it is interesting to note that in Afghanistan the word for country and home is used interchangeably—*watan*. When Afghan refugee women talk of going home, they talk about going back to their *watan*. Home is thus intricately woven into the idea of belonging, belonging to a place and a community. In this sense, a person derives her/his sense of self from home, hence the saying "to be at home." Refugees and migrants are never quite at home in the countries and places they live in because the sense of belonging is missing; home also represents a way of life, a way of being, a culture, and a way of thinking. Salman Rushdie, writing about refugees and migrants in his novel *Shame,* expresses their angst: "We have come unstuck from more than land. We have floated upwards from history, from memory, from Time." [10] Leaving home is thus not a simple act of changing one's place of residence. It is a parting of ways with a life with which one is familiar and comfortable; one derives one's identity from one's sense of home.

Rosemary George relies on the psychoanalytical theory of Jung to demonstrate these connections. Jung, she writes, "regarded an individual's home as the universal archetypal symbol of the self." [11] According to Jung, the different rooms in a house represent a person's different selves and states of consciousness. This identification with the house is deeply embedded in the human psyche. George explains that this identification is a two-way process, whereby the home not only represents how one perceives one's self but also stands for how others may perceive a person. Therefore, home is crucial for the perception of identity, and many women consider it to be an extension of their selves. This is why there is so much emphasis on teaching girls about housekeeping; slowly they learn to derive their identity and self-worth from the manner in which they keep their house clean and in order. The way one furnishes and decorates one's home—the furniture, the crockery, the cutlery, and other material objects—also has representational value, as it reflects social and economic status:

> . . . Our family left their homes just like that and didn't even carry a single spoon or a cup. We still don't have anything proper as we came to Peshawar with only the clothes that we were wearing at that time.

When refugees are forced to leave home, the space that they took great pains to build into a reflection of themselves, they suddenly feel bereft of identity. In many interviews one senses that this loss is embedded in the objects left behind:

> We left everything that we owned and came towards Pakistan in the midst of a snowfall. With a broken heart we came towards Pakistan, leaving everything behind. All we had were just a few blankets.

The hardships of homelessness impair a sense of personal efficacy as well, as revealed in the story of another refugee woman who undergoes the common experience of helplessness in protecting one's family and difficulty in securing a satisfactory living situation:

> In Pakistan we ended up in Nasir Bagh refugee camp; at the time my son had pneumonia. I didn't know where to go, but God bless a Pakistani policeman who gave me a reference, due to which my child received medical attention. During our early days we were living in tents. Living in tents was very hard because it provided little protection from the harsh storms and summer heat. It took us a long time to get used to living in a tent. It was very hard for my children to live in a tent during the scorching heat of the summer. Due to such hard conditions we were forced to rent a house, but our neighbors kept bothering us because my husband had worked in the communist regime.

This woman also suggests the multiple problems connected with the location of a house. She was a second-wave refugee who had fled Kabul after the *Mujahedeen* took over; as such, first-wave refugees who had fled the Russians and procommunist regimes perceived her and her family as the enemy who were responsible for their plight. Thus the renting of a house did not ease her problems. Instead, her countrymen and women made her doubly uncomfortable in a second country due to the job her husband had held with the government.

The locale of home thus is not devoid of the larger politics of the country of origin. Since refugees either live in camps or settle in similar neighborhoods, they tend to reproduce the politics of their homeland in the host country. Sometimes families get enmeshed in these politics—a politics that can easily take a violent or threatening turn.

The presence of loyal friends and relatives in close proximity to the location of home is important for psychological security. On home ground, people often have contacts and relatives or friends upon whom they rely in times of crisis. As aliens without any reliable structures for protection, refugees lament the loss of informal networks of friends and relatives. As one woman put it:

> We had a good life in Afghanistan when there was still peace. We had property and every-
> thing. Most importantly, we had relatives. Now we have no one. I lost my son. . . .

For this respondent, the presence of relatives and her son are more important than the ownership of property for a good life. For many Afghan women refugees, home is associated with a sense of security that is nourished through the existence of loved ones who will take care of one in times of need. Equally important, there is a sense of happiness connected with one's relatives as they are also a source of love and shared experiences of sadness and laughter. Given Afghan women's restricted mobility and limited knowledge of the outside world, their dependence upon these relationships is pivotal to their well-being.

While many Afghan women refugees' experiences of life were restricted to the home, this did not mean that the home was a prison. Even as they are physically restricted to the "refuge of the father" [12] they were frequently able to transcend the confines of home. This is so because this space for refuge is protected in patriarchal societies by the figure of the father. The physical leaving of home implies entrance into uncertainty as one crosses into unprotected terrain. This is why it is often assumed to be acceptable if women are harassed outside their home, as the underlying logic is that they should not have left the refuge of the father. In other words, they are assumed to have "asked for it."

In much the same way, the loss of country is also synonymous with the loss of home and in the case of refugee women, both occur simultaneously. The deep psychological insecurity, therefore, exists at multiple levels. As they leave their home, they leave behind various familial relationships; as they leave their country, they leave behind the larger familial metaphor represented by nation, culture, history and identity. As they enter a new country, the sense of exposing themselves to the danger of the unknown, to harassment in a male domain for which they were neither prepared nor trained, takes on frightening proportions. The patriarch who protects, the interchangeable father and the state, is absent and unable to protect. Again, displacement is not a simple fact of changing one's place and country of residence. It has deep-seated psychological repercussions.

The deep psychological sense of security associated with home is not only turned on its head. The home, which provides nourishment, becomes the very place that leads to death. It becomes a metaphor for the grave.[13] Furthermore, the constantly changing forms of the "enemy" (ranging from the Russians and Soviet-supported governments to the *Mujahedeen,* the *Taliban,* the Northern Alliance, and most recently the Americans) make it hard to single out one identifiable phenomenon and associate it with insecurity. In the case of Afghanistan, there are multiple enemies and one does not know which one is worse or which one will strike. The following quote, where the respondent could not tell whose rockets and bombs were killing them, makes this very clear:

> Missiles came and landed. What was it! It was a kind of war. Our home was down the mound. On one side was Tina Pass mound and on the other side we had the Bala Hisar, and on another side the Special Guard . . . we were surrounded from all four sides. Bombs from all sides landed on our area. Many people died in our area. In every home, if there were four persons, all four died; if there were five, five died; if there were six, six died; if there was one, that one died. People lost their assets as well as lives.
>
> Day and night the planes kept coming and conducted bombardment, which destroyed our homes. Nothing was left. Wealth and property was destroyed. We were left with nothing, not even enough to cross over to Pakistan. There were also children. On one occasion, the bullets would come from the *Mujahedeen* while on the other from the government's soldiers. There was heavy war. . . .

The inability to identify one single enemy makes the experience of displacement harder. When everyone becomes the enemy, "othering" for peace becomes increasingly difficult. Practical and implementable options become hard to visualize. Under such conditions, women are unable to provide or envision strategies for peace and reconstruction.

More generally one is struck in the interviews by how creativity is disrupted by violence and dislocation. Home is a place from where the imagination can take off without fear—from where one can undertake multiple journeys that are inexhaustible in their scope and width. This is how many Afghan women are able to express their ideas and concerns and communicate with the outside world. For many women, writing and creativity are possible only when there is a secure and settled life ensured through the existence of a stable unthreatened home. The forced retreat from home affects women's creativity. In a bid to save their lives and their loved ones, refugees are preoccupied entirely with escaping into safety:

> I was in such a hurry that I cannot remember the way I came through here from Afghanistan. I was anxious. How could I remember the poetic collection? I was not sure of survival here.

It is not just visions of peace that atrophy under conditions of war and displacement, but the very capacity and need to be creative: to imagine, to write, to narrativize, to hold on to one's thoughts.

Envisioning objectives for peace is further hampered by the experience of having to flee one's country twice and sometimes thrice. It would be very hard to go through the devastating experience of violence two or three times and still stay optimistic about the future. The following is a moving account, and I include it here not because it is a solitary voice but because it is representative of many other similar voices. This particular narrative is about the double trauma of going back to Afghanistan only to find out that conditions did not change with a change in government, and hence the respondent's decision to come back to Pakistan.

We went. When the Islamic government took over, our whole family went back. Our home was in Kabul. We had been punished enough. We had seen many hardships during our refugee life and gone through helplessness and loneliness. We thought perhaps we would find peace in our homeland. But when we went, rockets were launched on the very first day. Our father had told us that there would be peace but there was fighting everywhere. Not for a single day did we have happiness. We spent the whole night in fear as rockets were being launched constantly. These were engineer sahib's rockets. At that time they were known as engineer sahib's rockets.[14]

. . . One day rockets were launched constantly and towards the late afternoon my cousin came and told my mother that my uncle had been martyred. . . . All our family has been destroyed in this revolution . . . we were all frightened. My father was left with small children and we were so grief stricken that we didn't know what to do. When they left my brother and we (three sisters) remained in the house. Toward the afternoon our houses and our whole colony was taken under siege. When we inquired we were told that war between Shoravi (pro-Russian government) and the Hizb-Islami had broken out. This is what our neighbors said. We were surprised and confused about the war. What if it never ended? If they broke into our house what would we do? We used to buy bread from the market and that day there was not a single piece in the house. We didn't know what to do especially with the small children. We were having feelings of regret. We wished that we had gone back and had not stayed here. We stayed hungry in the house with the children for two days and two nights. Rockets were constantly launched. No one could go out nor could anyone come in from outside. We had no hope for life. We always thought that any time a rocket would fall and hit our heads. After two days the siege was over. They went away after satisfying themselves. Many people died or were injured. We told our father that it was better to be without a homeland than to be living in such a homeland. So we came back to Pakistan.

The respondent goes on to describe the final event that convinced her father to return once again as a refugee:

I told my father that we wanted to go back to Pakistan but he did not agree. He said that the war would be over one day. When he did not agree with us, we prepared ourselves to combat the rockets and stay . . . when I was coming back [from my uncle's house] towards my house, which was located on a roadside, a rocket fell and hit a bus and then a taxi. Both burst into flames. . . . I have a habit that I always wear white clothes. When I looked at my clothes they had shreds of human flesh on them. It looked like raindrops. . . . I could not tolerate it anymore and I ran towards my house when another rocket came and hit our house. I was injured again. I was very seriously injured because when I regained consciousness I was in a hospital in Peshawar, Pakistan.

This woman's experience of displacement is unusual if we compare it to non-refugee populations. However, for Afghan refugees, such stories have acquired "normalcy" in that they are so common. An addition to the double trauma—of going back, only to return to the country of refuge again—is the constant relocation of the refugees within the host country. Shifting from camps to homes and from there to other cities in search of safety and livelihoods is an inhospitable experience, as the host population looks upon the refugees as anathema. While there were those who shifted back and forth in the hope of settling back in their country eventually, there are others whose villages were completely destroyed and who are unable to relate to a country to go back to:

> But that [Afghanistan] is also not our country (*watan*). We are not only refugees here [in Pakistan] but also there [in Afghanistan]. We have no village (*watan*) anywhere. Today we are here and tomorrow there. Now the landlord has asked us to vacate this place but we don't have money to shift.

Although the Afghan refugee women are unable to "make sense" of and narrativize[15] their collective experience at present, this does not preclude a vision of a golden past that they would like to recreate. They usually begin with emphasizing how good life was in Afghanistan. In fact, all respondents underscore this view. It comes repeatedly, irrespective of whether they were rich or poor. This is often done in great detail: descriptions of meals—breakfasts, entertainment when guests arrived—images of plenty. This past associates home with happiness—with plenty. It is a dreamlike memory of the homeland that no longer can be envisioned looking forward. This present inability to imagine a future is poetically explained by one respondent as a mistake in having forgotten to ask God for peace:

> What we regret mostly is that we wished to God that our visit to Afghanistan had brought us happiness and we could see what our country was like. . . . What did we see in our country? War and bloodshed! We only saw bloodshed and war in our homeland and we returned to Pakistan with these images in our minds.
>
> We had forgotten what happiness was. We prayed to God to give us our homeland but we did not ask for our peace and security there. Perhaps we had asked Him to give us our country but forgot to ask Him to grant peace along with it. This was a mistake that we made.

CONCLUSION

This chapter has focused on how women fare on the home-front during times of conflict. There are ruptures in the meaning of home as the result of war, and I have tried to highlight the depth and extent to which the multiple meanings of home impact women. Among these meanings, home can become a symbol of violence when it comes to a woman's relationship with a man and patriarchal authority. This has been the feminist view. However, for a woman, a house/home still represents a sanctuary—even if it is a patriarchal sanctuary. Home is the source of primary identity for women, not only because both are associated predominantly with the private sphere, but also because home is the locus of self, culture, and belonging. This is true for men as well as women; however, due to the historical role that women play in the making of home, they identify much more with it.

Aside from being a reflection of self and of social and economic status, home represents the space where women can be happy and secure, where they can be efficacious and creative, and where they enjoy familial support. But the extreme violence and destruction of the war mean that home and country are no longer the symbols of protection and security. Instead, home and country mirror the peril they contain for the very people they need to shelter and protect. This peril has often been experienced several times—the double and triple trauma as the Afghan refugees keep fleeing from their country and their homes in the face of constant bombings and fighting. This process has also rendered some women completely homeless so that they are unable to conceptualize the presence of a place that may be called home.

The themes that emerge from the interviews are about the destruction resulting from war, deaths due to rocket attacks and the yearning to go back to the place that was home and that lies destroyed. Many talk about the double trauma of returning only to find out that the same destruction and senseless war continued and they were as insecure as they had been previously. There is thus a sense of betrayal.

The experience of alienation in Pakistan only furthers this sense. For Afghan women, their house is not "home"—it is a place, a mud house, a rented house, a camp or a tent. It is not home. There are constant thoughts of returning home, and this prevents them from coming to terms with the present. Their refusal to accept their move as final (something their hosts also do not want them to do) makes them feel that the present is "temporary," even though it has affected their lives very deeply and permanently.

We conclude that displacement, whether within one's country or outside of it, generates anxieties not only about physical security but also about nonmaterial aspects that form the basis of our identities, of who we are. There are shifts in identities, ruptures in their meanings, and changes in our perceptions of ourselves and others' perceptions of us. For many women memory is an important coping mechanism. Memory serves to preserve their class and social identities but also their national identities and association with their country as something beautiful. But simultaneously, the memory of violence prevents them from narrativizing their individual experience into collective history or collective consciousness.

I do not wish to end on a note of pessimism. As a social scientist, I would like to see new spaces being created by Afghan refugee women in the midst of the tremendous violence they face. I am confident that these spaces and a new politics will eventually be formed; however, for the time being, we need to recognize that having undergone multiple traumas at multiple levels, they require respite and a breathing space—a space and time for personal and collective healing and for creativity to be restored. For us to expect towering narratives of courage and indigenous exotic wisdom, as well as survival, is to impose a new colonizing idea and discourse upon them.

24. MEMORIALIZING ABSENCE

MARITA STURKEN

It has been said quite often since September 11 that Americans are standing at a juncture of history, that, on that date, the world changed forever into a "before" and an "after." [1] Such proclamations of radical breaks in historical consciousness have happened before, of course. Writing in 1924 about the experience of modernity, Virginia Woolf stated, "on or about December 1910, human character changed." Many years later, Theodor Adorno wrote, "to write poetry after Auschwitz is barbaric," implying that cultural production was irrevocably changed in the wake of the Holocaust. There are many good arguments to reject the current version of the shock of history insofar as it is a particularly American-centric and provincial one, one that awards traumatic events in the U.S. more historical weight than those in the rest of the world. Yet, the feeling persists that this date will be forever understood as one that marks the end of one era and the beginning of another, indeed that September 11, 2001 will be remembered as the beginning of the new world of the twenty-first century.

In many ways, this before/after can be attributed to the aspects of this event that were so unanticipated, so unimaginable: The image of one plane, and then another, colliding into the twin towers of the World Trade Center, and the buildings' collapse, so quick and so controlled. As millions of witnesses watched, from Manhattan, Brooklyn, New Jersey, and throughout the nation and the world on their television sets, the shock of the spectacular image of the plane's impact was replaced by an equally unbelievable image—the absence of the twin towers in the skyline, the erasure of the two massive buildings anchoring lower Manhattan. How instantly had those two towers changed meaning, for never had they signified more than in their absence. Standing untouched, the World Trade Center had been invested with many meanings in its duration of almost 30 years—the folly of oversized public building projects, the banal glass towers of modernity's fading years, the symbol of New York tourism, and, later, the arrogance of American capital. Yet, once fallen, their absence spoke more profoundly than their presence ever could. To look now at the skyline is to experience absence; all images of the towers have taken on a poignancy that was, before September 11, unimaginable.

In the face of absence, especially an absence so violently and tragically wrought at the cost of so many lives, people feel a need to create a presence of some kind, and it may be for this reason that questions of memorialization have so quickly followed this event. It seemed as if people were already talking of memorials the day after, when the numbers and names of the missing were unknown and the search for survivors still the focus of national attention. What, we might ask, is behind this rush to memorialize? Could we imagine people talking of memorialization after the destruction of the Warsaw Ghetto, or the bombing of Hiroshima? Or, for that matter, that the people of Rwanda talked of memorialization after the massacres that killed hundreds of thousands there? Throughout history, public memorialization has most commonly taken place with the distance of time. After wars have been declared over, towns, cities, and nations have built memorials to name the dead and those sacrificed. In the U.S., historical figures such as Lincoln, Jefferson, and Roosevelt became the focus of memorials many decades after they died. Many of the most important memorials in the U.S. took decades to build, each the product of bureaucratic wrangling and conflicting agendas. In recent years, it is true, this process has accelerated. The Vietnam Veterans Memorial was built seven years after the end of U.S. participation in the war, and even then it was considered to be long overdue. The Oklahoma City National Memorial was opened five years after the April 1995 bombing that killed 168 people, and it was in many ways a memorial sped into existence by the presence of a powerful group of family members and survivors who participated in the memorialization process.[2] Now, the question of memorialization of September 11 has focused on what is called "Ground Zero" in New York City, completely overshadowing the sites of destruction at the Pentagon and in Western Pennsylvania, making it clear that the New York site is the symbolic center of this tragic event.

In 1984, French philosopher Michel de Certeau wrote in his essay "Walking in the City," that the observation deck of the World Trade Center promoted a god's eye view of the city, one that fulfilled "a lust to be a viewpoint and nothing more." De Certeau contrasted this view—in which "the gigantic mass [of the city] is immobilized before the eyes"—to the many meaningful acts that take place at street level, to the "speech acts" of pedestrians that make meaning of the city's landscape.[3] In many ways, the discussions that have taken place about how to memorialize the events of September 11 in New York City have furthered this split view of the city—the contrast between the towering skyscrapers and the smaller acts of meaning created at street level. In this sense, the memory of this event already indicates the conflicting visions of the monumental and the individual, intimate rituals of grief.

Much of the discussion of memorialization has been preoccupied with the gap that remains in the New York skyline. Discussions about how to redevelop the site have been tied up inevitably with feelings of concern about what the absence of the World Trade Center signifies, that is, the belief that to leave the skyline absent of its form, or any tall building, is an expression of weakness and defeat (to the best of my knowledge, the *New York Times* was the only publication to note that the World Trade Center already had a memorial, now lost in the rubble, to the six people who were killed in the 1993 bombing there).[4] In the weeks after September 11, a bevy of modern architects such as Philip Johnson and Robert A. M. Stern and Museum of Modern Art architecture curator Terence Riley stepped forward in stunning fashion to embrace the idea that the two towers should be rebuilt as they were, in the words of Bernard Tschumi, the dean of Columbia's architecture school, only "bigger and better"[5]—an idea that disregards some basic tenets of psychology (no one would want to work in a new terrorist target) and displays some historical and economic ignorance (the towers were built with public money by a public institution in a very different era of government funding) and disregard for safety (tall skyscrapers are notoriously difficult to evacuate). One can only imagine that they regret those words now, because, as months have passed, these assertions have been tempered by an increased understanding of the complexity of a project to reconceive the area and integrate it back into the city, and of the diverse set of interests in the site, from private investors to public officials to grieving families. Yet, in the immediate aftermath, only architects Elizabeth Diller and Ricardo Scofidio remarked upon the power of the skyline's transformation as its message: "Let's not build something that would mend the skyline, it is more powerful to leave it void. We believe it would be tragic to erase the erasure."[6]

New York has since become awash in memorial ideas and designs, which range from the amateur to the professional, from austerity to kitsch. Ironically, many of the concepts of memorialization that have been put forward have been specifically about memorializing the towers themselves. Indeed, many of the drawings that have peopled the city in the subsequent months have been attempts to replace the towers with their representation—children's drawings that reimagine them in their place, murals of the towers, tributes to the "twin brothers," and images placed strategically at lookout sites that attempt to insert the towers into views in which they are now missing—all a kind of vernacular intervention into their absence. New York's art world has also engaged with reimaging the towers aesthetically. Philippe de Montebello, director of the Metropolitan Museum of Art, suggested that the jagged fragment of the building that hovered over the destruction should be preserved and form part of a memorial.[7] In fact, this has been an aspect of many memorials in the past—most notably the Hiroshima Peace Memorial Park, which incorporates the skeletal ruins of a building, and many World War II memorials, such as Coventry Cathedral in England, that speak to history in their preservation of the ruins of destroyed structures.[8] For the most part, these memorials use the ruins of the past to convey a warning and a bitter message about the human capacity for violence. For de Montebello, this fragment was not only an icon of survival, but already a "masterpiece"—not only, one suspects, because it has created the haunting image of a modern ruin, but because it looks already like a modern work of art. Before they were dismantled and taken to the Fresh Kills landfill, these shards towered over the site like fragments of a Gothic cathedral—a strange reminder of the Gothic references of the "skin" of the towers' construction.

Others turned to the shadow of the towers' presence in the skyline for inspiration. Art Spiegelman created a cover of the *New Yorker* in which the towers were barely visible as black shadows on black, an image haunting in its somber familiarity. On the six-month anniversary of September 11, the *Tribute in Light,* a collaboration by six artists and architects, recreated the twin towers temporarily in blue light.[9] These "phantom towers" were designed like votive candles reaching skyward. This project was compelling in both its capacity to trace the shadow of the towers' memory, to evoke both their presence and absence, and in the project's own inevitable ephemerality—it too became simply a memory. Like the votive candles that appeared around New York in September, the *Tribute in Light* offered a kind of shadow of the tower's form, a palimpsest, a ghost. It is not incidental that this project was originally named "Towers in Light," but the name was changed when some families of September 11 protested that it should not be a memorial to the lost twin towers but to those who died there. This dispute over its naming encapsulates in many ways the conflicts of memorialization and the tensions between monumentality and mourning the individual dead. The *Tribute in Light* was ultimately an attempt to engage with the absence of the twin towers, not to reckon with the dead.

Yet the preoccupation with memorializing the twin towers and making sense of their absence seems inconsequential when seen in light of the profound loss of life that took place there. In the end, whatever memorial is built on the site of Ground Zero will be a memorial not to the twin towers of the World Trade Center but to the ordinary people whose lives were arbitrarily caught up in history on September 11. The fact that this site is inescapably a graveyard must factor into any memorial design, and awards significant power to the families of the dead in relation to the site. The public grappling with the absence of the twin towers is thus in many ways an attempt to ward off confronting the many lives lost within them.

A marking of the individual has been from the very beginning a part of the rituals surrounding those who died on September 11, with the lists of those lost published in full-page ads by corporations and in the "Portraits of Grief" of each one in the *New York Times,* a feature that ran daily through the end of the year. However, it was the posters for the missing that first transformed the cityscape into a space for remembrance. Flyers hurriedly made with photographs and descriptions were posted near hospitals, rescue centers, and on the streets of lower Manhattan, each reading first like a declaration of personal statistics—date of birth, place of work, clothing worn, where last seen, and unique physical characteristics—that was a desperate call for *recognition* of the individual lost. These were initially messages of hope, yet they became very quickly emblems of loss. The photographs were testimony to a time "before," when those photographed could not have imagined the unimaginable—nor for that matter could they have imagined the talisman that the photograph itself would become, conveying the pressing belief that a loved one was not gone but simply "lost."

The photographs in these missing posters signify in their very nature a rupture, images of a past—family gatherings, vacations—so distant, so unaware of the future. As Marianne Hirsch writes, "Violently yanked out of one context and inserted into a totally incongruous one, they exemplify what Roland Barthes describes as the retrospective irony of looking at photographs—the viewers possess the deadly knowledge that the subject of the image will not know."[10] In many ways the images that circulated throughout the streets of New York, in the train stations, near hospitals and rescue centers, by the subways, were attempts to counter the media images that had become synonymous with September 11—in this case, most specifically, the images of people falling/jumping from the first tower to their deaths.[11] The missing posters showed images of people smiling at the camera's gaze with thankful innocence, but the identifying text, originally intended to help find someone missing, soon took on chilling new meaning— "One World Trade Center, 100th Floor," "worked on the 93rd Floor," "Cantor and Fitzgerald employee"—that connected it back to other images, of the flames enveloping the building, of people falling through the sky.[12] For many months after September 11, these posters remained tenaciously throughout the city, worn by the weather and time, yet still capable of startling one back into remembrance of what had happened.

Photography has played a central role not only in the construction of September 11 as a global media event, but also in the struggle to produce presence in the face of absence. The photographic image promises to mediate absence in its rendering of the trace of the real and the aura of the absent one. We use photographs as substitutes for someone gone, as a means of feeling them present in our lives. Yet, photography has been associated since its origins with death, as Roland Barthes famously wrote, "Ultimately what I am seeking in the photograph taken of me . . . is Death. . . ."[13] It is precisely this paradox of the photograph, its capacity to conjure those absent and its rendering of everything before its gaze into the past, within mortality, that reveals to us the dilemma of such yearnings for presence. The presence of the absent one can never, of course, be fully realized in the image. The image promises a connection, a shadow of the missing one, but ultimately is a painful reminder of the absolute finality of such loss.

Yet the photograph's promise, however unrealized, allows it to play a central role in how we mediate loss. Initially, the site of Ground Zero was considered to be taboo for photographing, and visitors to the periphery were discouraged from taking pictures.[14] Yet, in the months after September 11, there were several open exhibitions around the city of photographs taken by amateurs, locals, and rescue workers that were hugely popular. The urges to both take photographs and to look at the images of disaster, some very mundane and others quite extraordinary, is clearly part of the process of assimilating this event. Photographs can serve to inspire awe and voyeurism through the spectacular, but they can also make catastrophe feel containable. In my experience of these exhibitions, part of their effect was the pleasure of seeing unusual views of Ground Zero, seemingly "secret" images, that appeared to be more visceral in their snapshot quality than the news images.

The rituals of mourning that involve the display or taking of photographs are part of a larger set of practices that provide comfort to those who are bereft. These are attempts to mediate the pain of loss through creating some form of presence—lighting candles as symbols of life, creating shrines, bringing something to a meaningful place or, finally, just doing something. The posters for the missing were the first stage of many small, individual acts of mourning and memorialization that took place throughout the city. These collective acts of mourning can be seen in the larger context of public mourning in the United States over the past 20 years. Whereas individual rituals of mourning and tributes to the dead have been practiced in private throughout history, they became a part of American national culture in the early 1980s when visitors to the Vietnam Veterans Memorial began to leave things there. These were spontaneous gestures at first, of scribbled notes and photographs left for the dead, which became more systematic over time, in particular as such rituals acts were recorded by the media and featured in coffee-table books. In Oklahoma City, people who were drawn to the site to look at the destruction began to leave things at a chain-link fence there: photographs, key chains, license plates, T-shirts with names written on them, and tributes to those killed. The fence was then publicized in media accounts and photos, and when the memorial was completed, it was incorporated into the memorial's design.

In New York, small and spontaneous memorials sprang up immediately around the city, in Union Square Park and at numerous fire stations, and more widely on numerous websites, as people felt the need to perform some kind of ritual to mark their loss. Leaving flowers, writing messages, and lighting candles are declarative acts that also serve to individualize the dead. As such, these objects and messages resist the transformation of the individual identity of the victims into a collective subjectivity, and thus resist the mass subjectivity of disaster in general. The destruction of the World Trade Center, like all disasters, created an image of injury to a mass body, what Michael Warner defines as "an already abstracted body" that is symbolized by the image of the destroyed towers. The mass body of disasters, Warner writes, such as natural disasters, airline disasters, and, inevitably, terrorist acts of mass destruction, is represented as a singular entity. Those killed are absorbed into this larger image of a collective dead, marked together by death into a singular subject. Warner writes, "disaster is popular, as it were, because it is a way of making mass subjectivity available, and it tells us something about the desirability of that mass subject."[15] Media representations are dependent, of course, on the image of disaster, which always, according to Warner, "commands a headline," and on creating a set of stories through which the individuals of that mass body can be typified. The small gestures of remembrance in rituals of mourning are attempts to prevent the absorption of the individual into this simple set of preestablished types.

Spontaneous rituals that provide comfort to people in the aftermath of traumatic events often become codified over a period of time, and, inevitably either fade away or become regulated as part of official memorials. The letters and objects left at the Vietnam Veterans Memorial, many of which are cryptic and anonymous messages to the dead presumably left by Vietnam veterans, are now placed almost immediately in plastic bags, gathered at the end of each day by the National Park Service, and relegated to a government archive. At the Oklahoma City Memorial, which has become a major tourist destination and already has an enormous archive, an elaborate set of rules governs the placement of objects on the memorial chairs and the chain-link fence. People now know before coming to these sites the role these objects of remembrance play. In New York, the media coverage of rituals of mourning has begun already to make them sites of tourism, on display for public fascination.[16]

Thus, the rituals of memory have become incorporated into the media spectacle of September 11, and the media has been in part a vehicle for mourning. Many people that I know began their days after September 11 reading the "Portraits of Grief" in the *New York Times* and weeping over the simple descriptions of those who died.[17] As an attempt to both democratize the exclusive pages of the *New York Times*'s obituary section and to work against traditional obituary form, these portraits were also forms of public grieving. Media coverage of the bereaved families and survivors both feeds a public desire to get closer to the pain of the event and to vicariously grieve through others. In this process, individuals are subsumed into particular kinds of cultural figures that foster media focus. The women whose husbands died on September 11, for instance, have since emerged as the "widows of 9/11." Just as the firefighters have been defined as the iconic victims of this event (in the way that the children were the iconic victims of Oklahoma City), the widows have emerged as the iconic figures of grief, posing, for example, in *People* magazine with their newborn children, now known as "post–9/11" babies. It is an inevitable consequence of the role that the media play in an event of this magnitude that people's grief is packaged into human interest stories for consumption—though not without producing ambivalence. As A. R. Torres, whose husband died at the World Trade Center, writes, "Now I am waiting for the WTC movie to come out, hoping it won't be about me."[18]

In addition to the ongoing production of human-interest stories, the commodification of September 11 now takes many forms: the transformation of Ground Zero into a site of tourism with viewing ramps and lines of onlookers, the transmutation of grief into patriotism in the form of advertising campaigns capitalizing on nationalist sentiment, the production of numerous commodities about the World Trade Center, and websites geared at online grieving rituals. Many of these forms inevitably spill over from mourning into kitsch. Writing about the proliferation of "haloed seraphim" and "teddy bears in firefighter helmets" in an essay on "The Kitschification of September 11," Daniel Harris asks, "Does an event as catastrophic as this one require the rhetoric of kitsch to make it less horrendous?"[19]

All this should bring us back to Adorno, whose statement needs to be understood not as a rejection of post-Holocaust representations so much as a cautionary warning about the potential aesthetic pleasure of such representations, and the subsequent narratives of redemption that they can provide. The central site at St. Paul's Chapel in lower Manhattan is filled with messages of solidarity and sympathy scribbled on sheets and papers, of photographs and expressions of loss. It is also a place where tourists pose for photographs with New York City policemen and take photographs of the devastation. When I have visited the site, I have felt a tremendous contradiction in the mixture of rituals of grief and tourism, the shock of a destroyed landscape tempered by the increasing theme-park quality. For the people I know who escaped with their lives that day, tourism is not an option.

Yet, consumerism and tourism are also means through which people are attempting to make sense of what happened. People make do with the symbols that they have at hand—teddy bears, symbols of sympathy—and the activities available to them, such as making pilgrimages to the site, to try and make sense of their loss. At the same time, a consumerism of grief can facilitate a glossing-over of the complexity of September 11 as a global event, reducing global politics to a simple statement of sentiment. Narratives of redemption tend to be politically regressive in that they are attempts to mediate loss through finding the good—a newfound patriotism, feelings of community—that has come from pain. As such, they have been used throughout history to justify political agendas—in the case of September 11, redemptive narratives have helped to render those who died in Afghanistan invisible.

Memorials, of course, are not separate from the workings of consumerism. Memorials are designed in part as sites of tourism and are quite often the source of commodities of mourning. The Oklahoma City Memorial, for instance, has a gift shop that sells not only tasteful renderings of the memorials and books about it, but also bumper stickers that read "On American Soil" and running shorts emblazoned with the memorial logo. It is inevitable that whatever memorial is built at Ground Zero will be a primary site of tourism and a central draw for that part of the city. A crucial issue in the memorial design will thus be the degree to which it mediates this relationship.

The question of how to properly represent the dead in memorializing them hovers over Ground Zero with increasing urgency as the months go by and design plans circulate. What aesthetic should dominate the memory of September 11? Throughout the history of memorials, figuration has been a primary mode of representation. Yet, in the tension between the concerns of modernism and the aesthetic styles of memorialization, there emerged in the twentieth century a very specific divide between memorial designs that favor realism and figuration and those that deploy abstraction. Furthermore, in the contemporary cultural context of pluralism and multiculturalism, the capacity of a lone figure to represent a larger collective has become quite problematic. This tension emerged in the aftermath of September 11, when a design for a memorial of firefighters was rejected by the firefighters themselves for "political correctness." The proposed memorial was a replica of a news photograph of three firefighters raising a flag at Ground Zero, an iconic image that refers back to the Marine Corps Memorial of men raising the flag of Iwo Jima (itself the replica of a well-known photograph). Yet, the firefighters rejected the design because the three white firefighters in the photograph had been transformed into a racially diverse group to metaphorically include the ethnicities of the firefighters who died.[20] (In fact, the New York City Fire Department is 94 percent white, itself a shocking statistic for a city that is less than 50 percent white.)[21]

This debate over aesthetics and representation had been played out previously with the design of the Vietnam Veterans Memorial, which was the source of a heated controversy before it was built because many veterans (and funder Ross Perot) felt that its modernist design of a low wall with names connoted shame and guilt. As a compromise, a second memorial of three soldiers was constructed nearby. Yet, the realist figures of those three soldiers, carefully crafted to be white, black, and Latino, immediately had the effect of making the women veterans feel excluded. Consequently, the women now have a realist statue of their own.[22] Figuration is thus about inclusion and exclusion, a problem in a society sensitive to issues of difference. The aesthetics of mourning is thus split between these two polar approaches, the realist statue epitomized by the Marine Corps War Memorial of Iwo Jima and derivative of iconic photographs, and the use of abstraction and naming to individualize the dead.

The most successful national memorials have been those that allow visitors a wide range of potential interactions and rituals, and, most importantly, allow people to create a space where they can speak to the dead. These memorials facilitate a conversation with the dead in part through naming those who died, and in so doing, separating them out as individuals from the mass body of disaster. At the Vietnam Veterans Memorial, people touch the names and make rubbings of them to take away; they leave objects and letters for the dead with the sense that the dead receive them. At the Oklahoma City National Memorial, each victim is represented by a bronze chair with a lighted base, providing a place for families to visit and for strangers to reflect on the meaning of an individual life. The chairs effectively evoke both the absence of the dead as they sit unoccupied, yet their presence as well, as families come to speak to their loved ones there.[23]

Naming is central to how people make meaning at memorials, but it is not without its problems. For instance, there were disputes about whose names were included on the Vietnam Veterans Memorial (including whether some of the dead had been killed within the proper "war zone"). It is already evident that there were workers killed at the World Trade Center who were there by chance, who did not have citizenship or working papers, and whose names may never be known. Yet, naming in a memorial is one means to attempt to counter the reality that our society awards more value to some lives over others. The media coverage of September 11 establishes a hierarchy of the dead, with, for instance, the privileging of the stories of public servants, such as firefighters over office workers, of policemen over security guards, and the stories of those with economic capital over those without, of traders over janitors. In addition, as the controversies over the awarding of money to families has shown, there are huge discrepancies when the values of capitalism (through equations of potential earning power) rather than need are the basis for the compensation awarded to grieving families. A memorial that names the dead as individuals can be more democratic and state in its very design that all lives are worth honoring equally. A name can tell us very little about someone's life, their hopes, the people who loved them. It can, however, remind us that each name was a life lived with meaning.

The building of a memorial at Ground Zero inevitably will have the effect of privileging the role of the public at the site. The space of Ground Zero is being symbolically reclaimed by the public through the dead who are forever lost there. This reclamation should have a constraining effect on the private interests in the site, given the symbolic power and moral authority of groups such as the 9-11 Widows and Victims' Families Association to garner public support and sway politicians.[24]

Ultimately, however, it is important that any process of memorialization of September 11 confront what memorials do well, and what they don't do. National memorials traditionally have been built with dual purposes: To act as forms of pedagogy about the nation and historical figures within it, and to honor the dead. Philosopher Charles Griswold has called them a "species of pedagogy."[25] Yet, this pedagogy is highly limited. Memorials do not teach well about history, since their role is to remember those who died rather than to understand *why* they died. One can visit the Vietnam Veterans Memorial and the Oklahoma City National Memorial without understanding, for instance, the fraught history of the Vietnam War and the reasons why American lives were lost in Vietnam, or what aspects of American society gave rise to the right-wing terrorists who bombed Oklahoma City. It is important that the sites that are created to mourn the dead do not foreclose on discussions about why lives were lost.

The memorials that resonate within a culture are those that allow debates to continue, that don't try to contain history and memory but create a space where they are generated in all their conflict. The challenge in New York will be to create a memorial where the World Trade Center once stood that provides a place to grieve for and speak to the dead, yet which does not allow for a smoothing-over of the search for meaning, or attempt to bring closure to an event that should not and cannot have closure.

NOTES

1. Religious Terror and Global War, *by Mark Juergensmeyer*

1. Mark Juergensmeyer, *The New Cold War? Religious Nationalism Confronts the Secular State* (Berkeley: University of California Press, 1993).

2. Mark Juergensmeyer, *Terror in the Mind of God: The Global Rise of Religious Violence* (Berkeley: University of California Press, 2000). Excerpts from this book are utilized for this essay.

3. Author's interview with Dr. Abdul Aziz Rantisi, cofounder and political leader of Hamas, Khan Yunis, Gaza, March 1, 1998.

4. Pierre Bourdieu, *Language and Symbolic Power,* trans. by Gino Raymond and Matthew Adamson (Cambridge, MA: Harvard University Press, 1991), p. 117.

5. One interpretation of the basic rules of nonviolent conflict resolution may be found in my book *Gandhi's Way: A Handbook of Conflict Resolution* (Berkeley: University of California Press, 2002).

6. Author's interview with Yoel Lerner, Director of the Sannhedrin Institute, Jerusalem, March 2, 1998.

7. Interview with Dr. Rantisi, March 2, 1998.

8. Natalie Zemon Davis, "The Rites of Violence: Religious Riots in Sixteenth-Century France," *Past and Present* 59 (May 1973) pp. 52–53.

9. Ibid., pp. 81–82.

10. Stanley Tambiah, *Leveling Crowds: Ethnonationalist Conflicts and Collective Violence in South Asia* (Berkeley: University of California Press, 1996), pp. 310–11.

11. Ibid., p. 311.

12. Pierre Bourdieu and Loic J. D. Wacquant, *An Invitation to Reflexive Sociology* (Chicago: University of Chicago Press, 1992), p. 131.

13. Author's interview with Mahmud Abouhalima, convicted codefendant in bombing of the World Trade Center, United States Penitentiary, Lompoc, California, August 19, 1997.

14. Author's interview with Dr. Muhammad Ibraheem el-Geyoushi, Dean of the Faculty of Dawah, Al-Azhar University, Cairo, May 30, 1990.

15. Interview with Dr. Rantisi, March 1, 1998.

16. Frantz Fanon, *The Wretched of the Earth* (New York: Grove Press, 1963).

17. Interview with Abouhalima, September 30, 1997.

18. Bourdieu, *Language and Symbolic Power,* pp. 72–76. See also his *Outline of a Theory of Practice,* trans. by Richard Nice (Cambridge: Cambridge University Press, 1977), pp. 171–83.

19. Jurgen Habermas, trans. by Thomas McCarthy, *Legitimation Crisis* (Boston: Beacon Press, 1975).

20. The phrase originates with historian Darrin McMahon in his fascinating book on the religious roots of the far right. McMahon, *Enemies of the Enlightenment: The French Counter-Enlightenment and the Making of Modernity* (New York: Oxford University Press, 2001).

21. Bourdieu, *Language and Symbolic Power*, p. 116.

22. For a forceful statement of this thesis, see Partha Chatterjee, *The Nation and Its Fragments: Colonial and Postcolonial Histories* (Princeton: Princeton University Press, 1993).

23. I describe this "loss of faith" at length in Juergensmeyer, *The New Cold War?*, pp. 11–25.

24. Jurgen Habermas, "Modernity—An Incomplete Project," reprinted in Paul Rabinow and William M. Sullivan, eds., *Interpretive Social Science: A Second Look* (Berkeley: University of California Press, 1987), p. 148.

25. See, for instance, Roger Friedland, "When God Walks in History: The Institutional Politics of Religious Nationalism," *International Sociology* (September 1999).

26. José Casanova, *Public Religions in the Modern World* (Chicago: University of Chicago Press, 1994), p. 211.

2. The Struggle for the Soul of Islam, *by Robert W. Hefner*

1. See Ibn Khaldun, *Muqaddimah* (2 vols.), trans. by F. Rosenthal (New York: Pantheon, 1958).

2. James P. Piscatori, *Islam in a World of Nation-States* (Cambridge, UK: Cambridge University Press, 1986), pp. 76–98.

3. See Benedict Anderson, *Imagined Communities: Reflections on the Origin and Spread of Nationalism*, 2nd edition (New York: Verso, 1991), esp. pp. 12–19; Ernest Gellner, *Nations and Nationalism* (Ithaca: Cornell University Press, 1983). For a critique of secularist views of nationalism, see Peter van der Veer, *Religious Nationalism: Hindus and Muslims in India* (Berkeley: University of California Press, 1994), pp. 15–16.

4. On the role of Protestantism in English nationalism, see Hugh McLeod, "Protestantism and British National Identity, 1815–1945," in Peter van der Veer and Hartmut Lehmann, eds., *Nation and Religion: Perspectives on Europe and Asia* (Princeton: Princeton University Press, 1999), pp. 44–70.

5. For the Muslim Middle East, see Olivier Roy, *The Failure of Political Islam* (Cambridge, MA: Harvard University Press, 1994); for Indonesia, see Robert W. Hefner, *Civil Islam: Muslims and Democratization in Indonesia* (Princeton: Princeton University Press, 2000).

6. See Dale F. Eickelman, "Mass Higher Education and the Religious Imagination in Contemporary Arab Societies," in *American Ethnologist* 19:4 (November 1992), pp. 1–13.

7. Anderson, *Imagined Communities*, pp. 37–46.

8. Ali Rahnema, "Ali Shariati: Teacher, Preacher, and Rebel," in Ali Rahnema, ed., *Pioneers of Islamic Revival* (London: Zed Books, 1994), pp. 208–250.

9. Dale F. Eickelman and James Piscatori, *Muslim Politics* (Princeton: Princeton University Press, 1996), p. 5.

10. Ibid., p. 132.

11. See Robert Wuthnow, *The Restructuring of American Religion: Society and Faith Since World War II* (Princeton: Princeton University Press, 1988).

12. On the thesis of a clash of civilizations, see Samuel P. Huntington, *The Clash of Civilizations and the Remaking of World Order* (New York: Simon & Schuster, 1996). For critical commen-

taries, see Fred Halliday, *Islam and the Myth of Confrontation: Religion and Politics in the Middle East* (London: I. B. Tauris, 1995), and Hefner, *Civil Islam*, pp. 3–36.

13. For discussions of civic pluralist approaches to Muslim politics, see Abdullahi Ahmed An-Na'im, *Toward an Islamic Reformation: Civil Liberties, Human Rights, and International Law* (Syracuse: Syracuse University Press, 1990); John L. Esposito and John O. Voll, *Islam and Democracy* (New York: Oxford University Press, 1996); and John Cooper, Ronald Nettler, and Mohamed Mahmoud, *Islam and Modernity: Muslim Intellectuals Respond* (London: I. B. Tauris, 1998).

14. For a discussion of *dhimmi* and citizenship, see An-Na'im, *Toward an Islamic Reformation,* and Abdolkarim Soroush, *Reason, Freedom, and Democracy in Islam* (Oxford: Oxford University Press, 2000).

15. For an incisive sociological analysis of this point, see José Casanova, *Public Religions in the Modern World* (Chicago: University of Chicago Press, 1994).

16. Robert D. Putnam, *Making Democracy Work: Civic Traditions in Modern Italy* (Princeton: Princeton University Press, 1993).

17. See Bahman Baktiari and Halez Vaziri, "Iran's Liberal Revolution?" in *Current History,* vol. 101, no. 651, pp. 17–21.

18. See Hefner, *Civil Islam;* and Mark R. Woodward, "Talking Across Paradigms: Indonesia, Islam, and Orientalism," in Mark R. Woodward, ed., *Toward a New Paradigm: Recent Developments in Indonesian Islamic Thought* (Tempe, AZ: Program for Southeast Asian Studies, Arizona State University, 1996), pp. 1–46.

19. Guillermo O'Donnell and Philippe C. Schmitter, *Transitions from Authoritarian Rule: Tentative Conclusions about Uncertain Democracies* (Baltimore: Johns Hopkins University Press, 1986), pp. 48–56.

20. Kees van Dijk, *A Country in Despair: Indonesia Between 1997 and 2000* (Leiden: KITLV Press, 2001), p. 298.

21. Peter Evans, "Government Action, Social Capital and Development: Reviewing the Evidence on Synergy," in *World Development,* vol. 24, no. 6, pp. 1119–1132.

3. "Traditionalist" Islamic Activism: Deoband, Tablighis, and Talibs, *by Barbara D. Metcalf*

1. I am grateful to Muhammad Khalid Masud, Academic Director, and Peter van der Veer, co-director, who invited me to give the annual lecture of the Institute for the Study of Islam in the Modern World, Leiden University, November 23, 2001. This essay is based on the lecture I gave on that occasion.

2. An example of the typically imprecise discussion of "deobandism" is: "a sect that propagates . . . a belief that has inspired modern revivals of Islamic fundamentalism." John F. Burns, "Adding Demands, Afghan Leaders Show Little Willingness to Give Up bin Laden," *New York Times,* September 19, 2001.

3. Conversation with "the ambassador at large" of the Taliban, Rahmatullah Hashemi, Berkeley California, March 6, 2001, in the course of his tour through the Middle East, Europe, and the United States.

4. See, for example, "A Long, Strange Trip to the Taliban," in *Newsweek,* December 17, 2001, and Don Lattin and Kevin Fagan, "John Walker's Curious Quest: Still a Mystery How the Young Marin County Convert to Islam Made the Transition from Spiritual Scholar to Taliban Soldier," *San Francisco Chronicle,* December 13, 2001.

5. Olivier Roy, "Has Islamism a Future in Afghanistan?" In William Maley, ed. *Fundamentalism Reborn? Afghanistan and the Taliban* (New York: NYU Press, 1998), p. 208.

6. Here I differ from Salman Rushdie, who uses the term too broadly: "These Islamists [here he speaks of "radical political movements"]—we must get used to this word, 'Islamists,' meaning those who are engaged upon such political projects, and learn to distinguish it from the more general and politically neutral 'Muslim'—include . . . the Taliban." Salman Rushdie, "Yes, This is About Islam," *New York Times,* November 2, 2001.

7. The Jamiyyat-i Islami was formed by Burhanuddin Rabbani and others who had studied at Al Azhar; the Hezb-i Islami of Gulbuddin Hekmatyar was more influenced by the Pakistani Jama'at-i Islami. On the original movements, see Seyyid Vali Reza Nasr, *The Vanguard of the Islamic Revolution: The Jama'at-i Islami of Pakistan* (Berkeley: University of California Press, 1994) and Richard Mitchell, *The Society of the Muslim Brothers* (London: Oxford University Press, 1969).

8. See my *Islamic Revival in British India: Deoband, 1860–1900* (Princeton: Princeton University Press, 1982).

9. For an evocative picture of the education of an *'alim* that, despite the *Shi'a* setting, resonates broadly with the kind of education briefly described here, see Roy P. Mottahedeh, *The Mantle of the Prophet: Religion and Politics in Iran* (New York: Simon and Schuster, 1985).

10. For a comparative view of the contexts of such movements see William R. Roff, "Islamic Movements: One or Many?" In William R. Roff, ed., *Islam and the Political Economy of Meaning* (London: Croom Helm and Berkeley: University of California Press, 1987), pp. 31–52.

11. For a general background to all these movements see Metcalf, 1982, op. cit. On the "Barelvis" (who call themselves Ahlu's-Sunnat wa'l-Jama'at in order to assert that they are true Muslims, not a sect), see Usha Sanyal, *Devotional Islam and Politics in British India: Ahmad Riza Khan Barelwi and His Movement, 1870–1920* (Delhi: Oxford University Press, 1996). For the experience of religious institutions in Pakistan, see Jamal Malik, *Colonization of Islam: Dissolution of Traditional Institutions in Pakistan* (New Delhi: Manonar, 1996) and Muhammad Qasim Zaman, "Religious Education and the Rhetoric of Reform: The Madrasa in British India and Pakistan" in *Comparative Studies in Society and History* 41:2 (April 1999), pp. 294–323 and "Sectarianism in Pakistan: The Radicalization of Shi'i and Sunni Identities" in *Modern Asian Studies* 32:3 (July 1998), pp. 689–716, as well as his forthcoming monograph from Princeton University Press. For the religious institutions of South Asian Muslims in Europe and North America, see Philip Lewis, *Islamic Britain: Religion, Politics, and Identity among British Muslims* (London: I. B. Tauris, 1994) and Barbara D. Metcalf, ed., *Making Muslim Space in North America and Europe* (Berkeley: University of California Press, 1996).

12. Yohanan Friedmann, "The Attitude of the Jam' iyyat-i 'Ulama'-i Hind to the Indian National Movement and the Establishment of Pakistan" in Gabriel Baer, ed., *The Ulama in Modern History* (Jerusalem: Israeli Oriental Society, Asian and African Studies, VII, 1971), pp. 157–83.

13. www.darululoom-deoband.com. The estimate of numbers to be accommodated in the mosque is in Rahul Bedi, "Taliban ideology lives on in India," *On-line Asia Times* (December 12, 2001; www.atimes.com/ind-pak/CL12Df01.html).

14. Many journalists traveled to Deoband in late 2001 in order to report on the source of Taliban religious training. See, for example, Luke Harding, "Out of India," *The Guardian* November 2, 2001; Kartikeya Sharma, "Scholar's Getaway," *The Week* (www.the-week.com/21ju101/life8.htm); Michael Fathers, "At the Birthplace of the Taliban," *Time Magazine* (September 21, 2001, reprinted on www.foil.org/resources/9–11/Fathers010921-Deoband.htm). On December 29, 2001 the search engine "Google" listed approximately 2,500 sites for "Deoband," many of them reporting on the links of the school to the Taliban.

15. The Madrasa Haqqania in Akhora Khatak trained the core Taliban leadership. See Jeffrey Goldberg, "Jihad U.: The Education of a Holy Warrior," *The New York Times Magazine,* June 25, 2000.

16. See my "Women and Men in a Contemporary Pietist Movement: The Case of the Tablighi Jama'at," in *Appropriating Gender: Women's Activism and Politicized Religion in South Asia,* Amrita Basu and Patricia Jeffery, eds. (New York: Routledge, 1998), pp. 107–121 and reprinted in retitled volume: *Resisting the Sacred and the Secular: Women's Activism and Politicised Religion in South Asia* (Delhi: Kali for Women, 1999).

17. I discuss the movement's publications in "Living Hadith in the Tablighi Jama'at," *The Journal of Asian Studies* 52,3 (1993), pp. 584–608.

18. See her forthcoming study of the regional Sufi cult of Zindapir, *Pilgrims of Love: The Anthropology of a Global Sufi Cult* (Bloomington: Indiana University Press, 2002). This study also exemplifies the positive accommodation to contemporary life offered by a transnational Sufi movement and explicitly distinguishes Werbner from those who explain Islamic religious movements as a reaction to frustration and failure.

19. A little-noted aspect of Osama bin Laden's leadership was his claim to authority, despite his lack of a traditional education, to issue *fatawa.* His call to make *jihad* incumbent on all Muslims deployed a technical distinction of Islamic legal thought, saying that *jihad* was an individual duty, *farz 'ain,* rather than a duty on some subset of the *umma* (e.g., political leaders, soldiers), *farz kifaya.*

20. Tempest Rone, "Huge Gathering of Moderate Muslims in Pakistan," *San Francisco Chronicle,* November 3, 2001. Also, Maulana Zubair-ul-Hassan: "[The Holy Prophet] said it is not bravery to kill the non-believers but to preach [to] them is the real task." Quote in "Tableeghi Ijtima Concludes," *The Frontier Post* (Peshawar), November 5, 2001 (www.frontierpost.com.pk).

21. Seyyed Vali Reza Nasr, op. cit., makes the important argument that it is by welcoming Islamist parties into the democratic process, as happened in Pakistan in the mid-1980s, that they become politically moderate.

22. See Sayyid A. S. Pirzada, *The Politics of the Jamiat Ulema-i-Islam Pakistan 1971–1977* (Karachi: Oxford University Press, 2000).

23. The target of this is Fazlur Rahman, head of the JUI (F). See Rick Bragg, "A Pro-Taliban Rally Draws Angry Thousands in Pakistan, Then Melts Away," *New York Times,* October 6, 2001.

24. See Seyyed Vali Reza, Nasr, "International Politics, Domestic Imperatives, and Identity Mobilization: Sectarianism in Pakistan, 1979–98," *Comparative Politics* 32:2 (January 2000), pp. 171–190.

25. Rashid is the definitive source for the history of the Taliban. Ahmed Rashid, *Taliban: Militant Islam, Oil, and Fundamentalism in Central Asia* (New Haven: Yale University Press, 2000), p. 88.

26. Roy, op. cit. p. 211.

27. The phrase "ethnic polarization" is Olivier Roy's. He uses this phrase to suggest that ethnic loyalties are complex and fluid, not ideologized. He further argues that these loyalties have shaped all parties in the Afghan competitions of recent years.

28. Hashemi, for example, attempted to establish common ground with his foreign interlocutors in the spring of 2001 (see note 3, above). He emphasized the desperate conditions inside his country, both the crisis of public order characterized by warlordism following the Soviet withdrawal in the early 1990s and the immediate extreme conditions produced by drought and famine, as partial explanation for the regime's severe policies. He insisted that the regime favored public employment and education for women, but in the conditions of the time needed "to protect" them. He tried to show that the destruction of the Bamian Buddhas was

understandable—if perhaps irrational, he almost suggested—as a reaction to offers of international aid to preserve antiquities rather than to avert starvation and disease.

29. For a sensitive analysis of the tension between the lure of this rhetoric and actual moderation in behavior on the part of most British Muslims, see Pnina Werbner, "The Predicament of Diaspora and Millennial Islam," *Times Higher Education Supplement,* December 14, 2001. The argument is suggestive for the behavior of many Muslims in a place like Pakistan as well.

30. See Thomas L. Friedman, "In Pakistan, It's Jihad 101," *New York Times,* November 13, 2001 and Jeffrey Goldberg, "Jihad U.: The Education of a Holy Warrior," *The New York Times Magazine,* June 25, 2000.

31. Mixed in with sites addressing current political issues are sites that primarily transfer the materials of polemical pamphlets to the Web. Thus, a site posting "Barelwi" perspectives excerpts Deobandi *fatawa* to show that they are guilty of the very insolence toward the Prophet that they condemn—the kind of condemnation current a hundred years ago. See www.schinan.com/jhangi. A particularly elaborate site, intended to show that Ahl-i Hadith beliefs alone are true, reviews the errors of many other groups, with a dozen and a half linked pages challenging issues of "Tableegi-Jama'at." See www.salaf.indiaaccess.com/tableegi_jamaat.

32. Nicholas Lemann, "What Terrorists Want," *The New Yorker,* October 29, 2001, p. 39.

4. The Religious Undertow of Muslim Economic Grievances, *by Timur Kuran*

1. On the objectives of Islamism, see the pertinent essays in the five-volume "Fundamentalism Project," published by the University of Chicago Press, 1991–95. See, in particular, Mumtaz Ahmad, "Islamic Fundamentalism in South Asia: The Jamaat-i-Islami and the Tablighi Jamaat," pp. 457–530 in *Fundamentalisms Observed,* ed. Martin E. Marty and R. Scott Appleby (Chicago: University of Chicago Press, 1991); and John O. Voll, "Fundamentalism in the Sunni Arab World," *ibid.,* pp. 345–402.

2. For a highly influential description of the "Islamic way of life," see Sayyid Abu'l-A'la Mawdudi, *Let Us Be Muslims,* ed. Khurram Murad (Kuala Lumpur: Noordeen, 1990; orig. Urdu ed., 1940).

3. See, for instance, Muhammad Baqir al-Sadr, *Iqtisaduna: Our Economics,* 4 vols. (Tehran: World Organization for Islamic Services, 1982–84; orig. Arabic ed., 1961); Afzal-ur-Rahman, *Economic Doctrines of Islam,* 2nd ed., 3 vols. (Lahore: Islamic Publications, 1980).

4. For a concise statement of what Islamic economics offers and demands, see M. Umer Chapra, *Islam and the Economic Challenge* (Leicester, U.K.: Islamic Foundation, 1992).

5. For an evaluation of various economic reforms carried out in the name of Islam, see Timur Kuran, "Islamic Economics and the Islamic Subeconomy," *Journal of Economic Perspectives,* 9 (1995), pp. 171–191; and Sohrab Behdad, "Property Rights in Contemporary Islamic Economic Thought: A Critical Perspective," *Review of Social Economy,* 47 (1989), pp. 185–211.

6. For an extensive account, see Timur Kuran, "The Genesis of Islamic Economics: A Chapter in the Politics of Muslim Identity," *Social Research,* 64 (1997), pp. 301–338.

7. There is a vast literature on Middle Eastern modernization drives. For a few examples, see Fazlur Rahman, *Islam and Modernity: Transformation of an Intellectual Tradition* (Chicago: University of Chicago Press, 1982); Bassam Tibi, *Islam and the Cultural Accommodation of Social Change,* trans. Clare Krojzl (Boulder, Colorado: Westview Press, 1990); Bernard Lewis, *The Emergence of Modern Turkey,* 2nd ed. (London: Oxford University Press, 1961); Cyril E. Black and L. Carl Brown, eds., *Modernization in the Middle East: The Ottoman Empire and Its Afro-Asian Successors* (Princeton: Darwin Press, 1992); and Augustus Richard Norton, ed., *Civil Society in the Middle East* (Leiden: Brill, 1995).

8. Hayyim J. Cohen, "The Economic Background and the Secular Occupations of Muslim Jurisprudents and Traditionists of the Classical Period of Islam (until the middle of the eleventh century)," *Journal of the Economic and Social History of the Orient*, 13 (1970), pp. 16–61.

9. F. E. Peters, *The Hajj: The Muslim Pilgrimage to Mecca and the Holy Places* (Princeton: Princeton University Press, 1994), esp. pp. 180–183, 291–293; and Suraiya Faroqhi, *Pilgrims and Sultans: The Hajj under the Ottomans, 1517–1683* (London: I. B. Tauris, 1994), esp. chap. 1.

10. S. D. Goitein, "The Four Faces of Islam," chapter 1 in his *Studies in Islamic History and Institutions* (Leiden: E. J. Brill, 1966), p. 8.

5. The Globalization of Informal Violence, Theories of World Politics, and "the Liberalism of Fear," *by Robert O. Keohane*

1. This chapter originally appeared in *Dialog IO*, the online version of *International Organization*. I am grateful for comments on earlier versions of this paper to Carol Atkinson, Hein Goemans, Peter Gourevitch, Nannerl O. Keohane, Lisa L. Martin, Joseph S. Nye, John Gerard Ruggie, and Anne-Marie Slaughter, as well as to participants at seminars at the University of Pennsylvania, October 18, 2001; at the University of Amsterdam, November 2, 2001; at Duke University, November 16, 2001; and at the University of Tokyo, December 10, 2001. At the Amsterdam colloquium I benefited particularly from the comments of Gerd Junne and at the Tokyo colloquium from the comments of Yasuaki Osuma.

2. Joseph Schumpeter, *Capitalism, Socialism and Democracy* (New York: Harper and Row, 1950), p. 137.

3. Statement by Osama bin Laden, *New York Times*, October 8, 2001, p. B7.

4. The best definitional discussion of terrorism that I know of is by Alex Schmid, who defines it as "an anxiety-inspiring method of repeated violent action, employed by (semi)clandestine individual, group or state actors, for idiosyncratic, criminal or political reasons, whereby—in contrast to assassination—the direct targets of violence are not the main targets." See "The Response Problem as a Definition Problem," Alex P. Schmid and Ronald D. Crelinsten, eds., *Western Responses to Terrorism* (London: Frank Cass; 1993), pp. 8, 12.

5. Judith N. Shklar, *Ordinary Vices* (Cambridge: Belknap Press of Harvard University Press, 1984).

6. David Held, Anthony McGrew, David Goldblatt, and Jonathan Perraton, *Global Transformations* (Stanford: Stanford University Press, 1999), p. 15.

7. Robert O. Keohane and Joseph S. Nye, *Power and Interdependence*, 3rd edition (New York: Addison Wesley Longman, 2001), p. 229.

8. Held et al., op. cit., p. 80; Keohane and Nye, op. cit., p. 237.

9. Walter Lippmann, *U.S. Foreign Policy: Shield of the Republic* (Boston: Little, Brown, 1943), pp. 88, 101.

10. John H. Herz, *International Politics in the Atomic Age* (New York: Columbia University Press, 1959), pp. 107–108.

11. Keohane and Nye, op. cit., pp. 243–45.

12. Herz, op. cit., p. 22.

13. Lippmann, op. cit., p. 9.

14. From a Fourth of July oration by John Quincy Adams at the Capitol in 1821. Bradford Perkins, *The Creation of a Republican Empire, 1776–1865*. Volume I of the *Cambridge History of American Foreign Relations* (Cambridge: Cambridge University Press, 1993), pp. 149–150.

15. A few pessimistic and prescient observers understood that terrorism could pose a threat to the United States homeland despite our dominance in military power. See Ashton B. Carter and William Perry, *Preventive Defense: A New Security Strategy for America* (Washington, D.C.: Brookings, 1999) and Gary Hart, Warren Rudman, et al., *Phase I Report on the Emerging Global Security Environment for the First Quarter of the 21st Century,* United States Commission on National Security/21st Century (Washington: September 15, 1999), Conclusion 1.

16. In 1977 Joseph Nye and I distinguished between two types of dependence, which we labeled (following the contemporary literature on economic interdependence) sensitivity and vulnerability dependence. Sensitivity dependence refers to "liability to costly effects imposed from outside before policies are altered to try to change the situation." Vulnerability dependence, in contrast, refers to "an actor's liability to suffer costs imposed by external events even after policies have been altered." This language seems inappropriate in the contemporary situation, since in ordinary language, the attacks on an unprepared United States on September 11 demonstrated how vulnerable the country was. But the distinction between levels of dependence before and after policy change remains important. See Keohane and Nye, op. cit., p. 11; the text is unchanged from the 1st edition, 1977.

17. Keohane and Nye, op. cit., p. 14

18. My colleague Ole Holsti has pointed out to me that in surveys conducted by the Chicago Council on Foreign Relations in 1994 and 1998, the public more often regarded international terrorism as a "critical" foreign policy issue than did leaders. Indeed, 69 percent and 84 percent, respectively, of the public regarded terrorism as a critical issue in those years, compared to 33 percent and 61 percent of the elites. See page 21 in Ole Holsti, "Public Opinion and Foreign Policy," in Robert Lieber, ed., *Eagle Rules?* (New York: Longman, 2000), pp. 16–46.

19. Kenneth N. Waltz, *Theory of International Politics* (Reading, MA: Addison-Wesley, 1979), p. 125.

20. Inis L. Claude, *The Changing United Nations* (New York: Random House, 1967).

21. Max Weber, *Economy and Society,* Guenther Roth and Claus Wittich, eds. (Berkeley: University of California Press, 1978), p. 954.

22. Douglass North links legitimacy to the costs of enforcing rules. "The costs of maintenance of an existing order are inversely related to the perceived legitimacy of the existing system. To the extent that the participants believe the system fair, the costs of enforcing the rules and property rights are enormously reduced." Douglass C. North, *Structure and Change in Economic History* (New York: W. W. Norton, 1981), p. 53.

23. Shklar, op. cit., pp. 4, 237.

24. Shklar, op. cit., p. 244.

25. It is tempting in hindsight to forget that the political systems of European countries were not terribly strong in 1947. Germany was still under occupation, Italy had recently been Fascist, and France and Italy had very large pro-Soviet communist parties. Nevertheless, these countries had relatively highly-educated populations, they had some history of democratic or at least liberal politics, and their administrative bureaucracies were quite effective.

26. Joseph S. Nye, Jr, *The Paradox of American Power* (New York: Oxford University Press, 2002).

27. This is a point that the late Susan Strange repeatedly emphasized.

6. Violence, Law, and Justice In a Global Age, *by David Held*

1. Two sections of this essay have been adapted from my previous writings. The first section draws on some material developed at much greater length in my "Law of states, law of peoples," *Legal Theory*, 8.2, 2002, forthcoming. The second section draws on my "Violence and justice in a global age" and, with Mary Kaldor, on "What hope for the future? Learning the lessons of the past." Both these pieces were made available initially through OpenDemocracy.net. I would like to thank Mary Kaldor for allowing me to draw on our joint essay and to adapt some of the material for this new piece. Her work on old and new wars has been an especially important influence on me here.

2. Barbara Kingsolver, "A pure, high note of anguish," *Los Angeles Times*, September 23, 2001.

3. Immanuel Kant, *Kant's Political Writings*, H. Reiss, ed. and intro. (Cambridge: Cambridge University Press, 1970), pp. 107–8.

4. See Held and McGrew, Goldblatt and Perraton, *Global Transformations: Politics, Economics and Culture* (Cambridge: Polity Press, 1999), Chapters 3–5; and Held and McGrew, *The Global Transformation Reader* (Cambridge: Polity Press, 2000), Chapter 25.

5. See Vincent, "Modernity and universal human rights," in A. McGrew and P. Lewis, eds., *Global Politics* (Cambridge: Polity Press, 1992), pp. 269–92.

6. A. Cassese, *Violence and Law in the Modern Age* (Cambridge: Polity Press, 1988), p. 132.

7. Y. Dinstein, "Rules of war," in J. Krieger, ed., *The Oxford Companion to Politics of the World* (Oxford: Oxford University Press, 1993), p. 968.

8. Cf. Chinkin, "International law and human rights," in T. Evans, ed., *Human Rights Fifty Years On: A Reappraisal* (Manchester: Manchester University Press, 1998) and "A Survey of Human Rights," *The Economist*, December 5, 1998.

9. Cf. J. Crawford, "Prospects for an international criminal court," in M. D. A. Freeman and R. Halson, eds. *Current Legal Problems 1995*, 48, part 2, collected papers (Oxford: Oxford University Press, 1995); J. Dugard, "Obstacles in the way of an international criminal court." *Cambridge Law Journal*, 56, 1997; and M. Weller, "The reality of the emerging universal constitutional order: putting the pieces together," *Cambridge Review of International Studies*, Winter/Spring 1997.

10. Chinkin, 1998, op. cit., pp. 118–9

11. David Held, "Law of states, law of peoples," *Legal Theory*, 2002, 8, 2.

12. Mary Kaldor, "Reconceptualizing organized violence," in D. Archibugi, D. Held, and M. Köhler eds., *Re-imagining Political Community: Studies in Cosmopolitan Democracy* (Cambridge: Polity Press, 1998); and Mary Kaldor, *New and Old Wars* (Cambridge: Polity Press, 1998).

13. See Kaldor, op. cit., Chapters 6 and 7.

14. F. Kirgis, "Terrorist attacks on the World Trade Center and the Pentagon," September 2001, www.asil.org/insights/insigh77.htm

15. See Jurgen Habermas, "Bestialität und humanität," *Die Zeit*, April 18, 1999.

16. Crawford and Marks, "The global democracy deficit: an essay on international law and its limits," in Archibugi et al eds. op. cit., p. 2; Weller, op. cit., p. 45.

17. Held, *Democracy and the Global Order: From the Modern State to Cosmopolitan Governance* (Cambridge: Polity Press, 1995), pp. 107–113.

18. See Held and McGrew, Goldblatt and Perraton, op. cit., Chapters 1 and 2.

19. C. Beitz, "Philosophy of international relations," in the *Routledge Encyclopedia of Philosophy* (London: Routledge 1998); cf. C. Beitz, *Political Theory and International Relations* (Princeton: Princeton University Press, 1979); T. Pogge, *Realizing Rawls* (Ithaca, N.Y.: Cornell University Press, 1989; T. Pogge, (1994a) "Cosmopolitanism and sovereignty," in C. Brown, ed., *Political Restructuring in Europe: Ethical Perspectives* (London: Routledge 1994; T. Pogge, "An egalitarian law of peoples," *Philosophy and Public Affairs,* 1994, 23, 3; and B. Barry, "Statism and nationalism: a cosmopolitan critique," in I. Shapiro and L. Brilmayer, eds., *Global Justice* (New York: New York University Press, 1999); and see below.

20. See Held (2002) op. cit.

21. UNDP, *Globalization with a Human Face: Human Development Report 1999* (New York: Oxford University Press, 1999).

22. G. Thompson, "Economic globalization?," in David Held, ed., *A Globalizing World?* (London: Routledge, 2000).

23. Thomas Pogge, "Economic Justice and National Borders," *Revision,* 1999, 22, 2, p. 27; see UNDP, *Human Development Report 1997* (New York: Oxford University Press, 1997); UNDP, op. cit.; and Held and McGrew, op. cit.

24. See Pogge, ibid.; and Leftwich, *States of Development* (Cambridge: Polity Press, 2000).

25. See Held, *Democracy and the Social Order,* part 3.

26. Bruce Ackerman, "Political liberalisms," *Journal of Philosophy,* 1994, 91, 7; Amartya Sen, *Inequality Reexamined* (Oxford: Clarendon Press, 1992); and Sen, *Development as Freedom* (Oxford: Oxford University Press, 1999).

27. Martha Nussbaum, "Kant and cosmopolitanism," in J. Bohman and M. Lutz-Bachmann, eds. *Perpetual Peace: Essays on Kant's Cosmopolitan Ideal* (Cambridge: MIT Press, 1997).

28. Cf. Juergensmeyer, this volume.

29. David Held and Mary Kaldor, "What hope for the future? Learning the lessons from the past," OpenDemocracy.net, 2001.

30. I. Khan, "Terrorists should be tried in court," *The Guardian,* October 12, 2001.

31. Z. Sardar, "My fatwa on the fanatics," *The Guardian,* September 22, 2001.

32. Quoted in Hugo Young, "It may not be PC to say," *The Guardian,* October 9, 2001.

33. Young, ibid.

34. B. Parekh, Interview, *The Guardian,* October 11, 2001.

35. Fred Halliday, "No man is an island," *The Observer,* September 16, 2001.

36. Karen Armstrong, "The war we should fight," *The Guardian,* October 13, 2001.

37. Sen, "Humanity and citizenship," in J. Cohen, ed., *For Love of Country* (Boston: Beacon Press, 1996), p. 118

38. Fred Halliday, *Islam and the Myth of Confrontation* (London: I. B. Tauris, 1996).

7. Governance Hotspots: Challenges We Must Confront in the Post-September 11 World, *by Saskia Sassen*

1. See Seyla Benhabib, "Unholy Wars. Reclaiming Democratic Virtues After September," in this volume.

2. See Robert O. Keohane, "The Globalization of Informal Violence, Theories of World Politics and the 'Liberalism of Fear,' " and David Held, "Violence, Law, and Justice in a Global Age," in this volume.

3. Some of these contradictions are described in Aristide R. Zolberg, "Guarding the Gates," in this volume.

4. There are multiple instances of this. Just to mention a personal note, after my editorial on which this chapter is based came out in *The Guardian* on September 12, *The Daily Telegraph* (September 19) referred to me and another author of an editorial in *The Guardian* as the equivalent of, among other not necessarily positive characterizations, "the enemy within."

5. There are two important qualifications, impossible to develop in this type of piece. I consider both crucial for good policy; but here I am making a different point. One is that there are moral arguments which could be read as demonstrating the utility of the more moral policy decision (see e.g., the work by Joseph Carens and by Thomas Pogge), and even some elements in the Jubilee campaign for debt cancellation. I see this as a different type of logic from what I try to present here. Secondly, there is a large literature that shows the advantages of immigration for highly developed economies e.g., Portes and Rumbaut *Immigrant America* (Berkeley: University of California Press, 2000). I distinguish this from the broader argument I present here about the utility of developing specialized multilateral and internationalist forms for governing cross-border migration flows and of handling the growing indebtedness of the global south.

6. I have developed some of this at greater length elsewhere: "Women's Burden: Countergeographies of Globalization and the Feminization of Survival," *Journal of International Affairs* 53, 2: pp. 503–524, (Spring, 2000); and "Beyond Sovereignty: De-Facto Transnationalism in Immigration Policy," *European Journal of Migration Law* 1, 1999, 1: vol. 1, nr. 1, pp. 177–198.

7. In this regard the 1997 financial crisis in Southeast Asia is illuminating. These were and remain highly dynamic economies. Yet they had to face high levels of indebtedness and economic failure among a broad range of enterprises and sectors. The financial crisis—both its architecture and its consequences—has brought with it the imposition of structural adjustment policies and a growth in unemployment and poverty due to widespread bankruptcies of small and medium-sized firms catering to both national and export markets. The $120 billion rescue package that allowed for the introduction of SAP provisions, which reduce the autonomy of these governments, went to compensate the losses of foreign institutional investors, rather than to solve the poverty and unemployment of a large number of the people. The management of the crisis through IMF policies has been seen by some as worsening the situation for the unemployed and poor. There are several additional elements that played a crucial role. For a brief examination, see Sassen pp. 77–83; and footnote 9 *The Global City,* new edition (Princeton: Princeton University Press, 2001).

8. By 1990 there were almost 200 such loans in place. During the 1980s also, the Reagan administration put enormous pressure on many countries in its sphere of influence to implement neoliberal policies which resembled the SAPs. For one of the best critical examinations of globalization and its negative impacts on the global north, see Richard C. Longworth, *Global Squeeze. The Coming Crisis for First-World Nations* (Chicago: Contemporary Books, 1998).

9. It is also the case that about 100 countries have had financial crises over the last 25 years, most associated with sharp policy changes. There is research showing a structural interaction effect between financial deregulation and subsequent financial crisis e.g., C.M. Reinhardt, with G. Kaminsky "The Twin Crises: The Causes of Banking and Balance of Payments Problems," *American Economic Review,* Vol. 89, No. 3, June 1999, pp. 473–500.

10. Even before the economic crisis of the 1990s, the debt of poor countries in the south grew from $507 billion in 1980 to $1.4 trillion by 1992. Debt-service payments alone had increased to

$1.6 trillion, more than the actual debt. Further, as has been widely recognized now, the south had already paid its debt several times over, and yet its debt grew by 250 percent. According to some estimates, from 1982 to 1998 indebted countries paid four times their original debts, and at the same time their debts stocks went up by four times. According to Susan George, the south has paid back the equivalent of six Marshall Plans to the north. See Asoka Bandarage, *Women, Population and Global Crisis* (London: Zed Books, 1997).

11. All of these countries have remained deeply indebted, with 41 of them formally declared as Highly Indebted Poor Countries in 1999.

12. Each country's crisis is a complex event. In the case of Argentina, the IMF has kept a rather low profile since default but has said that at the heart of the failure of its policies lies the fact that Argentina insisted on pegging its currency to the dollar for too long after control over inflation had been achieved. Many agree with this observation today, though it should be said that at the time, the enormous prosperity the peg brought to about 20 percent of households and to many economic sectors was celebrated by just about everyone supporting IMF policies. Few if any, however, agree with the IMF's prescription to cut costs and deflate the economy as it entered crisis mode. This prescription has generated extensive debate but overall is seen as a mistake on the part of the IMF and as going counter to past prescriptions. Finally, a crucial issue in the Argentine case is the enormous corruption of the Mennem government in the 1990s.

13. See Erik Toussaint, *Your Money or Your Life: The Tyranny of Global Finance* (London: Pluto Press, 1999).

14. Elsewhere ("Women's Burden") I have argued that there are systemic links between two sets of developments usually not seen as related: the growing presence of women from developing economies in a variety of global circuits, notably illegal trafficking for work and female migration, and the rise in unemployment and debt in those same economies. One way of articulating this in substantive terms is to posit that a) the shrinking opportunities for male employment in many of these countries, b) the shrinking opportunities for more traditional forms of profit-making in these same countries as they increasingly accept foreign firms in a widening range of economic sectors and are pressured to develop export industries, and c) the fall in revenues for the governments in many of these countries, partly linked to these conditions and to the burden of debt servicing, have all contributed to raise the importance of alternative ways of making a living, making a profit, and securing government revenue.

15. These funds include remittances from prostitutes' earnings and payments to organizers and facilitators in these countries.

16. Vulture funds illustrate the worst possible outcome for LDC's when they depend on private lenders without much protection from the inter-state system. Datz (2001) examines the role of these funds in sharpening the negative effects for indebted poor countries. These funds buy sovereign debt on the condition that they settle disputes in domestic U.S. courts, which allows them to take these sovereigns to court as if they were private parties (thereby rendering these cases highly visible). This has allowed vulture funds to claim often large payments from sovereigns who do not want to risk investor credibility, thereby further cutting into their budgets, including in principle, for social expenditures. See, Giselle Datz, "Vulture Funds and Latin American Government Debt" (Committee on International Relations, University of Chicago). On file with Author.

17. Although the data on migration flows are inadequate, there is a consensus among experts that at least half of all cross-border registered immigration happens among countries in the global south.

18. This has emerged as a crucial issue. See, e.g., Zolberg in this volume.

19. A big caveat here is the fact that demographic protections can be notoriously off the mark, though much less so in highly developed countries.

20. IIASA (International Institute for Applied Systems Analysis), *Special Report: Global Population* (Vienna: IIASA, 2001).

21. As is well known, several large European countries are now below reproduction levels, notably Italy and France.

22. Heinz Fassman and Rainer Munz, *European Migration in the Late 20th Century* (Frankfort and New York, Campus Books: 1996).

23. Portes and Rumbaut, op. cit.

24. See Steven Erlanger, "A Jumpy, Anti-Immigrant Europe Is Creeping Rightward," *New York Times*, January 30, 2002. The article describes rightward political shifts fueled by fear of immigrants and their putative association with crime in France, the Netherlands, Denmark, Germany, Spain, Norway, Belgium, Italy, and Austria. In many cases new legislation is hardening immigration laws, although as of this writing the outcome of a new German immigration law that liberalizes admissions is still not settled. In this volume, Ari Zolberg describes an increasingly repressive immigration regime in the United States.

25. There are two ways in which governments have secured benefits through these strategies. One of these is highly formalized and the other is simply a by-product of the migration process itself. Among the strongest examples of a formal labor-export program today is the Philippines.

26. Trafficking involves the forced recruitment and/or transportation of people within and across states for work or services through a variety of forms, all involving coercion.

27. See e.g., Janie Chuang, "Redirecting the Debate over Trafficking in Women: Definitions, Paradigms, and Contexts," *Harvard Human Rights Journal*, 10 (Winter 1998).

28. IOM (International Organization for Migration), *Trafficking in Migrants* (Quarterly Bulletin) (Geneva: IOM, 1998).

29. For a good critical analysis see S. Dayan, "Policy Initiatives in the U.S. against the Illegal Trafficking of Women for the Sex Industry" (Committee on International Relations, University of Chicago). On file with Author.

30. One process that captures this specific type of interdependence is the global migration of maids, nannies, and nurses. See Barbara Ehrenreich and Arlie Hochschild, eds., *Global Woman* (New York: Metropolitan Books, 2002).

31. CIA (Central Intelligence Agency), "International Trafficking in Women to the United States: A Contemporary Manifestation of Slavery and Organized Crime." Prepared by Amy O'Neill Richard. (Washington, D.C.: Center for the Study of Intelligence) www.cia.gov/csi/monograph/women/trafficking/pdf.

32. Global Survival Network, "Crime and Servitude: An Expose of the Traffic in Women for Prostitution from the Newly Independent States." www.globalsurvival.net/femaletrade.html (November, 1977). Global tourism is becoming a significant factor promoting trafficking of women for the sex industry. See, Nancy A. Wonders and Raymond Michalowski, "Bodies, Borders, and Sex Tourism in a Globalized World: A Tale of Two Cities—Amsterdam and Havana," *Social Problems* 48, 4, pp. 545–571, 2001.

33. There are various reports on the particular cross-border movements in trafficking. Malay brokers sell Malay women into prostitution in Australia. East European women from Albania and Kosovo have been trafficked by gangs into prostitution in London. European teens from Paris and other cities have been sold to Arab and African customers (see Shannon, Susan, "The Global Sex Trade: Humans as the Ultimate Commodity," *Crime and Justice International* [May, 1999], pp 5–25). In the U.S. the police broke up an international Asian ring that imported women from China, Thailand, Korea, Malaysia, and Vietnam (see Booth, William, "Thirteen charged in gang importing prostitutes," *The Washington Post*, August 21, 1999). The women

were charged between $30,000 and $40,000 in contracts to be paid through their work in the sex trade or needle trade. The women in the sex trade were shuttled around several states in the U.S. to bring "continuing variety to the clients."

34. For a description of these measures, see Sassen, "Women's Burden," and "Beyond Sovereignty."

8. The United States and the World Economy After September 11, by Barry Eichengreen

1. See Alan Greenspan, "Globalization." Speech delivered at the Institute of International Finance (October 24, 2001), www.iif.com.

2. Cited in *The Economist* (September 29, 2001), p. 14.

3. On the genesis of this foreign economic policy strategy, see DeLong, J. Bradford and Barry Eichengreen, "Between Meltdown and Moral Hazard: The International Monetary and Financial Policies of the Clinton Administration," in Jeffrey A. Frankel and Peter R. Orszag, (eds.), *American Economic Policy in the 1990s* (Cambridge: MIT Press), pp. 191–254.

4. See Barry Eichengreen, *Globalizing Capital: A History of the International Monetary System* (Princeton: Princeton University Press, 1996); and Kevin O'Rourke, and Jeffrey G. Williamson, *Globalization and History* (Cambridge: MIT Press, 1999).

5. Harold James, *The End of Globalization* (Cambridge: Harvard University Press, 2001).

6. Organization for Economic Cooperation and Development *OECD Economic Outlook* (Paris: OECD, 2002).

7. Maurice Obstfeld and Kenneth Rogoff, "The Six Major Puzzles in International Macroeconomics: Is There a Common Cause?" NBER Working Paper no. 7777 (July 2002).

8. IMF forecasts see the volume of trade recovering to just 2.1 percent in 2002.

9. The 60 percent rise in the prices of the stocks of security-related companies in the four weeks following September 11 confirms that the incentive for their development is there.

10. See David D. Hale, "Rethinking Safety and Security in Business and Government: Wartime Precedents for Insuring Terrorism Risk," Presentation to the Davos World Economic Forum, New York (February 2002).

11. United Nations, *World Investment Report 2001* (Geneva and New York: United Nations, 2001).

12. See Institute of International Finance (2002), "Capital Flows to Emerging Market Economies," www.iif.com (January 30, 2002). An additional reason for the projected fall in FDI between 2001 and 2002 is that the total was boosted in 2001 by a series of one-time transactions, notably foreign buyouts of Banacci in Mexico and De Beers in South Africa. Working in the other direction is the fact that declining demand worldwide will tend to stimulate the volume of merger- and acquisitions-related investment, as companies seek to rationalize excess capacity in various industries.

13. Cunningham, Dixon, and Hayes report evidence to this effect. Alistair Cunningham, Liz Dixon, and Simon Hayes, "Analyzing Yield Spreads on Emerging Market Bonds," *Financial Stability Review* (December 2001), pp. 175–186.

14. See International Monetary Fund, "IMF Managing Director Sees Impressive Commitment by Turkey to Economic Reforms: Executive Board Approves U.S. $16 Billion Standby Credit," Press Release 02/7 (Washington, D.C.: IMF, February 4, 2002).

15. Anne Krueger, "International Financial Architecture for 2002: A New Approach to Sovereign Debt Restructuring," address by Anne Krueger, first deputy managing director, International Monetary Fund, given at the National Economists' Club Annual Members' Dinner, American Enterprise Institute, Washington, D.C. (November 26, 2001), www.imf.org/external/np/speeches/2001/112601.htm.

16. Thomas C. Dawson, "A Contribution to an Online Discussion on Sovereign Debt Restructuring," www.imf.org/externalnp.vc/2002/020702.htm (February 7, 2002), p. 3.

17. The Quota Formula Review Group chaired by Professor Richard Cooper of Harvard University was convened in 1999 to provide the executive board with an independent review of quota formulas. See International Monetary Fund, "Alternative Quota Formulas: Considerations," www.imf.org (September 27, 2001).

18. An application of these ideas to the Middle East is Jeffrey Sachs, "Long-Term Perspectives on Economic Development in the Middle East," Eitan Berlas Lecture, Tel Aviv University (January 2001).

19. These too are themes of the recent research of Jeffrey Sachs, "Tropical Underdevelopment," NBER Working Paper no. 8119 (February 2001).

20. Thus, much of Afghanistan's (official) trade has traditionally had to transit through the port of Karachi.

21. There is also a school of thought that countries burdened by these geographic and climatic characteristics have weaker political institutions. See Daron Acemoglu, Simon Johnson, and James Robinson, "The Colonial Origins of Comparative Development: An Empirical Investigation," NBER Working Paper no. 7771 (June 2000). Their European colonialists, rather than settling in large numbers and creating a demand for representative political institutions, built "extractive colonies" characterized by a highly uneven distribution of income and wealth and political institutions that suppressed rather than amplified the voice of the masses. The unstable policies, unreliable rule of law, and weak contract enforcement that stand in the way of economic development reflect factors rooted deeply in countries' history and geography and explain the inability of globalization to dissolve the world's enduring inequalities.

22. This may seem a strange recommendation for a country like Afghanistan, whose economy is based almost entirely on agriculture and animal husbandry. In 1978, the last year of peace, it was a significant exporter of agricultural goods and exported only a few manufactures—textiles, medicines, and cement, for example. This, of course, is the same thing most observers would have said about South Korea, Taiwan, or Israel, for that matter, two generations ago. There will always be a market for Afghanistan's melons and pomegranates; the question is whether, given climatic conditions and water availability, agriculture provides a durable basis for economic development.

23. Here I draw on my own previous research on the Marshall Plan, notably the introduction to Barry Eichengreen, ed., Europe's Postwar Recovery (Cambridge: Cambridge University Press, 1995).

24. Norway, Sweden, and the UK had majority governments in 1948, the year that Marshall aid began to flow, while Austria, Belgium, France, and Italy all had oversized majorities. Only the Netherlands and Germany had fragile coalitions, and only Denmark had a single-party minority government.

25. Craig Burnside and David Dollar, "Aid, Policies and Growth," American Economic Review 90, 2000, pp. 847–868.

26. Andrew MacIntyre (1998), "Political Institutions and the Economic Crisis in Thailand and Indonesia," ASEAN Economic Bulletin 15, pp. 272–280.

27. See also Stephan Haggard and Andrew MacIntyre, "The Political Economy of the Asian Financial Crisis: Korea and Thailand Compared," in Gregory Noble and John Ravenhill, eds., *The Asian Financial Crisis and the Architecture of Global Finance* (Cambridge: Cambridge University Press, 2000), pp. 56–79.

28. Kristof reports that its shoes sell for 55 cents a pair in Afghanistan but $1.90 a pair in neighboring Pakistan because of the latter's high import duties. The remainder of this paragraph draws further on this excellent article. See Nicholas D. Kristof, "To Put Terror Out of Business, Give Afghans a Living," *International Herald Tribune*, December 16, 2001, p. 6.

29. Pakistani exporters, in turn, will be able to fill the demand for myriad products that are in short supply in neighboring Afghanistan.

30. India would be another desirable member.

31. See for example World Bank, *Global Economic Prospects* (Washington, D.C.: World Bank, 2000).

32. David D. Hale, "Trade Can Fight Terrorism," *The Financial Times*, October 17, 2001, p. 14.

33. Evidence as opposed to rhetoric speaks clearly. Thus, aggregate annual per-capita growth in countries that opened to the world accelerated steadily from 1 percent in the 1960s to 5 percent in the 1990s, while growth in nonglobalizers remained stagnant at only 1 percent. See Neil L. McCullock, Alan Winters and Xavier Cirera, "Trade Liberalization and Poverty: A Handbook," London: Centre for Economic Policy Research; and David Dollar and Aart Kraay, "Spreading the Wealth," *Foreign Affairs*, January/February, 2002.

9. States, Terrorists, and the Clash of Civilizations, *by Jack A. Goldstone*

1. I owe special thanks to Mark Woodward, whose insights stimulated many of the ideas in this paper. However, he is not responsible for any of the views expressed here.

2. Samuel Huntington, *The Clash of Civilizations and the Remaking of World Order* (New York: Simon and Schuster, 1996).

3. Mark Katz, *Revolutions and Revolutionary Waves* (New York: St. Martin's Press, 1997).

4. This section is based largely on Anwar al-Huq Ahady, "The Afghanistan Revolutionary Wars," in Jack A. Goldstone, ed. *Revolutions, Theoretical, Comparative, and Historical Studies*, 3rd edition (Fort Worth, TX: Harcourt College Publishers, 2003).

5. This section is based largely on Glenn E. Robinson, *Building a Palestinian State: The Incomplete Revolution* (Bloomington: Indiana University Press, 1997).

6. It deserves to be noted that despite the horrifying success of the 9/11 attacks, the outcome could have been much more severe. It is astounding that the World Trade Center collapse killed under 3,000 people, out of more than 10 times that many who were in the immediate area at the time of the attack. It is a stroke of luck that the attack on the Pentagon hit the one area of the building that had been recently reinforced by reconstruction to withstand attack. It is a blessing that the last plane, apparently also bound for Washington, D.C., was held on the ground for an unscheduled delay long enough for information to reach the passengers about the ongoing attacks, allowing them to act to prevent that plane from reaching its intended target. There may have been yet one more team of hijackers that was also on a plane that was held on the ground. In short, the potential for catastrophe was even greater than what actually transpired.

7. Robinson, op. cit., p. 143.

8. Jack A. Goldstone, *Revolutions: Theoretical, Comparative, and Historical Studies*, 3rd edition (Fort Worth: Harcourt College Publishers, 2003).

10. Beyond Militarism, Arms Races, and Arms Control, *by Mary Kaldor*

1. This essay was originally prepared for the Nobel Peace Prize Centennial Symposium, December 6–8, 2001.

2. Anthony Giddens, *The Consequences of Modernity* (Cambridge: Polity Press, 1990).

3. Charles Tilly, *Coercion, Capital and European States, AD 990–1992* (Cambridge: Blackwell, 1992).

4. See David Held, et al. *Global Transformations* (Cambridge: Polity Press, 1999).

5. Mary Kaldor, *New and Old Wars: Organised Violence in a Global Era* (Cambridge: Polity Press, 1999).

6. Stockholm International Peace Research Institute, *SIPRI Yearbook 2001: Armaments. Disarmament and International Security* (Oxford: Oxford University Press, 2001).

7. L. Freedman, "The Revolution in Strategic Affairs" *Adelphi Paper 318* (London: International Institute of Strategic Affairs, 1998).

8. Freedman, ibid., p. 70.

9. James Der Derian, M. Shapiro, eds., *International/Intertextual Relations: Postmodern Readings of World Politics* (Lexington, MA: Lexington Books, 1989). See also Der Derian's chapter in this volume.

10. H. Anheier, M. Glasius, M. Kaldor, eds., *Global Civil Society 2001* (Oxford: Oxford University Press, 2001).

11. Brahimi, *Report of the Panel on United Nations Peace Operations*, UN Doc.A/55/305-S/2000/809, 21 August (New York: United Nations, 2000).

12. Robert Cooper, *The Postmodern State and the World Order,* (London: Demos/Foreign Policy Centre, 2001).

13. Ian Clark, *Globalization and International Relations Theory* (Oxford: Oxford University Press, 1999).

14. Tony Blair, "Doctrine of the International Community," http://www.primeminister.gov.uk, April 23, 1999.

11. 9/11: Before, After, and In Between, *by James Der Derian*

1. This is not to single out the positivists: A few years later, on the very day of the *first* World Trade Center bombing in 1993, I was participating in a conference on sovereignty with several budding constructivists—and no one thought it appropriate to bring up this successful breaching of U.S. sovereign territory. See James Der Derian, "A Reinterpretation of Realism: Genealogy, Semiology, Dromology," *International Theory: Critical Investigations* (London: Macmillan, 1995), pp. 363–396.

2. Walter Benjamin, *A Lyric Poet in the Era of High Capitalism* (London: Verso, 1997).

3. For an earlier discussion of the ideological, epistemological, and ontological obstacles facing any inquiry into terrorism, see James Der Derian, "The Terrorist Discourse: Signs, States, and Systems of Global Political Violence," *Antidiplomacy: Spies, Terror, Speed, and War* (Cambridge, MA and Oxford, UK: Blackwell, 1992), pp. 92–126.

4. George W. Bush, The President's State of the Union Address, The United States Capitol, Washington, D.C. (January 29, 2002). http://www.whitehouse.gove/news/releases/2002/01/20020129-11.html.

5. Michael Ignatieff, "It's War—But It Doesn't Have to Be Dirty," *The Guardian,* October 1, 2001.

6. George Will, "On the Health of the State," *Newsweek,* October 1, 2001, p. 70.

7. Edward Rothstein, "Attacks on U.S. Challenge the Perspectives of Postmodern True Believers," September 22, 2001, p. A17.

8. Mark Edington, *The New York Times,* March 2, 1993.

9. *Newsweek,* March 8, 1993, p. 22.

10. *Sunday Times,* February 28, 1993, p. 10.

11. These quotes are drawn from earlier work calling for new approaches to IR after the first WTC bombing. See "A Reinterpretation of Realism: Genealogy, Semiology, Dromology," *International Theory: Critical Investigations* (London: Macmillan, 1995), pp. 363–396.

12. See James Der Derian, *Virtuous War: Mapping the Military-Industrial-Media-Entertainment Network* (Boulder, CO and Oxford, UK: Westview/Perseus, 2001).

13. See www.fbi.gov/mostwant/terrorists/fugitives.htm.

14. See abcnews.com, "Casualties of 'Enduring Freedom:' U.S. Personnel Killed in the Line of Duty," abcnews.go.com/sections/us/DailyNews/STRIKE_Casualties.html.

15. On the increased risks facing war reporters, see Scott Baldauf, "Risks Mount for Reporters Covering War on Terrorism," *The Christian Science Monitor,* January 30, 2002. www.csmonitor.com/2002/0130/p07s02-wosc.html.

16. By comparison, 35 of 148 U.S. troops killed in action in the Gulf War were hit by U.S. fire, with 11 killed by accidental U.S. air strikes; and of 467 U.S. military personnel wounded, 72 were hit by friendly fire.

17. See Marc W. Herold, "A Dossier on Civilian Victims of United States' Aerial Bombing of Afghanistan: A Comprehensive Accounting," December 2001. www.media-alliance.org/mediafile/20-5/dossier/herold12-6.html. On the difficulty of assessing civilian casualties in Afghanistan, see Karen DeYoung, "More Bombing Casualties Alleged," *The Washington Post,* January 4, 2002, p. A18, and "It's difficult to count dead in Afghan war: Various reasons spur confusion regarding toll," *The Arizona Republic,* January 25, 2002. http://www.arizonarepublic.com/news/articles/0125attacks-civilian 25.html.

18. Michael Herr, *Dispatches* (New York: Avon Books, 1991), p. 20.

19. Of the primetime network anchors, Peter Jennings of ABC did better than the rest in keeping up with the speed of the crisis.

20. Social scientists and even historians tend to tidy up events, and already most narrative accounts of 9/11 fail to mention the range of stories that were reported on radio and television that day, without substantiation, of multiple bombs going off on the Mall, at the State Department, and elsewhere in New York and Washington; of a "fifth plane" heading for the White House; and grossly inflated casualty figures. These reports surely contributed to the willingness to find order amidst the chaos, quickly and uncritically.

21. Jean Baudrillard, *Simulacra and Simulation,* trans. Sheila Glaser (Ann Arbor, MI: University of Michigan Press, 1994), p. 159.

22. *ABC Sunday News,* September 30, 2001.

23. Donald Rumsfeld, Department of Defense News Briefing, September 25, 2001. For the transcript of the Rumsfeld press conference, see www.defenselink.mil/news/Sep2001/t09252001_t0925sd.html.

24. George W. Bush, speech delivered at the Central Intelligence Agency, September 26, 2001. See www.washingtonpost.com/wp-srv/nation/specials/attacked/transcripts/bushtext_092601.html.

25. Rothstein, op cit.

26. George W. Bush, Presidential Address to the Nation, October 7, 2001. See www.white-house.gov/news/releases/2001/10/20011007-8.html.

27. CNN.com, "Bin Laden's sole post-September 11 TV interview aired: Fugitive Al Qaeda Leader Vows Fight to the Death," January 31, 2002. See www.cnn.com/2002/US/01/31/gen.binladen.interview/index.html.

28. United States House of Representatives, "House Resolution 3162: Uniting and Strengthening America by Providing Appropriate Tools Required to Intercept and Obstruct Terrorism Act," October 24, 2001.

29. In a videotape interview with the Arabic cable network, Al Jazeera (which they never aired but was partially seen January 31 on *CNN*), bin Laden displayed his affinity for information technology while scoffing at the White House "request" that American television networks not broadcast his statements:

> They made hilarious claims. They said that Osama's messages have codes in them to the terrorists. It's as if we were living in the time of mail by carrier pigeon, when there are no phones, no travelers, no Internet, no regular mail, no express mail and no electronic mail.

See Howard Kurtz, "U.S. Doomed, Bin Laden Says on Tape," *The Washington Post*, February 1, 2002, p. A13.

30. See *The Washington Post*, September 26, 2001.

31. Disclaimer: I provided the information to them. See Johnnie L. Roberts, "Big Media and the Big Story: Are Conglomerates up to the Job? Or Are They Doing Too Much of the Government's Bidding?" *Newsweek*, October 13, 2001. www.msnbc.com/news/642434.asp.

32. See "Virtuous War Goes to Hollywood," in Der Derian, *Virtuous War*, op. cit., pp. 153–178.

33. Fans of Kleiser might wonder why his classic work, "Honey I Blew Up the Kid" (about an amateur physicist who turns his son into a giant) went unmentioned in the press releases. Was it proof that the U.S. government might be embarrassed to have hooked up with B-list directors? Or was it part of an infowar campaign to keep the lid on "Operation Shrink bin Laden Back to Size"? When holy war comes to Hollywood, and terrorist dreams come up against true lies, the truth is even further out there. See Steve Gorman, "U.S. filmmakers mull terror scenarios for Army," *Variety*, October 9, 2001.

34. Yogi actually said "ain't what it used to be"; it was the French poet Paul Valery who said "isn't," but Yogi wasn't very big on footnotes.

35. See Der Derian, *Virtuous War*, pp. 123–151.

36. United States Department of Defense, News Release, "U.S. Releases Videotape of Osama bin Laden," December 13, 2001.

37. Paul Virilio, *The Information Bomb*, trans. Chris Turner (London and New York: Verso, 2000), p. 132.

38. C. Wright Mills, *The Power Elite* (New York: Oxford University Press, 1957), pp. 314–5.

39. *Pace*, Hitchens, Chomsky, and their polarized supporters.

12. Is Cyber Terror Next?, *by Dorothy E. Denning*

1. Jefferson Graham, "Hackers Strike Middle Eastern Sites," *USA Today*, September 26, 2001.

2. Information was obtained from YIHAT's website at kill.net, which has subsequently been taken down. See also kimble.org and Brian McWilliams, "Anti-Terror Hackers Seek Govt Blessing," *Newsbytes*, October 17, 2001.

3. This defacement is mirrored at defaced.alldas.de/mirror/2001/10/20/www.dtepi.mil/.

4. defaced.alldas.de/.

5. Gary C. Gambill, "Who's Winning the Arab-Israeli Cyber War?" *Middle East Intelligence Bulletin,* vol. 2, no. 11 (November 2000).

6. Israeli–Palestinian Cyber Conflict, iDefense Intelligence Services Report, January 3, 2000.

7. "Al-Qaida Cyber Capability," Office of Critical Infrastructure Protection and Emergency Preparedness, Government of Canada, www.epc-pcc.gc.ca/emergencies/other/TA01-001_E.html.

8. For the latest figures, see www.cert.org.

9. The Cooperative Association for Internet Data Analysis (CAIDA) has an analysis of the worm on their website at www.caida.org/analysis/security/code-red/. The cost estimate is from Computer Economics: www.computereconomics.com.

10. Reuters, March 11, 2000.

11. Bill Nelson, Rodney Choi, Michael Iacobucci, Mark Mitchell, and Greg Gagnon, "Cyberterror: Prospects and Implications," Center for the Study of Terrorism and Irregular Warfare, Monterey, CA, August 1999.

12. David Tucker, "The Future of Armed Resistance: Cyberterror? Mass Destruction?" Conference Report and Proceedings, Center for the Study of Terrorism and Irregular Warfare, Monterey, CA, October 2000.

13. "Al-Qaida Cyber Capability," Office of Critical Infrastructure Protection and Emergency Preparedness, Government of Canada, www.epc-pcc.gc.ca/emergencies/other/TA01-001_E .html.

14. Ibid.

15. Brian McWilliams, "Suspect Claims Al Qaeda Hacked Microsoft," *Newsbytes,* December 17, 2001.

13. Black September, Infantile Nihilism, and National Security, *by Bruce Cumings*

1. Pp. 8–9 of the 1980 Penguin Books edition.

2. An Afghan-American woman named Laili Helms knew Mullah Omar, and called him an "Afghan hillbilly." See Alessandra Stanley, "The Liaison: She Spoke for the Taliban And Now Pays a Price," *The New York Times,* November 27, 2001, p. B6.

3. See Cumings, *War and Television* (New York: Verso, 1992).

4. I was struck in reading a forthcoming book by Salim Yaqub, *Containing Arab Nationalism* (Chapel Hill: University of North Carolina Press, 2002), at his sweeping depiction of the Middle East in the 1950s, where one secular and developmental regime after another dotted the landscape—some led by nationalists like Gemal Abdel Nasser, others by forward-looking monarchies (see his introduction).

5. Don DeLillo, "In the Ruins of the Future: Reflections on Terror and Loss in the Shadow of September," *Harper's Magazine,* December, 2001, p. 39.

6. Gordon Prange, *At Dawn We Slept: The Untold Story of Pearl Harbor* (New York: Penguin Books, 1981), p. 539.

7. Akira Iriye, *Power and Culture* (Cambridge, MA: Harvard University Press, 1981), pp. 1, 28–29.

8. Bill Moyers, "Which America Will We Be Now?" *The Nation,* November 19, 2001, pp. 11–14.

9. When Clinton left office defense spending was about $265 billion. In early 2002 President Bush called for an increase to nearly $379 billion. ("President to Seek $48 Billion More for the Military," *New York Times*, January 24, 2002, p. A1.)

10. Thomas Shanker, "Conduct of War Is Redefined by Success of Special Forces," *New York Times*, January 21, 2002, p. A1.

11. Eric Schmitt and James Dao, "U.S. Is Building Up Its Military Bases in Afghan Region," *New York Times*, January 9, 2002, p. A1.

12. For example, Reuters, "War on Terrorism Spreads Around the Globe," *New York Times* website, January 24, 2002.

13. Cumings, *The Origins of the Korean War*, vol. 2 (Princeton: Princeton University Press, 1990), pp. 761–65.

14. *New York Times*, October 16, 2001, Op-Ed page.

15. This was evident throughout the 1990s in the quadrennial public-opinion surveys published by the Chicago Council on Foreign Relations. See for example John E. Reilly, ed., *American Public Opinion and U.S. Foreign Policy* (Chicago: Chicago Council on Foreign Relations, 1995); the American public had vastly different views from the foreign-policy elite after the Cold War ended and the USSR collapsed: on defense spending, NATO's continued viability, and the use of U.S. troops to defend allies like South Korea, Israel, and Saudi Arabia, (pp. 34–5).

16. No one put this tendency more eloquently than Louis Hartz, in the final chapter of his classic book, *The Liberal Tradition in America* (New York: Harcourt, Brace, 1955).

17. Mary Kaldor, *The Imaginary War* (Cambridge, MA: Blackwell, 1990), pp. 86–93.

18. For example Ahmed Rashid, *Taliban: Militant Islam, Oil, and Fundamentalism in Central Asia* (New Haven: Yale University Press, 2000). Rashid is a well-informed journalist who speaks several of the local languages, and whose reporting from Afghanistan was consistently excellent.

19. Various press accounts on January 24, 2002 said the FBI had launched a nationwide recruitment campaign to hire hundreds of new agents who can speak Arabic and other relevant languages.

20. According to Robert Baer, once the CIA station chief in Dushanbe, Tajikistan, who speaks Arabic and even Dari (a major language in the region), quoted in Thomas Powers, "The Trouble with the CIA," *New York Review of Books*, January 17, 2002, p. 31.

21. Ibid., pp. 30–31.

14. On War and Peace-building: Unfinished Legacy of the 1990s, *by Susan L. Woodward*

1. This latter was the optimism of Greek foreign minister George Pappandreou, in conversation with the U.S. talk show host Charlie Rose, in mid-October 2001.

2. A recent thesis is proposed by John Ikenberry, *After Victory: Institutions, Strategic Restraint, and the Rebuilding of Order after Major Wars* (Princeton: Princeton University Press, 2001).

3. A particularly striking argument on the changing international political economy of oil and its greater significance is in Edward L. Morse and James Richard, "The Battle for Energy Dominance," *Foreign Affairs*, vol. 81, no. 2 (March/April 2002), pp. 1–17.

4. For example, what was being called an emerging Bush Doctrine by the time of the first State of the Union address after September 11, on January 22, 2002, and the label by President George W. Bush of an "axis of evil" from North Korea through Iran to Iraq, was variously interpreted. Was its purpose, for example, to provide a rallying slogan and target (those developing nuclear and

biological weapons) for "Phase 2" of the antiterrorist campaign after Afghanistan, as it was widely viewed, or was it aimed at an older agenda, exploiting September 11 to generate support for Bush's pre-September goal of a national missile defense shield?

5. As Under Secretary-General in support of the Secretary-General in preventive diplomacy and conflict prevention, Brahimi also took on many short-term, trouble-shooting tasks.

6. Analyses of the humanitarian missions can be found in Antonio Donini, Eric Dudley, and Ron Ockwell, *Afghanistan: Coordination in a Fragmented State,* UN/DHA (Department of Humanitarian Affairs), December 1996, and more critically, Paula R. Newberg, "Politics at the Heart: The Architecture of Humanitarian Assistance to Afghanistan," *Working Papers: International Migration Policy Program,* Global Policy Program, Carnegie Endowment for International Peace, Number 2 (July 1999).

7. Letter of the Secretary-General to the President of the General Assembly and the President of the Security Council, dated August 21, 2000 (announcing the receipt of the report on August 17 of the panel convened on March 7, 2000), A/55/305-S/2000/809, United Nations.

8. *Strategic Framework for Afghanistan: Towards a Principled Approach to Peace and Reconstruction* (June 23, 1998). Two cases were selected, Afghanistan and Sierra Leone, but the resumption of war in Sierra Leone interrupted its role as a second test case. As for Afghanistan, Paula Newberg suggested in 1999 that "Afghanistan has been an unwitting laboratory for experimentation in international assistance. By virtue of its persistent conflicts, inconvenient location, and the unfortunate indifference of the post-cold-war world community to its current plight, it has become a test case for the viability of integrated assistance planning in complex political emergencies," "Politics at the Heart," op. cit., page 4.

9. A term coined in the mid-1980s, it became a nearly universal term for all cases in the post-Cold War period that provoked some humanitarian agencies to respond.

10. On the recommendation, see Part IV, Section B, paragraphs 198–217, of the *Report of the Panel on United Nations Peace Operations* (United Nations: A/55/305-S/2000/809). Details of its setup also reveal the influence of lessons drawn by departments within the Secretariat from the East Timor mission in 1999.

11. On the importance of "rapid and effective deployment," see Part III, especially Section A, paragraphs 86–91, of the *Report of the Panel on United Nations Peace Operations.*

12. Executive Summary for paragraphs 48–64 of the *Report of the Panel on United Nations Peace Operations.*

13. Barbara Walter, "The Critical Barrier to Civil War Settlement," *International Organization,* vol. 51, no. 3 (Summer 1997), pp. 335–64, and some suggested refinements of the argument by Stephen John Stedman in "Introduction," especially pp. 6–10, and Joanna Spear, "Disarmament and Demobilization," in Stephen John Stedman, Donald Rothchild, and Elizabeth Cousens, eds., *Ending Civil Wars: The Implementation of Peace Agreements* (Boulder: Lynne Rienner, 2002). See also Michael Doyle and Nicholas Sambanis, "International Peacebuilding: A Theoretical and Quantitative Analysis," *American Political Science Review,* vol. 94, no. 4 (December 2000), pp. 779–801.

14. The British commander, moreover, was a veteran of peacekeeping operations in Bosnia and Herzegovina.

15. *Agreement on Provisional Arrangements in Afghanistan Pending the Re-Establishment of Permanent Government Institutions,* signed at Bonn, Germany, December 5, 2001 (www.usip.org/library/pa/afghanistan/pa_afghan_12052001.html). The importance of this provision cannot be overemphasized, although its implementation will depend on much, including the resources that outsiders provide. The lessons of successful peace-building in the 1990s make this crystal clear, from the success in Mozambique to the failure, thus far, in Bosnia and Herzegovina.

16. Discontent was being voiced openly by early February 2002 by Europeans who felt they were no longer being consulted, particularly those such as EU Commissioner for External Affairs Chris Patten, regarding the implications of the "axis of evil" speech.

17. For example, Michael R. Gordon, " 'New' U.S. War: Commandos, Airstrikes and Allies on the Ground," *New York Times*, December 29, 2001, pp. A1, B4–B5.

18. Local troops were American-trained and equipped, of course, as were Croatian soldiers in Croatia and in Bosnia and KLA (Kosovo Liberation Army) soldiers in Kosovo; in the KLA case, assistance also came from British special forces, just as in the case of Northern Alliance troops in Afghanistan.

19. In their primary role as advisors, moreover, it is difficult to see how Thom Shanker can argue that "American Special Operations forces in Afghanistan . . . are reshaping war-fighting doctrine," given their role since the Vietnam War and before, however surprising may be their success (as he argues), or similarly, in their indispensable role in guiding bombers to their targets (tactical, or forward, air control personnel [TACP]), which make special forces crucial to any air campaign, whether employed in support of peacekeeping, as were European troops in UNPROFOR, or war as in Kosovo; see Thom Shanker, "Conduct of War Is Redefined By Success of Special Forces," *New York Times*, January 21, 2002, p. A1.

20. While these developments might argue in support of those predicting a "revolution in military affairs [RMA]" as a result of technology, the evidence suggests that substantial quantitative improvements have not yet made a revolution. On the argument for this role of the new technology in Afghanistan, see Eric Schmitt and James Dao, "Use of Pinpoint Air Power Comes of Age in New War," *New York Times*, December 24, 2001, pp. A1 and B3, and James Dao, "The New Air War: Fewer Pilots, More Hits and Scarcer Targets," *New York Times*, November 29, 2001, pp. B1 and B4. On the RMA, see Andrew Krepinevich, "Transforming the American Military," in H. W. Brands, ed., *The Use of Force after the Cold War* (College Station, TX: Texas A&M University Press, 2000), pp. 201–216, and "Cavalry to Computer: The Pattern of Military Revolutions," *The National Interest*, vol. 37 (Fall 1994). Lawrence Freedman also argues that the U.S. war strategy in Afghanistan has not yet amounted to an RMA, in "The Third World War?" *Survival*, vol. 43, no. 4 (Winter 2001), pp. 61–87.

21. Michael R. Gordon, "A Vigorous Debate on U.S. War Tactics," *New York Times*, November 4, 2001, p. A1.

22. "Bases and exercises," according to Deputy Secretary of Defense Paul D. Wolfowitz, will "send a message to everybody . . . that we have a capacity to come back in and will." Eric Schmitt and James Dao, "U.S. Is Building Up Its Military Bases In Afghan Region," *New York Times*, January 9, 2002, pp. A1 and A10. The bases in the Balkan theater include Taszar, Hungary; Slavonski Brod, Croatia; Livno range and Tuzla base in Bosnia and Herzegovina; Camp Bondsteel in Kosovo; and sites in Albania and Macedonia. In the Afghan theater, they include Manas airport in Kyrgyzstan; Khanabad air base in Uzbekistan; Jacobabad, Dalbandin, and Pasni air bases in Pakistan; and in Afghanistan itself, Forward Base Rhino, an airstrip southeast of Kandahar, Bagram air base north of Kabul, and the airport at Mazar-I-Sharif.

23. See, for example, Judy Dempsey, "Europeans Chafe at 'Picking up Pieces' After U.S.," *The Financial Times*, February 21, 2002, p. 2.

24. The debate is reproduced in Michael R. Gordon and Serge Schmemann, "British Are Set to Lead Force That Will Keep Peace in Kabul," *New York Times*, December 11, 2001, p. B1. One "American official who is sympathetic to the general's position" is quoted as saying, "We need unity of command. It has to be General Franks who is in charge. To have two separate commands in Afghanistan would not be acceptable. We want to make sure that we have freedom of action, anywhere and everywhere," whereas "some Defense Department officials, with a deep

aversion to peacekeeping" did not want the U.S. to take on that responsibility—"we don't want to own this thing."

25. Paragraphs 39, 40, and 47(b) of Section II, part D (Doctrine, Strategy and Decision-Making for Peace Operations: Implications for Peace-Building Strategy), and paragraphs 118–126 of Section III: D (United Nations capacities to deploy operations rapidly and effectively: Civilian Police), of the *Report of the Panel on United Nations Peace Operations.*

26. Joseph Kahn, "U.S. Rejects Bid to Double Foreign Aid to Poor Lands," *New York Times,* January 29, 2002, p. A11. Some softening on this issue did occur in March 2002, but only in response to pressure by the International Conference on Financing for Development held on March 18–22 in Monterrey, Mexico.

27. *The World Bank's Experience with Post-Conflict Reconstruction* (Washington, D.C.: World Bank Operations Evaluation Department, 1998), p. 8.

28. Ibid., p. ix.

29. New offices include the Emergency Response Division of UNDP, the Office of Transition Initiatives (OTI) within the USAID, the addition of the word "conflict" to the humanitarian affairs department (CHAD) of the UK's DFID, and the initiative on development and security of the DAC. Canada established a Peace-building Fund, and similar special budgetary lines for policy coordination under peace-building circumstances were introduced by Denmark, the Netherlands, and Norway, but by 2000, only Germany had changed its budgetary lines to end the inherited distinction between relief and development and resulting bureaucratic stovepipes that many argue hamper the adjustment of economic assistance to the particular needs of peacebuilding.

30. The article that gave prominence to the now widely accepted criticism, Alvaro de Soto and Graciana del Castillo, "Obstacles to Peace-building," *Foreign Policy* 94 (Spring 1994), pp. 69–93, identifies the difference in mandate and approach between those normally assuming the responsibility for peace-building, such as the United Nations or regional security organizations, and those normally given the task of economic reconstruction, above all the international financial institutions and regional development banks.

31. *The World Bank's Experience* (1998), p. 47, and Jonathan Stevenson, *Preventing Conflict; The Role of the Bretton Woods Institutions,* Adelphi Paper 336 (London: The International Institute for Strategic Studies, 2000), p. 61.

32. These conclusions were drawn by the OED study, *The World Bank's Experience* (1998).

33. The initial paper setting out parameters by the World Bank, *Afghanistan: World Bank Approach Paper,* is available on its website (www.worldbank.org).

34. Annex II, para. 6, *Agreement on Provisional Arrangements in Afghanistan.*

35. A useful source for such activities is the website of Human Rights Watch (www.hrw.org).

36. UN officials in Somalia as well as experts on both Somalia and Afghanistan see even greater parallels, and need to learn lessons, from a comparison with Somalia. See Mark Turner, "Somalia provides lesson in non-interference," *The Financial Times,* November 19, 2001, p. 3.

37. The Commission has published a wealth of reports, discussion papers, and books, as well as a summary of the state of knowledge about prevention in their final report. A list of these publications can be found on the Carnegie website: www.carnegie.org.

38. For one result of these millions, granted by Vice President Gore's office to Ted Robert Gurr and his team at the University of Maryland, see the results of the State Failure Task Force Project at www.bsos.umd.edu/cidcm/stfail/.

39. Richard K. Betts suggests caution on drawing the conclusion of an "intelligence failure" and need, therefore, for drastic reform, in "Fixing Intelligence," *Foreign Affairs,* vol. 81, no. 1 (January/February 2002), pp. 43–59.

40. For an explanation based on U.S. strategic doctrine and military training, see Freedman, "The Third World War?" op. cit., especially pp. 65–67.

41. In a prescient but ignored warning on September 27, 2001, Ashraf Ghani (an Afghan-born, U.S.–trained anthropologist employed at Johns Hopkins University and the World Bank) recommended a very different course of action for the war by which the political process of creating an alternative government in Afghanistan would precede the military stage; see "The Folly of Quick Action in Afghanistan," *The Financial Times,* September 27, 2001.

42. "The immediate operational requirements of the battle against Al Qa'eda and the Taliban have thus worked against the goal of consolidating the interim administration's authority," writes Barnett Rubin; "The Afghan administration will not be able to establish that authority unless financial and military aid to warlords ceases in favor of an effort to build national security forces." See "Putting an End to Warlord Government," *New York Times,* January 15, 2002.

43. On the concept of spoilers, see Stephen John Stedman, "Spoiler Problems in Peace Processes," *International Security,* vol. 22, no. 2 (Fall 1997), pp. 5–53.

44. Elizabeth Becker, "U.S. Questions Its Share of Reconstruction Costs," *New York Times,* December 18, 2001, p. B5.

45. The flood of analyses and conferences, workshops, and meetings among donors and experts on the lessons to be learned for the current reconstruction and peace-building programs in Afghanistan, available as early as October 2001 and continuing into the first quarter of 2002, demonstrated how rich is the stock of current knowledge. See in particular the study published in June 2001, four months *before* the war, by academic experts Barnett R. Rubin, Ashraf Ghani, William Maley, Ahmed Rashid, and Olivier Roy, *Afghanistan: Reconstruction and Peace-building in a Regional Framework* (KOFF Peacebuilding Reports, No. 1, 2001, Center for Peacebuilding of the Swiss Peace Foundation), and the study done for the Norwegian Ministry of Foreign Affairs by Astri Suhrke, Arne Strand, and Kristian Berg Harpviken, *Peacebuilding Strategies for Afghanistan: Part I: Lessons from Past Experiences in Afghanistan* (Bergen: Chr. Michelsen Institute, January 7, 2002).

46. This hope was a theme of nearly all of the large number of conferences, workshops, donors' meetings, and informal conversations mentioned above (note 45).

47. The Taliban stopped paying salaries to civil servants in July 2001, and then looted the central bank before Kabul fell to the Northern Alliance. Currency held in a Moscow warehouse after the Taliban seized Kabul in 1996 was returned to the government in January 2002 to pay the first salaries in six months. The UN Trust Fund was expected to take over future installments but had only mobilized $10 million of the $20 million it had hoped to raise. To pay all back salaries, the Afghan government estimated it would need $200 to 250 million. Mark Landler, "At Long Last, Paychecks for Afghan Civil Servants," *New York Times,* January 24, 2002, p. A14.

48. These vivid, descriptive labels made in criticism come from off-the-record meetings.

49. As one knowledgeable observer reports, "*Everyone* wants to build schools for girls."

50. As reported from the Tokyo conference by Jonathan Watts, "Kabul's £3bn aid package tied to democracy," *The Guardian,* January 23, 2002.

51. Many in this camp argue that this is the primary lesson from Bosnia and Herzegovina, but that is a misreading of the Bosnian experience where speed was also emphasized, and realized, in many ways similar to the current process, but where delays in realizing results for Bosnian citizens (six years after a very successful, four-year $5.1 billion reconstruction program, development has not begun) are due to other causes.

52. This author belongs to this second school. See Astri Suhrke and Susan L. Woodward, "Make Haste Slowly in Assistance for Afghanistan," *International Herald Tribune,* January 21, 2002. For

more elaboration of the issues of economic strategy in peace-building and lessons to be learned from the 1990s, see Susan L. Woodward, "Economic Priorities in Peace Implementation," pp. 235–282 in Stephen Stedman, Donald Rothchild, and Elizabeth Cousens, eds., *Ending Civil Wars: The Implementation of Peace Agreements* (Boulder: Lynne Rienner, forthcoming, 2002); a shorter version of the article is published as a policy brief by the International Peace Academy (2002).

53. According to a World Bank assessment in early 1999 of the international aid program for Bosnia and Herzegovina, however, "Implementation of the reconstruction program has been most effective in those sectors (e.g., in transport and energy) where priorities of donor assistance have been established jointly with the authorities." *Bosnia and Herzegovina: 1996–1998. Lessons and Achievements, Review of the Priority Reconstruction Program and Looking Ahead: Towards Sustainable Economic Development.* A Report Prepared for the May 1999 Donors Conference Co-Hosted by the European Commission and the World Bank, p. 6.

54. In demanding attention to human rights, Human Rights Watch does go part of the way in this direction by demanding at Tokyo that donors fund reconstruction of the judicial system and the ministries, such as the Ministry of Women's Affairs, that are relevant to human rights. "Afghanistan: Donors in Tokyo Must Fund Human Rights," press release, New York, January 18, 2002.

55. A good representation of this debate occurred at a discussion at the Carnegie Endowment for International Peace in Washington, D.C. on January 17, 2002, between Marina Ottaway, an Africanist and co-director of the Carnegie Endowment's Democracy and Rule of Law Project, and Martha Brill Olcott, a specialist on Central Asia at Carnegie, on the one hand, and Paula Newberg, an expert on Pakistan and Afghanistan, including operational experience in UN missions to Afghanistan; it is reproduced on their website, "Afghanistan and Beyond: The Challenges of Reconstruction," www.ceip.org/files/events/events.asp?EventID=442.

56. In "Afghanistan and Beyond," p. 4.

57. Ghani, "The Folly of Quick Action."

58. Arendt Lijphart, *Democracy in Plural Societies* (New Haven: Yale University Press, 1977); and Timothy Sisk, *Power Sharing and International Mediation in Ethnic Conflicts* (Washington, D.C.: United States Institute of Peace Press, 1996).

59. Suhrke, et al., *Peacebuilding Strategies for Afghanistan*, Part I, chapter 2, p. 8.

60. Rubin, et al., *Afghanistan*, pp. 8–9.

61. Ibid., p. 5.

62. Martha Brill Olcott, a specialist on Central Asia at the Carnegie Endowment for International Peace in Washington, D.C., has been urging recognition of this fact for Central Asia as well in discussions on reconstruction strategy for Afghanistan. See her *Preventing New Afghanistans: A Regional Strategy for Reconstruction*, Policy Brief #11, Carnegie Endowment for International Peace (Washington, D.C.: January 2002).

63. Rubin, et al., *Afghanistan*, p. 5 (and see also pp. 44–46).

64. I have warned about the consequences of such asymmetric warfare for American global power in my "Failed States: Warlordism and 'Tribal' Warfare," *Naval War College Review*, vol. 52, no. 2, sequence 366 (Spring 1999), pp. 55–68. Freedman, "Third World War?" op. cit., elaborates on the military details of this asymmetry in the Afghan case.

65. United Nations Security Council, S/Res/1368 (2001) passed on September 12. United Nations Security Council S/Res/1373 (2001) passed on September 28.

66. John Donnelly, "Fighting Terror, the Military Campaign: CIA Takes on Major New Military Role in Afghan War, Agents Initiate Attacks, Deals," *The Boston Globe,* January 20, 2002, third edition, p. A1.

67. This ironically reverses the decision of the first Bush administration in November 1990 to make NATO the core of post-Cold War transatlantic security relations at a time when alternatives such as the Organization of Security and Cooperation in Europe and a more cooperative approach to security were much discussed.

68. G. John Ikenberry, *After Victory* (Princeton: Princeton University Press, 2000), provides one institutionalist explanation for this resilience.

69. Judith Goldstein and Robert O. Keohane, eds., *Ideas and Foreign Policy: Beliefs, Institutions, and Political Change* (Ithaca: Cornell University Press, 1993).

70. William A. Niskanen, *Bureaucracy and Representative Government* (Chicago: Aldine, Atherton, 1971).

71. Cumings writes, "Korea is the best example in modern history of how easy it is to get into a war, and how hard it is to get out," in "Black September, Infantile Nihilism, and National Security," in this volume.

15. Unholy Wars. Reclaiming Democratic Virtues After September 11, *by Seyla Benhabib*

1. This chapter was originally published in *Constellations: An International Journal of Critical and Democratic Theory,* March 2002.

2. See Susan Sontag, "The Talk of the Town," *The New Yorker,* September 20, 2001; Fred Jameson, "September 11," *The London Review of Books,* October 4, 2001; and Slavoj Zizek, "The Desert of the Real: Is this the End of Fantasy?" *In These Times,* October 29, 2001.

3. Only, the analogy is not quite accurate, for the French, who were colonizers, eventually left Algeria. But despite all theories to the contrary, the Jewish population of Palestine are not colonizers in the traditional sense of the term. They are not there to exploit the indigenous population or their resources, but to establish a "Jewish homeland"—however problematic and tragic this vision may be. The refusal of much of the Arab world to understand the uniqueness of the dream which motivated the Zionist enterprise makes it easy for them to assimilate Israel to the model of the Western oppressor while presenting themselves as the colonized and the oppressed. Israel was not established to be a colonizing force; it has become so increasingly since the occupation of the West Bank, and since its growing dependence on Palestinian labor to run its expanding economy.

4. "However, the monopolization of legitimate violence by the political-territorial association and its rational consociations into an institutional order is nothing primordial, but a product of evolution." Max Weber, *Economy and Society,* vol. 2, Guenther Roth and Claus Wittich, eds. (Berkeley: University of California Press, 1978), pp. 904–905.

5. Hannah Arendt, *The Origins of Totalitarianism* (New York: Harcourt, Brace and Jovanovich, 1979[1951]), Part Three.

6. Roxanne Euben, "Killing (for) Politics: Jihad, Martyrdom and Political Action," lecture given in the Political Theory Colloquium, Yale University, October 16, 2001. Forthcoming, *Political Theory* (February 2002).

7. Ronald Dworkin, "The Threat to Patriotism," *The New York Review of Books,* vol. xlix, No. 3 (February 28, 2002), p. 44. Also in this volume, chapter 17.

8. Samuel Huntington, *The Clash of Civilizations and the Remaking of World Order* (New York: Simon and Schuster, 1996), p. 2.

9. Huntington spends considerable time drawing distinctions between culture, civilization, and race, and concludes "A civilization is the broadest cultural entity" (43). Yet he adds that "Civilizations have no clear-cut boundaries and no precise beginnings and endings. People can and do redefine their identities and, as a result, the composition and shape of civilizations change over time. The cultures of peoples interact and overlap. . . . Civilizations are nonetheless meaningful entities, and while the lines between them are seldom sharp, they are real" (43). Despite these socially constructivist premises, Huntington defends an essentialist view in the rest of the book in that he seeks a system of clear individuation of civilizations which can then serve as an explanation for global conflict and international realignments. "Peoples and countries with similar cultures are coming together. Peoples and countries with different cultures are coming apart" (125). There are major difficulties in this explanatory model: if one cannot clearly individuate the explanans, how can one use it at all? According to Huntington it is uncertain whether there are five, six, or eight civilizations in the contemporary world (Sinic, Japanese, Hindu, Islamic, and Western, with arguably Orthodox Russian civilization, Latin American, and perhaps African to be included in the list). But how can these unclearly delineated entities then serve as explanations for the primary source of conflict? We seem to have a claim of the kind, "Identity conflict is caused by civilizational differences." But this is tautological, since identities are themselves defined by the civilizations and cultures to which one belongs. The concept of cultural/civilizational identity is an explanans as well as an explanandum. See my forthcoming, *The Claims of Culture: Equality and Diversity in the Global Era* (Princeton: Princeton University Press, 2002) where I discuss the conceptual and explanatory difficulties of Huntington's theses in the Introduction.

10. Edward Said on Samuel Huntington, in *Al-Ahram Weekly On-Line,* October 11–17, 2001. No. 555.

11. Roxanne Euben observes that " 'Islamism' is another, slightly less controversial way of referring to Islamic fundamentalism." In "Killing (for) Politics: Jihad, Martyrdom and Political Action." Paper read at Yale Political Science Colloquium, October 16, 2001. Forthcoming, *Political Theory* (February 2002).

12. See Roxanne Euben's excellent book, *Enemy in the Mirror: Islamist Fundamentalism and the Limits of Modern Rationalism* (Princeton: Princeton University Press, 1999).

13. Euben, "Killing (for) Politics," p. 8.

14. See Sayres S. Rudy for an in-depth social theoretical analyses of some of these issues, "Globalization, Islamism and Modernity," forthcoming.

15. Max Weber, "Religious Rejections of the World and their Directions," *Economy and Society,* vol. 1.

16. At the end of the 1980s, when I first visited Germany as an Alexander von Humboldt Fellow in Munich, I was taken aback by the sale of cassettes and videotaped versions of chants from the Koran in big shopping centers. Recorded by well-known *Muezzins* (cantors), these tapes permitted the faithful to utilize the technology of the society around them, while remaining true to themselves. The irony is that the chanting of the Koran, like the reading of the Talmud, the Old Testament, and unlike the reading of the Bible, is supposed to be a communal and collective act of chanting, telling, and recalling. The medium of Western technology threatens this communal fabric. The result may be "religion a la carte," as this phenomenon has been called, for many Muslims as well.

17. Francoise Gaspard, and Farhad Khosrokhar, *Le Foulard et la Republique* (Decouverte: Paris, 1995), pp. 44–45. My translation.

18. I deal with the ethics of communication and multiculturalism in *The Claims of Culture,* ch. 5 (forthcoming).

16. Terrorism and the Assault on Politics, *by Peter Alexander Meyers*

1. My thanks to Joan Simpson Burns, Craig Calhoun, Daniel Cefai, Filippo de Vivo, Andrew Feffer, Ron Kassimir, Daniel Menaker, Doug Mitchell, Mary Piccone, Paul Price, Effie Rentzou, Morton Schapiro, Jim Sleeper, Nancy S. Struever, Ashley Timmer, for comments, criticisms, editorial acumen, and encouragement, all important in the making of this essay and the larger work from which it is abridged, *Defend Politics Against Terrorism* (Chicago: University of Chicago Press, 2003).

2. Aristotle, *Politics,* 1253a1 ff.

3. For an interesting twist, see Robert E. Goodin, Carole Pateman, and Roy Pateman "Simian Sovereignty," *Political Theory,* vol. 25 no. 6, December 1997, pp. 821–849.

4. Aristotle drives home this point at *Politics* 1253a1 ff. by deploying a topic found in Book IX of *The Iliad* of Homer. Homer goes further: He shows that beasts who confuse themselves with gods can cause a lot of damage but are also likely to get into trouble when they least expect it. See, for example, Ulysses' encounter with the Cyclops in Book IX of *The Odyssey.*

5. Reading journalistic discussions in the aftermath of September 11 may lead you to forget a crucial distinction: To identify desperation as a cause of violence is one thing, to claim that violence is justified by desperation is another.

6. Phrases in quotes are from Hannah Arendt, *Was ist Politik?* (München: Piper, 1992), p. 11. Hobbes makes supporting points in Chapter One of *De Cive.* Even in its most ancient form, the distinction (to state it roughly) between nature and culture comes and goes—it is not eternal. The word *phusis* occurs only once in Homer, but (later on) prominently in Heraclitus. The Sophists sharpened it into a *topos,* and the central political implications to which it was tied in the seventeenth century (i.e., "social contract theory") appeared first in Thucydides. Cp. Cynthia Farrar, *The Origins of Democratic Thinking* (Cambridge: Cambridge University Press, 1988), p. 115ff., especially on Antiphon. The exaggeration of certainty pushed by this distinction is discussed by Martin Ostwald, *From Popular Sovereignty to the Sovereignty of Law* (Berkeley: University of California Press, 1986), p. 305 ff. and—appropriately for present purposes—related to imperialism.

7. Is the notorious "three-fifths" clause of Article 1, Section 2 of the U.S. Constitution a counter-example? I do not believe so. If racist violence associated with this clause persists in the present, it is not an inherent quality of the Constitution but rather a failure of politics to block pernicious consequences that flow from it. Democracy, unfortunately, includes the possibility of malicious actions.

8. It is difficult not to think of the Oslo accords as the prime example of our day.

9. E.g. William E. Connolly, *Identity\Difference: Democratic Negotiations of Political Paradox* (Ithaca: Cornell University Press, 1991).

10. This is true both for social "identification with a group" and, paradoxically, for "personal identity." For this and other reasons, I am deeply skeptical about the way "identity" has entered political thinking in the last twenty-five or so years.

11. To recognize that these relations do not always work so smoothly, and that even a kind of "politics" may develop within them, does not diminish the basic point here. Cp. David Schnarch, *Passionate Marriage* (New York: Norton, 1997). Comparing practices of "love" and "justice," see

Luc Boltanski, *L'amour et la justice comme competences : trois essais de sociologie de l'action* (Paris: Metaillie, 1990).

12. While points like this posed problems for philosophers, the rhetoricians were more perspicacious: "L'essentiel à mon sens est de comprendre pourquoi on ne saurait pas se passer des sophistes, entre tous les présocratiques, pour penser le politique et la démocratie. A nouer dans la séquence vraiment incontournable, car, pour le dire signalétiquement, la moins grosse de danger totalitaire : 1) il y a du politique; 2) le politique est une affaire de *logos* et d'*homologia;* 3) l'*homologia* est une coincidence, voire un hypocrisie ou une homonymie, plutôt qu'un unisson." Barbara Cassin, *L'effet sophistique* (Paris: Gallimard, 1995), p. 153.

13. A neatly put version of this, if without sufficient elaboration: ". . . politics consider men as united in society, and dependent on each other." David Hume, *A Treatise of Human Nature* (Oxford: Clarendon, 1978, original 1739), p. XV. Recent discussions of politics have made much of a difference between (bad/asymmetrical) dependence and (good/symmetrical) interdependence. This distinction is deeply misleading. The word "interdependence" was introduced into English by Samuel Taylor Coleridge, the propagandist and plagiarist of German Idealism. It clearly aims to give in one word the result reached by Hegel in the so-called "Master and Slave" section of *Die Phänomenologie des Geistes*. This is the classic demonstration that dependence is necessarily a two-sided relationship that always has benefits and burdens for both parties. So, the addition of the prefix *inter-* is pleonastic. There is no way to determine if dependence is "symmetrical" or not. The distinction, moreover, sustains the image of dependence as static, one-sided and bad, and thereby obfuscates the real and exceedingly complex effects which flow from it. For how this relates to power, see Peter A. Meyers, *A Theory of Power: Political, Not Metaphysical* (Ann Arbor: UMI, 1989) and, eventually, my elaboration of these themes in a book entitled *Dancing on a Landslide: Micro-Practical Foundations for a Political Theory of Power* (forthcoming).

14. *Dancing on a Landslide,* op. cit., contains a survey of eight main groups of usage from everyday Modern English: Literal, Figurative, Logical, Positional, Legal, Familial, Social, Psychological, and Pathological.

15. Four of these are discussed in my *A Theory of Power:* 1) indeterminacy of effects, 2) relationship, 3) fear of instability, and 4) desire for affirmation. This enumeration of the basic aspects of dependence should not be confused with, for example, a calculus of "pleasure and pain," which are bodily states or the conditions of appetitive faculties; the terms "fear" and "desire" refer instead to a person's interpretation of his relations to things (including other people) outside himself. Roberto Unger, *Passion* (New York: Free Press, 1984), Part I, discusses this relation under the terms longing and jeopardy. Nancy Chodorow, *The Reproduction of Mothering* (Berkeley: University of California Press, 1978), p. 58ff, uses the terms "anxiety" and "continuity" to describe the early development of balanced dependence, e.g., what Erikson calls "basic trust."

16. The emergence of connectedness as an end in itself (as in the ideal of "communitarianism," or more frivolously, as in *The Dating Game*) is an ideological novelty related to supposed social disintegration since the Industrial Revolution. Religious admonition may be a significant exception to this point, as in the Christian notion of "fellowship." Nonetheless, when connection with others is urged in the Bible (e.g., *Genesis* 1:27–8, 2:18; *Proverbs* 18:22; *Ecclesiastes* 4:9; *Hebrews* 13:4), even when it does not have the glorification of God as its goal, it aims at the encouragement of some other end, like the easing of human labor. I am no expert, but I do not find in the Quran an urging to "fellowship" for its own sake.

17. The status and use of "unintended consequences of action" has been a central theme in the modern social sciences. However, as C. Wright Mills's notion of "sociological fate" aptly suggested, the idea that forces of human origin but neither directly made nor controlled by us must be taken into account by those who engage in political activity appears with equal or greater

prominence in Renaissance writers like Machiavelli. The specifically modern conditions under which "unintended consequences of action" become constitutive conditions of relationships of power is a central theme in my *A Theory of Power,* op. cit.

18. For one development of the spatial character of dependence, see Peter A. Meyers, "On the Geometry of Body-Space," *International Review of Sociology,* Vol. 6 No. 3, 1996, pp. 405–428.

19. *Publicizing* serves as a "starting mechanism" for politics which 1) identifies a problem for political deliberation by attaching specifically political significance to a dispute; 2) at the same time, gives to that deliberation a *locus communis,* a rhetorical commonplace, from which to begin; and thus 3) prepares a third party to align itself on this particular matter by providing a politically precise but propositionally general linkage through which the process by which the public "fits itself" to this dispute can begin. This changes the interests of those implicated in the problem by constraining them to undertake 1) above, in a manner backed by public reasons; and so the stage is set on which other political activities can go forward. This summarizes the main argument of my "Why is the private/public distinction important for politics?", a paper presented to the Annual Meetings of the American Political Science Association (1991), *Working Papers of the Berkshire Forum,* 1999–4, and in preparation for publication as a book.

20. See also Weber (1978: I.54). Whether Weber himself ultimately sticks to this view is another question. My insertions from the original are meant to show that Weber is more consistent than the translation suggests.

21. Even in Weber's qualifying phrase, it is the qualifier "legitimate" which leads toward politics.

22. Examples of inappropriately or illegally withheld "state secrets" are legion. Stopping the recount of ballots in a closely contested election is obstructionist in this way as well. The day on which I write this note brings another example: "People at the Defense Department and elsewhere are cringing at the news that the Pentagon's shadowy new Office of Strategic Influence is plotting to plant deliberately false stories in the foreign press, with both feral and friendly nations." (Maureen Dowd, *New York Times,* February 20, 2002). In an extraordinary twist, the office was closed later that week; see Matt Kelley "Rumsfeld: Pentagon Closing Office," AP wire (February 26, 2002).

23. *Essay on Man,* Epistle iii, line 303.

24. "Thought on Government" in George A. Peak, Jr., ed., *The Political Writings of John Adams* (New York: Liberal Arts Press, 1954), p. 84.

25. Hamilton cites Pope and paraphrases *Federalist* #68. Then, with typical vanity, he cites himself: "It has been observed in a former paper, that the true test of a good government is its aptitude and tendency to produce a good administration." (#76)

26. For example, Madison writes in *Federalist* #45: "The public good, the real welfare of the great body of the people, is the supreme object to be pursued; and that no form of government whatever has any other value than as it may be fitted for the attainment of this object."

27. See e.g., *Federalist* #71 by Hamilton. Cp. Sheldon S. Wolin, *The Presence of the Past* (Baltimore: Johns Hopkins University Press, 1989), p. 116 ff., and James MacGregor Burns, and Peter A. Meyers, "A 'Common Market' Called America: The Constitution, Markets, and Democracy," *Think* (special issue on the Constitution, September 1987).

28. Ibid. and *Federalist* #72: "The administration of government, in its largest sense, comprehends all the operations of the body politic, whether legislative, executive, or judiciary; but in its most usual, and perhaps its most precise signification, it is limited to executive details, and falls peculiarly within the province of the executive department." On the relation between Hamilton and Hobbes, see Gerald Stourzh, *Alexander Hamilton and the Idea of Republican Government* (Stanford: Stanford University Press, 1970).

29. Franklin speaking to the constitutional convention on Monday, June 4, 1787, as recorded by Madison. Max Farrand, ed., *The Records of the Federal Convention of 1787* (New Haven: Yale University Press, 1937), vol. I, p. 103.

30. *Federalist* #67 and #69.

31. Whether it *really* was unimportant is an entirely different matter.

32. This assertion seems to contradict the now much-discussed claim that civic associations in America were in decline between 1945 and September 2001; see especially Robert D. Putnam, *Bowling Alone: The Collapse and Revival of American Community* (New York: Simon and Schuster, 2000). In fact, it involves a shift in the frame of reference. Putnam's analysis assumes that civic associations are crucial for but prior to politics. My assertion, rather, concerns the more or less explicit solution of political problems within civil society (e.g., activities exemplified by but not limited to so-called "new social movements").

33. Another perspective sees in "civil society" a synonym for "diversity." As already stated, I find "plurality" a more useful notion. Jane Jacobs, *The Death and Life of Great American Cities* (New York: Basic Books, 1960) is extremely perspicuous in relating plurality to territory and thereby makes it easier to see its connection to politics. Hannah Arendt's *The Human Condition* (Chicago: University of Chicago Press, 1958) shows the specificity of political space, which is not territorial. I develop these ideas at length in my *Left Speechless* (Cambridge: Cambridge University Press, forthcoming).

34. It was the failure of other social forces or practices to limit the free operation of the market and profit-motive which eventually clarified the distinction between economy and society. Cp. Karl Polanyi, *The Great Transformation* (New York: Rinehart & Co., 1944).

35. This distinction may have been achieved in the application of mathematical methods to economic questions by Cournot's *Principes Mathématiques de la Théorie des Richesses,* or even in the formalizations undertaken by David Ricardo, but it arrives as, so to speak, a fact of life in Alfred Marshall's *Principles of Economics* (1890 & subsequent editions), where the project to separate the scientific study of economics from the study of politics is clearly marked out and was soon to be part of an effort to create distinct departments of study at Cambridge University.

36. David Easton, *The Political System* (New York: Knopf, 1953); Robert Morrison MacIver, *The Web of Government* (New York: Free Press, 1947).

37. A classic argument for this is developed by Jacobs, op. cit.

38. I view with some skepticism the idea that an "international civil society" is constituted within the network of nongovernmental organizations. The reasons are too complicated to enter into here.

39. Cp. James C. Scott, *Seeing Like a State* (New Haven: Yale University Press, 1998) and *Weapons of the Weak* (New Haven: Yale University Press, 1985). Oddly, it was precisely the historical delimitation of the State as the sole site of politics that had earlier transformed these activities into something "merely" social; they were political all along. It should also be said that opinions vary widely concerning the relation between "new social movements" and politics. Andrew Feffer reminds me that, as conceived by Alain Touraine, Alberto Melucci, and others, these movements are founded in the reformation of identity by "alternative codes" and thus are not especially political (perhaps even antipolitical) in the sense I developed above.

40. Certainly, the writings and life of Vaclav Havel are at the center of this historical fact and the role it has played in changing American thinking about politics.

41. Democracy is often associated with, and eventually mistaken for, concerns which are not strictly speaking political: It is not an ethical impulse to equality, nor a social concern with in-

clusion, nor a project to create personal opportunity, nor a pattern of economic organization like the "free-market system."

42. A vast literature examines the relation between violence and democracy. Americans interested in this subject would do well to return to Richard Slotkin's three books about "the myth of the frontier" and the centrality of violence to American political culture: *Regeneration Through Violence* (1973), *The Fatal Environment* (1986), and *Gunfighter Nation* (1992). On violence as public spectacle, see recently Sissela Bok, *Mayhem* (Boston: Addison-Wesley, 1998).

43. Peter A. Meyers, *Left Speechless: America in the Light of its Holocaust Museum*, addresses some of the cultural conditions of such failures.

44. That the inequality of women and slaves both weighed heavily on the American democratic project in the nineteenth century is interestingly reflected in their competing claims for political suffrage just after the Civil War, and especially in debates between Elizabeth Cady Stanton and Frederick Douglass.

45. An economy no longer directly dependent on forced labor opened the way to the realization of this ideal. Note that historical links between capitalism and democracy are one thing, and the claim that only a capitalist economy can sustain a democratic regime is another. In the past, this was false; whether it will be true in the future will only be known if and when a viable alternative comes along. Note, too, that the person crowned by pundits as the "defining analyst of the globalization system"—Thomas L. Friedman, *The Lexus and the Olive Tree: Understanding Globalization* (New York: Farrar, Straus and Giroux, 1999), p. 9—insisted that in the long run there is no necessary connection between democracy and capitalism. See Joseph Schumpeter, *Capitalism, Socialism, and Democracy* (New York: Harper, 1942).

46. Distinguishing different ways of organizing political life—regimes—has been a formal strategy at the center of political thinking from its inception. Identifying monarchy, aristocracy, or democracy—rule by the one, the few, or the many—is an effective topical point of departure for considering the ways of life which correspond to each regime. In fact, by classical criteria democracy and communism are better and worse forms of the same type of regime. The contemporary failure of analysis by "regime" corresponds to one of the central facts of modern politics—the oft-remarked continuity amongst "political systems" constituted by the rise of "mass society" in need of "administration"—and thus may not be the best way to analyze it. Something like this point is made in the concluding chapter of Hannah Arendt, *The Origins of Totalitarianism* (New York: Harcourt, Brace, 1951). Vaclav Havel's essay, "The Power of the Powerless," remains one of the best interrogations of the grotesque convergences between totalitarianism and democracy. Benjamin R. Barber, *Strong Democracy* (Berkeley: University of California Press, 1984) tries to reassert a kind of regime analysis by distinguishing types of democracy.

47. Many of the American Founders drew the conclusion that democracy was, in fact, obsolete as a form of government, and proposed a new form of republic which centered around representative institutions rather than direct citizen action. A recent and lucid treatment of this shift may be found in Bernard Manin, *The Principles of Representative Democracy* (Cambridge: Cambridge University Press, 1997). Only later did democracy become the American ideal. This is narrowly reflected by the creation of the Democratic Party in 1828, a history of which appears in Arthur M. Schlesinger, Jr., ed., *History of U.S. Political Parties* (New York: Chelsea House, 1973). It appears more broadly in the political debates studied in Marvin Meyers, *The Jacksonian Persuasion: Politics and Belief* (Stanford: Stanford University Press, 1957), which may be read as an historical supplement to Tocqueville. For the development of the democratic ideal in France, see e.g., Pierre Rosanvallon, *La démocratie inachevée* (Paris: Gallimard, 2000).

48. Reflecting on the heroism of New York's public servants on September 11, Jim Sleeper proposes a very different view of this visceral element in democracy in "The Power of Myths," *The New York Observer*, November 7, 2001.

49. I have developed these general points one way in *A Theory of Power* and another way in "The 'Ethic of Care' and the Problem of Power," *The Journal of Political Philosophy,* Vol. 6 no. 2 (1998), pp. 142–170. Anthropologist Mary Piccone reminds me that specific cultural circumstances (as, for example, in Japan) can bury the impulse to speak out almost completely.

50. An important account of this process in general is Jürgen Habermas, *Strukturwandel der Öffentlichkeit: Untersuchungen zu einer Kategorie der bürgerlichen Gesellschaft* (Neuwied: Luchterhand, 1962); cp. Craig Calhoun, ed. (1992), *Habermas and the Public Sphere* (Cambridge: MIT Press), where some authors pursue Habermas's themes in the American context.

51. This may include political intervention, and not just "self-correction." For one perspective, see Amartya Sen's studies showing a correlation between the lack of a free press and famine, e.g. *Development as Freedom* (New York: Knopf, 1999).

52. This paragraph is drawn from Peter A. Meyers, "Why should I talk to you? How *connaissance réciproque* may be served by free public talk," in *Actes du congrès Connaissance réciproque, Canton, Chine* (published in Chinese translation, 1992).

53. On the American myth of the Constitution as a "machine that would go of itself," see the book of that name by Michael Kammen (New York: Knopf, 1986). The tendency of regimes to exhaust themselves, to undermine their own operation by operating "correctly," was well-known to ancient writers like Polybius. Two modern authors already mentioned used this knowledge of the historical dynamics of political life with special lucidity: Giambattista Vico and Joseph Schumpeter.

54. See article entitled, without irony, "The United State of America" (on the cover), in *The American Prospect,* Vol. 13, No. 3, February 11, 2002.

55. Benjamin R. Barber (1984), op. cit., is a rare theorist to take seriously this aspect of reception in democratic deliberation.

56. If you think this is recent news from the science of communication, cp. J. B. S. Hardman's entry on "Terrorism" in the *Encyclopaedia of the Social Sciences* (1934: XIV.575–580): "The publicity value of the terroristic act is a cardinal point in the strategy of terrorism. If terror fails to elicit a wide response in circles outside of those at whom it is directly aimed, it is futile as a weapon in a social conflict."

57. More precisely, Descartes says our first passion is what he calls *admiration* in *Les Passions de l'Ame* (1644, especially in pp. 53, 59–77), and "astonishment is an excess of admiration," (p. 73).

58. The claim that representations of violence tend to undermine the capacities and dispositions of citizens for public speech is central to my forthcoming book, *Left Speechless,* op. cit.

59. E.g., President Bush's statement on September 12, 2001: "Those in authority should take appropriate precautions to protect our citizens. But we will not allow this enemy to win the war by changing our way of life or restricting our freedoms."

60. If there is any doubt about President Bush's *hubris of position,* consider the following: "We fight now because we will not permit the terrorists—these vicious and evil men—to hijack a peaceful religion and to impose their will on America and the world. We fight now, and we will keep on fighting until our victory is complete." Speech at Fort Campbell, Kentucky, November 21, 2001. One must wonder what a war for control over other people's religious beliefs would look like in the twenty-first century.

61. See my *A Theory of Power: Political, not Metaphysical* (Ann Arbor: UMI, 1989). An elaborated version of this argument will eventually appear as, *Dancing on a Landslide: Micro-Practical Foundations for a Political Theory of Power.*

62. This traditional problematic is, not surprisingly, replayed by Ronald Dworkin, in "The Threat to Patriotism," *New York Review of Books,* Volume XLIX, Number 3, February 28, 2002, pp. 44–49. His piece also appears in this volume, Chapter 17.

63. Public Law 107–56; October 25, 2001.

64. Nancy Chang, "The USA PATRIOT Act: What's So Patriotic About Trampling on the Bill of Rights?", Center for Constitutional Rights website: www.ccr-ny.org/whatsnew/usa_patriot_act.asp, March 1, 2002.

65. For example: "We are convinced that liberty and security need not be at odds"; letter signed by Laura W. Murphy, Director, ACLU Washington National Office & Timothy H. Edgar, ACLU Legislative Counsel; "We can have security and civil liberties in a time of crisis"; letter addressed to "Member of congress," signed by Phyllis Schlafly, President, Eagle Forum, October 2, 2001. The diversity of claims to liberty is an old *topos;* see, e.g., Montesquieu, *De l'esprit des lois* XI.2.

66. Thus, the centrality of the concept of *personality* in law.

67. I grant that this distinction works only on one level; viewed from another angle, a "right" is a double relation to the State. . . . *Within* politics a right is a form of relationship—it is the structuring of the relationship between the parties in dispute to a "third."

68. Affirmative action is an obvious example of this. While many affirmative action programs have been of enormous positive social value, the practice works against politics in the long run.

69. *Nota bene:* I fully recognize that other major historical factors have played into this development, including the contradictions of race relations in America, the ideological grounds for American mobilization in World War II, and the extraordinary appearance of viable claims and international fora concerning human rights.

70. I wrote above that "antipolitics" is a kind of politics. Also, please note that what I say here is entirely compatible with a positive assessment of all sorts of state regulatory intervention or social provision. I am only saying that these are matters of administrative and legal activity, not politics.

17. The Threat to Patriotism, *by Ronald Dworkin*

1. This chapter originally appeared in the *New York Review of Books* (February 28, 2002). An update of the article was published in the *New York Review* on April 25, 2002 ("The Trouble with the Tribunals"), and may be found at www.nybooks.com/articles/15284.

2. The bill the administration originally sent to Congress, on September 18, was even worse than the final act. It would have licensed the use in American courts against American citizens of information obtained through wiretaps abroad that would be unconstitutional here, permitted freezing all the assets of people accused of terrorism even before they were tried, and allowed indefinite detention when the Justice Department said only that it had "had reason to believe" rather than "reasonable grounds" for suspecting terrorism. Congress took longer than Attorney General John Ashcroft wanted to consider the bill—he said it would be dangerous to delay passage for more than a few days—and it deleted some of the bill's most objectionable features.

3. A CNN broadcast described the history and fate of some of the detainees. See *CNN Presents,* "The Enemy Within," January 12, 2002. According to that broadcast, Mazen al-Najjar, for example, a Palestinian, has an American Ph.D., has lived in America for over 20 years, and has three children born here. In 1997 he was arrested for overstaying his visa: the Justice Department claimed he had ties to terrorist organizations, but a judge decided there was no evidence of that, and ordered him released in 2000. Immediately after September 11, he helped to organize a blood drive for its victims, but was picked up on the street and taken back into detention. He is held in 23-hour lockdown solitary confinement, and the press is not allowed to interview him. The Justice Department has determined that it would threaten security to release him, but he has been allowed no hearing in which to attempt to rebut that claim.

On the same broadcast, an interviewer suggested to Viet Dinh, an assistant attorney general, that the agency was not particularly interested in the violations with which people like al-Najjar were actually charged. "Right," he said. "What we are doing is simply using our process or our discretion to the fullest extent to remove from the street those who we suspect to be engaging in terrorist activity."

4. Officials have steadily refused such information, citing security interests as justification. See Dan Eggen, "Delays Cited in Charging Detainees," *The Washington Post*, January 15, 2002, p. A1.

5. See Jeffrey Toobin, "Crackdown," *The New Yorker*, November 5, 2001, p. 56.

6. "The Military Tribunals on Trial," *New York Review of Books*, February 14, 2002.

7. See Neil A. Lewis, "Rules on Tribunal Require Unanimity on Death Penalty," *New York Times*, December 28, 2001.

8. As Kenneth Roth, the executive director of Human Rights Watch, pointed out in a letter to Condoleezza Rice, the national security advisor, America could have pursued the terrorists as criminals. "But since the United States government engaged in armed conflict in Afghanistan— by bombing and undertaking other military operations—the Geneva Conventions clearly do apply to that conflict."

9. See Laurie Goodstein, "Jewish Groups Endorse Tough Security Laws," *New York Times*, January 3, 2002.

10. Full poll data are available at ‹www.publicagenda.org/specials/terrorism/terror_pubopinion.htm›

11. Mike Allen and Susan Schmidt, "Bush Defends Secret Tribunals for Terrorism Suspects," *The Washington Post*, November 30, 2001, p. A28.

12. Laurence H. Tribe, "Trial by Fury," *The New Republic*, December 10, 2001, pp. 18, 20.

13. 533 U.S. 678 (2001).

14. *Ex Parte Quirin*, 317 U.S. 1 (1942).

15. *Korematsu v. United States*, 323 U.S. 214 (1944).

16. See David J. Danelski, "The Saboteurs' Case," *Journal of Supreme Court History 1996*, Vol. 1, p. 61.

17. The President's military tribunal order cited the joint resolution that Congress adopted on September 18 authorizing the President "to use all necessary and appropriate force" against the September 11 terrorists or nations or persons who harbored them. That language does not license or approve military tribunals, however, and the President's order, in any case, is not limited to suspected September 11 terrorists, but applies to all terrorists, broadly defined.

18. Tribe, "Trial by Fury."

19. For a general account of the structure of fairness in the criminal process, see Chapter 3, "Principle, Policy, Procedure," in my book, *A Matter of Principle* (Cambridge, MA: Harvard University Press, 1985).

20. See testimony of Ali al-Maqtari before the Senate Judiciary Committee, judiciary.senate.gov/te120401f-almaqtari.htm.

21. See "Justice Oversight: Preserving Our Freedoms While Defending Against Terrorism," a statement submitted by the American Civil Liberties Union to the Senate Judiciary Committee on November 28, 2001, available at www.aclu.org/congress/1112801a.html.

22. The Due Process Clause might well be thought to require individualized hearings testing extended detention orders at least in the case of aliens who are lawful permanent residents of the United States, and perhaps also certain other aliens. See the Ninth Circuit's recent decision in *Kim* v. *Ziglar,* Ninth Circuit Court of Appeals, decided January 9, 2002.

18. Guarding the Gates, *by Aristide R. Zolberg*

1. Kathleen Newland, codirector of the Migration Policy Institute, Washington, D.C., as cited in *Newsweek,* November 12, 2001.

2. Steven A. Caramota, Director of Research, Center for Immigration Studies, "Immigration and Terrorism," testimony prepared for the Senate Judiciary Committee Subcommittee on Technology, Terrorism and Government Information, October 12, 2001 (judiciary.senate.gov/te101201st-caramota.htm).

3. Annual admissions are from the *1998 Statistical Yearbook of the Immigration and Naturalization Service* (the latest available). With regard to illegal immigration, the most reliable estimate is 4,130,478 in 1990, and 8,705,419 in 2000; Joe Costanzo, et al., U.S. Census Bureau, *Working Paper Series No. 61, Evaluating components of international migration: The residual foreign born* (January 2002).

4. U.S. Census Bureau, *The Foreign-Born Population of the United States: Population Characteristics,* P20-534 (March 2000, issued January 2001); *The Washington Post,* October 25, 2001, p. A24.

5. Peter Andreas, *Border Games: Policing the U.S.–Mexico Divide* (Ithaca: Cornell University Press, 2000).

6. For an analytic framework that combines economic and cultural considerations in relation to immigration policy, see Aristide R. Zolberg, "Matters of State: Theorizing Immigration Policy," in *The Handbook of International Migration: The American Experience,* Charles Hirschman, Philip Kasinitz, and Josh De Wind, eds. (New York: Russell Sage, 1999), pp. 71–93.

7. Patrick J. Buchanan, "Tracking Down the Enemy Within," *WorldNet Daily,* October 26, 2001. www.worldnetdaily.com/news/article.asp?ARTICLE_ID=25087.

8. Patrick J. Buchanan, *The Death of the West* (New York: St. Martin's Press, 2002).

9. *New York Times,* Nov. 2, 2001, p. B7.

10. John Torpey, *The Invention of the Passport: Surveillance, Citizenship, and the State* (Cambridge: Cambridge University Press, 1999).

11. I trace the development of "remote control" in "The Archeology of Remote Control," in Patrick Weil, et al., eds., *From Europe to North America* (Berghahn Books, forthcoming, 2002).

12. These figures are taken from Annual Reports of the Immigration and Naturalization Service; I am grateful to Fred Cocozelli for his assistance in gathering the appropriate data.

13. This account is drawn from Melanie Nezer, "The New Antiterrorism Legislation: The Impact on Immigrants," (*Refugee Reports,* 22,11, November 2001), pp. 1–8.

14. Rosemary Jenks, "The USA PATRIOT Act of 2001: A Summary of the Anti-Terrorism Law's Immigration-Related Provisions" (Washington, D.C.: Center for Immigration Studies "Backgrounder," December 2001).

15. *New York Times,* November 10, 2001, p. B5.

16. *The Washington Post,* October 30, 2001, p. A1.

17. *New York Times,* November 12, 2001, p. B8.

18. *New York Times,* January 28, 2002, p. A1.

19. *The Washington Post,* October 25, 2001, p. A24; Kevin E. Deardorff, and Lisa M. Blumerman, U.S. Bureau of the Census, Population Division, *Working Paper No. 58, Evaluating Components of international migration: Estimates of the foreign-born population by migrant status in 2000* (December 2001). The bureau calculated that in 2000, there were some 8.7 million aliens in the United States who were neither temporary visitors nor legal immigrants; however, as the total includes some in a quasi-legal status, waiting to have their cases adjudicated, it reckoned illegal immigrants proper at between 7 and 8 million, which is close to the earlier INS estimate of 7.5 million.

20. Joe Costanzo, et al., U.S. Census Bureau, Population Division, Working Paper Series No. 61, *Evaluating components of international migration: The residual foreign born* (December 2001); *New York Times,* January 23, 2002, p. A10.

21. *Christian Science Monitor,* September 19, 2001, p. 1; *The San Diego Union-Tribune,* October 25, 2001.

22. *National Post,* October 10, 2001.

23. *New York Times,* October 26, 2001, p. A18.

24. Doris Meissner, "After the Attacks: Protecting Borders and Liberties," *Policy Brief* 8, November 2001 (Washington, D.C.: Carnegie Endowment for International Peace), pp. 5–6.

25. "Census had a variety of categories, but none tallied Arab or Muslims," by Nicholas Kulish, *The Wall Street Journal,* September 26, 2001; *New York Times,* October 15, 2001, p. B10 (according to Jon Alterman, Middle East specialist at the U.S. Institute of Peace).

26. Ishan Bagby, Paul M. Perl, and Bryan T. Froehle, *The Mosque in America: A National Portrait. A report from the Mosque Study Project* (Washington, D.C.: Council on American-Islamic Relations, April 28, 2001).

27. "Jewish group says estimates of U.S. Muslim population are too high," by Rachael Zoll, the Associated Press, October 22, 2001 (www.washingtonpost.com/wp-srv/aponline/200111022/aponline212753_000.htm).

28. *New York Times,* November 2, 2001, p. B10.

29. *New York Times,* November 3, 2001, p. B1. This was raised from 1,017 reported a few days earlier (*New York Times,* October 30, 2001, p. B1).

30. *New York Times,* November 3, 2001, p. B1.

31. *New York Times,* November 14, 2001, p. B8.

32. For example, as of late January local law enforcement officials in eastern Michigan reported having interviewed fewer than half the men assigned to them; *The New York Times,* January 24, 2002, p. A25.

33. *New York Times,* December 20, 2001, p. A3.

34. Meissner, "After the Attack," p. 4.

19. The Political Psychology of Competing Narratives: September 11 and Beyond, by Marc Howard Ross

1. I want to thank Kevin Avruch, Eileen Babbitt, Dan Bar-On, Daniel Bar-Tal, Katherine Conner, Ethan Conner-Ross, Jane Caplan, Susan Schaefer Davis, Marc Gopin, Louis Kriesberg, Clark McCauley and Michael Weinstein for comments and suggestions on earlier drafts of this paper.

2. Samuel P. Huntington, "The Clash of Civilizations," *Foreign Affairs,* 1993, pp. 22–49.

3. My interests here is solely in the narratives the parties in a conflict recount, not those that academic or other analysts develop to explain the unfolding of events.

4. Beth Roy, *Some Trouble with Cows: Making Sense of Social Conflict* (Berkeley and Los Angeles: University of California Press, 1994).

5. I use the term psychocultural because I am interested in interpretations of the world which are widely shared among people in a culture and which are transmitted through psychological processes. For further elaboration of this concept see Marc Howard Ross, *The Culture of Conflict: Interpretations and Interests in Comparative Perspective* (New Haven and London: Yale University Press, 1993); Marc Howard Ross, "Psychocultural Interpretation Theory and Peacemaking in Ethnic Conflicts," *Political Psychology*, 16, pp. 523–544; and Marc Howard Ross, "Culture and Identity in Comparative Political Analysis," in Mark I. Lichbach and Alan S. Zuckerman, eds., *Comparative Politics: Rationality, Culture and Structure* (Cambridge: Cambridge University Press, 1997), pp. 42–80.

6. The general argument is found in Robert A. LeVine and Donald T. Campbell, *Ethnocentrism: Theories of Conflict, Ethnic Attitudes and Group Behavior* (New York: John Wiley, 1972). A specific recent example is that although the U.S. is by far the world's strongest military power, a recently published book on the U.S. military is titled "America the Vulnerable": John F. Lehman and Harvey Sicherman, *America the Vulnerable: Our Military Problems and How to Fix Them* (Philadelphia: Foreign Policy Research Institute, 2002).

7. All religious traditions also have images of peacemaking as well as war. They can have a particularly important role in conflict termination and peacebuilding. See Marc Gopin, *Between Eden and Armageddon: The Future of World Religions, Violence and Peacemaking* (Oxford and New York: Oxford University Press, 2000).

8. Clifford Geertz, "Thick Description: Toward an Interpretive Theory of Culture," in Clifford Geertz, *The Interpretation of Cultures* (New York: Basic Books, 1973), pp. 8–30. Roy D'Andrade points out the radical shift in the social sciences from the view of culture as behavior which could be understood within a stimulus-response framework to culture as systems of meaning after the 1950s. See page 89 in Roy G. D'Andrade, "Cultural Meaning Systems," in Richard A. Schweder and Robert A. LeVine, eds., *Culture Theory: Essays on Mind, Self, And Emotion* (Cambridge: Cambridge University Press, 1984), pp. 88–119. A more complete discussion of culture as meanings and symbols can be found in the Schweder and LeVine book.

9. Melford E. Spiro, "Some Reflections on Cultural Determinism and Relativism with Special Reference to Emotion and Reason," in Richard A. Schweder and Robert A. LeVine, op. cit., pp. 323–346.

10. Ross, 1997, op. cit.

11. I eschew the term construction here as it implies a more self-conscious process than is often the case.

12. Yael Zerubavel, *Recovered Roots: Collective Memory and the Making of Israeli National Tradition* (Chicago: University of Chicago Press, 1995); T. Dunbar Moodie, *The Rise of Afrikanerdom: Power, Apartheid, and the Afrikaner Civil Religion* (Berkeley and Los Angeles: University of California Press, 1975); and Leonard Thompson, *The Political Mythology of Apartheid* (New Haven and London: Yale University Press, 1985).

13. Anthony Smith uses the term ethnocide to describe deliberate efforts to destroy a community's cultural icons. See Anthony D. Smith, *National Identity* (Reno: University of Nevada Press, 1991). In recent years examples of such attacks include the destruction of the mosque at Ayodhya in Northern India in 1992, of cultural treasures and mosques in Bosnia, and of the huge Buddhist statues in Afghanistan. See Michael Sells, *The Bridge Betrayed: Religion and Genocide in Bosnia* (Berkeley and Los Angeles: University of California Press, 1996).

14. This does not mean that once a narrative emerges, it is unchanging. Quite the opposite; as new events unfold, there can be questioning and conflict around, and change in, a narrative. When stress is very high, sometimes there are multiple narratives which arise along with the disintegration of social cohesion.

15. This is seen at the level of political elites as well. Just a few days before the outbreak of fighting, the Senate narrowly voted in favor of action. Within a few days, however, few Senators publicly offered significant criticism of the war effort.

16. Timur Kuran, *Private Truths, Public Lies: The Social Consequences of Preference Falsification* (Cambridge: Harvard University Press, 1995). Elisabeth Noelle-Neumann describes a different dynamic as "the spiral of silence" arguing that for many people the fear of social isolation is more important than holding an unpopular belief. Consequently, people are quite attuned to public opinion in their society and not only are less likely to speak out when they perceive themselves in a minority but also change their opinions as well. See Elisabeth Noelle-Neumann, *The Spiral of Silence: Public Opinion, Our Social Skin* (Chicago: University of Chicago Press, 1993).

17. Vamik D. Volkan, *Bloodlines: From Ethnic Pride to Ethnic Terrorism* (New York: Farrar, Straus and Giroux, 1997). Significant dates in a group's emotional history are often centuries old. For Protestants in Northern Ireland it is William of Orange's victory in the Battle of the Boyne in 1690, for Serbs it is Prince Lazar's defeat at Kosovo in 1389, while for Jews, the destruction of the Second Temple in 70 AD. Their significance, however, is the relevance of these events as lessons and warnings about the present. Volkan uses the terms "chosen traumas" and "chosen glories" to describe past events whose contemporary emotional significance is transmitted across generations.

18. Zerubavel, op. cit., 1995.

19. Anthony D. Smith, *The Ethnic Origin of Nations* (Oxford: Basil Blackwell, 1986); and Smith, 1991, op. cit.

20. Weber's masterful analysis of the transformation of identity in nineteenth-century France is very relevant here. He argues that in the countryside there was only a weak identification with the state and French culture as late as the middle of the century and that elites in Paris saw their mission as one of bringing civilization to the primitive peasants. His detailed account documents how peasants are transformed into patriotic Frenchmen and -women between 1870 and 1914 through improved transportation networks, universal primary education in French, and military service. The development of a strong shared identity in France, and elsewhere, produced a population ready to sacrifice in World War I. See Eugen Weber, *Peasants Into Frenchmen: The Modernization of Rural France, 1870–1914* (Stanford: Stanford University Press, 1976).

21. For many the most dramatic conflict occurred over the status of Ethiopian immigrants. Although there was widespread agreement that they were Jews and thereby eligible to migrate to Israel under its law of return, some orthodox religious authorities insisted that differences in their ritual practices required that they undergo conversion in Israel (including ritual male circumcision) before they could be fully accepted as Jewish citizens.

22. This is not an uncommon pattern. Europeans coming to North America saw it as empty and ready for settlement and "taming." The Russians had the same view of central Asia and continued to settle in the region under various "virgin lands" programs. The British arriving in the highlands in Kenya and the Boers moving to the interior of South Africa had no trouble seeing the land as unused and ripe for settlement either.

23. Benedict Anderson, *Imagined Communities: Reflections on the Origin and Spread of Nationalism* (London and New York: Verso, 1991).

24. Smith, 1991, op. cit.

25. Edward Linenthal, *The Unfinished Bombing: Oklahoma City in American Memory* (Oxford and New York: Oxford University Press, 2001).

26. Another narrative Linenthal discusses focuses on the role of trauma in the aftermath of the bombing. This account, he argues, dominated the response of health professionals and some government agencies and had the consequence of medicalizing and individualizing responses to the events, and providing health-care professionals with a standard, acceptable formula for treating those touched by them, (see Linenthal, op. cit., pp. 81–108). The issue of how governments and other authorities define problems in ways that are consistent with their worldviews that then render them amenable to a particular course of action is an important issue but one I will not treat here. See for example David A. Rochefort and Roger Cobb, *The Politics of Problem Definition: Shaping the Policy Agenda* (Lawrence, KS: University Press of Kansas, 1994).

27. Gary B. Nash, "American History Reconsidered: Asking New Questions about the Past," in Diane Ravitch and Maris A. Vinovskis, eds., *Learning from the Past: What History Teaches us about School Reform* (Baltimore. Johns Hopkins University Press, 1995); and National Center for History in the School, *National Standards for History* (Los Angeles, CA: National Center for History in the Schools, 1996).

28. Linenthal, op. cit.; Edward T. Linenthal, *Sacred Ground: Americans and Their Battlefields* (Urbana and Chicago: Illinois University Press, 1993); Edward T. Linenthal, *Preserving Memory: The Struggle to Create America's Holocaust Museum* (New York: Columbia University Press, 2001); and Edward T. Linenthal and Tom Engelhardt, eds., *History Wars: The Enola Gay and other Battles for the American Past* (New York: Henry Holt and Company, 1996).

29. Linenthal, 1993, ibid.

30. Linenthal, 1993, op. cit., p. 132.

31. It is interesting how often disastrous defeats are heroic (and traumatic) events for many groups. In addition to Masada and Little Big Horn, we could identify the Battle of Blood River in South Africa, the Serb defeat at Kosovo, and Crusaders' massacres of Muslims. Volkan's psychoanalytically informed analysis explains this in terms of trauma and the inability to mourn enormous loss—feelings that are transmitted from generation to generation as a group is unable to reverse narcissistic injury and humiliation. See Vamik D. Volkan, *The Need to Have Enemies and Allies: From Clinical Practice to International Relationships* (New York: Jason Aronson, 1988); and Volkan, 1997, op. cit.

32. Linenthal, 1993, op. cit., p. 148.

33. Although this is not my major focus here, it is worth pointing out that asking an administrative agency to mediate, and resolve, large cultural and identity conflicts is often problematic. These are political issues that political leaders often prefer to ignore, but handing them off to administrative officials is rarely adequate. This problem is seen in the management of disputes involving Loyal Order parades in Northern Ireland since 1995 (see Marc Howard Ross, "Psychocultural Interpretations and Dramas: Identity Dynamics in Ethnic Conflict," *Political Psychology*, 22, pp. 157–78).

34. Zerubavel, 1995, op. cit., especially Chapters 5 and 8.

35. "These concepts—autonomy, identity, national genius, authenticity, unity, and fraternity— form an interrelated language or discourse that has its expressive ceremonials and symbols. These symbols and ceremonies are so much part of the world we live in that we take them, for the most part, for granted. They include the obvious attributes of nations—flags, anthems, parades, coinage, capital cities, oaths, folk costumes, museums of folklore, war memorials, ceremonies of remembrance for the national dead, passports, frontiers—as well as more hidden aspects, such as national recreations, the countryside, popular heroes and heroines, fairy tales, forms of etiquette, styles of architecture, arts and crafts, modes of town planning, legal procedures, educa-

tional practices and military does—all those distinctive customs, mores styles and ways of acting and feeling that are shared by members of a community of historical cultures" (Smith, 1991, op. cit., p. 77).

36. For a consideration of the American flag, see Carolyn Marvin and David W. Ingle, *Blood Sacrifice and the Nation: Totem Rituals and the American Flag* (Cambridge: Cambridge University Press, 1999). Their analysis ought to provide a context to help understand the veneration of the tattered flag recovered from the World Trade Center site following the attacks.

37. Sanford Levinson, *Written in Stone: Public Monuments in Changing Societies* (Durham and London: Duke University Press, 1998); and Michael J. Martinez, et al., eds., *Confederate Symbols in the Contemporary South* (Gainesville: University Press of Florida, 2000).

38. See Linenthal, The Unfinished Bombing, op. cit., and John R. Gillis, *Commemorations: The Politics of National Identity* (Princeton: Princeton University Press, 1994), for further discussion of the politics of memorials and commemoration.

39. An important issue here is the total absence of public participation in the process of discussing and designing the memorial. Linenthal's analysis of Oklahoma City makes it clear how important a public process is following a traumatic event.

40. Although it is easiest to describe conflicts as involving two sides, complex conflicts like the current one include many more parties each with their own distinct interests and interpretations of the situation. Howard Raiffa's discussion of multiparty, multi-issue conflicts is very useful here. Howard Raiffa, *The Art and Science of Negotiation* (Cambridge: Belknap Press, 1982).

41. Huntington, 1993, op. cit.

42. Neil Smith, "Global Executioner: Scales of Terror," *After September 11: Perspectives from the Social Sciences,* website, www.ssrc.org/sept11/essays/nsmith.htm.

43. Linenthal, The Unfinished Bombing, op. cit.

44. David J. Finley, Ole R. Holsti, and Richard R. Fagen, "Cognitive Dynamics and Images of the Enemy: Dulles and Russia," *Enemies in Politics* (Chicago: Rand McNally, 1967), pp. 25–96.

45. See his discussion of "chosen traumas," in Vamik Volkan, "On Chosen Trauma," in *Mind and Human Interaction,* 3, 1991, p. 13.; and see also Volkan, 1997, op. cit., and 1988, op. cit.

46. Robert Jervis, *Perception and Misperception in International Politics* (Princeton: Princeton University Press, 1976).

47. Herbert C. Kelman, "The Political Psychology of The Israeli–Palestinian Conflict: How Can We Overcome The Barriers to a Negotiated Solution?" *Political Psychology,* 8, 1987, pp. 347–63; and Herbert C. Kelman, "Contributions of an Unofficial Conflict Resolution Effort to the Israeli-Palestinian Breakthrough," *Negotiation Journal,* 11, 1995, pp. 19–27.

48. Allister Sparks, *Tomorrow is Another: The Inside Story of South Africa's Road to Change* (Chicago: University of Chicago Press, 1995).

49. David Laitin, "National Revivals and Violence," *Archives Europeennes de Sociologie,* 36, 1995, pp. 3–43; and David Laitin, *Identity in Formation: The Russian-Speaking Populations in the Near Abroad* (Ithaca, NY: Cornell University Press, 1998).

50. Malcolm Gladwell, *The Tipping Point: How Little Things Can Make a Big Difference* (Boston: Little, Brown, 2000).

51. We have little good data on public opinion and its dynamics in conflict zones. However, surveys from Northern Ireland and the Middle East in recent years suggest that people are often "inconsistent" in that many express strong distrust of the other side and its leaders while supporting a peaceful settlement of the conflict. There is also some evidence that opinion is very volatile and

there are strong reactions to recent events such as movements toward peace as well as violent incidents that can overwhelm long-held positions.

52. Herbert C. Kelman, "Israelis and Palestinians: Psychological Prerequisites for Mutual Acceptance," *International Security*, 3, 1978, pp. 162–186; and Kelman, 1987, op. cit.

53. Springbok is a rugby team that for many epitomized white supremacy during the apartheid regime. Mandela's action, and the response to it, clearly signaled a new relationship in the country.

54. In divided societies, there are few shared symbols and rituals and often those that are strongly positive to one group have a completely opposite meaning for the other side. Examples of this are the Confederate flag in the southern United States for blacks and whites, and Independence Day in Israel which is called the *Nakba* ("catastrophe") by Palestinians.

55. Ross, 2001, op. cit.

56. Joyce Neu and Vamik Volkan, "Developing a Methodology for Conflict Prevention: The Case of Estonia," Atlanta: The Carter Center, 1999. Montville describes a "walk though history" which involves members from different groups visiting contested places from the past and explaining to each other what it is that is so emotionally important about the site and events that took place there for their own community. Joseph Montville, "Reconciliation as Realpolitik: Facing the Burdens of History in Political Conflict Resolution," in Ho-Won Jeong, ed., *Conflict Resolutions, Dynamics, Process and Structure* (Burlington, VT: Ashgate, 1999).

20. Ordinary Feelings, Extraordinary Events: Moral Complexity in 9/11, by Rajeev Bhargava

1. See Todd Gitlin, "The Ordinariness of American Feelings," OpenDemocracy, September, 2001, www.opendemocracy.net/forum/document_details.asp?CatID=98&DocID=723.

2. Ibid.

3. On the distinction and the relationship between ideology and political theory, see M. Freeden, *Ideologies and Political Theory* (Oxford: Clarendon Press, 1996).

4. On these issues, I have benefited from discussion on transnational justice with Thomas Pogge.

5. The article, sent by email by a friend, is published in *The American Prospect*, Volume 12, no. 18, October 22, 2001. Available online at www.prospect.org/print/V12/18/walzer-m.html.

6. Of course, there is a third agent recognized by Walzer, i.e., the people whom the terrorists allegedly represent. But they are not always political active, and hence not political agents in the sense in which I use the term.

7. See J. Murphie in Jeffrie Murphy and Jean Hampton, *Forgiveness and Mercy* (Cambridge, UK: Cambridge University Press, 1990).

8. On this, see Paul Rogers's insightful pieces on the war in Afghanistan in *OpenDemocracy*. In his December 10, 2001 piece, "The Tenth Week of the War," he writes "The casualties in the Afghanistan war are already likely to be well above the level of September 11 atrocities (3,000–4,000), with many of them civilians." www.opendemocracy.net/forum/document_details.asp?CatID=103&DocID=889.

9. A word on these intellectuals: Many of them remain personally committed to the best ethical ideals developed in the West and are close cultural cousins of a typical Western intellectual. In all probability, they are not even liked by the people whose message they so earnestly carry. Culturally estranged, they appear shallow and hypocritical to them. In aligning themselves with the op-

pressed, and in trying to communicate their feelings, these intellectuals sow in themselves the seeds of a permanent schizophrenia.

21. Close Encounters: Islam, Modernity, and Violence, *by Nilüfer Göle*

1. I would like to thank Lauren Berlant and Elizabeth Povinelli for inviting me to give a talk on September 11 in the workshop on "Violence and Redemption" at the University of Chicago, November 2001. A shorter version of this article was published in French in *Confluences Méditerranée*, 2001–2002. I owe special thanks to Levent Yilmaz, Soli Ozel, and Ludwig Amman for their valuable comments.

2. Hassan Mneimneh and Kanan Makiya, "Manual for a 'Raid,' " *New York Review of Books*, January 17, 2002.

3. Reinhart Koselleck, *Le Futur Passé, Contribution à la sémantique futur des temps historiques*, translated from German by Jochen Hoock and Marie-Claire Hoock (Paris: EHESS Press, 1990).

4. David Frisby, *Fragments of Modernity: Theories of Modernity in the Work of Simmel, Kracauer, and Benjamin* (Cambridge, UK: Polity, 1985), p. 6.

5. Jacques Revel, "Micro-analyse et construction du social," in *Jeux d' échelles, La micro-analyse à l'expérience*, Revel, ed., (Paris: Gallimard, Seuil, 1996).

6. Such a perspective on anger and injustice is not exclusively developed by social scientists, but also by literary figures. See for example the article written by the novelist Orhan Pamuk, "The Anger of the Damned," *New York Review of Books*, November 15, 2001.

7. *Sign Posts* is the title of a book written by an Egyptian radical Islamist, Sayyid Qotb, which became the most popular blueprint for radicalization of political Islam and was widely read among the Islamist youth of all Muslim countries during the 1970s.

8. Michel Wieviorka, "Reflexions sur le 11 Septembre et ses suites," in *Confluences Méditerranée*, No. 40, 2001–2002, p. 27–40.

9. Talal Asad, *Genealogies of Religion* (Baltimore and London: John Hopkins University Press, 1993), p. 219.

10. For a detailed analysis of *Jihad*, both as an outcome of history and doctrine, cf. Alfred Morabia, *Le Gihad dans l'Islam medieval* (Paris: Albin Michel, 1993).

11. H. Mnemneh, and K. Makiya, op. cit.

12. Michel Wieviorka, op. cit.

13. Eric Darton, *Divided We Stand: A Biography of New York's World Trade Center* (New York: Basic Books, 1999), p. 124.

14. Ibid., p. 118.

15. Under the rubric "Portraits of Grief" in *New York Times*.

16. Darton, op. cit., p. 119.

17. René Girard, *La Violence et le Sacré* (Paris: Bernard Grasset, 1972), p. 59–88.

18. Mary Douglas, *Purity and Danger: An Analysis of Concepts of Pollution and Taboo* (London: Routledge and Kegan Paul, 1966).

19. H. Mnemneh, and K. Makiya, op. cit.; and *Le Monde*, October 2, 2001.

20. Darton, op. cit., p. 128.

21. The title of my book, *The Forbidden Modern: Civilization and Veiling* (Ann Arbor: University of Michigan Press, 1996).

22. Nilüfer Göle, "Ingénieurs islamistes et étudiantes voilées en Turquie," *Intellectuels et militants de l'Islam contemporain,* Gilles Kepel and Yann Richard, eds., Seuil, Paris, 1990.

23. A term used by Farhad Khosrokhavar, "Les nouveaux martyrs d'Allah," *Le Monde* October 2, 2001.

24. Dick Howard, "Quand l'Amerique rejoint tragiquement le monde," in *Esprit,* Paris, October 2001.

25. Richard Powers, "The Smile," *New York Times,* September 23, 2001.

26. Reminding us of the photography work of Guy Peellaert. See Guy Peellaert and Nik Cohn, *20th Century Dreams* (New York: Alfred A. Knopf, 1999).

22. America and the World: The Twin Towers as Metaphor, by Immanuel Wallerstein

1. This essay originated as the Charles R. Lawrence II Memorial Lecture delivered at Brooklyn College, December 5, 2001.

2. Published in *Theory and Society,* XXI, 1, February 1992, pp. 1–28.

3. The authors are Jerry L. Martin and Anne Neal.

4. "Multiple Kingdoms," *London Review of Books,* July 19, 2001, p. 23.

5. Chinua Achebe, *Home and Exile* (New York: Anchor Books, 2000), p. 91.

6. Slavoj Zizek, *On Belief* (New York: Routledge, 2001), p. 152.

7. *New York Times,* November 28, 2001, p. E8.

8. Stephen Jay Gould, *Full House: The Spread of Excellence from Plato to Darwin* (New York: Three Rivers Press, 1996), p. 41.

9. Ilya Prigogine, *The End of Certainty: Time, Chaos, and the New Laws of Nature* (New York: Free Press, 1997), p. 72.

23. Violence and Home: Afghan Women's Experience of Displacement, by Saba Gul Khattak

1. A much shorter version of this chapter has appeared under the title "Home as place and home as space: Afghan women's experience of displacement" in *Development* 45:1 (forthcoming).

2. Farrukh Saleem, "Stop the bombing, please" in *The News,* November 4, 2001.

3. There are some excellent accounts though; e.g., Carolyn Nordstrom, *A Different Kind of War Story* (Philadelphia: University of Pennsylvania Press, 1997); Patricia Lawrence, in Veena Das, Arthur Kleinman, Mamphela Rampheles, and Pamela Reynolds, eds., *Violence and Subjectivity* (Berkeley: University of California Press, 2000); and Pamela Reynolds in Das, et al. (ibid).

4. See Laura L. O'Toole and Jessica R. Schiffman, *Gender Violence: Interdisciplinary Perspectives* (New York: NYU Press, 1997) for a comprehensive history of the issue as well as other issues related to domestic violence in section 3, (pp. 243–304).

5. I am grateful to Farzana Bari, Women's Studies Center, Quaid e Azam University, Islamabad, who pointed out that I was looking at the home in a very positive way, whereas the home is not always a positive space in women's lives. While I acknowledge that even in the present context Afghan refugee women feel that the home has become a place of confinement and imprisonment for them, there are also other overriding aspects of the issue that are generally neglected and therefore not a part of the dominant discourse. Also, because I have let women's voices guide

me rather than imposing my own narrative upon them, I have tried to analyze the themes that surface in their interviews.

6. These interviews with Afghan refugee women were conducted as part of an SDPI project entitled, "Women, security and conflict in Pakistan."

7. The Mujahedeen (literally freedom fighters) were a coalition of seven Pakistan-based Afghan political parties who took over from the Najibullah regime. The coalition of extremely conservative and centrist religious parties could not last as there was internal dissent over who could exercise power.

8. The Taliban (literally "students of religion"), supported and trained by the Pakistani Interservices Intelligence Agency (ISI), occupied more than 80 percent of the country and imposed a very conservative (mis)interpretation of Islam upon the country. Afghan women were affected in the most disastrous manner by these policies that restricted them to the home and denied them the right to earn a livelihood or acquire education.

9. Trinh T. Minh-ha, "Other than myself/my other self," in *Travellers' Tales: Narratives of Home and Displacement,* George Robertson, Melinda Mash, Lisa Tickner, Jon Bird, Barry Curtis, and Tim Putnam, eds., (London and New York: Routledge, 1994), p. 12.

10. Rosemary Marangoly George, *The Politics of Home: Postcolonial Relocations and Twentieth Century Fiction* (Berkeley: University of California Press, 1999), p. 173.

11. Ibid., p. 19.

12. Trinh T. Minh-ha, op. cit., p. 15.

13. Comparisons of the home with the grave occur in several interviews, e.g., the description below highlights the same feeling of being caught in a space from where escape becomes impossible in the face of unpredictable and long periods of rocket attacks.

14. The reference is to the *Mujahedeen* Prime Minister, Engineer Hikmatyar. Thus the implication is that ironically enough, the government itself was attacking and destroying the Afghan people.

15. I borrow the usage of this word from Katherine Pratt Ewing who writes about the denial of a narrative and women's inability to narrativize Turkish Muslim womanhood. Katherine Pratt Ewing, "The violence of non-recognition: becoming a 'conscious' Muslim woman in Turkey" in *Cultures under Siege: Collective Violence and Trauma,* Antonius C. G. Robben and Marcelo M. Suarez-Orozco, eds. (Cambridge: Cambridge University Press, 2000).

24. Memorializing Absence, *by Marita Sturken*

1. I would like to thank Dana Polan and Amelia Jones for insightful comments on earlier versions of this essay, and participants in my graduate seminar on Cultural Studies in Communication whose discussions of September 11 were very helpful in thinking about these issues.

2. For an in-depth analysis of the involvement of survivors and families in the design process of the Oklahoma City Memorial, see Edward T. Linenthal, *The Unfinished Bombing: Oklahoma City in American Memory* (New York: Oxford University Press, 2001).

3. Michel de Certeau, "Walking in the City," *The Practice of Everyday Life,* trans. Steven Rendall (Berkeley: University of California Press, 1984), pp. 91–92.

4. Jim Dwyer, "The Memorial That Vanished," *The New York Times Magazine* (September 23, 2001), p. 81.

5. "To Rebuild or Not: Architects Respond," *New York Times Magazine* (September 23, 2001), p. 81.

6. Ibid.

7. Philippe de Montebello, "The Iconic Power of an Artifact," *New York Times* (September 25, 2001), p. A29.

8. For an analysis of the memory debates and memorials of Hiroshima, see Lisa Yoneyama, *Hiroshima Traces: Time, Space, and the Dialectics of Memory* (Berkeley: University of California Press, 1999).

9. The project was begun immediately after September 11 by two artists, Julian LaVerdiere and Paul Myoda, who were working on an art project about the World Trade Center before the attacks, and two architects, John Bennett and Gustavo Bonevardi, who had also conceived a similar idea. They were later joined by architect Richard Nash Gould and lighting designer Paul Marantz. The project was produced by the Municipal Art Society and Creative Time, a public art organization. See the cover of the *New York Times Magazine* (September 23, 2001); "Update" *New York Times Magazine* (October 7, 2001), 12; and the Creative Time website: http://www.creativetime.org/towers/.

10. Marianne Hirsch, "The Day Time Stopped," *The Chronicle of Higher Education* (January 25, 2002).

11. In an essay about her husband's death on his second day of work at the World Trade Center, A. R. Torres writes "my tragedy is personal, but I am forced to discover its terrible dimensions on the nightly news, in the daily papers and in every publication on the newsstand. It may even be that I was forced to witness my husband's final moments on the printed page." She goes on to describe looking at the photographs of the figures falling from the towers and seeing one figure hanging from the building, about to jump, who she believes was her husband. She writes, "There he was, grim-expressioned, ready to sky-dive with no parachute." A. R. Torres, "The Reluctant Icon," Salon.com (January 25, 2002), www.salon.com/mwt/feature/2002/01/25/widow_speaks/.

12. See Marshall Sella, "Missing: How a Grief Ritual is Born," *The New York Times Magazine* (October 7, 2001), p. 48–51.

13. Roland Barthes, *Camera Lucida: Reflections on Photography,* trans. Richard Howard (New York: Hill and Wang, 1981), p. 15.

14. In "The Day Time Stopped," her essay on the role of photography in relation to September 11, Marianne Hirsch describes the various reasons given by rescue personnel to prohibit photographs in the first weeks: because the site is a graveyard, because it is a crime scene, and because Mayor Giuliani said so.

15. Michael Warner, "The Mass Public and the Mass Subject," in *The Phantom Public Sphere,* edited by Bruce Robbins (Minneapolis: University of Minnesota Press, 1993), p. 248.

16. Columbia University has established a World Trade Center Archive for documents related to September 11.

17. The "Portraits of Grief" are collected on *New York Times* website and in *Portraits 9/11/01: The Collected "Portraits of Grief"* (New York: Times Books, 2002).

18. A. R. Torres, "The Reluctant Icon."

19. Daniel Harris, "The Kitschification of September 11," Salon.com (January 25, 2002), www.salon.com/news/feature/2002/01/25/kitsch/.

20. Kevin Flynn, "Firefighters Block a Plan for Statue in Their Honor," *New York Times* (January 18, 2002), p. A21.

21. John Ydstie, host, Leon Wynter, reporter, "Story on the New York City Fire Department," *Weekend Edition Saturday,* National Public Radio, February 16, 2002.

22. See Marita Sturken, *Tangled Memories: The Vietnam War, the AIDS Epidemic, and the Politics of Remembering* (Berkeley: University of California Press, 1997), Chapter 2.

23. One family held a wedding at the Oklahoma City Memorial with a photograph of the bride's father, who was killed in the bombing, on the chair that bears his name.

24. Dan Barry, "As September 11 Widows Unite, Grief Finds a Political Voice," *New York Times* (November 25, 2001), p. A1.

25. Charles Griswold, "The Vietnam Veterans Memorial and the Washington Mall: Philosophical Thoughts on Political Iconography," *Critical Inquiry* 12 (Summer 1986), pp. 688–719.

CONTRIBUTORS

Seyla Benhabib is the Eugene Meyer Professor of Political Science and Philosophy at Yale University.

Rajeev Bhargava is a professor of Political Theory and Indian Political Thought at the University of Delhi and is honorary director, Program of Advanced Social and Political Theory, Center for the Study of Developing Societies, Delhi.

Craig Calhoun is the president of the Social Science Research Council and a professor of Sociology and History at New York University.

Bruce Cumings is the Norman and Edna Freehling Professor of History at the University of Chicago.

Dorothy E. Denning is the Patricia and Patrick Callahan Family Professor of Computer Science and the director of the Georgetown Institute for Information Assurance at Georgetown University.

James Der Derian is a Research Professor of International Relations at Brown University and a professor of Political Science at the University of Massachusetts at Amherst.

Ronald Dworkin is the Patricia and Patrick Callahan Family Professor of Law and Philosophy at New York University and the Quain Professor of Jurisprudence at University College, London.

Barry Eichengreen is the George C. Pardee and Helen N. Pardee Professor of Economics and Political Science at the University of California, Berkeley.

Jack A. Goldstone is a professor of Sociology at the University of California, Davis.

Nilüfer Göle is a professor of Sociology at the Ecole des Hautes Etudes en Sciences Sociales in Paris.

Robert W. Hefner is a professor of Anthropology and the associate director of the Institute for the Study of Economic Culture (ISEC) at Boston University.

David Held holds the Graham Wallas Chair in Political Science at the London School of Economics.

Mark Juergensmeyer is the director of Global and International Studies and a professor of Sociology and Religious Studies at the University of California, Santa Barbara.

Mary Kaldor is a professor of Political Science and the director of the Programme on Global Civil Society at the London School of Economics.

Robert O. Keohane is a professor of Political Science at Duke University.

Saba Gul Khattak is the deputy director of and research fellow at the Sustainable Development Policy Institute in Pakistan.

Timur Kuran is a professor of Economics and Law and King Faisal Professor of Islamic Thought and Culture at the University of Southern California.

Barbara D. Metcalf is a professor of History at the University of California, Davis.

Peter Alexander Meyers is a Chercheur Associé of the Groupe de Sociologie Politique et Morale (EHESS, Paris) and Maître de Conférences at the Université de Lille 3.

Paul Price is editor of the Social Science Research Council.

Marc Howard Ross is the William Rand Kenan, Jr. Professor of Political Science at Bryn Mawr College.

Saskia Sassen is the Ralph Lewis Professor of Sociology at the University of Chicago.

Marita Sturken is an associate professor at the Annenberg School for Communication at the University of Southern California.

Ashley S. Timmer is the program director of the Program in Applied Economics at the Social Science Research Council.

Immanuel Wallerstein is a Senior Research Scholar at Yale University.

Susan L. Woodward is a professor of Political Science at the Graduate Center of the City University of New York.

Aristide R. Zolberg is a professor of Political Science at the New School University.

INDEX

ABC (television), 9
abortion activism, 27, 38
Abouhalima, Mahmud, 34, 35–36
Abraham, Spencer, 295
Abu Sayef, 149
Academic inquiry into 9/11
  American understanding of history, 201–3
  and boundaries of infosphere, 178
  and counterterror dangers, 187–90
  and exceptionality of 9/11, 178–81
  and languages, 210–11, 405n19
  and media, 181–89
  and network wars, 181–84, 186–89,
    402nn19, 20
  nihilism and meaning, 183, 198–99
  and social sciences, 177–78, 189, 199,
    209–11
  and virtuous wars, 180–81, 189
Achebe, Chinua, 355
Acheson, Dean, 208
Ackerman, Bruce, 98
Adams, John, 259
Adorno, Theodor, 249, 374, 381
Advani, L. K., 38
Afghanistan
  agriculture and development in, 130,
    399n22, 400nn28, 29
  communist regime in, 54, 144–46, 364–65
  and culture of violence, 165
  and emergence of Taliban, 62–64, 145–46,
    389n28
  and Islamic terrorism, 144–46, 148
  Islamist education in, 155
  jihad movements, 54
  madrasas in, 62–63
  post-conflict operations in, 222, 226, 227
  as postmodern nation-state, 244
  and postwar administration, 215–16,
    229–32, 406n15
  refugees of, 62–63, 364–71

  Soviet invasion of, 81, 144, 250
  state building in, 156
  UN mission in, 213, 215, 216
  as UN test case for assistance, 214, 406n8
  and U.S. foreign policy, 81, 142, 206
  See also Afghanistan, post-9/11 war in; Al
    Qaeda; Taliban; women of Afghanistan
    and concept of home
Afghanistan, post-9/11 war in
  as "casualty-free war," 168, 169, 175–76
  and conflict prevention, 223–24
  and declaration of war, 27, 184, 243
  economic assistance and strategy, 226–29
  and international security presence, 86,
    219–20, 407n24
  and lessons of 1990s, 223–24, 226–34, 237
  local fighters used in, 218, 225, 407n18
  long-term consequences of, 205
  meaning of American bombing, 361
  and national sovereignty, 243–44
  and noncombatant casualties, 181, 329
  and post-Taliban government, 215–16,
    229–32, 406n15
  and postwar policy in, 131, 132–33,
    220–28, 409nn41, 42
  regional dimension of, 232–34, 410n62
  swiftness of, 205
  uncertain resolution of, 176, 329–30
  U.S. and Great Britain, 86
  U.S. and UN, 86, 219–20, 234–35
  U.S. military tactics, 218, 219–20, 224–26,
    407nn18, 22, 24
Africa, 110, 126, 233. See also individual
  countries
African National Congress (South Africa),
  141, 273, 315
African Trade Insurance Agency, 113
Ahl-i Hadith (Islamic reformist school), 57,
  390n31
airline travel, 124–25

airplane hijackings, 95
Al Jazeera, 8–9, 30, 184, 185, 344, 403n29
Al Qaeda
  as antiglobalists, 39
  bin Laden and terrorist assaults on U.S.,
    149–50
  and communications technologies, 185,
    186
  cultural narrative of, 310
  and cyber terrorism, 196
  defeat of, 329
  differences from mainstream Islam, 28,
    151
  founding of, 149
  global vision of, 29–30, 34, 39
  hawala and, 67, 185
  and Islamic terrorism, 149–52, 157–58
  and Islamist party factions, 54
  recruitments by, 150, 151
  and secular world, 36, 39, 82
  sophisticated and creative operations,
    151–52
  suicidal nature of 9/11 attacks, 82
  as transnational organization, 30, 39, 150
  as united by war, 27
  war waged on, 175–76
Albright, Madeleine, 209, 322
Algeria, 27, 34, 38, 246
Algerian War (1950s), 242, 411n3
Allende, Salvador, 3, 353
American Civil Liberties Union (ACLU), 269,
  273, 291, 356, 419n65
American Council of Trustees and Alumni
  (ACTA), 351
American Jewish Committee, 296
American Prospect (magazine), 326
American Red Cross, 7
American self-image
  and advanced technology, 346–47
  and American hegemony, 352, 358
  certainty and uncertainty, 357–60
  and dialogue with nations, 358–59
  effects of terrorist attacks on, 348–51
  as greatest country in world, 346–47
  and high culture, 348
  ideals and privilege, 355–57, 359
  and "less-ness" of rest of world, 346–48
  and liberty, freedom, and democracy, 347
  liberty and security issues, 350
  military superiority, 11, 352, 354
  and moral complexity of 9/11, 322–23

  as most civilized, 348
  as most efficient, 347
  nationalism, 10, 346
  'no reservations' requirement, 351
  others' perspectives on, 11–12
  and traditional values, 359
  and understanding of history, 201–3
  and U.S. foreign policy, 352–55
  and war on terrorism, 350–51
  and weapons of other nations, 354–55
  and world power, 352–55, 358–59
America's Most Wanted (television), 186
Anderson, Benedict, 43, 44–45
André, Maj. John, 279
Annan, Kofi, 235
anthrax scare, 6, 14
Anti-Ballistic Missile Treaty (1972), 204
Arab-American Institute, 295
Arab Americans, 295–96
Arab nationalism, secular, 142
Arafat, Yasir, 31, 34, 147, 199, 315
Arendt, Hannah, 244, 417n46
Argentina, 109, 114, 126, 127, 128, 396n12
Aristotle, 255, 258, 413n4
Asahara, Shoko, 28
Ashcroft, Attorney General John, 184, 247,
  276, 277, 291, 357, 419n2
Asian Development Bank, 226
Ataturk, Mustafa Kemal, 43, 249
Atef, Muhammed, 149
Atta, Mohammed, 5, 246, 341
Aum Shinrikyo, 29–30, 38, 194
Ausaf (newspaper), 196
Ayodya, mosque at, 423n13
Al-Azhar school (Cairo), 34, 388n7

Ba'ath regimes, 249, 250, 252
Bachelard, Gaston, 340
Baer, Robert, 405n20
Bangladesh, 65, 116
Barber, Benjamin R., 417n46, 418n55
"Barelvi" (Islamist school), 57, 388n11,
  390n31
Barr, Rep. Bob, 275
Barthes, Roland, 378, 379
Basque ETA-PM, 195, 245, 280
Baudrillard, Jean, 168, 183
BBC, 8
Beirut, 207
Benhabib, Seyla, 106
Benjamin, Walter, 177

Bennett, John, 431n9
Berra, Yogi, 187, 403n34
Bhindranwale, Sant Jarnail Singh, 38
Bhutto, Benazir, 62
bin Laden, Osama
  on American moral depravity, 348–49
  appropriation of American public sphere,
    200, 267
  atavism and irrelevance of, 203
  attraction to violence and bravado, 200
  consensus regarding, 314
  contrasted to Cold War enemies, 202
  and cyber terrorism, 191, 193, 195, 196
  as defender of faith, 36
  fatawa of, 104, 389n19
  and Islamic nationalism, 43
  nihilism of message, 245–46
  as not representative of Islam, 28
  and Palestine conflict, 199
  and Saudi Arabia, 199–200
  study in West, 9
  and Taliban, 53, 63–64, 342
  television persona, 200
  videotaped speeches of, 163, 184, 188, 199,
    242, 403n29
  See also Al Qaeda
biological weapons, 152, 354–55
Biological Weapons Convention, 174
Black September (1970), 249
Blair, Prime Minister Tony, 13, 172, 203, 204,
  219, 346
Bonevardi, Gustavo, 431n9
Bonn process and postwar Afghanistan,
  215–16, 219, 222, 225, 228, 229, 230–31,
  406n15
"border patrol" and immigration policy, 286,
  287, 288–90, 292–95, 299
Bosnia and Herzegovina
  and Al Qaeda, 151
  and citizens' defensive militias, 165
  economic assistance, 22, 227, 409n51,
    410n53
  lessons of, 221, 223, 227, 230, 231, 232, 233,
    236
  militarized gangs of, 107
  "new war" and, 95, 164, 165
  as postmodern nation-state, 244
  postwar government in, 225
  and Powell Doctrine, 217
  regional dimension of conflict, 233
  state building in, 156

  UN peacekeeping failures in, 214, 215, 221,
    406n15
  U.S. operations in, 217, 218, 407n18
  and virtuous war, 180
  and war crimes tribunals, 94
  See also Yugoslavia
Bourdieu, Pierre, 30, 33, 36, 37
Brahimi, Lakhdar, 213, 214–15, 216, 222, 225,
  228, 234–35, 236, 406n5
Brahimi Report, 213–16, 219, 220, 232, 237
Branch Davidian sect, 38
Brazil, 126
Breyer, Justice Stephen, 278
British Department for International
  Development (DFID), 221, 408n29
Brodie, Bernard, 79
Buchanan, Patrick, 287, 298
Buddhism, 28
Buddhist statues, Taliban destruction of, 337,
  389n28, 423n13
Burgiba, Habib, 249
Burnside, Craig, 132
Bush, Pres. George H. W., 181, 206
Bush, Pres. George W.
  and Al Qaeda and Taliban prisoners, 247,
    276
  amazement at Muslim hatred, 320
  and "Bush Doctrine," 217, 405n4
  certainty of, 357
  Crusades reference, 319
  declaration of war, 27, 184, 243
  on evil and axis of evil, 178, 217, 405n4,
    407n16
  hubristic statements, 266, 418n60
  on immigration, 286–87, 288, 294–95, 296
  and Israel-Palestine conflict, 12
  joking behavior, 183
  language of, 100
  and military tribunals, 268, 274–76, 277,
    280, 420n17
  post-attack State of the Union speech, 122,
    178
  religionization of 9/11, 29, 212, 418n60
  trade liberalization and fast-track, 129
  USA PATRIOT Act signing, 291
  and war on terrorism, 12, 175
  war statements, binaries in, 184
Bush administration
  and Al Qaeda and Taliban prisoners, 247,
    275–76, 304
  and balance of powers, 268

Bush administration (*cont.*)
and defense budget, 204, 405n9
and extension of war on terrorism to Iraq,
12, 86, 204
foreign aid budget, 135
and international institutions, 83, 86
and missile defense, 204
multilateralism of, 14, 204
post-9/11 foreign policy, 14, 84, 85–86,
203–5, 236
and state building in Afghanistan, 156
and UN role, 83, 84, 85–86
unilateralism of, 14, 83, 203, 204
and war on terrorism, 3, 102, 127, 203–4,
316, 350–51

Canada, 124, 172–73, 221, 293–94, 295,
408n29
Cantor and Fitzgerald, 14
capitalism, 68, 125, 249–52, 338, 412n16,
417n45. *See also* globalization and world
economy
Carnegie Commission on Preventing Deadly
Conflict, 223, 408n37
Carter administration, 147
Casanova, Jose, 40
Cebrowski, Arthur, 187–88
Center for Constitutional Rights (New York
City), 269
Center for the Study of Terrorism and
Irregular Warfare at the Naval
Postgraduate School (NPS), 194–95
Centers for Disease Control (CDC), 6
Central Asia, 206, 208, 235
Central Intelligence Agency (CIA), 117–18,
210–11, 224, 235, 288, 325
Chang, Nancy, 269
charitable organizations, 7
Chechnya, 100, 170, 176, 195, 244
chemical weapons, 152, 354–55
Cheney, Lynne, 351
Chicago Council on Foreign Relations,
392n18, 405n15
Chile, 353
China, 3, 169, 170, 203, 204, 286, 316, 354
Chomsky, Noam, 351
Chrétien, Prime Minister Jean, 294
Christianity, 28, 29–30, 33, 38
Churchill, Winston, 83
Civil War, American, 201
Claude, Inis L., 84

Clausewitz, 159, 163, 203
Clinton, Pres. Bill, 117, 119
Clinton administration, 121, 204, 236, 286,
405n9
CNN, 9, 30, 185, 201, 403n29, 419n3
CNN Presents, "The Enemy Within," 419n3
Coalition Against Trafficking in Women, 117
Code Red worm, 192, 193
Cold War
analogies of 9/11 to, 201–2
arms control in, 173
and challenge to secular state, 37
and hybrid terrorist movements, 141
intelligence in, 210
and "liberalism of fear," 89
and modern war, 159–60
and new global war, 27–28
peacekeeping roles in, 171
and Revolution in Military Affairs, 166
Colley, Linda, 352
Collins, Joseph, 226
Commonwealth of Independent States (CIS),
171
communism, 68, 140–41, 142, 144–46, 156,
208, 353
Computer Emergency Response Team
Coordination Center (CERT/CC), 192
Condit, Gary, 200
Conrad, Joseph, 198
Constitution, U.S., 264, 269, 278, 356, 413n7,
421n22
Convention on Offenses and Certain Other
Acts Committed on Board Aircraft
(1963), 95
Cooper, Richard, 399n17
Council on American-Islamic Relations,
"Mosque Report," 295–96
Coventry Cathedral (England), 377
Crusades, 12, 150, 319
Cuban Missile Crisis, 201
Cumings, Bruce, 237, 411n71
Custer, Gen. George, 309
cyber terrorism, 5, 191–97

The Daily Telegraph, 395n4
Dal Khalsa ("army of the faithful"), 33
Dallaire, Gen. Romeo, 172
D'Andrade, Roy, 423n8
Danner, Mark, 207–8, 209
Darton, Eric, 339–40
Datz, Giselle, 396n16

Daud, Mohammed, 144
Davis, Natalie Zemon, 32
Dayton accord, 215, 230, 236
de Certeau, Michel, 375
de Montebello, Philippe, 376, 377
The Death of the West (Buchanan), 287
death penalty and military tribunals, 284, 350
debt crisis, 106–7, 108–14
   debts and debt-service ratios, 110–11,
     110t, 396n14
   and despair, 108–11
   and globalization, 109, 395nn7–10,
     396nn11, 12
   and IMF, 109, 111, 114, 395n7
   and inter-state/international banks, 114
   and lenders of first resort, 113–14, 396n16
   remedies for, 113–14
   social costs, 111–13, 112t, 396n14
   and structural adjustments, 109, 395nn7–9
   and trafficking in people, 113, 396n14
   and unemployment, 111, 113, 396n14
"Defending Civilization: How Our
   Universities Are Failing America and
   What Can Be Done About It" (ACTA),
   351
defense spending, 204, 405n9
Defensive Action, 38
democracy and democratization
   of American public life, 45–46
   and authoritarianism, 50
   and capitalism, 417n45
   challenges of 9/11, 14–15, 246–47
   and equality, 263, 417n44
   and freedom, 263–64
   of Muslim society and culture, 45–50, 51
   and politics, 262–65, 416n41, 417n46
   and religion in public life, 47
   and sovereignty, 243–44
   and speech, 264–65
   violence and, 262, 417n42
   and war, 14–15, 246–47
Democracy in America (Tocqueville),
   260–61
Denmark, 408n29
Deobandism
   and Islamist movements, 53–58, 387n2,
     388n7
   origin of, 53, 55–58
   and politics, 57–58, 64–65
   present-day schools, 58, 388n14
   and Sufism, 56, 60

   and Tablighi Jama'at, 53–54, 58–59
   and Taliban, 53, 62–63, 387n2, 388n14,
     389n15
Der Derian, James, 168
development
   "developmentalist" policies, 354
   humanitarian, 226–29, 409n45
   and post-conflict operations, 221–22, 227,
     408nn29, 30
   See also foreign aid
Development Assistance Committee (DAC)
   of the OECD, 221
Diller, Elizabeth, 376
Dispatchers (hacker group), 191
Dollar, David, 132
Donini, Antonio, 213
Dostum, Gen. Abdel Rashid, 225
Due Process Clause, 278, 421n22
Dulles, John Foster, 314, 315
Dworkin, Ronald, 247

Eagle Forum, 269, 419n65
East African embassy bombings (1998), 53,
   63, 150
East Timor, 172, 215, 216
Economic Community of West African States
   (ECOWAS), 171
economy. *See* globalization and world
   economy; Islam and economics
education in the Islamic world, 44–45, 71,
   154–56. *See also madrasas*
Egypt, 38, 49, 104, 200, 249
   Islamist movements in, 44, 54, 144, 148,
     155
   and religious terrorism, 27, 34, 142, 143,
     149
Egyptian Brotherhood, 246
Egyptian Jihad, 150
Eickelman, Dale F., 45
Eisenhower, Pres. Dwight, 189, 208
embassy bombings in East Africa (1998), 53,
   63, 150
Enlightenment, 37
entertainment industry, 30, 186–87, 189,
   251–52, 403n33
Estonia, 317
ETA (Spain), 140, 141
Euben, Roxanne, 412n11
Europe
   demographic deficits and immigration,
     115, 116, 397n24

Europe (*cont.*)
Marshall Plan and postwar recovery of, 88, 131, 132, 248, 399n24
modern urban civilization of, 209
post-9/11 role, 217
reactions to 9/11 in, 13
terrorist cells in, 9
See also individual countries
European Commission, 227
European Convention for the Protection of Human Rights and Fundamental Freedoms, 96, 275
European Union (EU), 13, 96, 97, 294
Evans, Peter, 50
Ex Parte Quirin ("Saboteurs Case"), 278–80

Fagen, Richard R., 314
Fanon, Frantz, 34
FARC (Revolutionary Armed Forces of Columbia), 140, 195
Farouk, King (Egypt), 199
fatawa (judgments), 56, 104, 389n19
Fateh, 34
FBI, 279, 283, 288, 290–91, 292, 293, 296, 405n19
fedayyeen, 250
Federalist Papers, 415nn25, 26, 28
Feingold, Sen. Russ, 281
Feinstein, Sen. Dianne, 293
Ferren, Bran, 188
Fifth Amendment, Due Process Clause, 278, 421n22
finance industry and effects of 9/11, 6–7
Finley, David J., 314
First Amendment, 264, 356
Fisher, Nigel, 222
Fleischer, Ari, 183
foreign aid
and Bush administration, 131, 135
and conditionality, 227, 228–29
and development community, 221–22, 226–27, 234–35, 408nn29, 30
donor competition/rivalries, 226–27, 234–35
economic assistance strategies for Afghanistan, 131–33, 226–29
failures of, 132
and globalization, 131–33, 134–35
and human rights, 97
and humanitarian development, 226–29, 409n45
as instrument against terrorism, 135
and Marshall Plan, 131, 132, 135, 248, 399n24
politics before aid, 227–28, 409n41, 410n53
and post-conflict operations, 221–22, 227, 408nn29, 30
speed of assistance, 227, 409n51
and weak governments, 132
foreign direct investment (FDI), 125–27, 398n12
Foreign Terrorist Tracking Force, 288
founders, American, 259–60, 415nn25, 26, 28, 417n47
Fox, Vicente, 124, 287, 295
Framework for World Bank Involvement in Post-Conflict Countries (World Bank), 221
France, 32, 220, 354, 392n25, 424n20
Frankfurter, Justice Felix, 279
Franklin, Benjamin, 259
Franks, Gen. Tommy, 220, 407n24
Free Trade Area of the Americas, 121
Friedman, Thomas, 417n45
fundamentalism, 46–47, 53–55, 412n11.
See also Islamic reform movements

Gandhi, Mahatma, 58
Garzón, Baltazar, 275
Gaspard, Francoise, 252
GATT, 118, 119, 354
Gaza Jericho Agreement of 1994, 146–47
Gellner, Ernest, 43
Gemeaha, Sheik Muhammad, 296
Geneva Conventions
and military tribunals, 276, 281, 420n8
and post-World War II humanitarian law, 174
and prisoners of post-9/11, 223, 247, 276, 304, 311, 420n8
and USA PATRIOT Act, 276, 420n8
Genocide Convention of 1948, 174
George, Rosemary, 366–67
Germany, 13, 206, 207, 227, 392n25, 408n29
GForce Pakistan (cyber terrorism group), 191
Ghani, Ashraf, 229, 409n41
Giddens, Anthony, 159
Global Survival Network, 118, 397n32
globalization
and cosmopolitan principles, 105
defining, 78–79

and developing countries, 133–34, 400n33
and "developmentalist" policies, 354
and entertainment industry, 30, 251–52
and geographical space, 78, 81
and globalism, 78–79
and governance, 106–20
and human rights, 94–95, 97, 101–2
and immigration, 9–10, 106–7, 114–19,
    285, 298
and informal violence, 77–91
and interdependence, 81–83, 90, 107, 111,
    117, 119, 120, 160, 392n16, 397n30
and Islam, 51–52, 73–74, 103–5, 251–52,
    312, 344
and Islamic economic system, 67–68, 69
and Islamic reform movements, 68, 73,
    104, 251–52
and Islamic technical modernization,
    251–52, 335–36, 412n16
law and justice in, 93–105
and localism, 355, 357
and moral arguments, 107, 395n5
and religious worldviews, 251–52
and responses to 9/11, 8–10, 336
and specialized multilateralisms, 118–19,
    120
and terrorism, 38–39, 107–8, 121–22,
    244–46, 335–36
U.S. role in, 121–22
and warfare, 159–76
See also globalization and world economy
globalization and world economy, 121–35
and capital flows, 126–27, 134
and debt crisis, 109, 395nn7–10, 396nn11,
    12
developing countries, 130, 133–34,
    399nn21, 22, 400n33
and economic integration, 18–19, 78–79,
    89, 97–98
effects of 9/11, 14, 121–22, 124, 134
and foreign aid, 131–33, 134–35
foreign trade, investment, and migration,
    122–24, 395n7
and free-trade areas, 132–33, 400nn28–30
and IMF, 121–22, 127–28
and immigration policy, 285, 298
and international investment, 123, 125–27,
    133, 134, 398n9, 398n12
and Islamic technical modernization,
    251–52, 412n16
predictions of economic collapse, 122, 133

and secular state, 37–38
security and, 123–24, 133, 353–54, 398n9
and trade liberalization, 128–30, 134
Gorazde, 172
Gore, Vice Pres. Al, 408n38
Gould, Richard Nash, 431n9
Gould, Stephen Jay, 357, 359
Gray, John, 121
Great Britain, 12, 13, 86, 216, 219–20, 354
Greenspan, Alan, 121
Griswold, Charles, 384
Guantánamo Bay, Cuba, 247, 275–76
The Guardian, 103, 395n4
Guatemala, 221, 222
Gulf War
    cultural narratives of, 307, 424n15
    military strategics, 168–69, 181, 206
    and Muslim resentment, 312
    and Palestinians, 249
    and Powell Doctrine, 217
    U.S. casualties, 181, 402n16
Gurr, Ted Robert, 408n38

Habermas, Jurgen, 36
hadith, 55, 56, 57, 59, 61
Hague Convention for the Suppression of
    Unlawful Seizure of Aircraft (1970), 95
Hale, David, 133
Halliday, Fred, 104
Hamas, 29, 34, 146, 147, 148, 149, 153, 242
Hamburg, David, 223
Hamilton, Alexander, 259, 260, 415n25
Hamza, Iman, 103
Haq, Ziaul, 62
Hardman, J. B. S., 418n56
Harris, Daniel, 381
Hashemi, Rahmatullah, 389n28
Havel, Vaclav, 416n40, 417n46
hawala, 67, 185, 251
Hebrew Bible, 33
Hegel, G. W. F., 260
Heidegger, Martin, 249
Hekmatyar, Gulbuddin, 388n7
Held, David, 106
Herold, Marc, 181
Herr, Michael, 181–82
Herz, John, 79–80
Hezb-i Islami, 388
Hezbollah, 148, 149, 192, 242
Hiroshima Peace Memorial Park, 377
Hirsch, Marianne, 378, 431n14

History of Political Theory (Sabine), 261
Hobbes, Thomas, 259, 263
Hollywood, 186–87, 189, 251–52, 403n33
Holsti, Ole, 314, 392n18
home. *See* women of Afghanistan and
    concept of home
"homeland security," 6
Hoover, J. Edgar, 279
Horkheimer, Max, 249
human rights
    and Afghan and Al Qaeda prisoners, 223
    and Bonn agreement, 222
    controlling war through, 173–76
    and globalization, 94–95, 97, 101–2
    and international law, 94–95, 97
    "new war" and violations of, 162, 164
    and postwar Afghanistan, 222
    and UN Declaration, 105
Human Rights Watch, 410n54, 420n8
humanitarian law, 173–76. *See also*
    peacekeeping and peace-building
Huntington, Samuel, 10, 248, 303, 312, 320,
    412n9
Hussein, Saddam, 169, 202, 208, 249

Ibn Khaldun, 41, 42
iDefense, 192
Ignatieff, Michael, 178, 182, 183
Illegal Immigration Reform and Immigrant
    Responsibility Act of 1996 (IIRIRA), 290
Ilyes Kandhlawi, Maulana Muhammad, 59
immigration, world regime of, 106–7, 114–19
    civil liberties and, 114
    and demographic deficits in global north,
        114, 115–17, 119, 396n19, 397n24
    and immigration flows, 116, 118, 119,
        396n17
    and multilateral policies, 118–19, 120
    and remittances, 116, 397n25
    and restrictive immigration, 114–15,
        397n24
    and terrorists, 9
    and trafficking in people, 107, 108, 113,
        114, 116–18, 396nn14, 15, 397n26
    See also immigration policy, U.S.
Immigration and Naturalization Service
    (INS), 278, 288, 290, 292, 293
immigration policy, U.S., 285–99
    admissions policies, 10, 285–87, 288
    anti-immigration advocacy, 287
    Arab and Muslim nationals, 292, 295–97

and "border patrol," 286, 287, 288–90,
    292–95, 299
and Canada, 293–94, 295
deportations, 291
and detentions, 291, 296–97
and global economy, 285, 298
government restraint, 287–88
and hijackers of 9/11, 285, 289, 290, 294
illegal immigration, 286, 293, 421n3,
    422n19
and "Integrated Entry and Exit Data
    System," 290, 292
and intelligence, 298–99
labor immigration, 286, 294–95
and mandatory identity documentation,
    297–98
and Mexico, 124, 286–87, 293, 294–95
post-9/11, 287–88, 290, 291, 292, 293
public opinion of, 287
and security perimeters, 294, 295
and USA PATRIOT Act, 291–92
and visa exemptions, 290, 292
and visas, 288, 290–91, 292–93
See also immigration, world regime of
India
    and American war on terrorism, 233,
        315–16
    antimodernist movements, 38
    colonial, 12, 57–58, 70
    Deobandism in, 53, 55–56, 57–58, 64, 65
    Islamist movements in, 53, 54, 55–56,
        57–58, 64, 65
    and Kashmir, 12, 13
    neo-modern militarism of, 169
    nuclear capacity, 169, 354
    and Pakistan, 315–16
    religious violence in, 27
    religious war tradition in, 33
Indonesia, 44, 46, 48–50, 51, 132, 142, 155,
    206
Institute for Creative Technology (ICT) at
    University of Southern California,
    186–87
Institute of International Economics, 121
Institute of International Finance, 125,
    398n12
institutionalist theory, 83–84, 85
intellectuals, 45, 47–49, 322–27, 330, 427n9
International Conference on Financing for
    Development (Monterrey), 135,
    408n26

International Criminal Court, 13, 94, 95, 105, 174
International Islamic Terrorism (IIT), 142–58
  Afghanistan and Mujahedeen, 144–46, 148
  aims of, 147, 149
  and Al Qaeda, 149–52, 157–58
  approaches and responses to, 152–58
  and communism, 156
  and Islamic education, 154–56
  and Islamist movements, 143–49
  military action against, 157–58
  networks of, 149
  as NGO, 156–57
  origins of, 143, 147
  and Palestine, 146–47, 152–53
  and poverty, 153–54
  and propaganda, 158
  and secular regimes, 142–43
  and state building, 156–57
  threat to U.S., 149–50, 152
International Monetary Fund (IMF), 109, 111, 114, 121–22, 127–28, 395nn7, 8, 399n17
International Red Cross, 174, 218
International Security Assistance Force (ISAF), 216, 220, 221, 226
International Tribunal at Nuremberg, 93–94
Internet. *See* cyber terrorism
intifada, 29, 146–47, 148, 242, 411n3
IRA (Irish Revolutionary Army), 140, 141, 245, 273, 280
Iran
  and Afghan groups, 144–45, 148
  antimodernism and religious nationalism, 38, 39
  democratization of, 48, 51
  and "economic Islamization," 69
  and Hezbollah, 148
  and Iraq, 148
  and Islamic terrorism, 143, 147–49
  Islamist education in, 155
  Islamist movements, 144, 147–48
  and modernizing leaders, 249
  revolution in, 29, 48, 54, 147–49, 312, 337
  secular regime, 142
  Shi'a minority, 148
  and Taliban, 63
Iranian revolution, 29, 48, 54, 147–49, 312, 337

Iraq
  and Ba'ath regimes, 249, 250
  extension of war on terrorism to, 12, 86, 204
  and Gulf War, 181, 217
  high-tech warfare against, 168
  and Iran, 148
  and modernizing leaders, 249
  secular Arab-nationalist regime, 142
  U.S. policies in, 319
Iriye, Akira, 202
Iron Guard (cyber terrorism group), 192
Islam and economics, 67–74, 251–52
  and export barriers, 71
  and globalization, 67–68, 69, 251–52
  and historical Islam, 72–73
  Islamic banking system, 67, 68–69, 70–71, 251
  Islamists and, 68–74
  religion and marketplace, 251–52
  and secular education, 71
  and solutions to current world crisis, 71–72
  and technical modernization, 251–52, 412n16
  and trade justifications, 73–74
  and Western multiculturalism, 71–72
  and Westernization, 69
Islamic Cultural Center of New York, 296
Islamic Jihad, 146, 147, 149
Islamic law *(shari'a)*, 47, 54, 249, 251, 337
Islamic reform movements, 41–50, 53–58
  and anger toward the West, 55
  and apoliticism, 65
  and clashes within Muslim cultures, 46–50, 51–52, 249–50
  colonial period, 53, 55–58, 57
  and concern with other Muslims, 65, 390n31
  and democratization, 45–50, 51
  and Deobandism, 53–58, 387n2, 388n7
  and education, 44–45, 155 (*see also madrasas*)
  and fear of sameness, 342
  and fundamentalism, 46–47, 53–55, 412n11
  and globalization, 68, 73, 104, 251–52
  hierarchical authority in, 342
  as ideological amalgam, 342
  and Islamic economic system, 68–69
  and Islamic resurgence, 44–46

Islamic reform movements (*cont.*)
    and Islamic terrorism, 143–49, 342
    and *jihad* movements, 33, 54, 61, 388n7
    leadership and "laicization," 61
    and modernity, 249–50, 342–43
    and nationalism, 43–46
    and politics, 34, 54–55, 57–58, 62, 64–65,
        388n6, 389n21
    religion and collective empowerment, 337
    revival of, 249–50
    "Salafism," 46–47
    sources of legitimacy in activism, 342
    and Tablighi Jama'at, 53–54, 58–61
    Western influences, 42–43, 249
    and women's veiling, 342–43
    See also Taliban
Islamic Salvation Front (Algeria), 38
Islamic world
    challenges of terrorism for, 103–5
    and collective imaginary, 335–38
    cultural narratives of, 310, 312, 313,
        318–19
    democratization and, 45–50, 51
    differences within, 11–12, 46–50, 51–52,
        104, 249, 313
    education in, 44–45, 71, 154–56 (*see also*
        madrasas)
    global awareness of, 344
    and globalization, 51–52, 73–74, 103–5,
        251–52, 312, 344
    Islamic sovereignty, 104
    migration and, 252
    military modernization of, 249
    modernity and, 42–46, 249, 251–53,
        335–38, 341–44, 412n16
    phobias and fears in, 340–42
    pluralization and authority in, 42–46
    and political crises, 104
    religion and marketplace, 251–52
    technical modernization of, 251–52,
        335–36, 412n16
    views of 9/11 attacks, 11–12, 336
    views of U.S. war in Afghanistan, 11
    Western dialogue with, 253
    Western policies toward, 51
    women's roles in, 251–52, 341, 342–43
Islamists. *See* Islamic reform movements
Israel, 169, 249, 307–8, 312, 354, 424n21
Israel-Palestine conflict
    appropriate responses to, 152–53
    and breakdown of rule of law, 101
    as conflict related to 9/11, 12
    and cultural narratives, 315, 317, 427n54
    and cyber terrorism, 192
    and destruction of normal life, 242,
        411n3
    and Hamas, 29, 34, 146, 147, 148, 149, 153,
        242
    and human rights, 176
    and *intifada*, 29, 146–47, 148, 242, 411n3
    Israeli occupation, 249
    and Muslim anger at U.S., 199
    necessity of resolution, 51, 319
    and Palestinian Authority, 34, 147
    religious terrorism, 29, 31, 38, 146–47,
        152–53
    and suicide attacks, 12, 27, 242, 246
    and U.S. support for Israel, 312
    Zionism and, 307–8, 424n21
Italy, 392n25

Jackson, Jesse, 351
Jackson, Justice Robert, 280
Jacobsson, Per, 131
jahiliyya, 249
Jama'at-i Islami, 54, 65, 388n7
Jameson, Fredric, 241
Jamiat Ulema-i-Islam (JUI), 62–63, 64, 65
Jamiyyat-i Islami, 388n7
Japan
    demographic deficit in, 115
    and international trade and investment, 97
    modern urban civilization of, 209
    and peacekeeping roles, 172–73
    post-conflict operations in Afghanistan,
        227
    Tokyo gas attacks, 27, 194
    U.S. containment in, 206
    U.S. relationship with, 316
Japanese-Americans, internment of, 277, 279,
    287
Jazeera. *See* Al Jazeera
Jennings, Peter, 402n19
jihad
    and bin Laden, 242, 389n19
    and clashes within Islamic cultures, 249
    and conversion mission, 245
    as heir of Islamist thought, 54, 388n7
    and individual obligation, 61, 389n19
    and martyrdom, 338
    as nihilistic, 244–45
    in opposition to Soviets, 54

as political use of religious thought, 337, 338
as spiritual warfare, 33
and Tablighi Jama'at, 61, 389n20
Jinnah, Mohammad Ali, 72
John Paul II, Pope, 319, 346
Johnson, Philip, 376
Jordan, 104, 249
Jubilee campaign, 108, 395n5
Jung, Carl, 366–67
Justice Department, U.S., 273, 274, 275, 296–97, 419nn2, 3

Kaldor, Mary, 101, 209
Kant, Immanuel, 92, 102, 104
Karadzic, Radovan, 176
Karzai, Hamid, 221
Kashmir, 12, 13, 169, 170, 233
Kelly, Kevin, 182, 188
Kelman, Herbert, 315
Kennedy, Sen. Edward M., 288
Keohane, Robert O., 14, 106
Keynes, John Maynard, 114
Khan, Imran, 101
Khatami, Pres. Mohammad, 48
Khomeini, Ayatollah, 38, 337
Khosrokhar, Farhad, 252
Khruschev, Nikita, 314
Kingsolver, Barbara, 92, 98
Kirgis, Frederic, 95
Kissinger, Henry, 127
Kleiser, Randal, 187, 403n33
Korea, 205, 207, 411n71
Korean War, 166, 205, 207
Kosovo
    and Al Qaeda, 151
    human rights in, 95, 176
    lessons of, 223, 224, 225, 230, 231, 232, 233
    narratives of Serb defeat at, 308, 424n17, 425n31
    and new warfare, 95
    peacekeeping in, 172
    postwar government in, 225
    and regional dimension of conflict, 233
    and trafficking of women, 397n33
    UN operations in, 215, 216, 218–19
    U.S. operations in, 218, 407n18
    and virtuous war, 180
    war and modern communications in, 163
    and war crimes tribunals, 94
    See also Yugoslavia

Kristof, Nicholas D., 400n28
Krueger, Anne, 127–28
Kuran, Timor, 307

Laitin, David, 316
Land Mines Convention, 174
Laskar Jihad (jihad militias), 46
Latin America, 3, 110, 141, 231
LaVerdiere, Julian, 431n9
law, international, 93–98
    and democracy, 97
    and human rights, 94–95, 97
    Kantian heritage of, 92, 102, 104
    state law and sovereignty, 93–97
Law and Order (television), 350
Lawyers' Committee for Human Rights, 291
Le Monde, 344
Lebanon, 231
Lemann, Nicholas, 65
Leviathan (Hobbes), 259
"liberalism of fear," 78, 87, 89
Liberation Tigers of Tamil Eelan (LTTE), 140, 141, 195
Lieberman, Sen. Joseph, 351
Linenthal, Edward, 308, 309, 313, 425n26, 426n39
Lippmann, Walter, 79, 80
Little Big Horn, 309, 425n31
Locke, John, 37, 259
Los Angeles Times, 92
loya jirga, 215

Macedonia, 223
MacIntyre, Andrew, 132
Madison, James, 259, 415n26
Madjid, Nurcholish, 47
Madrasa Haqqania, 63, 389n15
madrasas
    and Al Qaeda, 150
    and Deobandism, 53, 55–56, 58, 62–63, 64, 389n15
    and Islamic economic system, 251
    proliferation of, 155
    and Taliban, 59, 62–63, 64
Maher, Bill, 183
Mandela, Nelson, 315, 317
al-Maqtari, Ali, 283
Marantz, Oaul, 431n9
Marine Corps War Memorial of Iwo Jima, 383
Marshall Plan, 88, 131, 132, 135, 248, 399n24

"Marshall Plan" for Afghanistan, 131, 132, 248
Marx, Karl, 260
Masada, 307, 309, 425n31
Massoud, Ahmed Shah, 230
The Matrix (film), 182–83
Matthews, Chris, 356
McDonald's corporation, 121
McVeigh, Timothy, 15, 28, 68, 140
Mecca, pilgrimage to, 73
media
  academic inquiry into, 181–89
  Al Jazeera, 8–9, 30, 184, 185, 344, 403n29
  and bin Laden, 184, 188, 199, 200
  and critical thought, 182, 183–84
  Hollywood and war effort, 186–87, 189, 403n33
  images, 181–83, 184–85, 200, 402n20
  and interpretation, 2
  and memorials, 381, 383–84
  and MIME-NET, 187, 189
  mimetic war of images, 184–85
  network wars, 181–84, 186–89, 402nn19, 20
  nihilism, 183
  restrictions of thought, 183–84
  terrorism in, 266, 418n56
  transnational, 30
  war statements and programming, 184–85, 188
Meissner, Doris, 295, 299
memorials at Ground Zero, 374–84
  and absence, 374–75, 376
  aesthetics and representation, 382–83
  competing needs in, 310, 426n39
  concepts for, 310, 376–77
  and consumerism, 382
  and dual purposes of honor and pedagogy, 384
  and individual victims, 377–78, 383–84
  and kitsch, 381, 382
  and media, 381, 383–84
  and naming, 383–84
  need for public memorialization, 375
  and *New York Times* "Portraits of Grief," 378, 381
  and photographs, 378–79, 431nn11, 14
  public participation in design, 426n39
  and split view of city, 375
  and spontaneous rituals of mourning, 379–80

  and tourism, 380, 381–82
  and *Tribute to Light*, 377, 431n9
Metropolitan Museum of Art, 376
Mexico, 124, 126, 134, 286–87, 293, 294–95
Meyers, Gen. Richard, 184
Michigan National Guard, 293–94
Microsoft, 196–97
Middle East Intelligence Bulletin, 191
militarism, 159–76
  armed forces, 161–65, 173
  and arms control, 160–61, 173
  and arms races, 160–61
  and asymmetric threats, 166
  and "casualty-free war," 168–69
  and communications technology, 163, 218
  controlling war, 173–76
  and cultures of violence, 30–32, 164–65
  destructiveness of modern war, 160
  high-tech warfare and "rogue states," 168
  and human rights, 162, 164, 173–76
  interconnectedness and modern state, 160
  neo-modern militarism, 165–70, 173
  new American militarism, 165–69, 180–81, 218, 407n20
  and "new war," 161–65
  and peacekeeping, 170–73
  and political ideologies, 162–64
  post-Cold War changes, 159–61
  and Revolution in Military Affairs, 100, 166–68, 181, 189, 407n20
  and "rites of violence," 30, 32–33
  and terrorism, 30–35, 244–45
  and transnationalism, 30
  weapons systems, 166–68, 218
military tribunals, 274–84
  arguments for, 280–81, 283
  and balance of security and freedom, 281–83
  Bush and, 268, 274–76, 277, 280, 420n17
  and death penalty, 284, 350
  and Due Process Clause, 278, 421n22
  and extradition, 275
  and fairness of treatment, 280–81
  and Geneva Conventions, 276, 281, 420n8
  and presumption of guilt, 277
  and rights of accused, 278, 280–84, 421n22
  and "Saboteurs Case," 278–80
militia movements, 29–30, 38
Mills, C. Wright, 189, 414n17
Milosevic, Slobodan, 94, 224

MIME-NET (military-industrial-media-entertainment network), 187
Minh-ha, Trinh T., 365
Mir, Hadmid, 196
Mladic, Ratko, 176
Monroe Doctrine, 79
Montville, Joseph, 427n56
moral complexity and 9/11, 321–31
  and ambivalent messages, 321–23, 325–26
  and American actions in Afghanistan, 329–30
  and American intellectuals, 322, 323, 325–27, 330
  and collective dimensions of tragedy, 331
  and critiques of America, 322, 323–25, 330
  and failures of moderates, 326–27
  good and evil, 321, 326
  and ideological apology for American policies, 326
  and individuals, 331
  and non-Western intellectuals, 324–25, 330, 427n9
  and oppressor-oppressed relationships, 327
  and reasons underlying terrorism, 322–23
  and vengeance motives, 328–30
Morgenthau, Hans J., 80
Morocco, 49
Moussaoui, Zacarias, 275
Moyers, Bill, 202–3
Mozambique, 406n15
Mubarak, Hosni, 34, 249
al-Muhajiroun (cyber terrorism group), 192
Muhammad, 56
Mujahedeen, 144–46, 148, 250, 365, 430n7
multiculturalism, 71–72
Murphy, Jeffrie, 328
Museum of Modern Art, 376
Musharaff, Pervez, 13
Muslim Brethren, 146
Muslim Brothers (Egypt), 54
Muslim intellectuals, 45, 47–48, 49
Mutiny of 1857 (India), 57–58
Myoda, Paul, 431n9

NAFTA, 97, 119, 121, 124, 295
al-Najjar, Mazen, 419n3
narratives and cultures, 303–20
  alternative/competing narratives, 308, 310–14, 425n26
  community identity and history, 307–10, 424nn17, 20
  conflict resolution and de-escalation, 314–17, 426n51, 427n56
  and culture, 305–6, 308, 423n8
  defined, 303–4, 305, 423n5
  as exacerbators of conflict, 315–16
  and historical narratives, 309–10, 425n31
  identity and group consensus, 306–7, 314–15, 316, 423n13, 424nn14, 15
  images and metaphors of, 307–8, 424n17
  and Muslim anger, 312, 313, 318–19
  needs and vulnerability, 305, 423n6
  psychocultural narratives, 305–10
  reflections of worldviews, 314–15
  religious narratives, 305, 423n7
  and rituals, 309–10, 317, 425n35, 427nn53, 54, 56
  as shaping actions, 314
  and tipping points, 316
  and U.S. relations with the Muslim world, 317–20
Nasr, Seyyed Vali Reza, 389n21
Nasser, Gamal Abdel, 38, 249, 250, 404n4
The Nation, 186, 202, 269
nation-states, 243–45
National Islamic Front, 149
National Missile Defense Program (NMD), 100, 168, 204, 405n4
National Security Agency (NSA), 210
National Security Education Program, 210
nationalism, 10, 29–30, 36–39, 43–46, 346
Native Americans, 309
NATO, 83, 84, 171, 203, 235, 248, 411n67
Naval Postgraduate School (NPS), 194–95
Naval War College, 188
Nazism, 13, 140
Nehru, Jawaharlal, 38
Neier, Aryeh, 275
"neo-Salafism," 46–47
Netanyahu, Benjamin, 31
Netherlands, 227, 231, 408n29
New Testament, 33
New York City Fire Department, 383
New York Review of Books, 275
New York Times, 83, 178, 179, 183, 275, 344, 376, 378, 381
New Yorker, 183, 377
Newberg, Paula, 229, 406n8, 410n55
Newsbytes, 196
Newsweek, 42, 179, 186

NGOs (nongovernmental organizations),
117, 139, 141, 156–57, 171, 416n38
Nietzsche, Friedrich, 249
nihilism, 183, 198–99, 244–46
9–11 Widows and Victims' Families
Association, 384
Noelle-Neumann, Elisabeth, 424n16
North, Douglass, 392n22
North Korea, 166, 207, 208, 355
Northern Alliance, 169, 175, 205, 219, 225,
230, 365, 407n18, 409n47
Northern Ireland, 307, 316, 317, 424n17,
425n33, 426n51
Norway, 227, 408n29
Now, Let Me Tell You What I Really Think
(Matthews), 256
Nuclear Nonproliferation Treaty, 96
nuclear weapons, 79–80, 152, 167–68,
169–70, 173, 354
Nuremberg war crimes tribunals, 93–94, 174
Nye, Joseph, 392n16

Observer (London), 165
Obstfeld-Rogoff model, 123
O'Donnell, Guillermo, 49
OECD (Organization for Economic
Cooperation and Development), 122,
123, 129, 221
Office of Homeland Security, 349
Oklahoma City bombing, 27, 140, 308, 335,
425n26
Oklahoma City National Memorial, 375, 380,
382, 383, 384, 432n23
Olcott, Martha Brill, 410nn55, 62
Omar, Mullah, 145, 200, 203, 404n2
O'Neill, Sect. Paul, 127
Oppenheimer, J. Robert, 349–50
Organization of Security and Cooperation in
Europe (OSCE), 172, 411n67
Oslo accords, 31, 146, 153, 413n8
Ottaway, Marina, 410n55
Ottoman Empire, 43, 72–73, 150–51, 153,
251

Pahlavi, Reza Shah, 38, 147–48, 249
Pakistan
and culture of violence, 165
and Deobandism, 58, 62, 64
economic development in, 132–33,
400nn28, 29
and economic Islamization, 69, 70

and IMF, 127
and Islamic terrorism, 142, 149
Islamist education in, 155
Islamist movements and parties, 58, 62, 64,
65–66, 144, 148, 389n21
and Kashmir, 13
and Mujahedeen, 144–45
nationalism in, 44
and neo-modern militarism, 169–70, 354
secular regime in, 142
and Taliban, 62–63, 233
U.S. policies in, 145, 206
and war against Taliban, 233
Pakistan People's Party (PPP), 62
Pakistani Interservices Intelligence Agency
(ISI), 430n8
Palestine
and Black September, 249
and cyber terrorism, 192
and development agencies, 222
and Hamas, 146, 147, 148, 153
human rights violations in, 176
intifada, 29, 146–47, 148, 242, 411n3
and Islamic terrorism, 146–47, 152–53
Islamist education in, 155
and Palestinian Authority, 34, 147
and religious terrorism, 29, 31, 38
Zionism and, 307–8, 424n21
See also Israel-Palestine conflict
Palestine Liberation Organization (PLO),
142, 146–47, 153, 195, 317
Palestinian Authority (PA), 34, 147
Panel on United Nations Peace Operations
and Brahimi Report, 213–14
Pappandreou, George, 405n1
Parekh, Bhikhu, 103–4
Pashtuns, 62, 65, 145, 210, 233
Patten, Chris, 407n16
peacekeeping and peace-building, 170–73,
213–20
and Bonn talks on postwar Afghanistan,
215–16, 222, 228, 406n15
and Brahimi Report, 213–16, 219, 220,
232, 237
changes since Cold War, 171
dilemma of mandates and resources, 172,
219–20, 407n24
failures, 172, 214, 215, 221, 406nn8, 15
frameworks for intervention, 214, 406n8
and humanitarian emergencies, 214,
406n9

and humanitarian law, 175
and legacy of 1990s, 213–20
new tasks and roles of, 171–72
and organizational structure, 171, 216, 235
and postmodern, globalizing states,
 172–73
successes of, 172
UN operations, 170–72, 213–16, 218–20,
 235, 406n15
and U.S. roles, 216–20, 407n24
and use of force, 218–19
See also United Nations peacekeeping
Pearl, Daniel, 5
Pearl Harbor attacks (1941), 90, 175, 201,
 202–3, 210, 211, 287
Pentagon attack, 4–5, 338, 400n6
People magazine, 381
Perot, Ross, 383
Philippines, 116, 141, 142, 206, 316, 397n25
Pinochet, Augusto, 174, 353
Piscatori, James, 45
Politically Incorrect (television), 183
politics, 254–72
 and administrative control, 259–60,
  415nn25, 26, 28
 American disdain for, 260, 261–62
 and capitalism, 417n45
 and civil society, 260, 261–62, 264–65, 270,
  416nn32, 33, 416nn38, 39
 defining, 255–58
 and democracy, 262–65, 416n41, 417n46
 dependence and "connectedness," 257–58,
  414nn12–17
 depoliticization, 259, 415n22
 and economics, 260, 416nn34, 35
 and equality, 263, 417n44
 and freedom, 263–64
 fundamental conditions for, 256–58
 and government usurpations of power,
  268–69
 and Islamic reform movements, 34, 54–55,
  57–58, 62, 64–65, 388n6, 389n21
 and love, 257, 258, 413n11
 and modern state, 258–62, 268–71
 and plurality, 256–57, 258, 269, 413nn10,
  11
 and the public, 258, 269, 415n19
 regimes and organizations of political life,
  264, 417n46
 and rights, 269–71, 419nn67, 68
 security and liberty issues, 267–69

and speech, 255, 258, 264–65, 266, 271–72
and terrorism, 265–72
and violence, 255–56, 259, 262, 413nn5, 7,
 417n42
Politics and Vision (Wolin), 261
Politics (Aristotle), 255, 413n4
Pope, Alexander, 259, 415n25
poverty and political violence, 153–54
Powell, Colin, 204, 217, 276
Powell Doctrine, 217
power sharing, 230–32
Prigogine, Ilya, 357
Protestant reformation, 42
Putin, Vladimir, 170, 204
Putnam, Robert, 47, 266

Qaeda. *See* Al Qaeda
Qutb, Sayyid, 38, 249, 428n7

Rabbani, Burhanuddin, 388n7
Rabin, Yitzhak, 31
Radikal (Turkish daily), 344
Rahman, Fazlur, 62, 389n23
Rahman, Sheik Omar Abdul, 38
Rashid, Ahmed, 63, 389n25, 405n18
Rawls, John, 259
Razzak, Mohammad Afroze Abdul, 197
Reagan, Pres. Ronald, 204
religion
 and America's view of 9/11, 29, 212
 and cosmic war metaphor, 28–30
 and extremism, 28
 and nationalism, 29–30, 36–39, 43
 and "rites of violence," 30, 32–33
 and secularism, 27–28, 35, 36–39, 40,
  250–52
 See also Islamic reform movements;
  terrorism, religious
Ressam, Ahmed, 196
Reuters news agency, 183
Revolution in Military Affairs (RMA), 100,
 166–68, 181, 189, 407n20
Rice, Condoleezza, 186, 420n8
Ridge, Tom, 295
Riley, Terence, 376
Roosevelt, Pres. Franklin, 208, 279
Roth, Kenneth, 420n8
Rothstein, Edward, 178, 183–84
Rousseau, Jean-Jacques, 37, 259
Roy, Olivier, 54, 63, 389n27
Rubin, Barnett, 230, 232, 233, 409n42

Rumsfeld, Donald, 9, 168, 183, 184, 188, 204, 276
Rushdie, Salman, 337, 366, 388n6
Russia
    financial crisis and foreign investment, 100
    and global war on terrorism, 3, 203, 204, 316
    and missile treaty, 204
    and neo-modern militarism, 100, 169–70, 354
    and new war in Afghanistan, 235
    social confusion of, 38, 39
    U.S. relationship with, 316
    See also Soviet Union
Russian Stock Exchange, 195
Rwanda, 94, 163, 165, 172, 174, 214, 222, 236, 244

Sadat, Anwar, 249, 317, 337
Safire, William, 269, 275
Said, Edward, 248, 295
Salafism and "neo-Salafism," 46–47
Salvation Army, 33
Sardar, Ziauddin, 103
Saudi Arabia
    Al Qaeda attack on U.S. in, 150
    and anti-communist struggle in Afghanistan, 145
    and bin Laden, 104
    and economic Islamization, 70
    and Islamic nationalism, 44
    and Islamic terrorism, 142, 149
    Islamist education in, 155
    Islamist movements, 144, 148
    and Mujahedeen, 144, 145
    and Muslim hatred of U.S., 199–200
    and post-conflict operations in Afghanistan, 227
    and Salafy, 46
    U.S. troops in, 206
Schelling, Thomas, 79
Schmid, Alex, 391n4
Schmitter, Philippe, 49
Schumpeter, Joseph, 77, 418n53
Scofidio, Ricardo, 376
secularism, 27–28, 35, 36–39, 40, 43–44, 250–52
Sendero Luminoso (Peru), 140
Senghor, Léopold-Sédar, 359
Serbia, 163. See also Yugoslavia
Shah, King Zahir, 144, 147

Shame (Rushdie), 366
Shanker, Thom, 407n19
shari'a (Islamic law), 47, 54, 249, 251, 337
Shariati, Dr. Ali, 45
Sharon, Ariel, 174, 199, 315
Shi'a Islam, 53, 145, 148
Shklar, Judith N., 78, 87, 89
Sierra Leone, 406n8
Signposts (Qutb), 428n7
Sikhism, 33
Simulacra and Simulation (Baudrillard), 183
Skowcroft, Brent, 206
Smith, Adam, 265
Smith, Anthony, 423n13
Smith, Neil, 313
Somalia, 150, 207, 214, 408n36
Sontag, Susan, 241
Soros Foundation, 248
Soroush, Abdolkarim, 47, 48
South Africa, 172–73, 315, 316, 317, 354
South Asia, 3, 32, 57, 60, 70. See also individual countries
Southeast Asia, 118, 126, 205–6, 395n7, 397n33. See also individual countries
sovereignty and law, 93–97
Soviet Union
    and Afghanistan, 81, 144–46, 250, 364–65
    and Cold War, 201
    collapse of, 68, 81, 141, 166, 250
    and Dulles, 314
    and Islamist revival, 250
    and new American militarism, 166
    nuclear capacity, 354
    and U.S. foreign security policy, 353
    See also Russia
Spiegelman, Art, 377
Srebrenica massacre, 172, 176
Sri Lanka, 33, 165
St. Paul's Chapel (New York City), 381–82
Starbucks, 121
state building, 156–57
State Department, U.S., 288, 290, 292
Steering Group for Reconstruction of Afghanistan, 227
Stern, Robert A. M., 376
Stimson, Henry, 208
Stone, Chief Justice Harlan Fiske, 279
Strategic Framework for Afghanistan (UN), 214, 406n8
Structural Adjustment Loans, 109

Structural Adjustment Programs (SAPs), 109, 111, 395nn7, 8
student visas, 288, 292–93
Sudan, 69
Sufism, 56, 60–61, 389n18
Suharto regime (Indonesia), 48–49, 132, 142
suicide bombings, 12, 27, 242, 246
Sunday Times (London), 179
Sunni Islam, 53, 57, 148
Sununu, John, 295
Supreme Court, U.S., 278–80, 356
Sweden development agency (SIDA), 221
Symbionese Liberation Army, 143
Syria, 49, 142, 143, 148, 249, 250

Tablighi Jama'at, 58–61, 64–66, 389n20
Taliban
    anti-Americanism of, 63
    and bin Laden, 53, 63–64, 342
    commentators' descriptions of, 53, 387n2
    and Deobandism, 53, 62–63, 387n2, 388n14, 389n15
    destruction of Bamian Buddhas, 337, 389n28, 423n13
    early goals in Afghanistan, 64
    and early U.S. interests, 63, 146
    emergence of, 62–64, 145–46, 389n28, 430n8
    and international spotlight, 53
    and Islamists, 146, 388n6
    and Jamiat Ulema-i-Islam, 62–63, 64
    and politics, 64–65
    pragmatic and moderate voices in, 64, 389n28
    and salaries to civil servants, 409n47
    and Tablighi Jama'at, 53–54
    unassured defeat of, 329–30
    and women, 63, 64, 342, 365, 430n8
Tambiah, Stanley, 32–33
Tamil Tigers (Sri Lanka), 140, 141, 195
Tenet, George, 183, 224
terrorism
    and accountability, 245
    in American consciousness, 349–50
    approaches/responding to, 99–102, 152–58, 166, 273–76, 277–84
    appropriating of public sphere, 266–68
    and asymmetries, 81–83, 184–85
    breeding grounds for, 107–8
    and challenges to democracies, 246–47
    and challenges to globalization, 121–22

    and "clash of civilizations," 139, 248–50
    and competing cultural narratives, 310–11, 315–16
    cyber terrorism, 191–97
    defining, 77–78, 391n4
    emotional responses to, 98–99
    foreign aid and, 135
    global ideologies of, 244–46
    and globalization, 38–39, 107–8, 121–22, 244–46, 335–36
    and government usurpations of power, 268–69
    historical-causal understandings of, 336
    hybrid movements (type III), 141–42, 146, 147, 148, 152
    International Islamic Terrorism, 142–58
    and Islamic collective imaginary, 335–38
    and *jihad,* 245–46
    justice, freedom, and war, 98–103
    and lines between crime and war, 246–47
    and media, 266, 418n56
    and modernity, 335–36
    and moral complexity, 326–28
    movements aimed at system overthrow (type II), 140–41, 152
    national or regional liberation movements (type I), 140, 141–42, 146, 148, 152
    and new American militarism, 166
    as new kind of war, 99–100, 245
    and "New Left" of 1960s, 143
    and NGOs, 139, 156–57
    nihilism of, 245–46
    and normalcy, destruction of, 242, 244
    and politics, 265–72
    public concern about, pre-9/11, 392n18
    and speech, 266, 271–72
    state-centric categories, 247
    state terrorism, 244–45
    and tacit consent to 9/11, 336
    as totalitarianism, 244
    types of, 139–42, 152
    U.S. fostering of, 142
    and U.S.-led coalition against, 3, 102, 127, 203–4, 316, 350–51
    See also terrorism, religious; violence
terrorism, religious, 29–35, 39–40
    and antimodernist movements, 38–39
    and "crisis of legitimacy," 36–38
    and culture of war, 30–33
    and cyber terrorism, 194
    and global war, 30–35

terrorism, religious (*cont.*)
  and globalization, 38–39
  and International Islamic Terrorism,
    142–58
  and Islamic reform movements, 143–49,
    342
  and political rule based on religious law, 34
  as postmodern terror, 39–40
  as public performance of violence, 30–31,
    32–33, 39–40
  and religion in society, 35
  and religiosity, 28, 35–36
  and religious nationalism, 29–30
  and "rites of violence," 30–31, 32–33
  and secularism, 27, 35, 36–39
  and symbolic empowerment, 33–35
  and transnationalism, 30
  violence and religion in, 39–40
Thailand, 132
Tilly, Charles, 159
Tocqueville, Alexis de, 260–61, 286
Tokyo conference on rebuilding Afghanistan
    (January 2002), 222, 226–29, 410n54
Tokyo nerve gas attacks, 27, 194
Torres, A. R., 381, 431n11
trafficking in people, 116–18
  and debt crisis, 113, 396n14
  defined, 397n26
  and globalization, 117, 397nn30, 32
  of migrants, 117–18
  and restrictive immigration, 116
  of women, 117, 396n14, 397nn30, 32, 33
Tribe, Laurence, 277, 280
Tribute to Light, 377, 431n9
Truman, Pres. Harry, 208
Truth, Sojourner, 359
Tschumi, Bernard, 376
Tunisia, 249
Turkey, 43, 72, 127, 142, 150, 153, 249

'ulama, 45, 53, 54, 56–58, 59, 60, 62, 64–65
UNESCO, 354
United Nations
  in Afghanistan, 213, 215, 216
  and Brahimi, 213–14
  and Bush administration, 83, 84
  and foreign aid after 9/11, 131
  and global terrorism, 30
  lessons of 1990s, 213–17, 226–29, 235–37
  Security Council, 77, 83–85, 214, 216
  See also United Nations peacekeeping

United Nations Charter, 84, 85, 96, 171,
    219
United Nations Declaration of Human
    Rights (1948), 105
United Nations Development Programme
    (UNDP), 171, 221, 226
United Nations High Commission for
    Refugees (UNHCR), 116, 171
United Nations Mission for Assistance to
    Afghanistan (UNAMA), 216
United Nations peacekeeping, 170–72,
    213–16
  and Bonn process, 215–16
  and Brahimi Report, 213–16, 219
  failures of, 172, 214, 215, 221, 406n15
  and frameworks for intervention, 214,
    406n8
  lessons of 1990s, 213–17, 235, 236–37
  mandates and resources, 219–20, 407n24
  and organizational structure, 216, 235
  and U.S. role, 216, 219–20, 407n24
  and use of force, 218–19
United Nations Security Council, 77, 83–85,
    214, 216
United States
  and anti-communist struggle in
    Afghanistan, 145
  demographic deficits, 115, 116
  and early Taliban, 63, 146
  founders, 259–60, 415nn25, 26, 28, 417n47
  and lessons of 1990s, 223–24
  and multilateral institutions, 83–84, 85–86
  role in globalization, 121–22
  and war in Kosovo, 219
  and world economy post-9/11, 128–30
  See also American self-image; Bush
    administration; immigration policy,
    U.S.; United States foreign security
    policy
United States Agency for International
    Development (USAID), 221, 408n29
United States foreign security policy
  after World War II, 79–80, 208
  and American hegemony, 352–55
  antiterrorism policies as military
    campaigns, 220–21
  and asymmetrical powers, 81–82
  and concept of security, 220–21
  and containment, 205–9, 223, 352, 405n15
  and geographical space, 80–81
  and geopolitical changes, 353–54

and globalization of informal violence,
79–81, 87–89, 392n15
and immigration, 285–99
and intelligence, 210–11, 224
and "liberalism of fear," 87–89
militarization of peace and security,
236–37
military lessons of 1990s, 216–20
and Muslim anger, 312, 313, 319
and neutralization, 353
and peacekeeping, 220–21
post-9/11, 203–5
and Powell Doctrine, 217
and public concern about terrorism,
392n18
public opinions of, 209, 405n15
and Realism, 80, 87, 88
redefinition of interests, 88–89
relationship with Muslim world, 319
and unfinished legacy of 1990s, 236–37
and vulnerability to terrorism, 81–82
and war on terrorism, 3, 102, 127, 203–4,
316, 350–51
pre–World War II, 79
See also Afghanistan, post-9/11 war in
UNITY (cyber terrorism group), 192
UNPROFOR, 221
U.S. Atomic Energy Commission, 349
USA PATRIOT Act
and Ashcroft, 419n2
and border patrol, 292
and civil rights, 276–77
definition of terrorism in, 273, 291–92
detention of aliens, 273, 275–76, 291,
419nn2, 3
and Geneva Conventions, 276, 420n8
and government searches, 274, 292
habeas corpus under, 284, 292
and immigration policy, 291–92
little domestic protest over, 276
and military tribunals, 274–76
and monitoring of conversations, 274
original version of, 419n2
passing of, 186, 419n2
problems of, 247–48, 268, 273–74, 419n2
and right to counsel, 247–48, 274
and rights of detainees, 247–48, 274–76,
284, 291–92
and "roving wiretaps," 186
U.S.S. Cole, attack on, 150
Uzbekistan, 206, 316

Variety (magazine), 186
Vattel, Emerich de, 289
veiling of Muslim women, 337–38, 342–43
Vendrell, Francesc, 213, 222
Vietnam, 100
"Vietnam Syndrome," 181, 217
Vietnam War, 205–6, 217, 247, 353
Vietnam War Memorial, 309–10, 375, 379,
380, 383, 384
violence
and Afghan refugees, 362–64, 370–71, 372
crime and war, 246–47
defining, 79
and democracy, 262, 417n42
and desperation, 255, 413n5
formal violence, 79–80
and geographical space, 78–81
and globalism, 78–79, 89
globalization of informal, 77–91
institutions and legitimacy, 83–86, 392n22
interdependence and power, 81–83, 90,
392n16
and international relations theory, 14, 90
and "liberalism of fear," 78, 87–89, 91
and politics, 255–56, 259, 262, 413nn5, 7,
417n42
and religious war, 30–32
and speech, 266
and the state, 259
and U.S. foreign security policy, 79–81,
87–89, 392n15
and visual sense, 334–35
See also militarism; terrorism
Virilio, Paul, 189
"virtuous wars," 180–81, 402n16
Voice of America, 186
Volkan, Vamik D., 315, 317, 424n17, 425n31

Wahabism, 57, 200, 246
Waltz, Kenneth N., 80, 83
Walzer, Michael, 326, 327, 427n6
war. See Afghanistan, post-9/11 war in;
violence
war crimes tribunals, 93–94, 101, 174
Warner, Michael, 380
Weather Underground, 143
Weber, Max, 84, 243, 250, 258–59, 411n4,
415nn20, 21, 424n20
Wellstone, Sen. Paul, 117
Werbner, Pnina, 60, 389n18
Will, George, 178, 183

Wired (magazine), 182, 186, 188
Wohlstetter, Albert, 79
Wolfensohn, James, 221
Wolfowitz, Paul D., 407n22
Wolin, Sheldon S., 261
women
    illegal trafficking of, 117, 396n14,
        397nn30, 32, 33
    and Islam, 251–52, 337–38, 341, 342–43
    and Taliban, 63, 64, 342, 365, 430n8
women of Afghanistan and concept of home,
        361–73
    and creativity, 369–70
    as metaphor for grave, 369, 430n13
    public and private spaces, 362–64
    refugees and insecurity, 364–66, 368–69,
        372–73
    and Taliban, 63, 64, 365, 430n8
    and war/violence, 362–64, 370–71, 372
    and women's identities, 364, 366–67, 368,
        372, 429n5
Women's Rights Advocacy Program,
        Initiative Against Trafficking in Persons,
        117
Woolf, Virginia, 374
World Bank, 109, 111, 133, 214, 221–22, 226,
        227
World Trade Center
    architectural design of, 339–40
    first attack on (1993), 27, 35, 150, 179, 376,
        401n1
    international citizens killed, 30, 322
    symbolic significance of, 125, 338–41,
        374–75
    towers and absence, 374–75
    towers as metaphor, 348, 351, 353, 357, 360
    See also memorials at Ground Zero
World Trade Organization (WTO), 118, 325,
        354
World War II
    and American military victory, 206
    analogies/parallels to 9/11, 201, 202–3

    blurring of military and civilian targets,
        241–42
    and humanitarian law, 174
    Marshall Plan and postwar recovery, 88,
        130–31, 132, 248, 399n24
    and military tribunals, 278–80
    and nature of war, 100, 160
    and offensive maneuvers, 167
    and U.S. containment policy, 208
    war memorials, 377
Wye River accord, 31

Yalta Agreement, 353
Yamasaki, Minori, 339
Yaqub, Salim, 404n4
Yassin, Sheik Ahmed, 38
Yemen, 150
Young, Hugo, 103
Young Intelligent Hackers Against Terror
        (YIHAT), 191
Yugoslavia
    high-tech warfare against, 168
    lessons learned in, 217, 218, 407nn18, 22
    lessons not learned in, 223, 224, 225, 227,
        230, 231, 232, 233
    patterns of violence in, 95
    peacekeeping in, 172, 173, 214, 215, 221,
        406n15
    and Powell Doctrine, 217
    and state terrorism, 244
    U.S. operations in, 217, 218, 236, 407n18
    war crimes tribunals, 94, 174, 222
    See also Bosnia and Herzegovina; Kosovo

Zadvydas v. *Davis*, 278
Zakariyya Kandhlawi, Maulana Muhammad,
        60
Zepa, 172
Zerubavel, Yael, 307–8, 309
Zionism, 307–8, 424n21
Zizek, Slavoj, 241, 355, 357
Zolberg, Aristide, 397n24